SEVENTH-DAY ADVENTISTS

BELIEVE...

A Biblical Exposition of Fundamental Doctrines

The Ministerial Association of the General Conference of Seventh-day Adventists assumes full responsibility for the accuracy of the camera-ready copy of this book. Editing, copy editing, and proofreading for this book was done under the direction of the Ministerial Association. Due to technical limitations, vowel points and diacritical marks have not been included when transliterating foreign words.

More than 580,000 copies in print
Second Edition, second printing: February 2006

Library of Congress Assigned No.: BX6155.7 S482.7

ISBN: 1-57847-041-2

CONTENTS

A Word About the Fundamental Beliefs of
Seventh-day Adventists v
To the Readers of This Book vii

THE DOCTRINE OF GOD
1. The Word of God 11
2. The Godhead 23
3. God the Father 35
4. God the Son 43
5. God the Holy Spirit 69

THE DOCTRINE OF MAN
6. Creation 79
7. The Nature of Man 91

THE DOCTRINE OF SALVATION
8. The Great Controversy 113
9. The Life, Death, and Resurrection of Christ 121
10. The Experience of Salvation 133
11. Growing in Christ 149

THE DOCTRINE OF THE CHURCH
12. The Church 163
13. The Remnant and Its Mission 181
14. Unity in the Body of Christ 201
15. Baptism 211
16. The Lord's Supper 225
17. Spiritual Gifts and Ministries 237
18. The Gift of Prophecy 247

THE DOCTRINE OF THE CHRISTIAN LIFE
19. The Law of God 263
20. The Sabbath 281
21. Stewardship 301
22. Christian Behavior 311
23. Marriage and the Family 329

THE DOCTRINE OF LAST THINGS

24. Christ's Ministry in the Heavenly Sanctuary 347
25. The Second Coming of Christ 371
26. Death and Resurrection 387
27. The Millennium and the End of Sin 403
28. The New Earth 417

Index 429

A WORD ABOUT THE FUNDAMENTAL BELIEFS OF SEVENTH-DAY ADVENTISTS

THROUGH THE YEARS, SEVENTH-DAY ADVENTISTS have been reluctant to formalize a creed, in the usual sense of that term. However, from time to time, for practical purposes, we have found it necessary to summarize our beliefs in an organized structure.

In 1872 the Adventist press at Battle Creek published a "synopsis of our faith" in twenty-five propositions. This document, slightly revised and expanded to twenty-eight sections, appeared in the denominational *Yearbook* of 1889 and was inserted again in the years 1905-1914. Later, in response to an appeal from church leaders in Africa for "a statement which would help government officials and others to a better understanding of our work," a committee of four, including the president of the General Conference, prepared a statement encompassing "the principal features" of belief as they may be summarized. This statement of twenty-two fundamental beliefs, first printed in the 1931 *Yearbook*, stood until the 1980 General Conference session replaced it with a similar but more comprehensive summary in twenty-seven paragraphs, published under the title, "Fundamental Beliefs of Seventh-day Adventists."

Even in publishing that 1980 summary, the church took steps to assure that it would not come to be viewed as an unchangeable creed. The preamble to the statement of fundamental beliefs reads:

> "Seventh-day Adventists accept the Bible as their only creed and hold certain fundamental beliefs to be the teachings of the Holy Scriptures. These beliefs, as set forth here, constitute the church's understanding and expression of the teaching of Scripture. Revision of these statements may be expected at a General Conference session when the church is led by the Holy Spirit to a fuller understanding of Bible truth or finds better language to express the teachings of God's Holy Word."

Such an expansion and revision occurred at the 2005 Session of the General Conference of Seventh-day Adventists in St. Louis, Missouri, USA, when an additional fundamental belief was voted, not to add new or previously unknown material, but better to express the church's understanding of God's power to give victorious life over the powers of evil to believers in Jesus Christ (see chapter 11).

This present volume is based on these short summary statements, which appear at the beginning of each chapter. Our aim in this book is to present for our members, friends, and other interested individuals—in an expanded, readable, and practical manner—these doctrinal convictions and their significance for Adventist Christians in today's society. Although this volume is not an officially voted statement (only the summary statements have been officially voted by the General Conference in session), it may be viewed as representative of "the truth as it is in Jesus" (Ephesians 4:21) that Seventh-day Adventists around the globe cherish and proclaim.

We gratefully acknowledge the vision of former General Conference President Neal C. Wilson and other denominational officers, who originally authorized and encouraged the Ministerial Association to undertake preparation of this volume's first edition in 1988 in order to furnish reliable information on the beliefs of our church. We also acknowledge several scholars and technicians who provided the basic manuscript for the first edition: P. G. Damsteegt, Norman Gulley, Laurel Damsteegt, Mary Louise McDowell, David Jarnes, Kenneth Wade, and my immediate predecessor as Ministerial Association Secretary, W. Floyd Bresee. A select committee of 194 individuals from all of the church's world divisions plus a smaller editorial committee of leaders, theologians, and pastors gave additional supervision to the preparation of the 1988 edition. We also gratefully acknowledge the writing and editorial skills of John M. Fowler in preparation of this second, expanded edition—particularly the additional chapter (number 11) entitled "Growing in Christ."

Finally, special tribute should be paid to J. Robert Spangler, former Ministerial Association Secretary and long-time editor of *Ministry* magazine, who initiated the concept and funding for this project. Dreams too seldom become tangible. His did. You hold it in your hands. Without his vision this book would not likely have been conceived. Without his persistence, it would not have been published.

We pray that as you consider each of these fundamental beliefs, you will clearly see Jesus and His plan of abundance for your personal life.

James A. Cress
Ministerial Association Secretary
General Conference of Seventh-day Adventists

TO THE READERS OF THIS BOOK...

WHAT DO YOU BELIEVE ABOUT GOD? Who is He? What does He expect of us? What is He really like?

God told Moses that no man could see His face and live. But Jesus told Philip that anyone who had seen Him had seen the Father (John 14:9). Since He walked among us—indeed, became one of us—we are able to perceive who God is and what He is like.

We have written this exposition of our major beliefs to reveal how Seventh-day Adventists perceive God. This is what we believe about His love, kindness, mercy, grace, justice, benevolence, purity, righteousness, and peace. Through Jesus Christ, we see God benevolently holding children on His lap. We see Him weeping as He shares the sorrow of the mourners at the tomb of Lazarus. We see His love as He cries, "Forgive them, for they do not know what they do" (Luke 23:34).

We have written this book to share our vision of Christ—a vision that finds its focus at Calvary, where "mercy and truth have met together; righteousness and peace have kissed each other" (Ps. 85:10). At Calvary, He became sin for us—He who knew no sin—"that we might become the righteousness of God in Him" (2 Cor. 5:21).

We have written this book believing that every doctrine, every belief, must reveal the love of our Lord. Here is a Person with an unconditional love and commitment unparalleled in human history. Recognizing that He who is the incarnation of truth is infinite, we humbly confess that there is still much truth to be discovered.

We have written this book conscious of our indebtedness to the rich biblical truths we have received from the Christian church of history. We acknowledge the noble line of witnesses—such as Wycliffe, Huss, Luther, Tyndale, Calvin, Knox, and Wesley—whose advance into new light led the church forward to a fuller understanding of God's character. And that understanding is ever progressive. "The path of the just is as the shining light, that shineth more and more unto the perfect day" (Prov. 4:18, KJV). Yet as we find new facets of God's revelation, they will harmonize perfectly with the united testimony of the Scriptures.

We have written this book with the guidance of a clear directive continually reminding us that "if you search the Scriptures to vindicate your own opinions, you will never reach the truth. Search in order to learn what the

Lord says. If conviction comes as you search, if you see that your cherished opinions are not in harmony with the truth, do not misinterpret the truth in order to suit your own belief, but accept the light given. Open mind and heart that you may behold wondrous things out of God's Word" (Ellen G. White, *Christ's Object Lessons,* Mountain View, CA: Pacific Press Pub. Assn., 1900, p. 112).

We have not written this book to serve as a creed—a statement of beliefs set in theological concrete. Adventists have but one creed: "The Bible, and the Bible alone."

We have not written this book to titillate the imagination. This is not a speculative work—unless one considers the Bible to be that! Rather, it is a thorough, biblically based, Christ-centered exposition of what we believe. And the beliefs expressed are not the product of a studious afternoon; they represent more than 100 years of prayer, study, prayer, reflection, prayer... In other words, they are the product of Adventist growth "in the grace and knowledge of our Lord and Saviour Jesus Christ" (2 Peter 3:18).

We have written this book aware that some will ask if doctrine is really important in an age that finds itself struggling to survive the threat of nuclear annihilation, an age preoccupied with the explosive growth of technology, an age in which Christian endeavor tries vainly to press back the brooding specters of poverty, hunger, injustice, and ignorance.

We have written this book with the deep conviction that all doctrines, when properly understood, center on Him—the Way, the Truth, and the Life—and are extremely important. Doctrines define the character of the God we serve. They interpret events, both past and present, establishing a sense of place and purpose in the cosmos. They describe the objectives of God as He acts. Doctrines are a guide for Christians, giving stability in what otherwise would be unbalancing experiences, injecting certainty into a society that denies absolutes. Doctrines feed the human intellect and establish goals that inspire Christians and motivate them with concern for other persons.

We have written this book to lead Adventist believers into a deeper relationship with Christ through a study of the Bible. Knowing Him and His will is vitally important in this age of deception, doctrinal pluralism, and apathy. Such a knowledge is the Christian's only safeguard against those who, "like savage wolves," will come speaking perverse things in order to subvert the truth and destroy the faith of God's people (see Acts 20:29, 30). Especially in these last days, to keep from being "carried about with every wind of doctrine, by the trickery of men" (Eph. 4:14), all must have a right concept of God's character, government, and purposes. Only those who have fortified their minds with the truth of the Scriptures will be able to stand in the final conflict.

We have written this book to assist those who are interested in knowing why we believe what we believe. This study, written by Adventists themselves, is not just window dressing. Carefully researched, it represents an authentic exposition of Adventist beliefs.

Finally, we have written this book recognizing that Christ-centered doctrine performs three obvious functions: first, it edifies the church; second, it preserves the truth; and third, it communicates the gospel in all its richness.

True doctrine calls for far more than mere belief—it calls for action. Through the Holy Spirit, Christian beliefs become loving deeds. A true knowledge of God, His Son, and the Holy Spirit is "saving knowledge." That is the theme of this book.—Editors.

The Word of God

1

The Holy Scriptures, Old and New Testaments, are the written Word of God, given by divine inspiration through holy men of God who spoke and wrote as they were moved by the Holy Spirit. In this Word, God has committed to man the knowledge necessary for salvation. The Holy Scriptures are the infallible revelation of His will. They are the standard of character, the test of experience, the authoritative revealer of doctrines, and the trustworthy record of God's acts in history. (2 Pet. 1:20, 21; 2 Tim. 3:16, 17; Ps. 119:105; Prov. 30:5, 6; Isa. 8:20; John 17:17; 1 Thess. 2:13; Heb. 4:12.)

NO BOOK HAS BEEN SO LOVED, SO HATED, so revered, so damned as the Bible. People have died for the Bible. Others have killed for it. It has inspired man's greatest, noblest acts and been blamed for his most damnable and degenerate. Wars have raged over the Bible, revolutions have been nurtured in its pages, and kingdoms crumbled through its ideas. People of all viewpoints—from liberation theologians to capitalists, from fascists to Marxists, from dictators to liberators, from pacifists to militarists—search its pages for words with which to justify their deeds.

The Bible's uniqueness does not come from its unparalleled political, cultural, and social influence but from its source and its subject matter. It is God's revelation of the unique God-man: the Son of God, Jesus Christ—the Saviour of the world.

Divine Revelation

While throughout history some have questioned God's existence, many have confidently testified that He exists and that He has disclosed Himself. In what ways has God revealed Himself, and how does the Bible function in His revelation?

General Revelation. The insight into God's character that history, human behavior, conscience, and nature provide is frequently called "general revelation" because it is available to all and appeals to reason.

For millions, "The heavens declare the glory of God; and the firmament shows His handiwork" (Ps. 19:1). The sunshine, rain, hills, and streams, all testify of a loving Creator. "For since the creation of the world His invisible attributes are clearly seen, being understood by the things that are made, even His eternal power and Godhead, so that they are without excuse" (Rom. 1:20).

Others see evidence of a caring God in the happy relationships and extraordinary love between friends, family members, husband and wife, parents and children. "As one whom his mother comforts, so I will comfort you" (Isa. 66:13). "As a father pities his children, so the Lord pities those who fear Him" (Ps. 103:13).

Yet the same sunshine that testifies of a loving Creator can turn the earth into a parched desert, bringing starvation. The same rain can turn into a rush of water that drowns families; the same lofty hill can crack, crumble—and then crush. And human relationships often involve jealousy, envy, anger, and even hatred that leads to murder. The world around us gives mixed signals, presenting more questions than it answers. It reveals a conflict between good and evil but does not explain how and why the conflict started, who is fighting, why, or who will ultimately win.

Special Revelation. Sin obscures God's self-revelation through creation by limiting our ability to interpret God's testimony. In love, God gave a special revelation of Himself to help us get answers to these questions. Through both the Old and New Testament He disclosed Himself to us in a specific way, leaving no questions about His character of love. At first His revelation came through prophets; then His ultimate revelation, through the person of Jesus Christ (Heb. 1:1, 2).

The Bible both contains propositions that declare the truth about God and reveals Him as a person. Both areas of revelation are necessary: We need to know God through Jesus Christ (John 17:3), as well as "the truth that is in Jesus" (Eph. 4:21, NIV). And by means of the Scriptures God breaks through our mental, mortal, and spiritual limitations, communicating His eagerness to save us.

The Focus of the Scriptures

The Bible reveals God and exposes humanity. It exposes our predicament and reveals His solution. It presents us as lost, estranged from God, and reveals Jesus as the one who finds us and brings us back to God.

Jesus Christ is the focus of Scripture. The Old Testament sets forth the Son of God as the Messiah, the world's Redeemer; the New Testament reveals Him as Jesus Christ, the Saviour. Every book, either through symbol or reality, reveals some phase of His work and character. Jesus' death on the cross is the ultimate revelation of God's character.

The cross makes this ultimate revelation because it brings together two extremes: man's unfathomable evil and God's inexhaustible love. What could give us greater insight into human fallibility? What could better reveal sin? The cross reveals a God who allowed His only Son to be killed. What a sacrifice! What greater revelation of love could He have made? Indeed, the focus of the Bible is Jesus Christ. He is at the center stage of the cosmic drama. Soon His triumph at Calvary will culminate in the elimination of evil. Human beings and God will be reunited.

The theme of God's love, particularly as seen in Christ's sacrificial death on Calvary—the grandest truth of the universe—is the focus of the Bible. All major Bible truths, therefore, should be studied from this perspective.

Authorship of the Scriptures

The Bible's authority for faith and practice rises from its origin. Its writers viewed the Bible as distinct from other literature. They referred to it as "Holy Scriptures" (Rom. 1:2), "sacred writings" (2 Tim. 3:15, RSV), and the "oracles of God" (Rom. 3:2; Heb. 5:12).

The uniqueness of the Scriptures is based on their origin and source. The Bible writers claimed they did not originate their messages but received them from divine sources. It was through divine revelation that they were able "to see" the truths they passed on (see Isa. 1:1; Amos 1:1; Micah 1:1; Hab. 1:1; Jer. 38:21).

These writers pointed to the Holy Spirit as the One who communicated through the prophets to the people (Neh. 9:30; cf. Zech. 7:12). David said, "The Spirit of the Lord spoke by me, and His word was on my tongue" (2 Sam. 23:2). Ezekiel wrote, "the Spirit entered me," "the Spirit of the Lord fell upon me," "the Spirit took me up" (Eze. 2:2; 11:5, 24). And Micah testified, "I am full of power by the Spirit of the Lord" (Micah 3:8).

The New Testament recognized the role of the Holy Spirit in the production of the Old Testament. Jesus said that David was inspired by the Holy Spirit (Mark 12:36). Paul believed that the Holy Spirit spoke "through Isaiah" (Acts 28:25). Peter revealed that the Holy Spirit guided all the prophets, not just a few (1 Peter 1:10, 11; 2 Peter 1:21). At times the writer faded completely into the background, and only the real author—the Holy Spirit—was acknowledged: "The Holy Spirit says..." "By this the Holy Spirit indicates..." (Heb. 3:7; 9:8, RSV).

The New Testament writers recognized the Holy Spirit as the source of their own messages also. Paul explained, "Now the Spirit expressly says that in latter times some will depart from the faith" (1 Tim. 4:1). John spoke of being "in the Spirit on the Lord's day" (Rev. 1:10). And Jesus commissioned His apostles through the agency of the Holy Spirit (Acts 1:2; cf. Eph. 3:3-5).

So God, in the person of the Holy Spirit, has revealed Himself through the Holy Scriptures. He wrote them, not with His hands, but with other hands—about forty pairs—over a period of more than 1,500 years. And since God the Holy Spirit inspired the writers, God, then, is its author.

Inspiration of the Scriptures

"All Scripture," Paul says, "is given by inspiration of God" (2 Tim. 3:16). The Greek word *theopneustos*, translated as "inspiration," literally means, "God-breathed." God "breathed" truth into men's minds. They, in turn, expressed it in the words found in the Scriptures. Inspiration, therefore, is the process through which God communicates His eternal truth.

The Process of Inspiration. Divine revelation was given by inspiration of God to "holy men of God" who were "moved by the Holy Spirit" (2 Peter 1:21). These revelations were embodied in human language with all its limitations and imperfections, yet they remained God's testimony. God inspired men—not words.

Were the prophets as passive as tape recorders that replay exactly what is recorded? In some instances writers were commanded to express the exact words of God, but in most cases God instructed them to describe to the best of their ability what they saw or heard. In these latter cases, the writers used their own language, patterns, and style.

Paul observed that "the spirits of the prophets are subject to the prophets" (1 Cor. 14:32). Genuine inspiration does not obliterate the prophet's individuality, reason, integrity, or personality. To some degree, Moses and Aaron's relationship illustrates that between the Holy Spirit and the writer. God said to Moses, "I have made you as God to Pharaoh, and Aaron your brother shall be your prophet" (Ex. 7:1; cf. 4:15, 16). Moses informed Aaron of God's messages, and, in turn, Aaron communicated them in his own vocabulary and style to Pharaoh. Likewise, Bible writers conveyed divine commands, thoughts, and ideas in their own style of language. It is because God communicates in this way that the vocabulary of the different books of the Bible varied and reflects the education and culture of the writers.

The Bible "is not God's mode of thought and expression.... Men will often say such an expression is not like God. But God has not put Himself in words, in logic, in rhetoric, on trial in the Bible. The writers of the Bible were God's penmen, not His pen."[1] "Inspiration acts not on the man's words or his expressions but on the man himself, who, under the influence of the Holy Ghost, is imbued with thoughts. But the words receive the impress of the individual mind. The divine mind and will is combined with the human mind and will; thus the utterances of the man are the word of God."[2]

In one instance we have God speaking and writing the exact words, the Ten Commandments. They are of divine, not human composition (Ex. 20:1-17; 31:18; Deut. 10:4, 5), yet even these had to be expressed within the limits of human language.

The Bible, then, is divine truth expressed in human language. Imagine trying to teach quantum physics to a baby. This is the type of problem God faces in His attempt to communicate divine truths to sinful, limited humanity. It is our limitations that restrict what He can communicate to us.

A parallel exists between the incarnate Jesus and the Bible: Jesus was God and man combined, the divine and the human in one. So the Bible is the divine and human combined. As it was said of Christ, so it can be affirmed of the Bible, that "the Word became flesh and dwelt among us" (John 1:14). This divine-human combination makes the Bible unique among literary works.

Inspiration and the Writers. The Holy Spirit prepared certain persons to communicate divine truth. The Bible does not explain in detail how He qualified these individuals, but in some way He formed a union between the divine and the human agent.

Those who had a part in writing the Bible were not chosen because of natural talents. Nor did divine revelation necessarily convert the person or assure him of eternal life. Balaam proclaimed a divine message under inspiration while acting contrary to God's counsels (Numbers 22-24). David, who was used by the Holy Spirit, committed great crimes (cf. Psalm 51). All the writers of the Bible were men with sinful natures, needing God's grace daily (cf. Rom. 3:12).

The inspiration the biblical writers experienced was more than illumination or divine guidance, for these come to all who seek truth. In fact, the biblical writers sometimes wrote without fully understanding the divine message they communicated (1 Peter 1:10-12).

The writers' responses to the messages they bore were not uniform. Daniel and John said they were greatly perplexed over their writings (Dan. 8:27: Rev. 5:4), and 1 Peter 1:10 indicates that other writers searched for the meaning of their messages or those of others. Sometimes these individuals feared to proclaim an inspired message, and some even debated with God (Habakkuk 1; Jonah 1:1-3; 4:1-11).

The Method and Content of Revelation. Frequently, the Holy Spirit communicated divine knowledge by means of visions and dreams (Num. 12:6). Sometimes He spoke audibly or to the inner senses. God spoke to Samuel "in his ear" (1 Sam. 9:15). Zechariah received symbolic representations with explanations (Zechariah 4). The visions of heaven that Paul and John received were accompanied by oral instructions (2 Cor. 12:1-4, Revelation 4, 5). Ezekiel observed events transpiring in another location (Ezekiel 8). Some writers participated in their visions, performing certain functions as part of the vision itself (Revelation 10).

As to contents, to some the Spirit revealed events yet to occur (Daniel 2, 7, 8, 12). Other writers recorded historical events, either on the basis of personal experience or through selecting materials from existing historical records (Judges, 1 Samuel, 2 Chronicles, the Gospels, Acts).

Inspiration and History. The biblical assertion that "All Scripture is inspired by God" or "God-breathed," profitable and authoritative for moral and spiritual living (2 Tim. 3:15, 16, RSV; NIV) leaves no question about divine guidance in the selection process. Whether the information came from personal observation, oral or written sources, or direct revelation, it all came to the writer through the Holy Spirit's guidance. This guarantees the Bible's trustworthiness.

The Bible reveals God's plan in His dynamic interaction with the human race, not in a collection of abstract doctrines. His self-revelation stands rooted in real events that occurred in a definite time and place. The reliability of the historical accounts is extremely important because they form the framework of our understanding of God's character and His purpose for us. An accurate understanding leads to eternal life, but an incorrect view leads to confusion and death.

God commanded certain men to write a history of His dealings with Israel. These historical narratives, written from a viewpoint different from that of secular history, comprise an important part of the Bible (cf. Num. 33:1, 2; Joshua 24:25, 26; Eze. 24:2). They provide us with accurate, objective history, from a divine perspective. The Holy Spirit gave the writers special insights so that they could record events in the controversy between good and evil that demonstrate the character of God and guide people in their quest for salvation.

These historical incidents are "types" or "examples" "written for our admonition, on whom the ends of the ages have come" (1 Cor. 10:11). Paul says, "For everything that was written in the past was written to teach us, so that through endurance and the encouragement of the Scriptures we might have hope" (Rom. 15:4, NIV). The destruction of Sodom and Go-morrah serves as "an example" or warning (2 Peter 2:6; Jude 7). Abraham's experience of justification is an example for every believer (Rom. 4:1-25; James 2:14-22). Even Old Testament civil laws, filled with deep spiritual meaning, are written for our benefit today (1 Cor. 9:8, 9).

Luke mentions that he wrote his Gospel because he wanted to give an account of Jesus' life, "that you may know the certainty of those things in which you were instructed" (Luke 1:4). John's criterion for selecting which incidents of Jesus' life to include in his Gospel was "that you may believe that Jesus is the Christ, the Son of God, and that believing you may have life in His name" (John 20:31). God led the Bible writers to present history in a way that would guide us to salvation.

The biographies of biblical personalities provide another evidence of divine inspiration. These accounts carefully delineate both the weaknesses and strengths of their characters. They faithfully depict their sins, as well as successes.

No cover-up shrouds Noah's lack of self-control or Abraham's deception. The fits of temper that Moses, Paul, James, and John exhibited are recorded.

Bible history exposes the failures of Israel's wisest king and the frailties of the twelve patriarchs and twelve apostles. Scripture makes no excuses for them, nor does it attempt to minimize their guilt. It portrays them all for what they were and what they became or failed to become by the grace of God. Without divine inspiration no biographer could write such a perceptive analysis.

The Bible's writers viewed all the historical narratives it contains as true historical records, not as myths or symbols. Many contemporary skeptics reject the stories of Adam and Eve, Jonah, and the Flood. Yet Jesus accepted them as historically accurate and spiritually relevant (Matt. 12:39-41; 19:4-6; 24:37-39).

The Bible does not teach partial inspiration or degrees of inspiration. These theories are speculations that rob the Bible of its divine authority.

The Accuracy of the Scriptures. Just as Jesus "became flesh and dwelt among us" (John 1:14), so, in order for us to understand truth, the Bible was given in the language of humanity. The inspiration of the Scriptures guarantees their trustworthiness.

How far did God safeguard the transmission of the text beyond assuring that its message is valid and true? It is clear that while the ancient manuscripts vary, the essential truths have been preserved.[3] While it is quite possible that copyists and translators of the Bible made minor mistakes, evidence from biblical archeology reveals that many alleged errors were really misunderstandings on the part of scholars. Some of these problems arose because people were reading biblical history and customs through Western eyes. We must admit that humans only know in part—their insight into divine operations remains fragmentary.

Perceived discrepancies, then, should not erode confidence in the Scriptures; they often are products of our inaccurate perceptions rather than actual mistakes. Is God on trial when we come across a sentence or text that we cannot fully understand? We may never be able to explain every text in Scripture, but we do not have to. Fulfilled prophecies verify the Scripture's reliability.

In spite of attempts to destroy it, the Bible has been preserved with amazing, even miraculous, accuracy. Comparison of the Dead Sea scrolls with later manuscripts of the Old Testament demonstrates the carefulness with which it has been transmitted.[4] They confirm the trustworthiness and reliability of the Scriptures as the infallible revelation of God's will.

The Authority of the Scriptures

The Scriptures have divine authority because in them God speaks through the Holy Spirit. Thus the Bible is the written evidence for the Word of God. Where is the evidence for this claim, and what are implications for our lives and our pursuit of knowledge?

The Claims of the Scriptures. The Bible writers testify that their messages come directly from God. It is "the word of the Lord" that came to Jeremiah, Ezekiel, Hosea, and others (Jer. 1:1, 2, 9; Eze. 1:3; Hosea 1:1; Joel 1:1; Jonah 1:1). As messengers of the Lord (Haggai 1:13; 2 Chron. 36:16), God's prophets were commanded to speak in His name, saying, "Thus says the Lord" (Eze. 2:4; cf. Isa. 7:7) His words constitute their divine credentials and authority.

At times the human agent God is using recedes into the background. Matthew alludes to the authority behind the Old Testament prophet he quotes with the words, "all this was done that it might be fulfilled which was spoken by the Lord through the prophet" (Matt. 1:22). He sees the Lord as the direct agency, the authority; the prophet is the indirect agency.

Peter classifies Paul's writings as Scripture (2 Peter 3:15, 16). And Paul testifies regarding what he wrote, "I did not receive it from man, nor was I taught it, but it came through a revelation of Jesus Christ" (Gal. 1:12, RSV). New Testament writers accepted the words of Christ as Scripture and regarded them as having the same authority as the Old Testament writings (1 Tim. 5:18; Luke 10:7).

Jesus and the Authority of Scripture. Throughout His ministry, Jesus stressed the authority of the Scriptures. When tempted by Satan or battling His opponents, "It is written" was His defense and offense (Matt. 4:4, 7, 10; Luke 20:17). "Man shall not live by bread alone," He said, "but by every word that proceeds from the mouth of God" (Matt. 4:4). When asked how one could enter into eternal life, He answered, "What is written in the law? What is your reading of it?" (Luke 10:26).

Jesus placed the Bible above human traditions and opinions. He rebuked the Jews for setting aside the authority of the Scriptures (Mark 7:7-9) and appealed to them to study the Scriptures more carefully, saying, "Haven't you ever read what the Scriptures say?" (Matt. 21:42, TEV; cf. Mark 12:10, 26).

He strongly believed in the authority of the prophetic word and revealed that it pointed to Himself. The Scriptures, He said, "testify of me." "If you believe Moses, you would believe Me; for he wrote about Me" (John 5:39, 46). Jesus' most convincing assertion that He had a divine mission issued from His fulfillment of Old Testament prophecy (Luke 24:25-27).

So without reservation Christ accepted the Holy Scriptures as the authoritative revelation of God's will for the human race. He saw the Scriptures as a body of truth, an objective revelation, given to lead humanity out of the darkness of faulty traditions and myths into the true light of a saving knowledge.

The Holy Spirit and the Authority of Scripture. During Jesus' life the religious leaders and the careless crowd did not discern His true identity. Some felt He was a prophet like John the Baptist, Elijah, or Jeremiah—merely a man. When Peter confessed that Jesus was "the Christ, the Son of the living God," Jesus pointed out that it was divine illumination that made possible his confession (Matt. 16:13-17). Paul emphasizes this truth: "No one can say that Jesus is Lord except by the Holy Spirit" (1 Cor. 12:3).

So it is with the written Word of God. Without the Holy Spirit's illumination of our minds we could never correctly understand the Bible or even acknowledge it as God's authoritative will.[5] Because "no one knows the things of God except the Spirit of God" (1 Cor. 2:11), it follows that "the natural man does not receive the things of the Spirit of God, for they are foolishness to him; nor can he know them, because they are spiritually discerned" (1 Cor. 2:14). Consequently, "the message of the cross is foolishness to those who are perishing" (1 Cor. 1:18).

Only with the aid of the Holy Spirit, who searches "the deep things of God" (1 Cor. 2:10), can one become convicted of the authority of the Bible as a revelation of God and His will. It is then that the cross becomes "the power of God" (1 Cor. 1:18) and one can join Paul's testimony, "Now we have received, not the spirit of the world, but the Spirit who is from God, that we might know the things that have been freely given to us by God" (1 Cor. 2:12).

The Holy Scriptures and the Holy Spirit can never be separated. The Holy Spirit is both the author and the revealer of biblical truth.

The Scriptures' authority in our lives increases or decreases in accord with our concept of inspiration. If we perceive the Bible as being merely a collection of human testimonies or if the authority we grant it in some way depends on how it moves our feelings or emotions, we sap its authority in our lives. But when we discern God's voice speaking through the writers, no matter how weak and human they may have been, the Scriptures become the absolute authority in matters of doctrine, reproof, correction, and instruction in righteousness (2 Tim. 3:16).

The Scope of Scriptural Authority. Contradictions between Scripture and science are frequently the result of speculation. When we cannot harmonize science with Scripture, it is because we have "an imperfect comprehension of either science or revelation...but rightly understood, they are in perfect harmony."[6]

All human wisdom must be subject to the authority of Scripture. The Bible truths are the norm by which all other ideas must be tested. Judging the Word of God by finite human standards is like trying to measure the stars with a yardstick. The Bible must not be subjected to human norms. It is superior to all human wisdom and literature. Rather than our judging the Bible, all will be judged by it, for it is the standard of character and test of all experience and thought.

Finally, the Scriptures retain authority even over the gifts that come from the Holy Spirit, including guidance through the gift of prophecy or speaking in tongues (1 Corinthians 12: 14:1; Eph. 4:7-16). The gifts of the Spirit do not supercede the Bible; indeed, they must be tested by the Bible, and if not in accord with it, they must be discarded as not genuine. "To the law and to the testimony! If they do not speak according to this word, it is because there is no light in them" (Isa. 8:20). (See chapter 18 of this book.)

The Unity of the Scriptures

A superficial reading of the Scriptures will yield a superficial understanding of it. Read in such a way, the Bible may appear to be a jumble of stories, sermons, and history. Yet, those open to the illumination of the Spirit of God, those willing to search for the hidden truths with patience and much prayer, discover that the Bible evidences an underlying unity in what it teaches about the principles of salvation. The Bible is not monotonously uniform. Rather, it comprises a rich and colorful diversity of harmonious testimonies of rare and distinct beauty. And because of its variety of perspectives it is better able to meet human needs through all times.

God has not revealed Himself to humanity in a continuous chain of unbroken utterances, but little by little, through successive generations. Whether penned by Moses in a Midian field or Paul in a Roman prison, its books reveal the same Spirit-inspired communication. An understanding of this "progressive revelation" contributes to an understanding of the Bible and its unity.

Though written generations apart, the truths of the Old and New Testaments remain inseparable; they do not contradict each other. The two testaments are one, as God is one. The Old Testament, through prophecies and symbols, reveals the gospel of the Saviour to come; the New Testament, through the life of Jesus, reveals the Saviour who came—the gospel in reality. Both reveal the same God. The Old Testament serves as foundation for the New. It provides the key to unlock the New, while the New explains the mysteries of the Old.

God graciously calls us to become acquainted with Him by searching His Word. In it we can find the rich blessing of the assurance of our salvation. We can discover for ourselves that the Scriptures are "profitable for doctrine, for reproof, for correction, for instruction in righteousness." Through them we "may be complete, thoroughly equipped for every good work" (2 Tim. 3:16, 17).

References

1. Ellen G. White, *Selected Messages* (Washington, D.C.: Review and Herald, 1958), book 1, p. 21.

2. *Ibid.*

3. For a reason for some variant readings, see White, *Early Writings* (Washington, D.C.: Review and Herald, 1945), pp. 220, 221.

4. See Siegfried H. Horn, *The Spade Confirms the Book*, rev. ed. (Washington, D.C.: Review and Herald, 1980).

5. For the general Seventh-day Adventist understanding of biblical interpretation, see General Conference Committee, Report of the General Conference Committee Annual Council, Oct. 12, 1986, "Methods of Bible Study," Distributed by the Biblical Research Institute, General Conference of Seventh-day Adventists, 6840 Eastern Ave., N.W., Washington, D.C. 20012. See also *A Symposium on Biblical Hermeneutics*, ed. G. M. Hyde (Washington, D.C.: Review and Herald, 1974); Gerhard F. Hasel, *Understanding the Living Word of God* (Mountain View, CA: Pacific Press, 1980). Cf. P. Gerard Damsteegt, "Interpreting the Bible" (Paper prepared for the Far Eastern Division Biblical Research Committee Meeting, Singapore, May 1986).

6. White, *The Story of Patriarchs and Prophets* (Mountain View, CA: Pacific Press, 1958), p. 114.

The Godhead

2

There is one God: Father, Son, and Holy Spirit, a unity of three co-eternal Persons. God is immortal, all-powerful, all-knowing, above all, and ever present. He is infinite and beyond human comprehension, yet known through His self-revelation. He is forever worthy of worship, adoration, and service by the whole creation. (Deut. 6:4; Matt. 28:19; 2 Cor. 13:14; Eph. 4:4-6; 1 Pet. 1:2; 1 Tim. 1:17; Rev. 14:7.)

AT CALVARY ALMOST EVERYONE REJECTED JESUS. Only a few recognized who Jesus really was—among them, the dying thief who called Him Lord (Luke 23:42) and the Roman soldier who said, "Truly this Man was the Son of God!" (Mark 15:39).

When John wrote, "He came unto His own, and His own did not receive Him" (John 1:11), he was thinking not merely of the crowd at the cross, or even of Israel, but of every generation that has lived. Except for a handful, all humanity, like that raucous crowd at Calvary, has failed to recognize in Jesus their God and Saviour. This failure—humanity's greatest and most tragic— shows that humanity's knowledge of God is radically deficient.

Knowledge of God

The many theories attempting to explain God, and the many arguments for and against His existence, show that human wisdom cannot penetrate the divine. Depending on human wisdom alone to learn about God is like using a magnifying glass to study the constellations. Hence, to many, God's wisdom is a "hidden wisdom" (1 Cor. 2:7). To them, God is a mystery. Paul wrote, "None of the rulers of this age knew; for had they known, they would not have crucified the Lord of glory" (1 Cor. 2:8).

One of the most basic commandments of Scripture is to love "God with all your heart, with all your soul, and with all your mind" (Matt. 22:37; cf. Deut. 6:5). We cannot love someone we know nothing about, yet we cannot by searching find out the deep things of God (Job 11:7). How then can we come to know and love the Creator?

God Can Be Known. Realizing the human predicament, God, in His love and compassion, reached out to us through the Bible. It reveals that "Christianity is not a record of a man's quest for God; it is the product of God's revelation of Himself and His purposes to man."[1] This self-revelation is designed to bridge the gulf between a rebellious world and a caring God.

The manifestation of God's greatest love came through His supreme revelation, Jesus Christ, His Son. Through Jesus we can know the Father. As John states, "The Son of God has come and has given us an understanding, that we may know Him who is true" (1 John 5:20).

And Jesus said, "This is eternal life, that they may know You, the only true God, and Jesus Christ whom You have sent" (John 17:3).

This is good news. Although it is impossible to know God completely, the Scriptures afford a practical knowledge of Him that is sufficient for us to enter into a saving relationship with Him.

Obtaining a Knowledge of God. Unlike other knowledge, the knowledge of God is as much a matter of the heart as it is of the brain. It involves the whole person, not just the intellect. There must be an openness to the Holy Spirit and a willingness to do God's will (John 7:17; cf. Matt. 11:27). Jesus said, "Blessed are the pure in heart, for they shall see God" (Matt. 5:8).

Unbelievers, therefore, cannot understand God. Paul exclaimed, "Where is the wise man? Where is the scholar? Where is the philosopher of this age? Has not God made foolish the wisdom of the world? For since in the wisdom of God the world through its wisdom did not know him, God was pleased through the foolishness of what was preached to save those who believe" (1 Cor. 1:20, 21, NIV).

The way we learn to know God from the Bible differs from all other methods of acquiring knowledge. We cannot place ourselves above God and treat Him as an object to be analyzed and quantified. In our search for a knowledge of God we must submit to the authority of His self-revelation—the Bible. Since the Bible is its own interpreter, we must subject ourselves to the principles and methods it provides. Without these biblical guidelines we cannot know God.

Why did so many of the people of Jesus' day fail to see God's self-revelation in Jesus? Because they refused to subject themselves to the guidance of the Holy Spirit through the Scriptures, they misinterpreted God's message and crucified their Saviour. Their problem was not one of intellect. It was their closed hearts that darkened their minds, resulting in eternal loss.

The Existence of God

There are two major sources of evidence for the existence of God—the book of nature and the Scriptures.

Evidence From Creation. Everyone can learn of God through nature and human experience. David wrote, "The heavens declare the glory of God; and the firmament shows His handiwork" (Ps. 19:1). John maintained that God's revelation, including nature, enlightens everyone (John 1:9). And Paul claimed, "Since the creation of the world His invisible attributes are clearly seen, being understood by the things that are made" (Rom. 1:20).

Human behavior also gives evidence for God's existence. In the Athenian worship of the "unknown God," Paul saw evidence of a belief in God. Said he, "The One whom you worship without knowing, Him I proclaim to you" (Acts 17:23). Paul also said the behavior of non-Christians revealed the witness of "their conscience" and showed that God's law is written "in their hearts" (Rom. 2:14, 15). This intuition that God exists is found even among those who have no access to the Bible. This general revelation of God led to a number of classical rational arguments for the existence of God.[2]

Evidence From Scripture. The Bible does not prove God's existence. It assumes it. Its opening text declares, "In the beginning God created the heavens and the earth" (Gen. 1:1). The Bible describes God as the Creator, Sustainer, and Ruler of all creation. God's revelation through creation is so powerful that there is no excuse for atheism, which arises from a suppression of divine truth or from a mind that refuses to acknowledge the evidence that God exists (Ps. 14:1; Rom 1:18-22, 28).

There are enough evidences for God's existence to convince anyone who seriously tries to discover the truth about Him. Yet faith is a prerequisite, for "without faith it is impossible to please Him, for he who comes to God must believe that He is, and that He is a rewarder of those who diligently seek Him" (Heb. 11:6).

Faith in God, however, is not blind. It is based on sufficient evidence found both in God's revelations through the Scriptures and through nature.

The God of the Scriptures

The Bible reveals God's essential qualities through His names, activities, and attributes.

God's Names. At the time the Scriptures were written, names were important, as they still are in the Near East and Orient. There, a name is considered to reveal the character of the bearer—his true nature and identity. The importance of God's names, disclosing His nature, character, and qualities, are revealed in His command, "You shall not take the name of the Lord your God in vain" (Ex. 20:7). David sang: "Praise to the name of the Lord Most High" (Ps. 7:17). "Holy and awesome is His name" (Ps. 111:9) "Let them praise the name of the Lord, for His name alone is exalted" (Ps. 148:13).

The Hebrew names *El* and *Elohim* ("God") reveal God's divine power. They depict God as the strong and mighty One, the God of Creation (Gen. 1:1; Ex. 20:2; Dan. 9:4). *Elyon* ("Most High") and *El Elyon* ("God Most High") focus on His exalted status (Gen: 14:18-20; Isa. 14:14). *Adonai* ("Lord") pictures God as Almighty Ruler (Isa. 6:1; Ps. 35:23). These names emphasize the majestic and transcendent character of God.

Other names reveal God's willingness to enter into a relationship with people. *Shaddai* ("Almighty") and *El Shaddai* ("God Almighty") portray the Almighty God, the source of blessing and comfort (Ex. 6:3; Ps. 91:1). The name *Yahweh*,[3] translated *Jehovah* or LORD, stresses God's covenant faithfulness and grace (Ex. 15:2, 3; Hosea 12:5, 6). In Exodus 3:14, Yahweh describes Himself as "I am who I am," or "I shall be what I shall be," indicating His unchangeable relation to His people. On occasions God even revealed Himself more intimately as "Father" (Deut. 32:6; Isa. 63:16; Jer. 31:9; Mal. 2:10), calling Israel "My Son, and My firstborn" (Ex. 4:22; cf. Deut. 32:19).

Except for *Father*, the New Testament names for God carry equivalent meanings to those of the Old Testament. In the New Testament, Jesus used *Father* to bring us into a close and personal relationship with God (Matt. 6:9; Mark 14:36; cf. Rom. 8:15; Gal. 4:6).

God's Activities. Bible writers spend more time describing God's activities than His being. He is introduced as Creator (Gen 1:1; Ps. 24: 1, 2), Upholder of the world (Heb. 1:30), and Redeemer and Saviour (Deut. 5:6; 2 Cor. 5:19), carrying the burden for humanity's ultimate destiny. He makes plans (Isa. 46:11), predictions (Isa. 46:10), and promises (Deut. 15:6; 2 Peter 3:9). He forgives sins (Ex. 34:7) and consequently deserves our worship

(Rev. 14:6, 7). Ultimately, the Scriptures reveal God as Ruler, "the King eternal, immortal, invisible, the only God" (1 Tim. 1:17, NIV). His actions confirm that He is a personal God.

God's Attributes. The writers of Scripture provide additional information on the essence of God through testimonies about His divine attributes.

God's incommunicable attributes comprise aspects of His divine nature not given to created beings. God is self-existent, for He has "life in Himself" (John 5:26). He is independent in will (Eph. 1:5) and in power (Ps. 115:3). He is omniscient, knowing everything (Job 37:16; Ps. 139:1-18; 147:5; 1 John 3:20), because, as Alpha and Omega (Rev. 1:8), He knows the end from the beginning (Isa. 46:9-11).

God is omnipresent (Ps. 139:7-12; Heb. 4:13), transcending all space. Yet He is fully present in every part of space. He is eternal (Ps. 90:2; Rev. 1:8), exceeding the limits of time, yet is fully present in every moment of time.

God is all-powerful, omnipotent. That nothing is impossible to Him assures us that He accomplishes whatever he purposes (Dan. 4:17, 25, 35; Matt. 19:26; Rev. 19:6). He is immutable—or unchangeable—because He is perfect. He says, "I am the Lord, I do not change" (Mal. 3:6; see Ps. 33:11, James 1:17). Since, in a sense, these attributes define God, they are incommunicable.

God's communicable attributes flow from His loving concern for humanity. They include love (Rom. 5:8), grace (Rom. 3:24), mercy (Ps. 145:9), patience (2 Peter 3:15, NIV), holiness (Ps. 99:9), righteousness (Ezra 9:15; John 17:25), justice (Rev. 22:12), and truth (1 John 5:20). These gifts come only with the Giver Himself.

The Sovereignty of God

The Scriptures clearly teach God's sovereignty. "He does according to His will...No one can restrain His hand" (Dan. 4:35). "For You created all things, and by Your will they exist and were created" (Rev. 4:11). "Whatever the Lord pleases He does, in heaven and in earth" (Ps. 135:6). So Solomon could say, "The king's heart is in the hand of the Lord, like the rivers of water; He turns it wherever He wishes" (Prov. 21:1). Paul, aware of God's sovereignty, wrote, "I will return again to you, God willing" (Acts 18:21; see Rom 15:32), while James admonished, "You ought to say, 'If the Lord wills'" (James 4:15).

Predestination and Human Freedom. The Bible reveals God's full control over the world. He "predestined" people "to be conformed to the image of His Son" (Rom. 8:29, 30), to be adopted as His children, and to obtain an inheritance (Eph. 1:4, 5, 11, 12). What does such sovereignty imply for human freedom?

The verb *to predestinate* means "to determine beforehand." Some assume these passages teach that God arbitrarily elects some to salvation and others to damnation, irrespective of their own choice. But study of the context of these passages shows that Paul does not speak about God's capriciously excluding anyone.

The thrust of these texts is *inclusive*. The Bible clearly states that God "desires all men to be saved and to come to the knowledge of the truth" (1 Tim. 2:4). He is "not willing that any should perish but that all should come to repentance" (2 Peter 3:9). There is no evidence that God has decreed that some persons should be lost; such a decree would deny Calvary, where Jesus dies for everyone. The *whoever* in the text, "For God so loved the world that He gave His only begotten Son, that *whoever* believes in Him should not perish but have everlasting life" (John 3:16), means that anyone can be saved.

"That man's free will is the determining factor in his personal destiny is evident from the fact that God continually presents the results of obedience and disobedience, and urges the sinner to choose obedience and life (Deut. 30:19; Joshua 24:15; Isa. 1:16, 20; Rev. 22:17); and from the fact that it is possible for the believer, having once been a recipient of grace, to fall away and be lost (1 Cor. 9:27; Gal. 5:4; Heb. 6:4-6; 10:29).

"God may foresee each individual choice that will be made, but His foreknowledge does not determine what that choice shall be....Bible predestination consists in the effective purpose of God that all who choose to believe in Christ shall be saved (John 1:12; Eph. 1:4-10)."[4]

Then what does Scripture mean when it says that God loved Jacob and hated Esau (Rom. 9:13) and that He hardened Pharaoh's heart (vv. 17, 18; cf. vv. 15, 16; Ex. 9:16; 4:21)? The context of these texts shows that Paul's concern is mission and not salvation. Redemption is available to anyone—but God chooses certain persons for special assignments. Salvation was equally available to Jacob and Esau, but God chose Jacob, not Esau, to be the line through whom He would take the message of salvation to the world. God exercises sovereignty in His mission strategy.

When Scripture says that God hardened Pharaoh's heart, it is merely crediting Him with doing what He allows and not implying that He ordains it. Pharaoh's negative response to God's call actually illustrates God's respect for his freedom to choose.

Foreknowledge and Human Freedom. Some believe that God relates to persons without knowing their choices until they are made—that God knows certain future events such as the Second Advent, the millennium, and the restoration of the earth but has no idea who will be saved. They feel that God's dynamic relationship with the human race would be in jeopardy if He knew everything that would transpire from eternity to eternity. Some suggest that He would be bored if He knew the end from the beginning.

But God's knowledge about what individuals will do does not interfere with what they actually choose to do any more than a historian's knowledge of what people did in the past interferes with their actions. Just as a camera records a scene but does not change it, foreknowledge looks into the future without altering it. The foreknowledge of the Godhead never violates human freedom.

Dynamics Within the Godhead

Is there only one God? What of Christ and the Holy Spirit?

The Oneness of God. In contrast to the heathen of surrounding nations, Israel believed there was only one God (Deut. 4:35; 6:4; Isa. 45:5; Zech. 14:9). The New Testament makes the same emphasis on the unity of God (Mark 12:29-32; John 17:3; 1 Cor. 8:4-6; Eph. 4:4-6; 1 Tim. 2:5). This monotheistic emphasis does not contradict the Christian concept of the triune God or Trinity—Father, Son, and Holy Spirit; rather, it affirms that there is no pantheon of various deities.

The Plurality Within the Godhead. Although the Old Testament does not explicitly teach that God is triune, it alludes to a plurality within the Godhead. At times God employs plural pronouns such as: "Let Us make man in Our image" (Gen. 1:26); "Behold the man has become like one of Us" (Gen. 3:22); "Come, let Us go down" (Gen. 11:7). At times the Angel of the Lord is identified with God. Appearing to Moses, the Angel of the Lord said, "I am the God of your Father—the God of Abraham, the God of Isaac, and the God of Jacob" (Ex. 3:6).

Various references distinguish the Spirit of God from God. In the Creation story, "the Spirit of God was hovering over the face of the waters" (Gen. 1:2). Some texts not only refer to the Spirit but include a third person in God's work of redemption: "And now the Lord God [the Father] and His Spirit [the Holy Spirit] have sent Me [the Son of God]" (Isa. 48:16); "I [the Father] have put My Spirit upon Him [the Messiah]; He will bring forth justice to the Gentiles" (Isa. 42:1).

The Relationship Within the Godhead. The first advent of Christ gives us a much clearer insight into the triune God. John's Gospel reveals that the Godhead consists of God the Father (see chapter 3 of this book), God the Son (chapter 4), and God the Holy Spirit (chapter 5)—a unity of three co-eternal persons having a unique and mysterious relationship.

1. A *loving relationship*. When Christ cried out, "My God, My God, why have You forsaken Me?" (Mark 15:34), He was suffering from the estrangement from His Father that sin had caused. Sin broke humanity's original relationship with God (Gen. 3:6-10; Isa.59:2). In His last hours, Jesus, the One who knew no sin, became sin for us. In taking our sin, our place, He experienced the separation from God that was our lot—and died in consequence.

Sinners will never comprehend what Jesus' death meant to the Godhead. From eternity He had been with His Father and the Spirit. They had lived as coeternal, coexistent in utter self-giving and love for one another. To be together for so long bespeaks the perfect, absolute love that existed within the Godhead. "God is love" (1 John 4:8) means that each so lived for the others that they experienced complete fulfillment and happiness.

Love is defined in 1 Corinthians 13. Some may wonder how the qualities of longsuffering or patience would apply within the Godhead, who had a perfect, loving relationship. Patience was first needed when dealing with rebel angels and later with wayward humans.

There is no distance between the persons of the triune God. All three are divine, yet they share their divine powers and qualities. In human organizations final authority rests in one person—a president, king, or prime minister. In the Godhead, final authority resides in all three members.

While the Godhead is not one in person, God is one in purpose, mind, and character. This oneness does not obliterate the distinct personalities of the Father, the Son, and the Holy Spirit. Nor does the separateness of personalities within the Deity destroy the monotheistic thrust of Scripture that the Father, Son, and Holy Spirit are *one God*.

2. A *working relationship*. Within the Godhead an economy of function exists. God does not unnecessarily duplicate work. Order is the first law of heaven, and God works in orderly ways. This orderliness issues from and preserves the union within the Godhead. The Father seems to act as source, the Son as mediator, and the Spirit as actualizer or applier.

The incarnation beautifully demonstrated the working relationship of the three persons of the Godhead. The Father gave His Son, Christ gave Himself, and the Spirit gave Jesus birth (John 3:16; Matt. 1:18, 20). The angel's testimony to Mary clearly indicates the activities of all three in the mystery of God becoming man. "The Holy Spirit will come upon you, and the power of the Highest will overshadow you; therefore, also, that Holy One who is to be born will be called the Son of God" (Luke 1:35).

Each member of the Godhead was present at the baptism of Christ: the Father giving encouragement (Matt. 3:17), Christ giving Himself to be baptized as our example (Matt. 3:13-15), and the Spirit giving Himself to Jesus to empower Him (Luke 3:21, 22).

Toward the end of His earthly life Jesus promised to send the Holy Spirit as counselor or helper (John 14:16). Hours later, hanging on the cross, Jesus cried out to His Father, "My God, My God, why have You forsaken Me?" (Matt. 27:46). In those climactic moments for salvation history the Father, Son, and Holy Spirit were all part of the picture.

Today the Father and the Son reach out to us through the Holy Spirit. Jesus said, "When the Helper comes, whom I shall send to you from the Father, He will testify of Me" (John 15:26). The Father and Son send the Spirit to reveal Christ to each person. The great burden of the Trinity is to bring God and a knowledge of Christ to everyone (John 17:3) and to make Jesus present and real (Matt. 28:20; cf. Heb. 13:5). Believers are elected to salvation, Peter said, "according to the foreknowledge of God the Father, in sanctification of the spirit, for obedience and sprinkling of the blood of Jesus Christ" (1 Peter 1:2).

The apostolic benediction includes all three persons of the Godhead. "The grace of the Lord Jesus Christ, and the love of God, and the communion of the Holy Spirit be with you all" (2 Cor. 13:14). Christ heads the list. God's point of contact with humanity was and is through Jesus Christ—the God who became man. Though all three members of the Trinity work together to save, only Jesus lived as a man, died as a man, and became our Saviour (John 6:47; Matt. 1:21; Acts 4:12). But because "God was in Christ reconciling the world to Himself" (2 Cor. 5:19), God could also be designated as our Saviour (cf. Titus 3:4), for He saved us through Christ the Saviour (Eph. 5:23; Phil. 3:20; cf. Titus 3:6).

In the economy of function, different members of the Godhead perform distinct tasks in saving man. The work of the Holy Spirit does not add anything to the adequacy of the sacrifice that Jesus Christ made at the cross. Through the Holy Spirit the objective atonement at the cross is subjectively applied as the Christ of the atonement is brought within. Thus Paul speaks of "Christ in you, the hope of glory" (Col. 1:27).

Focus on Salvation

The early church baptized believers in the name of the Father, Son, and Holy Spirit (Matt. 28:19). But since it was through Jesus that God's love and purpose were revealed, the Bible focuses on Him. He is the hope foreshadowed in the Old Testament sacrifices and festivals. He is the One who occupies center stage in the Gospels. He is the Good News proclaimed by the disciples in sermons and writings—the Blessed Hope. The Old Testament looks forward to His coming; the New Testament reports His first advent and looks forward to His return.

Christ, the mediator between God and us, thus unites us to the Godhead. Jesus is "the way, the truth, and the life" (John 14:6). The good news is centered in a Person and not merely a practice. It has to do with a relationship, not just rules—for Christianity is Christ. We find Him the core, content, and context for all truth and life.

Looking at the cross, we gaze into the heart of God. On that instrument of torture He poured out His love for us. Through Christ the love of the Godhead fills our aching, empty hearts. Jesus hung there as God's gift and our substitute. At Calvary God descended to earth's lowest point to meet us; but it is the highest place where we can go. When we go to Calvary we have ascended as high as we can toward God.

At the cross the Trinity made a full revelation of unselfishness. There was our most complete revelation of God. Christ became man to die for the race. He valued selflessness more than self-existence. There Christ became our "righteousness and sanctification and redemption" (1 Cor. 1:30). Whatever value or meaning we have or ever will have comes from His sacrifice on that cross.

The only true God is the God of the cross. Christ unveiled to the universe the Godhead's infinite love and saving power; He revealed a triune God who was willing to go through the agony of separation because of unconditional love for a rebel planet. From this cross God proclaims His loving invitation to us: Be reconciled, "and the peace of God, which transcends all understanding, will guard your hearts and your minds in Christ Jesus" (Phil. 4:7, NIV).

References

1. Gordon R. Lewis, *Decide for Yourself: A Theological Workbook* (Downers Grove, IL: Inter Varsity Press, 1978), p. 15.

2. They are the cosmological, teleological, ontological, anthropological, and religion arguments. See, e.g., T. H. Jemison, *Christian Beliefs* (Mountain View, CA: Pacific Press, 1959), p. 72; Richard Rice, *The Reign of God* (Berrien Springs, MI: Andrews University Press, 1985), pp. 53-56. These arguments do not prove God's existence but show that there is a strong possibility that God exists. Ultimately, however, belief in God's existence is based on faith.

3. *Yahweh* is "a conjectural transliteration" of the sacred name of God in the Old Testament (Ex. 3:14, 15; 6:3). The original Hebrew contained the four consonants YHWH. In time, out of fear of profaning God's name, the Jews refused to read this name aloud. Instead, wherever YHWH appeared, they would read the word *Adonai*. In the seventh or eighth century A.D., when vowels were added to the Hebrew words, the Masoretes supplied the vowels of Adonai to the consonants YHWH. The combination produced the

word *Jehovah*, which is used in the KJV. Other translations prefer the word *Yahweh* (Jerusalem Bible) or LORD (RSV, NIV, NKJV). (See Siegfried H. Horn, *Seventh-day Adventist Bible Dictionary*, Don F. Neufeld, ed., rev. ed., [Washington, D.C.: Review and Herald, 1979] pp. 1192, 1193).

4. "Predestination," *Seventh-day Adventist Encyclopedia*, Don F. Neufeld, ed., rev. ed., (Washington, D.C.: Review and Herald, 1976), p. 1144.

God the Father

3

God the eternal Father is the Creator, Source, Sustainer, and Sovereign of all creation. He is just and holy, merciful and gracious, slow to anger, and abounding in steadfast love and faithfulness. The qualities and powers exhibited in the Son and the Holy Spirit are also revelations of the Father. (Gen. 1:1; Rev. 4:11; 1 Cor. 15:28; John 3:16; 1 John 4:8; 1 Tim. 1:17; Ex. 34:6, 7; John 14:9.)

THE GREAT DAY OF JUDGMENT BEGINS. Fiery thrones with burning wheels move into place. The Ancient of Days takes His seat. Majestic in appearance, He presides over the court. His awesome presence pervades the vast courtroom audience. A multitude of witnesses stand before Him. The judgment is set, the books are opened, and the examination of the record of human lives begins (Dan. 7:9, 10).

The entire universe has been waiting for this moment. God the Father will execute His justice against all wickedness. The sentence is given: "A judgment was made in favor of the saints" (Dan. 7:22). Joyful praises and thanksgiving reverberate across heaven. God's character is seen in all its glory, and His marvelous name is vindicated throughout the universe.

Views of the Father

God the Father is frequently misunderstood. Many are aware of Christ's mission to earth for the human race and of the Holy Spirit's role within the individual, but what has the Father to do with us? Is He, in contrast to the gracious Son and Spirit, totally removed from our world, the absentee Landlord, the unmoved First Cause?

Or is He, as some think of Him, the "Old Testament God"—a God of vengeance, characterized by the dictum "an eye for an eye, and a tooth for a tooth" (Matt. 5:38; cf. Ex. 21:24); an exacting God who requires perfect works—or else! A God who stands in utter contrast to the New Testament's portrayal of a loving God who stresses turning the other cheek and going the second mile (Matt. 5:39-41).

God the Father in the Old Testament

The unity of the Old and New Testaments and of their common plan of redemption is revealed by the fact that it is the same God who speaks and acts in both Testaments for the salvation of His people. "God, who at various times and in different ways spoke in time past to the fathers by the prophets, has in these last days spoken to us by His Son, whom He has appointed heir of all things, through whom also He made the worlds" (Heb. 1:1, 2). Although the Old Testament alludes to the Persons of the Godhead, it doesn't distinguish Them. But the New Testament makes clear that Christ, God the Son, was the active agent in Creation (John 1:1-3, 14; Col. 1:16) and that He was the God who led Israel out of Egypt (1 Cor. 10:1-4; Ex. 3:14; John 8:58). What the New Testament says of Christ's role in Creation and the Exodus suggests that even the Old Testament often conveys to us its portrait of God the Father through the agency of the Son. "God was in Christ reconciling the world to Himself" (2 Cor. 5:19). The Old Testament describes the Father in the following terms:

A God of Mercy. No sinful human being has ever seen God (Ex. 33:20). We have no photograph of His features. God demonstrated His character by His gracious acts and by the word picture He proclaimed before Moses: "The Lord, the Lord God, merciful and gracious, long-suffering, and abounding in goodness and truth, keeping mercy for thousands, forgiving iniquity and transgression and sin, by no means clearing the guilty, visiting the iniquity of the fathers upon the children and the children's children to the third and fourth generation" (Ex. 34:6, 7; cf. Heb. 10:26, 27). Yet mercy does not blindly pardon but is guided by the principle of justice. Those who reject His mercy reap His punishment on iniquity.

At Sinai God expressed His desire to be Israel's friend—to be with them. He said to Moses, "Let them make Me a sanctuary, that I may dwell among them" (Ex. 25:8). Because it was God's earthly dwelling place, this sanctuary became the focal point of Israel's religious experience.

A Covenant God. Eager to establish lasting relations, God made solemn covenants with people such as Noah (Gen. 9:1-17) and Abraham (Gen. 12:1-3, 7; 13:14-17; 15:1, 5, 6; 17:1-8; 22:15-18—see chapter 7 in this book). These covenants reveal a personal, loving God interested in His people's concerns. To Noah He gave assurance of regular seasons (Gen. 8:22) and that there never would be another worldwide flood (Gen 9:11); to Abraham He promised numerous descendants (Gen. 15:5-7) and a land wherein he and his descendants could dwell (Gen. 15:18; 17:8).

A Redeemer God. As God of the Exodus, He miraculously led a nation of slaves to liberty. This great redemptive act is the backdrop for the entire Old Testament and an example of His longing to be our Redeemer. God is not a distant, detached, uninterested person but One very much involved in our affairs.

The Psalms particularly were inspired by the depth of God's loving involvement: "When I consider Your heavens, the work of Your fingers, the moon and the stars, which You have ordained, what is man that You are mindful of him, and the son of man that You visit him?" (Ps. 8:3, 4). "I will love You, O Lord, my strength. The Lord is my rock and my fortress and my deliverer; My God, my strength, in whom I will trust; My shield and the horn of my salvation, my stronghold" (Ps. 18:1, 2). "For He has not despised nor abhorred the affliction of the afflicted" (Ps. 22:24).

A God of Refuge. David saw God as One in whom we can find refuge— very much like the six Israelite cities of refuge, which harbored innocent fugitives. The Psalms' recurrent theme of "refuge" pictures both Christ and the Father. The Godhead was a refuge. "For in the time of trouble He shall hide me in his pavilion; in the secret place of His tabernacle He shall hide me; He shall set me high upon a rock" (Ps. 27:5). "God is our refuge and strength, a very present help in trouble" (Ps. 46:1). "As the mountains surround Jerusalem, so the Lord surrounds His people from this time forth and forever" (Ps. 125:2).

The psalmist expressed a longing for more of his God: "As the deer pants for the water brooks, so pants my soul for You, O God. My soul thirsts for God, for the living God" (Ps.42: 1, 2). From experience, David testified, "Cast your burden on the Lord, and He shall sustain you; He shall never permit the righteous to be moved" (Ps. 55:22). "Trust in Him at all times, you people; pour out your heart before Him; God is a refuge for us" (Ps. 62:8)—"a God full of compassion, and gracious, longsuffering and abundant in mercy and truth" (Ps. 86:15).

A God of Forgiveness. After his sins of adultery and murder, David earnestly entreated, "Have mercy upon me, O God, according to Your lovingkindness; according to the multitude of Your tender mercies." "Do not cast me away from Your presence, and do not take Your Holy Spirit from me" (Ps. 51:1, 11). He was comforted by the assurance that God is wonderfully merciful. "For as the heavens are high above the earth, so great is His mercy toward those who fear Him; as far as the east is from the west, so far has He removed our transgressions from us. As a father pities those who fear Him. For He knows our frame; He remembers that we are dust" (Ps. 103:11-14).

A God of Goodness. God is the One who "executes justice for the oppressed, who gives food to the hungry. The Lord gives freedom to the prisoners. The Lord opens the eyes of the blind; the Lord raises those who are bowed down; the Lord loves the righteous. The Lord watches over the strangers; He relieves the fatherless and widow" (Ps. 146:7-9). What a great picture of God is given in the Psalms!

A God of Faithfulness. In spite of God's greatness, Israel wandered away from Him most of the time (Leviticus 26, Deuteronomy 28). God is depicted as loving Israel as a husband loves his wife. The book of Hosea poignantly illustrates God's faithfulness in the face of flagrant unfaithfulness and rejection. God's continuing forgiveness reveals His character of unconditional love.

Though God permitted her to experience the calamities caused by her unfaithfulness—attempting to correct Israel's ways—He still embraced her with His mercy. He assured her, "You are My servant, I have chosen you and have not cast you away: Fear not, for I am with you; be not dismayed, for I am your God. I will strengthen you, yes, I will help you, I will uphold you with My righteous right hand" (Isa. 41:9, 10). In spite of their unfaithfulness, He tenderly promised, "If they confess their iniquity and the iniquity of their fathers, with their unfaithfulness in which they were unfaithful to Me,... if their uncircumcised hearts are humbled, and they accept their guilt—then I will remember My covenant with Jacob...with Isaac... with Abraham" (Lev. 26:40-42; cf. Jer. 3:12).

God reminds His people of His redemptive attitude: "O Israel, you will not be forgotten by Me! I have blotted out, like a thick cloud, your transgressions, and like a cloud, your sins. Return to Me, for I have redeemed you" (Isa. 44:21, 22). No wonder He could say, "Look to Me, and be saved, all you ends of the earth! For I am God, and there is no other" (Isa. 45:22).

A God of Salvation and Vengeance. The Old Testament description of God as a God of vengeance must be seen in the context of the destruction of His faithful people by the wicked. Through "the day of the Lord" theme the prophets reveal God's actions on behalf of His people at the end of time. It is a day of salvation for His people, but a day of vengeance on their enemies, who will be destroyed. "Say to those who are fearful-hearted, 'Be strong, do not fear! Behold, your God will come with vengeance; with the recompense of God; He will come and save you'" (Isa. 35:4).

A Father God. Addressing Israel, Moses referred to God as their Father, who had redeemed them: "Is He not your Father, who bought you?" (Deut. 32:6). Through redemption, God adopted Israel as His child. Isaiah wrote, "O Lord, you are our Father" (Isa. 64:8; cf. 63:16). Through Malachi, God affirmed, "I am the Father" (Mal. 1:6). Elsewhere, Malachi related God's fatherhood to His role as Creator: "Have we not all one Father? Has not one God created us?" (Mal. 2:10). God is our Father through both Creation and redemption. What a glorious truth!

God the Father in the New Testament

The God of the Old Testament does not differ from the God of the New Testament. God the Father is revealed as the originator of all things, the father of all true believers, and in a unique sense the father of Jesus Christ.

The Father of All Creation. Paul identifies the Father, distinguishing Him from Jesus Christ: "There is only one God, the Father, of whom are all things,...and one Lord Jesus Christ, through whom are all things, and through whom we live" (1 Cor. 8:6; cf. Heb. 12:9; John 1:17). He testifies, "I bow my knees to the Father of our Lord Jesus Christ, from whom the whole family in heaven and earth is named" (Eph. 3:14, 15).

The Father of All Believers. In New Testament times this spiritual father-child relationship exists not between God and the nation of Israel but between God and the individual believer. Jesus provides the guidelines for this relationship (Matt. 5:45; 6:6-15), which is established through the believer's acceptance of Jesus Christ (John 1:12, 13).

Through the redemption Christ has wrought, believers are adopted as God's children. The Holy Spirit facilitates this relationship. Christ came "to redeem those who were under the law, that we might receive the adoption as sons. And because you are sons, God has sent forth the Spirit of His Son into your hearts, crying out, 'Abba, Father!'" (Gal. 4:5, 6; cf. Rom. 8:15, 16).

Jesus Reveals the Father. Jesus, God the Son, provided the most profound view of God the Father when He, as God's self-revelation, came in human flesh (John 1:1, 14). John states, "No one has seen God at any time. The only begotten Son...has declared Him" (John 1:18). Jesus said, "I have come down from heaven" (John 6:38): "He who has seen Me has seen the Father" (John 14:9). To know Jesus is to know the Father.

The Epistle to the Hebrews stresses the importance of this personal revelation: "God, who at various times and in different ways spoke in time past to the fathers by the prophets, has in these last days spoken to us by His Son, whom He has appointed heir of all things, through whom also He made the worlds;...being the brightness of His glory and the express image of His person" (Heb. 1:1-3).

1. *A God who gives*. Jesus revealed His Father as a *giving* God. We see His giving at Creation, at Bethlehem, and at Calvary.

In creating, the Father and the Son acted together. God gave us life in spite of knowing that doing so would lead to the death of His own Son.

At Bethlehem, He gave Himself as He gave His Son. What pain the Father experienced when His Son entered our sin-polluted planet! Imagine the Father's feeling as He saw His Son exchange the love and adoration of angels for the hatred of sinners; the glory and bliss of heaven for the pathway of death.

But it is Calvary that gives us the deepest insight into the Father. The Father, being divine, suffered the pain of being separated from His Son—in life and death—more acutely than any human being ever could. And He suffered *with* Christ in like measure. What greater testimony about the Father could be given! The cross reveals—as nothing else can—the truth about the Father.

2. *A God of love.* Jesus' favorite theme was the tenderness and abundant love of God. "Love your enemies," He said, "bless those who curse you, do good to those who hate you, and pray for those who spitefully use you and persecute you, that you may be sons of your Father in heaven; for He makes His sun rise on the evil and on the good, and sends rain on the just and the unjust" (Matt. 5:44, 45).

"And your reward will be great, and you will be sons of the Highest. For He is kind to the unthankful and evil. Therefore be merciful, just as your Father also is merciful" (Luke 6:35, 36).

In stooping down and washing the feet of His betrayer (John 13:5, 10-14), Jesus revealed the loving nature of the Father. When we see Christ feeding the hungry (Mark 6:39-44; 8:1-9), healing the deaf (Mark 9:17-29), giving speech to the dumb (Mark 7:32-37), opening the eyes of the blind (Mark 8:22-26), lifting up the palsied (Luke 5:18-26), curing the lepers (Luke 5:12, 13), raising the dead (Mark 5:35-43; John 11:1-45), forgiving sinners (John 8:3-11), and casting out demons (Matt. 15:22-28; 17:14-21), we see the Father mingling among men, bringing them His life, setting them free, giving them hope, and pointing them to a restored new earth to come. Christ knew that revealing the precious love of His Father was the key to bringing people to repentance (Rom 2:4).

Three of Christ's parables portray God's loving concern for lost humanity (Luke 15). The parable of the lost sheep teaches that salvation comes through God's initiative and not because of our searching after Him. As a shepherd loves his sheep and risks his life when one is missing, so in even greater measure does God manifest His yearning love for every lost person.

This parable also has cosmic significance—the lost sheep represents our rebellious world, a mere atom in God's vast universe. God's costly gift of His Son to bring our planet back into the fold indicates that our fallen world is as precious to Him as the rest of His creation.

The parable of the lost coin emphasizes what immense value God places on us sinners. And the parable of the prodigal son shows the enormous love of the Father, who welcomes home penitent children. If there is joy in heaven over one sinner who repents (Luke 15:7), imagine the joy the universe will experience at our Lord's second coming.

The New Testament makes clear the Father's intimate involvement with His Son's return. At the Second Advent the wicked cry to the mountains and rocks, "Fall on us and hide us from the face of Him who sits on the throne and from the wrath of the Lamb!" (Rev. 6:16). Jesus said, "For the Son of Man will come in the glory of His Father with His angels" (Matt. 16:27), and "you will see the son of Man sitting at the right hand of the Power [the Father], and coming on the clouds of heaven" (Matt. 26:64).

With a longing heart the Father anticipates the Second Advent, when the redeemed will finally be brought into their eternal home. Then His sending of "His only begotten Son into the world, that we might live through Him" (1 John 4:9) will clearly not have been in vain. Only unfathomable, unselfish love explains why, though we were enemies, "we were reconciled to God through the death of His Son" (Rom. 5:10). How could we spurn such love and fail to acknowledge Him as our Father?

God the Son

4

God the eternal Son became incarnate in Jesus Christ. Through Him all things were created, the character of God is revealed, the salvation of humanity is accomplished, and the world is judged. Forever truly God, He became also truly man, Jesus the Christ. He was conceived of the Holy Spirit and born of the virgin Mary. He lived and experienced temptation as a human being but perfectly exemplified the righteousness and love of God. By His miracles He manifested God's power and was attested as God's promised Messiah. He suffered and died voluntarily on the cross for our sins and in our place, was raised from the dead, and ascended to minister in the heavenly sanctuary on our behalf. He will come again in glory for the final deliverance of His people and the restoration of all things. (John 1:1-3, 14; Col. 1:15-19; John 10:30; 14:9; Rom. 6:23; 2 Cor. 5:17-19; John 5:22; Luke 1:35; Phil. 2:5-11; Heb. 2:9-18; 1 Cor. 15:3, 4; Heb. 8:1, 2; John 14:1-3.)

THE WILDERNESS HAD BECOME A NIGHTMARE of vipers. Snakes slithered under cooking pots; coiled around tent pegs. They lurked among children's toys; lay in wait in the sleeping pallets. Their fangs sank deep, injecting deadly poison.

The wilderness, which once had been Israel's refuge, became its graveyard. Hundreds lay dying. Realizing their predicament, terrorized parents hurried to Moses' tent, pleading for help. "Moses prayed for the people" (Num. 21:7).

God's answer? Mold a serpent and lift it high—and all who looked on it would live. "So Moses made a bronze serpent, and put it on a pole; and ... if a serpent had bitten anyone, when he looked at the bronze serpent, he lived" (Num. 21:9).

The serpent has always been Satan's symbol (Genesis 3; Revelation 12), representing sin. The camp had been plunged into Satan's hands. God's remedy? Not looking at a lamb on the sanctuary altar, but beholding a bronze serpent.

It was a strange symbol of Christ. Just as the likeness of the serpents that stung was lifted up on a pole, Jesus, made in the likeness of the serpents that stung, was lifted up on a pole. Jesus, made "in the likeness of sinful flesh" (Rom. 8:3), was to be lifted up on the shameful cross (John 3:14, 15). He became sin, taking upon Himself all the sins of everyone who has lived or will live. "For He made Him who knew no sin to be sin for us, that we might become the righteousness of God in Him" (2 Cor. 5:21). By looking to Christ, hopeless humanity can find life.

How could the incarnation bring salvation to humanity? What effect did it have on the Son? How could God become a human being, and why was it necessary?

The Incarnation: Predictions and Fulfillment

God's plan to rescue those who strayed from His all-wise counsel (John 3:16; 1 John 4:9) convincingly demonstrates His love. In this plan His Son was "foreordained before the foundation of the world" as the sacrifice for sin, to be the hope of the human race (1 Peter 1:19, 20). He was to bring us back to God and provide deliverance from sin through the destruction of the works of the devil (1 Peter 3:18; Matt. 1:21; 1 John 3:8).

Sin had severed Adam and Eve from the source of life and should have resulted in their immediate death. But in accordance with the plan laid before the foundation of the world (1 Peter 1:20, 21), the "counsel of peace" (Zech. 6:13), God the Son stepped between them and divine justice, bridging the gulf and restraining death. Even before the cross, then, His grace kept sinners alive and assured them of salvation. But to restore us fully as sons and daughters of God, He had to become a man.

Immediately after Adam and Eve sinned, God gave them hope by promising to introduce a supernatural enmity between the serpent and the woman—between his seed and hers. In the cryptic statement of Genesis 3:15 the serpent and its offspring represent Satan and his followers; the woman and her seed symbolize God's people and the Saviour of the world. This statement was the first assurance that the controversy between good and evil would end in victory for God's Son.

The victory, however, would be painful: "He [the Saviour] shall bruise your [Satan's] head, and you [Satan] shall bruise His [the Saviour's] heel"(Gen. 3:15). No one would come out unscathed.

From that moment, mankind looked for the Promised One. The Old Testament unfolds that search. Prophecies foretold that when the Promised One arrived, the world would have evidence to confirm His identity.

A Prophetic Dramatization of Salvation. After sin entered, God instituted animal sacrifices to illustrate the mission of the Saviour to come (see Gen. 4:4). This symbolic system dramatized the manner in which God the Son would eradicate sin.

Because of sin—the transgression of God's law—the human race faced death (Gen. 2:17; 3:19; 1 John 3:4; Rom. 6:23). God's law demanded the life of the sinner. But in His infinite love God gave His Son, "that whoever believes in Him should not perish but have everlasting life" (John 3:16). What an incomprehensible act of condescension! God, the eternal Son Himself, pays vicariously the penalty for sin, so that He can provide us forgiveness and reconciliation to the Godhead.

After Israel's exodus from Egypt, the sacrificial offerings were conducted in a tabernacle as part of a covenant relationship between God and His people. Built by Moses according to a heavenly pattern, the sanctuary and its services were instituted to illustrate the plan of salvation (Ex. 25:8, 9, 40; Heb. 8:1-5).

To obtain forgiveness, a repentant sinner brought a sacrificial animal that had no blemishes—a representation of the sinless Saviour. The sinner then would place his hand upon the innocent animal and confess his sins (Lev. 1:3, 4). This act symbolized the transfer of the sin from the guilty sinner to the innocent victim, depicting the substitutionary nature of the sacrifice.

Since "without shedding of blood there is no remission" of sins (Heb. 9:22), the sinner then killed the animal, making the deadly nature of sin evident. A sorrowful way to express hope, but the sinner's only way to express faith.

After the priestly ministry (Leviticus 4-7), the sinner received forgiveness of sins through his faith in the substitutionary death of the coming Redeemer, which the animal sacrifice symbolized (cf. Lev. 4:26, 31, 35). The New Testament recognizes Jesus Christ, the Son of God, as "the Lamb of God who takes away the sin of the world" (John 1:29). Through His precious blood, "as of a lamb without blemish and without spot" (1 Peter 1:19), He obtained for the human race redemption from the ultimate penalty of sin.

Predictions About a Saviour. God promises that the Saviour-Messiah—

the Anointed One—would come through Abraham's line: "In your seed all the nations of the earth shall be blessed" (Gen. 22:18; cf. 12:3).

Isaiah prophesied that the Saviour would come as a male child and would be both human and divine: "For unto us a Child is born, unto us a Son is given; and the government will be upon His shoulder. And His name will be called Wonderful, Counselor, Mighty God, Everlasting Father, Prince of Peace" (Isa. 9:6). This Redeemer would ascend the throne of David and establish an everlasting government of peace (Isa. 9:7). Bethlehem would be His birthplace (Micah 5:2).

The birth of this divine-human person would be supernatural. Citing Isaiah 7:14, the New Testament states, "Behold, a virgin shall be with child, and bear a Son, and they shall call His name Immanuel, which is translated, 'God with us'" (Matt. 1:23).

The Saviour's mission is expressed in these words: "The Spirit of the Lord God is upon Me, because the Lord has anointed Me to preach good tidings to the poor; He has sent Me to heal the broken-hearted, to proclaim liberty to the captives, and opening of the prison to those who are bound; to proclaim the acceptable year of the Lord" (Isa. 61:1, 2; cf. Luke 4:18, 19).

Amazingly, the Messiah would suffer rejection. He would be perceived as "a root out of dry ground." "He has no form or comeliness, and when we see Him, there is no beauty that we should desire Him....Despised and rejected by men, a man of sorrows and acquainted with grief....We did not esteem Him" (Isa. 53:2-4).

A close friend would betray Him (Ps. 41:9) for thirty pieces of silver (Zech. 11:12). During His trial He would be spat upon and beaten (Isa. 50:6). Those who executed Him would gamble for the very clothes He wore (Ps. 22:18). None of His bones were to be broken (Ps. 34:20), but His side was to be pierced (Zech. 12:10). In His afflictions He would not resist, but "as a sheep before its shearers is silent, so He opened not His mouth" (Isa. 53:7).

The innocent Saviour would suffer immensely for sinners. "Surely He has borne our griefs and carried our sorrows;...He was wounded for our transgressions, He was bruised for our iniquities; the chastisement for our peace was upon Him and by His stripes we are healed....And the Lord has laid on Him the iniquity of us all....He was cut off from the land of the living; for the transgressions of My people He was stricken" (Isa. 53:4-8).

The Saviour Identified. Only Jesus Christ has fulfilled these prophecies. Scriptures trace His genealogy to Abraham, calling Him the Son of Abraham (Matt. 1:1), and Paul affirms that the promise to Abraham and his seed was fulfilled in Christ (Gal. 3:16). The Messianic title *Son of David* was widely applied to Him (Matt. 21:9). He was identified as the promised Messiah, who would occupy the throne of David (Acts 2:29, 30).

Jesus' birth was miraculous. The virgin Mary "was found with child of the Holy Spirit" (Matt. 1:18-23). A Roman decree brought her to Bethlehem, the predicted birthplace (Luke 2:4-7).

One of Jesus' names was Immanuel, or "God With Us," which reflected His divine-human nature and illustrated God's identification with humanity (Matt. 1:23). His common name, Jesus, focused on His mission of salvation: "And you shall call His name Jesus, for He will save His people from their sins" (Matt. 1:21).

Jesus identified His mission with that of the Messiah predicted in Isaiah 61:1, 2: "Today this Scripture is fulfilled in your hearing" (Luke 4:17-21).

Although He made a profound impact on His people, His message was generally rejected (John 1:11; Luke 23:18). With few exceptions He was not recognized as the world's Saviour. Instead of acceptance, He met death threats (John 5:16; 7:19; 11:53).

Toward the end of Jesus' three-and-a-half-year ministry, Judas Iscariot, a disciple, betrayed Him (John 13:18; 18:2) for thirty pieces of silver (Matt. 26:14, 15). Instead of resisting, He rebuked His disciples for trying to defend Him (John 18:4-11).

Though innocent of any crime, less than twenty-four hours after He was arrested He had been spat upon, beaten, tried, condemned to death, and crucified (Matt. 26:67; John 19:1-16; Luke 23:14, 15). Soldiers gambled for His clothing (John 19:23, 24). During His crucifixion none of His bones was broken (John 19:32, 33, 36), and after He died soldiers pierced His side with a spear (John 19:34, 37).

Christ's followers recognized His death as the only sacrifice of avail to sinners. "God demonstrates His own love toward us, in that while we were still sinners, Christ died for us" (Rom. 5:8). "Walk in love," he wrote, "as Christ also has loved us and given Himself for us, an offering and a sacrifice to god for a sweet-smelling aroma" (Eph. 5:2).

The Time of His Ministry and Death. The Bible reveals that God sent His Son to earth in "the fullness of the time" (Gal. 4:4). When Christ began His ministry, He proclaimed, "The time is fulfilled" (Mark 1:15). These references to time indicate that the Saviour's mission proceeded in harmony with careful prophetic planning.

More than five centuries earlier, through Daniel, God had prophesied the exact time of the beginning of Christ's ministry and the time of His death.[1]

Toward the end of the seventy years of Israel's captivity in Babylon, God told Daniel that He had allocated to the Jews and the city of Jerusalem a probationary period of seventy weeks.

During this time, by repenting and preparing themselves for the Messiah's coming, the Jewish nation was to fulfill God's purpose for them.

Daniel also wrote of "reconciliation for iniquity" and a bringing in of "everlasting righteousness" as marking this period. These Messianic activities indicate that the Saviour was to come within this time (Dan. 9:24).

Daniel's prophecy specified that the Messiah would appear "seven weeks and sixty-two weeks," or a total of sixty-nine weeks, after "the going forth of the command to restore and build Jerusalem" (Dan. 9:25). After the sixty-ninth week the Messiah would be "cut off, but not for Himself" (Dan. 9:26)—a reference to His vicarious death. He was to die in the middle of the seventieth week, bringing "an end to sacrifice and offering" (Dan. 9:27).

The key to understanding time prophecies lies in the biblical principle that a day in prophetic time is equivalent to a literal solar year (Num. 14:34; Eze. 4:6).[2] According to this year-day principle, the seventy weeks (or 490 prophetic days) then represent 490 literal years.

Daniel states that this period was to begin with "the going forth of the command to restore and build Jerusalem" (Dan. 9:25). This decree, giving the Jews full autonomy, was issued in the seventh year of the Persian King Artaxerxes and became effective in the fall of 457 B.C. (Ezra 7:8, 12-26; 9:9).[3] According to the prophecy, 483 years (sixty-nine prophetic weeks) after the decree "Messiah the Prince" would appear. Four hundred and eighty-three years after 457 B.C. brings us to the fall of A.D. 27, when Jesus was baptized and began His public ministry.[4] Accepting these dates of 457 B.C. and A.D. 27, Gleason Archer comments that this was "a most remarkable exactitude in the fulfillment of such an ancient prophecy. Only God could have predicted the coming of His Son with such amazing precision; it defies all rationalistic explanation."[5]

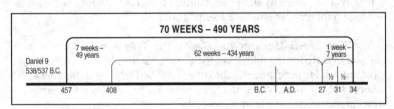

At His baptism in the Jordan, Jesus was anointed by the Holy Spirit and received God's recognition as the "Messiah" (Hebrew) or the "Christ" (Greek)—both meaning the "anointed one" (Luke 3:21, 22; Acts 10:38; John 1:41). Jesus' proclamation, "the time is fulfilled" (Mark 1:15) refers to the fulfillment of this time prophecy.

In the middle of the seventieth week, in the spring of A.D. 31, exactly three and one-half years after Christ's baptism, the Messiah brought the system of sacrifices to an end by giving His life. At the moment of His death the veil of the Temple was supernaturally "torn in two from top to bottom" (Matt. 27:51), indicating the divine abolition of all Temple services.

All the offerings and sacrifices had pointed forward to the all-sufficient sacrifice of the Messiah. When Jesus Christ, the true Lamb of God, was sacrificed at Calvary as a ransom for our sins (1 Peter 1:19), type met antitype, and shadow melded into reality. The earthly sanctuary services were no longer necessary.

At the exact time prophesied during the Passover festival, He died. "Indeed," Paul said, "Christ, our Passover, was sacrificed for us" (1 Cor. 5:7). This amazingly accurate time prophecy gives one of the strongest evidences of the fundamental historic truth that Jesus Christ is the long-predicted Saviour of the world.

The Resurrection of the Saviour. The Bible predicted not only the Saviour's death but also His resurrection. David prophesied "that His soul was not left in Hades, nor did His flesh see corruption" (Acts 2:31; cf. Ps. 16:10). Although Christ had raised others from the dead (Mark 5:35-42; Luke 7:11-17; John 11), His own resurrection demonstrated the power behind His claim to be Saviour of the world: "I am the resurrection and the life. He who believes in Me, though he may die, he shall live. And whoever lives and believes in Me shall never die" (John 11:25, 26).

After His resurrection He proclaimed, "Do not be afraid; I am the First and the Last. I am He who lives, and was dead, and behold, I am alive forevermore. Amen. And I have the keys of Hades and of Death" (Rev. 1:17, 18).

The Two Natures of Jesus Christ

In stating, "The Word became flesh and dwelt among us" (John 1:14), John set forth a profound truth. The incarnation of God the Son is a mystery. Scripture calls God's being manifested in the flesh "the mystery of godliness" (1 Tim 3:16).

The Creator of worlds, He in whom was the fullness of the Godhead became the helpless babe in the manger. Far superior to any of the angels, equal with the Father in dignity and glory, He yet condescended to wear the garb of humanity!

One can barely grasp the meaning of this sacred mystery, and then only by calling on the Holy Spirit for enlightenment. In trying to comprehend the incarnation it is well to remember that "the secret things which are revealed belong to us and to our children" (Deut. 29:29).

Jesus Christ Is Truly God. What is the evidence that Jesus Christ is divine? How did He perceive Himself? Did people recognize His divinity?

1. His divine attributes. Christ possesses divine attributes. He is omnipotent. He said the Father has given Him "all authority...in heaven and on earth" (Matt. 28:18; John 17:2).

He is omniscient. In Him, Paul said, "are hidden all the treasures of wisdom and knowledge" (Col. 2:3).

Jesus asserted His omnipresence with the assurances "Lo, I am with you always, even to the end of the age" (Matt. 28:20) and "Where two or three are gathered together in My name, I am there in the midst of them" (Matt. 18:20).

Although His divinity has the natural ability of omnipresence, the incarnate Christ has voluntarily limited Himself in this respect. He has chosen to be omnipresent through the ministry of the Holy Spirit (John 14:16-18).

Hebrews attests to His immutability, stating, "Jesus Christ is the same yesterday, today, and forever" (Heb. 13:8).

His self-existence was evident when He claimed life in Himself (John 5:26), and John testified, "In Him was life, and the life was the light of men" (John 1:4). Christ's announcement, "I am the resurrection and the life" (John 11:25) affirmed that in Him is "life, original, unborrowed, underived."[6]

Holiness is a part of His nature. At the annunciation, the angel said to Mary, "The Holy Spirit will come upon you, and the power of the Highest will overshadow you; therefore, also, that Holy One who is to be born will be called the Son of God" (Luke 1:35). At the sight of Jesus demons cried out, "Let us alone!...I know who You are—the Holy One of God" (Mark 1:24).

He is love. "By this we know love," John wrote, "because He laid down His life for us" (1 John 3:16).

He is eternal. Isaiah called Him "Everlasting Father" (Isa. 9:6). Micah referred to Him as the One "whose goings forth have been from of old, from everlasting" (Micah 5:2). Paul dated His existence "before all things" (Col. 1:17), and John concurred: "He was in the beginning with God. All things were made through Him, and without Him nothing was made that was made" (John 1:2, 3).[7]

2. His divine powers and prerogatives. The works of God are ascribed to Jesus. He is identified as both the Creator (John 1:3; Col. 1:16) and the Sustainer or Upholder—"in Him all things consist" (Col. 1:17; Heb. 1:3). He is able to raise the dead with His voice (John 5:28, 29) and will judge the world at the end of time (Matt. 25:31, 32). He forgave sin (Matt. 9:6; Mark 2:5-7).

3. His divine names. His names reveal His divine nature. Immanuel means "God with us" (Matt 1:23). Both believers and demons addressed Him as Son of God (Mark 1:1; Matt. 8:29; cf. Mark 5:7). The sacred Old Testament name of God—Jehovah, or *Yahweh*—is applied to Jesus. Matthew used the words of Isaiah 40:3, "Prepare the way of the Lord," to describe the preparatory work for Christ's mission (Matt. 3:3). And John identified Jesus with the Lord of hosts sitting on His throne (Isa. 6:1, 3; John 12:41).

4. His divinity acknowledged. John depicted Jesus as the divine Word that "became flesh" (John 1:1, 14). Thomas acknowledged the resurrected Christ as "My Lord and my God!" (John 20:28). Paul referred to Him as the One "who is over all, the eternally blessed God" (Rom. 9:5); and Hebrews addressed Him as God and Lord of Creation (Heb. 1:8, 10).[8]

5. His personal testimony. Jesus Himself claimed equality with God. He identified Himself as the "I AM" (John 8:58)—the God of the Old Testament. He called God "My Father" instead of "our Father" (John 20:17). And His statement "I and my Father are one" (John 10:30) sets forth the claim that He was of "one substance" with the Father, "Possessing the same attributes."[9]

6. His equality with God assumed. His equality with God the Father is taken for granted in the baptismal formula (Matt. 28:19), the full apostolic benediction (2 Cor. 13:14), His parting counsel (John 14-16), and Paul's exposition of the spiritual gifts (1 Cor. 12:4-6). Scripture describes Jesus as the brightness of God's glory and "the express image of His person" (Heb. 1:3). And when asked to reveal God the Father, Jesus replied, "He who has seen Me has seen the Father" (John 14:9).

7. He is worshiped as God. People worshiped Him (Matt. 28:17; cf. Luke 14:33). "All the angels of God worship Him" (Heb. 1:6). Paul wrote that "at the name of Jesus every knee should bow,…and that every tongue should confess that Jesus Christ is Lord" (Phil. 2:10, 11). Several benedictions accord to Christ the "glory forever and ever" (2 Tim. 4:18; Heb. 13:21; cf. 2 Peter 3:18).

8. His divine nature a necessity. Christ reconciled humanity to God. People needed a perfect revelation of God's character in order to develop a personal relationship with Him. Christ filled this need by displaying God's glory (John 1:14). "No one has seen God at any time. The only begotten Son, who is in the bosom of the Father, He has declared Him" (John 1:18; cf. 17:6). Jesus testified, "He who has seen Me has seen the Father" (John 14:9).

In total dependence on the Father (John 5:30), Christ used divine power to reveal God's love. With divine power He revealed Himself as the loving Saviour sent by the Father to heal, restore, and forgive sins (Luke 6:19; John 2:11; 5:1-15, 36; 11:41-45; 14:11; 8:3-11). Never, however, did He perform a miracle to spare Himself from the personal hardship and sufferings that other people would have experienced if placed in similar circumstances.

Jesus Christ is "one in nature, in character, in purpose" with God the Father.[10] He truly is God.

Jesus Christ Is Truly Man. The Bible testifies that in addition to His divine nature, Christ has a human nature. The acceptance of this teaching is crucial. Every one who "confesses that Jesus Christ has come in the flesh is of God," and every one who does not "is not of God" (1 John 4:2, 3). Christ's human birth, development, characteristics, and personal testimony provide evidence of His humanity.

1. His human birth. "The Word became flesh and dwelt among us" (John 1:14). Here *flesh* means "human nature"—a nature inferior to His heavenly one. In plain language Paul says, "God sent forth His Son, born of a woman" (Gal. 4:4; cf. Gen. 3:15). Christ was made in "the likeness of men" and "in human form" (Phil. 2:7, 8, RSV). This manifestation of God in human nature is "the mystery of godliness" (1 Tim. 3:16).

Christ's genealogy refers to Him as "the Son of David" and "the Son of Abraham" (Matt. 1:1). According to His human nature He "was born of the seed of David" (Rom. 1:3; 9:5) and was the "Son of Mary" (Mark 6:3). Though He was born of a woman as is every other child, there was a great difference, a uniqueness. Mary was a virgin, and this Child was conceived of the Holy Spirit (Matt. 1:20-23; Luke 1:31-37). He could claim true humanity through His mother.

2. His human development. Jesus was subject to the laws of human development; He "grew and became strong in spirit, filled with wisdom" (Luke 2:40, 52). At the age of 12 He became aware of His divine mission (Luke 2:46-49). Throughout His boyhood He was subject to His parents (Luke 2:51).

The road to the cross was one of constant growth through suffering, which played an important role in His development. "He learned obedience by the things which He suffered. And having been perfected, He became the author of eternal salvation to all who obey" (Heb. 5:8, 9; 2:10, 18). Yet though He experienced development, He did not sin.

3. He was called a "man." John the Baptist and Peter refer to Him as "a Man" (John 1:30; Acts 2:22). Paul speaks of "the grace of the one Man, Jesus Christ" (Rom. 5:15). He is the "Man" who brought "the resurrection of the dead" (1 Cor. 15:21); the "one Mediator between God and men, the Man Christ Jesus" (1 Tim. 2:5). In addressing His enemies, Christ refers to Himself as Man: "You seek to kill Me, a Man who has told you the truth which I heard from God" (John 8:40).

Jesus' favorite self-designation, one He used seventy-seven times, was "Son of Man" (cf. Matt. 8:20; 26:2). The title Son of God focuses the attention on His relationship within the Godhead. The name Son of man emphasizes His solidarity with the human race through His incarnation.

4. His human characteristics. God made humans "a little lower than the angels" (Ps. 8:5). Similarly, Scripture presents Jesus as One "who was made a little lower than the angels" (Heb. 2:9). His human nature was created and did not possess superhuman powers.

Christ was to be truly human; this was part of His mission. Being so required that He possess the essential characteristics of human nature—He was "flesh and blood" (Heb. 2:14). "In all things," Christ was made "like" His fellow human beings (Heb. 2:17). His human nature possessed the same mental and physical susceptibilities as the rest of humanity: hunger, thirst, weariness, and anxiety (Matt. 4:2; John 19:28; 4:6; cf. Matt. 26:21; 8:24).

In His ministry to others He revealed compassion, righteous anger, and grief (Matt. 9:36; Mark 3:5). At times He felt troubled, and sorrowful, and He even wept (Matt. 26:38; John 12:27; 11:33, 35; Luke 19:41). He prayed with cries and tears, once to the point of perspiring blood (Heb. 5:7; Luke 22:44). His life of prayer expressed His complete dependence on God (Matt. 26:39-44; Mark 1:35; 6:46; Luke 5:16; 6:12).

Jesus experienced death (John 19:30, 34). He was resurrected, not as a spirit, but with a body (Luke 24:36-43).

5. The extent of His identification with human nature. The Bible reveals that Christ is the second Adam; He lived "in the likeness of sinful flesh" or "in the likeness of sinful man" (Rom. 8:3, NIV). To what extent did He identify with or become identical to fallen humanity? A correct view of the expression "the likeness of sinful flesh" or "sinful man" is crucial. Inaccurate views have brought dissension and strife throughout the history of the Christian church.

a. He was "in the likeness of sinful flesh." The uplifted serpent in the desert, described earlier, provides an understanding of Christ's human nature. As the brass image made in the likeness of the poisonous serpents was lifted up for the people's healing, so the Son of God, made "in the likeness of sinful flesh," was to be the Saviour of the world.

Before the incarnation Jesus was "in the form of God;" that is to say, the divine *nature* was His from the beginning (John 1:1; Phil. 2:6, 7 NIV, NEB). In taking the "form of a servant" He laid aside divine prerogatives. He became His Father's servant (Isa. 42:1), to carry out the Father's will (John 6:38; Matt. 26:39, 42). He clothed His divinity with humanity, He was made in the "likeness of sinful flesh," or "sinful human nature," or "fallen human nature," (cf. Rom. 8:3).[11] This in no way indicates that Jesus Christ was sinful or participated in sinful acts or thoughts. Though made in the form or likeness of sinful flesh, He was sinless, and His sinlessness is beyond questioning.

b. He was the second Adam. The Bible draws a parallel between Adam and Christ, calling Adam the "first man" and Christ the "last Adam" or "second Man" (1 Cor. 15:45, 47). But Adam had the advantage over Christ. At the Fall he lived in paradise. He had a perfect humanity, possessing full vigor of body and mind.

Not so with Jesus. When He took on human nature, the race had already deteriorated through 4,000 years of sin on a sin-cursed planet. So that He could save those in the utter depths of degradation, Christ took a human nature that, compared with Adam's unfallen nature, had decreased in physical and mental strength—though He did so without sinning.[12]

When Christ took the human nature that bore the consequences of sin, He became subject to the infirmities and weaknesses that all experience. His human nature was "beset by weakness" or "compassed with infirmity" (Heb. 5:2, KJV; Matt. 8:17; Isa. 53:4). He sensed His weakness. He had to offer "prayers and supplications, with vehement cries and tears to Him who was able to save Him from death" (Heb. 5:7), thus identifying Himself with the needs and weaknesses so common to humanity.

Thus "Christ's humanity was not the Adamic humanity, that is, the humanity of Adam before the fall; nor fallen humanity, that is, in every respect the humanity of Adam after the fall. It was not the Adamic, because it had the innocent infirmities of the fallen. It was not the fallen, because it had never descended into moral impurity. It was, therefore, most literally our humanity, but without sin."[13]

c. His experience with temptations. How did temptations affect Christ? Was it easy or difficult for Him to resist them? The way He experienced temptations proves that He was truly human.

i. "In all points tempted as we are." That Christ was "in all points tempted as we are" (Heb. 4:15) shows that He was a partaker of human nature. Temptation and the possibility of sinning were real to Christ. If He could not sin He would have been neither human nor our example. Christ took human nature with all its liabilities, including the possibility of yielding to temptation.

How could He have been tempted "in all points" as we are?

Obviously, "in all points" or "in every way" (NIV) does not mean that He met the identical temptations we meet today. He was never tempted to watch demoralizing TV programs or to break the speed limit in an automobile.

The basic issue underlying all temptations is the question of whether to surrender to the will of God. In His encounter with temptation Jesus always maintained His allegiance to God. Through continual dependence on divine power He successfully resisted the fiercest temptations, even though He was human.

Christ's victory over temptation qualified Him to sympathize with human weaknesses. Our victory over temptation comes by maintaining dependence upon Him. "God is faithful, who will not allow you to be tempted beyond what you are able, but with the temptation will also make the way of escape, that you may be able to bear it" (1 Cor. 10:13).

It must be recognized that in the end "it is a mystery that is left unexplained to mortals that Christ could be tempted in all points like as we are, and yet be without sin."[14]

ii. "Suffered, being tempted." Christ suffered while subjected to temptation (Heb. 2:18). He was made "perfect through sufferings" (Heb. 2:10). Because He Himself faced the power of temptation, we can know that He understands how to help anyone who is tempted. He was one with humanity in suffering the temptations to which human nature is subjected.

How did Christ suffer under temptation? Though He had "the likeness of sinful flesh," His spiritual faculties were free from any taint of sin. Consequently, His holy nature was extremely sensitive. Any contact with evil pained Him. So, because He suffered in proportion to the perfection of His holiness, temptation brought more suffering to Jesus than to anyone else.[15]

How much did Christ suffer? His experience in the wilderness, Gethsemane, and Golgotha reveal that He resisted temptation to the point of shedding His blood (cf. Heb. 12:4).

Christ not only suffered more in proportion to His holiness, He faced stronger temptations than we humans have to. B. F. Wescott notes, "Sympathy with the sinner in his trial does not depend on the experience of sin but on the experience of the strength of the temptation to sin which only the sinless can know in its full intensity. He who falls yields before the last strain."[16] F. F. Bruce concurs by stating, "Yet He endured triumphantly every form of testing that man could endure, without any weakening of His faith in God or any relaxation of His obedience to Him. Such endurance involves more, not less than ordinary human suffering."[17]

Christ also faced a powerful temptation never known to man—the temptation to use His divine power on His own behalf. E.G. White states, "He had received honor in the heavenly courts, and was familiar with absolute power. It was as difficult for Him to keep the level of humanity as it is for men to rise above the low level of their depraved natures, and be partakers of the divine nature."[18]

d. Could Christ sin? Christians differ on the question of whether Christ could sin. We agree with Philip Schaff, who said, "Had he [Christ] been endowed from the start with *absolute* impeccability, or with the impossibility of sinning, he could not be a true man, nor our model for imitation: his holiness, instead of being his own self-acquired act and inherent merit, would be an accidental or outward gift, and his temptations an unreal show."[19] Karl Ullmann adds, "The history of the temptation, however it may be explained, would have no significancy; and the expression in the epistle to the Hebrews 'he was tempted in all points as we,' would be without meaning."[20]

6. The sinlessness of Jesus Christ's human nature. It is self-evident that the divine nature of Jesus was sinless. But what about His human nature?

The Bible portrays Jesus' humanity as sinless. His birth was supernatural—He was conceived of the Holy Spirit (Matt. 1:20). Before His birth, He was described as "that Holy One" (Luke 1:35). He took the nature of man in its fallen state, bearing the consequences of sin, not its sinfulness. He was one with the human race, except in sin.

Jesus was "in all points tempted as we are, yet without sin," being "holy, harmless, undefiled, separate from sinners" (Heb. 4:15; 7:26). Paul wrote that He "knew no sin" (2 Cor. 5:21). Peter testified that He "committed no sin, nor was guile found in His mouth" (1 Peter 2:22), and compared Him with "a lamb without blemish and without spot" (1 Peter 1:19; Heb. 9:24). "In Him," John said, "there is no sin....He is righteous" (1 John 3:5-7).

Jesus took upon Himself our nature with all its liabilities, but He was free from hereditary corruption or depravity and actual sin. He challenged

His opponents, "Which of you convicts Me of sin?" (John 8:46). When facing His severest trial, He declared, "The ruler of this world is coming, and he has nothing in Me" (John 14:30). Jesus had no evil propensities or inclinations or even sinful passions. None of the avalanche of temptations could break His allegiance to God.

Jesus never made a confession of sin or offered a sacrifice. He did not pray, "Father, forgive Me," but rather, "Father, forgive them" (Luke 23:34). Always seeking to do His Father's will, not His own, Jesus constantly maintained His dependence on the Father (cf. John 5:30).

Unlike that of fallen humanity, Jesus' "spiritual nature" is pure and holy, "free from every taint of sin."[21] It would be a mistake to think He is "altogether human" as we are. He is the second Adam, the unique Son of God. Nor should we think of Him "as a man with the propensities of sin." While His human nature was tempted in all points in which human nature is tempted, He never fell, He never sinned. Never was there in Him an evil propensity.[22]

Indeed, Jesus is humanity's highest, holiest example. He is sinless, and all He did demonstrated perfection. Truly, He was the perfect example of sinless humanity.

7. The necessity of Christ's taking human nature. The Bible gives various reasons as to why Christ had to have a human nature.

a. To be the high priest for the human race. As Messiah, Jesus had to occupy the position of high priest or mediator between God and man (Zech. 6:13; Heb. 4:14-16). This function required human nature. Christ met the qualifications: (i) He could have "compassion on those who are ignorant and going astray" because He was "beset by weaknesses" or "compassed with infirmity" (Heb. 5:2, KJV). (ii) He is "merciful and faithful" because He was in all things made "like His brethren" (Heb. 2:17). (iii) He "is able to aid them who are tempted" because "He Himself has suffered, being tempted" (Heb. 2:18). (iv) He sympathizes with weaknesses because He "was in all points tempted as we are, yet without sin" (Heb. 4:15).

b. To save even the most degraded person. To reach people where they are and rescue the most hopeless, He descended to the level of a servant (Phil. 2:7).

c. To give His life for the sins of the world. Christ's divine nature cannot die. In order to die, then, Christ had to have a human nature. He became man and paid the penalty for sin, which is death (Rom. 6:23; 1 Cor. 15:3). As a human being, He tasted death for everyone (Heb. 2:9).

d. To be our example. To set the example as to how people should live, Christ must live a sinless life as a human being. As the second Adam, He dispelled the myth that humans cannot obey God's law and have victory over sin. He demonstrated that it is possible for humanity to be faithful to God's will. Where the first Adam fell, the second Adam gained the victory over sin and Satan and became both our Saviour and our perfect example. In His strength, His victory can be ours (John 16:33).

By beholding Him, people "are being transformed into the same image from glory to glory" (2 Cor. 3:18). "Let us fix our eyes on Jesus, the author and perfecter of our faith....Consider him who endured such opposition from sinful men, so that you will not grow weary and lose heart" (Heb. 12:2, 3, NIV). Truly, Christ "suffered for us, leaving us an example, that you should follow His steps" (1 Peter 2:21; cf. John 13:15).

The Union of the Two Natures

The person of Jesus Christ has two natures: divine and human. He is the God-man. But note that the incarnation involved the eternal Son of God taking on Himself human nature, not the man Jesus acquiring divinity. The movement is from God to man, not man to God.

In Jesus, these two natures were merged into one person. Note the following biblical evidence:

Christ Is a Union of Two Natures. The plurality associated with the triune God is not present in Christ. The Bible describes Jesus as one person, not two. Various texts refer to the divine and human nature, yet speak of only one person. Paul described the person Jesus Christ as God's Son (divine nature) who is born of a woman (human nature; Gal. 4:4). Thus Jesus, "being in the form of God, did not consider it robbery to be equal with God" (divine nature), "but made Himself of no reputation, taking the form of a servant, and coming in the likeness of man" (human nature; Phil. 2:6, 7).

Christ's dual nature is not composed of an abstract divine power or influence that is connected with His humanity. "The Word," John said, "became flesh and dwelt among us, and we beheld His glory, the glory as of the only begotten of the Father, full of grace and truth" (John 1:14). Paul wrote, God sent "His own Son in the likeness of sinful flesh" (Rom. 8:3); "God was manifest in the flesh" (1 Tim. 3:16; 1 John 4:2).

The Blending of the Two Natures. At times the Bible describes the Son of God in terms of His human nature. God purchased His church with His own blood (Acts. 20:28; cf. Col. 1:13, 14). At other instances it characterizes the Son of Man in terms of His divine nature (cf. John 3:13; 6:62; Rom. 9:5).

When Christ came into the world, "a body" had been prepared for Him (Heb. 10:5). When He took upon Himself humanity, His divinity was clothed with humanity. This was not accomplished by changing humanity into divinity or divinity into humanity. He did not go out of Himself to another nature but took humanity into Himself. Thus divinity and humanity were combined.

When He became incarnate, Christ did not cease to be God, nor was His divinity reduced to the level of humanity. Each nature kept its standing. "In Him," Paul says, "dwells all the fullness of the Godhead bodily" (Col. 2:9). At the crucifixion His human nature died, not His deity, for that would have been impossible.

The Necessity of the Union of the Two Natures. An understanding of the interrelationship of Christ's two natures gives a vital insight into Christ's mission and our very salvation.

1. To reconcile humanity with God. Only a divine-human Saviour could bring salvation. At the incarnation Christ, in order to impart His divine nature to believers, brought humanity into Himself. Through the merits of the blood of the God-man believers can partake of the divine nature (2 Peter 1:4).

The ladder in Jacob's dream, symbolizing Christ, reaches us where we are. He took human nature and overcame, that we, through taking His nature, might overcome. His divine arms grasp the throne of God, while His humanity embraces the race, connecting us with God, earth with heaven.

The combined divine-human nature makes effective Christ's atoning sacrifice. The life of a sinless human being or even an angel could not atone for the sins of the human race. Only the divine-human Creator could ransom humanity.

2. To veil divinity with humanity. Christ veiled His divinity with the garb of humanity, laying aside His celestial glory and majesty so that sinners would be able to exist in His presence without being destroyed. Though He was still God, He did not appear as God (Phil. 2:6-8).

3. To live victoriously. Christ's humanity alone could never have endured the deceptions of Satan. But in Him dwelt "all the fullness of the Godhead bodily" (Col. 2:9). He was able to overcome sin because He relied completely upon the Father (John 5:19, 30; 8:28), and "divine power combined with humanity gained in behalf of man an infinite victory."[23]

Christ's experience in victorious living is not His exclusive privilege. He exercised no power that humanity cannot exercise. We may also "be filled with all the fullness of God" (Eph. 3:19). Through Christ's divine power we can have access to "all things that pertain to life and godliness."

The key to this experience is faith in the "exceeding great and precious promises" through which we "may be partakers of the divine nature, having escaped the corruption that is in the world through lust" (2 Peter 1: 3, 4). He offers the same power by which He overcame so that all may faithfully obey and have a victorious life.

Christ's comforting promise is one of victory: "To him who overcomes I will grant to sit with Me on My throne, as I also overcame and sat down with My Father on His throne" (Rev. 3:21).

The Offices of Jesus Christ

The offices of prophet, priest, and king were unique, generally requiring a consecration service through anointing (1 Kings 19:16; Ex. 30:30, 2 Sam. 5:3). The coming Messiah, the Anointed One—prophecies pointed out—was to hold all three of these offices. Christ performs His work as mediator between God and us through the offices of prophet, priest, and king. Christ the Prophet proclaims God's will to us, Christ the Priest represents us to God and vice versa, and Christ the King wields God's gracious authority over His people.

Christ the Prophet. God revealed Christ's prophetic office to Moses: "I will raise up for them a Prophet like you from among their brethren, and will put My words in His mouth, and He shall speak to them all that I command Him" (Deut. 18:18). Christ's contemporaries recognized the fulfillment of this prediction (John 6:14; 7:40; Acts 3:22, 23).

Jesus referred to Himself as "prophet" (Luke 13:33). He proclaimed with prophetic authority (Matt. 7:29) the principles of God's kingdom (Matthew 5-7; 22:36-40) and revealed the future (Matt. 24:1-51; Luke 19:41-44).

Before His incarnation Christ filled the Bible writers with His Spirit and gave them prophecies about His sufferings and subsequent glories (1 Peter 1:11). After His ascension He continued to reveal Himself to His people. Scripture says He gives His "testimony"—"the spirit of prophecy"—to His faithful remnant (Rev. 12:17; 19:10—see chapter 18 of this book).

Christ the Priest. A divine oath firmly established the Messiah's priesthood: "The Lord has sworn and will not relent, 'You are a priest forever according to the order of Melchizedek'" (Ps. 110:4). Christ was not a descendant of Aaron. Like Melchizedek, His right to the priesthood came by divine appointment (Heb. 5:6, 10—see chapter 7). His mediating priesthood had two phases: an earthly and a heavenly.

1. Christ's earthly priesthood. The priest's role at the altar of burnt offering symbolized Jesus' earthly ministry. Jesus qualified perfectly for the
office of priest: He was truly man, and He was "called by God" and acted
"in things pertaining to God" with the special task of offering "gifts and
sacrifices for sins" (Heb. 5:1, 4, 10).

The priest was to reconcile the worshipers to God through the sacrificial system, which represented the provision of atonement for sin (Lev. 1:4;
4:29, 31, 35; 5:10; 16:6; 17:11). Thus the continual sacrifices at the altar of
burnt offering symbolized the availability of continual atonement.

These sacrifices were not sufficient. They could not make the offerer
perfect, take away sins, or produce a clear conscience (Heb. 10:1-4; 9:9).
They were simply a shadow of the good things to come (Heb. 10:1; cf. 9:9,
23, 24). The Old Testament said that the Messiah Himself would take the
place of these animal sacrifices (Ps. 40:6-8; Heb. 10:5-9). These sacrifices, then, pointed to the vicarious sufferings and atoning death of Christ
the Saviour. He, the Lamb of God, became sin for us, a curse for us; His
blood cleanses us from all sins (2 Cor. 5:21; Gal. 3:13; 1 John 1:7; cf. 1 Cor.
15:3).

So during His earthly ministry Christ was both priest and offering. His
death on the cross was part of His priestly work. After His sacrifice at Golgotha, His priestly intercession centered in the heavenly sanctuary.

2. Christ's heavenly priesthood. The priestly ministry Jesus began on
earth, He completes in heaven. His humiliation on earth as God's suffering servant qualified Him to be our High Priest in heaven (Heb. 2:17; 18;
4:15; 5:2). Prophecy reveals that the Messiah was to be a priest on God's
throne (Zech. 6:13). After His resurrection the humiliated Christ was exalted. Now our High Priest sits "at the right hand of the throne of the Majesty in the heavens," ministering in the heavenly sanctuary (Heb. 8:1, 2; cf.
1:3; 9:24).

Christ began His intercessory work immediately following His ascension. The ascending cloud of incense in the holy place of the Temple typi-
fies Christ's merits, prayers, and righteousness, which makes our worship
and prayers acceptable to God. Incense could be offered only on coals tak-
en from the altar of burnt offering, which reveals an intimate connection
between intercession and the atoning sacrifice of the altar. Thus Christ's
intercessory work is built on the merits of His completed sacrificial atonement.

Christ's intercession offers encouragement to His people: He is "able to
save to the uttermost those who come to God through Him, since He ever
lives to make intercession for them" (Heb. 7:25). Because Christ mediates
for His people, all of Satan's accusations have lost their legal basis (1 John
2:1; cf. Zech. 3:1). Paul asked rhetorically, "Who is he who condemns?"

Then he offered the assurance that Christ Himself is at God's right hand, interceding for us (Rom. 8:34). Affirming His role as Mediator, Christ said, "Most assuredly, I say to you, whatever you ask the Father in My name He will give you" (John 16:23).

Christ the King. God "has established His throne in heaven, and His kingdom rules over all" (Ps. 103:19). It is self-evident that the Son of God, as one of the Godhead, shares in this divine government over the whole universe.

Christ, as the God-man, will exercise His kingship over those who have accepted Him as Lord and Saviour. "Your throne, O God," Scripture says, "is forever and ever; a scepter of righteousness is the scepter of your kingdom" (Ps. 45:6; Heb. 1:8, 9).

Christ's kingdom was not established without strife, for "the kings of the earth set themselves, and the rulers take counsel together, against the Lord and against His Anointed [Messiah]" (Ps. 2:2). But their schemes fail. God will establish the Messiah on His throne by decree: "I have set My king on My holy hill of Zion"; He has declared, "You are My Son, today I have begotten You" (Ps. 2:6, 7; Heb. 1:5). The name of the King who is to occupy the throne of David is "THE LORD OUR RIGHTEOUSNESS" (Jer. 23:5, 6). His rule is unique, for He is to function on the heavenly throne as both priest and king (Zech 6:13).

To Mary the angel Gabriel announced that Jesus was to be that Messianic ruler, saying, "He will reign over the house of Jacob forever, and of His kingdom there will be no end" (Luke 1:33). His kingship is portrayed by two thrones, symbolizing His two kingdoms. The "throne of grace" (Heb. 4:16) represents the kingdom of grace; the "throne of His glory" (Matt. 25:31) stands for the kingdom of glory.

1. The kingdom of grace. Immediately after the first human had sinned, the kingdom of grace was instituted. It existed by the promise of God. Through faith people could become its citizens. But it was not fully established until the death of Christ. When He cried out on the cross, "It is finished," the requirements for the plan of redemption were met and the new covenant ratified (cf. Heb. 9:15-18).

Jesus' proclamation, "The time is fulfilled, and the kingdom of God is at hand" (Mark 1:15) was a direct reference to the kingdom of grace soon to be established by His death. Founded on the work of redemption, not Creation, this kingdom receives its citizens through regeneration—the new birth. Jesus ruled, "Unless one is born of water and the Spirit, he cannot enter the kingdom of God" (John 3:5; cf. 3:3). He compared its growth to the phenomenal development of a mustard seed and the effect of yeast on flour (Mark 4:22-31; Matt. 13:33).

The kingdom of grace is not seen in outward show but by its effect on the heart of the believers. This kingdom, Jesus taught, "does not come with observation; nor will they say, "See here!" or "See there!" For indeed, the kingdom of God is within you" (Luke 17:20, 21). It is not a kingdom of this world, He said, but a kingdom of truth. "I am a king. For this cause I was born, and for this cause I have come into the world, that I should bear witness to the truth. Every one who is of the truth hears My voice (John 18:37). Paul said this kingdom is Christ's kingdom of "righteousness and peace and joy in the Holy Spirit," into which believers have been transferred (Rom. 14:17; Col. 1:13).

The establishment of this kingdom was an excruciating experience, affirming that there is no crown without a cross. At the close of His public ministry Jesus, the Messiah, the God-man, came to Jerusalem as the rightful heir to the throne of David. Seated on a donkey as was the Jewish custom for a royal entry (Zech. 9:9), He accepted the masses' spontaneous, enthusiastic display of support. During His triumphal entry into the royal city "a very great multitude" spread their clothes to form a royal carpet, cutting down palm branches and shouting, "Hosanna to the Son of David! Blessed is He who comes in the name of the Lord!" (Matt. 21:8, 9) thus fulfilling Zechariah's prophecy. Now Christ presented Himself as the Messianic king.

Unfortunately, His claim to the throne did not go unopposed. Satanic hatred against the "sinless One" reached its culmination. In a twelve-hour period the defenders of the faith, the Sanhedrin, had Him arrested secretly, put Him to trial, and condemned Him to death.

During His trial, Jesus publicly affirmed that He was the Son of God and King of His people (Luke 23:3; John 18:33-37). In response to His claim He was scornfully clothed in a royal robe and crowned, not with a crown of gold, but of thorns (John 19:2). His reception as king was sheer mockery. Beating Him up, the soldiers scoffed, "Hail, King of the Jews!" (John 19:3). And when the Roman governor, Pilate, presented Him to the nation, saying,"Behold your King!" His own people unanimously rejected Him, crying out, "Away with Him, away with Him! Crucify Him!" (John 19:14, 15).

Through the deepest humiliation—death on the cross—Christ established the kingdom of grace. Soon afterward exaltation ended His humiliation. Upon His ascension He was enthroned in heaven as Priest and King, sharing His Father's throne (Ps. 2:7, 8; cf. Heb. 1:3-5; Phil. 2:9-11; Eph. 1:20-23). This enthronement did not give Him, as the divine Son of God, any power that was not already His. But now, as the divine-human Mediator, His human nature participated in the heavenly glory and power for the first time.

2. The kingdom of glory. A representation of the kingdom of glory was given at the Mount of Transfiguration. There, Christ presented Himself in His glory. "His face shone like the sun, and His clothes became white as light" (Matt. 17:2). Moses and Elijah represented the redeemed—Moses representing those who have died in Christ and will be resurrected, and Elijah representing believers who will be taken to heaven without experiencing death at the Second Advent.

The kingdom of glory will be established with cataclysmic events at Christ's return (Matt. 24:27, 30, 31; 25:31, 32). Following the judgment, when the Son of man's mediatorial work in the heavenly sanctuary has ended, the "Ancient of Days"—God the Father—will bestow upon Him "dominion and glory and a kingdom" (Dan. 7:9, 10, 14). Then the "kingdom and dominion, and the greatness of the kingdoms under the whole heaven, shall be given to the people, the saints of the Most High. His kingdom is an everlasting kingdom, and all dominions shall serve and obey Him" (Dan. 7:27).

The kingdom of glory will finally be established on earth at the end of the millennium, when the New Jerusalem will descend from heaven (Revelation 20, 21). By accepting Jesus Christ as our Saviour, we can become citizens of His kingdom of grace today and the kingdom of glory at His second coming. Before us lies a life with unlimited possibilities. The life Christ offers is not a life filled with failure and scattered hopes and dreams—but one of growth—a successful walk with the Saviour. It is a life that increasingly displays genuine love, joy, peace, longsuffering, kindness, goodness, faithfulness, gentleness, and self-control (Gal. 5:22, 23)—the fruits of the relationship Jesus offers to all who commit their lives to Him. Who can resist such an offer?

References

1. Seventy-week prophecy, see *70 Weeks, Leviticus, and the Nature of Prophecy,* ed., Frank B. Holbrook (Washington, D.C.: Biblical Research Institute, General Conference of Seventh-day Adventists, 1986), pp. 3-127.

2. On the biblical foundations of the year-day principle, see William H. Shea, *Selected Studies on Prophetic Interpretation* (Washington, D.C.: Review and Herald, 1982), pp. 56-93.

3. The dates for the reign of Artaxerxes have been firmly established by the Olympiad dates, the Ptolemy's Canon, the Elephantine Papyri, and the Babylonian Cuneiform tablets.

4. See also C. Mervyn Maxwell, *God Cares* (Mountain View, CA: Pacific Press, 1981), vol. 1, pp. 216-218.

5. Gleason L. Archer, *Encyclopedia of Bible Difficulties* (Grand Rapids, MI: Zondervan, 1982), p. 291.

6. White, *The Desire of Ages* (Mountain View, CA: Pacific Press, 1940), p. 530.

7. That Scripture alludes to Jesus as the "only begotten" and the "first born" and speaking of the day of His begetting does not deny His divine nature and eternal existence. The term *only begotten* (John 1:14; 1:18; 3:16; 1 John 4:9) comes from the Greek word *monogenes* and reveals that its range of meaning extends to "only" or "unique," depicting a special relationship, not an event in time. Isaac, for example, is called Abraham's "only begotten son," although he was not Abraham's only son or even his firstborn son (Gen. 16:16; 21:1-21; 25:1-6). Isaac was the unique son, the only one of his kind, destined to become Abraham's successor. "Jesus Christ, the pre-existent God, the divine creative Word, at His incarnation became in a unique sense the Son of God—which is why He is designated 'monogenes,' the only one of His kind, altogether unique in many aspects of His being and life. No other child of the human race was so compacted in his being, had so unequaled a relation to the Godhead, or did such a work as is true of Him. So 'monogenes' describes a relation between God the Father and Jesus Christ the Son as separate Persons of the Godhead. This is a relation that belongs to Christ's complex, divine-human personality, in connection with the economy of the plan of salvation." (Committee on Problems in Bible Translation, *Problems in Bible Translation* [Washington, D.C.: Review and Herald, 1954], p. 202). Likewise, when Christ is called the *firstborn* (Heb. 1:6; Rom. 8:29; Col. 1:15, 18; Rev. 1:5), the term does not refer to a point of time. Rather, it emphasizes importance or priority (cf. Heb. 12:23). In Hebrew culture, the firstborn received the family privileges. So Jesus, as the firstborn among men, won back all the privileges man had lost. He became the new Adam, the new "firstborn" or head of the human race. The biblical reference to the day in which Jesus was begotten is based on a similar concept to those of the only begotten and the firstborn. Depending on its context, the Messianic prediction, "You are My Son, today I have begotten you" (Ps. 2:7), refers to Jesus': incarnation (Heb. 1:6), resurrection (Acts. 13:33, cf. v. 30), or enthronement (Heb. 1:3, 5).

8. Additional evidence is found in laws of Greek grammar. (1) The anarthrous use of "Lord" (used without a definite article). The LXX translates YHWH with an anarthrous *kurios*. Very often, when one finds an anarthrous *kurios* in the New Testament, it indicates God (e. g. Matt. 7:21; 8:2, 6, 25). (2) A single article qualifies two substantives. Thus, e.g., Christ is described as God in the phrases "our great God and Saviour Jesus Christ" (Titus 2:13), "the righteousness of our God and Saviour Jesus Christ" (2 Peter 1:1). (3) When there are two substantives and the second is in the genitive case without an article, for either substantive, the quality of the one is attributed to the other. Thus in the same way that Rom. 1:17, 18 speaks of "righteousness of God" and "wrath of God," so Jesus is described as "Son of God" (Luke 1:35).

9. White, "The True Sheep Respond to the Voice of the Shepherd," *Signs of the Times*, Nov. 27, 1893, p. 54.

10. White, *Patriarchs and Prophets*, p. 34.

11. These expressions have often been used by Seventh-day Adventist writers to describe Jesus' identity with the human race, but never do they imply that He was in any way sinful. Throughout its history the official church position has been to uphold the absolute sinlessness of the Lord Jesus Christ.

12. Christ took upon Him "the same susceptibilities, mental and physical" as His contemporaries (White, "Notes of Travel," *Advent Review and Sabbath Herald*, Feb. 10, 1885, p. 81)—a human nature that had decreased in "physical strength, in mental power, in moral worth"—though not morally depraved, but totally sinless (White, "In All Points Tempted Like As We Are," *Signs*, Dec. 3, 1902, p. 2; White, *Desire of Ages*, p. 49).

13. Henry Melvill, in *Sermons by Henry Melvill*, B.D., ed., C. P. McIlvaine (New York, N.Y.: Stanford and Swords, 1844), p. 47. By "innocent infirmities," he meant hunger, pain, sorrow, etc. He called this view of the pre- and post-Fall nature of Christ "the orthodox doctrine" (*ibid.*).

14. White, Letter 8, 1895 in *The Seventh-day Adventist Bible Commentary*, ed., Francis D. Nichol, rev. ed. (Washington, D. C.: Review and Herald, 1980), vol. 5, pp. 1228, 1129; cf. *SDA Bible Commentary*, rev. ed., vol. 7, p. 426.

15. Cf. White, "In Gethsemane," *Signs*, Dec. 9, 1897, p. 3; White in *SDA Bible Commentary*, rev. ed., vol. 7, p. 927.

16. Brooke F. Wescott, *The Epistle to the Hebrews* (Grand Rapids, MI: Wm. B. Eerdmans, 1950), p. 59.

17. F. F. Bruce, *Commentary on the Epistle to the Hebrews* (Grand Rapids, MI: Wm. B. Eerdmans, 1972), pp. 85, 86.

18. White, "The Temptation of Christ," *Review and Herald*, April 1, 1875, p. 3.

19. Philip Schaff, *The Person of Christ* (New York, NY: George H. Doran, 1913), pp. 35, 36.

20. Karl Ullman, *An Apologetic View of the Sinless Character of Jesus*, The Biblical Cabinet; or Hermeneutical Exegetical, and Philological Library (Edinburgh, Thomas Clark, 1842), vol. 37, p. 11.

21. White, "In Gethsemane," *Signs*, Dec. 9, 1897, p. 3; cf. White, *Desire of Ages*, p. 266.

22. White, Letter 8, 1895, in *SDA Bible Commentary*, vol. 5, pp. 1128, 1129. In E. G. White's time the following definitions of *Propensity* were used; "Propensity;" from the Latin *propensus*, is defined as "Natural inclination; bias, bent" (*Webster's Collegiate Dictionary*, 3rd ed., [Springfield, MA: G. & C. Merrimam Co., 1916]); cf. *Nuttall's Standard Dictionary of the English Language* (Boston, MA: De Wolfe, Fiske & Co., 1886). *Webster's Unabridged Dictionary* defines it as "the quality or state of being propense [leaning toward, in a moral sense]; natural inclination; disposition to do good or evil; bias; bent, tendency" (*Webster's International Dictionary of the English Language* [Springfield, MA: G. & C. Merriam & Co., 1890]). One of E. G. White's fa-

vorite authors, Henry Melvill, wrote, "But whilst he took humanity with the innocent infirmities, he did not take it with the sinful propensities. Here Deity interposed. The Holy Ghost overshadowed the Virgin, and, allowing weakness to be derived from her, forbade wickedness; and so caused that there should be generated a sorrowing and a suffering humanity, but nevertheless an undefiled and a spotless; a humanity with tears, but not with stains; accessible to anguish, but not prone to offend; allied most closely with the produced misery, but infinitely removed from the producing cause (Melvill, p. 47). See Tim Poirier, "A Comparison of the Christology of Ellen White and Her Literary Sources" (Unpublished MS, Ellen G. White Estate, Inc., General Conference of Seventh-day Adventists, Washington, D. C. 20012).

23. White, "Temptation of Christ," *Review and Herald*, Oct. 13, 1874, p. [1]; cf. White in *SDA Bible Commentary*, vol. 7, pp. 907, 904; vol. 5, p. 1113.

God the Holy Spirit

5

God the eternal Spirit was active with the Father and the Son in Creation, incarnation, and redemption. He inspired the writers of Scripture. He filled Christ's life with power. He draws and convicts human beings; and those who respond He renews and transforms into the image of God. Sent by the Father and the Son to be always with His children, He extends spiritual gifts to the church, empowers it to bear witness to Christ, and in harmony with the Scriptures leads it into all truth. (Gen. 1:1, 2; Luke 1:35; 4:18; Acts 10:38; 2 Pet. 1:21; 2 Cor. 3:18; Eph. 4:11, 12; Acts 1:8; John 14:16-18, 26; 15:26, 27; 16:7-13.)

THOUGH THE CRUCIFIXION HAD bewildered, anguished, and terrified Jesus' followers, the resurrection brought morning to their lives. When Christ broke the shackles of death, the kingdom of God dawned in their hearts.

Now unquenchable fire burned within their souls. Differences that a few weeks earlier had erected nasty barriers among the disciples melted. They confessed their faults to one another and opened themselves more fully to receive Jesus, their ascended King.

The unity of this once-scattered flock grew as they spent day after day in prayer. One unforgettable day they were praising God when a noise like the roar of a tornado ripped through their midst. As though the burning in their hearts were becoming visible, fiery flames descended on each head. Like a rampaging fire, the Holy Spirit descended upon them.

Filled with the Spirit, the disciples could not contain their new, ardent love and joy in Jesus. Publicly and enthusiastically, they began to proclaim the good news of salvation. Alerted by the sound, a multitude of local citizens along with pilgrims from many nations flocked to the building. Filled with amazement and confusion, they heard—in their own language—powerful testimonies to God's mighty works spoken by unsophisticated Galileans.

"I don't understand," said some, "What does this mean?" Others tried to pass it off with, "They're drunk." "Not so," Peter cried above the noise of the crowd. "It's only nine o'clock in the morning. What you have heard and seen is taking place because the resurrected Jesus Christ has been exalted to the right hand of God and is giving us the Holy Spirit now" (Acts 2).

Who Is the Holy Spirit?

The Bible reveals that the Holy Spirit is a person, not an impersonal force. Statements such as, "It seemed good to the Holy Spirit, and us" (Acts 15:28), reveal that the early believers viewed Him as a person. Christ also spoke of Him as a distinct person. "He will glorify Me," He said, "for He will take of what is Mine and declare it for you" (John 16:14). Scriptures referring to the triune God describe the Spirit as a person (Matt. 28:19; 2 Cor. 13:14).

The Holy Spirit has personality. He strives (Gen. 6:3), teaches (Luke 12:12), convicts (John 16:8), directs church affairs (Acts 13:2), helps and intercedes (Rom. 8:26), inspires (2 Peter 1:21), and sanctifies (1 Peter 1:2). These activities cannot be performed by a mere power, influence, or attribute of God. Only a person can do them.

The Holy Spirit Is Truly God

Scripture views the Holy Spirit as God. Peter told Ananias that, in lying to the Holy Spirit, He had lied not "to men but to God" (Acts 5:3, 4). Jesus defined the unpardonable sin as "blasphemy against the Spirit," saying, "Anyone who speaks a word against the Son of Man, it will be forgiven him; but whoever speaks against the Holy Spirit, it will not be forgiven him, either in this age or in the age to come" (Matt. 12:31, 32). This could be true only if the Holy Spirit is God.

Scripture associates divine attributes with the Holy Spirit. He is life. Paul referred to Him as the "Spirit of life" (Rom. 8:2). He is truth. Christ called Him the "Spirit of truth" (John 16:13). The expressions "love of the Spirit" (Rom. 15:30) and "the Holy Spirit of God" (Eph. 4:30) reveal that love and holiness are part of His nature.

The Holy Spirit is omnipotent. He distributes spiritual gifts "to each one individually as He wills" (1 Cor. 12:11). He is omnipresent. He will "abide" with His people "forever" (John 14:16). None can escape His influence (Ps. 139:7-10). He also is omniscient, because "the Spirit searches all things, yes, the deep things of God" and "no one knows the things of God except the Spirit of God" (1 Cor. 2:10, 11).

The works of God are also associated with the Holy Spirit. Creation and resurrection both involve Him. Said Elihu, "The Spirit of God has made me, and the breath of the Almighty gives me life" (Job 33:4). And the psalmist said, "You send forth Your Spirit, they are created" (Ps. 104:30). Paul claimed, "He who raised Christ from the dead will also give life to your mortal bodies through His Spirit who dwells in you" (Rom. 8:11).

Only an omnipresent personal God, not an impersonal influence, nor a created being, could perform the miracle of bringing the divine Christ to one individual, Mary. At Pentecost, the Spirit made the one God-man, Jesus, universally present to all willing recipients.

The Holy Spirit is considered equal with the Father and the Son in the baptismal formula (Matt. 28:19), the apostolic blessing (2 Cor. 13:14), and the spiritual gifts discourse (1 Cor. 12:4-6).

The Holy Spirit and the Godhead

From eternity, God the Holy Spirit lived within the Godhead as the third member. The Father, Son, and Spirit are equally self-existent. Though each is equal, an economy of function operates within the Trinity (see chapter 2 of this book).

The truth about God the Holy Spirit is best understood as seen through Jesus. When the Spirit comes to believers, He comes as the "Spirit of Christ"—He does not come in His own right, carrying His own credentials. His activity in history centers on Christ's mission of salvation. The Holy Spirit was actively involved in Christ's birth (Luke 1:35), confirmed His public ministry at baptism (Matt. 3:16, 17), and brought the benefits of Christ's atoning sacrifice and resurrection to humanity (Rom. 8:11).

In the Godhead, the Spirit seems to fulfill the role of executor. When the Father gave His Son to the world (John 3:16), He was conceived of the Holy Spirit (Matt. 1:18-20). The Holy Spirit came to complete the plan, to make it a reality.

The Holy Spirit's intimate involvement in creation is seen in His presence at Creation (Gen. 1:2). Life's origin and maintenance depends on His operation; His departure means death. Said the Bible, if God "should gather to Himself His Spirit and His breath, all flesh would perish together, and man would return to dust" (Job 34:14, 15; cf. 33:4). We can see reflections of the Spirit's creative work in His re-creative work within each person who is open to God. God carries out His work within individuals through the Creator Spirit. So in incarnation, creation, and re-creation, the Spirit comes to bring God's intention to fulfillment.

The Promised Spirit

We were intended to be dwelling places of the Holy Spirit (see 1 Cor. 3:16). Adam and Eve's sin separated them from both the Garden and the indwelling Spirit. That separation continues—the enormity of wickedness before the Flood led God to declare, "My Spirit shall not strive with man forever" (Gen. 6:3).

In Old Testament times the Spirit equipped certain individuals to perform special tasks (Num. 24:2; Judges 6:34; 1 Sam. 10:6). At times He is "in" persons (Ex. 31:3; Isa. 63:11). Undoubtedly, genuine believers have always had an awareness of His presence, but prophecy predicted a pouring out of the Spirit "on all flesh" (Joel 2:28)—a time when a greater manifestation of the Spirit would usher in a new age.

While the world remained in the hands of the usurper, the pouring out of the fullness of the Spirit had to wait. Before the Spirit could be poured out upon all flesh, Christ must carry out His earthly ministry and make the atoning sacrifice. Pointing to Christ's ministry as a Spirit ministry, John the Baptist said, "I indeed baptize you with water" but He "will baptize you with the Holy Spirit" (Matt. 3:11). But the Gospels do not reveal Jesus baptizing with the Holy Spirit. Just hours before His death, Jesus promised His disciples, "I will pray the Father, and He will give you another Helper, that He may abide with you forever, even the Spirit of truth" (John 14:16, 17). Was the promised baptism of the Spirit received at the cross? No dove appeared on crucifixion Friday—only darkness and bolts of lightning.

Not until after His resurrection did Jesus breathe the Spirit on His disciples (John 20:22). He said, "Behold, I send the Promise of My Father upon you; but tarry in the city of Jerusalem until you are endued with power from on high" (Luke 24:49). This power would be received "when the Holy Spirit has come upon you," making believers His witnesses to the ends of the earth (Acts 1:8).

John wrote, "The Holy Spirit was not yet given, because Jesus was not yet glorified" (John 7:39). The Father's acceptance of Christ's sacrifice was the prerequisite for the outpouring of the Holy Spirit.

The new age broke in only when our victorious Lord was seated on Heaven's throne. Only then could He send the Holy Spirit in His fullness. After "being exalted to the right hand of God," Peter said, He "poured out" the Holy Spirit (Acts 2:33) upon His disciples who, anxiously anticipating this event, had gathered "with one accord in prayer and supplication" (Acts 1:5, 14). At Pentecost, fifty days after Calvary, the new age burst forth with all the power of the Spirit's presence. "And suddenly there came a sound from heaven, as of a rushing mighty wind, and it filled the whole house where they [the disciples] were sitting....And they were all filled with the Holy Spirit" (Acts 2:2-4).

The missions of both Jesus and the Holy Spirit were totally interdependent. The fullness of the Holy Spirit could not be given until Jesus had completed His mission. And Jesus, in turn, was conceived of the Spirit (Matt. 1:8-21), baptized by the Spirit (Mark 1:9, 10), led by the Spirit (Luke 4:1), performed His miracles through the Spirit (Matt. 12:24-32), offered Himself at Calvary through the Spirit (Heb. 9:14, 15) and was, in part, resurrected by the Spirit (Rom. 8:11).

Jesus was the first person to experience the fullness of the Holy Spirit. The astounding truth is that our Lord is willing to pour out His Spirit on all who earnestly desire Him.

The Mission of the Holy Spirit

The evening before Christ's death His words about His impending departure greatly troubled His disciples. He immediately assured them that they would receive the Holy Spirit as His personal representative. They would not be left as orphans (John 14:18).

The Origin of the Mission. The New Testament reveals the Holy Spirit in a unique way. He is called the "Spirit of Jesus" (Acts 16:7, NIV), "Spirit of His Son" (Gal. 4:6), "Spirit of God" (Rom. 8:9), the "Spirit of Christ" (Rom. 8:9; 1 Peter 1:11), and the "Spirit of Jesus Christ" (Phil. 1:19). Who originated the Holy Spirit's mission—Jesus Christ or God the Father?

When Christ revealed the origin of the Holy Spirit's mission to a lost world, He mentioned two sources. First, He referred to the Father: "I will pray the Father, and He will give you another Helper" (John 14:16; cf. 15:26, "from the Father"). The baptism with the Holy Spirit He called "the Promise of the Father" (Acts 1:4). Second, Christ referred to Himself: "I will send Him [the Spirit] to you" (John 16:7). Thus, the Holy Spirit proceeds from both the Father and the Son.

His Mission to the World. We can acknowledge Christ's Lordship only through the influence of the Holy Spirit. Said Paul, "No one can say that Jesus is Lord except by the Holy Spirit" (1 Cor. 12:3).

We are given the assurance that, through the Holy Spirit, Christ, "the true Light, "illuminates "every man who comes into the world" (John 1:9). His mission is to "convict the world of sin, and of righteousness, and of judgment" (John 16:8).

First, the Holy Spirit brings to us a deep conviction of sin, especially the sin of not accepting Christ (John 16:9). Second, the Spirit urges all to accept the righteousness of Christ. Third, the Spirit warns us of judgment, a powerful tool in stirring up sin-darkened minds to the need of repentance and conversion.

When we have repented we can be born again through the baptism of water and the Holy Spirit (John 3:5). Then ours is a new life, for we have become the dwelling place of the Spirit of Christ.

His Mission for Believers. The majority of texts concerning the Holy Spirit pertain to His relationship with God's people. His sanctifying influence leads to obedience (1 Peter 1:2), but no one continues to experience His abiding presence without meeting certain conditions. Peter said God has given the Spirit to those who continuously obey Him (Acts 5:32).[1] Thus, believers are warned about resisting, grieving, and quenching the Spirit (Acts 7:51; Eph. 4:30; 1 Thess. 5:19).

What does the Spirit do for believers?

1. He assists believers. When introducing the Holy Spirit, Christ called Him "another *Parakletos*" (John 14:16). This Greek word has been translated as "Helper" (NKJV), "Comforter" (KJV), "Counselor" (RSV), and can mean also "Intercessor," "Mediator," or "Advocate."

The only other *Parakletos* mentioned in Scripture is Christ Himself. He is our Advocate, or Intercessor, before the Father. "My little children, these things I write to you, that you may not sin. And if anyone sins, we have an Advocate with the Father, Jesus Christ the righteous" (1 John 2:1).

As Intercessor, Mediator, and Helper, Christ presents us to God and reveals God to us. Similarly, the Spirit guides us to Christ and manifests Christ's grace to us. This explains why the Spirit is called the "Spirit of grace" (Heb. 10:29). One of His greatest contributions is the application of Christ's redeeming grace to people (see 1 Cor. 15:10; 2 Cor. 9:14; James 4:5, 6).

2. He brings the truth of Christ. Christ called the Holy Spirit the "Spirit of truth" (John 14:17; 15:26; 16:13). His functions include bringing "to your remembrance all things that I said to you" (John 14:26) and guiding "you into all truth" (John 16:13). His message testifies to Jesus Christ (John 15:26). "He will not speak on His own authority," Christ said, "but whatever He hears He will speak; and He will tell you things to come. He will glorify Me, for He will take of what is Mine and declare it to you" (John 16:13, 14).

3. He brings the presence of Christ. Not only does He bring the message about Christ, He brings the very presence of Christ. Jesus said, "It is to your advantage that I go away; for if I do not go away, the Helper [Holy Spirit, John 14:16, 17] will not come to you; but if I depart, I will send Him to you" (John 16:7).

Cumbered with humanity, the Man Jesus was not omnipresent, which was why it was expedient that He depart. Through the Spirit, He could be everywhere all the time. Jesus said, "I will pray the Father, and He will give you another Helper, that He may abide with you forever, even the Spirit of truth." He gave the assurance that the Spirit was to dwell "with you and will be in you. I will not leave you orphans; I will come to you" (John 14:17, 18). "The Holy Spirit is Christ's representative, but divested of the personality of humanity, and independent thereof."[2]

At the incarnation, the Holy Spirit brought the presence of Christ to a person—Mary. At Pentecost, the Spirit brought the victorious Christ to the world. Christ's promises—"I will never leave you nor forsake you" (Heb. 13:5) and "I am with you always, even to the end of the age" (Matt. 28:20)—are realized through the Spirit. For this reason, the New Testament gives the Spirit a title never used of Him in the Old Testament—"the Spirit of Jesus" (Phil. 1:19).

Just as it is through the Spirit that both the Father and the Son make believers their home (John 14:23), so the only way believers can abide in Christ is through the Spirit.

4. He guides the operation of the church. Since the Holy Spirit brings the very presence of Christ, He is the true vicar of Christ on earth. As the abiding center of authority in matters of faith and doctrine, the ways in which He leads the church accord fully with the Bible. "The distinctive feature of Protestantism is that the Holy Spirit is the true vicar or successor of Christ on earth. To depend on organization, or leaders, or wisdom of men, is to put the human in place of the divine."[3]

The Holy Spirit was intimately involved in administering the apostolic church. In selecting missionaries, the church obtained His guidance through prayer and fasting (Acts 13:1-4). The individuals selected were known for their openness to the Spirit's leading. The book of Acts describes them as "filled with the Holy Spirit" (Acts 13:9, cf. 52). Their activities were under His control (Acts 16:6, 7). Paul reminded church elders that they had been put into their position by the Holy Spirit (Acts 20:28).

The Holy Spirit played an important role in resolving serious difficulties that threatened the unity of the church. Indeed, Scripture introduces the decisions of the first church council with the words "It seemed good to the Holy Spirit, and to us..." (Acts 15:28).

5. He equips the church with special gifts. The Holy Spirit has bestowed special gifts on God's people. In Old Testament times, "the Spirit of the Lord" came "upon" individuals, giving them extraordinary powers to lead and deliver Israel (Judges 3:10; 6:34; 11:29; etc.) and the ability to prophesy (Num. 11:17, 25, 26; 2 Sam. 23:2). The Spirit came upon Saul and

David when they were anointed as rulers of God's people (1 Sam. 10:6; 10; 16:13). To some people, the infilling of the Spirit brought unique artistic skills (Ex. 28:3; 31:3; 35:30-35).

In the early church, as well, it was through the Holy Spirit that Christ bestowed His gifts on the church. The Spirit distributed as He saw fit, thus benefiting the whole church (Acts 2:38; 1 Cor. 12:7-11). He provided the special power necessary for proclaiming the gospel to the ends of the earth (Acts 1:8—see chapter 17 of this book).

6. He fills the hearts of believers. Paul's query to the disciples at Ephesus, "Did you receive the Holy Spirit when you believed?" (Acts 19:2), is a crucial question for every believer.

When Paul received a negative reply, he laid hands on those disciples, and they received the baptism of the Holy Spirit (Acts 19:6).

This incident indicates that the conviction of sin brought about by the Holy Spirit and the Spirit's infilling of the life are two different experiences.

Jesus pointed out the necessity of being born of water and of the Spirit (John 3:5). Just before His ascension, He commanded new believers to be baptized "in the name of the Father and of the Son and of the Holy Spirit" (Matt. 28:19). In harmony with this command, Peter preached that "the gift of the Holy Spirit" is to be received at baptism (Acts 2:38). And Paul confirms the importance of the baptism of the Holy Spirit (see chapter 15 of this book) with an urgent appeal that believers "be filled with the Spirit" (Eph. 5:18).

The infilling of the Holy Spirit, transforming us into the image of God, continues the work of sanctification begun at the new birth. God has saved us according to His mercy "through the washing of regeneration and renewing of the Holy Spirit, whom He poured out on us abundantly through Jesus Christ our Saviour" (Titus 3:5, 6).

"It is the absence of the Spirit that makes the gospel ministry so powerless. Learning, talent, eloquence, every natural or acquired endowment may be possessed; but, without the presence of the Spirit of God, no heart will be touched, no sinner won to Christ. On the other hand, if they are connected with Christ, if the gifts of the Spirit are theirs, the poorest and most ignorant of His disciples will have a power that will tell upon hearts. God makes them channels for the out-flowing of the highest influence in the universe."[4]

The Spirit is vital. All of the changes Jesus Christ effects in us come through the ministry of the Spirit. As believers, we should be constantly aware that without the Spirit we can accomplish nothing (John 15:5).

Today, the Holy Spirit directs our attention to the greatest gift of love God proffers in His Son. He pleads that we not resist His appeals, but that we accept the only way whereby we can be reconciled to our loving and gracious Father.

References

1. See Arnold V. Wallenkampf, *New by the Spirit* (Mountain View, CA: Pacific Press, 1978), pp. 49, 50.

2. Ellen G. White, *The Desire of Ages*, p. 669.

3. LeRoy E. Froom, *The Coming of the Comforter*, rev. ed. (Washington, D.C.: Review and Herald, 1949), pp. 66, 67.

4. White, *Testimonies for the Church* (Mountain View, CA: Pacific Press, 1948), vol. 8, pp. 21, 22.

Creation

6

God is Creator of all things and has revealed in Scripture the authentic account of His creative activity. In six days the Lord made "the heaven and the earth" and all living things upon the earth and rested on the seventh day of that first week. Thus He established the Sabbath as a perpetual memorial of His completed creative work. The first man and woman were made in the image of God as the crowning work of Creation, given dominion over the world, and charged with responsibility to care for it. When the world was finished, it was "very good," declaring the glory of God. (Gen. 1:2; Ex. 20:8-11; Ps. 19:1-6; 33:6, 9; 104; Heb. 11:3.)

THE BIBLE ACCOUNT IS SIMPLE. At the creative command of God, the "heaven and the earth, the sea, and all that is in them" (Ex. 20:11) appeared instantly. A mere six days saw the change from "without form, and void" to a lush planet teeming with fully mature creatures and plant forms. Our planet was adorned with clear, pure, bright colors, shapes, and fragrances, put together with superb taste and exactness of detail and function.

Then God "rested," stopping to celebrate, to enjoy. Forever, the beauty and majesty of those six days would be remembered because of His stopping. Let us steal a quick look at the Bible's account of the Beginning.

"In the beginning, God created the heavens and the earth." The earth was shrouded with water and darkness. On the first day, God separated the light from the darkness, calling the light "day" and the darkness "night."

On day two, God "divided the waters," separating the atmosphere from the water clinging to the earth, making conditions suitable for life. On the third day, God gathered the waters together into one place, establishing land and sea. Then God clothed the naked shores, hills, and valleys; "the land produced vegetation: plants bearing seed according to their kinds and trees bearing fruit with seed in it according to their kinds" (Gen. 1:12, NIV).

On the fourth day, God established the sun, moon, and stars "for signs and seasons, and for days and years." The sun was to govern the day, the moon, the night (Gen. 1:14-16).

God fashioned the birds and marine life on the fifth day. He created them "according to their kind" (Gen. 1:21)—an indication that the creatures He created would consistently reproduce after their own kinds.

On the sixth day, God made the higher forms of animal life. He said, "Let the earth bring forth the living creature according to its kind: cattle and creeping thing and beast of the earth, each according to its kind" (Gen. 1:24).

Then, as the crowning act of Creation, God made man "in His own image; in the image of God He created him; male and female He created them" (Gen. 1:27). God saw everything He had created and "indeed it was very good" (Gen. 1:31).

The Creative Word of God

"By the word of the Lord," the psalmist wrote, "the heavens were made, and all the host of them by the breath of His mouth" (Ps. 33:6). How did this creative word operate?

The Creative Word and Preexisting Matter. The words of Genesis, "God said," introduce the dynamic divine command responsible for the majestic events of the six days of Creation (Gen. 1:3, 6, 9, 11, 14, 20, 24). Each command came charged with a creative energy that transformed a planet "without form, and void" into a paradise. "He spoke, and it was done; He commanded and it stood fast" (Ps. 33:9). Truly, "the worlds were framed by the word of God" (Heb. 11:3).

This creative word was not dependent upon preexisting matter (ex nihilo): "By faith we understand that the universe was formed at God's command, so that what is seen was not made out of what was visible" (Heb. 11:3, NIV). Though at times God did use preexisting matter—Adam and the beasts were formed of the earth, and Eve was made from Adam's rib (Gen. 2:7, 19, 22)—ultimately, God created all matter.

The Creation Story

Many questions have been asked about the Genesis account of Creation. Do the two Creation narratives the first book of the Bible contains contradict each other, or are they consistent? Are the days of Creation literal, or do they represent large time periods? Were the heavens—the sun, moon, and even the stars—really made only 6,000 years ago?

The Creation Account. The Bible's two reports of Creation—one in Genesis 1:1 to 2:3 and the other in Genesis 2:4-25—harmonize.

The first narrative recounts, in chronological order, the creation of all things.

The second narrative begins with the words, "These are the generations of..." (KJV), an expression that, in Genesis, introduces a family history (cf. Gen. 5:1; 6:9; 10:1). This narrative describes man's place in Creation. It is not strictly chronological, but reveals that everything served to prepare the environment for man.[1] It gives more details of the creation of Adam and Eve and of the environment God provided in the garden of Eden than does the first. In addition, it informs us of the nature of humanity and of divine government. Only if these two Creation accounts are accepted as literal and historical do they harmonize with the rest of Scripture.

The Creation Days. The days of the Bible's Creation account signify literal twenty-four-hour periods. Typical of how the Old Testament people of God measured time, the expression "the evening and the morning" (Gen. 1:5, 8, 13, 19, 23, 31) specifies individual days with the day beginning at evening, or sunset (see Lev. 23:32; Deut. 16:6). There is no justification for saying that this expression meant one literal day in Leviticus, for instance, and thousands or millions of years in Genesis.

The Hebrew word translated "day" in Genesis 1 is *yom*. When yom is accompanied by a definite number, it always means a literal, 24-hour day (e.g. Gen. 7:11; Ex. 16:1)—another indication that the Creation account speaks of literal twenty-four-hour days.

The Ten Commandments offers another evidence that the Genesis Creation account involves literal days. In the fourth commandment, God says, "Remember the Sabbath day, to keep it holy. Six days you shall labor and do all your work, but the seventh day is the Sabbath of the Lord your God. In it you shall do no work;...for in six days the Lord made the heavens and the earth, the sea, and all that is in them, and rested the seventh day. Therefore the Lord blessed the Sabbath day and hallowed it" (Ex. 20:8-11).

Succinctly, God retells the Creation story. Each day (yom) was filled with creative activity; then the Sabbath climaxed the Creation week. The twenty-four-hour Sabbath day, therefore, commemorates a literal week of Creation. The fourth commandment would be meaningless were each day stretched into aeons.[2]

Those who cite 2 Peter 3:8, "With the Lord one day is as a thousand years," trying to prove that the days of Creation were not literal twenty-four-hour days, overlook the fact that the same verse ends with "a thousand years" are "as one day." Those who read into the days of Creation thousands of years or large indefinite periods of millions, or even billions, of years are questioning the validity of God's word—just as the serpent tempted Eve to do.

What Are the "Heavens"? Some people are puzzled, and understandably so, by the verses that say that God "created the heavens and the earth" (Gen. 1:1; cf. 2:1; Ex. 20:11) and that He made the sun, moon, and stars on the fourth day of Creation week 6,000 years ago (Gen. 1:14-19). Were all heavenly bodies brought into existence at that time?

Creation week did not involve the heaven that God has dwelt in from eternity. The "heavens" of Genesis 1 and 2 probably refer to our sun and its system of planets.

Indeed, the earth, instead of being Christ's first creation, was most likely His last one. The Bible pictures the sons of God, probably the Adams of all the unfallen worlds, meeting with God in some distant corner of the universe (Job 1:6-12). So far, space probes have discovered no other inhabited planets. They, apparently, are situated in the vastness of space—well beyond the reach of our sin-polluted solar system, quarantined against the infection of sin.

The God of Creation

Just what kind of God is our Creator? Is such an infinite personage interested in us—minute specks of life in a distant corner of His universe? After creating the earth, did He go on to bigger and better things?

A Caring God. The Bible's Creation account begins with God and moves to human beings. It implies that, in creating the heavens and the earth, God was preparing the perfect environment for the human race. Mankind, male and female, was His glorious masterpiece.

The account reveals God as a careful planner with a concern for His creation. He planted a special garden home for them and gave them the responsibility of cultivating it. He created human beings so they could have a relationship with Him. This was not to be a forced, unnatural relationship; He created them with freedom of choice and capacity to love and serve Him.

Who Was the Creator God? All the members of the Godhead were involved in Creation (Gen. 1:2, 26). The active agent, however, was the Son of God, the preexisting Christ. In the prologue to his Creation account, Moses wrote, "In the beginning God created the heavens and the earth." Recalling those words, John specified Christ's role in Creation: "in the beginning was the Word, and the Word was with God, and the Word was God....All things were made through Him, and without Him nothing was made that was made" (John 1:1-3). Subsequently, in the same passage John makes abundantly clear of whom he was writing: "The Word became flesh and dwelt among us" (John 1:14). Jesus was the Creator, the One who spoke the earth into existence (see also Eph. 3:9; Heb. 1:2).

A Display of God's Love. How deep is God's love! When Christ, with loving care, knelt over Adam, shaping this first man's hand, He must have known that men's hands would someday abuse and ultimately nail Him to the cross. In a sense, Creation and the cross merge, since Christ the Creator was slain from the foundation of the world (Rev. 13:8). His divine foreknowledge[3] did not stop Him. Under the ominous cloud of Calvary, Christ breathed into Adam's nostrils the breath of life, knowing that this creative act would deprive Him of His breath of life. Incomprehensible love is the basis of Creation.

The Purpose of Creation

Love motivates all that God does, for He is love (1 John 4:8). He created us not only so we could love Him but so that He could love us, too. His love led Him to share, in Creation, one of the greatest gifts that He can confer—existence. Has the Bible, then, indicated for what purpose the universe and its inhabitants exist?

To Reveal God's Glory. Through His created works, God discloses His glory: "The heavens declare the glory of God; the skies proclaim the work of His hands. Day after day they pour forth speech; night after night they display knowledge. There is no speech or language where their voice is not heard. Their voice goes out into all the earth, their words to the end of the world" (Ps. 19:1-4, NIV).

Why such a display of God's glory? Nature functions as a witness for God. He intends His created works to direct individuals to their Creator. "For since the creation of the world," Paul says, "God's invisible qualities—His eternal power and divine nature—have been clearly seen, being understood from what has been made, so that men are without excuse" (Rom. 1:20, NIV).

As we are drawn to God through nature, we learn more about the qualities of God—qualities that can be incorporated into our own lives. And, by reflecting God's character, we bring glory to Him, thus fulfilling the purpose for which we are created.

To Populate the World. The Creator did not intend the earth to be a lonely, empty planet; it was to be inhabited (Isa. 45:8). When the first man felt the need of a companion, God created the woman (Gen. 2:20; 1 Cor. 11:9). Thus, He established the marriage institution (Gen. 2:22-25). And the Creator not only gave the couple dominion over this newly created world—but, with the words "Be fruitful and multiply" (Gen. 1:28), He gave them the privilege of participating in its creation.

The Significance of Creation

People are tempted to ignore the doctrine of Creation. "Who cares," they ask, "how God created the earth? What we need to know is how to get to heaven." Yet the doctrine of a divine Creation forms "the indispensable foundation for Christian and biblical theology."[4] A number of fundamental biblical concepts are rooted in the divine Creation.[5] Indeed, a knowledge of how God created "the heavens and the earth" can ultimately help one find his way to the new heaven and earth John the Revelator speaks of. What, then, are some of the implications of the doctrine of Creation?

The Antidote to Idolatry. God's creatorship distinguishes Him from all other gods (1 Chron. 16:24-27; Ps. 96:5, 6; Isa. 40:18-26; 42:5-9; 44). We should worship the God who made us, and not the gods we have made. By virtue of His creatorship, He deserves our total allegiance. Any relationship that interferes with this allegiance is idolatry and subject to divine judgment. Thus, faithfulness to the Creator is a life-or-death matter.

The Foundation of True Worship. Our worship of God is based on the fact that He is our Creator and we are His creatures (Ps. 95:6). The importance of this theme is indicated by its inclusion in the call extended to earth's inhabitants just before Christ's return—to worship the One "who made heaven and earth, the sea and springs of water" (Rev. 14:7).

The Sabbath—a Memorial of Creation. God established the seventh-day Sabbath so that we would have a weekly reminder that we are creatures of His making. The Sabbath was a gift of grace, speaking not of what we did, but of what God has done. He especially blessed this day and sanctified it so we would never forget that, besides work, life should include communion with the Creator, rest, and celebration of God's marvelous creative works (Gen. 2:2, 3). To emphasize its importance, the Creator placed the injunction to remember this sacred memorial of His creative power in the center of the moral law as an everlasting sign and symbol of Creation (Ex. 20:8-11; 31:13-17; Eze. 20:20—see chapter 20 of this book).

Marriage—a Divine Institution. During the Creation week, God established marriage as a divine institution. He intended this sacred union between two individuals to be indissoluble: The man was to "be joined to his wife," and they were to "become one flesh" (Gen. 2:24; see also Mark 10:9; see chapter 23 of this book).

The Basis for True Self-worth. The Creation account states that we were made in God's image. This understanding provides a true concept of the worth of the individual. It leaves no room for a low estimate of ourselves. Indeed, we have been given a unique place in creation, with the special privilege of constant communication with the Creator and the opportunity of becoming more like Him.

The Basis for True Fellowship. God's creatorship establishes His fatherhood (Mal. 2:10) and reveals the brotherhood of all humanity. He is our Father; we are His children. Regardless of sex, race, education, or position, all have been created in God's image. Understood and applied, this concept would eliminate racism, bigotry, and any other form of discrimination.

Personal Stewardship. Since God created us, we belong to Him. This fact implies that we have the sacred responsibility to be faithful stewards of our physical, mental, and spiritual faculties. Acting in complete independence of the Creator is the epitome of ungratefulness (see chapter 21 of this book).

Responsibility for the Environment. At Creation God placed the first man and woman in the garden (Gen. 2:8). They were to cultivate the earth and to "have dominion" over all animal life (Gen. 1:28). This indicates that we have the divinely bestowed responsibility of preserving the quality of our environment.

Dignity of Manual Labor. The Creator asked Adam "to tend and keep" the Garden of Eden (Gen. 2:15). His assigning mankind this useful occupation in a perfect world reveals the dignity of manual labor.

The Worth of the Physical Universe. At each stage of Creation God said what He had made was "good" (Gen. 1:10, 12, 17, 21, 25), and when He had finished creating, He pronounced the whole "very good" (Gen. 1:31). Thus, created matter is not intrinsically evil, but good.

The Remedy for Pessimism, Loneliness, and Meaninglessness. The Creation narrative reveals that, rather than coming into existence because of chance evolution, everything was created with a purpose. The human race was designed for an everlasting relationship with the Creator Himself. When we understand that we were created for a reason, life becomes meaningful and rich, and the painful emptiness and dissatisfaction that so many express vanishes, replaced by the love of God.

The Holiness of God's Law. God's law existed before the Fall. In their unfallen state human beings were subject to it. It was to warn against self-destruction, to reveal the limits of freedom (Gen. 2:17), and to safeguard the happiness and peace of the subjects of God's kingdom (Gen. 3:22-24— see chapter 19 of this book).

The Sacredness of Life. The Creator of life continues to be involved in the formation of human life, thereby making life sacred. David praises God because of His involvement in his birth: "You have formed my inward parts; You have covered me in my mother's womb. I will praise You, for I am fearfully and wonderfully made; ...my frame was not hidden from You, when I was made in secret, and skillfully wrought in the lowest parts of the earth. Your eyes saw my substance, being yet unformed. And in Your book they all were written" (Ps. 139: 13-16). In Isaiah the Lord identifies Himself as the One "who formed you from the womb" (Isa. 44:24). Because life is a gift of God, we must respect it; in fact, we have a moral duty to preserve it.

God's Creative Work Continues

Has God finished His Creation? The Creation narrative ends with the statement, "Thus the heavens and the earth, and all the host of them, were finished" (Gen. 2:1). The New Testament affirms that God's Creation was completed at the "foundation of the world" (Heb. 4:3). Does this mean that Christ's creative energy is no longer in operation? Not at all. The creative word still operates in various ways.

1. Christ and His creative word. Four thousand years after Creation a centurion said to Christ, "Only speak a word, and my servant will be healed" (Matt. 8:8). Just as He had done at Creation, Jesus spoke—and the servant was healed. Throughout Jesus' earthly ministry the same creative energy that brought life to Adam's lifeless body raised the dead and brought new life to the afflicted who requested His help.

2. The creative word today. Neither this world nor the universe operates on any inherent power of its own. The God who created them preserves and sustains them. He "covers the heavens with clouds," "prepares rain for the earth," and "makes grass to grow on the mountains. He gives to the beast its food, and to the young ravens that cry" (Ps. 147:8, 9; cf. Job 26:7-14). He upholds all things by His word, and "in Him all things consist" (Col. 1:17; cf. Heb. 1:3).

We are dependent upon God for the function of every cell of our bodies. Every breath, every heartbeat, every blink of the eye speaks of the care of a loving Creator. "In Him we live and move and have our being" (Acts 17:28).

God's creative power is involved not only in Creation, but in redemption and restoration. God re-creates hearts (Isa. 44:21-28; Ps. 51:10). "We are His workmanship," Paul said, "created in Christ Jesus for good works" (Eph. 2:10). "If anyone is in Christ, he is a new creation" (2 Cor. 5:17). God, who hurled the many galaxies across the cosmos, uses that same power to re-create the most degraded sinner into His own image.

This redeeming, restoring power is not limited to changing human lives. The same power that originally created the heavens and the earth will, after the final judgment, re-create them—make of them a new and magnificent creation, a new heavens and a new earth (Isa. 65:17-19, Revelation 21, 22).

Creation and Salvation

So, in Jesus Christ, Creation and salvation meet. He created a majestic universe and a perfect world. Both the contrasts and the parallels between Creation and salvation are significant.

The Duration of Creation. At Creation Christ commanded, and it was instantly accomplished. Rather than vast periods of metamorphosis, His powerful word was responsible for Creation. In six days He created all. Yet why did it take even six days? Could not He have spoken just once and brought everything into existence in a moment?

Perhaps He took delight in the unfolding of our planet in those six days. Or perhaps this "extended" time has more to do with the value He placed on each created thing, or with His desire to reveal the seven-day week as a model for the cycle of activity and rest He intended for man.

But Christ does not just speak salvation into existence. The process of saving people stretches over millennia. It involves the old and new covenants, Christ's thirty-three and one-half years on earth and His nearly 2,000 years of subsequent heavenly intercession. Here is a vast span of time—according to Scripture chronology, about 6,000 years since Creation—and people still have not been returned to the Garden of Eden.

The contrast between the time required for Creation and for re-creation demonstrates that God's activities are always in the best interest of the human race. The shortness of Creation reflects His eagerness to bring about fully developed individuals who could enjoy His creation. Delaying the completion of Creation by making it dependent on a process of gradual development over long periods of time would have been contrary to the character of a loving God. The amount of time allowed for re-creation reveals God's loving desire to save as many people as possible (2 Peter 3:9).

Christ's Creative Work. In Eden Christ spoke the creative word. In Bethlehem, the "Word became flesh and dwelt among us" (John 1:14)—the Creator became part of Creation. What utter condescension! Though no one witnessed Christ's creation of the world, many did witness the power that gave sight to the blind (John 9:6, 7), speech to the dumb (Matt. 9:32, 33), healing to lepers (Matt 8:2, 3), and life to the dead (John 11:14-45).

Christ came as the second Adam, the new beginning for the race (Romans 5). He gave man the Tree of Life in Eden; man hung Him on a tree at Calvary. In Paradise, man stood tall in the image of God; at Calvary, Man hung limp in the image of a criminal. On both Creation Friday and crucifixion Friday, "It is finished" spoke of a completed creative work (Gen. 2:2, John 19:30)—one Christ accomplished as God, the other as Man; one in swift power, the other in human suffering; one for a time, the other for eternity; one subject to the Fall, the other in victory over Satan.

It was the perfect, divine hands of Christ that first gave man life; and it is the hands of Christ, pierced and blood-stained, that will give man eternal life. For man is not only created; he may be re-created. Both creations are equally the work of Christ—neither has come from within through natural development.

Created in the image of God, we have been called to glorify God. As the crowning act of His Creation, God invites each of us to enter into communion with Him, daily seeking the regenerating power of Christ so that, to God's glory, we will be able to reflect His image more fully.

References

1. L. Berkhof, *Systematic Theology*, 4th rev. ed. (Grand Rapids, MI: Wm. B. Eerdmans, 1941), p. 182.

2. Even considering that each day of Creation was a mere 1,000 years in length would cause problems. With such a schema, by the evening of the sixth "day"—his very first "day" of life—Adam would have been much older than the total life span the Bible allots him (Gen. 5:5). See Jemison, *Christian Beliefs*, pp. 116, 117.

3. See chapter 4 of this book.

4. "Creation," *SDA Encyclopedia*, p. 357.

5. Ibid.; Arthur J. Ferch, "What Creation Means to Me," *Adventist Review*, Oct. 9, 1986, pp. 11-13.

The Nature of Man

7

Man and woman were made in the image of God with individuality, the power and freedom to think and to do. Though created free beings, each is an indivisible unity of body, mind, and spirit, dependent upon God for life and breath and all else. When our first parents disobeyed God, they denied their dependence upon Him and fell from their high position under God. The image of God in them was marred and they became subject to death. Their descendants share this fallen nature and its consequences. They are born with weaknesses and tendencies to evil. But God in Christ reconciled the world to Himself and by His Spirit restores in penitent mortals the image of their Maker. Created for the glory of God, they are called to love Him and one another, and to care for their environment. (Gen. 1:26-28; 2:7; Ps. 8:4-8; Acts 17:24-28; Gen. 3; Ps. 51:5; Rom. 5:12-17; 2 Cor. 5:19, 20; Ps. 51:10; 1 John 4:7, 8, 11, 20; Gen. 2:15.)

AND GOD SAID, "LET US MAKE MAN in Our image, according to Our likeness." God did not speak into existence His crowning creation. Instead, He lovingly stooped to shape this new creature from the dust of the earth.

Earth's most creative sculptor could never carve out such a noble being. Perhaps a Michelangelo could fashion a stunning exterior, but what of
the anatomy and physiology carefully designed for function, as well as for
beauty?

The perfect sculpture lay completed with every hair, eyelash, and nail in
place, but God was not finished. This man was not to collect dust, but to
live, to think, to create, and to grow in glory.

Stooping over this magnificent form, the Creator "breathed into his
nostrils the breath of life; and man became a living being" (Gen. 2:7; cf.
1:26). Realizing man's need for companionship, God made "him a helper
comparable to him." God caused "a deep sleep" to come over Adam and,
as Adam slept, God extracted one of Adam's ribs and made it into a woman (Gen. 2:18, 21, 22). "So God created man in His own image; in the image of God He created him; male and female He created them." Then God
blessed them, and God said to them, "Be fruitful and multiply; fill the earth
and subdue it; have dominion over the fish of the sea, over the birds of the
air, and over every living thing that moves on the earth." A garden home
more splendid than the finest on earth today was given Adam and Eve.
There were trees, vines, flowers, hills, valleys—all adorned by the Master
Himself. Two special trees, the Tree of Life and the Tree of Knowledge of
Good and Evil, were there. God gave Adam and Eve permission to eat freely of every tree except the Tree of Knowledge of Good and Evil (Gen. 2:8,
9, 17).

Thus, the crowning event of creation week was accomplished. And "God
saw everything that He had made, and indeed it was very good" (Gen.
1:31).

The Origin of Man

Though today many believe that human beings originated from the lower forms of animal life and are the result of natural processes that took billions of years, such an idea cannot be harmonized with the biblical record.
That human beings have been subject to a process of degeneration is crucial to the biblical view of the nature of man.[1]

God Created Man. The origin of the human race is found in divine
council. God said, "Let Us make man" (Gen. 1:26). The plural "Us" refers
to the Trinitarian Godhead—God the Father, God the Son, and God the
Holy Spirit (see chapter 2 of this book). Of one purpose, then, God began
to create the first human being (Gen. 1:27).

Created From the Dust of the Ground. God formed man from "the
dust of the ground" (Gen. 2:7), using preexisting matter but not other
forms of life, such as marine or land animals. Not until He had formed ev-

ery organ and put it in its place did He introduce the "breath of life" that made man a living person.

Created After a Divine Type. God created each of the other animals—fishes, birds, reptiles, insects, mammals, etc.—"according to its kind" (Gen. 1:21, 24, 25). Each species had a typical form of its own and the ability to reproduce its specific kind. Man, however, was created after the divine type, not after a type of the animal kingdom. God said, "Let Us make man in Our image, according to Our likeness" (Gen. 1:26). There is a clear discontinuity between human beings and the animal kingdom. Luke's genealogical entry describing the origin of the human race expresses this difference simply, but profoundly: "Adam, the son of God." (Luke 3:38).

Man's Exalted Position. The creation of man was the zenith of all Creation. God put man, created in the image of the sovereign God, in charge of Planet Earth and all animal life. L. Berkhof states of Adam, "It was his duty and privilege to make all the nature and all created beings that were placed under his rule, subservient to his will and purpose, in order that he and his whole glorious dominion might magnify the almighty Creator and Lord of the universe" (Gen. 1:28; Ps. 8:4-9).[2]

The Unity of the Human Race. The genealogies in Genesis demonstrate that the successive generations after Adam and Eve all descended from this first pair. As humans, we all share the same nature which constitutes a genetic or genealogical unity. Paul said, "From one man he [God] made every nation of men, that they should inhabit the whole earth" (Acts 17:26, NIV).

Furthermore, we see other indications of the organic unity of our race in the biblical assertions that Adam's transgression brought sin and death upon *all*, and in the provision of salvation for *all* through Christ (Rom. 5:12, 19; 1 Cor. 15:21, 22).

The Unity of Man's Nature

What are the characteristic parts of human beings? Are they made up of several independent components, such as a body, a soul, and a spirit?

The Breath of Life. God "formed man of the dust of the ground, and breathed into his nostrils the breath of life; and man became a living being" (Gen. 2:7).

When God changed the elements of earth into a living being, He "breathed" the "breath of life" into the nostrils of Adam's lifeless body. This breath of life is "the breath of the Almighty" that gives life (Job 33:4)—the spark of life. We might compare it with the streams of electricity that, when they flow through various electrical components, transform a quiet, gray panel of glass in a box into a pulsating splash of color and action—when we flip the switch on a color TV. The electricity brings sound and motion where once there was nothing.

Man—a Living Soul. What did the breath of life do? When God formed the human being from the elements of the earth, all the organs were present: the heart, lungs, kidneys, liver, spleen, brain, etc.—all perfect, but lifeless. Then God breathed into this lifeless matter the breath of life, and "man became a living being."

The scriptural equation is straightforward: the dust of the ground (earth's elements) + the breath of life = a living being, or living soul. The union of earth's elements with the breath of life resulted in a living being, or soul.

This "breath of life" is not limited to people. Every living creature possesses it. The Bible, for example, attributes the breath of life to both those animals that went into Noah's ark and those that did not (Gen. 7:15, 22).

The Hebrew term in Genesis 2:7 that has been translated "living being" or "living soul" is *nephesh chayyah*. This expression does not exclusively designate man, for it also refers to marine animals, insects, reptiles and beasts (Gen. 1:20, 24; 2:19).

Nephesh, translated as "being" or "soul," comes from *naphash*, meaning "to breathe." Its Greek equivalent in the New Testament is *psuche*. "Inasmuch as breath is the most conspicuous evidence of life, *nephese* basically designates man as a living being, a person."[3] When used of animals, as in the Creation story, it describes them as living creatures that God created.

It is important to note the Bible says that man *became* a living soul. Nothing in the creation account indicates that man *received* a soul—some kind of separate entity that, at Creation, was united with the human body.

An Indivisible Unity. The importance of the Creation account for properly understanding the nature of man cannot be overestimated. By stressing his organic unity, Scripture portrays man as a whole. How then do the soul and spirit relate to the nature of man?

1. The biblical meaning of soul. As we have already mentioned, in the Old Testament "soul" is a translation of the Hebrew *nephesh*. In Genesis 2:7 it denotes man as a living being after the breath of life entered into a physical body formed from the elements of the earth. "Similarly, a new soul comes into existence whenever a child is born, each 'soul' being a new unit of life uniquely different and separate from other similar units. This quality of individuality in each living being, which constitutes it a unique entity, seems to be the idea emphasized by the Hebrew term *nephesh*. When used in this sense, *nephesh* is not a part of the person; it is the person and, in many instances, is translated 'person' (see Gen. 14:21; Num. 5:6; Deut. 10:22; cf. Ps. 3:2) or 'self' (Lev. 11:43; 1 Kings 19:4; Isa. 46:2; etc.).

"On the other hand, expressions such as 'my soul,' 'your soul,' 'his soul,' etc., are generally idioms for the personal pronouns 'I,' 'me,' 'you,' 'he,' etc. (see Gen. 12:13; Lev. 11:43, 44; 19:8; Joshua 23:11, Ps. 3:2; Jer. 37:9; etc.). In more than 100 of 755 occurrences in the Old Testament the KJV translates *nephesh* as 'life' (Gen. 9:4, 5; 1 Sam. 19:5; Job 2:4, 6; Ps. 31:13; etc.).

"Often *nephesh* refers to desires, appetites, or passions (cf. Deut. 23:24; Prov. 23:2; Eccl. 6:7), and is sometimes translated 'appetite' (Prov. 23:2; Eccl. 6:7). It may refer to the seat of the affections (Gen. 34:3; Song of Sol. 1:7; etc.), and at times it represents the volitional part of man, as when translated 'pleasure' (KJV) in Deuteronomy 23:24; Psalm 105:22; Jeremiah 34:16. In Numbers 31:19 the nephese is 'killed,' and in Judges 16:30 (translated 'me') it dies. In Numbers 5:2 ('the dead') it refers to a corpse (cf. Lev. 19:28; Num. 9:7, 10).

"The usage of the Greek word *psuche* in the New Testament is similar to that of *nephesh* in the Old Testament. It is used of animal life as well as human life (Rev. 16:3). In the KJV it is translated forty times simply as 'life' or 'lives' (see Matt. 2:20; 6:25; 16:25; etc.). In some instances it is used to mean simply 'people' (see Acts 7:14; 27:37; Rom. 13:1; 1Peter 3:20; etc.), and in others it is equivalent to the personal pronoun (see Matt. 12:18; 2 Cor. 12:15; etc.). Sometimes it refers to the emotions (Mark 14:34; Luke 2:35), to the mind (Acts 14:2; Phil. 1:27), or to the heart (Eph. 6:6)."[4]

The *psuche* is not immortal but subject to death (Rev. 16:3). It can be destroyed (Matt. 10:28).

Biblical evidence indicates that sometimes *nephesh* and *psuche* refer to the whole person and at other times to a particular aspect of man such as the affections, emotions, appetites, and feelings. This usage, however, in no way shows that man is a being made up of two separate and distinct parts. The body and the soul exist together; together they form an indivisible union. The soul has no conscious existence apart from the body. There is no text indicating that the soul survives the body as a conscious entity.

2. The biblical meaning of spirit. Whereas the Hebrew word *nephesh*, translated *soul*, denotes individuality or personality, the Old Testament Hebrew word *ruach*, translated *spirit*, refers to the energizing spark of life essential to individual existence. It stands for the divine energy, or life principle, that animates human beings.

"*Ruach* occurs 377 times in the Old Testament and most frequently is translated 'spirit,' 'wind,' or 'breath' (Gen. 8:1, etc.). It is also used to denote vitality (Judges 15:19), courage (Joshua 2:11), temper or anger (Judges 8:3), disposition (Isa. 54:6), moral character (Eze. 11:19), and the seat of the emotions (1 Sam. 1:15).

"In the sense of breath, the *ruach* of men is identical with the *ruach* of animals (Eccl. 3:19). The *ruach* of man leaves the body at death (Ps. 146:4) and returns to God (Eccl. 12:7; cf. Job 34:14). *Ruach* is used frequently of the Spirit of God, as in Isaiah 63:10. Never in the Old Testament, with respect to man, does *ruach* denote an intelligent entity capable of sentient existence apart from a physical body.

"The New Testament equivalent of *ruach* is *pneuma*, 'spirit,' from *pneo*, 'to blow,' or 'to breathe.' As with *ruach*, there is nothing inherent in the word *pneuma* denoting an entity in man capable of conscious existence apart from the body, nor does New Testament usage with respect to man in any way imply such a concept. In such passages as Romans 8:15; 1 Corinthians 4:21; 2 Timothy 1:7; 1 John 4:6 *pneuma* denotes 'mood,' 'attitude,' or 'state of feeling.' It is also used of various aspects of the personality, as in Galatians 6:1; Romans 12:11; etc. As with *ruach*, the *pneuma* is yielded to the Lord at death (Luke 23:46; Acts 7:59). Like *ruach*, *pneuma* is also used of the Spirit of God (1 Cor. 2:11, 14; Eph. 4:30; Heb. 2:4; 1 Peter 1:12; 2 Peter 1:21; etc.)."[5]

3. Unity of body, soul, and spirit. What is the relationship between body, soul, and spirit? What is the influence of this relationship on the unity of man?

a. A twofold union. Although the Bible views the nature of man as a unity, it does not precisely define the relationship among body, soul, and spirit. At times soul and spirit are used interchangeably. Notice their parallelism in Mary's expression of joy following the annunciation: "My soul magnifies the Lord, and my spirit has rejoiced in God my Saviour" (Luke 1:46, 47).

In one instance man is characterized by Jesus as body and soul (Matt. 10:28) and in another instance by Paul as body and spirit (1 Cor. 7:34). In the former, *soul* refers to the higher faculty of man, presumably the mind through which he communicates with God. In the latter, *spirit* refers to this higher faculty. In both instances the body includes the physical, as well as the emotional, aspects of a person.

b. A threefold union. There is one exception to the general characterization of man as comprising a twofold union of body and spirit, also spoken of in terms of a threefold union. He states, "Now may the God of peace Himself sanctify you completely; and may your whole spirit, soul, and body be preserved blameless at the coming of our Lord Jesus Christ" (1 Thess. 5:23). This passage conveys Paul's desire that none of these aspects of the person be excluded from the sanctification process.

In this instance *spirit* may be understood as the higher principle of intelligence and thought with which man is endowed, and with which God can communicate by His Spirit (see Rom. 8:16). It is by the renewing of the mind through the activities of the Holy Spirit that the individual is transformed into Christ's likeness (see Rom. 12:1, 2).

"By 'soul'...when distinguished from spirit, may be understood that part of man's nature that finds expression through the instincts, emotions, and desires. This part of one's nature can be sanctified, too. When, through the working of the Holy Spirit, the mind is brought into conformity with God's mind, and sanctified reason bears sway over the lower nature, the impulses, which would otherwise be contrary to God, become subject to His will."[6]

The body, which is controlled by either the higher or the lower nature, is the physical constitution—the flesh, blood, and bones.

Paul's sequence of first the spirit, then the soul, and finally the body is no coincidence. When the spirit is sanctified, the mind is under divine control. The sanctified mind, in turn, will have a sanctifying influence on the soul, i.e., the desires, feelings, and emotions. The person in whom this sanctification takes place will not abuse his body, so his physical health will flourish. Thus, the body becomes the sanctified instrument through which the Christian can serve His Lord and Saviour. Paul's call for sanctification is clearly rooted in the concept of the unity of human nature and reveals that effective preparation for Christ's second advent necessitates the preparation of the whole person—spirit, soul, and body.

c. An indivisible, sympathetic union. It is clear that each human being is an indivisible unit. The body, soul, and spirit function in close cooperation, revealing an intensely sympathetic relationship among a person's spiritual, mental and physical faculties. Deficiencies in one area will hamper the other two. A sick, impure, confused spirit or mind will have a detrimental effect on one's emotional and physical health, as well. The reverse is also true. A weak, sick, or suffering physical constitution will generally impair one's emotional and spiritual health. The impact the faculties have on each other means that each individual has a God-given responsibility to maintain the faculties in the best possible condition. Doing so is a vital part of being restored into the image of the Creator.

Man in the Image of God

The living beings that God created on the sixth day of Creation were made "in the image of God" (Gen. 1:27). What does being created in God's image imply?

Created in the Image and Likeness of God. It is frequently suggested that human moral and spiritual dimensions reveal something about God's moral and spiritual nature. But since the Bible teaches that man comprises an indivisible unity of body, mind, and soul, man's physical features must also, in some way, reflect God's image. But isn't God a spirit? How could a spirit being be associated with any form or shape?

A brief study of the angels reveals that they, like God, are spiritual beings (Heb. 1:7, 14). Yet they always appear in human form (Gen. 18:1-19:22; Dan. 9:21; Luke 1:11-38; Acts 12:5-10). Could it be that a spiritual being may have a "spiritual body" with a form and features (cf. 1 Cor. 15:44)?

The Bible indicates that some people have seen parts of God's person. Moses, Aaron, Nadab, Abihu, and the seventy elders saw His feet (Ex. 24:9-11). Although He refused to show His face, after covering Moses with His hands God revealed His back to him as He passed by (Ex. 33:20-23). God appeared to Daniel in a judgment-scene vision as the Ancient of Days seated on a throne (Dan. 7:9, 10). Christ is described as "the image of the invisible God" (Col. 1:15) and "the express image of His person" (Heb. 1:3). These passages seem to indicate that God is a personal being and has a personal form. This should come as no surprise, for man was created in the image of God.

Man was created a "little lower than the angels" (Heb. 2:7), an indication that he must have been endowed with mental and spiritual gifts. Although Adam lacked experience, insight, and character development, he was made "upright" (Eccl. 7:29), a reference to moral uprightness.[7] Being in the moral image of God, he was righteous, as well as holy (cf. Eph. 4:24), and was part of the creation God pronounced "very good" (Gen. 1:31).

Since man was created in the moral image of God, he was given the opportunity to demonstrate love and loyalty to his Creator. Like God, he had the power of choice—the freedom to think and act according to moral imperatives. Thus he was free to love and obey or to distrust and disobey. God risked man's making the wrong choice, because only with the freedom to choose could man develop a character that would fully display the principle of love that is the essence of God Himself (1 John 4:8). His destiny was to reach the highest expression of the image of God: to love God with all his heart, soul, and mind and to love others as himself (Matt. 22:36-40).

Created for Relationships With Others. God said, "It is not good that man should be alone" (Gen. 2:18), and He made Eve. Just as the three members of the Godhead are united in a loving relationship, so we were created for the fellowship found in friendship or marriage (Gen. 2:18). In these relationships we have the opportunity to live for others. To be genuinely human is to be relationship oriented. The development of this aspect of the image of God is an integral part of the harmony and prosperity of the kingdom of God.

Created to Be Stewards of the Environment. God said, "Let Us make man in Our image, according to Our likeness; let them have dominion over the fish of the sea, over the birds of the air, and over the cattle; over all the earth and over every creeping thing that creeps on the earth" (Gen. 1:26). Here God mentions man's divine image and his dominion over the lower creation in one breath. It was as God's representative that man was placed over the lower created orders. The animal kingdom cannot understand the sovereignty of God, but many animals are capable of loving and serving man.

David, in referring to man's dominion, states, "You have made him to have dominion over the works of Your hands; You have put all things under his feet" (Ps. 8:6-8). Man's exalted position was indicative of the glory and honor with which he was crowned (Ps. 8:5). His was the responsibility to rule graciously over the world, imaging or reflecting God's beneficent rule over the universe. So we are not the victim of circumstances, dominated by environmental forces. Rather, God has commissioned us to make a positive contribution by shaping the environment, using each situation in which we are placed as an opportunity to accomplish God's will.

These insights provide the key to improving human relationship in a world in which brokenness abounds. They also hold the answer to the selfish consumption of earth's natural resources and the inconsiderate pollution of air and water that lead to an increasing deterioration of the quality of life. Adoption of the biblical perspective on human nature provides the only assurance of a prosperous future.

Created to Imitate God. As human beings, we are to act like God because we were made to be like God. Though we are human, and not divine, we are to reflect our Maker within our dominion in every way possible. The fourth commandment appeals to this obligation: we are to follow our Maker's example in working the first six days of the week and resting on the seventh (Ex. 20:8-11).

Created With Conditional Immortality. At Creation, our first parents were given immortality, though their possession of it was conditioned upon obedience. Having access to the Tree of Life, they were destined to live forever. The only way they could jeopardize their state of immortality was through transgressing the command that forbade them to eat of the Tree of Knowledge of Good and Evil. Disobedience would lead to death (Gen. 2:17; cf. 3:22).

The Fall

Though created perfect and in God's image, and placed in a perfect environment, Adam and Eve became transgressors. How did such a radical—and terrible—transformation come about?

The Origin of Sin. If God created a perfect world, how could sin develop?

1. God and the origin of sin. Is God the Creator also the author of sin? Scripture points out that by nature God is holy (Isa. 6:3) and there is no unrighteousness in Him. "His work is perfect; for all His ways are just; righteous and upright is He" (Deut. 32:4). Scripture states, "Far be it from God to do wickedness, and from the Almighty to commit iniquity" (Job 34:10). "God cannot be tempted by evil, nor does He Himself tempt anyone" (James 1:13); He hates sin (Ps. 5:4; 11:5). God's original creation was "very good" (Gen. 1:31). Far from being the author of sin, He is "the author of eternal salvation to all who obey Him" (Heb. 5:9).

2. The author of sin. God could have prevented sin by creating a universe of robots that would do only what they were programmed to do. But God's love demanded that He create beings who could respond freely to His love—and such a response is possible only from beings who have the power of choice.

Providing His creation with this kind of freedom, however, meant that God must take the risk that some created beings would turn from Him. Unfortunately, Lucifer, a high-ranking being in the angelic world, became proud (Eze. 28:17; cf. 1 Tim. 3:6). Dissatisfied with his position in God's government (cf. Jude 6), he began to covet God's own place (Isa. 14:12-14). In an attempt to take control of the universe, this fallen angel sowed seeds of discontent among his fellow angels, and won the allegiance of many. The resulting heavenly conflict ended when Lucifer, now known as Satan, the adversary, and his angels were expelled from heaven (Rev. 12:4; 7-9; see also chapter 8 of this book).

3. The origin of sin in the human race. Undeterred by his expulsion from heaven, Satan determined to entice others to join his rebellion against God's government. His attention was drawn to the newly created human race. How could he lead Adam and Eve to rebel? They lived in a perfect world, with all their needs provided for by their Creator. How could they ever become discontented and distrust the One who was the source of their happiness? The account of the first sin gives the answer.

In his assault on the first human beings, Satan decided to catch them off guard. Approaching Eve when she was near the Tree of Knowledge of Good and Evil, Satan—in the guise of a serpent—questioned her about God's prohibition against eating of the tree. When Eve affirmed that God had said that they would die by eating of the tree, Satan challenged the divine prohibition, saying, "You will not surely die." He aroused her curiosity by suggesting that God was trying to keep her from a wonderful new experience—that of being like God (Gen. 3:4, 5). Immediately, doubt about God's word took root. Eve became infatuated with the grand possibilities the fruit was said to offer. The temptation began to play havoc with her sanctified mind. Belief in God's word now changed to belief in Satan's word. Suddenly, she imagined that "the tree was good for food, that it was pleasant to the eyes, and a tree desirable to make one wise." Dissatisfied with her position, Eve yielded to the temptation of becoming like God. "She took of its fruit and ate. She also gave to her husband with her, and he ate" (Gen. 3:6).

In trusting her senses rather than God's word, Eve severed her dependence upon God, fell from her high position, and plunged into sin. The fall of the human race, therefore, was first and foremost characterized by a breakdown in faith in God and His word. This unbelief led to disobedience, which in turn resulted in a broken relationship and finally to a separation between God and man.

The Impact of Sin. What were the immediate and long-term consequences of sin? How did it affect human nature? And what is the prospect of eliminating sin and improving human nature?

1. The immediate consequences. The first consequence of sin was a change in human nature that affected interpersonal relationships, as well as man's relationship with God. The new, exhilarating, eye-opening experience brought Adam and Eve only feelings of shame (Gen. 3:7). Instead of becoming God's equals, as Satan had promised, they became afraid and attempted to hide (Gen. 3:8-10).

When God questioned Adam and Eve about their sin, instead of admitting their fault, they tried to pass the blame along. Adam said, "The woman whom You gave to be with me, she gave me of the tree, and I ate" (Gen. 3:12). His words imply that both Eve and, indirectly, God were responsible for his sin, clearly showing how his sin had broken his relationship with his wife and his Creator. Eve, in turn, blamed the serpent (Gen. 3:13).

The dire consequences that came of it reveal the seriousness of their transgression. God cursed Satan's medium, the serpent, condemning it to move on its belly, as a perpetual reminder of the Fall (Gen. 3:14). To the woman God said, "I will greatly multiply your sorrow and your conception; in pain you shall bring forth children; your desire shall be for your husband, and he shall rule over you" (Gen. 3:16). And because Adam listened to his wife instead of to God, the earth was cursed to increase the anxiety and toil of his labors: "Cursed is the ground for your sake; in toil you shall eat of it all the days of your life. Both thorns and thistles it shall bring forth for you, and you shall eat the herb of the field. In the sweat of your face you shall eat bread till you return to the ground, for out of it you were taken" (Gen 3:17-19).

In reaffirming the unchangeableness of His law and that any transgression leads to certain death, God said: "Dust you are, and to dust you shall return" (Gen. 3:19). He executed this verdict by expelling the transgressors from their Edenic home, severing their direct communication with God (Gen. 3:8), and preventing them from partaking of the Tree of Life, the source of eternal life. Thus Adam and Eve became subject to death (Gen. 3:22).

2. The character of sin. Many scriptural passages, including particularly the account of the Fall, make it clear that sin is a moral evil—the result of a free moral agent's choosing to violate the revealed will of God. (Gen. 3:1-6; Rom. 1:18-22).

a. The definition of sin. Biblical definitions of sin include: "the transgression of the law" (1 John 3:4, KJV), a failure to act by anyone "who knows the good he ought to do and doesn't do it" (James 4:17, NIV), and "whatever is not from faith" (Rom. 14:23). One broad, inclusive definition of sin is: "Any deviation from the known will of God, either of neglect to do what He has specifically commanded or of doing what He has specifically forbidden."[8]

Sin knows no neutrality. Christ states, "He who is not with Me is against Me" (Matt. 12:30). Failure to believe in Him is sin (John 16:9). Sin is absolute in its character because it is rebellion against God and His will. Any sin, small or great, results in the verdict "guilty." Thus "whoever shall keep the whole law, and yet stumbles in one point, he is guilty of all" (James 2:10).

b. Sin involves thoughts, as well as actions. Frequently, sin is spoken of only in terms of concrete and visible acts of lawbreaking. But Christ said that being angry with someone violates the sixth commandment of the Decalogue, "You shall not kill" (Ex. 20:13, RSV), and that lustful desires transgress the command "You shall not commit adultery"

(Ex. 20:14). Sin, therefore, involves not only overt disobedience in actions but also thoughts and desires.

c. Sin and guilt. Sin produces guilt. From the biblical perspective, guilt implies that the one who has committed sin is liable to punishment. And because all are sinners, the whole world is "guilty before God" (Rom. 3:19).

If not cared for properly, guilt devastates the physical, mental, and spiritual faculties. And ultimately, if not resolved, it produces death—for "the wages of sin is death" (Rom. 6:23).

The antidote for guilt is forgiveness (Matt. 6:12), which results in a clear conscience and peace of mind. This forgiveness God is eager to grant repentant sinners. To the sin-burdened, guilt-ridden race, Christ graciously calls, "Come to Me, all you who labor and are heavy laden and I will give you rest" (Matt. 11:28).

d. The control center of sin. The seat of sin is in what the Bible calls the heart—what we know as the mind. From the heart "spring the issues of life" (Prov. 4:23). Christ reveals that it is the person's thoughts that defile, "for out of the heart proceed evil thoughts, murders, adulteries, fornications, thefts, false witness, blasphemies" (Matt. 15:19). It is by the heart that the entire person—the intellect, will, affections, emotions, and body—is influenced. Because the heart is "deceitful above all things, and desperately wicked" (Jer. 17:9), human nature can be described as corrupt, depraved, and thoroughly sinful.

3. Sin's effect on humanity. Some may feel that the sentence of death was too severe a penalty for eating the forbidden fruit. But we can only gauge the seriousness of the transgression in the light of the effect of Adam's sin on the human race.

Adam and Eve's first son committed murder. Their descendants soon violated the sacred marriage union by engaging in polygamy, and it was not long before wickedness and violence filled the earth (Gen. 4:8, 23; 6:1-5, 11-13). God's appeals for repentance and reformation went unheeded, and only eight persons were saved from the Flood waters that destroyed the unrepentant. The history of the race after the Flood is, with few exceptions, a sad account of the outworkings of the sinfulness of human nature.

a. The universal sinfulness of humanity. History reveals that Adam's descendants share the sinfulness of his nature. In prayer David said, "In Your sight no one living is righteous" (Ps. 143:2; cf. 14:3). "There is no one who does not sin" (1 Kings 8:46). And Solomon said, "Who can say,

"I have made my heart clean, I am pure from my sin?" (Prov. 20:9; Eccl. 7:20). The New Testament is equally clear, stating that "all have sinned and fall short of the glory of God" (Rom. 3:23) and that "if we say we have no sin, we deceive ourselves, and the truth is not in us" (1 John 1:8).

b. Is sinfulness inherited or acquired? Paul said, "In Adam all die" (1 Cor. 15:22). In another place he noted, "Through one man sin entered the world, and death through sin, and thus death spread to all men, because all sinned" (Rom. 5:12).

The human heart's corruption affects the total person. In this light Job exclaims, "Who can bring a clean thing out of an unclean? No one!" (Job 14:4). David said, "Behold, I was brought forth in iniquity, and in sin my mother conceived me" (Ps. 51:5). And Paul stated that "the carnal mind is enmity against God; for it is not subject to the law of God, nor indeed can be. So then, those who are in the flesh cannot please God" (Rom. 8:7, 8). Before conversion, he pointed out, believers were "by nature children of wrath," just like the rest of humanity (Eph. 2:3).

Although as children we acquire sinful behavior through imitation, the above text affirms that we inherit our basic sinfulness. The universal sinfulness of humanity is evidence that by nature we tend toward evil, not good.

c. The eradication of sinful behavior. How successful are people in removing sin from their lives and from society?

Every effort to achieve a righteous life through one's own strength is doomed. Christ said that everyone who has sinned is "a slave of sin." Only divine power can emancipate us from this slavery. But Christ has assured us, "If the Son make you free, you shall be free indeed" (John 8:36). You can only produce righteousness, He said, if "you abide in Me" because "without Me you can do nothing" (John 15:4, 5).

Even the apostle Paul failed to live a righteous life on his own. He knew the perfect standard of God's law but he was not able to achieve it. Recounting his efforts, he said, "I do not understand my own actions. For I do not do what I want, but I do the very thing I hate." "I do not do the good I want, but the evil I do not want is what I do." Then he pointed to the impact of sin in his life: "Now if I do what I do not want, it is no longer I that do it, but sin which dwells within me." In spite of his failures he admired God's perfect standard, saying, "I delight in the law of God, in my inmost self, but I see in my members another law at war with the law of my mind and making me captive to the law of sin which dwells in my members. Wretched man that I am! Who will deliver me from this body of death?" (Rom. 7:15, 19, 20, 22-24, RSV).

Paul finally acknowledged that he needed divine power to be victorious. Through Christ he put aside a life according to the flesh and began a new life according to the Spirit (Rom. 7:25, 8:1).

This new life in the Spirit is the transforming gift of God. Through divine grace, we who are "dead in trespasses and sins" become victorious (Eph. 2:1, 3, 8-10). The spiritual rebirth so transforms the life (John 1:13, John 3:5) that we can speak of a new creation—the "old things have passed away" and "all things have become new" (2 Cor. 5:17). The new life, however, does not exclude the possibility of sinning (1 John 2:1).

4. Evolution and man's fall. Ever since creation Satan has confused many by weakening confidence in the scriptural accounts of the origins of the human race and man's fall. One could call evolution the "natural" view of humanity, a view based on the assumption that life began by chance and that humans, through a long evolutionary process, have emerged from the lower forms of life. Through a process of survival of the fittest, they evolved to their present status. Not yet having reached their potential, they are still evolving.

A growing number of Christians have adopted theistic evolution, which claims that God used evolution in bringing about the Genesis creation. Those accepting theistic evolution do not view the first chapters of Geneses as literal but as allegory or myth.

a. The biblical view of man and evolution. Creationist Christians are concerned about the impact of the evolutionary theory on the Christian faith. James Orr wrote: "Christianity is met today, not by piecemeal attacks upon its doctrines...but by a positively-conceived counterview of the world, claiming to rest on scientific grounds, ably constructed and defended, yet in its fundamental ideas striking at the roots of the Christian system."[9]

The Bible rejects the allegorical or mythical interpretation of Genesis. The Bible writers themselves interpret Geneses 1-11 as literal history. Adam, Eve, the serpent, and Satan are all seen as historical characters in the drama of the great controversy (see Job 31:33; Eccl. 7:29; Matt. 19:4, 5; John 8:44; Rom. 5:12, 18, 19; 2 Cor. 11:3; 1 Tim. 2:14; Rev. 12:9).

b. Calvary and evolution. Evolution in whatever form or shape contradicts the basic foundations of Christianity. As Leonard Verduin asserted, "In the place of the story of a 'Fall' has come the story of an *ascent*."[10] Christianity and evolution are diametrically opposed. Either our first parents were created in the image of God and experienced a fall into sin or they did not. If they did not, then why be Christian?

Calvary most radically questions evolution. If there has been no fall, why would we need Christ to die in our behalf? Not just death in general, but Christ's death for us proclaims that humanity is not "OK." Left to ourselves, we would continue to deteriorate until the human race is annihilated.

Our hope rests upon the Man who hung from the cross. His death alone opens up the possibility of a better, fuller life that will never end. Calvary declares that we need a substitute to liberate us.

c. The incarnation and evolution. Perhaps the Creation-versus-evolution question is best answered by viewing the creation of humanity from the perspective of the incarnation. In bringing the second Adam, Christ, into history God was creatively at work. If God could bring about this supreme miracle, there is no question as to His ability to form the first Adam.

d. Has man come of age? Frequently, evolutionists have pointed to the enormous scientific advances in the last few centuries as evidence that man seems to be the arbiter of his own destiny. With science supplying his needs, given enough time, he will solve all the world's problems.

Yet technology's messianic role is meeting increasing skepticism, because technology has thrust the planet to the brink of annihilation. Humanity has utterly failed to subdue and control the sinful heart. Consequently, all the scientific progress has only made the world more dangerous.

Increasingly, philosophies of nihilism and despair appear valid. Alexander Pope's dictum, "Hope springs eternal in the human breast," rings hollow today. Job has a better grasp of reality—time trudges on "day after hopeless day" (Job 7:6, LB). Man's world is running down. Someone had to come from beyond human history, invade it, and bring a new reality into it.

Rays of Hope. How great was the depravity of humanity? At the cross humans murdered their Creator—the ultimate parricide! But God has not left mankind without hope.

David contemplated humanity's position in Creation. At first impressed with the vastness of the universe, he thought man insignificant. Then he became aware of humanity's true position. Speaking of man's present relation to God, he said, "You have made him a little lower than the angels, and You have crowned him with glory and honor. You have made him to have dominion over the works of Your hands" (Ps. 8:5, 6; cf. Heb. 2:7).

In spite of the Fall, there remains a sense of human dignity. Although marred, the divine likeness was not completely obliterated. Though fallen, corrupt, and sinful, man is still God's representative on earth. His nature is less than divine, yet he holds a dignified position as God's caretaker of earthly creation. When David realized this, he responded with praise and thanksgiving: "O Lord, our Lord, how excellent is Your name in all the earth" (Ps. 8:9).

The Covenant of Grace

Through transgression the first pair had become sinful. No longer able to resist Satan, could they ever be free, or were they left to perish? Was there any hope?

The Covenant Given at the Fall. Before God pronounced the punishment on the fallen pair's sins He gave them hope by introducing the covenant of grace. He said, "I will put enmity between you [Satan] and the woman, and between your seed and her Seed; He shall bruise your head, and you shall bruise His heel" (Gen. 3:15).

God's message brought encouragement because it announced that though Satan had brought humanity under his evil spell, ultimately he would be defeated. The covenant was made between God and humanity. First, God promised through His grace a bulwark against sin. He would create a hatred between the serpent and the woman; between Satan's followers and God's people. This would disrupt man's relationship with Satan and open the way for a renewed relationship with God.

Through the centuries war was to continue between God's church and Satan. The conflict would reach its culmination in the death of Jesus Christ, who was the prophesied personification of the Seed of the woman. At Calvary, Satan was defeated. Bruised though the Seed of the woman was, the author of evil was defeated.

All who accept God's offer of grace will know an enmity in the battle with Satan. Through faith they will share in the Saviour's victory at Calvary.

The Covenant Established Before Creation. The covenant of grace was not developed after the Fall. The Scriptures bring out that even before Creation the members of the Godhead had covenanted among Themselves to rescue the race if it should fall into sin. Paul said God "chose us in Him [Christ] before the foundation of the world, that we should be holy and without blame before Him in love, having predestined us to adoption as sons by Jesus Christ to Himself, according to the good pleasure of His will, to the praise and glory of His grace" (Eph. 1:4-6; cf. 2 Tim. 1:9). Speaking about Christ's atoning sacrifice, Peter said, "He indeed was foreordained before the foundation of the world" (1 Peter 1:20).

The covenant was based on an unshakable foundation: the promise and oath of God Himself (Heb. 6:18). Jesus Christ was the surety of the covenant (Heb. 7:22). A surety is someone who assumes any debt or obligation in the event of a default of another person. Christ's serving as the surety meant that if the human race would fall into sin He would bear their punishment. He would pay the price of their redemption; He would make the atonement for their sin; He would meet the demands of God's violated law. No human being or angel could assume that responsibility. Only Christ the Creator, the representative head of the race, could take that responsibility (Rom. 5:12-21; 1 Cor. 15:22).

The Son of God is not only the surety of the covenant, He is also its mediator or executor. His description of His mission as incarnate Son of man reveals this aspect of His role. He said, "I have come down from heaven, not to do My own will, but the will of Him who sent Me" (John 6:38; cf. 5:30, 43). The will of the Father is "that everyone who sees the Son and believes in Him may have everlasting life" (John 6:40). "And this is eternal life," He said, "that they may know You, the only true God, and Jesus Christ whom You have sent" (John 17:3). At the end of His mission He testified about His execution of the Father's commission, saying, "I have glorified You on the earth. I have finished the work which You have given Me to do" (John 17:4).

At the cross Jesus fulfilled His pledge to be humanity's surety in the covenant. His cry "It is finished!" (John 19:30), marked the completion of His mission. With His own life He had paid the penalty God's violated law required, guaranteeing the salvation of the repentant human race. At that moment Christ's blood ratified the covenant of grace. Through faith in His atoning blood, repentant sinners would be adopted as sons and daughters of God, thus becoming heirs of eternal life.

This covenant of grace demonstrates God's infinite love for humanity. Established before Creation, the covenant was revealed after the Fall. At that time, in a special sense, God and humanity became partners.

The Covenant Renewal. Unfortunately mankind rejected this magnificent covenant of grace both before the Flood and after it (Gen. 6:1-8; 11:1-9). When God offered the covenant again, He did so through Abraham. Again He affirmed the promise of redemption: "In your Seed all the nations of the earth shall be blessed, because you have obeyed My voice" (Gen. 22:18; cf. 12:3; 18:18).

The Scriptures particularly highlight Abraham's faithfulness to the covenant conditions. Abraham believed God, and He "accounted it to him for righteousness" (Gen. 15:6). That Abraham's participation in the covenant blessings, while grounded in the grace of God, was also contingent upon his obedience reveals that the covenant upholds the authority of God's law (Gen. 17:1, 26:5).

Abraham's faith was of such quality that he was given the title "the father of all those who believe" (Rom. 4:11). He is God's model of the righteousness by faith that reveals itself in obedience (Rom. 4:2, 3; James 2:23, 24). The covenant of grace does not automatically bestow its blessing on Abraham's natural descendants but only on such as follow Abraham's example of faith. "Only those who are of faith are sons of Abraham" (Gal. 3:7). Every individual on earth can experience the covenant promises of salvation by meeting the condition: "If you are Christ's, then you are Abraham's seed, and heirs according to the promise" (Gal. 3:29). From the Godward side the Sinaitic covenant (also called the first covenant) was a renewal of the Abrahamic covenant of grace (Heb. 9:1). But Israel perverted it into a covenant of works (Gal. 4:22-31).

The New Covenant. Later scriptural passages speak of "a new or better covenant."[11] But they do so, not because the everlasting covenant was changed but because (1) through Israel's unfaithfulness God's everlasting covenant had been perverted into a system of works; (2) it was associated with a new revelation of God's love in Jesus Christ's incarnation, life, death, resurrection, and mediation (cf. Heb. 8:6-13); and (3) it was not until the cross that it was ratified by the blood of Christ (Dan. 9:27; Luke 22:20; Rom 15:8; Heb. 9:11-22).[12]

What this covenant offers those who accept it is enormous. Through God's grace it offers them the forgiveness of their sins. It offers the Holy Spirit's work of writing the Ten Commandments on the heart, and restoring repentant sinners into the image of their Maker (Jer. 31:33). The new-covenant, new-birth experience brings the righteousness of Christ and the experience of justification by faith.

The renewal of the heart it affords transforms individuals so that they will bring forth the fruits of the Spirit: "love, joy, peace, longsuffering, kindness, goodness, faithfulness, gentleness, self-control" (Gal. 5:22, 23). Through the power of Christ's saving grace they may walk as Christ walked, daily enjoying the things that please God (John 8:29). Fallen humanity's only hope is to accept God's invitation to enter into His covenant of grace. Through faith in Jesus Christ we can experience this relationship that assures our adoption as children of God and heirs with Christ to His kingdom.

References

1. *The doctrine of man* has long been a theological term used to discuss the components of the human family. In this discussion man does not necessarily mean male, excluding female, but has been used for ease of discussion

and continuity with theological tradition and semantics.

2. Berkhof, *Systemic Theology*, p. 183.

3. "Soul," *SDA Encyclopedia*, rev. ed., p. 1361.

4. "Soul," *SDA Bible Dictionary*, rev. ed., p. 1061.

5. *Ibid.*, p. 1064.

6. *SDA Bible Commentary*, rev. ed., vol. 7, p. 257.

7. *Ibid.*, rev. ed., vol. 3, p. 1090.

8   "Sin, I" *SDA Bible Dictionary*, rev. ed., p. 1042.

9. James Orr, *God's Image in Man* (Grand Rapids, MI: Wm. B. Eerdmans, 1948), pp. 3, 4.

10. Leonard Verduin, *Somewhat Less than God: The Biblical View of Man* (Grand Rapids, MI: Wm. B. Eerdmans, 1970). P. 69.

11. The New Testament associates the experience of Israel at Mount Sinai with the old covenant (Gal. 4:24, 25). At Sinai God renews His everlasting covenant of grace to His people who had been liberated (1 Chron. 16:14-17; Ps. 105:8-11; Gal. 3:15-17). God promises them, "If you will indeed obey My voice and keep My covenant, then you shall be a special treasure to Me above all people; for all the earth is Mine. And you shall be to Me a kingdom of priests and a holy nation" (Ex. 19:5, 6; cf. Gen. 17:7, 9, 19). The covenant was based on righteousness by faith (Rom. 10:6-8; Deut. 30:11-14) and the law was to be written in their heart (Deut. 6:4-6; 30:14).

    The covenant of grace is always subject to perversion by the believers' turning it into a system of salvation by works. Paul used Abraham's failure to trust God—his depending on his own works to solve his problems—as an illustration of the old covenant (Genesis 16; 12:10-20; 20; Gal. 4:22-25). In fact the experience of righteousness by works has existed ever since sin entered this world and the everlasting covenant was broken (Hosea 6:7).

    Throughout Israel's history the majority tried "to establish their own righteousness" through "the works of the law" (Rom. 9:30-10:4). They lived according to the letter, not according to the Spirit (2 Cor. 3:6). Trying to justify themselves by the law (Gal. 5:4), they lived under the condemnation of the law and are in bondage, not in freedom (Gal. 4:21-23). Thus they perverted the Sinai covenant.

    The book of Hebrews applies the first, or old, covenant to the history of Israel since Sinai and reveals its temporary nature. It shows that the Levitical priesthood was to be temporary, performing a symbolic function until the reality in Christ had arrived (Hebrews 9; 10). Sadly enough, many failed to see that in themselves the ceremonies were worthless (Heb. 10:1). Adherence to this system of "shadows" when type had met antitype, shadow had met reality, distorted the true mission of Christ. Hence the strong language used to stress the superiority of the better, or new, covenant over Sinai.

The old covenant, therefore, can be described in negative and positive terms. Negatively, it refers to the people's perversion of God's everlasting covenant. Positively, it stands for the temporary earthly ministry designed by God to meet the emergency created by this human failure. See also White, *Patriarchs and Prophets*, pp. 370-73; White, "Our Work," *Review and Herald*, June 23, 1904, p. 8; White, "A Holy Purpose to Restore Jerusalem" *Southern Watchman*, March 1, 1904, p. 142; Hasel, *Covenant in Blood* (Mountain View, CA: Pacific Press, 1982); cf. Wallenkampf, *Salvation Comes From the Lord* (Washington, D. C.: Review and Herald, 1983), pp. 84-90.

12. Cf. Hasel, *Covenant in Blood*.

8 *The Great Controversy*

All humanity is now involved in a great controversy between Christ and Satan regarding the character of God, His law, and His sovereignty over the universe. This conflict originated in heaven when a created being, endowed with the freedom of choice, in self-exaltation became Satan, God's adversary, and led into rebellion a portion of the angels. He introduced the spirit of rebellion into this world when he led Adam and Eve into sin. This human sin resulted in the distortion of the image of God in humanity, the disordering of the created world, and its eventual devastation at the time of the worldwide flood. Observed by the whole creation, this world became the arena of the universal conflict, out of which the God of love will ultimately be vindicated. To assist His people in this controversy, Christ sends the Holy Spirit and the loyal angels to guide, protect, and sustain them in the way of salvation. (Rev. 12:4-9; Isa. 14:12-14; Ezek. 28:12-18; Gen. 3; Rom. 1:19-32; 5:12-21; 8:19-22; Gen. 6:8; 2 Pet. 3:6; 1 Cor. 4:9; Heb. 1:14.)

SCRIPTURE PORTRAYS A COSMIC BATTLE between good and evil, God and Satan. Understanding this controversy, which has involved the entire universe, helps answer the question, Why did Jesus come to this planet?

A Cosmic View of the Controversy

Mystery of mysteries, the conflict between good and evil began in heaven. How could sin possibly originate in a perfect environment?

Angels, beings of a higher order than humans (Ps. 8:5), were created to enjoy intimate fellowship with God (Rev. 1:1; 3:5; 5:11). Of superior strength and obedient to God's Word (Ps. 103:20), they function as servants or "ministering spirits" (Heb. 1:14). Though generally invisible, at times they appear in human form (Genesis 18, 19, Heb. 13:2). It was through one of these angelic beings that sin was introduced to the universe.

The Origin of the Controversy. Using the kings of Tyre and Babylon as figurative descriptions for Lucifer, Scripture illuminates how this cosmic controversy began. "Lucifer, son of the morning," the anointed covering cherub, resided in the presence of God (Isa. 14:12; Eze. 28:14).[1] Scripture says, "You were the seal of perfection, full of wisdom and perfect in beauty….You were perfect in your ways from the day you were created, till iniquity was found in you" (Eze. 28:12, 15).

Although sin's rise is inexplicable and unjustifiable, its roots can be traced to Lucifer's pride: "Your heart was lifted up because of your beauty; you corrupted your wisdom for the sake of your splendor" (Eze. 28:17). Lucifer refused to be content with the exalted position his Creator had given him. In selfishness he coveted equality with God Himself: "You have said in your heart; "I will ascend into heaven, I will exalt my throne above the stars of God…I will be like the Most High""(Isa. 14:12-14). But though he desired God's position, he did not want His character. He grasped for God's authority but not His love. Lucifer's rebellion against God's government was the first step in his transformation into Satan, "the adversary."

Lucifer's covert actions blinded many angels to God's love. The resulting discontent and disloyalty to God's government grew until one third of the angelic host joined him in rebellion (Rev. 12:4). The tranquility of God's kingdom was shattered, and "war broke out in heaven" (Rev. 12:7). The celestial warfare resulted in Satan—depicted as the great dragon, the ancient serpent, and the devil—being "cast to the earth, and his angels were cast out with him" (Rev. 12:9).

How Did Human Beings Become Involved? Upon his expulsion from heaven, Satan spread his rebellion to our earth. Disguised as a speaking serpent and using the same arguments that had led to his own downfall, he effectively undermined Adam and Eve's trust in their Creator (Gen. 3:5). Satan aroused in Eve discontent regarding her assigned position. Infatuated by the prospect of equality with God, she believed the tempter's word—and doubted God's. Disobeying God's command, she ate the fruit and influenced her husband to do the same. In believing the serpent's word over that of their Creator, they betrayed their trust in and loyalty to God. Tragically, the seeds of the controversy that had begun in heaven took root in Planet Earth (see Genesis 3).

In seducing our first parents to sin, Satan ingeniously wrested from them their dominion over the earth. Now claiming to be the "prince of this world," Satan challenged God, His government, and the peace of the whole universe from his new headquarters—Planet Earth.

The Impact on the Human Race. The effects of the struggle between Christ and Satan soon became apparent as sin distorted the image of God in humanity. Though God offered His covenant of grace to the human race through Adam and Eve (Gen. 3:15; see chapter 7 of this book), their first child, Cain, murdered his brother (Gen. 4:8). Wickedness continued to multiply until in sorrow God had to say of man "that every intent of the thoughts of his heart was only evil continually" (Gen. 6:5).

God used a great flood to cleanse the world of its unrepentant inhabitants and give the human race a new start (Gen. 7:17-20). But before long the descendants of faithful Noah departed from God's covenant. Although God had promised never again to destroy the entire earth with a flood, they blatantly concretized their distrust of Him by erecting the tower of Babel in an attempt to reach heaven and thus have a means of escape from any ensuing flood. This time God quashed man's rebellion by confounding his universal language (Gen. 9:1, 11; 11).

Sometime later, with the world in near total apostasy, God extended His covenant to Abraham. Through Abraham, God planned to bless all nations of the world (Gen. 12:1-3; 22:15-18). However, the successive generations of Abraham's descendants proved faithless to God's gracious covenant. Entrapped in sin, they aided Satan in achieving his objective in the great controversy by crucifying the Author and Surety of the covenant, Jesus Christ.

Earth—the Theater of the Universe. The account in the book of Job of a cosmic convocation involving representatives from various parts of the universe gives additional insight into the great controversy. The account begins, "Now there was a day when the sons of God came to present themselves before the Lord, and Satan also came among them. And the Lord said to Satan, 'From where do you come?' So Satan answered the Lord and said, 'From going to and fro on the earth, and from walking back and forth on it'" (Job 1:6, 7; cf. 2:1-7).

Then the Lord, in effect, said, "Satan, look at Job. He faithfully obeys My law. He is perfect!" (see Job 1:8).

When Satan countered, "Yes, but he's perfect only because it pays to serve You. Don't You protect him?" Christ responded by permitting Satan to test Job in any way short of taking his life (see Job 1:9-2:7).

The cosmic perspective the book of Job affords provides powerful proof of the great controversy between Christ and Satan. This planet is the stage on which this dramatic struggle between right and wrong is being played out. As Scripture states, "We have been made a spectacle to the world, both to angels, and to men" (1 Cor. 4:9).

Sin severed the relationship between God and man, and "whatever is not from faith is sin" (Rom 14:23). The breaking of God's commandments, or laws, is the immediate result of a lack of faith, the evidence of a ruptured relationship. In turn, by the plan of salvation God intends to restore the trust in the Creator that leads to a loving relationship manifested by obedience. As Christ noted, love leads to obedience (John 14:15).

In our lawless age absolutes are neutralized, dishonesty is praised, bribery is a way of life, adultery is rampant, and agreements—both international and personal—lie shattered. It is our privilege to look beyond our desperate world to a caring, omnipotent God. This larger view reveals to us the importance of our Saviour's atonement, which is bringing this universal controversy to an end.

The Cosmic Issue

What is the pivotal issue in this life-and-death struggle?

God's Government and Law. God's moral law is just as essential to the existence of His universe as are the physical laws that hold it together and keep it functioning. Sin is "the transgression of the law" (1 John 3:4, KJV), or "lawlessness" as the Greek word *anomia* indicates. Lawlessness issues from a rejection of God and His government.

Rather than admitting responsibility for the lawlessness in the world, Satan lays the blame on God. He says God's law, which he alleges is arbitrary, infringes on individual freedom. Furthermore, he charges, since it is impossible to obey it, that law works against the best interests of created beings. Through this constant and insidious undermining of the law, Satan attempts to overthrow God's government and even God Himself.

Christ and the Issue of Obedience. The temptations Christ faced during His earthly ministry revealed the seriousness of the controversy over obedience and surrender to God's will. In meeting those temptations, which prepared Him to be "a merciful and faithful High Priest" (Heb. 2:17), He met in single combat a deadly foe. In the wilderness after Christ fasted forty days, Satan tempted Him to change stones to bread to prove He really was the Son of God (Matt. 4:3). As Satan had tempted Eve to doubt God's word in Eden, so now he tried to cause Christ to doubt the validity of what God had said at His baptism: "This is My beloved Son, in whom I am well pleased" (Matt. 3:17). Had Christ taken matters into His own hands, creating bread out of stones to prove His divine sonship, He would have, like Eve, revealed a lack of trust in God. His mission would have ended in failure.

But Christ's highest priority was to live by His Father's word. In spite of His great hunger, He answered Satan's temptation with "Man shall not live by bread alone, by every word that proceeds from the mouth of God" (Matt. 4:4).

In another attempt to defeat Christ, Satan gave Him a panoramic view of the kingdoms of the world, promising, "All these things I will give You if You will fall down and worship me" (Matt. 4:9). He implied that by doing so Christ could regain the world thus completing His mission without enduring the agony of Calvary. Without a moment's hesitation, and in absolute loyalty to God, Jesus commanded, "Away with you, Satan!" Then, using Scripture, the most effective weapon in the great controversy, He said, "You shall worship the Lord your God, and Him only you shall serve" (Matt. 4:10). His words ended the battle. Through retaining His total dependence on the Father, Christ had defeated Satan.

Showdown at Calvary. This cosmic controversy comes into its clearest focus at Calvary. Satan intensified his efforts to abort Jesus' mission as the time approached for it to close. Satan was especially successful in using the religious leaders of the time, whose jealousy over Christ's popularity caused such trouble that He had to end His public ministry (John 11:45-54). Through betrayal by one of His disciples and perjured testimony, Jesus was arrested, tried, condemned to death (Matt. 26:63, 64; John 19:7). In absolute obedience to His Father's will, Jesus remained faithful until death.

The benefits of both Christ's life and His death reach beyond the limited world of the human race. Speaking of the cross, Christ said, "Now the prince of this world [Satan] will be driven out" (John 12:31, NIV).

The cosmic controversy came to its climax at the cross. The love and faithful obedience Christ demonstrated there in the face of Satan's cruelty undermined Prince Satan's position, assuring his ultimate downfall.

Controversy About Truth as It Is in Jesus

Today the great controversy raging furiously around Christ's authority involves not only His law but His word—the Scriptures. Approaches to the interpretation of the Bible have been developed that allow little or no room for divine revelation.[2] Scripture is treated as if it were no different from any other ancient document and analyzed with the same critical methodology. A growing number of Christians, including theologians, no longer view the Scriptures as the Word of God, the infallible revelation of His will. Consequently, they have come to question the biblical view of the person of Jesus Christ—His nature, virgin birth, miracles, and resurrection are widely debated.[3]

The Most Crucial Question. When Christ asked, "Who do men say that I, the Son of Man, am?" the disciples replied, "Some say John the Baptist, some Elijah, and others Jeremiah or one of the prophets" (Matt. 16:13, 14). In other words, most of His contemporaries considered Him as a mere man. Scripture continues the account: Jesus asked His twelve, "But who do you say that I am?"

"And Simon Peter answered and said, 'You are the Christ, the Son of the living God.'

"Jesus answered and said to him, 'Blessed are you, Simon Bar-Jonah, for flesh and blood has not revealed this to you, but My Father who is in heaven'" (Matt. 16:15-17).

Today everyone faces the same question Christ asked His disciples. One's answer to this life-or-death question depends on one's faith in the testimony of God's Word.

The Center of Bible Doctrines. Christ is the focus of the Scriptures. God invites us to comprehend the truth as it is in Jesus (Eph. 4:21), for He is the truth (John 14:5). One of Satan's strategies in the cosmic conflict is to convince people that they can understand truth apart from Jesus. So several centers of truth have been proposed, either individually or in combination: (1) man, (2) nature, or the observable universe, (3) Scriptures, and (4) the church.

While these all have their part in revealing truth, Scripture presents Christ as the Creator of each of the above and transcending each. They all find real meaning only in the One from whom they came. Divorcing Bible doctrines from Him leads to a misunderstanding regarding "the way, the truth, and the life" (John 14:6). It suits both the nature and the purpose of the antichrist to suggest other centers of truth than Christ. (In the original Greek, *antichrist* may mean not only "against" Christ but "in the place of" Christ). By substituting some other center than Christ in the church's doctrines, Satan achieves his goal of directing attention away from the One who is the only hope of humanity.

The Function of Christian Theology. The cosmic view unveils Satan's attempt to remove Christ from His rightful place, both in the universe and in truth. Theology, by definition a study of God and His relationship with His creatures, must unfold all doctrines in the light of Christ. The mandate of Christian theology is to inspire confidence in the authority of the Word of God and to replace all other suggested centers of truth with Christ. When it does so, true Christian theology serves the church well, for it goes to the root of the cosmic controversy, exposes it, and meets it with the only incontrovertible argument—Christ as revealed in the Scriptures. From this perspective God can use theology as an effective instrument for aiding humanity in opposing Satan's efforts on earth.

The Significance of the Doctrine

The doctrine of the great controversy reveals the tremendous battle that affects every person born in the world—that, in fact, touches every corner of the universe. Scripture says, "We do not wrestle against flesh and blood, but against principalities, against powers, against the rulers of the darkness of this age, against spiritual hosts of wickedness in the heavenly places" (Eph. 6:12).

The Doctrine Produces a Constant State of Watchfulness. An understanding of this doctrine convicts one of the need to combat evil. Success is possibly only through dependence on Jesus Christ, the Captain of the hosts, the One "strong and mighty, the Lord mighty in battle" (Ps. 24:8). As Paul said, accepting Christ's survival strategy entails taking up "the whole armor of God, that you may be able to withstand in the evil day, and having done all, to stand. Stand therefore, having girded your waist with truth, having put on the breastplate of righteousness, and having shod your feet with the preparation of the gospel of peace; above all, taking the shield of faith with which you will be able to quench all the fiery darts of the wicked one. And take the helmet of salvation, and the sword of the Spirit, which is the word of God; praying always with all prayer and supplication in the Spirit, being watchful to this end with all perseverance and supplication for all the saints" (Eph. 6:13-18). What a privilege for true Christians to live a life characterized by patience and faithfulness and—a readiness at all times for the conflict (Rev. 14:2), manifesting a constant dependence upon One who has made us "more than conquerors" (Rom. 8:37).

It Explains the Mystery of Suffering. Evil did not originate with God. He who "loved righteousness and hated lawlessness" (Heb. 1:9) is not to blame for the world's misery. Satan, a fallen angel, is responsible for cruelty and suffering. We can better understand robberies, murders, funerals, crimes, and accidents—however heartbreaking—when we see them in the framework of the great controversy.

The cross testifies to both the destructiveness of sin and the depths of God's love for sinners. Thus the great controversy theme teaches us to hate sin and to love the sinner.

It Displays Christ's Present Loving Concern for the World. Upon His return to heaven, Christ did not leave His people orphans. In great compassion He provided us with every possible aid in the battle against evil. The Holy Spirit was commissioned to "fill in" for Christ—to be our constant companion until Christ would return (John 14:16; cf. Matt. 28:20). The angels were also commissioned to be involved in His saving work (Heb. 1:14). Our victory is assured. We can have hope and courage as we face the future, because our Master is in control. Our lips can utter praises for His saving work.

It Reveals the Cosmic Significance of the Cross. The salvation of humanity was at stake in Christ's ministry and death, for He came to give His life for the remission of our sins. In doing so He vindicated His Father's character, law, and government, against which Satan had cast false aspersions.

Christ's life vindicated God's justice and goodness and demonstrated that God's law and government were fair. Christ revealed the groundlessness of Satan's attack on God, showing that through total dependence on God's power and grace repentant believers could rise above the daily temptations and live victorious over sin.

References

1. "Lucifer" comes from the Latin, *Lucifer*, meaning "light bearer." The phrase "son of the morning" was a common expression meaning "morning star"—Venus. "A literal rendering of the Hebrew expression translated 'Lucifer, son of the morning' would be 'shining one, son of dawn.' The figurative application of the brilliant planet Venus, brightest of all the heavenly luminaries, to Satan before his fall...is most appropriate as a graphic illustration of the high estate from which Lucifer fell" ("Lucifer," *SDA Bible Dictionary*, rev. ed., p. 683).

2. See General Conference Committee, "Methods of Bible Study," 1986: Hasel, *Biblical Interpretation Today* (Washington, D.C., Biblical Research Institute [of the General Conference of Seventh-day Adventists], 1985).

3. See, e.g., K. Runia, *The Present-day Christological Debate* (Downers Grove, IL: Inter-varsity Press, 1984); G.C. Berkouwer, *The Person of Christ* (Grand Rapids, MI: Wm. B. Eerdmans, 1954), pp. 14-56.

9

The Life, Death, and Resurrection of Christ

In Christ's life of perfect obedience to God's will, His suffering, death, and resurrection, God provided the only means of atonement for human sin, so that those who by faith accept this atonement may have eternal life, and the whole creation may better understand the infinite and holy love of the Creator. This perfect atonement vindicates the righteousness of God's law and the graciousness of His character; for it both condemns our sin and provides for our forgiveness. The death of Christ is substitutionary and expiatory, reconciling and transforming. The resurrection of Christ proclaims God's triumph over the forces of evil, and for those who accept the atonement, assures their final victory over sin and death. It declares the Lordship of Jesus Christ, before whom every knee in heaven and on earth will bow. (John 3:16; Isa. 53; 1 Pet. 2:21, 22; 1 Cor. 15:3, 4, 20-22; 2 Cor. 5:14, 15, 19-21; Rom. 1:4; 3:25; 4:25; 8:3, 4; 1 John 2:2; 4:10; Col. 2:15; Phil. 2:6-11.)

121

AN OPEN DOOR LEADS INTO THE CENTER of the universe, heaven. A voice calls, "Come in and see what goes on here!" In the Spirit, the apostle John looks into the throne room of God.

A dazzling emerald rainbow encircles the central throne, and lightning, thunder, and voices issue from it. Dignitaries—arrayed in white garments and wearing golden crowns—are seated on lesser thrones. As a doxology fills the air, the elders prostrate themselves in adoration, casting their golden crowns before the throne.

An angel, bearing a scroll sealed with seven seals, cries: "Who is worthy to open the scroll and to loose its seals?" (Rev. 5:2). With dismay John sees that no one in heaven or earth is worthy to open the scroll. His dismay turns to weeping until one of the elders consoles: "Do not weep. Behold, the Lion of the tribe of Judah, root of David, has prevailed to open the scroll and to loose its seven seals" (Rev. 5:5).

Looking again to the majestic throne, John sees a Lamb that had been slain but now is alive and empowered with the Spirit. As this lowly Lamb takes the scroll, the living creatures and elders strike up a new anthem: "You are worthy to take the scroll and to break open its seals. For you were killed, and by your sacrificial death you bought for God people from every tribe, language, nation, and race. You have made them a kingdom of priests to serve our God, and they shall rule on the earth" (Rev. 5:9, 10, TEV). Every created being in heaven and on earth joins their song: "Blessing and honor and glory and power be to Him who sits on the throne, and to the Lamb, forever and ever!" (Rev. 5:13).

What is so important about this scroll? It records the rescue of the human from its enslavement to Satan and portrays the ultimate victory of God over sin. It reveals a salvation so perfect that those captive to sin can be released from their prison house of doom simply through their choice. Long before His birth in Bethlehem the Lamb cried out: "Behold, I come; in the scroll of the Book it is written of me. I delight to do Your will, O my God, and Your law is within my heart" (Ps. 40:7, 8; cf. Heb. 10:7). The coming of the Lamb slain from the foundation of the world effected the redemption of humanity (Rev. 13:8).

God's Saving Grace

The Scriptures reveal a God who has an overwhelming concern for the salvation of humanity. The members of the Godhead are allied in the work of bringing people back into a union with their Creator. Jesus highlighted God's saving love, saying, "For God so loved the world that He gave His only begotten Son, that whoever believes in Him should not perish but have everlasting life" (John 3:16).

The Scriptures declare that "God is love" (1 John 4:8). He reaches out to humanity "with an everlasting love" (Jer. 31:3). The God who extends the invitation to salvation is all-powerful, but His love necessitates His permitting each person to have freedom of choice in responding (Rev. 3:20, 21). Coercion, a method contrary to His character, can have no part in His strategy.

The Divine Initiative. When Adam and Eve sinned, God took the initiative in searching for them. The guilty pair, hearing the sound of their Creator, did not run joyfully to meet Him as they had done before. Instead, they hid. But God did not abandon them. Ever so persistently He called, "Where are you?"

With deep sorrow, God outlined the consequences of their disobedience—the pain, the difficulties that they would encounter. Yet in their absolutely hopeless situation He revealed a wonderful plan promising ultimate victory over sin and death (Gen. 3:15).

Grace or Justice? Later, following Israel's apostasy at Sinai, the Lord revealed His benevolent-but-just character to Moses, proclaiming, "The Lord, the Lord God, merciful and gracious, longsuffering, and abounding in goodness and truth, keeping mercy for thousands, forgiving iniquity and transgression and sin, by no means clearing the guilty, visiting the iniquity of the fathers upon the children and children's children to the third and fourth generation" (Ex. 34:6, 7).

God's character reveals a unique blending of grace and justice, of a willingness to clear the guilty. Only in the person of Christ can we understand how these qualities of character can be reconciled to each other.

To Forgive or to Punish? During the times of Israel's apostasy, God often pleaded longingly for His people to acknowledge their iniquity and return to Him (Jer. 3:12-14). But they spurned His gracious invitations (Jer. 5:3). An unrepentant attitude that mocks forgiveness makes punishment inevitable (Ps. 7:12).

Though God is merciful, He cannot forgive those who cling to sin (Jer. 5:7). Pardon has a purpose. God wants to change sinners into saints: "Let the wicked forsake his way, and the unrighteous man his thoughts; Let him return to the Lord, and He will have mercy on him; and to our God, for He will abundantly pardon" (Isa. 55:7). His message of salvation clearly sounds throughout the world: "Look to Me, and be saved, all you ends of the earth! For I am God, and there is no other" (Isa. 45:22).

God's Wrath Against Sin. The original transgression created in the human mind a disposition of enmity against God (Col. 1:21). Consequently, we deserve the displeasure of God, who is "a consuming fire" against sin (Heb. 12:29; cf. Hab. 1:13). The solemn truth is that "all have sinned" (Rom.

3:23)—all are "by nature children of wrath" (Eph. 2:3; cf. 5:6) and subject to death, "for the wages of sin is death" (Rom 6:23).

Divine wrath is what Scripture calls God's reaction to sin and unrighteousness (Rom. 1:18). Deliberate rejection of God's revealed will—His law—provokes His righteous anger or wrath (2 Kings 17:16-18; 2 Chron. 36:16). G. E. Ladd wrote, "Men are ethically sinful; and when God counts their trespasses against them, he must view them as sinners, as enemies, as the objects of the divine wrath; for it is an ethical and religious necessity that the holiness of God manifests itself in wrath against sin."[1] Yet at the same time, God yearns to save the rebellious world. While He hates every sin, He has a loving concern for every sinner.

The Human Response. God's dealings with Israel culminated in the ministry of Jesus Christ, who gave the clearest insight into "the exceeding riches" of divine grace (Eph. 2:7). Said John, "We beheld His glory, the glory of the only begotten of the Father, full of grace and truth" (John 1:14). "Christ Jesus," Paul wrote, has become "for us wisdom from God—and righteousness and sanctification and redemption—that, as it is written, 'He who glories, let him glory in the Lord'" (1 Cor. 1:30, 31). Who therefore can despise "the riches of His goodness, forbearance, and longsuffering?" No wonder Paul points out that it is "the goodness of God" that leads to repentance (Rom. 2:4).

Even the human response to God's offer of salvation does not originate with human beings but with God. Our faith is but a gift of God (Rom. 12:3), as is our repentance (Acts 5:31). Our love arises in response to God's love (1 John 4:19). We cannot save ourselves from Satan, sin, suffering, and death. Our own righteousness is like filthy rags (Isa. 64:6). "But God, who is rich in mercy, because of His great love with which He loved us, even when we were dead in trespasses, made us alive together with Christ....For by grace you have been saved through faith, and that not of yourselves; it is a gift of God, not of works, lest anyone should boast" (Eph. 2:4; 5, 8, 9).

Christ's Ministry of Reconciliation

The good news is that "God was in Christ reconciling the world to Himself" (2 Cor. 5:19). His reconciliation restores the relationship between God and the human race. The text points out that this process reconciles sinners to God, not God to sinners. The key in leading sinners back to God is Jesus Christ. God's plan of reconciliation is a marvel of divine condescension. He had every right to let humanity perish.

As we have already noted, God took the initiative in restoring the broken relationship between humanity and Himself. "When we were enemies," Paul said, "we were reconciled to God through the death of His Son" (Rom. 5:10). Consequently, "we also rejoice in God through our Lord Jesus Christ, through whom we have now received the reconciliation" (Rom. 5:11).

The process of reconciliation has been associated with the term *atonement.* "The English word 'atonement' originally meant 'at-one-ment,' that is, a state of being 'at one,' or in agreement. Accordingly 'atonement' denoted harmony of a relationship, and when there had been estrangement this harmony would be the result of a process of reconciliation. Understood in terms of its original meaning 'atonement' properly denotes a state of reconciliation that terminated a state of estrangement."[2]

Many Christians limit the term *atonement* exclusively to the redeeming effects of Christ's incarnation, suffering, and death. In the sanctuary services, however, atonement not only involved the killing of the sacrificial lamb but also included the priestly ministering of its shed blood in the sanctuary itself (cf. Lev. 4:20, 26, 35; 16:15-18, 32, 33). According to this biblical usage, then, atonement can refer to both Christ's death and His intercessory ministry in the heavenly sanctuary. There, as High Priest, He applies the benefits of His complete and perfect atoning sacrifice to achieve the reconciliation of humans to God.[3]

Vincent Taylor also observed that the doctrine of atonement has two aspects "(a) the saving deed of Christ, and (b) the appropriation of His work by faith, both individual and communal. These two *together* constitute the Atonement." From this insight he concluded that "atonement is both accomplished *for us* and wrought *in us*."[4] This chapter focuses on the atonement as it relates to the death of Christ. The atonement associated with His High Priestly ministry will be discussed later (see chapter 24 of this book).

Christ's Atoning Sacrifice

Christ's atoning sacrifice at Calvary marked the turning point in the relationship between God and humanity. Though there is record of people's sins, as a result of the reconciliation God does not count their sins against them (2 Cor. 5:19). This does not mean that God dismisses punishment or that sin no longer arouses His wrath. Rather, it means that God has found a way to grant pardon to repentant sinners while still upholding the justice of His eternal law.

Christ's Death a Necessity. For a loving God to maintain His justice and righteousness, the atoning death of Jesus Christ became "a moral and legal necessity." God's "justice requires that sin be carried to judgment. God must therefore execute judgment on sin and thus on the sinner. In this execution the Son of God took our place, the sinner's place, according to God's will. The atonement was necessary because man stood under the righteous wrath of God. Herein lies the heart of the gospel of forgiveness of sin and the mystery of the cross of Christ: Christ's perfect righteousness adequately satisfied divine justice, and God is willing to accept Christ's self-sacrifice in place of man's death."[5]

Persons unwilling to accept the atoning blood of Christ receive no forgiveness of sin and are still subject to God's wrath. Said John, "He who believes in the Son has everlasting life; and he who does not believe the Son shall not see life, but the wrath of God abides on him" (John 3:36).

Therefore, the cross is a demonstration of both God's mercy and His justice. "God presented him [Christ] as a sacrifice of atonement, through faith in his blood. He did this to demonstrate his justice, because in his forbearance he had left the sins committed beforehand unpunished—he did it to demonstrate his justice at the present time, so as to be just and the one who justifies the man who has faith in Jesus" (Rom. 3:25, 26, NIV).

What Does the Atoning Sacrifice Accomplish? The Father Himself presented His Son as "a sacrifice of atonement" (Rom. 3:25, NIV; Greek, *hilasterion*), "a propitiation" (KJV, NKJV), "an expiation" (RSV). The New Testament use of *hilasterion* has nothing to do with the pagan notion of "placating an angry God" or "appeasing a vindictive, arbitrary, and capricious God."[6] The text reveals that "God in His merciful will presented Christ as the propitiation to His holy wrath on human guilt because He accepted Christ as man's representative and the divine Substitute to receive His judgment on sin."[7]

From this perspective one can understand Paul's description of Christ's death as "an offering and a sacrifice to God for a sweet smelling aroma" (Eph. 5:2; cf. Gen. 8:21; Ex. 29:18; Lev. 1:9). "Christ's self-sacrifice is *pleasing* to God because this sacrificial offering took away the barrier between God and sinful man in that Christ fully bore God's wrath on man's sin. Through Christ, God's wrath is not turned into love but is turned away from man and borne by Himself."[8]

Romans 3:25 also reveals that through Christ's sacrifice sin is expiated or purged. Expiation focuses on what the atoning blood does to the repentant sinner. He experiences forgiveness, removal of personal guilt, and cleansing from sin.[9]

Christ the Vicarious Sin-bearer. The Scriptures present Christ as the "sin-bearer" of the human race. In profound prophetic language Isaiah stated that "He was wounded for our transgressions, He was bruised for our iniquities; ...and the Lord has laid on Him the iniquity of us all. ...It pleased the Lord to bruise Him; He has put Him to grief,...[He was] an offering for sin,...and He bore the sin of many" (Isa. 53:5, 6, 10, 12; cf. Gal. 1:4). Paul had this prophecy in mind when he said, "Christ died for our sins according to the Scriptures" (1 Cor. 15:3).

These texts point to an important concept in the plan of salvation: The sins and guilt that have defiled us can be transferred to our Sin-bearer, making us clean (Ps. 51:10). The sacrificial ceremonies of the Old Testament sanctuary revealed this role of Christ. There, the transfer of sin from the repentant sinner to the innocent lamb symbolized its transfer to Christ, the Sin-bearer (see chapter 4 of this book).

What Is the Role of the Blood? The blood played a central role in the atoning sacrifices of the sanctuary service. God made provision for the atonement when He said, "The life of the flesh is in the blood, and I have given it to you...to make atonement for your souls," (Lev. 17:11). After the killing of the animal the priest had to apply its blood before forgiveness was granted.

The New Testament reveals that the Old Testament ceremonies for obtaining forgiveness, purification, and reconciliation through substitutionary blood were fulfilled in the atoning blood of Christ's Calvary sacrifice. In contrast to the old ways, the New Testament says, "How much more, then, will the blood of Christ, who through the eternal Spirit offered himself unblemished to God, cleanse our consciences from acts that lead to death, so that we may serve the Living God!" (Heb. 9:14, NIV). The shedding of His blood accomplished the expiation for sin (Rom. 3:25, RSV). John said that because of His love, God "sent His Son to be the propitiation [*hilasmos*] for our sins" (1 John 4:10; "expiation" RSV; "an atoning sacrifice" NIV).

In summary, "God's objective act of reconciliation has been accomplished through the propitiating and expiating blood (self-sacrifice) of Christ Jesus, His Son. Thus God "is both the provider and the recipient of the reconciliation."[10]

Christ the Ransom

When human beings came under the dominion of sin, they became subject to the condemnation and curse of God's law (Rom. 6:4; Gal. 3:10-13). Slaves of sin (Rom. 6:17), subject to death, they were unable to escape. "No man can redeem the life of another or give to God a ransom for him" (Ps. 49:7, NIV). Only God is invested with power to redeem. "I will ransom them from the power of the grave; I will redeem them from death" (Hosea 13:14).

How did God redeem them? Through Jesus, who testified that He "did not come to be served, but to serve, and to give His life a ransom for many" (Matt. 20:28; see 1 Tim. 2:6), God "purchased" the church with "His own blood" (Acts 20:28). In Christ "we have redemption through His blood, the forgiveness of sins" (Eph. 1:7; cf. Rom. 3:24). His death was to "redeem us from every lawless deed and purify for Himself His own special people, zealous for good works" (Titus 2:14).

What Did the Ransom Accomplish? Christ's death ratified God's ownership of humanity. Said Paul, "You are not your own; you were bought at a price" (1 Cor. 6:19, 20, NIV; see also 1 Cor. 7:23).

Through His death, Christ broke the dominion of sin, terminated the spiritual captivity, removed the condemnation and curse of the law, and made eternal life available to all repentant sinners. Peter said believers were redeemed from "aimless conduct received by tradition from your fathers" (1 Peter 1:18). Paul wrote that those delivered from the slavery of sin and its deadly fruit are now in the service of God with its "fruit to holiness, and the end, everlasting life" (Rom. 6:22).

To ignore or deny the ransom principle would be "to lose the very heart of the gospel of grace and to deny the deepest motive of our gratitude to the Lamb of God."[11] This principle is central to the doxologies sung in the heavenly throne room: "You were slain, and with your blood you purchase men for God from every tribe and language and people and nation. You have made them to be a kingdom and priests to serve our God, and they will reign on the earth" (Rev. 5:9, 10, NIV).

Christ the Representative of Humanity

Both Adam and Christ—"the last Adam," or "the second Man" (1 Cor. 15:45, 47)—represent all humanity. While the natural birth saddles each person with the results of Adam's transgression, everyone who experiences the spiritual birth receives the benefits of Christ's perfect life and sacrifice. "For as in Adam all die, even so in Christ all shall be made alive" (1 Cor. 15:22).

Adam's rebellion brought sin, condemnation, and death to all. Christ reversed the downward trend. In His great love, He subjected Himself to the divine judgment on sin and became humanity's representative. His substitutionary death provided the deliverance from the penalty of sin and the gift of eternal life for repentant sinners (2 Cor. 5:21; Rom. 6:23; 1 Peter 3:18).

Scripture clearly teaches the universal nature of Christ's substitutionary death. By "the grace of God," He experienced death for everyone (Heb. 2:9). Like Adam, all have sinned (Rom. 5:12), therefore, everyone experiences death—the first death. The death that Christ tasted for everyone was the second death—the full curse of death (Rev. 20:6—see chapter 27 of this book).

Christ's Life and Salvation

"For if when we were enemies we were reconciled to God through the death of His Son, much more, having been reconciled, we shall be saved by His life" (Rom. 5:10). It took Christ's life, as well as His death, to bridge the chasm gouged by sin. Both are necessary and contribute to our salvation.

What Can Christ's Perfect Life Do For Us? Jesus lived a pure, holy, and loving life, relying completely on God. This precious life He shares with repentant sinners as a gift. His perfect character is portrayed as a wedding garment (Matt. 22:11) or a robe of righteousness (Isa. 61:10) that He gives to replace the filthy rags of human attempts to achieve righteousness (Isa. 64:6).

In spite of our human corruption, when we submit ourselves to Christ, our heart is united with His heart, our will is merged in His will, our mind becomes one with His mind, our thoughts are brought into captivity to Him; we live His life. We are covered with His garment of righteousness. When God looks at the believing, penitent sinner He sees, not the nakedness or deformity of sin, but the robe of righteousness formed by Christ's perfect obedience to the law.[12] None can be truly righteous unless covered by this robe.

In the parable of the wedding garment the guest who arrived in his own clothes was not cast out because of unbelief. He had accepted the invitation to the banquet (Matt. 22:10). But his coming was not enough. He needed the wedding garment. Similarly, belief in the cross is not enough. To be presentable before the King, we also need Christ's perfect life—His righteous character.

As sinners we not only need the debt to be cancelled, we need our bank account restored. We need more than release from prison, we need to be adopted into the family of the King. The mediatorial ministry of the resurrected Christ has the twofold objective of forgiving and clothing—the application of His death and life to our life and our standing before God. Calvary's "It is finished" marked the completion of a perfect life and a perfect sacrifice. Sinners need both.

The Inspiration of Christ's Life. Christ's life on earth also gave humanity a model of how to live. Peter, for instance, recommends as an example to us the way Jesus responded to personal abuse (1 Peter 2:21-23). He who was made like us and was tempted in all points as we are demonstrated that those who depend on God's power have no need to continue in sin. Christ's life provides the assurance that we can live victoriously. Paul testified, "I can do all things through Christ who strengthens me" (Phil. 4:13).

Christ's Resurrection and Salvation

"If Christ is not risen," Paul said, "then our preaching is in vain and your faith is also vain" and "you are still in your sins!" (1 Cor. 15:14, 17). Jesus Christ was physically resurrected (Luke 24:36-43), ascended as the God-man to heaven, and began His crucial intercessory work as Mediator at the right hand of God the Father (Heb. 8:1, 2—see chapter 4 of this book).

Christ's resurrection gave a meaning to the cross that the shattered disciples could not see on crucifixion Friday. His resurrection transformed these men into a mighty force that changed history. The resurrection—never detached from the crucifixion—became central to their mission. They proclaimed the living, crucified Christ, who had triumphed over the forces of evil. Herein lay the power of the apostolic message.

"The resurrection of Christ," Philip Schaff wrote, "is emphatically a test question upon which depends the truth or falsehood of the Christian religion. It is either the greatest miracle or the greatest delusion which history records."[13] Wilbur M. Smith commented, "The resurrection of Christ is the very citadel of the Christian faith. This is the doctrine that turned the world upside down in the first century, that lifted Christianity preeminently above Judaism, and the pagan religions of the Mediterranean world. If this goes, so must almost everything else that is vital and unique in the Gospel of the Lord Jesus Christ: 'If Christ be not risen, then is your faith vain' (1 Cor. 15:17)."[14]

Christ's current ministry is rooted in His death and resurrection. While the atoning sacrifice at Calvary was sufficient and complete, without the resurrection we would have no assurance that Christ had successfully finished His divine mission on earth. That Christ has risen confirms the reality of life beyond the grave and demonstrates the truthfulness of God's promise of eternal life in Him.

The Results of Christ's Saving Ministry

Christ's atoning ministry affects not only the human race but the entire universe.

Reconciliation Throughout the Universe. Paul reveals the magnitude of Christ's salvation in and through the church: "His intent was that now, through the church, the manifold wisdom of God should be made known to the rulers and authorities in the heavenly realms" (Eph. 3:10, NIV). He further asserts that it pleased God through Christ "to reconcile all things to Himself...whether things on earth or things in heaven, having made peace through the blood of His cross" (Col. 1:20). Paul revealed the astounding results of this reconciliation: "At the name of Jesus every knee should bow, of those in heaven, and of those on earth, and of those under the earth, and that every tongue should confess that Jesus is Lord, to the glory of God the Father" (Phil. 2:10, 11).

The Vindication of God's Law. Christ's perfect, atoning sacrifice upheld the justice and goodness or righteousness of God's holy law as well as His gracious character. Christ's death and ransom satisfied the demands of the law (that sin needed to be punished), while justifying repentant sinners through His grace and mercy. Paul said, "He condemned sin in the flesh, that the righteous requirement of the law might be fulfilled in us who do not walk according to the flesh but according to the Spirit" (Rom. 8:3, 4).

Justification. Reconciliation becomes effective only when forgiveness is accepted. The prodigal son was reconciled with his father when he accepted his father's love and forgiveness.

"Those who accept by faith that God has reconciled the world to Himself in Christ and who submit to Him will receive from God the invaluable gift of *justification* with its immediate fruit of peace with God (Romans 5:1). No longer the object of God's wrath, justified believers have become the objects of God's favor. With full access to the throne of God through Christ, they receive the power of the Holy Spirit to break down all the barriers or dividing walls of hostility which exists between Jew and Gentile" (see Eph. 2:14-16).[15]

The Futility of Salvation by Works. God's ministry of reconciliation reveals the futility of human endeavors to obtain salvation through works of the law. Insight into divine grace leads to the acceptance of the justifying righteousness available through faith in Christ. The gratitude of those who have experienced forgiveness makes obedience a joy; works, then, are not the ground of salvation but its fruitage.[16]

A New Relationship With God. Experiencing God's grace—which offers Christ's perfect life of obedience—His righteousness, and His atoning death as a free gift leads to a deeper relationship with God. Gratitude, praise, and joy arise, obedience becomes a delight, the study of His Word a joy, and the mind a ready dwelling place of the Holy Spirit. A new relationship between God and the repentant sinner takes place. It is a fellowship based on love and admiration rather than fear and obligation (cf. John 15:1-10).

The more we understand God's grace in the light of the cross, the less self-righteousness we will feel, and the more we will realize how blessed we are. The power of the same Holy Spirit that was operative in Christ when He rose from the dead will transform our lives. Instead of failure, we will experience daily victory over sin.

The Motivation for Mission. The amazing love revealed in God's ministry of reconciliation through Jesus Christ motivates our sharing the gospel with others. When we have experienced it ourselves, we cannot keep secret the fact that God will not count sin against those who accept Christ's sacrifice for sins. We will pass on to others the moving gospel invitation "Be reconciled to God. For He made Him who knew no sin to be sin for us, that we might become the righteousness of God in Him" (2 Cor. 5:20, 21).

References

1. George E. Ladd, *A Theology of the New Testament* (Grand Rapids, MI: Wm. B. Eerdmans, 1974), p. 453.

2. "Atonement," *SDA Bible Dictionary*, rev. ed., p. 97.

3. For a full discussion of this biblical concept, see *Seventh-day Adventists Answer Questions on Doctrine* (Washington, D.C.: Review and Herald, 1957), pp. 341-355.

4. Vincent Taylor, *The Cross of Christ* (London: Macmillan, 1956), pp. 88, 89.

5. Hans K. LaRondelle, *Christ Our Salvation* (Mountain View, CA: Pacific Press, 1980), pp. 25, 26.

6. Raoul Dederen, "Atoning Aspects in Christ's Death," in *The Sanctuary and the Atonement*, eds., Arnold V. Wallenkampf and W. Richard Lesher, (Washington, D.C.: [Biblical Research Institute of the General Conference of Seventh-day Adventists], 1981), p. 295. He added: "Among the heathen propitiation was thought of as an activity by which the worshiper was able himself to provide that which would induce a change of mind in the deity. He simply bribed his god to be favorable to him. In the Scriptures expiation-propitiation is thought of as springing from the love of God" (*Ibid*, p. 317).

7. LaRondelle, p. 26.

8. *Ibid.*, pp. 26, 27.

9. Dederen, p. 295.

10. LaRondelle, p. 28. The quotation in this reference was from H.G. Link and C. Brown, "Reconciliation," *The New International Dictionary of New Testament Theology* (Grand Rapids, MI: Zondervan, 1978), vol. 3, p. 162.

11. LaRondelle, p. 30.

12. See White, *Christ's Object Lessons* (Washington, D.C.: Review and Herald, 1941), p. 312.

13. Philip Schaff, *History of the Christian Church* (Grand Rapids, MI: Wm. B. Eerdmans, 1962), vol. 1, p. 173.

14. Wilbur M. Smith, "Twentieth-Century Scientists and the Resurrection of Christ" *Christianity Today*, April 15, 1957, p. 22. For arguments for the historicity of the resurrection, see Josh McDowell, *Evidence That Demands a Verdict* (Campus Crusade for Christ, 1972), pp. 185-274.

15. LaRondelle, pp. 32, 33.

16. See Hyde, "What Christ's Life Means to Me," *Adventist Review*, Nov. 6, 1986, p. 19.

10 The Experience of Salvation

In infinite love and mercy God made Christ, who knew no sin, to be sin for us, so that in Him we might be made the righteousness of God. Led by the Holy Spirit, we sense our need, acknowledge our sinfulness, repent of our transgressions, and exercise faith in Jesus as Lord and Christ, as Substitute, and Example. This faith which receives salvation comes through the divine power of the Word and is the gift of God's grace. Through Christ we are justified, adopted as God's sons and daughters, and delivered from the lordship of sin. Through the Spirit we are born again and sanctified; the Spirit renews our minds, writes God's law of love in our hearts, and we are given the power to live a holy life. Abiding in Him, we become partakers of the divine nature and have the assurance of salvation now and in the judgment. (2 Cor. 5:17-21; John 3:16; Gal. 1:4; 4:4-7; Titus 3:3-7; John 16:8; Gal. 3:13, 14; 1 Pet. 2:21, 22; Rom. 10:17; Luke 17:5; Mark 9:23, 24; Eph. 2:5-10; Rom. 3:21-26; Col. 1:13, 14; Rom. 8:14-17; Gal. 3:26; John 3:3-8; 1 Pet. 1:23; Rom. 12:2; Heb. 8:7-12; Ezek. 36:25-27; 2 Pet. 1:3, 4; Rom. 8:1-4; 5:6-10.)

CENTURIES AGO, THE SHEPHERD OF HERMAS dreamed of a wrinkled old lady who had lived long. In his dream as time passed, she began to change: while her body was still old and her hair white, her face looked younger. Eventually, she was restored to her youth.

T. F. Torrance likened the woman to the church.[1] Christians cannot be static. If the Spirit of Christ reigns within (Rom. 8:9), they are in the process of change.

Paul said, "Christ loved the church and gave himself up for her, that he might sanctify her, having cleansed her by the washing of water with the word, that he might present the church to himself in splendor, without spot or wrinkle or any such thing, that she might be holy and without blemish" (Eph. 5:25-27, RSV). Such a cleansing is the goal of the church. Hence, the believers comprising the church can testify that "though our outer nature is wasting away, our inner nature is being renewed every day" (2 Cor. 4:16, RSV). "We all, with unveiled face, beholding as in a mirror the glory of the Lord, are being transformed into the same image from glory to glory, just as by the Spirit of the Lord" (2 Cor. 3:18). This transformation is the ultimate internal Pentecost.

Throughout Scripture the descriptions of the believer's experience—salvation, justification, sanctification, purification, and redemption—are spoken of as (1) already accomplished, (2) presently being realized, and (3) to be realized in the future. An understanding of these three perspectives helps solve the seeming tensions in emphasis relative to justification and sanctification. This chapter, therefore, is divided into three major sections dealing with salvation in the believer's past, present, and future.

The Experience of Salvation and the Past

A factual knowledge about God and His love and benevolence is insufficient. Trying, apart from Christ, to develop the good in oneself is counterproductive. The experience of salvation that reaches deep into the soul comes from God alone. Speaking of this experience, Christ said, "Unless one is born again, he cannot see the kingdom of God....Unless one is born of water and the Spirit, He cannot enter the kingdom of God" (John 3:3, 5).

Only through Jesus Christ can one experience salvation, "for there is no other name under heaven given among men by which we must be saved" (Acts 4:12). Jesus said, "I am the way, the truth, and the life. No one comes to the Father except through Me" (John 14:6).

The experience of salvation involves repentance, confession, forgiveness, justification, and sanctification.

Repentance. Not long before His crucifixion, Jesus promised His disciples the Holy Spirit, who would reveal Him by convicting "the world of sin, and of righteousness, and of judgment" (John 16:8). When at Pentecost the Holy Spirit did convict the people of their need of a Saviour, and they asked how they should respond, Peter replied, "Repent!" (Acts 2:37, 38; cf. 3:19).

1. What is repentance? The word *repentance* is a translation of the Hebrew *nachum*, "to be sorry," "to repent." The Greek equivalent, *metanoeo*, means "to change one's mind," "to feel remorse," "to repent." Genuine repentance results in a radical change in attitude toward God and sin. God's Spirit convicts those who receive Him of the seriousness of sin by bringing them to a sense of God's righteousness and of their own lost condition. They experience sorrow and guilt. Recognizing the truth that "he who covers his sins will not prosper, but whoever confesses and forsakes them will have mercy" (Prov. 28:13), they confess specific sins. Through the decided exercise of their wills, they surrender totally to the Saviour and renounce their sinful behavior. Thus repentance reaches its climax in conversion—a turning of the sinner toward God (from the Greek *epistrophe*, "a turning toward," cf. Acts 15:3).[2]

David's repentance of his sins of adultery and murder vividly exemplifies how this experience prepares the way for victory over sin. Convicted by the Spirit, he despised and mourned his sin and pleaded for purity: "I acknowledge my transgressions, and my sin is ever before me. Against You, You only, have I sinned, and done this evil in Your sight." "Have mercy upon me, O God, according to Your lovingkindness; according to the multitude of Your tender mercies, blot out my transgressions." Create in me a clean heart, O God, and renew a steadfast spirit within me" (Ps. 51:3, 1, 10). David's subsequent experience demonstrates that God's pardon not only provides forgiveness for sin but reclaims from sin.

Although repentance precedes forgiveness, the sinner cannot, by repentance, fit himself to secure the blessing of God. In fact, the sinner cannot even produce from within himself repentance—it is the gift of God (Acts 5:31; cf. Rom. 2:4). The Holy Spirit draws the sinner to Christ in order that he may find repentance—this heartfelt sorrow for sin.

2. Motivation for repentance. Christ said: "And I, if I am lifted up from the earth, will draw all peoples to Myself" (John 12:32). The heart is melted and subdued when we sense that Christ's death justifies us and delivers us from the penalty of death. Imagine the feelings of the prisoner in death row awaiting execution when suddenly a pardon is handed him.

In Christ the repentant sinner is not only pardoned but acquitted—declared righteous! He does not deserve and cannot earn such treatment. As Paul points out, Christ died for our justification, while we were weak, sinful, ungodly, and enemies of God (Rom. 5:6-10). Nothing so touches the depths of the soul as a sense of Christ's pardoning love. When sinners contemplate this unfathomable divine love, displayed on the cross, they receive the most powerful motivation possible to repent. This is the goodness of God that leads us to repentance (Rom. 2:4).

Justification. In His infinite love and mercy God made Christ, "who knew no sin to be sin for us, that we might become the righteousness of God in Him" (2 Cor. 5:21). Through faith in Jesus, the heart is filled by His Spirit. Through this same faith, which is a gift of God's grace (Rom. 12:3; Eph. 2:8), repentant sinners are justified (Rom. 3:28).

The term *justification* is a translation of the Greek *dikaioma*, meaning "righteous requirement, deed," "regulation," "judicial sentence," "act of righteousness," and *dikaiosis*, signifying, "justification," "vindication," "acquittal." The related verb *dikaioo*, meaning "be pronounced and treated as righteous," "be acquitted," "be justified," "be set free, made pure," "justify," "vindicate," "do justice," gives additional insights into the term's meaning.[3]

In general, *justification*, as used theologically, is "the divine act by which God declares a penitent sinner righteous or regards him as righteous. Justification is the opposite of condemnation (Rom. 5:16)."[4] The basis for this justification is not our obedience, but Christ's, for "through one Man's righteous act the free gift came to all men, resulting in justification of life.... By one Man's obedience many will be made righteous" (Rom. 5:18, 19). He gives this obedience to those believers who are "justified freely by His grace" (Rom. 3:24). "Not by works of righteousness which we have done, but according to His mercy He saved us" (Titus 3:5).

1. The role of faith and works. Many wrongly believe that their standing before God depends on their good or bad deeds. Addressing the question of how persons are justified before God, Paul unequivocally stated that he "suffered the loss of all things,...that I may gain Christ and be found in Him, not having my own righteousness,...but that which is through faith in Christ, the righteousness which is from God by faith" (Phil. 3:8, 9). He pointed to Abraham, who "believed God, and it was accounted ["credited," NIV] to him for righteousness" (Rom. 4:3; Gen. 15:6). He was justified before he underwent circumcision, not on account of it (Rom. 4:9, 10).

What kind of faith did Abraham have? The Scriptures reveal that "by faith Abraham obeyed" when God called him, leaving his homeland and traveling "not knowing where he was going" (Heb. 11:8-10; cf. Gen. 12:4; 13:18). That he had a genuine, living faith in God was demonstrated by his obedience. It was on the basis of this dynamic faith that he was justified.

The apostle James warned about another incorrect understanding of justification by faith—that one can be justified by faith without manifesting corresponding works. He showed that genuine faith cannot exist without works. Like Paul, James illustrated his point from Abraham's experience. Abraham's offering of Isaac his son (James 2:21) demonstrated his faith. "Do you see," James asked, "that faith was working together with his works, and by works faith was made perfect?" (James 2:22). "Faith by itself, if it does not have works, is dead" (James 2:17).

Abraham's experience revealed that works are the evidence of a true relationship with God. The faith that leads to justification is, therefore, a living faith that works (James 2:24).

Paul and James agreed on justification by faith. While Paul addressed the fallacy of obtaining justification through works, James dealt with the equally dangerous concept of claiming justification without corresponding works. Neither works nor a dead faith lead to justification. It can be realized only by a genuine faith that works by love (Gal. 5:6) and purifies the soul.

2. The experience of justification. Through justification by faith in Christ, His righteousness is imputed to us. We are right with God because of Christ our Substitute. God, Paul said, "made Him who knew no sin to be sin for us, that we might become the righteousness of God in Him" (2 Cor. 5:21). As repentant sinners, we experience full and complete pardon. We are reconciled to God!

Zechariah's vision about Joshua the high priest beautifully illustrates justification. Joshua stands before the angel of the Lord clothed in filthy garments, which represents sin's defilement. As he stands there, Satan calls for his condemnation. Satan's accusations are correct—Joshua does not deserve acquittal. But God, in divine mercy, rebukes Satan: "Is this not a brand plucked from the fire?" (Zech. 3:2). Is this not my precious one whom I am preserving in a special way?

The Lord orders the soiled attire to be removed speedily and declares: "See, I have removed your iniquity from you, and I will clothe you with rich robes" (Zech. 3:4). Our loving, all-merciful God sweeps Satan's charges aside, justifying the trembling sinner, covering him with robes of Christ's righteousness. As Joshua's dirty robes represented sin, so the new robe represented the believer's new experience in Christ. In the process of justification, confessed and forgiven sin is transferred to the pure and holy Son of God, the sin-bearing Lamb. "The undeserving repentant believer, however, is dressed with the imputed righteousness of Christ. This exchange of clothes, this divine, saving transaction, is the Biblical doctrine of justification." [5] The justified believer has experienced forgiveness and been purified of his sins.

The Results. What are the results of repentance and justification?

1. Sanctification. The word *sanctification* is a translation of the Greek *hagiasmos*, meaning "holiness," "consecration," "sanctification," from *hagiazo*, "to make holy," "to consecrate," "to sanctify," "to set apart." The Hebrew equivalent is *qadash*, "to separate from common use."[6]

True repentance and justification lead to sanctification. Justification and sanctification are closely related,[7] distinct but never separate. They designate two phases of salvation: Justification is what God does *for* us, while sanctification is what God does *in* us.

Neither justification nor sanctification is the result of meritorious works. Both are solely due to Christ's grace and righteousness. "The righteousness by which we are justified is imputed; the righteousness by which we are sanctified is imparted. The first is our title to heaven, the second is our fitness for heaven."[8]

The three phases of sanctification the Bible presents are: (1) an accomplished act in the believer's past; (2) a process in the believer's present experience; (3) and the final result that the believer experiences at Christ's return.

As to the believer's past, at the moment of justification the believer is also sanctified "in the name of the Lord Jesus and by the Spirit of our God" (1 Cor. 6:11). He or she becomes a "saint." At that point the new believer is redeemed and belongs fully to God.

As a result of God's call (Rom. 1:7), believers are called "saints," for they are "in Christ" (Phil. 1:1; see also John 15:1-7), not because they have achieved a state of sinlessness. Salvation is a present experience. "His mercy," Paul said, has "saved us, through the washing of regeneration and renewing of the Holy Spirit" (Titus 3:5), setting us apart and consecrating us to a holy purpose and walk with Christ.

2. Adoption into God's family. At the same time new believers have received the "Spirit of adoption." God has adopted them as His children, which means that believers are sons and daughters of the King! He has made them His heirs, "joint heirs with Christ" (Rom. 8:15-17). What a privilege, honor, and joy!

3. Assurance of salvation. Justification brings also the assurance of the believer's acceptance. It brings the joy of being reunited with God *now*. No matter how sinful one's past life, God pardons all sins, and we are no longer under the condemnation and curse of the law. Redemption has become a reality: "In Him we have redemption through His blood, the forgiveness of sins, according to the riches of His grace" (Eph. 1:7).

4. The beginning of a new and victorious life. The realization that the Saviour's blood covers our sinful past brings healing to body, soul, and mind. Feelings of guilt may be dispensed with, for in Christ all is forgiven, all is new. By daily bestowing His grace, Christ begins transforming us into the image of God.

As our faith in Him grows, our healing and transformation progress, and He gives us increasing victories over the powers of darkness. His overcoming the world guarantees our deliverance from the slavery of sin (John 16:33).

5. The gift of eternal life. Our new relationship with Christ brings with it the gift of eternal life. John affirmed, "He who has the Son has life; he who does not have the Son of God does not have life" (1 John 5:12). Our sinful past has been cared for; through the indwelling Spirit we can enjoy the blessings of salvation.

The Experience of Salvation and the Present

Through Christ's blood bringing purification, justification, and sanctification, the believer is "a new creation; the old things have passed away; behold, all things have become new" (2 Cor. 5:17).

A Call to a Life of Sanctification. Salvation includes living a sanctified life on the basis of what Christ accomplished at Calvary. Paul appealed to believers to live a life consecrated to ethical holiness and moral conduct (1 Thess. 4:7). To enable them to experience sanctification, God gives believers the "Spirit of holiness" (Rom. 1:4). "According to the riches of his glory," Paul said, God "may grant you to be strengthened with might through His Spirit in the inner man, and that Christ may dwell in your hearts through faith" (Eph. 3:16, 17, RSV).

As a new creation, believers have new responsibilities. "Just as you presented your members as slaves of uncleanness, and of lawlessness leading to more lawlessness," Paul said, "so now present your members as slaves of righteousness for holiness" (Rom. 6:19). Now they are to live "in the Spirit" (Gal. 5:25).

Spirit-filled believers "do not walk according to the flesh, but according to the Spirit" (Rom. 8:1, cf. 8:4). They are transformed, since "to be carnally minded is death, but to be spiritually minded is life and peace" (Rom. 8:6). Through the indwelling of the Spirit of God they "are not in the flesh but in the Spirit" (Rom. 8:9).

The highest goal of the Spirit-filled life is to please God (1 Thess. 4:1). Sanctification is God's will, Paul said. Therefore "you should abstain from sexual immorality" and "no one should take advantage of and defraud his brother in this manner....For God did not call us to uncleanness, but in holiness" (1 Thess. 4:3, 6, 7).

The Internal Change. At the Second Advent we will be changed physically. This corruptible mortal body will put on immortality (1 Cor. 15:51-54). However, our characters must undergo transformation in preparation for the Second Advent.

Character transformation involves the mental and spiritual aspects of the image of God—the "inner nature" that is to be renewed daily (2 Cor. 4:16, RSV; cf. Rom. 12:2). Thus, like the old lady in the Shepherd of Hermas story, the church is growing younger within—each fully surrendered Christian is being changed from glory to glory, until, at the Second Advent, his or her transformation into the image of God will be completed.

1. The involvement of Christ and the Holy Spirit. Only the Creator can accomplish the creative work of transforming our lives (1 Thess. 5:23). However, He does not do so without our participation. We must place ourselves in the channel of the Spirit's working, which we can do by beholding Christ. As we meditate on Christ's life, the Holy Spirit restores the physical, mental, and spiritual faculties (cf. Titus 3:5). The Holy Spirit's work involves revealing Christ and restoring us into Christ's image (cf. Rom. 8:1-10).

God desires to live within His people. Because He had promised "I will dwell in them:" (2 Cor. 6:16; cf. 1 John 3:24; 4:12), Paul could say: "Christ lives in me" (Gal. 2:20; cf. John 14:23). The Creator's indwelling daily revives the believers inwardly (2 Cor. 4:16), renewing their minds (Rom. 12:2; see also Phil. 2:5).

2. Partaking of the divine nature. Christ's "exceeding great and precious promises" pledge His divine power to complete the transformation of our characters (2 Peter 1:4). This access to divine power allows us diligently to "add to . . . faith virtue, to virtue knowledge, to knowledge self-control, to self-control perseverance, to perseverance godliness, to godliness brotherly kindness, and to brotherly kindness love" (2 Peter 1:5-7). "If these things be in you, and abound," Peter says, "they make you that ye shall neither be barren nor unfruitful in the knowledge of our Lord Jesus Christ. But he that lacketh these things is blind" (2 Peter 1:8,9, KJV).

a. Only through Christ. What transforms humans into the image of their Creator is the putting on or partaking of the Lord Jesus Christ (Rom. 13:14; Heb. 3:14)—the "renewing of the Holy Spirit" (Titus 3:5). It is the perfecting of God's love in us (1 John 4:12). Here is a mystery akin to that of the incarnation of the Son of God. As the Holy Spirit enabled the divine Christ to partake of human nature, so that Spirit enables us to partake of the divine character traits. This appropriation of the divine nature renews the inner person, making us Christlike, though on a different level: Whereas Christ became human, believers do not become divine. Rather, they become Godlike in character.

b. A dynamic process. Sanctification is progressive. By prayer and study of the Word, we constantly grow in fellowship with God.

A mere intellectual understanding of the plan of salvation will not suffice. "Unless you eat the flesh of the Son of Man and drink His blood," Christ revealed, "you have no life in you. Whoever eats My flesh and drinks My blood has eternal life, and I will raise him up at the last day. For My flesh is food indeed, and My blood is drink indeed. He who eats My flesh and drinks My blood abides in Me, and I in him" (John 6:53-56).

His imagery vividly conveys that believers are to assimilate Christ's words. Jesus said, "The words that I speak to you are spirit, and they are life" (John 6:63; see also Matt. 4:4).

Character is composed of what the mind "eats and drinks." When we digest the bread of life, we become transformed into the likeness of Christ.

3. The two transformations. In 1517, the same year in which Luther nailed his ninety-five theses to the castle-church door in Wittenburg, Germany, Rafael began painting his famous Transfiguration picture in Rome. These two events had something in common. Luther's acts marked the birth of Protestantism, and Rafael's painting, albeit unintentionally, epitomized the spirit of the Reformation.

The painting shows Christ standing on the mountain with the demoniac looking hopefully to Him from the valley (cf. Mark 9:2-29). The two groups of disciples—one on the mountain, the other in the valley—depict two types of Christian.

The disciples on the mountain wanted to remain with Christ, seemingly unconcerned about the needs in the valley below. Through the centuries many have built on "mountains" far removed from the needs of the world. Their experience is prayer without works.

On the other hand, the disciples in the valley worked without prayer—and their efforts to cast out the demon were unsuccessful. Multitudes have been imprisoned either in the trap of working for others without power or in that of praying much without working for others. Both of these kinds of Christian need to have the image of God restored in them.

a. The true transformation. God hopes to change fallen beings into His image by transforming their wills, minds, desires, and characters. The Holy Spirit brings to believers a decided change of outlook. His fruits, "Love, joy, peace, longsuffering, kindness, goodness, faithfulness, gentleness, self-control" (Gal. 5:22, 23), now constitute their life-style—even though they remain corruptible mortals till Christ's return.

If we do not resist Him, Christ "will so identify Himself with our thoughts and aims, so blend our hearts and minds into conformity to His will, that when obeying Him we shall be but carrying out our own impulses. The will, refined and sanctified, will find its highest delight in doing His service."[9]

b. The two destinations. Christ's transfiguration reveals another striking contrast. Christ was transfigured, but, in a sense, so was the boy in the valley. The boy was transfigured into a demonic image (see Mark 9:1-29). Here we see illuminated two contrasting plans—God's plan to restore us and Satan's to ruin us. Scripture says God is able to keep us "from falling" (Jude 24, KJV). Satan, on the other hand, does his utmost to keep us in a fallen state.

Life involves constant change. There is no neutral ground. We are either being ennobled or degraded. We are either "slaves of sin" or "slaves of righteousness" (Rom. 6:17, 18). Whoever occupies our minds occupies us. If, through the Holy Spirit, Christ occupies our minds, we will become Christlike people—a Spirit-filled life brings "every thought into captivity to the obedience of Christ" (2 Cor. 10:5). But to be without Christ cuts us off from the source of life and change and makes our ultimate destruction inevitable.

The Perfection of Christ. What is biblical perfection? How can it be received?

1. Biblical perfection. The words *perfect* and *perfection* are translations of the Hebrew *tam* or *tamim*, which mean "complete," "right," "peaceful," "sound," "wholesome," or "blameless." Generally, the Greek *teleios* means "complete," "perfect," "full-grown," "mature," "fully developed," and "having attained its purpose."[10]

In the Old Testament, when used of humans, the word has a relative sense. Noah, Abraham, and Job were each described as perfect or blameless (Gen. 6:9; 17:1; 22:18; Job 1:1, 8), though each had imperfections (Gen. 9:21; 20; Job 40:2-5).

In the New Testament *perfect* often describes mature persons who have lived up to the best available light and attained the potential of their spiritual, mental, and physical powers (cf. 1 Cor. 14:20; Phil. 3:15; Heb. 5:14). Believers are to be as perfect in their finite sphere, Christ said, as God is perfect in His infinite and absolute sphere (cf. Matt. 5:48). In God's sight, a perfect person is one whose heart and life are wholly surrendered to the worship and service of God, who is constantly growing in divine knowledge, and who is, through God's grace, living up to all the light he has received while rejoicing in a life of victory (cf. Co. 4:12; James 3:2).

2. Full perfection in Christ. How may we become perfect? The Holy Spirit brings us to the perfection of Christ. By faith, Christ's perfect character becomes ours. People can never claim that perfection independently, as if it were their innate possession or theirs by right. Perfection is a gift of God.

Apart from Christ human beings cannot obtain righteousness. "He who abides in Me, and I in him" He said, "bears much fruit; for without Me you can do nothing" (John 15:5). It is Christ "who became for us wisdom from God—and righteousness and sanctification and redemption" (1 Cor. 1:30).

In Christ these qualities constitute our perfection. He completed, once for all, our sanctification and redemption. No one can add to what He has done. Our wedding garment, or robe of righteousness, was wrought out by Christ's life, death, and resurrection. The Holy Spirit now takes the finished product and works it out in the Christian's life. In this way we can "be filled with all the fullness of God" (Eph. 3:19).

3. Move on to perfection. What role do we, as believers, play in all of this? Through the indwelling Christ we grow up to spiritual maturity. Through God's gifts to His church we can develop "to a perfect man, to the measure of the stature of the fullness of Christ" (Eph. 4:13). We need to grow beyond our spiritual childhood experience (Eph. 4:14)—beyond the basic truths of Christian experience—moving on to the "solid food" prepared for mature believers (Heb. 5:14). "Therefore," Paul said, "leaving the discussion of the elementary principles of Christ, let us go on to our perfection" (Heb. 6:1). "This is my prayer," he said, "that your love may abound more and more in knowledge and depth of insight, so that you may be able to discern what is best and may be pure and blameless until the day of Christ, filled with the fruit of righteousness that comes through Jesus Christ—to the glory and praise of God" (Phil. 1:9-11, NIV).

The sanctified life is not a life without severe difficulties and obstacles. Paul admonished believers to "work out your own salvation with fear and trembling." But he added the encouraging words, "For it is God who works in you both to will and to do for His good pleasure" (Phil. 2:12, 13).

"Exhort one another daily," he said, "lest any of you be hardened through the deceitfulness of sin. For we have become partakers of Christ if we hold the beginning of our confidence steadfast to the end" (Heb. 3:13, 14; cf. Matt. 24:13).

But, Scripture warns, "If we deliberately keep on sinning after we have received the knowledge of the truth, no sacrifice for sin is left, but only a fearful expectation of judgment" (Heb. 10:26, 27, NIV).

These exhortations make evident that Christians "need more than a purely legal justification or sanctification. They need holiness of character even though salvation is always by faith. The title to heaven rests on the righteousness of Christ only. In addition to justification, God's plan of salvation provides through this title a *fitness* for heaven by the indwelling Christ. This fitness must be revealed in man's moral character as evidence that salvation 'has happened.'"[11]

What does this mean in human terms? Continual prayer is indispensable for living a sanctified life that is perfect at every stage of its development. "For this reason we...do not cease to pray for you,...that you may have a walk worthy of the Lord, fully pleasing Him, being fruitful in every good work and increasing in the knowledge of God" (Col. 1:9, 10).

Daily Justification. All believers who are living the Spirit-filled sanctified life (Christ-possessed) have a continuing need for daily justification (Christ-bestowed). We need this because of conscious transgressions and because of errors we may commit unwittingly. Realizing the sinfulness of the human heart, David requested forgiveness for his "hidden faults" (Ps. 19:12, RSV; cf. Jer. 17:9). Speaking specifically of the sins of believers, God assures us that "if anyone sins, we have an Advocate with the Father, Jesus Christ the righteous" (1 John 2:1).

The Experience of Salvation and the Future

Our salvation is finally and fully accomplished when we are either glorified in the resurrection or translated to heaven. Through glorification God shares with the redeemed His own radiant glory. This is the hope that all of us, as God's children, anticipate. Said Paul, "And we rejoice in our hope of sharing the glory of God" (Rom. 5:2, RSV).

It is fulfilled at the Second Advent when Christ appears "to bring salvation to those who are waiting for Him" (Heb. 9:28, NIV).

Glorification and Sanctification. The indwelling of Christ in our hearts is one of the conditions for future salvation—the glorification of our mortal bodies. "Christ in you," Paul said, is "the hope of glory" (Col. 1:27), explaining in another place, "If the Spirit of Him who raised Jesus from the dead dwells in you, He who raised Christ from the dead will also give life to your mortal bodies through His Spirit who dwells in you" (Rom. 8:11). Paul assures us, God "chose you for salvation through sanctification by the Spirit and belief in the truth...for the obtaining of the glory of our Lord Jesus Christ" (2 Thess. 2:13, 14).

In Him, we are already in the throne room of heaven (Col. 3:1-4). Those who are "partakers of the Holy Spirit" have in actuality tasted "the powers of the age to come" (Heb. 6:4, 5). By contemplating the Lord's glory and fixing our eyes on the attractive loveliness of Christ's character, we "are being transformed into his likeness with ever-increasing glory" (2 Cor. 3:18, NIV)—we are being prepared for the transformation we will experience at the Second Advent.

Our final redemption and adoption as a child of God takes place in the future. Paul says, "The creation eagerly waits for the revealing of the sons of God," adding that "even we ourselves groan within ourselves, eagerly waiting for the adoption, the redemption of our body" (Rom. 8:19, 23; cf. Eph. 4:30).

This climactic event takes place at "the times of restoration of all things" (Acts 3:21). Christ calls it "the regeneration" (Matt. 19:28; "renewal of all things," NIV). Then "the creation itself also will be delivered from the bondage of corruption into the glorious liberty of the children of God" (Rom. 8:21).

The scriptural view that in one sense adoption and redemption—or salvation—have "already" been accomplished and that in another sense they have not yet been accomplished has confused some. A study of the full scope of Christ's work as Saviour provides the answer. "Paul related our *present salvation* to the *first* coming of Christ. In the historic cross, resurrection, and heavenly ministry of Christ our justification and sanctification are secured once and for all. Our *future salvation*, the glorification of our *bodies*, Paul related, however, to the *second* coming of Christ.

"For this reason Paul can say simultaneously: 'We are saved,' in view of the cross and resurrection of Christ in the past; and 'we are not yet saved,' in view of the future return of Christ to redeem our bodies."[12]

To emphasize our present salvation to the exclusion of our future salvation creates an incorrect, unfortunate understanding of Christ's complete salvation.

Glorification and Perfection. Some incorrectly believe that the ultimate perfection that glorification will bring is already available to humans. But of himself, Paul, that dedicated man of God, wrote near the end of his life, "Not that I have already attained, or am already perfected; but I press on, that I may lay hold of that for which Christ Jesus has also laid hold of me. Brethern, I do not count myself to have apprehended; but one thing I do, forgetting those things which are behind and reaching forward to those things which are ahead, I press toward the goal for the prize of the upward call of God in Christ Jesus" (Phil. 3:12-14).

Sanctification is a lifelong process. Perfection now is ours only in Christ, but the ultimate, all-comprehensive transformation of our lives into the image of God will take place at the Second Advent. Paul cautions: "Let him who thinks he stands take heed lest he fall" (1 Cor. 10:12). The history of Israel and the lives of David, Solomon, and Peter are serious warnings for all. "As long as life shall last, there is need of guarding the affections and the passions with a firm purpose. There is inward corruption, there are outward temptations, and wherever the work of God shall be advanced, Satan plans so to arrange circumstances that temptation shall come with overpowering force upon the soul. Not one moment can we be secure only as we are relying upon God, the life hid with Christ in God."[13]

Our final, creative transformation is accomplished when incorruptibility and immortality become ours—when the Holy Spirit completely restores the original creation.

The Ground of Our Acceptance With God

Neither Christlike character traits nor faultless behavior is the ground of our acceptance with God. Saving righteousness comes from the one righteous Man, Jesus, and is conveyed to us by the Holy Spirit. We can contribute nothing to Christ's gift of righteousness—we can only receive it. No one other than Christ is righteous (Rom. 3:10); independent human righteousness is only filthy rags (Isa. 64:6; see also Dan. 9:7, 9, 11, 20; 1 Cor. 1:30).[14]

Even what we do in response to Christ's saving love cannot form the basis of our acceptance with God. That acceptance is identified with the work of Christ. In bringing Christ to us, the Holy Spirit brings that acceptance.

Is our acceptance based on Christ's justifying righteousness or His sanctifying righteousness—or both? John Calvin pointed out that as "Christ cannot be divided into parts, so the two things, justification and sanctification, which we perceive to be united together in him, are inseparable."[15] Christ's ministry has to be seen in its totality. This makes it paramount to avoid speculation about these two terms by "trying to define minutely the fine points of distinction between justification and sanctification...Why try to be more minute than is Inspiration on the vital questions of righteousness by faith?"[16]

Just as the sun has light and heat—inseparable, yet with unique functions—so Christ has become to us righteousness as well as sanctification (1 Cor. 1:30). Not only are we fully justified but also fully sanctified in Him.

The Holy Spirit brings the "It is finished" of Calvary within, applying the only experience of God's acceptance of humanity to us. This "It is finished" of the cross calls into question all other human attempts to gain acceptance. In bringing the Crucified within, the Spirit brings the only ground of our acceptance with God, providing the only genuine title to and fitness for salvation available to us.

References

1. T. F. Torrance, *Royal Priesthood, Scottish Journal of Theology Occasional Papers*, no. 3 (Edinburgh: Oliver and Boyd, 1963), p. 48.

2. See "Conversion" and "Repent, Repentance," *SDA Bible Dictionary*, rev. ed., pp. 235, 933.

3. W.E. Vine, *An Expository Dictionary of the New Testament Words* (Old Tappan, NJ: Fleming H. Revell, 1966), pp. 284-86; William F. Arndt and F. Wilbur Gingrich, *A Greek English Lexicon of the New Testament and Other Early Christian Literature* (Chicago, IL: University of Chicago Press, 1973), p. 196.

4. "Justification," *SDA Bible Dictionary*, rev. ed., p. 635.

5. LaRondelle, p. 47.

6. "Sanctification," *SDA Bible Dictionary*, rev. ed., p. 979.

7. *Ibid.*

8. Ellen G. White, *Messages to Young People* (Nashville, TN: Southern Publishing Assn., 1930), p. 35.

9. White, *The Desire of Ages*, p. 668.

10. "Perfect, Perfection," *SDA Bible Dictionary*, rev. ed., p. 864.

11. LaRondelle, p. 77.

12. *Ibid.*, p. 89.

13. White, in *SDA Bible Commentary*, rev. ed., vol. 2, p. 1032.

14. Commenting on Christ our High Priest, White said, "The religious services, the prayers, the praise, the penitent confession of sin ascend from true believers as incense to the heavenly sanctuary, but passing through the corrupt channels of humanity, they are so defiled that unless purified by blood, they can never be of value with God. They ascend not in spotless purity, and unless the Intercessor, who is at God's right hand, presents and purifies all by His righteousness, it is not acceptable to God. All incense from earthly tabernacles must be moist with the cleansing drops of the blood of Christ" (*Selected Messages*, book 1, p. 344).

15. J. Calvin, *Institutes of the Christian Religion* (Grand Rapids: Associated Publishers and Authors, Inc. n.d.), III, 11, 6.

16. White, in *SDA Bible Commentary*, rev. ed., vol. 6, p. 1072.

Growing in Christ

11

By His death on the cross Jesus triumphed over the forces of evil. He who subjugated the demonic spirits during His earthly ministry has broken their power and made certain their ultimate doom. Jesus' victory gives us victory over the evil forces that still seek to control us, as we walk with Him in peace, joy, and assurance of His love. Now the Holy Spirit dwells within us and empowers us. Continually committed to Jesus as our Saviour and Lord, we are set free from the burden of our past deeds. No longer do we live in the darkness, fear of evil powers, ignorance, and meaninglessness of our former way of life. In this new freedom in Jesus, we are called to grow into the likeness of His character, communing with Him daily in prayer, feeding on His Word, meditating on it and on His providence, singing His praises, gathering together for worship, and participating in the mission of the church. As we give ourselves in loving service to those around us and in witnessing to His salvation, His constant presence with us through the Spirit transforms every moment and every task into a spiritual experience. (Ps. 1:1, 2; 23:4; 77:11, 12; Col. 1:13, 14; 2:6, 14, 15; Luke 10:17-20; Eph. 5:19, 20; 6:12-18; 1 Thess. 5:23; 2 Pet. 2:9; 3:18; 2 Cor. 3:17, 18; Phil. 3:7-14; 1 Thess. 5:16-18; Matt. 20:25-28; John 20:21; Gal. 5:22-25; Rom. 8:38, 39; 1 John 4:4; Heb. 10:25.)

BIRTH IS A MOMENT OF JOY. A seed germinates, and the appearance of those first two leaves makes the gardener happy. A baby is born, and its first scream announces to the world that here is a new life to reckon with. The mother forgets all her pain and joins the rest of the family in joy and celebration. A nation is born to be free, and an entire people throng the streets and fill the city squares, waving symbols of their newfound joy. But imagine: Those two leaves do not turn into four but rather remain the same or vanish away; a year later the little baby neither smiles nor takes a first step but remains frozen in the simplicity of its entrance into the world; the newly freed nation for a short while turns within, into a prison house of fear, torture, and captivity.

The joy of the gardener, the ecstasy of the mother, and the promise of a freedom-filled future turn into disappointment, grief, and mourning. Growth—continual, constant, maturing, and fruit-bearing growth—is essential to life. Without it birth has no meaning or purpose or destiny.

To grow is an inseparable equation of life—both physical and spiritual. Physical growth demands proper nourishment, environment, nurture, exercise, education, training, and a purpose-filled life. But the issue under consideration here is spiritual growth. How do we grow in Christ and mature as Christians? What are the hallmarks of spiritual growth?

Life Begins With Death

Perhaps the most basic and unique principle about Christian life is that it begins with death—indeed, with two events of death. First, the death of Christ on the cross makes possible our new life—free from the dominion of Satan (Col. 1:13, 14), free from the condemnation of sin (Rom. 8:1), free from death the penalty of sin (Rom. 6:23)—and it brings reconciliation with God and humans. Second, the death of self makes it possible for us to take up the life that Christ offers. As a result, third, we walk in newness of life.

Death of Christ. The cross is central to God's plan of salvation. Without it Satan and his demonic forces would not have been defeated, the problem of sin would not have been solved, and death would not have been crushed. The apostle tells us: "The blood of Jesus Christ His Son cleanses us from all sin" (1 John 1:7). "For God so loved the world," says the Bible's most favorite passage. If God's love conceived and originated the plan of salvation, the execution of the plan is explained in the second part of that passage: "that He gave His only begotten Son." The uniqueness of God's gift was not that He gave His Son but that He gave Him to die for our sins. Without the cross there could be no forgiveness of sins, no eternal life, and no victory over Satan.

Through His death on the cross, Christ triumphed over Satan. From the fiery temptations in the wilderness on through the agony of Gethsemane, Satan mercilessly led the attack against the Son of God—to weaken His will, to cause His way to falter, to lead Him to distrust His Father, and to pressure Him to detour from the path of bearing the bitter cup of humanity's sin as a vicarious sacrifice. The cross was the final onslaught. There, "Satan with his angels, in human form, was present,"[1] to carry the great warfare against God to its ultimate end, hoping that Christ would even now come down from the cross and fail to fulfill God's redemptive purpose of offering His Son as a sacrifice for sin (John 3:16). But Christ, by giving up His life on the cross, crushed the power of Satan, "disarmed principalities and powers," and "made a public spectacle of them, triumphing over them in it" (Col. 2:15). On the cross, "the battle had been won. His [Christ's] right hand and His holy arm had gotten Him the victory. As a Conqueror He planted His banner on the eternal heights. . . . All heaven triumphed in the Saviour's victory. Satan was defeated, and knew that his kingdom was lost."[2]

The apostle's graphic description in Colossians is noteworthy. First, Christ disarmed the principalities and powers of evil. The Greek for *disarmed* literally means "stripped." Because of the cross, Satan stands stripped of all his demonic power over God's people, as long as they place their trust in the One who brought about that victory on the cross. Second, the cross made Satan and his cohorts "a public spectacle" before the universe. The one who once boasted that he would "be like the Most High" (Isa. 14:14) is now made a cosmic spectacle of shame and defeat. Evil no longer holds power over believers, who have passed from the kingdom of darkness to the kingdom of light (Col. 1:13). Third, the cross has ensured final, eschatological victory over Satan, sin, and death.

Thus the cross of Christ has become an instrument of God's victory over evil:

- A means whereby forgiveness of sins becomes possible (Col. 2:13)

- A cosmic exhibit of universal reconciliation (2 Cor. 5:19)

- An assurance of the present possibilities of a victorious life and growth in Christ, whereby sin shall not reign in our mind or body (Rom. 6:12)—and our status as sons and daughters of God (Rom. 8:14)

- An eschatological certainty that this world of evil, once the usurped dominion of Satan, will be cleansed of the presence and power of sin (Rev. 21:1)

At every step of this ladder of redemption and victory, we see the fulfillment of Christ's own prophecy, "I beheld Satan as lightning fall from heaven" (Luke 10:18).

The Christ of the cross is God's redemptive action for the problem of sin. Lest we forget that fact, Jesus asserted that His blood was to be "poured out for many for the forgiveness of sins" (Matt. 26:28). That shedding of the blood is crucial for the experience and appreciation of salvation. For one thing, it speaks about sin. Sin is real. Sin is costly. Sin's grip is so immense and deadly that forgiveness of sin and freedom from its power and guilt are impossible without the "precious blood of Christ" (1 Pet. 1:19). This truth about sin needs to be said again and again, because we live in a world that denies the reality of sin or remains indifferent to it. But at the cross we are confronted with the diabolical nature of sin, which can be cleansed only by that blood "poured out for many for the forgiveness of sins" (Matt. 26:28).

Let us never forget or be indifferent to the fact that Jesus died for our sins and that without His death, there could be no forgiveness. It is our sins that drove Jesus to the cross. As Paul states, "For when we were still without strength, in due time Christ died for the ungodly....in that while we were still sinners, Christ died for us" (Rom. 5:6, 8). Or, as Ellen White states, sin "weighed heavily upon Christ, and the sense of God's wrath against sin was crushing out His life."[3] There is no escape from affirming and proclaiming the "once for all" (see Rom. 6:10; Heb. 7:27; 10:10) sacrificial and substitutionary nature of the death of Jesus.

We are not saved by Christ the good man, by Christ the God-man, by Christ the great Teacher, or by Christ the impeccable Example. We are saved by the Christ of the cross: "Christ was treated as we deserve, that we might be treated as He deserves. He was condemned for our sins, in which He had no share, that we might be justified by His righteousness, in which we had no share. He suffered the death which was ours, that we might receive the life which was His. 'With His stripes we are healed.'"[4]

The blood of Jesus, then, assures forgiveness from sin and casts the seed for newness of growth. One of the first aspects of this newness and growth in the Christian life is reconciliation. The cross is God's instrument for effecting human's reconciliation with Him. "God was in Christ," says the apostle Paul, "reconciling the world unto himself" (2 Cor. 5:19). Because of what He did on the cross, we are able to stand before God without sin and without fear. That which estranged us from God has been dealt with. "As far as the east is from the west, so far has He removed our transgressions from us" (Ps. 103:12). The Man on the cross has opened a new way into the very presence of God. "It is finished," He announced on the cross, and then He urged His followers to enter into an ever-abiding fellowship of God.

Reconciliation with God immediately opens up the second phase of the redemptive growth process: reconciliation with our fellow humans. One of the beautiful pictures at the cross is the variety of people who crowded around there. Not all were admirers of Jesus. Not all were saints. But look at the people. There were Egyptians who prided themselves in their business acumen; there were Romans who boasted in civilization and culture; there were Greeks who excelled in their learning; there were Jews who considered themselves as God's chosen people; there were Pharisees who thought they were the chosen of the chosen; there were Sadducees who thought they were doctrinally pure; there were slaves who sought freedom; there were free men who indulged in the luxury of leisure; there were men, women, and children.

But the cross made no distinction between all these. It judged all of them as sinners; it offered to all of them the divine path of reconciliation. At the foot of the cross the ground is level. All are brought together—and nothing divides humanity anymore. A new brotherhood is launched. A new fellowship begins. East merges with west, north comes down to south, white shakes hands with black, rich leaps over to clasp the hands of the poor. The cross bids all to the fountain of the blood—to taste the sweetness of life, to share the experience of grace, and to proclaim to the world the emergence of a new life, a new family (Eph. 2:14-16). Thus the cross initiated victory over Satan and sin, and consequently, brought new life in Christ.

Death to self. A second important aspect of Christian newness and growth is death to the old self. You cannot read the New Testament without coming to grips with this fundamental aspect of the new life of the Christian. Read Galatians 2:20, 21: "I have been crucified with Christ; it is no longer I who live, but Christ lives in me; and the life which I now live in the flesh I live by faith in the Son of God, who loved me and gave Himself for me." Or read Romans 6:6-11: "Our old man was crucified with Him, that the body of sin might be done away with, that we should no longer be slaves of sin.... reckon yourselves to be dead indeed to sin, but alive to God in Christ Jesus our Lord." Or read Jesus' enunciation of the new life principle: "Unless a grain of wheat falls into the ground and dies, it remains alone; but if it dies, it produces much grain " (John 12:24).

Christian life, thus, does not begin with birth. It begins with death. Until self dies, until self is crucified, there is no beginning at all. There must be a radical, deliberate, total surgery of self. "Therefore, if anyone is in Christ, he is a new creation; old things have passed away; behold, all things have become new" (2 Cor. 5:17). "The Christian's life is not a modification or improvement of the old, but a transformation of nature. There is a death to self and sin, and a new life altogether. This change can be brought about only by the effectual working of the Holy Spirit."[5] The apostle underscores both death to sin and resurrection to a new life through the experience of baptism: "Do you not know that as many of us as were baptized into Christ Jesus were baptized into His death? Therefore we were buried with Him through baptism into death, that just as Christ was raised from the dead by the glory of the Father, even so we also should walk in newness of life" (Rom. 6:3, 4). Baptism thus symbolically opens the door of new life and bids us to grow in Christ.

Something happens to a person who accepts Jesus as Saviour and Master. Simon the waverer becomes Peter the courageous. Saul the persecutor becomes Paul the proclaimer. Thomas the doubter becomes the missionary of the frontier. Cowardice gives place to courage. Unbelief gives way to a torch of faith. Jealousy is swallowed up by love. Self-interest vanishes into brotherly concern. Sin has no room in the heart. Self stands crucified. Hence Paul wrote, "Put off the old man with his deeds. . . put on the new man who is renewed in knowledge according to the image of Him who created him" (Col. 3:9, 10).

Jesus insisted: "If anyone desires to come after Me, let him deny himself, and take up his cross, and follow Me" (Matt. 16:24; cf. Luke 9:23). In Christian life, the death of self is not an option but a necessity. The cross and its claims—both immediate and ultimate—must confront Christian discipleship and demand absolute response. Dietrich Bonhoeffer's powerful commentary is worthy of note: "If our Christianity has ceased to be serious about discipleship, if we have watered down the gospel into emotional uplift which makes no costly demands and which fails to distinguish between natural and Christian existence, then we cannot help regarding the cross as an ordinary everyday calamity, as one of the trials and tribulations of life....When Christ calls a man, he bids him come and die. ...it is the same death every time—death in Jesus Christ, the death of the old man at his call."[6]

So the call to Christian life is a call to the cross—to continually deny self its persistent desire to be its own savior and to adhere fully to the Man of the cross, in order that our "faith might not rest in the wisdom of men but in the power of God" (1 Cor. 2:5, RSV).

Living a new life. A third aspect of growing in Christ is living the new life. One of the great misunderstandings of Christian life is that salvation is a free gift of God's grace—and that's the end of the story. It is not. Yes, it is true that in Christ "we have redemption through His blood, the forgiveness of sins, according to the riches of His grace" (Eph. 1:7). It is also true that "by grace you have been saved through faith, and that not of yourselves; it is the gift of God, not of works, lest anyone should boast" (Eph. 2:8, 9).

Yes, grace is free. But grace cost God His Son's life. Free grace does not mean cheap grace. To quote Bonhoeffer again: "Cheap grace is the preaching of forgiveness without requiring repentance, baptism without church discipline, Communion without confession, absolution without personal confession. Cheap grace is grace without discipleship, grace without the cross, grace without Jesus Christ, living and incarnate."[7]

Cheap grace has nothing to do with the call of Jesus. When Jesus calls a person, He offers him or her a cross to carry. To be a disciple is to be a follower, and being a follower of Jesus is no cheap trick. To the Corinthians Paul writes forcefully of the obligations of grace. First, he speaks of his own experience: "By the grace of God I am what I am, and his grace toward me was not in vain. On the contrary, I worked harder than any of them [the apostles], though it was not I, but the grace of God which is with me" (1 Cor. 15:10). Thus Paul acknowledges the supremacy of God's grace in his life. And immediately he adds that this grace was not given to him in vain. The Greek *eis kenon* literally translates "for emptiness." That is to say, Paul did not receive grace in order to lead a vain, empty life—but rather a life filled with the fruit of the Spirit, and even that, not in his own strength, but by the power of the indwelling grace. Similarly, he pleads with the believers "not to accept the grace of God in vain" (2 Cor. 6:1).

The grace of God has not come to redeem us from one kind of emptiness, to place us in another kind of emptiness. God's grace is His activity to reconcile us to Himself, to make us a part of the family of God. Having come into the family, we live in the family, bearing the fruits of God's love through the power of His amazing grace.

Growing in Christ, therefore, is a growth in maturity so that day by day we reflect the will of Christ and walk the way of Christ. Hence the question: what are the hallmarks of this mature life and the signs of its constant growth? Without exhausting the list, we can reflect on seven such hallmarks.

Hallmarks of Growing in Christ

1. A life of Spirit. Jesus told Nicodemus, "Unless one is born of water and the Spirit, he cannot enter the kingdom of God" (John 3:5). Without the regenerating power of the Holy Spirit, the Christian life cannot even begin. He is the Spirit of truth (John 14:17). He guides us in all truth (John

16:13) and makes us understand the will of God as revealed in the Scriptures. He brings a conviction of sin, righteousness, and judgment (John 16:7, 8), without which we cannot fathom the present and eternal consequences of our actions and the life we lead. It is the transforming power and presence of the Spirit in our lives that makes us sons and daughters of God (Rom. 8:14). It is through the Spirit that Christ "abides in us" (1 John 3:24). With the indwelling of the Spirit comes a new life—new in that it rejects the old ways of thought, action, and relationship that were against God's will; new also in that it makes of us a new creation, reconciled and redeemed, freed from sin in order to grow in righteousness (Rom. 8:1-16) and to reflect the image of Jesus "from glory to glory" (2 Cor. 3:17, 18). "When the Spirit of God takes possession of the heart, it transforms the life. Sinful thoughts are put away, evil deeds are renounced; love, humility, and peace take the place of anger, envy, and strife. Joy takes the place of sadness, and the countenance reflects the light of heaven. No one sees the hand that lifts the burden, or beholds the light descend from the courts above. The blessing comes when by faith the soul surrenders itself to God. Then that power which no human eye can see creates a new being in the image of God."[8]

The Spirit makes us "heirs of God and joint heirs with Christ, if indeed we suffer with Him, that we may also be glorified together" (Rom. 8:17). The life of the Spirit is thus a call to spiritual action: Reject the old order of sin and be sharers of Christ's sufferings in the present life in order that we may be sharers with Him of future glory. Christian spirituality is thus not a flight into a world of fantasy and mysticism. It is a call to suffer, share, witness, worship, and live the life of Christ in this world, in our communities, and in our homes. This is possible only by the indwelling presence of the Spirit. The prayer of Jesus is that even as we are in the world we should not be of the world (John 17:15). We must live in the world—that's our habitation, and that's the arena of our mission. But we do not belong to the world, for our citizenship and hope are in the world to come (Phil. 3:20).

Paul describes this Spirit-empowered life as one that is spiritually growing and maturing. Such maturity will reject the works of the flesh—"adultery, fornication, uncleanness, lewdness, idolatry, sorcery, hatred, contentions, jealousies, outbursts of wrath, selfish ambitions, dissensions, heresies, envy, murders, drunkenness, revelries, and the like" (Gal. 5:19-21)—and embrace and produce the fruit of the Spirit: "love, joy, peace, longsuffering, kindness, goodness, faithfulness, gentleness, self-control" (Gal. 5:22, 23).

2. A life of love and unity. Christian life is a life of unity, a life reconciled to God, on the one hand, and reconciled to one's fellow human beings, on the other. Reconciliation is the healing of a breach in relationships, and the primary cause of this breach in relationship is sin. Sin has separated us from God (Isa. 59:2) and has splintered humanity into a multitude of factions—racial, ethnic, gender, nationalities, color, caste, etc. The gospel of Jesus deals with this problem of sin and all the breaching factors associated with it and creates a new order of unity and reconciliation. Hence Paul could say, God "has reconciled us to Himself through Jesus Christ" (2 Cor. 5:18). Out of this reconciliation is born a new community—a redeemed community marked by vertical unity with God and horizontal unity with one's fellow beings. Indeed this life of love and unity is the kernel of the gospel. Did not Jesus say so in His high priestly prayer: "That they all may be one, as You, Father, are in Me, and I in You; that they also may be one in Us, that the world may believe that You sent Me" (John 17:20, 21)? The entire redemptive mission of Jesus and the power of His gospel cry out for vindication in love and a unity that must bind the members of the redeemed community. There is no Christian growth without such love and unity. And where this unity and love prevail, all the dividing walls between people will come tumbling down. Barriers of race, national origin, gender, caste, color, and other divisive factors stand abolished in the life of the person who has experienced the new creation, a new humanity (Eph. 2:11-16). As that person grows and matures, the glorious truth of reconciliation, love, and unity shines brighter and brighter in both individual and corporate expressions of Christian life.

The love factor in Christian growth is unique to the gospel. Jesus called it the new commandment (John 13:34), but the newness does not refer to love but to the object of love. People love, but they love the lovable—they love their own. But Jesus introduced a new factor: "Just as I have loved you, you should also love one another." That is to say, just as universal, as sacrificial, and as complete as Jesus' love is, so should our love be. The new love erects no barrier; it is inclusive; it loves even the enemy. On that type of love "hangs all the law and the prophets" (Matthew 22:37-40).

The command to love our neighbor leaves no room for modification. We do not select whom we love; we are called upon to love all. As children of one Father, we are expected to love one another. In the parable of the Good Samaritan, Christ has shown that "your neighbor does not mean merely one of the church or faith to which we belong. It has no reference to race, color, or class distinction. Our neighbor is every person who needs our help. Our neighbor is every soul who is wounded and bruised by the adversary. Our neighbor is everyone who is the property of God."[9]

True neighborly love penetrates the color of the skin and confronts the humanness of the person; it refuses to take shelter under caste but contributes to the enrichment of the soul; it rescues the dignity of a person from the prejudices of dehumanization; it delivers human destiny from the philosophic holocaust of thing-ism. In effect, true love sees in each face the image of God—potential, latent, or real. A growing, mature Christian will possess that kind of love, which is indeed the basis of all Christian unity.

3. A life of study. Food is a basic essential for growth. The function of any living organism requires adequate and constant nutrition. So it is in spiritual growth. But where do we find our spiritual food? Primarily from two sources: constant communion with God through the study of His Word and through cultivating a life of prayer. Nowhere is the importance of God's Word for spiritual life as clearly taught as in the words of Jesus Himself: "Man shall not live by bread alone, but by every word that proceeds from the mouth of God" (Matt. 4:4). Jesus provides a perfect example of how He used the Word to face Satan. "Jesus met Satan with the words of Scripture. 'It is written,' He said. In every temptation the weapon of His warfare was the word of God. Satan demanded of Christ a miracle as a sign of His divinity. But that which is greater than all miracles, a firm reliance upon a 'Thus saith the Lord,' was a sign that could not be controverted. So long as Christ held to this position, the tempter could gain no advantage."[10]

So it is with us. Says the Psalmist: "Your word I have hidden in my heart, that I might not sin against You!" (Ps. 119:12). To this, add the promise provided by the apostle: "For the word of God is living and powerful, and sharper than any two-edged sword, piercing even to the division of soul and spirit, and of joints and marrow, and is a discerner of the thoughts and intents of the heart" (Heb. 4:12). When the Christian uses this sharp, two-edged sword of the Spirit to fend off Satan's attacks, he or she is on the winning side of the battle. The believer is empowered to penetrate and cut through every obstacle to spiritual growth, to discern right from wrong so that a consistent choice can made on the right side, and to distinguish between the voice of God and the whispers of the devil. That's what makes the Word an irreplaceable tool for spiritual growth.

"All Scripture," Paul wrote, "is given by inspiration of God, and is profitable for doctrine, for reproof, for correction, for instruction in righteousness, that the man of God may be complete, thoroughly equipped for every good work" (2 Tim. 3:16, 17). Do you want to grow in understanding truth and doctrine? Do you want to know how to keep your soul on track for God? Do you want to know what God has in store for you today, tomorrow, or the day after? Reach for the Bible. Study it daily. Approach it with prayer. There's no better way to know God's will and seek His way.

4. A life of prayer. God speaks to us through His Word. Knowing His will is part of spiritual growth—part of communing with Him. Another aspect of this communion with God and growing in Him is prayer. If God's

Word is the bread that nourishes our soul, prayer is the breath that keeps our soul alive. Prayer is speaking with God, listening to His voice, kneeling in surrender, and rising up in the full empowerment of God's strength. It demands nothing of ourselves—except that we deny self, lean on His strength, and wait upon Him. Out of that waiting flows the power with which we can walk the Christian journey and fight the spiritual warfare. The prayer of Gethsemane assures the victory of the cross.

Paul considers prayer so important in Christian life and growth that he mentions six fundamental principles: "Pray always;" "pray with supplication in the Spirit;" "pray in the spirit;" "pray watchfully;" "pray with perseverance; and "pray ... for all saints" (Eph. 6:18). Like the Pharisee (Luke 18:11), we are often tempted to pray for a show, for ourselves, or simply as a routine. But effective prayer is self-denying, Spirit-filled, intercessory, pleading for the needs of others, even as we pray for the fulfillment of God's will on earth by being His faithful witnesses. Prayer is a perpetual communion with God; it is the oxygen of the soul, and without it the soul atrophies and dies. "Prayer," says Ellen White, "is one of the most essential duties. Without it you cannot maintain a Christian walk. It elevates, strengthens, and ennobles; it is the soul talking with God."[11]

5. *A life of fruit-bearing.* "By their fruits," Jesus said, "you will know them" (Matt. 7:20). Fruit-bearing is an important aspect of Christian growth. Salvation by grace is often misunderstood as denial of obedience and fruit-bearing. Nothing can be farther from biblical truth. Yes, we are saved freely by faith in what God's grace has done through Christ, and we have nothing of which to boast in ourselves (Eph. 2:7, 8; John 3:16). But we are not saved to do what we please; we are saved to live in accordance with God's will. There is nothing legalistic and hence unnecessary about obedience to the law, but it is the natural sequence to God's gracious liberation from sin. Hence, "faith by itself, if it does not have works, is dead" (James 2:17).

Consider Jesus' assertion and hope in John 14 and 15. The assertion is His relationship with the Father, and the hope is for the relationship of His disciples with Him. In the first, Jesus asserts, "I have kept my Father's commandments and abide in his love" (John 15:10). The obedience of Jesus to the Father is not a legalistic compliance but an outgrowth of His abiding in the Father's love. The intimate relationship between the Father and the Son is based on love and love alone, and it is this love that led the Son to accept the Father's will and taste the bitterness of Gethsemane and Calvary.

Jesus uses the Father-Son relationship of love as an illustration of the kind of relationship His disciples should have with Him. Just as the relationship of Jesus with the Father preceded His obedience to the Father, so should the relationship of the disciples with Jesus precede their obedience to Him. "If you love me, you will keep my commandments" (John 14:15). "I do as the Father has commanded me, so that the world may know that I love the Father" (verse 31).

Observe the hope Jesus has for His disciples. He does as the Father commanded so that the world may know His relationship of love with the Father. The love relationship precedes the doing of the Father's will. He loves His Father and therefore willingly does His Father's will. Likewise, Jesus anticipates a love foundation for His own disciples. "Abide in me," He says, "as I abide in you. Just as the branch cannot bear fruit by itself unless it abides in the vine, neither can you unless you abide in me" (John 15:4). Fruit-bearing, obedience, and living in accordance with God's will are thus essential signs of spiritual growth. The absence of fruit indicates the absence of abiding in Christ.

6. A life of spiritual warfare. Christian discipleship is not a journey of ease. We are engaged in a warfare that is real and dangerous. As Paul says, "For we do not wrestle against flesh and blood, but against principalities, against powers, against the rulers of the darkness of this age, against spiritual hosts of wickedness in the heavenly places. Therefore take up the whole armor of God, that you may be able to withstand in the evil day, and having done all, to stand" (Eph. 6:12, 13).

In this warfare, supernatural forces are arraigned against us. Just as the angels of the Lord are engaged in the ministry of serving His followers, delivering them from evil, and guiding them in spiritual growth (Ps. 34:7; 91:11, 12; Acts 5:19, 20; Heb. 1:14; 12:22), so are the fallen angels deeply plotting to turn us away from the demands of discipleship. The Bible asserts that Satan and his angels are in rage against the followers of Jesus (Rev. 12:17) and the devil himself is walking "about like a roaring lion, seeking whom he may devour" (1 Pet. 5:8, 9). The road to spiritual growth is filled with the devil's traps, and it is here that our spiritual warfare takes on its ferocity. Hence Paul uses some strong words of action: Stand! Take up! Put on! Be strong! (Eph. 6:12, 13). "The Christian life is a battle and a march. In this warfare there is no release; the effort must be continuous and persevering. It is by unceasing endeavor that we maintain the victory over the temptations of Satan. Christian integrity must be sought with resistless energy and maintained with a resolute fixedness of purpose. . . . All must engage in this warfare for themselves; no one else can fight our battles. Individually we are responsible for the issues of the struggle."[12]

God, however, has not left us alone in this warfare. He has provided us victory in and through Christ Jesus (1 Cor. 15:57). He has given us well-tested armor with which to face the enemy. Paul describes this armor as consisting of the girdle of truth, the breastplate of righteousness, the shoes of the gospel of peace, the shield of faith, the helmet of salvation, the sword of the Spirit, and the unfailing power of prayer (Eph. 6:13-18). Guarded with such armor, dependent completely on the unfailing power of the Spirit, we cannot but grow in spiritual valor and win the warfare in which we are engaged.

7. A life of worship, witness, and hope. Christian growth does not take place in a vacuum. It takes place, on the one hand, within the community of the redeemed, and on the other, as a witness to the community that needs to be redeemed. Observe the apostolic community. Soon after the ascension of Christ and accompanied by the power of the Holy Spirit, the early church both individually and corporately manifested its growth and maturity in worship, fellowship, study, and witness (Acts 2:42-47; 5:41, 42; 6:7). Without corporate worship, we miss the identity and arena of our fellowship, and it is in this fellowship and interpersonal relationship with others that we mature and grow. Hence the apostle's counsel: "And let us consider one another in order to stir up love and good works, not forsaking the assembling of ourselves together, as is the manner of some, but exhorting one another, and so much the more as you see the Day approaching" (Heb. 10:24, 25).

The more we grow in worship, study, and fellowship, the more we are urged to serve and witness. Christian growth demands growth in service (Matt. 20:25-28) and a growth toward witness. "As the Father has sent me," Jesus said, "I also send you" (John 20:21). Christian life is never meant to be a life within the circle of the self, but always to be poured out in service and witness to others. The Great Commission of Matthew 28 charges the Christian to be mature enough to take the gospel of forgiveness to the world around in order that all may know the redemptive grace of God. The sign of the life of the Spirit and Christian growth is a life of ever-expanding witness—Jerusalem, Judea, Samaria, and the uttermost part of the world (Acts 1:8)

We live, worship, fellowship, and witness in time—and for the Christian, time anticipates the future. "I press on," says Paul, "toward the goal for the prize of the upward call of God in Christ Jesus" (Phil. 3:12-14). Lead a sanctified life, says the same apostle, in order that "your whole spirit, soul, and body [may] be preserved blameless at the coming our Lord Jesus Christ" (1 Thess. 5:23). Growing in Christ is thus a growing in anticipation, in hope, of the final consummation of the redemptive experience in the Kingdom to come. "To the humble, believing soul, the house of God on earth is the gate of heaven. The song of praise, the prayer, the words spoken by Christ's representatives, are God's appointed agencies to prepare a people for the church above, for that loftier worship into which there can enter nothing that defileth."[13]

References

1. Ellen G. White, *The Desire of Ages,* pp. 746, 749.

2. Ibid., p. 758.

3. Ibid., p. 687.

4. Ibid., p. 25.

5. Ibid., p. 172.

6. Dietrich Bonhoeffer, *The Cost of Discipleship* (New York: The Macmillan Company, 1959), pp. 78, 79.

7. Ibid., *p.* 47.

8. White, *The Desire of Ages,* p. 173.

9. Ibid., p. 503.

10. Ibid., p. 120.

11. White, *Testimonies for the Church,* vol. 2, p. 313.

12. _____, *The Ministry of Healing,* p. 453.

13. _____, *Testimonies,* vol. 5, p. 491.

The Church

12

The church is the community of believers who confess Jesus Christ as Lord and Saviour. In continuity with the people of God in Old Testament times, we are called out from the world; and we join together for worship, for fellowship, for instruction in the Word, for the celebration of the Lord's Supper, for service to all mankind, and for the worldwide proclamation of the gospel. The church derives its authority from Christ, who is the incarnate Word, and from the Scriptures, which are the written Word. The church is God's family; adopted by Him as children, its members live on the basis of the new covenant. The church is the body of Christ, a community of faith of which Christ Himself is the Head. The church is the bride for whom Christ died that He might sanctify and cleanse her. At His return in triumph, He will present her to Himself as a glorious church, the faithful of all the ages, the purchase of His blood, not having spot or wrinkle, but holy and without blemish. (Gen. 12:3; Acts 7:38; Eph. 4:11-15; 3:8-11; Matt. 28:19, 20; 16:13-20; 18:18; Eph. 2:19-22; 1:22, 23; 5:23-27; Col. 1:17, 18.)

163

OVERCOME BY ANGER, THE ELDERLY MAN pounds the rod he carries against the boulder. Drawing it back, he swings again and shouts: "Hear now, you rebels! Must we bring water for you out of this rock?"

A stream of water gushes out of the rock, meeting Israel's need. But in taking credit to himself for the gift of water instead of ascribing it to *the* Rock, Moses had sinned. And because of that sin, he would not enter the Promised Land (see Num. 20:7-12).

That Rock was Christ, the foundation on which God established His people both individually and corporately. This imagery runs throughout Scripture.

In the last sermon Moses preached to Israel, perhaps recalling this incident, he used the metaphor of the rock to picture God's stability and dependability:

"Ascribe greatness to our God.
He is the Rock, His work is perfect;
For all His ways are justice,
A God of truth and without injustice;
Righteous and upright is He" (Deut. 32:3, 4).

Centuries later, David echoed the same theme—His Saviour as the rock:

"In God is my salvation and my glory;
The rock of my strength,
And my refuge, is in God" (Ps. 62:7).

Isaiah used the same imagery of the coming Messiah: "A stone for a foundation, a tried stone, a precious cornerstone, a sure foundation" (Isa. 28:16).

Peter testified that Christ fulfilled this prediction, not as a common stone but a "living stone, rejected indeed by men, but chosen by God and precious" (1 Peter 2:4). Paul identified Him as the only sure foundation, saying, "No other foundation can anyone lay than that which is laid, which is Jesus Christ" (1 Cor. 3:11). Referring to the rock that Moses struck, he said, "And all drank the same spiritual drink. For they drank of that spiritual Rock that followed them, and that Rock was Christ" (1 Cor. 10:4).

Jesus Christ Himself used the image directly, when He declared, "On this rock I will build My church, and the gates of Hades shall not prevail against it" (Matt. 16:18). He established the Christian church on Himself, the Living Rock. His own body was to be sacrificed for the sins of the world—the striking of the Rock. Against a church built on the solid foundation He provides, nothing can prevail. From this Rock the healing waters would flow to the thirsty nations (cf. Eze. 47:1-12; John 7:37, 38; Rev. 22:1-5).

How feeble and weak the church was when Christ made that pronouncement! It consisted of a few tired, doubting, self-promoting disciples, a handful of women, and the fickle multitude that vanished when the Rock was struck. Yet the church was built, not on frail human wisdom and ingenuity but on the Rock of Ages. Time would reveal that nothing could destroy His church or deter it from its mission of glorifying God and leading men and women to the Saviour (cf. Acts 4:12, 13, 20-33).

The Biblical Meaning of "Church"

In the Scriptures the word *church*[1] is a translation of the Greek *ekklesia*, which means "a calling out." This expression was commonly used of any assembly summoned by the practice of calling people to meet.

The Septuagint, the Greek version of the Hebrew Old Testament popular in Jesus' time, used *ekklesia* to translate the Hebrew *qahal*, which stood for "gathering," "assembly," or "congregation" (Deut. 9:10; 18:16; 1 Sam. 17:47; 1 Kings 8:14; 1 Chron. 13:2).[2]

This usage was broadened in the New Testament. Note how it uses the term *church*: (1) believers assembled for worship in a specific place (1 Cor. 11:18; 14:19, 28); (2) believers living in a certain locality (1 Cor. 16:1; Gal. 1:2; 1 Thess. 2:14); (3) a group of believers in the home of an individual (1 Cor. 16:19; Col. 4:15; Philemon 2); (4) a group of congregations in a given geographic area (Acts 9:31);[3] (5) the whole body of believers throughout the world (Matt. 16:18; 1 Cor. 10:32; 12:28; cf. Eph. 4:11-16); (6) the whole faithful creation in heaven and on earth (Eph. 1:20-22; cf. Phil. 2:9-11).

The Nature of the Church

The Bible portrays the church as a divine institution, calling it "the church of God" (Acts 20:28; 1 Cor. 1:2). Jesus invested the church with divine authority (Matt. 18:17, 18). We can understand the nature of the Christian church by viewing its Old Testament roots and the various metaphors the New Testament uses in speaking of it.

The Roots of the Christian Church. The Old Testament portrays the church as an organized congregation of God's people. From the earliest times God-fearing families in the lineage of Adam, Seth, Noah, Shem, and Abraham were the guardians of His truth. These households, in which the father functioned as the priest, could be considered the church in miniature. To Abraham, God gave the rich promises through which this household of God gradually became a nation. Israel's mission was simply an extension of that given Abraham: To be a blessing to all nations (Gen. 12:1-3), showing God's love for the world.

The nation God brought out of Egypt was called "the church [or "congregation," RSV, NIV] in the wilderness" (Acts 7:38, KJV). Its members were considered "a kingdom of priests and a holy nation" (Ex 19:6), God's "holy people" (Deut. 28:9; cf. Lev. 26:12)—His church.

God placed them in Palestine, the center of the major civilizations of the world. Three great continents—Europe, Asia, and Africa—met in Palestine. Here, the Jews were to be "servants" to other nations, to extend the invitation to others to join them as God's people. In short, God called them out in order to call the nations in (Isa. 56:7). He desired, through Israel, to create the largest church on earth—a church where representatives of all nations of the world would come to worship, learn of the true God, and return to their own people with the message of salvation.

In spite of God's continual care for His people, Israel became involved in idolatry, isolationism, nationalism, pride, and self-centeredness. God's people failed to fulfill their mission.

In Jesus, Israel came upon a watershed. God's people were looking for a Messiah to free their nation but not a Messiah to set them free from themselves. At the cross, Israel's spiritual bankruptcy became evident. By crucifying Christ, they demonstrated outwardly the decay within. When they shouted, "We have no king but Caesar!" (John 19:15), they were refusing to allow God to rule over them.

At the cross two opposite missions came to a climax: the first, that of a church gone awry, so centered upon itself that it was blinded to the very One who had given it its existence—the second, that of Christ, so centered on love for people that He perished in their place to give them eternal existence.

While the cross signified the end of Israel's mission, Christ's resurrection inaugurated the Christian church and its mission—the proclamation of the gospel of salvation through the blood of Christ. When the Jews lost their mission, they became just another nation and ceased to be God's church. In their place God established a new nation—a church—that would carry forward His mission for the world (Matt. 21:41, 43).

The New Testament church, closely related to ancient Israel's community of faith,[4] is made up of both converted Jews and Gentiles who believe in Jesus Christ. Thus true Israel is all those who by faith accept Christ (see Gal. 3:26-29). Paul illustrates the new organic relationship of these diverse peoples by the imagery of two trees—a good and a wild olive tree, Israel and Gentiles, respectively. The Jews who do not accept Christ are no longer the children of God (Rom. 9:6-8) and are represented by branches broken off of the good tree, while those Jews who received Christ remain attached.

Paul portrays the Gentiles who accept Christ as branches from the wild olive tree grafted into the good tree (Rom. 11:17-25). He instructs these new Gentile Christians to respect the divine heritage of God's chosen instruments: "If the root is holy, so are the branches. And if some of the branches were broken off, and you, being a wild olive tree, were grafted in among them, and with them became a partaker of the root and fatness of the olive tree, do not boast against the branches. But if you boast, remember that you do not support the root, but the root supports you" (Rom. 11:16-18).

The New Testament church differs significantly from its Old Testament counterpart. The apostolic church became an independent organization, separate from the nation of Israel. National boundaries were discarded, giving the church a universal character. Instead of a national church, it became a missionary church, existing to accomplish God's original plan, which was restated in the divine mandate of its founder, Jesus Christ: "Make disciples of all nations" (Matt. 28:19).

Metaphoric Descriptions of the Church.

The metaphoric descriptions of the New Testament church illuminate the nature of the church.

1. *The church as a body.* The metaphor of the body stresses the unity of the church and the functional relationship of each member to the whole. The cross reconciles all believers "to God in one body" (Eph. 2:16). Through the Holy Spirit they are "baptized into one body" (1 Cor. 12:13)—the church. As a body, the church is nothing less than Christ's body (Eph. 1:23). It is the organism through which He imparts His fullness. Believers are the members of His body (Eph. 5:30). Consequently, He gives spiritual life through His power and grace to every true believer. Christ is "the head of the body" (Col. 1:18), the "head of the church" (Eph. 5:23).

In His love, God has given to each member of His church body at least one spiritual gift that enables that member to accomplish a vital function. Just as what each organ does is vital to the human body, the successful completion of the church's mission depends on the functioning of each of the spiritual gifts given members. What good is a body without a heart, or how much less efficient is it without eyes, or a leg? If its members withhold their gifts the church will be deaf, or blind, or at least crippled. However, these special, God-assigned gifts are not an end in themselves (see chapter 17 of this book).

2. *The church as a temple.* The church is "God's building," "the temple of God" in which the Holy Spirit dwells. Jesus Christ is its foundation and the "chief cornerstone" (1 Cor. 3:9-16; Eph. 2:20). This temple is not a dead structure—it displays dynamic growth. As Christ is the "living stone," Peter said, so believers are "living stones" that make up a "spiritual house" (1 Peter 2:4-6).

The building is not yet completed. New living stones are constantly added to the temple that is "being built together to become a dwelling in which God lives by His Spirit" (Eph. 2:22, NIV). Paul urges believers to use the best building materials in this temple so that it will endure the fiery test at the Day of Judgment (1 Cor. 3:12-15).

The temple metaphor emphasizes both the holiness of the local congregation and of the church at large. God's temple is holy, said Paul. "If any one defiles the temple of God, God will destroy him" (1 Cor. 3:17). Close alliances with unbelievers are contrary to its holy character, Paul noted, and should be avoided, "for what fellowship has righteousness with lawlessness?...And what agreement has the temple of God with idols?" (2 Cor. 6:14, 16). (His counsel pertains to both business and marriage relations.) The church is to be held in great respect, for it is the object on which God bestows His supreme regard.

3. The church as a bride. The church is represented as a bride—the Lord as the bridegroom. The Lord solemnly pledges, "I will betroth you to Me forever; yes, I will betroth you to Me in righteousness and justice, in lovingkindness and mercy" (Hosea 2:19). Again He assures, "I am married to you" (Jer. 3:14).

Paul uses the same imagery: I "present you as a chaste virgin to Christ" (2 Cor. 11:2). Christ's love for His church is so deep and lasting that He "gave Himself for it" (Eph. 5:25). He made this sacrifice "that He might sanctify and cleanse it with the washing of water by the word" (Eph. 5:26).

Through the sanctifying influence of the truth of God's Word (John 17:17) and the cleansing that baptism provides, Christ can purify the members of the church, taking away their filthy garments and clothing them in the robe of His perfect righteousness. Thus He can prepare the church to be His bride—"a glorious church, not having spot or wrinkle or any such thing, but...holy and without blemish" (Eph. 5:27). The church's full glory and splendor will not be seen until Christ returns.

4. The church as "Jerusalem above." The Scriptures call the city of Jerusalem Zion. There, God dwells with His people (Ps. 9:11); it is from Zion that salvation comes (Ps. 14:7; 53:6). That city was to be the "joy of the whole earth" (Ps. 48:2).

The New Testament sees the church as the "Jerusalem above"—the spiritual counterpart of the earthly Jerusalem (Gal. 4:26). The citizens of this Jerusalem have their "citizenship in heaven" (Phil. 3:20). They are the "children of promise," who are "born according to the Spirit," enjoying the liberty by which Christ has made them free (Gal. 4:28, 29; 5:1). The citizens of this city are no longer in the bondage of attempting to be "justified by the law" (Gal. 4:22, 26, 31; 5:4); "through the Spirit" they eagerly wait for "the hope of righteousness by faith." They realize that in Christ Jesus it is "faith working through love" that gives them citizenship (Gal. 5:5, 6).

Those who are part of this glorious company "have come to Mount Zion and to the city of the living God, the heavenly Jerusalem, to an innumerable company of angels, to the general assembly and church of the firstborn who are registered in heaven" (Heb. 12:22, 23).

5. The church as a family. The church in heaven and on earth is considered a family (Eph. 3:15). Two metaphors are used to describe how people join this family: adoption (Rom. 8:14-16; Eph. 1:4-6) and the New Birth (John 3:8). Through faith in Christ, those who are newly baptized are no longer slaves but children of the heavenly Father (Gal. 3:26-4:7) who live on the basis of the new covenant. Now they belong to the "household of God" (Eph. 2:19)—the "household of faith" (Gal. 6:10).

Members of His family address God as "Father" (Gal. 4:6) and relate to one another as brother and sister (James 2:15; 1 Cor. 8:11; Rom. 16:1). Because he brought many into the church family, Paul sees himself as a spiritual father. "In Christ Jesus," he said, "I became your father through the gospel" (1 Cor. 4:15, NIV). He refers to those he brought in as "my beloved children" (1 Cor. 4:14; cf. Eph. 5:1).

A special characteristic of the church as family is fellowship. Christian fellowship (*koinonia* in Greek) is not merely socialization but a "fellowship in the gospel" (Phil. 1:5). It involves genuine fellowship with God the Father, His Son, and the Holy Spirit (1 John 1:3; 1 Cor. 1:9; 2 Cor. 13:14, RSV, NIV), as well as with believers (1 John 1:3, 7). Members, then, give anyone who becomes a part of the family "the right hand of fellowship" (Gal. 2:9).

The metaphor of family reveals a caring church "where people are loved, respected, and recognized as somebody, a place where people acknowledge that they need each other. Where talents are developed. Where people grow. Where everybody is fulfilled."[5] It also implies accountability, a respect for spiritual parents, and a watching out for spiritual brothers and sisters. Finally, it means that each member will have toward other members a love that engenders a deep loyalty that undergirds and strengthens.

Membership in a church family enables individuals who vary greatly, in nature and disposition, to enjoy and support one another. Church family members learn to live in unity while not losing their individuality.

6. The church as the pillar and foundation of truth. The church of the living God is "the pillar and foundation of the truth" (1 Tim. 3:15, NIV). It is the depository and citadel of truth, protecting truth from the attacks of its enemies. Truth, however, is dynamic, not static. If members claim to have new light—a new doctrine or a new interpretation of the Scriptures—those of experience should test the new teaching by the standard of Scripture (see Isa. 8:20). If the new light meets this standard, then the church must accept it; if not, it should reject it. All members should yield to this Bible-based judgment, for "in the multitude of counselors there is safety" (Prov. 11:14).

Through spreading the truth, i.e., through its witness, the church becomes "the light of the word," "a city that is set on a hill" that "cannot be hidden," and "the salt of the earth" (Matt. 5:13-15).

7. The church as an army—militant and triumphant. The church on earth is like an army engaged in battle. It is called to war against spiritual darkness: "We do not wrestle against flesh and blood, but against principalities, against powers, against the rulers of the darkness of this age, against spiritual hosts of wickedness in the heavenly places" (Eph. 6:12). Christians must "take up the whole armor of God" that they "may be able to withstand in the evil day, and having done all, to stand" (Eph. 6:13).

Throughout the centuries the church has had to fight against the enemy, both within and without (see Acts 20:29, 30; 1 Tim. 4:1). It has made remarkable progress and obtained victories, but it is not yet the church triumphant. Unfortunately, the church still has great defects. By means of another metaphor, Jesus explained the imperfections within the church: "The kingdom of heaven is like a man who sowed good seed in his field. But while everyone was sleeping, his enemy came and sowed weeds among the wheat, and went away" (Matt. 13:24, 25, NIV). When the servants wanted to pull up the weeds, the farmer said that when "you are pulling the weeds, you may root up the wheat with them. Let both grow together until the harvest" (Matt. 13:29, 30, NIV). Weeds and wheat both flourished in the field. While God leads the converted to the church, Satan brings in the unconverted. These two groups influence the whole body—the one working for purification, the other for corruption. The conflict between them—within the church—will continue till the harvest, the Second Advent.

The church's external warfare is not over yet, either. Tribulation and strife lie ahead. Knowing that he has a but a short time, Satan is angry with God's church (Rev. 12:12, 17) and will bring against it "a time of trouble, such as never was since there was a nation." But Christ will intervene on behalf of His faithful people, who will be "delivered, everyone who is found in the book" (Dan. 12:1). Jesus assures us that "he who endures to the end shall be saved" (Matt. 24:13).

At Christ's return, the church triumphant will emerge. At that time He will be able to present "to Himself a glorious church," the faithful of all ages, the purchase of His blood, "not having spot or wrinkle, but holy and without blemish" (Eph. 5:27).

The Church Visible and Invisible. The terms *visible* and *invisible* have been used to distinguish the two aspects of the church on earth. The metaphors we have discussed above particularly apply to the visible church.

1. The visible church. The visible church is God's church organized for service. It fulfills Christ's great commission to carry the gospel to the world (Matt. 28:18-20) and prepares people for His glorious return (1 Thess. 5:23; Eph. 5:27).

Christ's specially chosen witness, it illumines the world and ministers as He did, preaching the gospel to the poor, healing the brokenhearted, preaching deliverance to the captives and recovering of sight to the blind, setting at liberty those who are oppressed, and preaching the acceptable year of the Lord (Luke 4:18, 19).

2. The invisible church. The invisible church, also called the church universal, is composed of all God's people throughout the world. It includes the believers within the visible church and many who, though they do not belong to a church organization, have followed all the light Christ has given them (John 1:9). This latter group includes those who have never had the opportunity to learn the truth about Jesus Christ but who have responded to the Holy Spirit and "by nature do the things contained in the law" of God (Rom. 2:14).

The existence of the invisible church reveals that worship of God is, in the highest sense, spiritual. "The true worshipers," Jesus said, "will worship the Father in spirit and truth; for the Father is seeking such to worship Him" (John 4:23). Because of the spiritual nature of true worship, human beings cannot calculate precisely who is and who is not a part of God's church.

Through the Holy Spirit, God leads His people from the invisible church into union with His visible church. "I have other sheep that are not of his sheep pen, I must bring them also. They too will listen to my voice, and there shall be one flock and one shepherd" (John 10:16, NIV). It is only in the visible church that they can fully experience God's truth, love, and fellowship, because He has given to the visible church the spiritual gifts that edify its members corporately and individually (Eph. 4:4-16). When Paul was converted, God put him in touch with His visible church and then appointed him to lead out in the mission of His church (Acts 9:10-22). Just so today, He intends to lead His people into His visible church, characterized by loyalty to God's commandments and possessing the faith of Jesus, so they may participate in finishing His mission on earth (Rev. 14:12; 18:4; Matt. 24:14—see chapter 13 of this book).

The concept of the invisible church has also been considered to include the united church in heaven and on earth (Eph. 1:22, 23) and the church in hiding during times of persecution (Rev. 12:6, 14).

The Organization of the Church

Christ's mandate of carrying the gospel to the whole world involves also the nurturing of those who have already accepted the gospel. New members are to be established in the faith and taught to use their God-given talents and gifts in mission. Since "God is not the author of confusion" but desires that all things should be done "decently and in order" (1 Cor. 14:33, 40), the church must have a simple but effective organization.

The Nature of the Organization. Let us consider church membership and organization.

1. Church membership. When they have met certain qualifications, converts become new members of the new covenant community of faith. Membership involves the acceptance of new relationships toward other people, the state, and God.

a. Membership qualifications. People who wish to become members of His church must accept Jesus Christ as Lord and Saviour, repent of their sins, and be baptized (Acts. 2:36-41; cf. 4:10-12). They should have experienced the new birth and accepted Christ's commission to teach others to observe all things He commanded them (see Matt. 28:20).

b. Equality and service. In harmony with Christ's declaration that "you are all brethren" and "he who is the greatest among you shall be your servant" (Matt. 23:8, 11), members are committed to relate to one another on the basis of equality. Yet they must also realize that following Christ's example means they are to minister to the needs of others, leading them to the Master.

c. Priesthood of all believers. With Christ's ministry in the heavenly sanctuary the efficacy of the Levitical priesthood came to an end. Now the church has become "a holy priesthood" (1 Peter 2:5). "You," Peter said, "are a chosen generation, a royal priesthood, a holy nation, His own special people, that you may proclaim the praises of Him who called you out of darkness into His marvelous light" (1 Peter 2:9).

This new order, the priesthood of all believers, does not authorize each individual to think, believe, and teach as he or she chooses without accountability to the body of the church. It means that each church member has a responsibility to minister to others in the name of God and can communicate directly with Him without any human intermediary. It emphasizes the interdependence of church members, as well as their independence. This priesthood makes no qualitative distinction between clergy and laity, although it leaves room for a difference in function between these roles.

d. Allegiance to God and state. The Bible recognizes God's hand in the establishment of government and commits believers to respecting and obeying civil authorities. The one who holds civil authority is "God's minister, an avenger to execute wrath on him who practices evil." Church members, therefore, render "taxes to whom taxes are due, customs to whom customs, fear to whom fear, honor to whom honor" (Rom. 13:4, 7).

In their attitudes to the state, members are guided by Christ's principle: "Render therefore to Caesar the things that are Caesar's, and to God the things that are God's" (Matt. 22:21). But if the state should interfere with a divine command their highest allegiance is to God. Said the apostles, "We ought to obey God rather than men" (Acts 5:29).

2. The major function of church organization. The church was organized to accomplish God's plan to fill this planet with the knowledge of God's glory. Only the visible church can provide a number of the functions vital to meeting this end.

a. Worship and exhortation. Throughout history the church has been God's agency for gathering believers to worship the Creator on the Sabbath. Christ and His apostles followed this worship practice, and the Scriptures admonish believers today not to forsake "the assembling of ourselves together,…but exhorting one another, and so much the more as you see the Day approaching" (Heb. 10:25; cf. 3:13). Congregational worship brings the worshiper refreshment, encouragement, and joy.

b. Christian fellowship. Through the church the members' deepest needs for fellowship are fully satisfied. "Fellowship in the gospel" (Phil. 1:5) transcends all other relations, for it provides an intimate relationship with God, as well as with others of like faith (1 John 1:3, 6, 7).

c. Instruction in the Scriptures. Christ gave to the church "the keys of the kingdom of heaven" (Matt. 16:19). These keys are the words of Christ—all the words of the Bible. More specifically, they include "the key of knowledge" regarding how to enter the kingdom (Luke 11:52). Jesus' words are spirit and life to all who receive them (John 6:63). They bring eternal life (John 6:68).[6]

When the church proclaims the truths of the Bible, these keys to salvation have the power to bind and to loose, to open and shut heaven,

because they declare the criteria by which people are received or rejected, saved or lost. Thus the church's gospel proclamation exudes "the fra-
grance of life" or "the smell of death" (2 Cor. 2:16, NIV).

Jesus knew the importance of living "by every word that proceeds
from the mouth of God" (Matt. 4:4). Only by doing so can the church
fulfill Jesus' mandate to teach all nations "to observe all things that I
have commanded you" (Matt. 28:20).

d. Administering of the divine ordinances. The church is God's
instrument for the administration of the ordinance of baptism, the rite
of entrance to the church (see chapter 15 of this book), and the ordinances of foot washing and the Lord's Supper (see chapter 16 of this
book).

e. Worldwide proclamation of the gospel. The church is organized for mission service to fulfill the work Israel failed to do. As seen in
the life of the Master, the greatest service the church provides the world
is in being fully committed to completing the gospel "witness to all nations" (Matt. 24:14), empowered by the baptism of the Holy Spirit.

This mission includes proclaiming a message of preparation for
Christ's return that is directed both to the church itself (1 Cor. 1:7, 8; 2
Peter 3:14; Rev. 3:14-22; 14:5) and to the rest of humanity (Rev. 14:6-12;
18:4).

The Government of the Church

After Jesus' ascension the leadership of the church rested in the hands
of the apostles. Their first organizational act, in counsel with other believers, was to elect another apostle to take Judas' place (Acts 1:15-26).

As the church grew, the apostles realized the impossibility of both
preaching the gospel and caring for the church's temporal affairs. So they
turned the church's practical business over to seven men whom the church
appointed. Though the church distinguished between the "ministry of the
word" and "serving tables" (Acts 6:1-4), it made no attempt to separate
clergy from laity in discharging the mission of the church. In fact, two of
the seven, Stephen and Philip, were noted for their effective preaching and
evangelism (Acts 7 and 8).

The church's expansion into Asia and Europe called for additional steps
in organization. With the establishment of numerous new churches, elders
were ordained "in every church" to ensure stable leadership (Acts 14:23).

When a major crisis developed, the parties involved were allowed to
state their respective positions to a general council comprised of apostles
and elders representing the church at large. The decisions of this council
were seen as binding upon all parties and were accepted as the voice of

God (Acts 15:1-29). This incident illustrates the fact that when it is a matter of issues affecting the entire church, counsel and authority on a much broader level than that of the local church are necessary. In this case the decision of the council grew out of the agreement reached by the representatives of all parties involved (Acts 15:22, 25).

The New Testament makes clear that as the need arose, God guided the leadership of His work. With His direction and in counsel with the church, they formed a church government that, if followed today, will help safeguard the church from apostasy and enable it to fulfill its great commission.

Biblical Principles of Church Government.

1. Christ is the head of the church. Christ's headship over the church is based primarily on His mediatorial work. Since His victory over Satan on the cross, Christ has been given "all authority" in "heaven and on earth" (Matt. 28:18). God has put "all things under His feet, and gave Him to be head over all things to the church" (Eph. 1:22; cf. Phil. 2:10, 11). He is therefore "Lord of lords and King of kings" (Rev. 17:14).

Christ also is the Head of the church, because the church is His body (Eph. 1:23; Col. 1:18). Believers are "members of His body, of His flesh and of His bones" (Eph. 5:30). They must have an intimate connection with Him, because from Him the church is "nourished and knit together by joints and ligaments" (Col. 2:19).

2. Christ is the source of all its authority. Christ demonstrates His authority in (a) the establishment of the Christian church (Matt. 16:18), (b) the institution of ordinances the church must administer (Matt. 26:26-30; 28:19, 20; 1 Cor. 11:23-29; John 13:1-17), (c) the endowment of the church with divine authority to act in His name (Matt. 16:19; 18:15-18; John 20:21-23), (d) the sending of the Holy Spirit to guide His church under His authority (John 15:26; 16:13-15), and (e) the appointment within the church of special gifts so that individuals can function as apostles, prophets, evangelists, pastors (shepherds), and teachers to prepare its members for service and to build up "the body of Christ" till all experience unity in the faith and reflect "the fullness of Christ" (Eph. 4:7-13).

3. The Scriptures carry Christ's authority. Though Christ guides His church through the Holy Spirit, the Word of God is the sole standard by which the church operates. All its members are to obey that Word, because it is law in the absolute sense. All human traditions, customs, and cultural practices are subject to the authority of the Scriptures (2 Tim. 3:15-17).

4. Christ's authority and the offices of the church. Christ exercises His authority through His church and its specially appointed servants, but He never transfers His power. No one has any independent authority apart from Christ and His Word.

Seventh-day Adventist congregations elect their officers. But while these officers function as representatives of the people, their authority comes from Christ. Their election simply confirms the call they received from Christ. The primary duty of the elected officers is to see that biblical instructions for worship, doctrine, discipline, and gospel proclamation are followed. Since the church is the body of Christ, they are to seek its counsel regarding their decisions and actions.

The New Testament Officers of the Church. The New Testament mentions two church offices—those of the elder and the deacon. The importance of these offices is underscored by the high moral and spiritual requirements set for those who would fill them. The church recognized the sacredness of the calling to leadership through ordination, the laying on of hands (Acts 6:6; 13:2, 3; 1 Tim. 4:14; 5:22).

1. The elders.

    a. What is an elder? The "elders" (Greek, *presbuteros*) or "bishops" (*episkopos*) were the most important officers of the church. The term *elder* means older one, implying dignity and respect. His position was similar to that of the one who had supervision of the synagogue. The term *bishop* means "overseer." Paul used these terms interchangeably, equating *elders* with *overseers* or *bishops* (Acts 20:17, 28; Titus 1:5, 7).

    Those who held this position supervised the newly formed churches. *Elder* referred to the status or rank of the office, while *bishop* denoted the duty or responsibility of the office—"overseer."[7] Since the apostles also called themselves elders (1 Peter 5:1; 2 John 1; 3 John 1), it is apparent that there were both local elders and itinerant elders, or elders at large. But both kinds of elder functioned as shepherds of the congregations.

    b. The qualifications. To qualify for the office of elder a person must be "blameless, the husband of one wife, temperate, soberminded, of good behavior, hospitable, able to teach; not given to wine, not violent, not greedy for money, but gentle, not quarrelsome, not covetous; one who rules his own house well, having his children in submission with all reverence (for if a man does not know how to rule his own house, how will he take care of the church of God?); not a novice, lest being puffed up with pride he fall into the same condemnation as the devil. Moreover he must have a good testimony among those who are outside, lest he fall into reproach and the snare of the devil" (1 Tim. 3:1-7; cf. Titus 1:5-9).

Before appointment to the office, therefore, the candidate must have demonstrated his leadership ability in his home. "The family of the one suggested for office should be considered. Are they in subjection? Can the man rule his own house with honor? What character have his children? Will they do honor to the father's influence? If he has no tact, wisdom, or power of godliness at home, in managing his own family, it is safe to conclude that the same defects will be carried into the church, and the same unsanctified management will be seen there."[8] The candidate, if married, should demonstrate leadership in the home before being trusted with the responsibility of leadership of "God's household" (1 Tim. 3:15, NIV).

Because of the importance of the office Paul charged, "Do not lay hands on anyone hastily" (1 Tim. 5:22).

c. The elder's responsibility and authority. An elder is first and foremost a spiritual leader. He is chosen "to shepherd the church of God" (Acts 20:28). His responsibilities include supporting weak members (Acts 20:35), admonishing the wayward (1 Thess. 5:12), and being alert for teachings that would create divisions (Acts 20:29-31). Elders must model the Christian lifestyle (Heb. 13:7; 1 Peter 5:3) and set examples of liberality (Acts 20:35).

d. The attitude toward the elders. To a large extent, effective church leadership depends on the loyalty of the membership. Paul encourages believers to respect their leaders and "to esteem them very highly in love for their work's sake" (1 Thess. 5:13). "Let the elders who rule well," he said, "be counted worthy of double honor, especially those who labor in the word and doctrine" (1 Tim. 5:17).

Scripture makes clear the need to respect church leadership: "Obey those who rule over you, and be submissive, for they watch out for your souls, as those who must give account" (Heb. 13:17; cf. 1 Peter 5:5). When members make it difficult for the leaders to perform their God-assigned responsibilities, both will experience grief and miss the joy of God's prosperity.

Believers are encouraged to observe the leaders' Christlike lifestyles. "Consider the outcome of their way of life and imitate their faith" (Heb. 13:7, NIV). They should pay no attention to gossip. Paul warned, "Do not receive an accusation against an elder except from two or three witnesses" (1 Tim. 5:19).

2. The deacons and deaconesses. The name *deacon* comes from the Greek *diakonos*, meaning "servant," or "helper." The office of deacon was instituted to enable the apostles to give themselves fully "to prayer and to the ministry of the word" (Acts 6:4). Although deacons were to care for the temporal affairs of the church, they were also to be actively involved in evangelistic work (Acts 6:8; 8:5-13, 26-40).

The feminine form of the term appears in Romans 16:1.[9] Translators have rendered this word either as "servant," (KJV, NIV), or "deaconess" (RSV). "The word and its usage in this text suggest that the office of deaconess may have been established in the church at the time Paul wrote the book of Romans."[10]

Like elders, deacons are also selected by the church on the basis of moral and spiritual qualifications (1 Tim. 3:8-13).

The Discipline of the Church. Christ gave the church the authority to discipline its members and provided the proper principles for doing so. He expects the church to implement these principles whenever necessary to maintain its lofty calling of being a "holy priesthood" and "holy nation" (cf. Matt. 18:15-18; 1 Peter 2:5, 9). Yet the church must also attempt to impress upon the erring members their need of amending their ways. Christ commends the church of Ephesus because it "cannot bear those who are evil" (Rev. 2:2), but He rebukes the churches of Pergamus and Thyatira for tolerating heresies and immorality (Rev. 2:14, 15, 20). Note the following biblical counsel on discipline:

1. Dealing with private offenses. When one member wrongs another (Matt. 18:15-17), Christ counsels the wronged person to approach the offender—the sheep that went astray—and persuade him to change his behavior. If unsuccessful he should make a second attempt, accompanied by one or two unbiased witnesses. If this attempt fails, the matter should be brought before the entire church.

If the erring member rejects the wisdom and authority of Christ's church he severs himself from its fellowship. In disfellowshipping the guilty person, the church simply confirms his or her condition. If, under the guidance of the Holy Spirit, the church has carefully followed the biblical counsel, its decisions have been acknowledged in heaven. Said Christ, "Whatever you bind on earth will be bound in heaven, and whatever you loose on earth will be loosed in heaven" (Matt. 18:18).

2. Dealing with public offenses. Though "all have sinned and fall short of the glory of God" (Rom. 3:23), flagrant and rebellious offenses bringing a reproach on the church should be immediately dealt with by disfellowshipping the offender.

Disfellowshipping removes the evil—which otherwise would work like leaven. And it restores the purity of the church and acts as a redemptive remedy for the offender. Upon learning of a case of sexual immorality in the Corinthian church, Paul urged immediate action. "In the name of our Lord Jesus Christ," he said, "when you are gathered together, along with my spirit, with the power of our Lord Jesus Christ, deliver such a one to Satan for the destruction of the flesh that his spirit may be saved in the day of the Lord Jesus....Purge out the old leaven, that you may be a new lump" (1 Cor. 5:4, 5, 7). Do not associate with anyone who calls himself a believer, he said, "but is sexually immoral or greedy, an idolater or slanderer, a drunkard or a swindler. With such a man do not even eat.... 'Expel the wicked man from among you'" (1 Cor. 5:11, 13, NIV).

3. Dealing with divisive persons. A member who causes "divisions and offenses" (Rom. 16:17), "who walks disorderly," refusing to obey biblical counsel, should be avoided so that "he may be ashamed" of his attitude. "Yet do not count him as an enemy," Paul said, "but admonish him as a brother" (2 Thess. 3:6, 14, 15). If the "divisive man" refuses to listen to the "second admonition" of the church, he should be rejected, "knowing that such a person is warped and sinning, being self-condemned" (Titus 3:10, 11).

4. Restoration of offenders. Church members should not despise, shun, or neglect the disfellowshipped. Rather, they should attempt to restore their relationship with Christ through repentance and a new birth. Disfellowshipped individuals can be restored to church fellowship when they reveal sufficient evidence of genuine repentance (2 Cor. 2:6-10).

Especially through restoring sinners to the church, God's power, glory, and grace are revealed. He longs to liberate the captives of sin, transferring them from the kingdom of darkness into the kingdom of light. God's church, the theater of the universe, displays the power of Christ's atoning sacrifice in the lives of men and women.

Today, Christ, through His church, invites all to become a part of His family. "Behold," He says, "I stand at the door and knock. If any one hears My voice and opens the door, I will come in to him and dine with him, and he with Me" (Rev. 3:20).

References

1. On the origin of the term *church* Berkhof wrote, "The names 'Church', 'Kerk' and 'Kirche' are not derived from the word *ekklesia*, but from the word *kuriake*, which means 'belonging to the Lord'. They stress the fact that the

Church is the property of God. The name *to kuriakon* or *he kuriake* first of all designated the place where the Church assembled. This place was conceived of as belonging to the Lord, and was therefore called *to kuriakon*" (*Systematic Theology*, p. 557).

2. "Church, Nature of," *SDA Encyclopedia*, rev. ed., p. 302; "Church," *SDA Bible Dictionary*, rev. ed., p. 224.

3. According to the modern translations that accept the Tisschendorf reading of the singular, based on the Codex Sinaiticus, Alexandrinus, Vaticanus, and Ephraemi Rescriptus.

4. Except for their teaching about Jesus, the beliefs of the early church were very similar to those of Judaism. Both Jewish and Gentile Christians continued to worship in the synagogues on the Sabbath, listening to the Old Testament being explained (Acts 13:42-44; 15:13, 14, 21). The rending of the Temple veil signified that the rituals had met their antitypical fulfillment. The book of Hebrews intends to turn Christian minds away from the *types* to the underlying reality of the types—the atoning death of Jesus, His priesthood in heaven, and His saving grace. The New Testament era was a transitional time, and although the apostles sometimes participated in the Old Testament rituals, the decision of the first Jerusalem council shows that they perceived no saving value in them.

5. Charles E. Bradford, "What the Church Means to Me," *Adventist Review*, Nov. 20, 1986, p. 15.

6. See *SDA Bible Commentary*, rev. ed., vol. 5, p. 432.

7. See *SDA Bible Commentary*, rev. ed., vol. 6, pp. 26, 38.

8. Ellen G. White, *Testimonies*, vol. 5, p. 618.

9. *Diakonos* can be either male or female in gender; therefore, the gender in this case is determined by the context. Because Phoebe who is "our sister" is also a *diakonos*, this word must be feminine even though it is spelled as a masculine noun.

10. "Deaconess," *SDA Bible Dictionary*, rev. ed., p. 277. In New Testament times the term *diakonos* had a broad meaning. "It was still employed to describe all who served the church in any capacity. Paul, though an apostle, frequently described himself (see 1 Cor. 3:5; 2 Cor. 3:6; 6:4; 11:23; Eph. 3:7; Col. 1:23) and Timothy...(see 1 Tim. 4:6), as *diakonoi* (plural of *diakonos*)." (*SDA Bible Commentary*, rev. ed., vol. 7, p. 300). In these instances it has been translated as "ministers" or "servants" instead of "deacons."

The Remnant and Its Mission

13

The universal church is composed of all who truly believe in Christ, but in the last days, a time of widespread apostasy, a remnant has been called out to keep the commandments of God and the faith of Jesus. This remnant announces the arrival of the judgment hour, proclaims salvation through Christ, and heralds the approach of His Second Advent. This proclamation is symbolized by the three angels of Revelation 14; it coincides with the work of judgment in heaven and results in a work of repentance and reform on earth. Every believer is called to have a personal part in this worldwide witness. (Rev. 12:17; 14:6-12; 18:1-4; 2 Cor. 5:10; Jude 3, 14; 1 Pet. 1:16-19; 2 Pet. 3:10-14; Rev. 21:1-14.)

THE GREAT RED DRAGON CROUCHES, ready. Already, it has brought about the downfall of one third of heaven's angels (Rev. 12:4, 7-9). Now, if it can devour the infant about to be born, it will have won the war.

The woman standing before it is garbed with the sun and has the moon under her feet and wears a crown of twelve stars. The male Child to whom she gives birth is destined to "rule all nations with a rod of iron."

The dragon pounces, but its efforts to kill the Child are in vain. Instead, the Child is "caught up to God and to His throne." Enraged, the dragon turns its wrath against the mother, who is miraculously given wings and is taken to a remote place specially prepared by God, where He nourishes her for a time and time and half a time—three and a half years, or 1260 prophetic days (Rev. 12:1-6, 13, 14).

In biblical prophecy, a pure woman represents God's faithful church.[1] A woman depicted as a fornicator or adulteress represents God's people who have apostasized (Ezekiel 16; Isa. 57:8; Jer. 31:4, 5; Hosea 1-3; Rev. 17:1-5).

The dragon, the "serpent of old, called the Devil and Satan," was waiting to devour the male Child, the long-expected Messiah, Jesus Christ. Satan, warring against his archenemy Jesus, used as his instrument the Roman empire. Nothing, not even death on the cross, could deter Jesus from His mission as Saviour of humanity.

At the cross, Christ defeated Satan. Speaking of the crucifixion, Christ said, "Now is the judgment of this world; now the ruler of this world will be cast out" (John 12:31). Revelation describes heaven's hymn of victory: "Now salvation, and strength, and the kingdom of our God, and the power of His Christ have come, for the accuser of our brethren, who accused them before our God day and night, has been cast down....Therefore rejoice, O heavens, and you who dwell in them!" (Rev. 12:10-12). Satan's expulsion from heaven restricted his works. No longer could Satan accuse God's people before the heavenly beings.

But while heaven rejoices, earth must take warning: "Woe to the inhabitants of the earth and the sea! For the devil has come down to you, having great wrath, because he knows that he has a short time" (Rev. 12:12).

To vent his anger Satan began persecuting the woman—the church (Rev. 12:13), which, though it suffered greatly, nevertheless survived. Sparsely populated areas of the earth—"the wilderness"—provided refuge for God's faithful during the 1260 prophetic days or 1260 literal years (Rev. 12:14-16—see chapter 4 on the year-day principle.)[2]

At the end of this wilderness experience God's people emerge in response to signs of the soon return of Christ. John identifies this faithful group as "the remnant...which keep the commandments of God, and have the testimony of Jesus Christ." The devil particularly hates this remnant (Rev. 12:17, KJV).

When and where did this persecution take place? How did it come about? When did the remnant begin to appear? What is its mission? The answer to these questions requires a review of both Scripture and history.

The Great Apostasy

The persecution of the Christian church was brought about at first by pagan Rome, then by apostasy within its own ranks. This apostasy was no surprise—John, Paul, and Christ predicted it.

During His last major discourse, Jesus warned His disciples of the coming deception. "Take heed that no one deceives you," He said, "for false Christs and false prophets will arise and show great signs and wonders, so as to deceive, if possible, even the elect" (Matt. 24:4, 24). His followers would experience a period of "great tribulation," but they would survive (Matt. 24:21, 22). Impressive signs in nature would mark the end of this persecution and would reveal the nearness of Christ's return (Matt. 24:29, 32, 33).

Paul too warned: "After my departure, savage wolves will come in among you, not sparing the flock. Also from among yourselves men will rise up, speaking perverse things, to draw away the disciples after themselves" (Acts 20:29, 30). These "wolves" would lead the church to "the apostasy," or "falling away."

This apostasy must occur before Christ's return, Paul said. It was such a certainty that the fact that it had not yet taken place was a sure sign that Christ's coming was not yet imminent. "Let no one deceive you by any means," he said, "for that Day will not come unless the falling away [apostasy] comes first, and the man of sin [lawlessness] is revealed, the son of perdition, who opposes and exalts himself above all that is called God or that is worshiped, so that he sits as God in the temple [church] of God, showing himself that He is God" (2 Thess. 2:3, 4).

Even during Paul's time this apostasy was already at work in a limited way. His method of operation was satanic, "with all power, signs and lying wonders, and with all unrighteous deception" (2 Thess. 2:9, 10). Before the end of the first century John stated that "many false prophets have gone out into the world." Indeed, he said, "the spirit of the Antichrist" is "already in the world" (1 John 4:1, 3).

How did this apostate system come about?

The Ascendancy of the "Man of Sin." "As the church left its 'first love' (Rev. 2:4), it forfeited its purity of doctrine, its high standards of personal conduct, and the invisible bond of unity provided by the Holy Spirit. In worship, formalism replaced simplicity. Popularity and personal power came more and more to determine the choice of leaders who first assumed increasing authority within the local church, then sought to extend their authority over neighboring churches.

"Administration of the local church under the guidance of the Holy Spirit eventually gave way to ecclesiastical authoritarianism at the hands of a single official, the bishop, to whom every church member was personally subject and through whom alone he had access to salvation. Henceforth leadership thought only of ruling the church instead of serving it, and the 'greatest' was no longer one who considered himself 'servant of all.' Thus, gradually, developed the concept of a priestly hierarchy that interposed between the individual and his Lord."[3]

As the importance of the individual and the local church eroded, the bishop of Rome emerged as the supreme power in Christianity. With the assistance of the emperor this highest bishop, or pope,[4] was recognized as the visible head of the universal church, invested with supreme authority over all church leaders throughout the world.

Under the leadership of the papacy,[5] the Christian church plunged into yet deeper apostasy. The increasing popularity of the church accelerated its decline. Lowered standards caused the unconverted to feel comfortable in the church. Multitudes knowing very little of genuine Christianity joined the church in name only, bringing their pagan doctrines, images, modes of worship, celebrations, feasts, and symbolism with them.

These compromises between paganism and Christianity led to the formation of the "man of sin"—a gigantic system of false religion, a mixture of truth and error. The prophecy of 2 Thessalonians 2 does not condemn individuals but exposes the religious system responsible for the great apostasy. Many believers within this system, however, belong to God's universal church, because they live according to all the light that they have.

The Suffering Church. With the decline of spirituality, the church of Rome developed a more secular profile with closer ties to the imperial government. Church and state were united in an unholy alliance.

In his classic *The City of God*, Augustine, one of the most influential church Fathers, set forth the Catholic ideal of a universal church in control of a universal state. Augustine's thinking laid the foundation of medieval papal theology.

In A.D. 533, in a letter incorporated in the Code of Justinian, the emperor Justinian declared the bishop of Rome head over all the churches.[6] He also recognized the pope's influence in eliminating heretics.[7]

When Justinian's general Belisarius liberated Rome in A.D. 538, the bishop of Rome was freed from the control of the Ostrogoths, whose Arianism had resulted in their restricting the developing Catholic Church. Now the bishop could exercise the prerogatives Justinian's decree of A.D. 533 had granted him; he could increase the authority of the "Holy See." Thus began the 1260 years of persecution as Bible prophecy had foretold (Dan. 7:25; Rev. 12:6, 14; 13:5-7).

Tragically, the church, with the assistance of the state, tried to force its decrees and teachings on all Christians. Many surrendered their beliefs out of fear of persecution, while those faithful to the scriptural teachings experienced severe persecution. The Christian world became a battlefield.

Many were imprisoned or executed in the name of God! During the 1260-year persecution millions of faithful believers experienced great suffering, while many paid for their loyalty to Christ with death.[8]

Every drop of blood spilled put a stain on the name of God and Jesus Christ. Nothing has done more harm to the cause of Christianity than this ruthless persecution. The grossly distorted view of the character of God given by these actions of the church and the doctrines of purgatory and eternal torment led many to reject Christianity altogether.

Long before the Reformation, voices within the Catholic Church protested against its merciless killing of opponents, its arrogant claims and demoralizing corruption. The church's unwillingness to reform gave birth to the Protestant Reformation in the sixteenth century. Its success was a great blow to the authority and prestige of the church of Rome. Through the Counter-Reformation the papacy carried on a bloody struggle to crush the Reformation, but it gradually lost the battle against the forces striving for civil and religious freedom.

Finally, in 1798, 1260 years after A.D. 538, the Roman Catholic Church received a deadly blow (cf. Rev. 13:3).[9] The spectacular victories of Napoleon's armies in Italy placed the pope at the mercy of the French revolutionary government, which saw the Roman religion as the irreconcilable enemy of the Republic. The French government directed Napoleon to take the pope prisoner. At his orders General Berthier entered Rome and proclaimed the political rule of the papacy at an end. Taking the pope captive, Berthier carried him off to France, where he died in exile.[10]

The overthrow of the papacy was the culmination of a long series of events associated with its progressive decline. That event marks the end of the prophetic period of 1260 years. Many Protestants interpreted this event as a fulfillment of prophecy.[11]

The Reformation

Unscriptural doctrines based on tradition, relentless persecution of dissenters, corruption, and the spiritual declension of many of the clergy were among the major factors that caused people to cry out for reforms within the established church.

The Doctrinal Issues. The following are examples of the unbiblical doctrines that helped foster the Protestant Reformation and still separate Protestants and Roman Catholics.

1. The head of the church on earth is the vicar of Christ. This doctrine claims that only the bishop of Rome is the vicar or representative of Christ on earth and the visible head of the church. In contrast to the biblical view of church leadership (see chapter 12 of this book), this doctrine was based on the assumptions that Christ made Peter the visible head of the church and that the pope is Peter's successor.[12]

2. The infallibility of the church and its head. The doctrine that contributed most strongly to the prestige and influence of the church of Rome was that of its infallibility. The church claimed it had never erred and never would. It based this teaching on the following reasoning, which finds no biblical support: Because the church is divine, one of its inherent attributes is infallibility. In addition, since God intended, through this divine church, to lead all people of good will to heaven, she must be infallible in teaching faith and morals.[13] Christ, then, will preserve her from all error through the power of the Holy Spirit.

The logical corollary, which denies the basic corruptness of humans (see chapter 7 of this book), is that the church's leader must also be infallible.[14] Accordingly, Catholic literature claimed divine prerogatives for its leader.[15]

3. The eclipse of Christ's high-priestly mediatorial ministry. As the influence of the church of Rome increased, the attention of believers was shifted away from Christ's continual mediatorial work as High Priest in heaven—the antitype of the continual daily sacrifices of the Old Testament sanctuary services (see chapters 4 and 24 of this book)—to an earthly priesthood with its leader in Rome. Instead of trusting in Christ for forgiveness of sins and eternal salvation (see chapters 9 and 10 of this book), believers placed their faith in popes, priests, and prelates. Contradicting the New Testament teaching of the priesthood of all believers, the clergy's ministry of absolution was now believed to be vital for salvation.

Christ's priestly ministry in heaven, where He constantly applies the benefits of His atoning sacrifice to repentant believers, was effectually negated when the church substituted the mass for the Lord's Supper. Unlike the Lord's Supper—a service that Jesus instituted to commemorate His death and to foreshadow His coming kingdom (see chapter 16 of this book)—the Catholic Church claims the mass to be a human priest's unbloody sacrifice of Christ to God. Because Christ is offered again, as He was at Calvary, the mass was considered to bring special grace to believers and the deceased.[16]

Ignorant of the Scriptures, knowing only the mass conducted by a human priesthood, multitudes lost the blessing of direct access to our Mediator, Jesus Christ. Thus the promise and invitation, "Let us therefore come boldly to the throne of grace, that we may obtain mercy and find grace to help in time of need" (Heb. 4:16), was obliterated.

4. The meritorious nature of good works. The prevalent view that by doing good works a person could obtain the merit vital for salvation—that faith could not save—contradicted the New Testament's teaching (see chapters 9 and 10 of this book). The Catholic Church taught that the good works that were the result of grace infused into the sinner's heart were meritorious, which meant that they gave an individual a just claim to salvation. In fact, one could perform more good works than were necessary for salvation—as was the case with the saints—and thus accumulate extra merits. This extra merit could be used for the benefit of others. Because the church held that sinners were justified on the basis of the righteousness infused into their hearts, good works played an important role in a person's justification.

Meritorious works also played an important role in the doctrine of purgatory, which asserts that those who are not perfectly pure must bear a cleansing, temporal punishment for their sins in purgatory before they enter into the joys of heaven. By their prayers and good works, living believers could shorten the duration and the intensity of the suffering of those in purgatory.

5. *The doctrine of penance and indulgences.* Penance is the sacrament by which Christians may obtain forgiveness for sins committed after baptism. This forgiveness of sins is accomplished through the absolution of a priest, but before it can be obtained, Christians must examine their consciences, repent for their sins, and resolve to nevermore offend God. Then they must confess their sins to the priest and perform the penance—some task assigned by the priest.

Penance, however, did not completely release sinners. They still had to bear the temporal punishment either in this life or in purgatory. To take care of this punishment the church instituted indulgences, which provided the remission of the temporal punishment that remained due on account of sin after the guilt had been absolved. Indulgences, which could benefit both the living and those in purgatory, were granted on condition of penitence and the performance of prescribed good works, often in the form of payment of money to the church.

It was the extra merits of the martyrs, saints, apostles, and especially Jesus Christ and Mary, that made indulgences possible. Their merits were deposited in a "treasury of merit" and were transferable to those believers whose accounts were deficient. The pope, as the alleged successor of Peter, was in control of the keys of this treasury and could release people from temporal punishment by assigning them credit from the treasury.[17]

6. *Ultimate authority resides in the church.* Throughout the centuries the established church adopted many pagan beliefs, holy days, and symbols. When voices cried out against these abominations, the church of

Rome assumed the sole right to interpret the Bible. The church, not the Bible, became the final authority (see chapter 1 of this book). The church argued that two sources of divine truth existed: (1) The sacred Scriptures and (2) the Catholic tradition, which consisted of the writings of the Church Fathers, the decrees of church councils, approved creeds, and ceremonies of the church. Whenever church doctrines were supported by tradition but not by Scripture, tradition took precedence. Common believers had no authority to interpret the doctrines God had revealed in Scripture. That authority resided only in the Catholic Church.[18]

The Dawn of a New Day. In the fourteenth century John Wycliffe called for a reformation of the church, not only in England, but in all Christendom. During a time when few copies of the Bible existed, he provided the first translation of the whole Bible into English. His teachings of salvation through faith in Christ alone and that only the Scriptures were infallible laid the foundation of the Protestant Reformation. As the morning star of the Reformation, he tried to free Christ's church from the bonds of paganism that chained it in ignorance. He inaugurated a movement that was to liberate the individual minds and to free whole nations from the clutches of religious error. Wycliffe's writings touched the souls of Huss, Jerome, Luther, and many others.

Martin Luther—fiery, impulsive, uncompromising—was perhaps the most powerful personality of the Reformation. More than any other man, he led people back to the Scriptures and the great gospel truth of justification by faith, while he railed against salvation by works.

Declaring that believers should receive no authority other than the Scriptures, Luther turned people's eyes upward, from human works, priests, and penance, to Christ as their only Mediator and Saviour. It was impossible, he said, by human works to lessen the guilt of sinning or to avoid its punishment. Only repentance toward God and faith in Christ can save sinners. Because it is a gift, freely given, His grace cannot be purchased. Humans can have hope, therefore, not because of indulgences, but because of the shed blood of a crucified Redeemer.

Like an archaeological expedition finding treasures buried beneath the accumulated discards of the centuries, the Reformation uncovered long-forgotten truths. Justification by faith, the great principle of the gospel, was rediscovered, as was a new appreciation for the once-for-all atoning sacrifice of Jesus Christ and His all-sufficient mediatorial priesthood. Many unbiblical teachings, such as prayers for the dead, veneration of saints and relics, celebration of the mass, worship of Mary, purgatory, penance, holy water, celibacy of the priesthood, the rosary, the inquisition, transubstantiation, extreme unction, and dependence upon tradition, were repudiated and abandoned.

The Protestant Reformers were nearly unanimous in identifying the papal system as the "man of sin," the "mystery of iniquity," and the "little horn" of Daniel—the entity that was to persecute God's true people during the 1260 years of Revelation 12:6, 14, and 13:5 before the Second Coming.[19]

The doctrine of the Bible and the Bible only as the norm of faith and morals became basic to Protestantism. The Reformers considered all human traditions subject to the final and higher authority of the Scriptures. In matters of religious faith no authority—pope, councils, church Fathers, kings, or scholars—was to rule the conscience. Indeed, the Christian world was beginning to awake from its slumber, and eventually, in many lands, religious liberty was proclaimed.

The Stagnated Reformation

The reformation of the Christian church should not have ended in the sixteenth century. The Reformers had accomplished much but had not rediscovered all the light lost during the apostasy. They had taken Christianity out of utter darkness, but it still stood in the shadows. While they had broken the iron hand of the medieval church, given the Bible to the world, and restored the basic gospel, they had failed to discover other important truths. Baptism by immersion, immortality as a gift bestowed by Christ at the resurrection of the just, the seventh-day as the Bible Sabbath, and other truths (see chapters 7, 15, 20, and 26 of this book) were still lost in the shadows.

But instead of advancing the Reformation, their successors consolidated its achievements. They focused their attention on the Reformers' words and opinions instead of on Scripture. A few discovered new truths, but the majority refused to advance beyond what the early Reformers believed. Consequently, the Protestant faith degenerated into formalism and scholasticism, and errors that should have been discarded were enshrined. The flame of the Reformation gradually died out, and Protestant churches themselves became cold, formal, and in need of reform.

The post-Reformation era buzzed with theological activity, but little spiritual progress was made. Frederic W. Farrar wrote that in this period "liberty was exchanged for bondage; universal principles for beggarly elements; truth for dogmatism; independence for tradition; religion for system. A living reverence for Scripture was superseded by a dead theory of inspiration. Genial orthodoxy gave place to iron uniformity and living thought to controversial dialectics."[20] And although the "Reformation had broken the leaden scepter of the Old Scholasticism," the Protestant churches introduced "a new Scholasticism whose rod was of iron."[21] Robert M. Grant called this new scholasticism "as rigid as any medieval theological construction."[22] The Protestants "practically bound themselves by the limits of their current confessions."[23]

Controversies erupted. "There never was an epoch in which men were so much occupied in discovering each other's errors, or in which they called each other by so many opprobrious names."[24] Thus the good news became a war of words. "Scripture no longer speaks to the heart but to the critical intellect."[25] "Dogmas were orthodox, but spirituality was extinguished. Theology was triumphant, but love was quenched."[26]

The Remnant

In spite of the apostasy and tribulation of the 1260 years, some believers continued to reflect the purity of the apostolic church. When the 1260 years of oppression ended in A.D. 1798, the dragon had failed to eradicate entirely God's faithful people. Against these Satan continued to direct his destructive efforts. Said John, "And the dragon was enraged with the woman, and went to make war with the rest of her offspring, who keep the commandments of God and have the testimony of Jesus Christ" (Rev. 12:17).

What Is the Remnant? In John's description of the dragon's battle with the woman and her descendants, he used the expression "the rest of her offspring" (Rev. 12:17). That expression means "remaining ones" or "remnant" (Rev. 12:17, KJV). The Bible portrays the remnant as a small group of God's people who, through calamities, wars, and apostasy, remain loyal to God. This faithful remnant were the rootstock God used to propagate His visible church on earth (2 Chron. 30:6; Ezra 9:14, 15; Isa. 10:20-22; Jer. 42:2; Eze. 6:8; 14:22).

God commissioned the remnant to declare His glory and lead His scattered people throughout the world to His "holy mountain Jerusalem," "Mount Zion" (Isa. 37:31, 32; 66:20; cf. Rev. 14:1). Of those thus gathered together Scripture states, "These are the ones who follow the Lamb wherever He goes" (Rev. 14:4).

Revelation 12:17 contains a description of the last remnant in God's chosen line of loyal believers—His loyal witnesses in the last days before Christ's second coming. What are the remnant's characteristics?

The Characteristics of the Remnant. The remnant at the time of the end cannot be easily mistaken. John describes this group in specific terms. Appearing after the 1260 years of persecution, they are made up of those "who keep the commandments of God and have the testimony of Jesus Christ" (Rev. 12:17).

They have the responsibility of proclaiming, just before Christ's return, God's final warning to all the world—the three angels' messages of Revelation 14 (Rev. 14:6-12). These messages themselves contain a description of the remnant—they are "those who keep the commandments of God and the faith of Jesus" (Rev. 14:12). Let us consider more closely each of these characteristics.

1. *The faith of Jesus.* God's remnant people are characterized by a faith similar to that which Jesus had. They reflect Jesus' unshakable confidence in God and the authority of Scripture. They believe Jesus Christ is the Messiah of the prophecy, the Son of God, who came as the world's Saviour. Their faith encompasses all the truths of the Bible—those which Christ believed and taught.

God's remnant, then, will proclaim the everlasting gospel of salvation by faith in Christ. They will warn the world that the hour of God's judgment has arrived and they will prepare others to meet their soon-coming Lord. They will be engaged in a worldwide mission to complete the divine witness to humanity (Rev. 14:6, 7; 10:11; Matt. 24:14).

2. *The commandments of God.* Genuine faith in Jesus commits the remnant to follow His example. "He who says he abides in Him," John said, "ought himself also to walk just as He walked" (1 John 2:6). Since Jesus kept His Father's commandments, they too will obey God's commandments (John 15:10).

Particularly, since they are the remnant, their actions must harmonize with their profession—otherwise, it is worthless. Jesus said, "Not everyone who says to Me, 'Lord, Lord' shall enter the kingdom of heaven, but he who does the will of My Father in heaven" (Matt. 7:21). Through the strength Christ gives them, they obey God's requirements, including all ten of the commandments, God's unchanging moral law (Ex. 20:1-17; Matt. 5:17-19; 19:17; Phil. 4:13).

3. *The testimony of Jesus.* John defines "the testimony of Jesus" as "the spirit of prophecy" (Rev. 19:10). The remnant will be guided by the testimony of Jesus conveyed through the gift of prophecy.

This gift of the Spirit was to function continuously throughout the history of the church, until "all come to the unity of the faith and the knowledge of the Son of God, to a perfect man, to the measure of the stature of the fullness of Christ" (Eph. 4:13). It is, therefore, one of the major characteristics of the remnant.

Such prophetic guidance makes the remnant a people of prophecy who proclaim a prophetic message. They will understand prophecy and teach it. The revelation of truth that comes to the remnant helps them accomplish their mission of preparing the world for Christ's return (see chapter 18 of this book).

The Emergence of the Remnant of the Last Days. The Bible indicates that the remnant appears on the world's stage after the time of great persecution (Rev. 12:14-17). The earth-shaking events of the French Revolution, which led to the captivity of the pope at the end of the 1260-year period (A.D. 1798), and the fulfillment of the three great cosmic signs—in which the earth, sun, moon, and stars testified of the nearness of Christ's return (see chapter 25 of this book)—led to a major revival of the study of prophecy. A widespread expectation of the imminent coming of Jesus arose. Throughout the world many Christians recognized that "the time of the end" had arrived (Dan. 12:4).[27]

The fulfillment of Bible prophecies during the second half of the eighteenth and the first half of the nineteenth century brought about a powerful interconfessional movement centered on the Second Advent hope. In every church believers in the imminent return of Christ could be found, all praying, working, and anticipating the climax of the ages.

The Advent hope brought a deep spirit of unity among its adherents, and many joined together to warn the world about Christ's soon return. The Advent movement was a truly biblical interconfessional movement centered on the Word of God and the Advent hope.

The more they studied the Bible, the more convinced they became that God was calling a remnant to continue the stagnated Reformation of the Christian church. They had themselves experienced the absence of the true spirit of the Reformation in their respective churches and a lack of interest in the study of and preparation for the Second Advent. Their Bible study revealed that the trials and disappointments God had led them through constituted a deeply spiritual, purifying experience that brought them together as God's remnant. God had commissioned them to continue the Reformation that had brought so much joy and power to the church. With gratitude and humility they accepted their mission, realizing that God's commission had not come to them because of any inherent superiority, and that only through Christ's mercy and power could they in any way be successful.

The Mission of the Remnant

The prophecies of the book of Revelation clearly outline the mission of the remnant. The three angels' messages of Revelation 14:6-12 reveal the proclamation of the remnant that will bring a full and final restoration of the gospel truth.[28] These three messages comprise God's answers to the overwhelming satanic deception that sweeps the world just before Christ's return (Rev. 13;3, 8, 14-16). Immediately following God's last appeal to the world Christ returns to reap the harvest (Rev. 14:14-20).

The First Angel's Message

"Then I saw another angel flying in the midst of heaven, having the everlasting gospel to preach to those who dwell on the earth—to every nation, tribe, tongue, and people—saying with a loud voice, 'Fear God and give glory to Him, for the hour of His judgment has come; and worship Him who made heaven and earth, the sea and springs of water'" (Rev. 14:6, 7).

The first angel symbolizes God's remnant carrying an everlasting gospel to the world. This gospel is the same good news of God's infinite love that the ancient prophets and apostles proclaimed (Heb. 4:2). The remnant do not present a different gospel—in view of the judgment they reaffirm that everlasting gospel that sinners can be justified by faith and receive Christ's righteousness.

This message calls the world to repentance. It summons all to "fear," or reverence, God and to give "glory," or honor, to Him. We were created for this purpose, and we can give honor or glory to God in our words and actions: "By this My Father is glorified, that you bear much fruit" (John 15:8).

John predicts that the movement preparing the world for Christ's return will give a renewed emphasis to the biblical concern for glorifying God. As never before, it will present the New Testament appeal for the sacred stewardship of our lives: "Your body is the temple of the Holy Spirit." We do not have exclusive rights to our physical, moral, and spiritual powers; Christ bought these with His blood at Calvary. "Therefore glorify God in your body and in your spirit, which are God's" (1 Cor. 6:19, 20). "Therefore, whether you eat or drink, or whatever you do, do all to the glory of God" (1 Cor. 10:31).

The fact that "the hour of His judgment" has arrived adds urgency to the call to repent (see chapter 24 of this book). In Revelation 14:7, the word *judgment* translates the Greek *krisis*, the act of judging, not the sentence of judgment (*krima*). It refers to the entire process of judgment, including the arraignment of people before the divine judgment bar, the investigation of life records, the verdict of acquittal or conviction, and the bestowal of eternal life or the sentence of death (see Matt. 16:27; Rom. 6:23; Rev. 22:12). The judgment-hour message also proclaims God's judgment on all apostasy (Dan. 7:9-11, 26; Revelation 17, 18).

The judgment-hour message points particularly to the time when, as the last phase of His high-priestly ministry in the heavenly sanctuary, Christ entered upon His work of judgment (see chapter 24 of this book).

This message also calls on all to worship the Creator. God's call to worship must be seen in contrast to the summons to worship the beast and his image (Rev. 13:3, 8, 15). Soon everyone will have to make a choice between true and false worship—between worshiping God on His terms (righteousness by faith) or on our terms (righteousness by works). By commanding us "to worship Him who made heaven and earth, the sea and springs of water" (Rev. 14:7; cf. Ex. 20:11), this message calls attention to the fourth commandment. It leads people into true worship of the Creator, an experience that involves honoring His memorial of Creation—the seventh-day Sabbath of the Lord, which He instituted at Creation and affirmed in the Ten Commandments (see chapter 20 of this book). The first angel's message, therefore, calls for the restoration of true worship by presenting before the world Christ the Creator and Lord of the Bible Sabbath. This is the sign of God's Creation—a sign neglected by the vast majority of His created beings.

Providentially, the proclamation of this message calling attention to the Creator-God began at the stage of history when the evolutionary philosophy received a major boost from the publication of Charles Darwin's *Origin of Species* (1859). The preaching of the first angel's message constitutes the greatest bulwark against the progress of the theory of evolution.

Finally, this call implies the restoration of the honor of God's holy law, which has been trampled upon by the "man of lawlessness" (2 Thess. 2:3, RSV). Only when true worship is restored and believers live the principles of God's kingdom can God be glorified.

The Second Angel's Message

"Babylon is fallen, is fallen, that great city, because she has made all nations drink of the wine of the wrath of her fornication" (Rev. 14:8).

From early history, the city of Babylon symbolized defiance of God. Its tower was a monument to apostasy and a center of rebellion (Gen. 11:1-9). Lucifer (Satan) was its invisible king (Isa. 14:4, 12-14), and it appears that he wanted to make Babylon the agency of his master plan for ruling the human race. Throughout the Bible the struggle between God's city, Jerusalem, and Satan's city, Babylon, illustrates the conflict between good and evil.

During the early Christian centuries, when the Romans were oppressing both Jews and Christians, Jewish and Christian literature referred to the city of Rome as *Babylon*.[29] Many believe that Peter used *Babylon* as a pseudonym for Rome (1 Peter 5:13). Because of its apostasy and persecution, most Protestants of the Reformation and post-Reformation era referred to the church of Rome as spiritual Babylon (Revelation 17), the enemy of God's people.[30]

In Revelation, *Babylon* refers to the wicked woman, the mother of harlots, and her impure daughters (Rev. 17:5). It symbolizes all apostate religious organizations and their leadership, though it refers especially to the great apostate religious alliance between the beast and his image that will bring about the final crisis described in Revelation 13:15-17.

The second angel's message brings out the universal nature of the Babylonian apostasy and her coercive power, saying that "she has made all nations drink of the wine of the wrath of her fornication." The "wine" of Babylon represents her heretical teachings. Babylon will pressure the powers of state to enforce universally her false religious teachings and decrees.

The "fornication" mentioned represents the illicit relationship between Babylon and the nations—between the apostate church and civil powers. The church is supposed to be married to her Lord; in seeking instead the support of the state, she leaves her spouse and commits spiritual fornication (cf. Eze. 16:15; James 4:4).

This illicit relationship results in tragedy. John sees the inhabitants of the earth "drunk" with false teachings and Babylon herself "drunk with the blood of the saints and with the blood of the martyrs of Jesus," who refuse to accept her unscriptural doctrines and submit to her authority (Rev. 17:2, 6).

Babylon falls because she rejects the first angel's message—the gospel of righteousness by faith in the Creator. As during the first few centuries the church of Rome apostatized, many Protestants today have departed from the great Bible truths of the Reformation. This prophecy of Babylon's fall especially finds its fulfillment in the departure of Protestantism at large from the purity and simplicity of the everlasting gospel of righteousness by faith that once so powerfully impelled the Reformation.

The second angel's message will have increasing relevance as the end draws near. It will meet its complete fulfillment with the alliance of the various religious organizations that have rejected the first angel's message. The message of the fall of Babylon is repeated in Revelation 18:2-4, which announces the complete downfall of Babylon and calls on those of God's people who are still in the various religious bodies comprising Babylon to separate from them. Says the angel, "Come out of her, my people, lest you share in her sins, and lest you receive of her plagues" (Rev. 18:4).[31]

The Third Angel's Message

"If anyone worships the beast and his image, and receives his mark on his forehead or on his hand, he himself shall also drink of the wine of the wrath of God, which is poured out full strength into the cup of His indignation. And he shall be tormented with fire and brimstone in the presence of the holy angels and in the presence of the Lamb. And the smoke of their torment ascends forever and ever; and they have no rest day or night, who worship the beast and his image, and whoever receives the mark of his name. Here is the patience of the saints; here are those who keep the commandments of God and the faith of Jesus" (Rev. 14:9-12).

The first angel's message proclaims the everlasting gospel and calls for the restoration of the true worship of God as Creator because the judgment hour has arrived. The second angel warns against all humanly originated forms of worship. Finally, the third angel proclaims God's most solemn warning against worshiping the beast and his image—which all who reject the gospel of righteousness by faith ultimately will do.

The beast described in Revelation 13:1-10 is the church-state union that dominated the Christian world for many centuries and was described by Paul as the "man of sin" (2 Thess. 2:2-4) and by Daniel as the "little horn" (Dan. 7:8, 20-25; 8:9-12, KJV). The image of the beast represents that form of apostate religion that will be developed when churches, having lost the true spirit of the Reformation, shall unite with the state to enforce their teachings on others. In uniting church and state they will have become a perfect image to the beast—the apostate church that persecuted for 1260 years. Hence the name *image of the beast.*

The third angel's message proclaims the most solemn and fearful warning in the Bible. It reveals that those who submit to human authority in earth's final crisis will worship the beast and his image rather than God. During this final conflict two distinct classes will develop. One class will advocate a gospel of human devisings and will worship the beast and his image, bringing upon themselves the most grievous judgments. The other class, in marked contrast, will live by the true gospel and "keep the commandments of God and the faith of Jesus" (Rev. 14:9, 12). The final issue involves true and false worship—the true and the false gospel. When this issue is clearly brought before the world, those who reject God's memorial of creatorship—the Bible Sabbath—choosing to worship and honor Sunday in the full knowledge that it is not God's appointed day of worship, will receive the "mark of the beast." This mark is a mark of rebellions; the beast claims its change of the day of worship shows its authority even over God's law.[32]

The third message directs the world's attention to the consequence of refusing to accept the everlasting gospel and God's message of the restoration of true worship. It pictures vividly the final result of people's choices regarding worship. The choice is not an easy one, for whatever one chooses will involve suffering. Those who obey God will experience the wrath of the dragon (Rev. 12:17) and eventually be threatened with death (Rev. 13:15), while those who choose to worship the beast and his image will incur the seven last plagues and finally "the lake of fire" (Rev. 15, 16; 20:14, 15).

But while both choices involve suffering, their outcomes differ. The worshipers of the Creator will escape the deadly wrath of the dragon and stand together with the Lamb on Mount Zion (Rev. 14:1; 7:2, 4). The worshipers of the beast and his image, on the other hand, receive the full wrath of God and die in the presence of the holy angels and the Lamb (Rev. 14:9, 10; 20:14).

Every person will have to choose whom to worship. Either one's choice of righteousness by faith will be revealed as one participates in a form of worship God has endorsed, or one's effectual choice of righteousness by works will be revealed as one participates in a form of worship God has forbidden but which the beast and his image command, a man-made worship. God cannot accept this latter form of worship, because it gives priorities to the commandments of men and not to those of God. It seeks justification through the works of man and not by faith that comes through a total surrender to God as Creator, Redeemer, and Re-creator. In this sense, then, the message of the third angel is the message of justification by faith.

God has His children in all churches, but through the remnant church He proclaims a message that is to restore His true worship by calling His people out of the apostasy and preparing them for Christ's return. Recognizing that many of God's people have yet to join them, the remnant sense their inadequacies and weaknesses when they try to fulfill this solemn mission. They realize that it is only through God's grace that they can accomplish their momentous task.

In light of the soon coming of Christ and the need to prepare to meet Him, God's urgent, compassionate call comes home to each of us: "Come out of her, my people, lest you share in her sins, and lest you receive of her plagues. For her sins have reached to heaven, and God has remembered her iniquities" (Rev. 18:4, 5).

References

1. The dazzling brilliance of the sun surrounding the pure woman (Rev. 12:1) represents, according to various commentators, the light of the New Testament gospel, which empowered and gave unction to the early church. The moon, mirroring the light of the sun, fitly symbolizes the Old Testament's reflection of the light of the gospel through the predictions and rites that pointed forward to the cross and the One to come. The crown of the twelve stars represents the church's roots, arising in the Old Testament in the fathers of the twelve tribes and extending in the New through the twelve apostles.

2. The use of the year-day principle to calculate prophetic time was mentioned earlier in reference to the Messianic prophecy of Daniel 9. See chapter 4 of this book.

3. *SDA Bible Commentary*, vol. 4, p. 835.

4. The name *pope* literally comes from the Low Latin *papa*, Low Greek, *papas*, "father," "bishop"; Greek *pappas*, "father." The pope is "the bishop of Rome; the head of the Roman Catholic Church." (*Webster's New Universal Unabridged Dictionary*, 2nd ed. [New York, NY: Simon & Schuster, 1979]).

5. The papacy can be defined as the system of ecclesiastical government in which supreme authority is vested in the pope.

6. Letter, Justinian to Pope John, quoted in Letter, Pope John to Justinian, in Codex Justinianus (Code of Justinian), book I, title 1, 8, *Corpus Juris Civilis*, comp., Paulus Krueger, 12th ed. (Berlin: Weidmannsche Verlaglsbuchhandlung, 1959), vol. 2, p. 11, in *The Civil Law*, ed. and trans. S. P. Scott, (Cincinnati, OH: Central Trust Comp., 1932), vol. 12, pp. 11-13. Cf. *Justiniani Novellae* (Justinian's New Constitutions), 131st New Constitution, Chap. 2, *Corpus Juris Civilis*, comps. Rudolfus Schoell and Guilelmus Kroll, 7th ed., vol. 3, p. 665, in *Civil Law*, vol. 17, p. 125. See also Don Neufeld and Julia Neuffer, eds., *Seventh-day Adventist Bible Student's Source Book* (Washington, D. C.: Review and Herald, 1962), pp. 684, 685.

7. Letter, Justinian to Archbishop Epiphanius of Constantinople, March 26, 533, in Codex Justinianus, Book I, title 1, 7, *Corpus Juris Civilis*, Krueger's ed., vol. 2, p. 8 as quoted in *Source Book*, p. 685.

8. See, e.g., "Persecution," *Encyclopedia of Religion and Ethics*, ed. James Hastings (New York, NY: Charles Scribner's Sons, 1917), vol. 9, pp. 749-57; John Dowling, *The History of Romanism: From the Earliest Corruptions of Christianity to the Present Time*, 10th ed. (New York, NY: Edward Walker, 1846), pp. 237-616.

9. This blow severely damaged the prestige of the papacy but did not end its influence. Revelation 13:3 speaks of a healing of the "deadly wound," indicating a revival of the papal influence. In the last days it becomes the most powerful religious influence of the world.

10. George Trevor, *Rome: From the Fall of the Western Empire* (London: The Religious Tract Society, 1868), pp. 439, 440; John Adolphus, *The History of France From the Year 1790 to the Peace Concluded in Amiens in 1802* (London: George Kearsey, 1803), vol. 2, pp. 364-369. See also *Source Book*, pp. 701, 702.

11. Leroy E. Froom, *The Prophetic Faith of Our Fathers* (Washington, D. C.: Review and Herald, 1948), vol. 2, pp. 765-782.

12. Peter Geiermann, *The Convert's Catechism of Catholic Doctrine* (St. Louis, MO: B. Herder Book Co., 1957), pp. 27, 28.

13. *Ibid.*, p. 27.

14. Later, the doctrine of papal infallibility was based on the assumption that (1) "infallibility as an attribute of a divine church is necessarily found in its fullness in her headship'" (2) Peter was infallible in teaching faith and morals, and (3) the pope has inherited from Peter the attributes of the divine church. It was concluded that when speaking *ex cathedra* "the Pope is an infallible Teacher in Faith and Morals" (Geiermann, p. 29). *Ex cathedra* in Latin literally means "from the chair." In reference to the pope it refers to his official pronouncements addressed to the Catholic Church.

15. For claims made for the papacy, see, e.g., Lucius Ferraris, "Papa," art. 2, in

Prompta Bibliotheca (Venice; Gaspar Storti, 1772), vol. 6, pp. 25-29 as quoted in *Source Book*, p. 680. For the claims of the papacy itself, see, e.g., Pope Leo XIII, Encyclical Letter, Jan. 10, 1890 and June 20, 1894 in *The Great Encyclical Letters of Pope Leo XIII* (New York, NY: Benziger Brothers, 1903), pp. 193, 304. See also *Source Book*, p. 614.

16. *Catechism of the Council of Trent for Parish Priests*, trans. by John A. McHugh and Charles J. Callan (New York, NY: Joseph F. Wagner, Inc., 1958 reprint), pp. 258, 259. See also *Source Book*, pp. 1041-1043.

17. *SDA Bible Commentary*, vol. 7, pp. 47, 48.

18. See Council of Trent, Session IV (April 8, 1546) as quoted in *The Creeds of Christendom*. Ed., Philip Schaff, 6th ed., rev. (Grand Rapids, MI: Baker, 1983), vol. 2, pp. 79-83. See also *Source Book*, pp. 1041-1043.

19. Froom, *Prophetic Faith of Our Fathers*, vol. 2, pp. 528-531.

20. Frederic W. Farrar, *History of Interpretation* (Grand Rapids, MI: Baker, 1979), p.358.

21. *Ibid.*

22. Robert M. Grant, *A Short History of Interpretation of the Bible* (Philadelphia, PA: Fortress Press, 1984), p. 97.

23. Farrar, p. 361.

24. *Ibid.*, 363.

25. Grant, p. 97.

26. Farrar, p. 365.

27. For the origin of the remnant, see Froom, *Prophetic Faith of Our Fathers*, vol. 4; P. Gerard Damsteegt, *Foundations of the Seventh-day Adventist Message and Mission* (Grand Rapids, MI: Wm. B. Eerdmans, 1977).

28. Cf. Damsteegt, "A Theology of Restoration" (paper presented at the Centennial Conference on Evangelism, Andrews University, May 4, 1974).

29. See Midrash Rabbah on Canticles I.6, 4; Tertullian, *Against Marcion*, III, 13; Tertullian, *Answer to the Jews*, 9.

30. Froom, *Prophetic Faith of Our Fathers*, vol. 2, pp. 531, 787.

31. *SDA Bible Commentary*, vol. 7, pp. 828-31.

32. The Catholic Church claims the authority to change the day of worship. "Q. *Which is the Sabbath day?* A. Saturday is the Sabbath day. Q. *Why do we observe Sunday instead of Saturday?* A. We observe Sunday instead of Saturday because the Catholic Church transferred the solemnity from Saturday to Sunday" (Geiermann, p. 50). See also *Source Book*, p. 886. This catechism received the "apostolic blessing" of Pope Pius X, Jan. 25, 1910 (*Ibid.*).

14

Unity in the Body of Christ

The church is one body with many members, called from every nation, kindred, tongue, and people. In Christ we are a new creation; distinctions of race, culture, learning, and nationality, and differences between high and low, rich and poor, male and female, must not be divisive among us. We are all equal in Christ, who by one Spirit has bonded us into one fellowship with Him and with one another; we are to serve and be served without partiality or reservation. Through the revelation of Jesus Christ in the Scriptures we share the same faith and hope and reach out in one witness to all. This unity has its source in the oneness of the triune God, who has adopted us as His children. (Rom. 12:4, 5; 1 Cor. 12:12-14; Matt. 28:19, 20; Ps. 133:1, 2; 2 Cor. 5:16, 17; Acts 17: 26, 27; Gal. 3:27, 29; Col. 3:10-15; Eph. 4:14-16; 4:1-6; John 17:20-23.)

JESUS, HAVING FINISHED HIS WORK ON EARTH (John 17:4), continued to agonize over the condition of His disciples, even the evening before His death.

Jealousy led to arguments over who was the greatest and who would be assigned the highest positions in Christ's kingdom. Jesus' explanation that humility was the substance of His kingdom and that true followers of His would be servants, willingly giving of themselves with no expectation of even thanks in return, seemed to have fallen on deaf ears (Luke 17:10). Even the example He set, stooping to wash their feet when none of them would do it because of the implications, seemed to have been in vain (see chapter 16 of this book).

Jesus is Love. It was His sympathy that kept the masses following Him. Not understanding this unselfish love, His disciples were filled with strong prejudices toward non-Jews, women, "sinners," and the poor, which blinded them to the all-encompassing love of Christ toward these detested ones. When the disciples found Him conversing with a Samaritan woman of ill repute, they had not yet learned that the fields, ripe for harvest, include grain of all varieties, ready to be reaped.

But Christ could not be swayed by tradition, public opinion, or even family control. His irrepressible love reached down and restored broken humanity. Such love, which would set them apart from the careless public, would be the evidence of being true disciples. As He loved, they were to love. The world would forever be able to distinguish Christians—not because of their profession, but because of the revelation of Christ's love in them (cf. John 13:34, 35).

So even in the Garden of Gethsemane the main thing on Christ's mind was the unity of His church—those who had come "out of the world" (John 17:6). He pleaded with His Father for a unity in the church similar to that which the Godhead experienced. I pray "that they all [His followers] may be one, as You, Father, are in Me, and I in You; that they also may be one in Us, that the world may believe that You sent Me" (John 17:21).

Such unity is the church's most powerful witnessing tool, for it gives evidence of Christ's unselfish love for humanity. Said He, "I in them, and You in Me; that they may be made perfect in one, and that the world may know that You have sent Me, and have loved them as You have loved Me" (John 17:23).

Bible Unity and the Church

What kind of unity did Christ have in mind for the visible church today? How is such love and unity possible? What is its foundation? What are its constituents? Does it demand uniformity or allow for diversity? How does unity function?

Unity of the Spirit. The Holy Spirit is the moving force behind church unity. Through Him all believers are led to the church. By Him they are "all baptized into one body" (1 Cor. 12:13). These baptized members are to have a unity Paul described as "the unity of the Spirit" (Eph. 4:3).

The apostle listed the basic components of the unity of the Spirit: "There is one body and one Spirit," he said, "just as you were called in one hope of your calling; one Lord, one faith, one baptism; one God and Father of all, who is above all, and through all, and in you all" (Eph. 4:4-6). The seven-fold repetition of the word *one* emphasizes the complete unity Paul envisioned.

Calling them from every nationality and race, the Holy Spirit baptizes people into one body—the body of Christ, the church. As they grow into Christ, cultural differences are no longer divisive. The Holy Spirit breaks down barriers between high and low, rich and poor, male and female. Realizing that in God's sight they are all equal, they hold one another in esteem.

This unity functions on the corporate level also. It means that local churches everywhere are equal, even though some are recipients of money and missionaries from other countries. Such a spiritual union knows no hierarchy. Nationals and missionaries are equal before God.

The united church has one hope—the "blessed hope" of salvation that will be realized at the "glorious appearing of our great God and Saviour Jesus Christ" (Titus 2:13). This hope is a source of peace and joy, and provides a powerful motive for united witness (Matt. 24:14). It leads to transformation, for "everyone who has this hope in Him purifies himself, just as He is pure" (1 John 3:3).

Through a common faith—personal faith in the atoning sacrifice of Jesus Christ—all become a part of the body. The one baptism that symbolizes Christ's death and resurrection (Rom. 6:3-6) perfectly expresses this faith, witnessing of a union with Christ's body.

Finally, Scripture teaches that there is one Spirit, one Lord, and one God and Father. All aspects of church unity find their foundation in the oneness of the triune God. "There are the diversities of gifts, but the same Spirit. There are differences of ministries, but the same Lord. And there are diversities of activities, but it is the same God who works all in all" (1 Cor. 12:4-6).

The Extent of Unity. Believers experience a unity of mind and judgment. Notice the following exhortations: "Now may the God of patience and comfort grant you to be like-minded toward one another, according to Christ Jesus, that you may with one mind and one mouth glorify the God and Father of our Lord Jesus Christ" (Rom. 15:5, 6). "Now I plead with you, brethren, by the name of our Lord Jesus Christ, that you all speak of the same thing, and that there be no divisions among you, but that you be perfectly joined together in the same mind and in the same judgment" (1 Cor. 1:10). "Be of good comfort, be of one mind, live in peace; and the God of love and peace will be with you" (2 Cor. 13:11).

God's church, then, ought to reveal a unity of feeling, thought, and action. Does this mean that members should have identical feelings, thoughts, and actions? Does biblical unity imply uniformity?

Unity in Diversity. Biblical unity does not mean uniformity. The biblical metaphor of the human body demonstrates that the church's unity exists in diversity.

The body has many organs, all contributing to the optimal performance of the body. Each fulfills a vital, though different, task; none is useless.

This same principle operates in the church. God distributes His gifts "to each one individually as He wills" (1 Cor. 12:11), creating a healthy diversity that benefits the congregation. Not all members think alike, nor are they qualified to perform the same work. All, however, function under the direction of the same Spirit, building up the church to the best of their God-given abilities.

To accomplish its mission, the church needs the contributions of all the gifts. Together, they provide a total evangelistic thrust. The success of the church does not depend on each member's being the same and doing the same as every other member; rather, it depends on all the members performing their God-assigned tasks.

In nature the vine with its branches provides an illustration of unity in diversity. Jesus used the metaphor of the vine to depict the believer's union with Himself (John 15:1-6). The branches, the believers, are the extensions of the True Vine—Christ. Like every branch and leaf, each individual Christian differs from the others, yet a oneness exists, since all receive their nourishment from the same source, the Vine. The branches of the vine are individually separate and do not blend into each other: yet each branch will be in fellowship with the others if they are joined to the same parent stalk. They all receive nourishment from the same source: assimilating the same life-giving properties.

So Christian unity depends on the grafting of the members into Christ. From Him comes the power that vitalizes Christian life. He is the source of the talent and power necessary to accomplish the church's task. Being linked to Him shapes the tastes, habits, and lifestyles of all Christians. Through Him, all members are linked to one another, and joined in a common mission. As the members abide in Him, selfishness is driven away and Christian unity is established, enabling them to accomplish His mission.

So while there are different temperaments in the church, all work under one Head. While there are many gifts, there is but one Spirit. Though the gifts differ, there is harmonious action. "It is the same God who works all in all" (1 Cor. 12:6).

Unity of Faith. Diversity of gifts does not mean a diversity of beliefs, however. In the last days God's church will be composed of a people who share a platform of the everlasting gospel—their lives characterized by the observance of the commandments of God and the faith of Jesus (Rev. 14:12). Together, they proclaim to the world God's invitation to salvation.

How Important Is Church Unity?

Unity is essential to the church. Without it the church will fail to accomplish its sacred mission.

Unity Makes the Church's Efforts Effective. In a world torn apart by dissent and conflict, the love and unity among church members of different personalities, temperaments, and dispositions witnesses to the church's message more powerfully than anything else could. This unity provides incontrovertible evidence of their connection with heaven and of the validity of their credentials as disciples of Christ (John 13:35). It proves the power of God's Word.

Conflict between professed Christians has raised disgust in unbelievers and has been perhaps the greatest obstacle to their acceptance of the Christian faith. True unity among believers defuses this attitude. It is a major evidence to the world, Christ said, that He is their Saviour (John 17:23).

Unity Reveals the Reality of God's Kingdom. A truly united church on earth reveals that its members are serious in their expectation of living together in heaven. Unity on earth demonstrates the reality of God's eternal kingdom. To those who live in this way the Scripture will be fulfilled, "How wonderful it is, how pleasant, for God's people to live together in harmony!" (Ps. 133:1, TEV).

Unity Shows the Strength of the Church. Unity brings strength; disunity, weakness. A church is truly prosperous and strong when its members are united with Christ and one another, working in harmony for the salvation of the world. Then and only then are they in the truest sense "God's fellow workers" (1 Cor. 3:9).

Christian unity challenges our increasingly disunited world, torn apart by loveless selfishness. The unified church exhibits the answer for a society divided by culture, race, sex, and nationality. A unified church will resist satanic attacks. Indeed, the powers of darkness are impotent against the church whose members love one another as Christ has loved them.

The positive and beautiful effect of a unified church can be compared with the performance of an orchestra. In the moments before the conductor appears, as the musicians tune their instruments and warm up, they produce a cacophony. When the conductor appears, however, the chaotic noise stops, and all eyes focus on him. Every member of the orchestra sits poised, ready to perform as he directs. Following the conductor's leading the orchestra produces beautiful, harmonious music.

"Unity in the body of Christ means blending the instrument of my life in the great orchestra of the called-out ones, under the baton of the divine Conductor. At His downbeat, following creation's original score, we have the privilege of performing for mankind the symphony of God's love."[1]

The Achievement of Unity

If the church is to experience unity, both the Godhead and believers must be involved in bringing it about. What is the source of unity—how can it be obtained? What role do believers play?

The Source of Unity. Scripture points out that unity finds its sources in (1) the keeping power of the Father (John 17:11), (2) the Father's glory that Christ gave to His followers (John 17:22), and (3) Christ's indwelling in the believers (John 17:23). The Holy Spirit, the "Spirit of Christ" in the midst of the body of Christ, is the cohesive power and presence that keeps each segment united.

Like the hub and spokes of a wheel, the closer church members (the spokes) come to Christ (the hub) the closer they come to each other. "The secret of true unity in the church and in the family is not diplomacy, not management, not a superhuman effort to overcome difficulties—though there will be much of this to do—but union with Christ."[2]

The Holy Spirit as Unifier. As the "Spirit of Christ" and the "Spirit of truth," the Holy Spirit brings about unity.

1. The focus of unity. As the Spirit enters believers, He causes them to transcend human prejudices of culture, race, sex, color, nationality, and status (see Gal. 3:26-28). He accomplishes this by bringing Christ within the heart. Those whom He inhabits will focus on Jesus, not themselves. Their union with Christ establishes the bond of unity among themselves—the fruit of the indwelling Spirit. They will then minimize their differences and unite in mission to glorify Jesus.

2. The role of the spiritual gifts in achieving unity. How attainable is the goal of church unity? When Christ began His mediatorial work at the side of His Father in heaven, He made certain that the goal of having His people united was not an illusion. Through the Holy Spirit He gave special gifts particularly intended to establish "the unity of the faith" among believers.

In discussing these gifts, Paul said, Christ "gave some to be apostles, some prophets, some evangelists, and some pastors and teachers." These gifts were given to the church for the "equipping of the saints for the work of ministry, for the edifying of the body of Christ, till we all come to the unity of the faith and of the knowledge of the Son of God, to a perfect man, to the measure of the stature of the fullness of Christ" (Eph. 4:11-13).

These unique gifts are designed to develop the "unity of the Spirit" into a "unity of faith" (Eph. 4:3, 13) so that believers would be mature and firm and "no longer be infants, tossed back and forth by the waves, and blown here and there by every wind of teaching and by the cunning and craftiness of men in their deceitful scheming" (Eph. 4:14, NIV—see chapter 17 of this book).

Through these gifts believers speak the truth in love and grow up into Christ, the Head of the church—developing a dynamic unity of love. In Christ, Paul said, "the whole body, joined and held together by every supporting ligament, grows and builds itself up in love, as each part does its work" (Eph. 4:16, NIV).

3. The basis for unity. It is as the "Spirit of truth" (John 15:26) that the Holy Spirit works to fulfill Christ's promise. His task is to guide believers into all truth (John 16:13). Clearly, then, Christ-centered truth is the basis of unity.

The Spirit's mission is to guide believers into the "truth as it is in Jesus." Such a study has a unifying effect. Yet study alone is not sufficient to bring about true union. Fellowship, spiritual gifts, and love are all very important, but their fullness comes through the One who said, "I am the way, the truth, and the life" (John 14:6). Christ prayed, "Sanctify them by Your truth. Your word is truth" (John 17:17). To experience unity, believers, then, must receive the light as it shines from the Word.

As this truth as it is in Jesus dwells in the heart, it will refine, elevate, and purify the life, eliminating all prejudice and friction.

Christ's New Commandment. Like man, the church was made in the image of God. As each member of the Godhead has love for the others, so will the members of the church love one another. Christ has commanded believers to demonstrate their love to God by loving others as themselves (Matt. 22:39).

Jesus Himself carried the principle of love to the ultimate at Calvary. Just before His death He extended the injunction He laid down earlier, giving His disciples a new commandment: "Love one another as I have loved you" (John 15:12; cf. 13:34). It was as if He were saying to them, "I'm asking you not to stand up for your rights, to see that you get your due, to sue if you don't. I'm asking you to bare your back to the whip, to turn your other cheek, to be falsely accused, mocked, derided, to be bruised, broken, nailed to a cross and buried, if it takes that to love others. For that is loving others as I love you."

1. The impossible possibility. How can we love as Christ loved? Impossible! Christ asks the impossible, but He can accomplish the impossible. He promises, "And I, if I am lifted up from the earth, will draw all peoples to Myself" (John 12:32). For unity in the body of Christ is incarnational—the unity of believers with God through the Word that became flesh. It is also relational—the unity of believers through their common roots in the Vine. And finally, it is rooted in the cross—the love of Calvary dawning within believers.

2. Unity at the cross. Church unity takes place at the cross. It is only as we realize that we cannot and do not love like Jesus that we admit our need of His abiding presence and believe Him when He said: "Without Me you can do nothing" (John 15:5). At the cross we realize that He did not die just for us but for every person on earth. This means He loves all nationalities, races, colors, and classes. He loves each equally, whatever their differences may be. That's why unity is rooted in God. Man's narrow vision tends to separate people. The cross breaks through human blindness and puts God's price tag on human beings. It shows that none are worthless. All are wanted. If Christ loves them, so should we.

When Christ predicted that His crucifixion would draw all to Him, He meant that the magnetic drawing power of Himself, the greatest of sufferers, would bring unity to His body, the church. The vast gulf between heaven and us—the gulf that Christ crossed—makes the small step across the street or town we must take to reach a brother insignificant.

Calvary means, "Carry each other's burdens" (Gal. 6:2, NIV). He bore the entire burden of all mankind, which crushed out His life so that He could give us life and set us free to help each other.

Steps to Unity. Unity does not come automatically. Believers must take steps to secure it.

1. Unity in the home. An ideal training ground for church unity is the home (see chapter 23 of this book). If we learn wise management, kindness, gentleness, patience, and love with the cross as its center, at home, we will be able to carry these principles out in the church.

2. Aim for unity. We will never attain unity unless we conscientiously work for it. And we can never complacently consider ourselves to have attained. We must daily pray for unity and carefully cultivate it.

We should minimize differences and avoid arguing about nonessentials. Instead of focusing on what divides us, we should talk about the many precious truths on which we agree. Talk of unity and pray that Christ's prayer will be fulfilled. By doing so we can realize the unity and harmony God wants us to have.

3. Work together toward a common goal. The church will not experience unity until, acting as one unit, it is involved in proclaiming the gospel of Jesus Christ. Such a mission provides an ideal training for learning harmony. It teaches believers that they are all individual parts of God's mighty family and that the happiness of the whole depends upon the well-being of each believer.

In His ministry Christ melded together the restoration of the soul and the restoration of the body. And when He sent His disciples on their mission He insisted on a similar emphasis: preaching and healing (Luke 9:2; 10:9).

So Christ's church must carry on both the work of preaching—the ministry of the Word—and medical missionary work. Neither of these phases of God's work is to be carried out independently or become all-absorbing. As in Christ's day, a balance, working together in harmony, should characterize our work for souls.

Those involved in the various phases of church work must cooperate closely if they wish to give the gospel invitation to the world in a powerful way. Some feel that unity implies consolidating for efficiency. However, the body metaphor indicates that each organ, large or small, is important. Cooperation—not rivalry—is God's plan for His worldwide work. Thus unity within the body of Christ becomes a demonstration of Christ's unselfish love so magnificently revealed at the cross.

4. Develop a global perspective. A church is not exhibiting true unity unless it is actively building up God's work in all parts of the earth. The church should do everything it can to avoid national, cultural, or regional isolationism. To achieve unity of judgment, purpose, and action, believers of different nationalities must mingle and serve together.

The church must take care not to foster separate national interests, which would harm its united, worldwide thrust. Church leadership should operate in such a way as to preserve equality and unity, taking care not to develop programs or facilities in any one area that must be financed at the expense of building the work in other areas of the world.

5. Avoid attitudes that divide. Attitudes of selfishness, pride, self-confidence, self-sufficiency, superiority, prejudice, criticism, denunciation, and faultfinding among believers contribute to disunity in the church. Often a loss of the first love in the Christian experience lies behind these attitudes. A fresh look at God's gift in Christ at Calvary can renew love for one another (1 John 4:9-11). The grace of God mediated by the Holy Spirit can subdue these sources of disunity in the natural heart.

When one New Testament church developed the problem of disunity, Paul counseled the church to "walk in the Spirit" (Gal. 5:16). Through constant prayer we are to seek the guidance of the Spirit, who will lead us into unity. Walking in the Spirit produces the fruit of the Spirit—love, joy, peace, patience, kindness, goodness, faithfulness, gentleness and self-control—which is an effective antidote to disunity (Gal. 5:22, 23).

James spoke out against another root of disunity—basing how we treat individuals on their wealth or status. In strong terms he denounced such favoritism: "If you show partiality, you commit sin, and are convicted by the law as transgressors" (James 2:9). Because God is impartial (Acts 10:34), we should not give deference to some church members more than to others because of position, wealth, or abilities. We may respect them, but we ought not consider them more precious to our heavenly Father than the lowliest child of God. Christ's words correct our perspective: "Whatever you did for one of the least of these brothers of mine, you did for me" (Matt. 25:40, NIV). He is represented in the person of the least, as well as in the most blessed of members. All are His children and hence equally important to Him.

Just as our Lord, the Son of man, became a brother to every son and daughter of Adam, so we His followers are called to reach out in unity of mind and mission in a redemptive way to our brothers and sisters from "every nation, tribe, tongue, and people" (Rev. 14:6).

References

1. Benjamin F. Reaves, "What Unity Means to Me," *Adventist Review*, December 4, 1986, p. 20.

2. Ellen G. White, *The Adventist Home* (Nashville, TN: Southern Publishing Assn., 1952), p. 179.

Baptism

15

By baptism, we confess our faith in the death and resurrection of Jesus Christ and testify of our death to sin and of our purpose to walk in newness of life. Thus we acknowledge Christ as Lord and Saviour, become His people, and are received as members by His church. Baptism is a symbol of our union with Christ, the forgiveness of our sins, and our reception of the Holy Spirit. It is by immersion in water and is contingent on an affirmation of faith in Jesus and evidence of repentance of sin. It follows instruction in the Holy Scriptures and acceptance of their teachings. (Rom. 6:1-6; Col. 2:12, 13; Acts 16:30-33; 22:16; 2:38; Matt. 28:19, 20.)

NYANGWIRA, WHO LIVED IN CENTRAL AFRICA, did not consider baptism to be merely an option. For more than a year she had eagerly studied the Bible. She longed to become a Christian.

One evening she shared with her husband the things she had learned. Outraged, he shouted, "I don't want this kind of religion in my home, and if you keep on studying, I'll kill you." Although she was crushed, Nyangwira continued studying and soon was ready for baptism.

Before leaving for the baptismal service Nyangwira knelt respectfully before her husband and told him she was to be baptized. He picked up his large hunting knife and shouted, "I have told you that I do not want you to be baptized. The day you are baptized, I will kill you."

But Nyangwira, determined to follow her Lord, left with her husband's threats resounding in her ears.

Before entering the water, she confessed her sins and dedicated her life to her Saviour, not knowing whether she would be laying down her life for her Lord that day, too. Peace filled her heart as she was baptized.

When she returned home, she brought the knife to her husband.

"Have you been baptized? he asked angrily.

"Yes," replied Nyangwira simply. "Here is the knife."

"Are you ready to be killed?"

"Yes, I am."

Amazed at her courage, the husband no longer had a desire to kill her.[1]

How Important Is Baptism?

Is baptism worth risking one's life for? Does God really require baptism? Does salvation hinge on whether one is baptized?

Jesus' Example. One day Jesus left the carpenter shop in Nazareth, bade His family farewell, and went to the Jordan, where His cousin John was preaching. Approaching John, He asked to be baptized. Amazed, John tried to dissuade Him, saying, "I have need to be baptized by You, and are You coming to me?"

"Permit it to be so now," Jesus answered, "for thus it is fitting for us to fulfill all righteousness" (Matt. 3:13-15).

Jesus' baptism forever gave this ordinance[2] divine sanction (Matt. 3:13-17; cf. Matt. 21:25). Baptism is an aspect of righteousness in which all can participate. Since Christ, the Sinless One, was baptized to "fulfill all righteousness," we, who are sinners, ought to do the same.

Jesus' Commandment. At the end of His ministry Christ commanded His disciples: "Go therefore and make disciples of all the nations, baptizing them in the name of the Father and of the Son and of the Holy Spirit, teaching them to observe all things that I have commanded you" (Matt. 28:19, 20).

In this commission Christ made clear that He required baptism of those who wished to become a part of His church, His spiritual kingdom. As, through the disciples' ministry, the Holy Spirit brought people to repent and to accept Jesus as their Saviour, they were to be baptized in the name of the triune God. Their baptism would demonstrate that they had entered into a personal relationship with Christ and were committed to living in harmony with the principles of His kingdom of grace. Christ concluded His mandate to baptize with assurance, "And lo, I am with you always, even to the end of the age."

After Christ's ascension the apostles proclaimed the necessity and urgency of baptism (Acts 2:38; 10:48; 22:16). In response, multitudes were baptized, forming the New Testament church (Acts 2:41, 47; 8:12) and accepting the authority of the Father, the Son, and the Holy Spirit.

Baptism and Salvation. Christ taught that "He who believes and is baptized will be saved" (Mark 16:16). In the apostolic church, baptism automatically followed acceptance of Christ. It was a confirmation of the new believer's faith (cf. Acts 8:12; 16:30-34).

Peter used the experience of Noah during the Flood to illustrate the relationship between baptism and salvation. In antediluvian times sin had reached such proportions that, through Noah, God warned the world to repent or face destruction. Only eight persons believed, entered the ark, and "were saved through water." "There is also an antitype which now saves us," Peter said, "namely baptism (not the removal of the filth of the flesh, but the answer of a good conscience toward God), through the resurrection of Jesus Christ" (1 Peter 3:20, 21).

Peter explained that we are saved by baptism as Noah and his family were saved through water. Of course God, not the flood waters, saved Noah. By analogy, it is the blood of Christ, not the water of baptism, that removes sin from the believer. "But baptism, like [Noah's] obedience in entering the ark, is 'the answer of a good conscience toward God.' When man by God's power gives "the answer," salvation provided 'by the resurrection of Jesus Christ' becomes effective."[3]

However, while baptism is vitally linked to salvation, it does not guarantee salvation.[4] Paul considered Israel's exodus experience to be a symbolic representation of baptism:[5] "I do not want you to be unaware that all our fathers were under the cloud, all passed through the sea, all were baptized into Moses in the cloud and in the sea, all ate the same spiritual food, and all drank the same spiritual drink." "Immersed" in water—the cloud above and the water on each side—the people of Israel were symbolically baptized as they passed through the Red Sea. Yet in spite of this experience "God was not well pleased" with most of them (1 Cor. 10:1-5). So today, baptism does not automatically assure salvation. Israel's experience was written for our "admonition, on whom the ends of the ages have come. Therefore let him who thinks he stands take heed lest he fall" (1 Cor. 10:11, 12).

"One Baptism"

The administration of baptism in the Christian world varies. Some employ *immersion*, or dipping; others *aspersion*, or sprinkling; and still others *affusion*, or pouring. Characteristic of the unity the Spirit brings in God's church is the practice of "one baptism" (Eph. 4:5).[6] What does the Bible reveal about the meaning of the term *to baptize*—about the practice itself and its spiritual significance?

The Meaning of the Word Baptize. The English word *baptize* comes from the Greek verb *baptize*, which implies immersion, since it is derived from the verb *bapto*, meaning "to dip in or under."[7] When the verb *to baptize* refers to water baptism it carries the idea of immersing, or dipping a person under water.[8]

In the New Testament the verb *to baptize* is used (1) to refer to water baptism (e.g., Matt. 3:6; Mark 1:9; Acts 2:41); (2) as a metaphor of Christ's suffering and death (Matt. 20:22, 23; Mark 10:38, 39; Luke 12:50); (3) to the coming of the Holy Spirit (Matt. 3:11; Mark 1:8; Luke 3:16; John 1:33; Acts 1:5; 11:16); and (4) of ablutions or the ritual washing of the hands (Mark 7:3, 4; Luke 11:38). This fourth usage simply denotes washings to cleanse from ceremonial impurities and does not legitimize baptism by pouring.[9] Scripture uses the noun *baptism* of both water baptism and Christ's death (Matt. 3:7; 20:22).

J. K. Howard observes that the New Testament offers "no evidence that sprinkling was ever an apostolic practice, indeed the evidence all points to it being a late introduction."[10]

Baptism in the New Testament. The incidents of water baptism the New Testament records involved immersion. We read that John baptized *in* the river Jordan (Matt. 3:6; cf. Mark 1:5) and "in Aenon near Salim, because there was much water there" (John 3:23). Only immersion would require "much water."

John immersed Jesus. He baptized Jesus "*in* the Jordan" and after the baptism Jesus "*came up out* of the water" (Mark 1:9, 10, RSV; cf. Matt. 3:16).[11]

The apostolic church baptized by immersion also. When Philip the evangelist baptized the Ethiopian eunuch, they both "went down into the water" and "came up out of the water" (Acts 8:38, 39).

Baptism in History. Before the Christian era the Jews baptized their proselytes by immersion. The Essenes at Qumran followed the practice of immersing both members and converts.[12]

Evidence from the paintings in catacombs and churches, from the mosaics on floors, walls, and ceilings, from sculptured reliefs, and from drawings in ancient New Testaments "overwhelmingly testifies to immersion as the normal mode of baptism in the Christian church during the first ten to fourteen centuries."[13] Baptisteries in the ancient cathedrals, churches, and ruins in North Africa, Turkey, Italy, France, and elsewhere still testify to the antiquity of this practice.[14]

The Meaning of Baptism

Baptism's meaning is intimately related to its mode. Alfred Plummer said, "It is only when baptism is administered by immersion that its full significance is seen."[15]

Symbol of Christ's Death and Resurrection. As covering by waters symbolized overwhelming trouble and afflictions (Ps. 42:7; 69:2; 124:4, 5), so Jesus' water baptism represented a prophetic enactment of His suffering, death, and burial (Mark 10:38; Luke 12:50), and His emergence from the water spoke of His subsequent resurrection (Rom. 6:3-5).

Baptism would have had no significance as a symbol of Christ's passion "if the apostolic church had practiced a mode of baptism other than immersion." Therefore "the strongest argument for baptism by immersion is a theological one."[16]

Symbol of Being Dead to Sin and Alive to God. In baptism believers enter into the passion experience of our Lord. Paul said, "Do you not know that as many of us as were baptized into Christ Jesus were baptized into His death? Therefore we were buried with Him through baptism into death, that just as Christ was raised from the dead...we also should walk in newness of life" (Rom. 6:3, 4).

The intimacy of the believer's relationship with Christ is revealed through expressions like "baptized into Christ Jesus," "baptized into His death," and "buried with Him through baptism." Howard noted, "In the symbolic act of baptism the believer enters into the death of Christ, and in a real sense that death becomes his death; and he enters into the resurrection of Christ, and that resurrection becomes his resurrection."[17] What does the believer's entering into the passion of our Lord imply?

1. Death to sin. In baptism believers "have been united together in the likeness of His [Christ's] death" (Rom. 6:5) and "crucified with Christ" (Gal. 2:20). This means "our old man was crucified with Him, that the old body of sin might be done away with, that we should no longer be slaves of sin. For he who has died has been freed from sin" (Rom. 6:6-8).

Believers have renounced their former lifestyle. They are dead to sin and confirm that the "old things have passed away" (2 Cor. 5:17), their lives being hid with Christ in God. Baptism symbolizes the crucifixion of the old life. It is not only a death but also a burial. We are "buried with Him in baptism" (Col. 2:12). As a burial follows a person's death, so when the believer goes down into the watery grave, the old life that passed away when he accepted Jesus Christ is buried.

In baptism believers renounce the world. In obedience to the command

"Come out from among them and be separate, says the Lord. Do not touch what is unclean" (2 Cor. 6:17), candidates make public their forsaking of Satan's service and their receiving of Christ into their lives.

In the apostolic church the call to repentance included the call to baptism (Acts 2:38). Thus baptism also marks true repentance. Believers die to their transgressing of the law and obtain forgiveness of sin through the cleansing blood of Jesus Christ. The baptismal ceremony is a demonstration of an inner cleansing—the washing away of sins that have been confessed.

2. Alive to God. Christ's resurrection power goes to work in our lives. It enables us to walk in newness of life (Rom. 6:4)—dead now to sin, "but alive to God in Christ Jesus our Lord" (Rom. 6:11). We testify that the only hope of a life victorious over the old nature is in the grace of a risen Lord who has provided a new spiritual life through the energizing power of the Holy Spirit. This new life lifts us to a higher plateau of human experience, giving us new values, aspirations, and desires that focus on a commitment to Jesus Christ. We are new disciples of our Saviour, and baptism is the sign of our discipleship.

Symbol of a Covenant Relationship. In Old Testament times circumcision marked the covenantal relationship between God and Abraham (Gen. 17:1-11).

The Abrahamic covenant had both spiritual and national aspects. Circumcision was a mark of national identity. Abraham himself and all the males of his family eight days old and older were to be circumcised (Gen. 17:10-14; 25-27). Any male not circumcised was to be "cut off" from God's people because he had broken the covenant (Gen. 17:14).

That the covenant was made between God and Abraham, an adult, reveals its spiritual dimension. Abraham's circumcision signified and confirmed his previous experience of justification by faith. His circumcision was "a seal of the righteousness of the faith which he had while still uncircumcised" (Rom. 4:11).

But circumcision alone did not guarantee entrance into the true spiritual dimension of the covenant. Frequently, God's spokesmen warned that nothing less than spiritual circumcision would suffice. "Circumcise the foreskin of your heart, and be stiff-necked no longer" (Deut. 10:16; cf. 30:6; Jer. 4:4). The "uncircumcised in the heart" were to be punished with the Gentiles (Jer. 9:25, 26).

When the Jews rejected Jesus as the Messiah, they broke their covenant relationship with God, terminating their special status as His chosen people (Dan. 9:24-27—see chapter 4 of this book). Although God's covenant and His promises remained the same, He chose a new people. Spiritual Israel replaced the Jewish nation (Ga. 3:27-29; 6:15, 16).

Christ's death ratified the new covenant. People entered this covenant through spiritual circumcision—a response of faith to Jesus' atoning death. Christians have "the gospel for the uncircumcised" (Gal. 2:7). The new covenant requires an "inward faith" and not an "outward rite" of those who would belong to spiritual Israel. One can be a Jew through birth, but one can be a Christian only through the new birth. "For in Christ Jesus neither circumcision nor uncircumcision avail anything, but faith working through love" (Gal. 5:6). What matters is "circumcision is that of the heart, in the Spirit" (Rom. 2:28, 29).

Baptism, the sign of a saving relationship with Jesus, represents this spiritual circumcision. "In Him you were also circumcised with the circumcision made without hands, by putting off the body of the sins of the flesh, by the circumcision of Christ, buried with Him in baptism, in which you also were raised with Him through faith in the working of God who raised Him from the dead" (Col. 2:11, 12).

"Having the 'body of flesh' removed through the spiritual circumcision performed by Jesus, the one baptized now 'puts on Christ' and enters into the covenant relationship with Jesus. As a result he is in line to receive the fulfillment of the covenant promises."[18] "For as many of you as were baptized into Christ have put on Christ....If you are Christ's, then you are Abraham's offspring, heirs according to promise" (Gal. 3:27-29, RSV). Those who have entered into this covenant relationship experience God's assurance, "I will be their God, and they shall be My people" (Jer. 31:33).

Symbol of Consecration to Christ's Service. At His baptism Jesus received a special outpouring of the Holy Spirit, signifying His anointing or dedication to the mission His Father had assigned Him (Matt. 3:13-17; Acts 10:38). His experience reveals that water baptism and Spirit baptism belong together, that a baptism void of the reception of the Holy Spirit is incomplete.

In the apostolic church the outpouring of the Holy Spirit generally followed water baptism. So today, when we are baptized in the name of the Father, the Son, and the Holy Spirit, we are dedicated, consecrated, and united with the three great powers of heaven and to the spreading of the everlasting gospel.

The Holy Spirit prepares us for this ministry by purifying our hearts from sin. John declared that Jesus "will baptize you with the Holy Spirit and fire" (Matt. 3:11). Isaiah revealed that God would cleanse His people from their impurities "by the spirit of judgment and by the spirit of burning" (Isa. 4:4). I will "thoroughly purge away your dross," God said, "and take away all your alloy" (Isa. 1:25). "God is a consuming fire" to sin (Heb. 12:29). The Holy Spirit will purify the lives of all who surrender to Him, consuming their sins.

Then the Holy Spirit provides them with His gifts. His gifts are "a special divine endowment, given at the time of baptism, to enable the believer to serve the church and to minister to those who have not yet accepted Jesus Christ."[19] The baptism of the Holy Spirit gave the early church the power to witness (Acts 1:5, 8), and only that same baptism will enable the church to complete its mission of proclaiming the everlasting gospel of the kingdom (Matt. 24:14; Rev. 14:6).

Symbol of Entrance Into the Church. As the sign of a person's regeneration or new birth (John 3:3, 5), baptism also marks that person's entrance into Christ's spiritual kingdom.[20] Since it unites the new believer to Christ, it always functions as the door to the church. Through baptism the Lord adds the new disciples to the body of believers—His body, the church (Acts 2:41, 47; 1 Cor. 12:13). Then they are members of God's family. One cannot be baptized without joining the church family.

Qualifications for Baptism[21]

Faith. One prerequisite for baptism is a faith in Jesus' atoning sacrifice as the only means of salvation from sin. Christ said, "He who believes and is baptized will be saved" (Mark 16:16). In the apostolic church only those who believed the gospel were baptized (Acts 8:12, 36, 37; 18:8).

Since "faith comes by hearing, and hearing by the word of God" (Rom. 10:17), instruction is an essential part of baptismal preparation. Christ's great commission confirms the importance of such instruction: "Go therefore and make disciples of all nations, baptizing them in the name of the Father and of the Son and of the Holy Spirit, teaching them to observe all things that I have commanded you" (Matt. 28:19, 20). Becoming a disciple involves thorough instruction.

Repentance. "Repent," said Peter, "and let every one of you be baptized" (Acts 2:38). Instruction in the Word of God produces not only faith but repentance and conversion. In response to God's call people see their lost condition, confess their sinfulness, submit themselves to God, repent of their sin, accept Christ's atonement, and consecrate themselves to a new life with Him. Without conversion they cannot enter a personal relationship with Jesus Christ. Only through repentance can they experience death to sin—a prerequisite for baptism.

Fruits of Repentance. Those who desire baptism must profess faith and experience repentance. But unless they also bring forth "fruits worthy of repentance" (Matt. 3:8) they will not have met the biblical requirements for baptism. Their lives ought to demonstrate their commitment to truth as it is in Jesus and express their love to God through obedience to His commandments. In preparing for baptism they ought to have surrendered erroneous beliefs and practices. The fruits of the Spirit displayed in their lives will reveal that the Lord abides in them and they in Him (John 15:1-8). Unless they give this evidence of their relationship with Christ, they are not yet ready to join the church.[22]

Examination of Candidates. Becoming a church member involves taking a spiritual step—it is not simply a matter of having one's name recorded in a book. Those administering baptism are responsible for determining the readiness of candidates for baptism. They must ascertain the candidate's understanding of the principles for which the church stands and give evidence of a new creation and an enjoyable experience in the Lord Jesus.[23]

Yet they must be careful not to judge the motives of those seeking baptism. "When a person presents himself as a candidate for church membership, we are to examine the fruit of his life, and leave the responsibility of his motive with himself."[24]

Some have been buried alive in the water of baptism. Self did not die. These did not receive a new life in Christ. Those who have joined the church in this way have brought with them the seeds of weakness and apostasy. Their "unsanctified" influence confuses those within and without the church and jeopardizes its witness.

Should Infants and Children Be Baptized? Baptism incorporates new believers into the church within the context of "being born again." Their conversion qualified them for baptism and church membership. Incorporation takes place at the "new birth," not at "infant birth." This is why *believers* were baptized—"both *men* and *women*" (Acts 8:12, 13, 29-38; 9:17, 18; 1 Cor. 1:14). "Nowhere in the New Testament," Karl Barth admitted, "is infant baptism either permitted or commanded."[25] G. R. Beasley-Murray confessed, "I find myself unable to recognize in infant baptism the baptism of the New Testament Church."[26]

Because infants and little children cannot experience conversion, they do not qualify for baptism. Does that mean that they are excluded from the new covenant community? Certainly not! Jesus did not exclude them from His kingdom of grace. "Let the little children come to Me, and do not forbid them," He said, "for of such is the kingdom of heaven.' And He laid His hands on them" (Matt. 19:14, 15). Believing parents fulfill a vital role in guiding their children into a relationship with Christ that will eventually lead them to baptism.

Jesus' positive response to the mothers who brought their children to Him to be blessed has led to the practice of child dedication. For this service parents bring their children to church to be presented or dedicated to God.

At what age should a person be ready for baptism? Individuals can be baptized if they (1) are old enough to understand the meaning of baptism, (2) have surrendered to Christ and converted, (3) understand the fundamental principles of Christianity, and (4) comprehend the significance of church membership. A person puts his salvation in jeopardy only when he has come to the age of accountability and then rejects the influence of the Holy Spirit.

Because individuals differ as to their spiritual maturity at any given age, some are ready for baptism at an earlier age than are others. So we can set no fixed minimum age for baptism. When parents consent to their children's being baptized at an early age, they must accept the responsibility for their spiritual growth and character development.

The Fruit of Baptism

The preeminent fruit baptism bears is a life lived for Christ. Goals and aspirations focus on Christ, not on self. "If then you were raised with Christ, seek those things which are above, where Christ is, sitting at the right hand of God. Set your mind on things above, not on things of the earth" (Col. 3:1, 2). Baptism is not the reaching of the highest peak attainable to the Christian. As we grow spiritually, we acquire Christian graces to be used in serving others on God's plan of multiplication: "Grace and peace be multiplied to you in the knowledge of God and of Jesus our Lord" (2 Peter 1:2). As we remain faithfully committed to our baptismal vows, the Father, Son, and Holy Spirit, in whose name we have been baptized, guarantee that we have access to divine power to assist in every emergency we may face in the postbaptismal life.

The second fruit is a life lived for Christ's church. We are no longer isolated individuals; we have become members of Christ's church. As living stones we make up God's temple (1 Peter 2:2-5). We maintain a special relationship to Christ, the head of the church, from whom we receive our daily graces for growth and development in love (Eph. 4:16). We assume responsibilities within the covenant community, the members of which, bear a responsibility for the newly baptized (1 Cor. 12:12-26). For their own good, as well as that of the church, these new members must be involved in a life of worship, prayer, and loving service (Eph. 4:12).

The final fruit is a life lived in and for the world. It is true that we who have been baptized hold our citizenship in heaven (Phil. 3:20). But we have been called out of the world simply to be trained within the body of Christ to return to the world as servants, participating in Christ's saving ministry. True disciples will not withdraw from the world into the church; we are born into Christ's kingdom as missionaries. Faithfulness to our baptismal covenant involves leading others into the kingdom of grace.[27]

Today God anxiously waits for us to enter into the abundant life He so graciously has provided. "And now why are you waiting? Arise and be baptized, and wash away your sins, calling on the name of the Lord" (Acts 22:16).

References

1. S. M. Samuel, "A Brave African Wife," *Review and Herald*, February 14, 1963, p. 19.

2. An ordinance is an established symbolic religious rite or observance that sets forth the central truths of the gospel and is of universal and perpetual obligation. Christ prescribed two ordinances—baptism and the Lord's Supper. An ordinance is not a sacrament in the sense of being an *opus operatum*—an act that in and of itself imparts grace and effects salvation. Baptism and the Lord's Supper are sacraments only in the sense of being like the *sacramentum*—the oath taken by Roman soldiers to obey their commander even unto death. These ordinances involve a vow of total allegiance to Christ. See Strong, *Systematic Theology* (Philadelphia, PA: Judson Press, 1954), p. 930; "Baptism," *SDA Encyclopedia*, rev. ed., pp. 128, 129.

3. Jemison, *Christian Beliefs*, p. 244.

4. "From the beginning SDA's, in common with their Protestant heritage, have rejected any view of baptism as an *opus operatum*, that is, as an act that, in and of itself, imparts grace and effects salvation" ("Baptism," *SDA Encyclopedia*, rev. ed., p. 128).

5. *SDA Bible Commentary*, rev. ed., vol. 6, p. 740.

6. At times individuals who have experienced baptism by immersion feel convicted that they should be rebaptized. Does this desire conflict with Paul's assertion that there is only "one baptism" (Eph. 4:5)? Paul's practice reveals that it does not. On a visit to Ephesus he met several disciples who had been baptized by John the Baptist. They had experienced repentance and expressed their faith in the coming Messiah (Acts 19:1-5).

These disciples had no clear understanding of the gospel. "When they received baptism at the hand of John, they were holding serious errors. But with clearer light they gladly accepted Christ as their Redeemer, and with this advance step came a change in their obligations. As they received a purer faith, there was a corresponding change in their life and character. In token of this change, and as an acknowledgement of their faith in Christ, they were rebaptized, in the name of Jesus."

"Many a sincere follower of Christ has had a similar experience. A clearer understanding of God's will, places man in a new relation to Him. New duties are revealed. Much which before appeared innocent, or even praiseworthy, is now seen to be sinful….His former baptism does not satisfy him now. He has seen himself a sinner, condemned by the law of God. He has experienced anew a death to sin, and he desires again to be buried with Christ by baptism, that he may walk in newness of life. Such a course is in harmony with the example of Paul in baptizing the Jewish converts. That incident was recorded by the Holy Spirit as an instructive lesson for the church" (White, *Sketches From the Life of Paul* [Battle Creek, MI: Review and Herald, 1883], pp. 132, 133; see also *Seventh-day Adventist Church Manual* [Washington, D. C.: General Conference of Seventh-day Adventists, 1986] rev. ed., p. 50; White, *Evangelism*, pp. 372-375).

Scripture says nothing that would deny rebaptism to individuals who have broken their covenant with God through grievous sin or apostasy and then experienced reconversion and desire a renewal of their covenant (see *Seventh-day Adventist Church Manual*, pp. 51, 162; White, *Evangelism*, p. 375).

7. See Albrecht Oepke, "Bapto, Baptizo," in *Theological Dictionary of the New Testament*, ed. Gerhard Kittel, trans. Geoffrey W. Bromiley (Grand Rapids: Wm. B. Eerdmans Publ. Co., 1964), vol. 1, p. 529. Vine noted that *bapto* "was used among the Greeks to signify the dyeing of a garment, or the drawing of water by dipping a vessel into another, etc." (W. E. Vine, *An Expository Dictionary of Biblical Words* [New York, NY: Thomas Nelson, 1985], p. 50). "To dip," appears three times in the New Testament, in each instance reflecting the meaning "to submerge." In the parable of the rich man and Lazarus, the rich man requested Abraham to permit Lazarus to *dip* the tip of his finger into cold water and bring a drop to moisten his tongue (Luke 16:24). On the night before the crucifixion Jesus identified His betrayer by *dipping* a morsel and handing it to Judas (John 13:26). And when John in vision saw Jesus riding forth as the commander of the armies of heaven, Jesus' garments appeared to John as though they had been *dipped* in blood (Rev. 19:13).

8. George E. Rice, "Baptism: Union With Christ," *Ministry*, May 1982, p. 20.

9. See Albrecht Oepke, "Bapto, Baptizo," in *Theological Dictionary of the New Testament*, vol. 1, p. 535. Cf. Arndt and Gingrich, *Greek-English Lexicon of the New Testament*, p. 131.

10. J.K. Howard, *New Testament Baptism* (London: Pickering & Inglis Ltd., 1970), p. 48.

11. Italics supplied.

12. Matthew Black, *The Scrolls and Christian Origins* (New York: Charles Scribner's Sons, 1961), pp. 96-98. See also "Baptism," *SDA Bible Dictionary*, rev. ed., pp. 118, 119.

13. G.E. Rice, "Baptism in the Early Church," *Ministry*, March 1981, p. 22. Cf. Henry F. Brown, *Baptism Through the Centuries* (Mountain View, CA: Pacific Press, 1965); William L. Lampkin, *A History of Immersion* (Nashville: Broadman Press, 1962); Wolfred N. Cotte, *The Archeology of Baptism* (London: Yates and Alexander, 1876).

14. Brown, *Baptism Through the Centuries*, pp. 49-90.

15. Alfred Plummer, *A Critical and Exegetical Commentary on the Gospel According to S. Luke, The International Critical Commentary*, ed., Samuel R. Driver, *et al.*, 5th ed. (Edinburgh: T. & T. Clark, 1981 reprint), p. 88.

16. "Baptism," *SDA Encyclopedia*, rev. ed., p. 128.

17. Howard, *New Testament Baptism*, p. 69.

18. G.E. Rice, "Baptism: Union With Christ," *Ministry*, May 1982, p. 21.

19. Gottfried Oosterwal, "Every Member a Minister? From Baptism to a Theological Base," *Ministry*, Feb. 1980, pp. 4-7. See also Rex D. Edwards, "Baptism as Ordination," *Ministry*, Aug. 1983, pp. 4-6.

20. White in *SDA Bible Commentary*, rev. ed., vol. 6, p. 1075.

21. If there are qualifications for baptism, how can one be "baptized for the dead"? The following interpretation preserves the harmony of the biblical message:

In 1 Corinthians 15 Paul stresses the significance of the resurrection from the dead and rejects the notion that there is no resurrection. He shows that if there is no resurrection the believer's faith is in vain and futile (1 Cor. 15:14, 17). Along the same lines he argues "what will they do who are baptized for the dead, if the dead do not rise at all? Why then are they baptized for the dead?" (1 Cor. 15:29).

Some have interpreted the expression "baptized for the dead" as a reference to vicarious baptism by believers for dead persons. In light of the biblical qualifications for baptism one cannot maintain such a view. W. Robertson Nicoll points out that what Paul is referring to was a "normal experience, that the death of Christians leads to the conversion of survivors, who in the first instance 'for the sake of the dead' (their beloved dead), and in the hope of reunion, turn to Christ." Paul describes such converts "baptized for the dead." The hope of future blessedness, allying itself with family affections and friendship, was one of the most powerful factors in the early spread of Christianity" (W. Robertson Nicoll, ed., *The Expositor's Greek Testament* [Grand Rapids, MI: Wm. B Eerdmans, 1956], vol. 2, p. 931. M. Raeder points out that the preposition "for" [*huper* in Greek] in the expression "baptized for the dead" is a preposition of purpose. This means that this baptism was "for the sake of" or "because of the dead for the purpose of being reunited with dead Christian relatives at the resurrection" [M. Raeder, "Vikariatstaufe in 1 K. 15:29?" *Zeitschrift fur die Neutestamentlich Wissenschaft*, 45 (1955), pp. 258-260 quoted by Harold Riesenfeld, "Huper," *Theological Dictionary of the New Testament*, vol. 8, p. 513-. Cf. Howard, *New Testament Baptism*, pp. 108, 109).

Howard states that in its context Paul's argument in 1 Corinthians 15:29 runs, "If Christ has not risen those who have died 'in Christ' have perished, and, with no hope, we become hopeless and wretched, especially those who have entered the Christian community and have been baptized for the sake of those who have died in Christ, hoping to be reunited with them" (Howard, "Baptism for the Dead: A Study of 1 Corinthians 15:29, *Evangelical Quarterly*, ed. F. F. Bruce [Exeter, Eng.: Paternoster Press], July – September, 1965, p. 141).

22. Cf. Damsteegt, "Reaping the Harvest," *Adventist Review*, October 22, 1987, p. 15.

23. See *SDA Church Manual*, p. 41.

24. White, *Evangelism*, p. 313.

25. Karl Barth, *Church Dogmatics*, trans. G. W. Bromiley (Edinburgh: T. & T. Clark, 1969), vol. 4/4, p. 179.

26. G. R. Beasley-Murray, *Baptism in the New Testament* (Grand Rapids, MI: Wm. B. Eerdmans, 1973), p. 392.

27. See Edwards, "Baptism."

The Lord's Supper

16

The Lord's Supper is a participation in the emblems of the body and blood of Jesus as an expression of faith in Him, our Lord and Saviour. In this experience of communion Christ is present to meet and strengthen His people. As we partake, we joyfully proclaim the Lord's death until He comes again. Preparation for the Supper includes self-examination, repentance, and confession. The Master ordained the service of foot washing to signify renewed cleansing, to express a willingness to serve one another in Christlike humility, and to unite our hearts in love. The communion service is open to all believing Christians. (1 Cor. 10:16, 17; 11:23-30; Matt. 26:17-30; Rev. 3:20; John 6:48-63; 13:1-17.)

WITH DUSTY FEET THEY ARRIVED at the upper room for the Passover. Someone had provided a pitcher of water, a basin, and a towel for the customary foot washing, but no one wanted to perform the menial task.

Aware of His impending death, Jesus said sorrowfully, "With fervent desire I have desired to eat this Passover with you before I suffer; for I say to you, I will no longer eat of it until it is fulfilled in the kingdom of God" (Luke 22:15, 16).

The jealousy the disciples harbored against one another filled Jesus' heart with sadness. He realized they were still contending as to who should be considered the greatest in His kingdom (Luke 22:24; Matt. 18:1; 20:21). It was their maneuvering for position, their pride and self-esteem, that prevented the disciples from humbling themselves, from substituting for the servant and washing the feet of others. Would they ever learn that in God's kingdom true greatness is revealed by humility and loving service?

"During supper" (John 13:2, 4, RSV)[1] Jesus quietly arose, took the servant's towel, poured water into the basin, knelt down, and began to wash the disciples' feet. The Master as servant! Understanding the unspoken rebuke, the disciples were filled with shame. When He had completed His work and returned to His place, He said, "If I then, your Lord and Teacher, have washed your feet, you also ought to wash one another's feet. For I have given you an example, that you should do as I have done to you. Truly, truly, I say to you, a servant is not greater than his master; nor is he who is sent greater than he who sent him. If you know these things, blessed are you if you do them" (John 13:14-17, RSV).

Jesus then instituted, in place of the Passover, the service that was to memorialize His great sacrifice: the Lord's Supper. Taking the unleavened bread, He "blessed it and broke it, and gave it to the disciples" and said, "Take, eat; this is My body which is broken for you; do this in remembrance of Me." Then He took the cup of blessing and "gave thanks, and gave it to them, saying, 'Drink from it, all of you. For this is My blood of the new covenant, which is shed for the remission of sins.... This do, as often as you drink it, in remembrance of Me.' For as often as you eat this bread and drink this cup, you proclaim the Lord's death till He comes" (see Matt. 26:26-28; 1 Cor. 11:24-26; 10:16).

The ordinances of foot washing and the Lord's Supper make up the Communion service. Thus, Christ instituted both of these ordinances to assist us with entering into communion with Him.

The Ordinance of Foot Washing

Custom demanded that in celebrating the Passover Jewish families remove all leaven, representing sin, from their homes before the first day of the Week of Unleavened Bread (Ex. 12:15, 19, 20). So believers must confess and repent of all sin—including pride, rivalry, jealousy, resentful feelings, and selfishness—before they can be in the right spirit to have communion with Christ at this deepest level.

To this end Christ instituted the ordinance of foot washing. Not only did He set an example but stated they ought to do the same, and promised them a blessing: "If you know these things, happy are you if you do them" (John 13:17). This ordinance, preceding the Lord's Supper, fulfills the injunction that all should examine themselves so as not to participate in that meal "in an unworthy manner" (1 Cor. 11:27-29).

The Meaning of the Ordinance. This ordinance reveals something about both Christ's mission and the participants' experience.

1. A memorial of Christ's condescension. The ordinance of foot washing memorializes Christ's humiliation in His incarnation and life of service.[2] Although He held a position with the Father amidst celestial glory, He "made Himself of no reputation, taking the form of a servant, and coming in the likeness of men" (Phil. 2:7).

It was humiliating for God's Son to give so selflessly, so lovingly, only to be rejected by the majority of those He came to save. Throughout Christ's earthly life Satan was determined to disgrace Him to the utmost at every turn. What mortification it must have brought Him—the innocent One— to be crucified as a criminal!

Christ lived a life of selfless service. He did not come "to be served, but to serve" (Matt. 20:28). Through the act of foot washing He showed that He would do any service, no matter how lowly, to save people. Thus He impressed His life of service and meekness on the minds of His followers.

In making this preparation ceremony an ordinance, Christ intended to lead believers into a state of tenderness and love that would move them to serve others. This ordinance encourages those who reflect on its significance to treat others with humility and sensitivity. By following Christ in foot washing we profess His spirit: "Through love serve one another" (Gal. 5:13).

Though participation in this service is humbling, it is far from degrading. Who would not feel privileged to bow before Christ and wash the very feet that were nailed to the cross? Jesus said, "Inasmuch as you did it to one of the least of these My brethren, you did it to Me." (Matt. 25:40).

2. A type of higher cleansing. The foot washing did more than clean feet. It represented a higher purification—a cleansing of the heart. When Peter asked Jesus to wash him all over, Jesus said, "He who is bathed needs only to wash his feet, but is completely clean." (John 13:10).

One who takes a bath is clean. However, open, sandaled feet soon became dusty and needed washing again. So it was with the disciples. Their sins had been washed away through baptism, but temptation had led them to cherish pride, jealousy, and evil in their hearts. They were not ready to have intimate communion with their Lord nor to accept the new covenant He was about to make with them. Through the foot washing, Christ desired to prepare them to take part in the Lord's Supper. Except for Judas, the betrayer, their hearts were cleansed by Christ's grace from selfishness and pride, and they were united in love for one another; through Jesus' selfless act they were humbled and became teachable.

Like the disciples, when we have accepted Christ and been baptized, we have been cleansed by His blood. But as we walk the Christian life, we fail. Our feet become dusty. We must come to Christ again and let His cleansing grace wash away the defilement. However, we do not need to be baptized again, for "he who is bathed needs only to wash his feet" (John 13:10).[3] Foot washing as an ordinance reminds us of our need for regular cleansing and that we are totally dependent upon the blood of Christ. Foot washing itself cannot cleanse from sin. Only Christ can purify us.

3. A fellowship of forgiveness. The attitude of forgiveness among the participants indicates that the cleansing this service symbolizes has become effective. Only as we forgive can we experience God's forgiveness. "If you forgive men their trespasses, your heavenly Father will also forgive you. But if you do not forgive men their trespasses, neither will your Father forgive your trespasses" (Matt. 6:14, 15).

Jesus said, "You also ought to wash one another's feet" (John 13:14). We need both to be willing to wash another's feet and to be willing to be washed by another. In the latter case we admit our need of spiritual help.

When the service is over, our faith assures us that we are clean because our sins have been washed away. By whom? By Christ. But it is fellow believers who administer to us the symbols of Christ's ministry and so this service becomes a fellowship of forgiveness.[4]

4. A fellowship with Christ and believers. This foot washing service demonstrates Christ's love for His followers "to the end" (John 13:1). When Peter refused to have his feet washed, Christ responded, "If I do not wash you, you have no part with Me" (verse 8). No cleansing, no fellowship. Those desiring continuing fellowship with Christ will participate in this ordinance.

That same evening Jesus said, "A new commandment I give to you, that you love one another; as I have loved you, that you also love one another" (verse 34). The message of the ordinance is clear: "Through love serve one another" (Gal. 5:13). Having this kind of love means that we will concede the highest place to our neighbors by esteeming others better than ourselves (Phil. 2:3). It mandates us to love those who differ with us. It allows us to hold neither feelings of supremacy nor partiality. Our lifestyles will reflect our love for fellow believers. Kneeling before them, washing their feet, we rejoice that we will live with them throughout eternity. All who follow Christ's example in this ordinance will in some way experience what it means to love as Christ loved. And such love can be a powerful witness.

A Buddhist monk once asked a missionary to suggest a scene that would represent Christianity. Artists were to decorate a hall on the monastery grounds with murals and reliefs that depicted major world religions. After some reflection the missionary began to share the account in John 13. The monk "said nothing as I read," the missionary recounted, "but I felt a strange, awesome quietness and power as the passage described Jesus' act of washing the disciples' feet." In that culture, discussing in public anything having to do with matters of the feet is considered very poor etiquette.

"When I finished reading, there was a moment of silence. He looked at me with incredulity and said, 'Do you mean to say that the Founder of your religion washed His students' feet?'

"Yes," I replied. The usually placid moon face with shaved eyebrows and head wrinkled up in shock and amazement. He was speechless—and so was I. I swallowed very hard several times, and we were both caught up in the drama of the scene. As I gazed at him, the look of incredulity on his face changed to a reverent awe. Jesus, the Founder of Christianity, had touched and washed dirty fishermen's feet! After a few moments he gained control of himself and rose to his feet. 'I see now the essence of Christianity.'"[5]

The Celebration of the Lord's Supper

Among Protestants the most common name for the Communion service is the "Lord's Supper" (1 Cor. 11:20). Other names are "the table of the Lord" (1 Cor. 10:21, RSV), "the breaking of bread" (cf. Acts 20:7; 2:42),[6] and the Eucharist—a reference to the thanksgiving and blessing aspect of the service (Matt. 26:26, 27; 1 Cor. 10:16; 11:24).

The Lord's Supper is to be a joyful season, not a time of sorrow. The preceding foot washing service provides an opportunity for self-examination, confession of sins, reconciliation of differences, and forgiveness. Having received the assurance of being cleansed by the blood of the Saviour, believers are ready to enter into special communion with their Lord. They turn to His table with joy, standing in the saving light, not the shadow, of the cross, ready to celebrate the redemptive victory of Christ.

The Meaning of the Lord's Supper. The Lord's Supper replaces the Passover festival of the old-covenant era. The Passover met its fulfillment when Christ the Paschal Lamb gave His life. Before His death Christ Himself instituted the replacement, the great festival of spiritual Israel under the new covenant. Thus, the roots of much of the symbolism of the Lord's Supper extend back into the Passover service.

1. Commemoration of the deliverance from sin. As the Passover festival commemorated Israel's deliverance from slavery in Egypt, the Lord's Supper commemorates deliverance from spiritual Egypt, the bondage of sin.

The Passover lamb's blood applied to the lintel and doorposts protected the inhabitants from death; the nourishment its flesh provided gave them the strength to escape from Egypt (Ex. 12:3-8). So Christ's sacrifice brings liberation from death; believers are saved through partaking of both His body and blood (John 6:54). The Lord's Supper proclaims that Christ's death on the cross provided our salvation, provided forgiveness, and guaranteed eternal life.

Jesus said, "Do this in remembrance of Me" (1 Cor. 11:24). This ordinance emphasizes the substitutionary dimension of Christ's atonement. "This is My body," Jesus said, "which is broken for you" (1 Cor. 11:24; cf. 53:4-12). At the cross the Innocent was substituted for the guilty, the Righteous for the unrighteous. This magnanimous act satisfied the demands of the law for the death of the sinner, providing forgiveness, peace, and the assurance of eternal life to repentant sinners. The cross removed our condemnation and provided us with the robe of Christ's righteousness and with the power to overcome evil.

a. The bread and the fruit of the vine. Jesus used many metaphors to teach different truths about Himself. He said, "I am the door" (John 10:7), "I am the way" (John 14:6), "I am the true vine" (John 15:1), and "I am the bread of life" (John 6:35). We cannot take any of these expressions literally, for He is not present in every door, way, or vine. Instead, they illustrate deeper truths.

At the time He miraculously fed the 5,000, Jesus revealed the deeper significance of His body and blood. As the true bread, He said, " 'Moses did not give you the bread from heaven, but My Father gives you the true bread from heaven. For the bread of God is He who comes down from heaven and gives life to the world.' Then they said to Him, 'Lord, give us this bread always.' And Jesus said to them, 'I am the bread of life. He who comes to Me shall never hunger, and he who believes in Me shall never thirst' " (John 6:32-35). He offered His body and blood to satisfy the hunger and thirst of our deepest needs and desires (John 6:50-54).

The Passover bread Jesus ate was unleavened, and the fruit of the vine unfermented.[7] Leaven (yeast), which produces fermentation that causes bread to rise, was considered a symbol of sin (1 Cor. 5:7, 8), so it was unfit to represent the Lamb "without blemish and without spot" (1 Peter 1:19).[8] Only unleavened or "unfermented" bread could symbolize the sinless body of Christ. Likewise, only the unspoiled fruit of the vine—the unfermented wine—appropriately symbolizes the spotless perfection of the cleansing blood of the Saviour.[9]

b. The eating and drinking. "Unless you eat the flesh of the Son of Man and drink His blood, you have no life in you. Whoever eats My flesh and drinks My blood has eternal life, and I will raise him up at the last day" (John 6:53, 54).

Eating Christ's flesh and drinking His blood is symbolic language for the assimilation of the Word of God, through which believers maintain communion with heaven and are enabled to have spiritual life. He says, "The words that I speak to you are spirit, and they are life" (John 6:63). "Man shall not live by bread alone, but by every word that proceeds from the mouth of God" (Matt. 4:4).

Believers feed on Christ, the bread of life, through partaking of the Word of life—the Bible. With that Word comes Christ's life-giving power. In the Communion service also we partake of Christ by assimilating His Word through the Holy Spirit. For this reason the preaching of the Word accompanies each Lord's Supper.

Since we appropriate the benefits of Christ's atoning sacrifice by faith, the Lord's Supper is much more than a mere memorial meal. Participation in the Communion service means a revitalization of our life through Christ's sustaining power, providing us with life and joy. In short, the symbolism shows that "we are as dependent on Christ for spiritual life as we are on food and drink for physical life."[10]

During the Communion service we "bless" the cup (1 Cor. 10:16). This means that as Christ "gave thanks" for the cup (Matt. 26:27), so we express gratitude for the blood of Jesus.

2. Corporate communion with Christ. In a world filled with strife and divisiveness, our corporate participation in these celebrations contributes to the unity and stability of the church, demonstrating true communion with Christ and one another. Stressing this communion, Paul said, "The cup of blessing which we bless, is it not a participation [or communion] in the blood of Christ? The bread which we break, is it not a participation [or communion] in the body of Christ? Because there is one bread, we who are many are one body, for we all partake of the one bread" (1 Cor. 10:16, 17, RSV).

"This is an allusion to the fact that the communion bread is broken into many pieces, which are eaten by the believers, and as all the pieces come from the same loaf, so all the believers who partake of the communion service are united in Him whose broken body is thus typified by the broken bread. By partaking together of this ordinance, Christians show publicly that they are united and belong to one great family, whose head is Christ."[11]

All church members should participate in this sacred Communion because there, through the Holy Spirit, "Christ meets His people, and energizes them by His presence. Hearts and hands that are unworthy may even administer the ordinances, yet Christ is there to minister to His children. All who come with their faith fixed upon Him will be greatly blessed. All who neglect these seasons of divine privilege will suffer loss. Of them it may appropriately be said, 'Ye are not all clean.'"[12]

We experience the strongest and deepest sense of community at the Lord's table. Here we meet on common ground, with the barriers that separate us broken down. Here we realize that while in society there is much to divide us, in Christ there is everything necessary to unite us. While sharing the Communion cup, Jesus committed the new covenant to His disciples. Said He, "Drink from it, all of you. For this is My blood of the new covenant which is shed for many for the remission of sins" (Matt. 26:27, 28; cf. Luke 22:20). As the old covenant was ratified by the blood of animal sacrifices (Ex. 24:8), so the new covenant was ratified by Christ's blood. At this ordinance believers renew their pledge of loyalty to their Lord, recognizing anew that they are a part of the amazing agreement by which, in Jesus, God bound Himself to humanity. Being a part of this covenant, they have something to celebrate. So the Lord's Supper is both a memorial and a thanksgiving of the sealing of the everlasting covenant of grace. The blessings received are in proportion to the faith of the participants.

3. Anticipation of the Second Advent. "For as often as you eat this bread and drink this cup, you proclaim the Lord's death *till He comes*" (1 Cor. 11:26). The Communion service spans the interim between Calvary and the Second Advent. It links the cross and the kingdom. It joins the "already" and the "not yet," which is the essence of the New Testament worldview. It holds together the Saviour's sacrifice and His second coming—salvation provided and salvation consummated. It proclaims that Christ is present through the Spirit till He comes visibly.

Christ's vow, "I will not drink of this fruit of the vine from now on until that day when I drink it new with you in My Father's kingdom" (Matt. 26:29) is prophetic. It directs our faith to a future celebration of the Communion meal with our Saviour in the kingdom. The occasion is the great festival of the "marriage supper of the Lamb" (Rev. 19:9).

In preparation for this event Christ instructed, "Let your waist be girded and your lamps burning; and you yourselves be like men who wait for their master, when he will return from the wedding, that when he comes and knocks they may open to him immediately. Blessed are those servants whom the master, when he comes, will find watching. Assuredly, I say to you that he will gird himself and have them sit down to eat, and will come and serve them" (Luke 12:35-37).

With His followers gathered at the banquet table Christ will celebrate the Supper as He did in Jerusalem. For so long He has waited for this occasion, and now all is ready. He arises from His throne and steps forward to serve. Amazement fills all. They feel totally unworthy of the honor of having Christ serve them. They protest, saying, "Let us serve!" But Christ quietly insists and has them sit down.

"Never was Christ truly greater on earth than on the memorable occasion of the Lord's Supper, when He took the place of a servant and humbled Himself. Never is Christ greater in heaven than when He ministers to His saints."[13] This is the climactic expectation to which the Lord's Supper points us—the joy of future glory through a personal fellowship with Christ in His everlasting kingdom.

Qualifications for Participation. Two great ordinances serve the Christian faith—baptism and the Lord's Supper. The former is the gateway into the church, and the latter benefits those who are members.[14] Jesus administered Communion only to His professed followers. The Communion service, therefore, is for believing Christians. Children do not customarily participate in these ordinances unless they are baptized.[15]

The Bible instructs believers to celebrate this ordinance with due reverence for the Lord, for the one who "eats this bread and drinks this cup…in an unworthy manner will be guilty of the body and blood of the Lord" (1 Cor. 11:27). This "unworthy manner" consists "either in unbecoming conduct (see verse 21) or in a lack of vital, active faith in the atoning sacrifice of Christ."[16] Such behavior shows disrespect to the Lord and can be considered a rejection of the Saviour and thus a sharing in the guilt of those who crucify Him.

Improper participation brings about God's displeasure. Those eating and drinking in an unworthy manner eat and drink "judgment" to themselves, "not discerning the Lord's body" (1 Cor. 11:29). They fail to distinguish between ordinary food and the consecrated emblems that symbolize Christ's atoning death. "Believers must not treat the ordinances as merely a commemorative ceremony of a happening in history. It is that, and much more; it is a reminder of what sin has cost God and what man owes to the Saviour. It is also a means of keeping fresh in mind the believer's duty to bear public witness to his faith in the atoning death of the Son of God."[17]

In view of these admonitions Paul counsels the believer to "examine himself" before participating in the Lord's Supper (1 Cor. 11:28). Before taking part, believers should prayerfully review their Christian experience, confessing their sins and restoring severed relationships.

The experience of the Adventist pioneers reveals what a blessing such an examination can provide: "When our numbers were few, the celebration of the ordinances was made a most profitable occasion. On the Friday before, every church member endeavored to clear away everything that would tend to separate him from his brethren and from God. Hearts were closely searched; prayers for a divine revelation of hidden sin were earnestly offered; confessions of over-reaching in trade, of ill-advised words hastily spoken, of sin cherished, were made. The Lord came near, and we were greatly strengthened and encouraged."[18]

This examination is a personal work. Others cannot do it, for who can read the heart or distinguish the weeds from the wheat? Christ, our example, rejected exclusiveness at the Supper. Though open sin excludes persons from participating (1 Cor. 5:11), Jesus Himself shared the meal with Judas—outwardly a professed follower but inwardly a thief and traitor.

What marks those who are qualified to participate in the Communion service, then, is the condition of the heart—a full commitment to Christ and faith in His sacrifice, not membership in any particular church. Consequently, believing Christians of all churches can take part in the Lord's Supper. All are invited to celebrate often this great festival of the new covenant, and through their participation to witness to their acceptance of Christ as a personal Saviour.[19]

References

1. See Robert Odom, "The First Celebration of the Ordinance of the Lord's House," *Ministry*, Jan. 1953, p. 20; Ellen G. White, *The Desire of Ages*, pp. 643-646.

2. *Ibid*, p. 650.

3. There is a relationship between baptism and the Lord's Supper. Baptism precedes church membership, while the foot washing serves those who already are church members. During this ordinance we may appropriately meditate on our baptismal vows.

4. See C. Mervyn Maxwell, "A Fellowship of Forgiveness," *Review and Herald*, June 29, 1961, pp. 6, 7.

5. Jon Dybdahl, *Missions: A Two-Way Street* (Boise, ID: Pacific Press, 1986), p. 28.

6. Though it is generally understood that in Acts 20:7 the expression refers to the celebration of the Lord's Supper, it does not exclusively refer to this ordinance. In Luke 24:35 it refers to a common daily meal.

7. On the assumption that the people of Bible times could not have preserved grape juice for an extended period of time in the warm climate of Israel from the time of the fall grape harvest until the Passover in the spring, it is taken for granted the Jews celebrated the Passover with fermented wine. This as-

sumption is unwarranted. Throughout the ancient world juices were often preserved in an unfermented state for extended periods through various methods. One method was to concentrate the juice to a syrup by boiling it. Stored in a cool place, this concentrate would not ferment. Simply diluting it with water yielded a non-alcoholic "sweet wine." See William Patton, *Bible Wines—Laws of Fermentation* (Oklahoma City, OK: Sane Press, n. d.), pp. 24-41; see also C. A. Christoforides, "More on Unfermented Wine," *Ministry*, April 1955, p. 34; Lael O. Caesar, "The Meaning of *Yayin* in the Old Testament" (Unpublished M.A. Thesis, Andrews University, 1986), pp. 74-77; White, *The Desire of Ages*, p. 653. The Passover wine could also be made from raisins (F. C. Gilbert, *Practical Lessons From the Experience of Israel for the Church of Today* [Nashville, TN: Southern Publ. Assn., 1972 ed.], pp. 240, 241).

8. In this light it is not without significance that Christ avoids using the usual word for wine (Greek, *oinos*) but employs the phrase "the fruit of the vine" (Mark 14:25). While *oinos* can refer to wine in its fermented as well as unfermented state, the fruit of the vine refers to the pure juice—a fitting symbol of the blood of Christ, who calls Himself the "True Vine" (John 15:1).

9. Yeast also causes the fermentation of grape juice. Yeast spores, carried freely through the air or by insects, attach themselves to the wax coat of the grape skins. When the grapes are crushed, the spores mix with the juice. At room temperature the yeast cells multiply rapidly, fermenting the wine (see Martin S. Peterson, Arnold H. Johnson, eds., *Encyclopedia of Food Technology* [Westport, CT: Avi Publishing Co., 1974], vol. 2, pp. 61-69; *Idem, Encyclopedia of Food Science* [Westport, CT: Avi Publishing Co., 1978] vol. 3, p. 878).

10. R. Rice, *Reign of God*, p. 303.

11. *SDA Bible Commentary*, rev. ed., vol. 6, p. 746.

12. White, *The Desire of Ages*, p. 656; cf. p. 661.

13. M.L. Andreasen, "The Ordinances of the Lord's House," *Ministry*, Jan. 1947, pp. 44, 46.

14. Cf. White, *Evangelism* (Washington, D.C.: Review and Herald, 1946), p. 273.

15. See, e.g., Frank Holbrook, "For Members Only?" *Ministry*, Feb. 1987, p. 13.

16. *SDA Bible Commentary*, rev. ed., vol. 6, p. 765.

17. *Ibid.*

18. White, *Evangelism*, p. 274; cf. *SDA Bible Commentary*, rev. ed., vol. 6, p. 765.

19. The Bible does not specify how frequently the Lord's Supper should be celebrated (see 1 Cor. 11:25, 26). Adventists have followed the practice of many Protestants to have this ordinance four times a year. "In adopting the quarterly plan, the early Advent believers felt that in holding the service more frequently there would be the danger of formality and failure to realize the

solemnity of the service." It seems to be a middle-of-the-road decision—between celebrating it too often and leaving it for too long a period, such as once a year (W. E. Read, "Frequency of the Lord's Supper," *Ministry*, April 1955, p. 43).

17

Spiritual Gifts and Ministries

God bestows upon all members of His church in every age spiritual gifts, which each member is to employ in loving ministry for the common good of the church and of humanity. Given by the agency of the Holy Spirit, who apportions to each member as He wills, the gifts provide all abilities and ministries needed by the church to fulfill its divinely ordained functions. According to the Scriptures, these gifts include such ministries as faith, healing, prophecy, proclamation, teaching, administration, reconciliation, compassion, and self-sacrificing service and charity for the help and encouragement of people. Some members are called of God and endowed by the Spirit for functions recognized by the church in pastoral, evangelistic, apostolic, and teaching ministries particularly needed to equip the members for service, to build up the church to spiritual maturity, and to foster unity of the faith and knowledge of God. When members employ these spiritual gifts as faithful stewards of God's varied grace, the church is protected from the destructive influence of false doctrine, grows with a growth that is from God, and is

built up in faith and love. (Rom. 12:4-8; 1 Cor. 12:9-11, 27, 28; Eph. 4:8, 11-16; Acts 6:1-7; 1 Tim. 3:1-13; 1 Pet. 4:10, 11.)

THE WORDS JESUS SPOKE JUST BEFORE He ascended to heaven were to change history. "Go into all the world," He ordered the disciples, "and preach the gospel to every creature" (Mark 16:15).

To all the world? To every creature? The disciples must have thought it an impossible task. Christ, sensing their helplessness, instructed them not to leave Jerusalem but "to wait for the Promise of the Father." Then He assured them, "You shall receive power when the Holy Spirit has come upon you; and you shall be witnesses to Me in Jerusalem, and in all Judea and Samaria, and to the end of the earth" (Acts 1:4, 8).

Following Jesus' ascension to heaven the disciples spent much time in prayer. Harmony and humility replaced the discord and jealousy that had marred much of their time with Jesus. The disciples were converted. Their close communion with Christ and the resulting unity were the necessary preparation for the outpouring of the Holy Spirit.

As Jesus received a special anointing with the Spirit to fit Him for His ministry (Acts 10:38), so the disciples received the baptism of the Holy Spirit (Acts 1:5) to enable them to witness. The results were electrifying. On the day they received the gift of the Holy Spirit, they baptized three thousand persons (see Acts 2:41).

The Gifts of the Holy Spirit

Christ illustrated the gifts of the Holy Spirit with a parable: "The kingdom of heaven is like a man traveling to a far country, who called his own servants and delivered his goods to them. And to one he gave five talents, to another two, and to another one, to each according to his own ability; and immediately he went on a journey" (Matt. 25:14, 15).

The man traveling to a far country represents Christ leaving for heaven. The man's "own servants" are His followers, who "were bought at a price" (1 Cor. 6:20)—"the precious blood of Christ" (1 Peter 1:19). Christ redeemed them for service, and they live "no longer for themselves, but for Him who died for them and rose again" (2 Cor. 5:15).

Christ gave goods to each servant according to his ability, and "to each his work" (Mark 13:34). Along with other gifts and abilities (see chapter 21 of this book), these goods represent the special gifts imparted by the Spirit.[1]

In a special sense, Christ gave these spiritual gifts to His church at Pentecost. "When He ascended on high," Paul said, He "gave gifts to men." Thus "to each one of us grace was given according to the measure of Christ's gift" (Eph. 4:7, 8). The Holy Spirit is the agent who distributes "to each one individually as He wills" (1 Cor. 12:11) these gifts that enable the church to do its assigned work.

The Purpose of Spiritual Gifts

The Holy Spirit gives a special ability to a member, enabling him to help the church fulfill its divine mission.

Harmony Within the Church. The Corinthian church did not lack any spiritual gift (1 Cor. 1:4, 7). Unfortunately, they bickered like children over which gifts were the most important.

Concerned about the divisions in their church, Paul wrote to the Corinthians about the true nature of these gifts and how they were meant to function. Spiritual gifts, he explained, are gifts of grace. From the same Spirit come "diversities of gifts," which lead to "differences of ministries" and "diversities of activities." But Paul emphasized that it is "the same God who works all in all" (1 Cor. 12:4-6).

The Spirit distributes gifts to every believer—for the edification, or building up, of the church. The needs of the Lord's work determine what the Spirit distributes and to whom. All do not receive the same gifts. Paul said the Spirit gives to one wisdom, to another knowledge, to another faith, to another miracles, to another prophecy, to another discerning of spirits, to another tongues, and to another the interpretation of tongues. "But one and the same Spirit works all these things, distributing to each one individually as He wills" (verse 11). Thankfulness for the working of a gift in the church should be directed to the Giver, not to the person who exercises the gift. And because the gifts are given for the church, not the individual, recipients should not consider the gifts their private property.

Since the Spirit distributes the gifts according as He sees fit, no gift is to be despised or belittled. No member of the church has a right to arrogance because of a particular appointment or function, nor should anyone feel inferior because of an assignment to a humble position.

1. The model of operation. Paul used the human body to illustrate harmony in the diversity of gifts. The body has many parts that each contribute in a unique way. "In fact God has arranged the parts in the body, every one of them, just as he wanted them to be" (verse 18, NIV).

No part of the body should say to another "I don't need you!" They all are dependent on one another and "those parts of the body that seem to be weaker are indispensable, and the parts that we think are less honorable we treat with special honor. And the parts that are unpresentable are treated with special modesty, while our presentable parts need no special treatment. But God has combined the members of the body and has given greater honor to the parts that lacked it" (verses 21-24, NIV).

The failure of any organ would affect the entire body. If the body had no brain the stomach would not function; and if it had no stomach the brain would be useless. So the church would suffer if any member, no matter how insignificant, was missing.

Certain parts of the body that are structurally weaker need special protection. One may function without a hand or leg but not without liver, heart, or lungs. We normally expose our faces and hands, but we cover other parts of the body with clothes for purposes of modesty or decency. Far from esteeming the lesser gifts lightly, we must treat them with greater care because the health of the church depends on them.

God intended the distribution of spiritual gifts in the church to prevent "division in the body" and to produce a spirit of harmony and dependency, so "its parts should have equal concern for each other. If one part suffers, every part suffers with it; if one part is honored, every part rejoices with it" (verses 25, 26, NIV). So when one believer suffers, the entire church should be made aware of it and should help alleviate the suffering. Only when this person is restored is the health of the church secure.

After discussing the value of each of the gifts, Paul listed a number of them: "God has appointed in the church first apostles, second prophets, third teachers, then workers of miracles, then healers, helpers, administrators, speakers in various kinds of tongues" (verse 28, RSV; cf. Eph. 4:11). Since no member has all the gifts, he encouraged all to "eagerly desire the greater gifts" (verse 31, NIV), referring to those most useful to the church.[2]

2. The indispensable dimension. The gifts of the Holy Spirit, however, are not sufficient by themselves. There is "a more excellent way" (verse 31). While the gifts of the Spirit will pass away at Christ's return, the fruit of the Spirit is eternal. It consists of the eternal virtue of love and the peace, goodness and righteousness that love brings with it (see Gal. 5:22, 23; Eph. 5:9). While prophecy, tongues, and knowledge will disappear, faith, hope, and love will remain. And "the greatest of these is love" (1 Cor. 13:13).[3]

This love God gives (*agape* in Greek) is a self-sacrificing and giving love (1 Cor. 13:4-8). It is "the higher type of love, which recognizes something of value in the person or object that is loved; love that is based on principle, not on emotion; love that grows out of respect for the admirable qualities of its object."[4] Gifts devoid of love cause confusion and divisiveness in the church. The more excellent way, therefore, is for each one with spiritual gifts to possess also this totally unselfish love. "Follow the way of love and eagerly desire spiritual gifts" (1 Cor. 14:1, NIV).

Living to God's Glory. Paul also spoke about spiritual gifts in his epistle to the Romans. Calling on every believer to live for God's glory (Rom. 11:36-12:2), Paul again used the parts of the body to illustrate the diversity and yet unity that characterize the believers who are joined together in the church (verses 3-6).

Recognizing that both faith and spiritual gifts have their source in God's grace, believers remain humble. The more gifts given a believer and the greater his spiritual influence, the greater should be his dependence upon God.

In this chapter Paul listed the following gifts: prophecy (inspired utterance, proclamation), ministry (service), teaching, exhortation (encouragement), giving (sharing), leadership, and mercy (compassion). As in 1 Corinthians 12, he ended his discussion with the greatest principle of Christianity—love (verse 9).

Peter presented the topic of spiritual gifts against the backdrop of the end of all things being "at hand" (1 Peter 4:7). The urgency of the hour dictates that believers must use the gifts. "As each one has received a gift," he said, "minister it to one another, as good stewards of the manifold grace of God" (verse 10). Like Paul, Peter taught that these gifts are not for self-glorification, but that "in all things God may be glorified" (verse 11). He also associated love with the gifts (verse 8).

The Growth of the Church. In Paul's third and final discussion of spiritual gifts, he urged believers "to live a life worthy of the calling you have received. Be completely humble and gentle; be patient, bearing with one another in love. Make every effort to keep the unity of the Spirit through the bond of peace" (Eph. 4:1-3, NIV).

Spiritual gifts contribute to fostering of a unity that causes the church to grow. Each believer has received "grace...according to the measure of Christ's gift" (verse 7).

Christ Himself "gave some to be apostles, some prophets, some evangelists, and some pastors and teachers." These gifts are service-oriented ministries given "for the equipping of the saints for the work of the ministry, for the edifying of the body of Christ, till we all come to the unity of faith and the knowledge of the Son of God, to a perfect man, to the measure of the stature of the fullness of Christ" (verses 11-13). Those who receive spiritual gifts are especially to serve believers, training them for the types of ministry according to their gifts. This builds up the church to a maturity that reaches the full stature of Christ.

These ministries increase spiritual stability and strengthen the church's defense against false doctrines, so that believers will "no longer be children, tossed to and fro and carried about with every wind of doctrine, by the trickery of men, in the cunning craftiness by which they lie in wait to deceive, but, speaking the truth in love, may grow up in all things into Him who is the head—Christ" (verses 14, 15).

Finally, in Christ, spiritual gifts bring about both the unity and the prosperity of the church. "From Him the whole body, joined and held together by every supporting ligament, grows and builds itself up in love, as each part does its work" (verse 16, NIV). In order for the church to experience the growth God intends, each member must use the gifts of grace He supplies.

As a result, the church experiences twofold growth—a growth in the number of members and an increase in individual spiritual gifts. Again, love is a part of this calling, for the church can realize this edification and growth only as it uses these gifts in love.

Implications of Spiritual Gifts

A Common Ministry. Scripture does not support the view that the clergy should minister while the laity merely warm the pews and wait to be fed. Both pastors and laity make up the church, "God's own people" (1 Peter 2:9, RSV). Together, they are responsible for the well-being of the church and its prosperity. They are called to work together, everyone according to his or her special, Christ-given gifts. The difference in gifts results in a variety of ministries or services, all united in their witness to extend the kingdom of God and prepare the world to meet their Saviour (Matt. 28:18-20; Rev. 14:6-12).

The Role of the Clergy. The doctrine of spiritual gifts places the responsibility for the training of the congregation on the shoulders of the minister. God has appointed apostles, prophets, evangelists, pastors, and teachers to equip His people for ministry. "Ministers should not do the work which belongs to the church, thus wearying themselves, and preventing others from performing their duty. They should teach the members how to labor in the church and in the community."[5]

The minister who does not have the gift of training does not belong to the pastoral ministry but to another part of God's work.[6] The success of God's plan for the church depends on the willingness and ability of its pastors to train the members to use their God-given gifts.

Gifts and Mission. God gives spiritual gifts to benefit the whole body, not simply the individuals who receive them. And, just as the recipient does not receive the gift for himself, so the church does not receive the totality of gifts for itself. God endows the church community with gifts to prepare it to fulfill the mission to the world He has assigned it.

Spiritual gifts are not rewards for a job well done—they are tools to do the job well. The Spirit usually gives gifts compatible with a person's natural gifts, though natural gifts alone are not spiritual gifts. It takes the new birth to energize a person with the Spirit. We must be born again to be endued with spiritual gifts.

Unity in Diversity, Not Uniformity. Some Christians try to make every other believer like themselves. This is a human plan, not God's. That the church remains united in spite of the diversity of spiritual gifts points to the complementary nature of the gifts. It indicates that the progress of God's church depends upon every believer. God intends that all gifts, ministries, and operations within the church blend together in the work of building on the foundation laid by the church of history. In Jesus Christ, the chief Cornerstone, "the whole building, being joined together, grows into a holy temple in the Lord" (Eph. 2:21).

Witnessing—the Purpose for Gifts. Believers receive a diversity of gifts, an indication that each has an individualized ministry. Yet every believer should be able to witness about his faith, sharing beliefs and telling others what God has done in his life. The purpose for which God gives each gift, no matter what it may be, is to enable its possessor to witness.

The Failure to Use Spiritual Gifts. Believers who refuse to employ their spiritual gifts will not only find that their gifts atrophy but also that they are jeopardizing their eternal life. In loving concern Jesus solemnly warned that the servant who did not use his talent was nothing less than a "wicked and lazy servant" who forfeited the eternal reward (Matt. 25:26-30).[7] The unfaithful servant freely admitted that his failure was deliberate and premeditated. Thus he had to bear the responsibility for his failure. "In the great final day of judgment those who have drifted along, dodging opportunities and shirking responsibilities, will be classed by the great Judge with evildoers."[8]

Discovering Spiritual Gifts

For members to be successfully involved in the church's mission they must understand their gifts. The gifts function as a compass, directing the possessor toward service and the enjoyment of the abundant life (John 10:10). To the extent that we "choose not to (or simply neglect to) recognize, develop, and exercise our gifts, the church is less than it could be. Less than God intended it to be."[9]

The process of discovering our spiritual gifts[10] should be characterized by the following:

Spiritual Preparation. The apostles prayed earnestly for a fitness to speak words that would lead sinners to Christ. They put away the differences and desires for supremacy that had stood between them. Confession of sin and repentance brought them into close fellowship with Christ. Those who accept Christ today need a similar experience in preparation for the baptism of the Holy Spirit.

The baptism of the Spirit is not a one-time event; we can experience it daily.[11] We need to plead with the Lord for that baptism, because it gives the church power to witness and to proclaim the gospel. To do this we must continually surrender our lives to God, abide fully in Christ, and ask Him for wisdom to discover our gifts (James 1:5).

Study the Scriptures. Our prayerful study of what the New Testament teaches about spiritual gifts allows the Holy Spirit to impress our minds with the specific ministry that He has for us. It is important that we believe that God has given us at least one gift to be used in His service.

Openness to Providential Guidance. We are not to use the Spirit, but He is to use us, for it is God who works in His people "to will and to work for his good pleasure" (Phil. 2:13, RSV). It is a privilege to be willing to work in any line of service that God's providence presents. We must give God the opportunity to work through others to solicit our help. So we ought to be ready to respond to the needs of the church whenever they present themselves. We should not be afraid to try new things, but we should also feel free to inform those requesting our help about our talents and experience.

Confirmation From the Body. Since God gives these gifts to build up His church, we may expect the final confirmation of our gifts to arise from the judgment of the body of Christ and not from our own feelings. Often it is more difficult to recognize one's own gifts than those of others. Not only must we be willing to listen to what others have to tell us about our gifts, but it is important that we recognize and confirm God's gifts in others.

Nothing is more exciting and fulfilling than to know that we are occupying the position or ministry or service that Providence has ordained for us. What a blessing is ours to employ in His service the special gift Christ has given to us through the Holy Spirit. Christ longs to share His gifts of grace. Today we can accept His invitation and discover what His gifts can do in a Spirit-filled life!

References

1. See, e g., Ellen G. White, *Christ's Object Lessons*, pp. 327, 328. We cannot always easily distinguish between the supernatural, the inherited, and the acquired abilities. In those who are under the control of the Spirit these abilities frequently seem to blend together.

2. See Richard Hammill, "Spiritual Gifts in the Church Today," *Ministry*, July, 1982, pp. 15, 16.

3. In the broadest sense love is a gift from God, for all good things come from Him (John 1:17). It is the fruit of the Spirit (Gal. 5:22) but not a spiritual gift in the sense that the Holy Spirit has distributed it to some believers and not to all. Everyone is to "pursue love" (1 Cor. 14:1).

4. *SDA Bible Commentary*, rev. ed., vol. 6, p. 778.

5. White, "Appeals for Our Missions" in *Historical Sketches of the Foreign Missions of the Seventh-day Adventists* (Basel, Switzerland: Imprimerie Polyglotte, 1886), p. 291. Cf. Rex D. Edwards, *A New Frontier—Every Believer a Minister* [Mountain View, CA: Pacific Press, 1979], pp. 58-73).

6. Cf. J. David Newmann, "Seminar in Spiritual Gifts," unpublished MS, p. 3.

7. On the seriousness of this condition, see White, "Home Discipline," *Review and Herald*, June 13, 1882, p. [1].

8. *SDA Bible Commentary*, rev. ed., vol. 5, p. 511.

9. Don Jacobsen, "What Spiritual Gifts Mean to Me," *Adventist Review*, December 25, 1986, p. 12.

10. See Roy C. Naden, *Discovering Your Spiritual Gifts* (Berrien Springs, MI: Institute of Church Ministry, 1982); Mark A. Finley, *The Way to Adventist Church Growth* (Siloam Springs, AR: Concerned Communications, 1982); C. Peter Wagner, *Your Spiritual Gifts Can Help Your Church Grow* (Glendale, CA: Regal Books, 1979).

11. Cf. White, *Acts of the Apostles*, p. 50; White, *Counsels to Parents, Teachers and Students* (Mountain View, CA: Pacific Press, 1943), p. 131.

The Gift of Prophecy

18

One of the gifts of the Holy Spirit is prophecy. This gift is an identifying mark of the remnant church and was manifested in the ministry of Ellen G. White—the Lord's messenger. Her writings are a continuing and authoritative source of truth which provide for the church comfort, guidance, instruction, and correction. They also make clear that the Bible is the standard by which all teaching and experience must be tested. (Joel 2:28, 29; Acts 2:14-21; Heb. 1:1-3; Rev. 12:17; 19:10.)

JEHOSHAPHAT, KING OF JUDAH, WAS DISTRESSED. Enemy troops were closing in, and the outlook seemed hopeless. "And Jehoshaphat...set himself to seek the Lord, and proclaimed a fast throughout all Judah" (2 Chron. 20:3). The people began streaming to the Temple to beg mercy and deliverance of God.

As Jehoshaphat led out in the prayer service, he called upon God to change the circumstances. He prayed, "Are You not God in heaven, and do You not rule over all the kingdoms of the nations, and in Your hand is there not power and might, so that no one is able to withstand You?" (verse 6). Hadn't God specially protected His own in the past? Hadn't He given this land to His chosen people? So Jehoshaphat pleaded, "O our God, will You not judge them? For we have no power...nor do we know what to do, but our eyes are upon You" (verse 12).

As all Judah stood before the Lord, one Jahaziel arose. His message brought courage and direction to the fearful people. He said, "Do not be afraid...for the battle is not yours, but God's....You will not need to fight in this battle. Position yourselves, stand still and see the salvation of the Lord,...for the Lord is with you" (verses 15-17). In the morning King Jehoshaphat told his troops to "Believe in the Lord your God, and you shall be established; *believe His prophets, and you shall prosper*" (verse 20).[1]

So fully did this king believe that little-known prophet, Jahaziel, that he replaced his front-line troops with a choir singing praise to the Lord and the beauty of holiness! As the anthems of faith filled the air, the Lord was at work bringing confusion among the armies allied against Judah. The slaughter was so great that "no one...escaped" (verse 24).

Jahaziel was God's mouthpiece for that special time.

Prophets played a vital role in both Old and New Testament times. But did prophecy cease to function with the closing of the biblical canon? To find the answer let us retrace prophetic history.

The Prophetic Gift in Bible Times

Though sin ended face-to-face communication between God and human beings (Isa. 59:2), God did not end His intimacy with humanity; instead, He developed other ways of communicating. He began sending His messages of encouragement, warning, and reproof through prophets.[2]

In the Scriptures a prophet is "one who receives communications from God and transmits their intent to His people."[3] Prophets did not prophesy on their own initiative, "for prophecy never came by the will of man, but holy men of God spoke as they were moved by the Holy Spirit" (2 Peter 1:21).

In the Old Testament the word *prophet* is generally a translation of the Hebrew *nabi*. Its meaning is expressed in Exodus 7:1, 2: "The Lord said to Moses: 'See, I have made you as God to Pharaoh, and Aaron your brother shall be your prophet [*nabi*]. You shall speak all that I command you. And Aaron your brother shall speak to Pharaoh.'" Moses' relationship to Pharaoh was like that of God to His people. And as Aaron communicated Moses' words to Pharaoh, so the prophet conveyed God's words to the people. The term *prophet*, then, designates a divinely appointed spokesperson for God. The Greek equivalent of the Hebrew *nabi* is *prophetes*, from which the English word *prophet* is derived.

"Seer," a translation of the Hebrew *roeh* (Isa. 30:10) or *chozeh* (2 Sam. 24:11; 2 Kings 17:13) is yet another designation for persons with the prophetic gift. The terms *prophet* and *seer* are closely related. Scripture explains, "Formerly in Israel, when a man went to inquire of God, he spoke thus: 'Come let us go to the seer'; for he who is now called a prophet was formerly called a seer" (1 Sam. 9:9). The designation *seer* emphasized the prophets' *reception* of a divine message. God opened to the "eyes," or minds, of the prophets information He wanted them to transmit to His people.

Through the years, God has given revelations of His will for His people through persons with the gift of prophecy. "Surely the Lord God does nothing, unless He reveals His secret to His servants the prophets" (Amos 3:7, cf. Heb. 1:1).

The Functions of the Prophetic Gift in the New Testament. The New Testament gives prophecy a prominent place among the gifts of the Holy Spirit, once ranking it first and twice second among the ministries most useful to the church (see Rom. 12:6; 1 Cor. 12:28; Eph. 4:11). It encourages believers to desire especially this gift (1 Cor. 14:1, 39).

The New Testament suggests that prophets had the following functions:[4]

1. They assisted in founding of the church. The church was "built on the foundation of the apostles and prophets, Jesus Christ Himself being the chief cornerstone" (Eph. 2:20, 21).

2. They initiated the church's mission outreach. It was through prophets that the Holy Spirit selected Paul and Barnabas for their first missionary journeys (Acts 13:1, 2) and gave direction as to where missionaries should labor (Acts 16:6-10).

3. They edified the church. "He who prophesies," Paul said, "edifies the church." Prophecies are spoken "to men for their upbuilding, and encouragement and consolation" (1 Cor. 14:, 3, 4, RSV). Along with other gifts, God gave prophecy to the church to prepare believers "for the work of ministry, for the edifying of the body of Christ" (Eph. 4:12).

4. They united and protected the church. Prophets helped to bring about "the unity of the faith," protect the church against false doctrines so believers would "no longer be infants tossed back and forth by the waves, and blown here and there by every wind of teaching and by the cunning and craftiness of men in their deceitful scheming" (Eph. 4:13, 14, NIV).

5. They warned of future difficulties. One New Testament prophet warned of an approaching famine. In response the church initiated a relief program to assist those who suffered because of that famine (Acts 11:27-

30). Other prophets warned of Paul's arrest and imprisonment in Jerusalem (Acts 20:23; 21:4, 10-14).

6. *They confirmed the faith in times of controversy.* At the first church council the Holy Spirit guided the church to a decision on a controversial issue dealing with the salvation of Gentile Christians. Then, through prophets, the Spirit reaffirmed the believers in the true doctrine. After conveying the council's decision to the membership, "Judas and Silas, who themselves were prophets, said much to encourage and strengthen ["confirm," KJV] the brothers" (Acts 15:32, NIV).

The Prophetic Gift in the Last Days

Many Christians believe that the gift of prophecy ceased at the close of the apostolic era. But the Bible reveals the church's special need for the divine guidance during the crisis at the time of the end; it testifies to a continuing need for and provision of the prophetic gift after New Testament times.

Continuation of Spiritual Gifts. There is no biblical evidence that God would withdraw the spiritual gifts He gave the church before they had completed their purpose, which, according to Paul, was to bring the church "to the unity of the faith and the knowledge of the Son of God, to a perfect man, to the measure of the stature of the fullness of Christ" (Eph. 4:13). Because the church has not yet reached this experience, it still needs all the gifts of the Spirit. These gifts, including the gift of prophecy, will continue to operate for the benefit of God's people until Christ returns. Consequently, Paul cautioned believers not to "quench the Spirit" or "despise prophecies" (1 Thess. 5:19, 20) and counseled, "Desire spiritual gifts, but especially that you may prophesy" (1 Cor. 14:1).

These gifts have not always manifested themselves abundantly in the Christian church.[5] After the death of the apostles, prophets enjoyed respectability in many circles until A.D. 300.[6] But the decline of spirituality in the church and the resultant apostasy (see chapter 13 of this book), led to a diminishing of both the presence and the gifts of the Holy Spirit. At the same time false prophets caused a loss of confidence in the prophetic gift.[7]

The decline of the prophetic gift during certain periods in church history did not mean that God had withdrawn the gift permanently. The Bible indicates that, as the end approaches, this gift will be present to assist the church through those difficult times. More than that, it points to an increased activity of this gift.

The Prophetic Gift Just Before the Second Advent. God gave the gift of prophecy to John the Baptist to announce Christ's first advent. In a similar way we may expect Him to send the prophetic gift again to proclaim the Second Advent so that everyone will have the opportunity to prepare to meet the Saviour.

In fact, Christ mentions the rise of false prophets as one of the signs that His coming is near (Matt. 24:11, 24). If there were to be no true prophets during the time of the end, Christ would have warned against anyone claiming that gift. His warning against false prophets implies that there would be true prophets, as well.

The prophet Joel predicted a special outpouring of the prophetic gift just before Christ's return. He said, "And it shall come to pass afterward that I will pour out My Spirit on all flesh; your sons and your daughters shall prophesy, your old men shall dream dreams, your young men shall see visions; and also on My menservants and on My maidservants I will pour out My Spirit in those days. And I will show wonders in the heavens and in the earth: Blood and fire and pillars of smoke. The sun shall be turned into darkness, and the moon into blood, before the coming of the great and terrible day of the Lord" (Joel 2:28-31).

The first Pentecost saw a remarkable manifestation of the Spirit. Peter, citing Joel's prophecy, pointed out that God had promised such blessings (Acts 2:2-21). However, we may ask whether Joel's prophecy reached its ultimate fulfillment in Pentecost or whether there must yet be another, more complete, fulfillment. We have no evidence that the phenomena in the sun and moon that Joel spoke of either preceded or followed that outpouring of the Spirit. These phenomena did not occur until many centuries later (see chapter 25 of this book).

Pentecost, then, was a foretaste of the full manifestation of the Spirit before the Second Advent. Like Palestine's early rain, which fell in the autumn, shortly after the crops were planted, the outpouring of the Holy Spirit at Pentecost inaugurated the dispensation of the Spirit. The complete and final fulfillment of Joel's prophecy corresponds to the latter rain, which, falling in the spring, ripened the grain (Joel 2:23). Likewise, the final bestowal of God's Spirit will take place just before the Second Advent, after the predicted signs in the sun, moon, and stars (cf. Matt. 24:29; Rev. 6:12-17; Joel 2:31). Like the latter rain, this final outpouring of the Spirit will ripen the harvest of the earth (Matt. 13:30, 39), and "whoever calls on the name of the Lord shall be saved" (Joel 2:32).

The Prophetic Gift in the Remnant Church. Revelation 12 reveals two major periods of persecution. During the first, which extended from A.D. 538 to A.D. 1798 (Rev. 12:6, 14—see chapter 13 of this book), loyal believers suffered intense persecution. Again, just before the Second Advent, Satan will attack "the remnant of her offspring," the remnant church that refuses to give up allegiance to Christ. Revelation characterizes the loyal believers who make up the remnant as they "who keep the commandments of God and have the testimony of Jesus Christ" (Rev. 12:17).

That the phrase "the testimony of Jesus" speaks of prophetic revelation is clear from later conversations between the angel and John.[8]

Near the end of the book the angel identifies himself as "your fellow servant, and of your brethren who have the testimony of Jesus" (Rev. 19:10) and "your fellow servant, and of your brethren the prophets" (Rev. 22:9). These parallel expressions make it clear that it is the prophets who have "the testimony of Jesus."[9] This explains the angel's statement that "the testimony of Jesus is the spirit of prophecy" (Rev. 19:10).

Commenting on this text, James Moffatt wrote, "For the testimony or witness of (*i.e.*, borne by) Jesus is (*i.e.*, constitutes) the spirit of prophecy." This... specially defines the brethren who hold the testimony of Jesus as possessors of prophetic inspiration. The testimony of Jesus is practically equivalent to Jesus testifying (xxii. 20). It is the self-revelation of Jesus (according to [Rev.] 1:1, due ultimately to God) which moves the Christian prophets."[10]

So the expression the *Spirit of Prophecy* can refer to (1) the Holy Spirit's inspiring the prophet with a revelation from God, (2) the operation of the gift of prophecy, and (3) the medium of prophecy itself.

The prophetic gift, Jesus' witness "to the church through the medium of prophecy,"[11] comprises a distinctive characteristic of the remnant church. Jeremiah linked the demise of this gift with lawlessness. "The Law is no more, and her prophets find no vision from the Lord" (Lam. 2:9). Revelation identifies the possession of the two as distinctive characteristics of the end-time church; its members "keep the commandments of God and have the testimony of Jesus Christ"—the prophetic gift (Rev. 12:17).

God gave the prophetic gift to the "church" of Exodus to organize, instruct, and guide His people (Acts 7:38, KJV). "By a prophet the Lord brought Israel out of Egypt, and by a prophet he was preserved" (Hosea 12:13). It comes as no surprise, then, to find that gift among those who are involved in the ultimate exodus—the escape from sin-polluted Planet Earth to the heavenly Canaan. This exodus, which will follow the Second Advent, is the final and complete fulfillment of Isaiah 11:11: "It shall come to pass in that day that the Lord shall set His hand again the second time to recover the remnant of His people who are left."

Help in the Final Crisis. The Scriptures reveal that God's people in the last days of Earth's history will experience the full wrath of the satanic dragon power as he engages in a final attempt to destroy them (Rev. 12:17). This will "be a time of trouble, such as never was since there was a nation" (Dan. 12:1). To help them survive this most intense conflict of the ages, God in His loving-kindness gave His people the assurance that they would not be alone. The testimony of Jesus, the Spirit of prophecy, would guide them safely to their final objective—unification with their Saviour at the Second Advent.

The following illustration explains the relationship between the Bible and postbiblical instances of the prophetic gift: "Suppose we are about to start upon a voyage. The owner of the vessel gives us a book of directions, telling us that it contains instructions sufficient for our whole journey, and that if we will heed them, we shall reach in safety our port of destination. Setting sail, we open our book to learn its contents. We find that its author lays down general principles to govern us in our voyage, and instructs us as far as practicable, judging the various contingencies that may arise till the end; but he also tells us that the latter part of the trip will be especially perilous; that the features of the coast are ever changing by reason of quicksands and tempests; "but for this part of the journey," says he, "I have provided you a pilot, who will meet you, and give you such directions as the surrounding circumstances and dangers may require; and to him you must give heed." With these directions we reach the perilous times specified, and the pilot, according to promise, appears. But some of the crew, as he offers his services, rise up against him. "We have the original book of directions," say they, "and that is enough for us. We stand upon that, and that alone; we want nothing of you." Who now heeds that original book of directions? Those who reject the pilot, or those who receive him as that book instructs them? Judge ye."[12]

Postbiblical Prophets and the Bible

The prophetic gift produced the Bible itself. In postbiblical times it is not to supersede or add to Scripture, because the canon of Scripture is now closed.

The prophetic gift functions in the end-time much as it did in the time of the apostles. Its thrust is to uphold the Bible as the basis of faith and practice, to explain its teachings, and to apply its principles to daily life. It is involved in establishing and edifying the church, enabling it to carry out its divinely appointed mission. The prophetic gift reproves, warns, guides, and encourages both individuals and the church, protecting them from heresy and unifying them on Bible truths.

Postbiblical prophets function much like prophets such as Nathan, Gad, Asaph, Shemaiah, Azariah, Eliezer, Ahijah, and Obed, Miriam, Deborah, Huldah, Simeon, John the Baptist, Agabus, Silas, Anna, and Philips's four daughters, who lived in Bible times, but whose testimonies never became a part of the Bible. The same God who spoke through the prophets whose writings are in the Bible inspired these prophets and prophetesses. Their messages did not contradict the previously recorded divine revelation.

Testing the Prophetic Gift. Because the Bible warns that before Christ's return false prophets will arise, we must investigate carefully all claims to the prophetic gift. "Do not treat prophecies with contempt," Paul said. "Test everything. Hold on to the good. Avoid every kind of evil" (1 Thess. 5:20-22, NIV; cf. 1 John 4:1).

The Bible specifies several guidelines by which we can distinguish the genuine prophetic gift from the spurious.

1. Does the message agree with the Bible? "To the law and to the testimony! If they do not speak according to this word, it is because there is no light in them" (Isa. 8:20). This text implies that messages of any prophet ought to be in harmony with God's law and testimony throughout the Bible. A later prophet must not contradict earlier prophets. The Holy Spirit never contradicts His previously given testimony, for God "does not change like shifting shadows" (James 1:17, NIV).

2. Do the predictions come true? "How can we know when a message has not been spoken by the Lord?" If what a prophet proclaims in the name of the Lord does not take place or come true, that is a message the Lord has not spoken. That prophet has spoken presumptuously. Do not be afraid of him" (Deut. 18:21, 22, NIV; cf. Jer. 28:9). Though predictions may comprise a comparatively small part of the prophetic message, their accuracy must be demonstrated.

3. Is Christ's incarnation recognized? "By this you know the Spirit of God: Every spirit that confesses that Jesus Christ has come in the flesh is of God, and every spirit that does not confess that Jesus Christ has come in the flesh is not of God" (1 John 4:2. 3). This test demands more than a simple acknowledgment that Jesus Christ lived on earth. The true prophet must confess the biblical teaching on Christ's incarnation—must believe in His deity and preexistence, His virgin birth, true humanity, sinless life, atoning sacrifice, resurrection, ascension, intercessory ministry, and second advent.

4. Does the prophet bear good or bad "fruit"? Prophecy comes through the Holy Spirit's inspiring "holy men of God" (2 Peter 1:21). We can discern false prophets by their fruits. "A good tree cannot bear bad fruit" Jesus said, "nor can a bad tree bear good fruit. Every tree that does not bear good fruit is cut down and thrown into the fire. Therefore by their fruits you will know them" (Matt. 7:16, 18-20).

This counsel is crucial in evaluating a prophet's claim. It speaks first of the prophet's life. It does not mean that the prophet must be absolutely perfect—Scripture says that Elijah was a man of "like passions as we are"

(James 5:17, KJV). But the prophet's life should be characterized by the fruit of the Spirit, not by works of the flesh (see Gal. 5:19-23).

Second, this principle pertains to the influence of the prophet on others. What results accrue in the lives of those who accept the messages? Do their messages equip God's people for missions and unify them in their faith (Eph. 4:12-16)?

Any person claiming to have the prophetic gift should be subjected to these biblical tests. If he or she measures up to these criteria we can have confidence that indeed the Holy Spirit has given that individual the gift of prophecy.

The Spirit of Prophecy in the Seventh-day Adventist Church

The gift of prophecy was active in the ministry of Ellen G. White, one of the founders of the Seventh-day Adventist Church. She has given inspired instruction for God's people living during the time of the end. The world of the early nineteenth century, when Ellen White began to deliver God's messages, was a man's world. Her prophetic call put her under critical scrutiny. Passing the biblical tests, she went on to minister through her spiritual gift for seventy years. From 1844, when she was 17, until 1915—the year of her death—she had more than 2,000 visions. During that time she lived and worked in America, Europe, and Australia, counseling, establishing new work, preaching, and writing.

Ellen White never assumed the title of prophetess, but she did not object when others called her by that title. She explained, "Early in my youth I was asked several times, Are you a prophet? I have ever responded, I am the Lord's messenger. I know that many have called me a prophet, but I have made no claim to this title....Why have I not claimed to be a prophet?—Because in these days many who boldly claim that they are prophets are a reproach to the cause of Christ; and because my work includes much more than the word 'prophet' signifies....To claim to be a prophetess is something that I have never done. If others call me by that name, I have no controversy with them. But my work has covered so many lines that I can not call myself other than a messenger."[13]

The Application of Prophetic Tests. How does Ellen White's ministry measure against the biblical tests of a prophet?

1. Agreement with the Bible. Her abundant literary production includes tens of thousands of Bible texts, coupled often with detailed expositions. Careful study has shown that her writings are consistent, accurate, and in full agreement with the Scriptures.

2. The accuracy of predictions. Ellen White's writings contain a relatively small number of predictions. Some are in the process of being fulfilled, while others still await fulfillment. But those that can be tested have been fulfilled with an amazing accuracy. Two instances that demonstrate her prophetic insights follow.

a. The rise of modern spiritualism. In 1850, when spiritualism—the movement that touts communication with the spirit world and the dead—had but just arisen, Ellen White identified it as a last-day deception and predicted its growth. Although at that time the movement was decidedly anti-Christian, she foresaw that this hostility would change and that it would become respectable among Christians.[14] Since that time spiritualism has spread worldwide, gaining millions of adherents. Its anti-Christian stance has changed; indeed, many call themselves Christian spiritualists, claiming that they have the true Christian faith and that "Spiritualists are the only religionists who have used the promised gifts of Christ, by which gifts they heal the sick, and demonstrate a future conscious and progressive existence."[15] They even assert that spiritualism "gives you the knowledge of all the great systems of religion, and still more, it gives you more knowledge of the Christian Bible than all the Commentaries combined. The Bible is a book of Spiritualism."[16]

b. A close cooperation between Protestants and Roman Catholics. During Ellen White's life a gulf existed between Protestants and Roman Catholics that seemed to preclude any cooperation between the two. Anti-Catholicism raged among Protestants. She prophesied that major changes within Protestantism would bring about a departure from the faith of the Reformation. Consequently, differences between Protestants and Catholics would diminish, leading to a bridging of the gulf separating the two.[17]

The years since her death have seen the rise of the ecumenical movement, the establishment of the World Council of Churches, the Catholic Church's Vatican II, and Protestant ignorance and even outright rejection of the Reformation views of prophetic interpretation.[18] These major changes have broken down barriers between Protestants and Catholics, leading to growing cooperation.

3. The acknowledgement of Christ's incarnation. Ellen White wrote extensively on the life of Christ. His role as Lord and Saviour, His atoning sacrifice at the cross, and His present intercessory ministry dominate her literary works. Her book *The Desire of Ages* has been acclaimed as one of the most spiritual treatises ever written on the life of Christ, while *Steps to Christ,* her most widely distributed book, has led millions to a deep relationship with Him.

Her works clearly portray Christ as fully God and fully man. Her balanced expositions fully agree with the biblical view, carefully avoiding the overemphasizing of one nature or the other—a problem that has caused so much controversy throughout the history of Christianity.

Her overall treatment of Christ's ministry is practical. No matter what aspect she deals with, her overriding concern is to bring the reader into a more intimate relationship with the Saviour.

4. The influence of her ministry. More than a century has passed since Ellen White received the prophetic gift. Her church and the lives of those who have heeded her counsels reveal the impact of her life and messages.

"Although she never held an official position, was not an ordained minister, and never received a salary from the church until after the death of her husband, her influence shaped the Seventh-day Adventist Church more than any other factor except the Holy Bible."[19] She was the moving force behind the establishment of the church's publishing work, schools, medical-missionary work, and the worldwide missionary outreach that has made the Seventh-day Adventist Church one of the largest and fastest-growing Protestant missionary organizations.

The material that she wrote fills more than eighty books, 200 tracts and pamphlets, and 4,600 periodical articles. Sermons, diaries, special testimonies, and letters comprise another 60,000 pages of manuscript materials.

The scope of this material is astounding. Ellen White's expertise was not limited to a few narrow fields. The Lord gave her counsel in matters of health, education, family life, temperance, evangelism, the publishing ministry, proper diet, medical work, and many other areas. Perhaps her writing in the field of health is the most amazing because of the way her insights, some given more than a century ago, have been verified by modern science.

Her writings focus on Jesus Christ and uphold the high moral and ethical values of the Judeo-Christian tradition.

Although many of her writings are directed to the Seventh-day Adventist Church, large portions have been appreciated by wider audiences. Her popular book *Steps to Christ* has been translated into more than 100 languages and has sold more than fifteen million copies. Her greatest work is the well-received five-volume Conflict of the Ages Series, which details the great controversy between Christ and Satan from the origin of sin until its eradication from the universe.

The impact of her writings on individuals is profound. Recently the Institute of Church Ministry of Andrews University did a study comparing the Christian attitude and behavior of Adventists who regularly read her books and those who do not. Their research strongly underscores the impact her writings have on those who read them. The study reached these conclusions: "Readers have a closer relationship with Christ, more certainty of their standing with God, and are more likely to have identified their spiritual gifts. They are more in favor of spending for public evangelism and contribute more heavily to local missionary projects. They feel more prepared for witnessing and actually engage in more witnessing and outreach programs. They are more likely to study the Bible daily, to pray for specific people, to meet in fellowship groups, and to have daily family worship. They see their church more positively. They are responsible for winning more converts."[20]

The Spirit of Prophecy and the Bible. The writings of Ellen White are not a substitute for Scripture. They cannot be placed on the same level. The Holy Scriptures stand alone—the unique standard by which her and all other writings must be judged and to which they must be subject.

1. The Bible the supreme standard. Seventh-day Adventists fully support the Reformation principle of *sola scriptura*—the Bible as its own interpreter and the Bible alone as the basis of all doctrines. The founders of the church developed fundamental beliefs through study of the Bible; they did not receive these doctrines through the visions of Ellen White. Her major role during the development of their doctrines was to guide in the understanding of the Bible and to confirm conclusions reached through Bible study.[21]

Ellen White herself believed and taught that the Bible was the ultimate norm for the church. In her first book, published in 1851, she said, "I recommend to you, dear reader, the Word of God as the rule of your faith and practice. By that Word we are to be judged."[22] She never changed this view. Many years later she wrote, "In His Word, God has committed to men the knowledge necessary for salvation. The Holy Scriptures are to be accepted as an authoritative, infallible revelation of His will. They are the standard of character, the revealer of doctrines, and the test of experience."[23] In 1909, during her last address to a general session of the church, she opened the Bible, held it up before the congregation, and said, "Brethren and sisters, I commend to you this Book."[24]

In response to believers who considered her writings an addition to the Bible, she wrote, saying, "I took the precious Bible and surrounded it with the several *Testimonies for the Church*, given for the people of God....You are not familiar with the Scriptures. If you had made God's word your study, with a desire to reach the Bible standard and attain to Christian perfection, you would not have needed the *Testimonies*. It is because you have neglected to acquaint yourselves with God's inspired Book that He has sought to reach you by simple, direct testimonies, calling your attention to the words of inspiration which you had neglected to obey, and urging you to fashion your lives in accordance with its pure and elevated teachings."[25]

2. A guide to the Bible. She saw her work as that of leading people back to the Bible. "Little heed is given to the Bible," she said, therefore "the Lord has given a lesser light to lead men and women to the greater light."[26] "The Word of God," she wrote, "is sufficient to enlighten the most beclouded mind and may be understood by those who have any desire to understand it. But notwithstanding all this, some who profess to make the Word of God their study are found living in direct opposition to its plainest teachings. Then, to leave men and women without excuse, God gives plain and pointed testimonies, bringing them back to the word that they have neglected to follow."[27]

3. A guide in understanding the Bible. Ellen White considered her writings a guide to a clearer understanding of the Bible. "Additional truth is not brought out; but God has through the *Testimonies,* simplified the great truths already given and in His own chosen way brought them before the people to awaken and impress the mind with them, that all may be left without excuse." "The written testimonies are not given to give new light, but to impress vividly upon the heart the truths of inspiration already revealed."[28]

4. A guide to apply Bible principles. Much of her writings apply the biblical counsels to everyday life. Ellen White said that she was "directed to bring out general principles, in speaking and in writing, and at the same time specify the dangers, errors, and sins of some individuals, that all might be warned, reproved, and counseled."[29] Christ had promised such prophetic guidance to His church. As Ellen White noted, "The fact that God has revealed His will to men through His Word, has not rendered needless the continued presence and guiding of the Holy Spirit. On the contrary, the Spirit was promised by our Saviour, to open the Word to His servants, to illuminate and apply its teachings."[30]

The Challenge to the Believer. Revelation's prophecy that the "testimony of Jesus" would manifest itself through the "spirit of prophecy" in the last days of earth's history challenges everyone not to take an attitude of indifference or disbelief, but to "test everything" and "hold on to the good." There is much to gain—or lose—depending on whether we carry out this biblically mandated investigation. Jehoshaphat said, "Believe in the Lord your God, and you shall be established; believe His prophets, and you shall prosper" (2 Chron. 20:20). His words ring true today, as well.

References

1. Italics supplied.

2. For biblical examples of female prophets, see Ex. 15:20; Judges 4:4; 2 Kings 22:14; Luke 2:36; Acts 21:9.

3. Frank B. Holbrook, "The Biblical Basis for a Modern Prophet," p. 1 (Shelf document, Ellen G. White Estate Inc., General Conference of Seventh-day Adventists, 6840 Eastern Ave., NW, Washington, D.C. 20012). Cf. Jemison, *A Prophet Among You* (Mountain View, CA: Pacific Press, 1955), pp. 52-55.

4. See Holbrook, "Modern Prophet," pp. 3-5.

5. Unfortunately, no complete records of what occurred throughout the Christian era are available.

6. Gerhard Friedrich, "Prophets and Prophecies in the New Testament" in *Theological Dictionary of the New Testament*, vol. 6, p. 859.

7. Cf. Friedrich, pp. 860, 861.

8. The expression "testimony of Jesus" is best understood as a subjective genitive, not an objective genitive. "Two translations are possible: a) The testimony (witness) *about* or *concerning* Jesus (objective genitive) = what Christians witness about Jesus. 'Who bear testimony to Jesus' (RSV). b) The testimony (witness) *from* or *by* Jesus (subjective genitive) = messages from Jesus to the church. The evidence from the use of this expression in the book of Revelation suggests that it should be understood as a subjective genitive (a testimony *from* or *by* Jesus), and that this testimony is given through prophetic revelation" (Holbrook, "Modern Prophet," p. 7).

   As one of the evidences Holbrook quotes Rev. 1:1, 2: "*The Revelation of Jesus Christ* which God gave unto him, *to shew* unto his servants...and *he sent and signified it* by his angel unto his servant John: who bare record of the Word of God, and of *the testimony of Jesus Christ*, and of all things that he saw." In this context it is evident that "the Revelation of Jesus" designates a revelation *from* or *by* Jesus to John. John bears record of this testimony/witness *from* Jesus. Both genitive expressions make the best sense in context as subjective genitives and agree with Christ's closing words in the book: "He *which testifieth* (witnesses) these things, saith, Surely I come quickly" (Revelation 22:20)" (*Ibid*. pp. 7, 8).

9. See *SDA Bible Commentary*, rev. ed., vol. 7, p. 812; T.H. Blincoe, "The Prophets Were Until John," *Ministry*, Supplement, July 1977, p. 24L; Holbrook, "Modern Prophet," p. 8.

10. James Moffatt in *Expositor's Greek Testament*, ed., W. Robertson Nicoll, vol. 5, p. 465.

11. "Spirit of Prophecy," *SDA Encyclopedia*, rev. ed., p. 1412. Those looking for the Second Advent, Paul said, have the testimony of Christ confirmed so that they come short in no gift (1 Cor. 1:6, 7).

12. Uriah Smith, "Do We Discard the Bible by Endorsing the Visions?" *Review and Herald*, Jan. 13, 1863, p. 52, quoted in *Review and Herald*, Dec. 1, 1977, p. 13.

13. White, "A Messenger," *Review and Herald*, July 26, 1906, p. 8. The title "the Lord's messenger" was given by inspiration (*Ibid*).

14. White, *Early Writings*, p. 59.

15. J.M. Peebles, "The Word Spiritualism Misunderstood," in *Centennial Book of Modern Spiritualism in America* (Chicago, IL: National Spiritualist Association of the United States of America, 1948), p. 34.

16. B.F. Austin, "A Few Helpful Thoughts," *Centennial Book of Modern Spiritualism*, p. 44.

17. White, *The Great Controversy Between Christ and Satan* (Mountain View, CA: Pacific Press, 1950), pp. 571, 588.

18. For the historicist view of Daniel's and Revelation's prophecies that dominated Protestantism from the Reformation until the nineteenth century, see Froom, *Prophetic Faith of Our Fathers*, vols. 2-4. See also chapter 13.

19. Richard Hammill, "Spiritual Gifts in the Church Today," *Ministry*, July 1982, p. 17.

20. Roger L. Dudley and Des Cummings, Jr., "A Comparison of the Christian Attitudes and Behaviors Between Those Adventist Church Members Who Regularly Read Ellen White Books and Those Who Do Not," 1982, pp. 41, 42. A research report of the Institute of Church Ministry, Andrews University, Berrien Springs, MI. The survey sampled more than 8,200 members attending 193 churches in the United States.

21. Jemison, *A Prophet Among You*, pp. 208-210; Froom, *Movement of Destiny* (Washington, D.C.: Review and Herald, 1971), pp. 91-132; Damsteegt, *Foundations of the Seventh-day Adventist Message and Mission*, pp. 103-293.

22. White, *Early Writings*, p. 78.

23. White, *Great Controversy*, p. vii.

24. William A. Spicer, *The Spirit of Prophecy in the Advent Movement* (Washington, D.C.: Review and Herald, 1937), p. 30.

25. White, *Testimonies*, vol. 5, pp. 664, 665.

26. White, "An Open Letter," *Review and Herald*, Jan. 20, 1903, p. 15, in White, *Colporteur Ministry* (Mountain View, CA: Pacific Press, 1953), p. 125).

27. White, *Testimonies*, vol. 5, p. 663.

28. *Ibid.*, p. 665.

29. *Ibid.*, p. 660.

30. White, *Great Controversy*, p. vii.

The Law of God

19

The great principles of God's law are embodied in the Ten Commandments and exemplified in the life of Christ. They express God's love, will, and purposes concerning human conduct and relationships and are binding upon all people in every age. These precepts are the basis of God's covenant with His people and the standard in God's judgment. Through the agency of the Holy Spirit they point out sin and awaken a sense of need for a Saviour. Salvation is all of grace and not of works, but its fruitage is obedience to the Commandments. This obedience develops Christian character and results in a sense of well-being. It is an evidence of our love for the Lord and our concern for our fellow men. The obedience of faith demonstrates the power of Christ to transform lives and therefore strengthens Christian witness. (Ex. 20:1-17; Ps. 40:7, 8; Matt. 22:36-40; Deut. 28:1-14; Matt. 5:17-20; Heb. 8:8-10; John 15:7-10; Eph. 2:8-10; 1 John 5:3; Rom. 8:3, 4; Ps. 19:7-14.)

ALL EYES FOCUSED ON THE MOUNTAIN. Its summit was covered with a thick cloud that, continuing to darken, swept downward until the entire mountain was engulfed in mystery. Lightning flashed from the darkness, while thunder echoed and reechoed. "Now Mount Sinai was completely in smoke, because the Lord descended upon it in fire. Its smoke ascended like the smoke of a furnace and the whole mountain quaked.... The blast of the trumpet sounded long and became louder and louder" (Ex. 19:18, 19). So powerful was this majestic revelation of God's presence that all Israel trembled.

Suddenly, the thunder and trumpet ceased, leaving an awesome silence. Then God spoke out of thick darkness that enshrouded Him as He stood on the mountain. Moved by deep love for His people, He proclaimed the Ten Commandments. Said Moses: "The Lord came from Sinai,...and He came with ten thousands of saints; from His right hand came a fiery law for them. Yes, He loves the people; all His saints are in Your hand; they sit down at Your feet; everyone receives Your words" (Deut. 33:2, 3).

When He gave the law at Sinai, God not only revealed Himself as the majestic supreme Authority of the universe. He also portrayed Himself as the Redeemer of His people (Ex. 20:2). It is because He is Saviour that He called not only Israel but all humanity (Eccl. 12:13) to obey ten brief, comprehensive, and authoritative precepts that cover the duty of human beings to God and to their fellow beings.

And God said:

"You shall have no other gods before Me.

"You shall not make for yourself any carved image or any likeness of anything that is in heaven above, or that is in the earth beneath, or that is in the water under the earth; you shall not bow down to them nor serve them. For I, the Lord your God, am a jealous God, visiting the iniquity of the fathers on the children to the third and fourth generations of those who hate Me, but showing mercy to thousands, to those who love Me and keep My commandments.

"You shall not take the name of the Lord Your God in vain, for the Lord will not hold him guiltless who takes His name in vain.

"Remember the Sabbath day, to keep it holy. Six days you shall labor and do all your work, but the seventh day is the Sabbath of the Lord your God. In it you shall do no work; you, nor your son, nor your daughter, nor your manservant, nor your maidservant, nor your cattle, nor your stranger who is within your gates. For in six days the Lord made the heavens and the earth, the sea and all that is in them, and rested on the seventh day. Therefore the Lord blessed the Sabbath day and hallowed it.

"Honor your father and your mother, that your days may be long upon the land which the Lord your God is giving you.

"You shall not murder.

"You shall not commit adultery.

"You shall not steal.

"You shall not bear false witness against your neighbor.

"You shall not covet your neighbor's house; you shall not covet your neighbor's wife, nor his manservant, nor his maidservant, nor his ox, nor his donkey, nor anything that is your neighbor's" (Ex. 20:3-17).

The Nature of the Law

As a reflection of God's character, the Ten Commandment law is moral, spiritual, and comprehensive, containing universal principles.

A Reflection of the Character of the Lawgiver. Scripture sees the attributes of God in His law. Like God, "The law of the Lord is perfect" and "the testimony of the Lord is pure" (Ps. 19:7, 8). "The law is holy, and the commandment holy and just and good" (Rom. 7:12). "Your commandments are truth. Concerning Your testimonies, I have known of old that You have founded them forever" (Ps. 119:151, 152). Indeed, "all Your commandments are righteousness" (Ps. 119:172).

A Moral Law. The Ten Commandments convey God's pattern of conduct for humanity. They define our relationship with our Creator and Redeemer and our duty to our fellow beings. Scripture calls the transgression of God's law sin (1 John 3:4, KJV).

A Spiritual Law. "The law is spiritual" (Rom. 7:14). Therefore, only those who are spiritual and have the fruit of the Spirit can obey it (John 15:4; Gal. 5:22, 23). It is God's Spirit that empowers us to do His will (Acts 1:8; Ps. 51:10-12). By abiding in Christ, we receive the power we need to bear fruit to His glory (John 15:5).

Human laws address only overt acts. But the Ten Commandments are "exceedingly broad" (Ps. 119:96), touching our most secret thoughts, desires, and emotions such as jealousy, envy, lust, and ambition. In the Sermon on the Mount, Jesus emphasized this spiritual dimension of the law, revealing that transgression begins in the heart (Matt. 5:21, 22, 27, 28; Mark 7:21-23).

A Positive Law. The Decalogue is more than just a short series of prohibitions; it contains far-reaching principles. It extends not only to the things we should not do but to the things we should do. We must not only refrain from evil acts and thoughts; we must learn to use our God-given talents and gifts for good. Thus every negative injunction has a positive dimension.

For example, the sixth commandment, "You shall not kill" has as its positive side "You shall promote life." "It is God's will that His followers seek to promote the well-being and happiness of everyone who comes within their sphere of influence. In a profound sense the gospel commission—the good news of salvation and eternal life in Jesus Christ—rests upon the positive principle embodied in the sixth precept."[1]

The Ten-Commandment law should not be seen "as much from the prohibitory side, as from the mercy side. Its prohibitions are the sure guarantee of happiness in obedience. As received in Christ, it works in us the purity of character that will bring joy to us through eternal ages. To the obedient it is a wall of protection. We behold in it the goodness of God, who by revealing to men the immutable principles of righteousness, seeks to shield them from the evils that result from transgression."[2]

A Simple Law. The Ten Commandments are profound in their simple comprehensiveness. They are so brief that even a child can quickly memorize them, yet so far-reaching that they cover every possible sin.

"There is not mystery in the law of God. All can comprehend the great truths which it embodies. The feeblest intellect can grasp these rules; the most ignorant can regulate the life, and form the character after the divine standard."[3]

A Law of Principles. The Ten Commandments are a summary of all right principles—they apply to all humanity at all times. Scripture says, "Fear God and keep His commandments, for this is the whole duty of man" (Eccl. 12:13).

The Decalogue—the Ten Words, or Ten Commandments (Ex. 34:28)—consists of two parts, indicated by the two tablets of stone upon which God wrote it (Deut. 4:13). The first four commandments regulate our duty to our Creator and Redeemer, and the last six regulate our duty toward people.[4]

This twofold division derives from the two great fundamental principles of love upon which God's kingdom operates: "You shall love the Lord your God with all your heart, with all your soul, with all your strength, and with all your mind," and "your neighbor as yourself" (Luke 10:27; cf. Deut. 6:4, 5; Lev. 19:18). Those who live these principles will be in full harmony with the Ten Commandments, for the commandments express these principles in more detail.

The first commandment directs the exclusive worship of the one true God. The second forbids idolatry.[5] The third prohibits irreverence and the perjury that involves the invoking of the divine name. The fourth calls for the observance of the Sabbath and identifies the true God as the Creator of heaven and earth.

The fifth commandment requires children to submit to their parents as God's appointed agents for the transmission of His revealed will to succeeding generations (see Deut. 4:6-9; 6:1-7). The sixth protects life as sacred. The seventh enjoins purity and safeguards the marital relationship. The eighth protects property. The ninth guards truth and proscribes perjury. And the tenth goes to the root of all human relationships by prohibiting the coveting of that which belongs to others.[6]

A Unique Law. The Ten Commandments have the unique distinction of being the only words God spoke audibly to an entire nation (Deut. 5:22). Not trusting this law to the forgetful minds of humans, God then engraved the commandments with His finger on two tablets of stone that were to be preserved inside the ark of the tabernacle (Ex. 31:18; Deut. 10:2).

To help Israel apply the commandments, God gave them additional laws detailing their relationship to Him and to each other. Some of these additional laws focused on the civil affairs of Israel (civil laws), others regulated the ceremonies of the sanctuary services (ceremonial laws). God communicated these additional laws to the people through an intermediary, Moses, who wrote them down in the "book of the law," and placed them "beside the ark of the covenant" (Deut. 31:25, 26)—not in the ark as he had done with God's supreme revelation, the Decalogue. These additional laws were known as "the Book of the Law of Moses" (Joshua 8:31; Neh. 8:1; 2 Chron. 25:4), or simply the "Law of Moses" (2 Kings 23:25; 2 Chron. 23:18).[7]

A Delightful Law. God's law is an inspiration to the soul. Said the psalmist: "Oh, how I love Your law! It is my meditation all the day." "I love Your commandments more than gold, yes than fine gold!" Even when "trouble and anguish have overtaken me," he said, "Your commandments are my delights" (Ps. 119:97, 127, 143). To those who love God, "His commandments are not burdensome" (1 John 5:3). Transgressors are the ones who consider the law a grievous yoke, for the sinful mind "does not submit to God's law, nor can it do so" (Rom. 8:7, NIV).

The Purpose of the Law

God gave His law to provide people with abundant blessings and to lead them into a saving relationship with Himself. Note the following specific purposes:

It Reveals God's Will for Humanity. As the expression of God's character and love, the Ten Commandments reveal His will and purpose for humanity. They demand perfect obedience, "for whoever shall keep the whole law, and yet stumble in one point, he is guilty of all" (James 2:10). Obedience to the law, as the rule of life, is vital to our salvation. Christ Himself said: "If you want to enter into life, keep the commandments" (Matt. 19:17). This obedience is possible only through the power the indwelling Holy Spirit provides.

It Is the Basis of God's Covenant. Moses wrote the Ten Commandments, with other explanatory laws, in a book called the book of the covenant (Exodus 20:1-24:8).[8] Later, he called the Ten Commandments "the tablets of the covenant," indicating their importance as the basis of the everlasting covenant (Deut. 9:9; cf. 4:13. For more on the covenants, see chapter 7 of this book).

It Functions as the Standard of Judgment. Like God, His "commandments are righteousness" (Ps. 119:172). The law, therefore, sets the standard of righteousness. Each of us will be judged by these righteous principles, not by our consciences. "Fear God and keep His commandments," Scripture says, "...for God will bring every work into judgment, including every secret thing, whether it is good or whether it is evil" (Eccl. 12:13, 14; cf. James 2:12).

Human consciences vary. Some consciences are "weak," while others are "defiled," "evil," or "seared with a hot iron" (1 Cor. 8:7, 12; Titus 1:15; Heb. 10:22; 1 Tim. 4:2). Like a watch, however well they may work, they must be "set" by some accurate standard to be of value. Our consciences tell us that we must do right, but they do not tell us what is right. Only consciences set by God's great standard—His law—can keep us from straying into sin.[9]

It Points Out Sin. Without the Ten Commandments people cannot see clearly God's holiness, their own guilt, or their need to repent.

When they do not know that they are in violation of God's law, they do not sense their lostness or their need of the atoning blood of Christ.

To help people see their true condition, the law functions like a mirror (see James 1:23-25). Those who "look" into it see their own character defects in contrast to God's righteous character. Thus the moral law demonstrates that all the world is guilty before God (Rom. 3:19), making everyone fully accountable to Him.

"Through the law we become conscious of sin" (Rom. 3:20, NIV) because "sin is the transgression of the law" (1 John 3:4, KJV). Indeed, Paul said, "I would not have known sin except through the law" (Rom. 7:7). Convicting sinners of their sin, it helps them realize that they are condemned under the judgment of God's wrath and that they are facing the penalty of eternal death. It brings them to a sense of their utter helplessness.

It Is An Agent in Conversion. God's law is the instrument the Holy Spirit uses to bring us to conversion: "The law of the Lord is perfect, converting the soul" (Ps. 19:7). When, after seeing our true character we realize that we are sinners, that we are on death row and without hope, we sense our need of a Saviour. Then the good news of the gospel becomes truly meaningful. Thus the law points us to Christ, the only one who can help us escape our desperate situation.[10] It was in this light that Paul referred to both the moral law and the ceremonial law as "our schoolmaster ["tutor," NKJV] to bring us unto Christ, that we might be justified by faith" (Gal. 3:24).[11]

While the law reveals our sin, it can never save us. Just as water is the means to cleanse a dirty face, so we, after having discovered our need in the mirror of God's moral law, reach for the fountain that is open "for sin and for uncleanness" (Zech. 13:1) and are cleansed by "the blood of the Lamb" (Rev. 7:14). We must look to Christ, "and as Christ [is] revealed to…[us] upon the cross of Calvary, dying beneath the weight of the sins of the whole world, the Holy Spirit shows…[us] the attitude of God to all who repent of their transgressions."[12] Then hope fills our souls, and in faith we reach out to our Saviour, who extends to us the gift of everlasting life (John 3:16).

It Provides True Freedom. Christ said that "whoever commits sin is a slave of sin" (John 8:34). When we transgress God's law, we have no liberty; but obedience to the Ten Commandments assures us true freedom. Living within the confines of God's law means liberty from sin. And it means freedom from that which accompanies sin—the continual worry, wounding of the conscience, and increasing guilt and remorse that wear out life's vital forces. Said the psalmist, "I will walk about in freedom, for I have sought out Your precepts" (Ps. 119:45, NIV). James referred to the Decalogue as "the royal law," "the perfect law of liberty" (James 2:8; 1:25).

That we might receive this freedom, Jesus invites us to come to Him with our burdens of sin. He offers us in their stead His yoke, which is easy (Matt. 11:29, 30). A yoke is an instrument of service. By dividing the load, the yoke makes it easier to perform tasks. Christ offers to be yoked together with us. The yoke itself is the law; "the great law of love revealed in Eden, proclaimed upon Sinai, and in the new covenant written in the heart, is that which binds the human worker to the will of God."[13] When we are yoked with Christ, He bears the heavy burden and makes obedience a joy. He enables us to succeed at what was impossible before. So that the law, written on our hearts, becomes a delight and a joy. We are free because we *want* to do as He commands.

If the law is presented without Christ's saving power, there is no freedom from sin. But God's saving grace, which does not nullify the law, brings the power that liberates from sin, for "where the Spirit of the Lord is, there is liberty" (2 Cor. 3:17).

It Restrains Evil and Brings Blessings. The increase in crime, violence, immorality, and wickedness that floods the world has resulted from disregard for the Decalogue. Where this law is accepted, it restrains sin, promotes right actions, and becomes a means of establishing righteousness. Nations that have incorporated its principles into their laws have experienced great blessing. On the other hand, abandonment of its principles brings about a steady decline.

In Old Testament times God often blessed nations and individuals in proportion to their obedience to His law. "Righteousness exalts a nation," Scripture says, and a "throne is established by righteousness" (Prov. 14:34; 16:12). Those who refused to obey God's commandments encountered calamities (Ps. 89:31, 32). "The curse of the Lord is on the house of the wicked, but He blesses the habitation of the just" (Prov. 3:33; cf. Lev. 26; Deut. 28). The same general principle is true today.[14]

The Perpetuity of the Law

Since the Ten Commandment moral law is a reflection of God's character, its principles are not temporal or situational but absolute, unchangeable, and of permanent validity for humanity. Christians through the centuries have firmly supported the perpetuity of God's law, strongly affirming its continuous validity.[15]

The Law Before Sinai. The law existed long before God gave the Decalogue to Israel. If it did not, there could have been no sin before Sinai, "for sin is the transgression of the law" (1 John 3:4, KJV). That Lucifer and his angels sinned gives evidence of the presence of the law even before Creation (2 Peter 2:4).

When God created Adam and Eve in His image, He implanted the moral principles of the law in their minds, making it natural for them to do His will. Their transgression introduced sin into the human family (Rom. 5:12).

Later, God said of Abraham that he "obeyed My voice and kept My charge, My commandments, My statutes, and My Laws" (Gen. 26:5). And Moses taught God's statutes and His laws before Sinai (Exodus 16; 18:16). A study of the book of Genesis shows that the Ten Commandments were known well before Sinai. That book makes clear that people realized that, before God gave the Decalogue, the acts it forbade were wrong.[16] This general understanding of the moral law shows that God must have provided humanity with knowledge of the Ten Commandments.

The Law at Sinai. During the long period of bondage in Egypt, a nation that did not recognize the true God (Ex. 5:2), the Israelites lived amid idolatry and corruption. As a consequence, they lost much of their understanding of God's holiness, purity, and moral principles. Their status as slaves made it difficult for them to worship.

Responding to their desperate cry for help, God remembered His covenant with Abraham and determined to deliver His people out of this "iron furnace" (Deut. 4:20) by bringing them to a country where "they might observe His statutes and keep His laws" (Ps. 105:43-45).

After their liberation He led them to Mount Sinai to give them the moral law that is the standard of His government and the ceremonial laws that were to teach them that the way of salvation is through the atoning sacrifice of the Saviour. At Sinai, then, God gave the law directly, in clear, simple terms, "because of transgressions" (Gal. 3:19), "so that sin through the commandments might become exceedingly sinful" (Rom. 7:13). Only by having God's moral law brought into sharp focus could the Israelites become conscious of their transgressions, discover their sense of helplessness, and see their need of salvation.

The Law Before Christ's Return. The Bible reveals that God's law is the object of Satan's attack and that his war against it will reach its climax just prior to the Second Advent. Prophecy indicates that Satan will lead the vast majority of people to disobey God (Rev. 12:9). Working through the "beast" power, he will direct the attention of the world toward the beast instead of God (Rev. 13:3; for more on these prophecies, see chapter 13 of this book).

1. The law under attack. Daniel 7 portrays this same power as a little horn. This chapter speaks of four great beasts, which, ever since the time of Christ, Bible commentators have identified as the world powers of Babylon, Medo-Persia, Greece, and Rome. The ten horns of the fourth beast represent the divisions of the Roman Empire at the time of its fall (A.D. 476).[17]

Daniel's vision centers on the little horn, a terrible and blasphemous power that arose among the ten horns, signifying the rise of an awesome power after the disintegration of the Roman Empire. This power would attempt to change God's law (Dan. 7:25) and would continue until Christ's return (see chapter 20 of this book). This attack is, in itself, evidence of the law's continuing significance in the plan of salvation. The vision ends by reassuring God's people that this power will not succeed in eliminating the law, because the judgment will destroy the little horn (Dan. 7:11, 26-28).

2. The saints defend the law. Obedience characterizes the saints who await the Second Advent. In the final conflict they rally to uphold God's law. Scripture describes them in these terms: They "keep the commandments of God and have the testimony of Jesus" (Rev. 12:17; 14:12) and are patiently looking forward to Christ's return.

In preparation for the Second Advent, these people proclaim the gospel, calling others to worship the Lord as Creator (Rev. 14:6, 7). Those who worship God in love will obey Him; as John said: "This is the love of God, that we keep His commandments. And His commandments are not burdensome" (1 John 5:3).

3. God's judgments and the law. God's judgment of the seven last plagues on the disobedient originates from the temple of "the tabernacle of Testimony" in heaven (Rev. 15:5). Israel was well acquainted with the phrase *the tabernacle of the testimony*; it designated the tabernacle that Moses built (Num. 1:50, 53; 17:8; 18:2, NIV). It was called this because the tabernacle housed the "ark of the Testimony" (Ex. 26:34), which contained the "two tablets of the Testimony" (Ex. 31:18). So the Ten Commandments are the "testimony"—the witness to humanity of the divine will (Ex. 34:28, 29).

But Revelation 15:5 refers to "the temple of the tabernacle of the testimony *in heaven*." Moses' tabernacle was merely a copy of the heavenly temple (Ex. 25:8, 40; cf. Heb. 8:1-5); the great original of the Ten Commandment law is kept there. That the final judgments are intimately related to the transgression of God's law adds to the evidence for the perpetuity of the Ten Commandments.

The book of Revelation also depicts the opening of the heavenly temple, which brings into view the "ark of His covenant" (Rev. 11:19). The phrase *ark of the covenant* designated the ark of the earthly sanctuary, which held the tablets containing "the words of the covenant, the Ten Commandments" (Ex. 34:27; cf. Num. 10:33; Deut. 9:9). The ark of the covenant in the heavenly sanctuary is the original ark containing the words of the everlasting covenant—the original Decalogue. Thus it is clear that the timing of God's final judgments on the world (Rev. 11:18) relates to the opening of this heavenly temple with its focus on the ark with the Ten Commandments—indeed, a fitting picture of the magnification of God's law as the standard of the judgment.

The Law and the Gospel

Salvation is a gift that comes by grace through faith, not by works of the law (Eph. 2:8). "No deed of the law, no effort however commendable, and no good works—whether they be many or few, sacrificial or not—can in any way justify the sinner (Titus 3:5; Rom. 3:20)."[18]

Throughout Scripture there is a perfect harmony between the law and the gospel, each upholding the other.

The Law and Gospel Before Sinai. When Adam and Eve sinned, they learned what guilt, fear, and need are (Gen. 3:10). God responded to their need, not by nullifying the law that condemned them, but instead by offering them the gospel that would restore them into fellowship and obedience to Him.

This gospel consisted of a promise of redemption through a Saviour, the seed of the woman, who would come someday and triumph over evil (Gen. 3:15). The system of sacrifices that God enjoined upon them taught them an important truth about the atonement: that forgiveness could be obtained only through the shedding of blood—the death of the Saviour. Believing that the animal sacrifice symbolized the Saviour's atoning death on their behalf, they obtained forgiveness of sin.[19] They were saved by grace.

This gospel promise was the center of God's everlasting covenant of grace offered to humanity (Gen. 12:1-3; 15:4, 5; 17:1-9). It was closely related to obedience to God's law (Gen. 18:18, 19; 26:4, 5). The surety of God's covenant was the Son of God, who, as the focal point of the gospel, was "the lamb slain from the foundation of the world" (Rev. 13:8). God's grace, then, began to operate as soon as Adam and Eve sinned. David said, "The mercy of the Lord is from everlasting to everlasting on those who fear Him,...to such as keep His covenant, and to those who remember His commandments to do them" (Ps. 103:17, 18).

The Law and Gospel at Sinai. There is a close relationship between the Decalogue and the gospel. The preamble to the law, for instance, refers to God as the Redeemer (Ex. 20:1). And following the proclamation of the Ten Commandments, God instructed the Israelites to erect an altar and begin offering the sacrifices that were to reveal His saving grace.

On Mount Sinai God gave Moses a large portion of the ceremonial law dealing with the building of the sanctuary, where God would dwell with His people and meet with them to share His blessings and forgive their sins (Ex. 24:9-31:18). This expansion of the simple system of sacrifices that had existed prior to Sinai foreshadowed Christ's mediatorial work for the redemption of sinners and the vindication of the authority and holiness of God's law.

God's dwelling place was in the Most Holy Place of the earthly sanctuary, over the mercy seat of the ark in which were kept the Ten Commandments. Every aspect of the sanctuary services symbolized the Saviour. The bleeding sacrifices pointed to His atoning death, which would redeem the human race from the condemnation of the law (see chapters 4 and 9).

While the Decalogue was placed inside the ark, the ceremonial laws, together with the civil regulations God gave, were written in the "Book of the Law" and placed beside the ark of the covenant as "a witness against" the people (Deut. 31:26). Whenever they sinned, this "witness" condemned their actions and provided elaborate requirements for reconciliation with God. From Sinai until Christ's death, transgressors of the Decalogue found hope, forgiveness, and cleansing by faith in the gospel portrayed by the sanctuary services of the ceremonial law.

The Law and the Gospel After the Cross. As many Christians have observed, the Bible indicates that while Christ's death abolished the ceremonial law, it affirmed the continued validity of the moral law.[20] Note the evidence:

1. The ceremonial law. When Christ died, He fulfilled the prophetic symbolism of the sacrificial system. Type met antitype, and the ceremonial law came to an end. Centuries earlier, Daniel had predicted that the death of the Messiah would "bring an end to sacrifice and offering" (Dan. 9:27—see chapter 4 of this book). When Jesus died, the veil of the temple was supernaturally torn in two from top to bottom (Matt. 27:51), indicating the end of the spiritual significance of the Temple services.

Although the ceremonial law filled a vital role before the death of Christ, it was deficient in many ways, being only " a shadow of the good things to come" (Heb. 10:1). It served a temporary purpose and was imposed on God's people until the coming of "the time of reformation" (Heb. 9:10; cf. Gal. 3:19)—until the time when Christ died as the true Lamb of God.

At the death of Christ the jurisdiction of the ceremonial law came to an end. His atoning sacrifice provided forgiveness for all sins. This act "wiped out the handwriting of requirements that was against us, which was contrary to us. And He has taken it out of the way, having nailed it to the cross" (Col. 2:14; cf. Deut. 31:26). Then it was no longer necessary to perform the elaborate ceremonies that were not, in any case, able to take away sins or purify the conscience (Heb. 10:4; 9:9, 14). No more worries about the ceremonial laws, with their complex requirements regarding food and drink offerings, celebrations of various festivals (Passover, Pentecost, etc.), new moons, or ceremonial Sabbaths (Col. 2:16; cf. Heb. 9:10), which were only a "shadow of things to come" (Col. 2:17).[21]

With Jesus' death, believers no longer had any need to deal with shadows—reflections of the reality in Christ. Now they could approach the Saviour Himself directly, for the "substance is of Christ" (Col. 2:17).

As interpreted by the Jews, the ceremonial law had become a barrier between them and other nations. It had become a great obstacle to their mission to enlighten the world with the glory of God. Christ's death abolished this "law of commandments contained in ordinances," breaking down "the middle wall of division" between Gentiles and Jews so as to create one family of believers reconciled into "one body through the cross" (Eph. 2:14-16).

2. The Decalogue and the cross. While Christ's death ended the authority of the ceremonial law, it established that of the Ten Commandments. Christ took away the curse of the law, thereby liberating believers from its condemnation. His doing so, however, did not mean that the law was abolished, giving us liberty to violate its principles. The abundant testimony of Scripture regarding the perpetuity of the law refutes such a view.

Calvin aptly stated that "we must not imagine that the coming of Christ has freed us from the authority of the law; for it is the eternal rule of a devout and holy life, and must, therefore, be as unchangeable as the justice of God."[22]

Paul described the relationship between obedience and the gospel of saving grace. Calling believers to holy living, he challenged them to present themselves "as instruments of righteousness to God. For sin shall have no dominion over you, for you are not under law but under grace" (Rom. 6:13, 14). So Christians do not keep the law to obtain salvation—those who try to do so will only find a deeper enslavement to sin. "As long as a man is under law he remains also under the dominion of sin, for law cannot save one from either the condemnation or the power of sin. But those who are under grace receive not only release from condemnation (Rom. 8:1), but also power to overcome (Rom. 6:14). Thus sin no longer will have dominion over them."[23]

"Christ," Paul added, "is the end of the law of righteousness to everyone who believes" (Rom. 10:4). Everyone, then, who believes in Christ realizes that He is the end of the law as a way of obtaining righteousness. In ourselves we are sinners, but in Jesus Christ we are righteous through His imputed righteousness.[24]

Yet being under grace does not give believers the license to "continue in sin that grace may abound" (Rom. 6:1). Rather, grace supplies the power that makes obedience and victory over sin possible. "There is therefore now no condemnation to those who are in Christ Jesus, who do not walk according to the flesh, but according to the Spirit" (Rom. 8:1).

Christ's death magnified the law, upholding its universal authority. If the Decalogue could have been changed, He would not have had to die. But because this law is absolute and immutable, a death was required to pay the penalty it imposed. This requirement Christ fully satisfied by His death on the cross, making eternal life available to all who accept His magnificent sacrifice.

Obedience to the Law

People cannot earn salvation by their good works. Obedience is the fruitage of salvation in Christ. Through His amazing grace, especially displayed at the cross, God has liberated His people from the penalty and curse of sin. Though they were sinners, Christ gave His life to provide them with the gift of eternal life. God's abundant love awakens in the repentant sinner a response that manifests itself in loving obedience through the power of the grace so abundantly bestowed. Believers who understand that Christ values the law and who understand the blessings of obedience will be strongly motivated to live Christlike lives.

Christ and the Law. Christ had the highest regard for the Ten Commandment law. As the great "I AM," He Himself proclaimed the Father's moral law from Sinai (John 8:58; Ex. 3:14—see chapter 4 of this book). Part of His mission on earth was to "magnify the law and make it honorable" (Isa. 42:21). A passage from the Psalms that the New Testament applies to Christ makes clear His attitude toward the law: "I delight to do Your will, O my God, and Your law is within my heart" (Ps. 40:8; cf. Heb. 10:5, 7).

His gospel produced a faith that firmly upheld the validity of the Decalogue. Asked Paul, do we "make void the law through faith? Certainly not! On the contrary, we establish the law" (Rom. 3:31).

So Christ came not only to redeem man but to vindicate the authority and holiness of the law of God, presenting its magnificence and glory before the people and giving them an example of how to relate to it. As His followers, Christians are called to magnify God's law in their lives. Having lived a life of loving obedience Himself, Christ stressed that His followers ought to be commandment keepers. When asked about the requirements for eternal life, He replied, "If you want to enter into life, keep the commandments" (Matt. 19:17). He also warned against the violation of this principle. "Not everyone who says to Me, 'Lord, Lord,' shall enter the kingdom of heaven, but he who does the will of My Father in heaven." Lawbreakers will be refused entrance (Matt. 7:21-23).

Christ Himself fulfilled the law, not by destroying it, but through a life of obedience. "Remember," He said, "that as long as heaven and earth last, not the least point nor the smallest detail of the Law will be done away with" (Matt. 5:18, TEV). Christ strongly emphasized that the grand object of God's law must always be kept in mind—to love the Lord your God with all your heart, soul, and mind, and your neighbor as yourself (Matt. 22:37, 38). However, He wanted His followers not to love one another as the world interprets love—selfishly or sentimentally. To explain the love He spoke of, Christ gave a "new commandment" (John 13:34). This new commandment was not to take the place of the Decalogue but to provide believers with "an example of what true, unselfish love really is—such love as had never before been witnessed on the earth. In this sense His commandment might be described as new. It charged them, not simply 'that ye love one another,' but 'that ye love one another, as I have loved you' (John 15:12). Strictly speaking, we have here simply one more evidence of how Christ magnified His Father's laws."[25]

Obedience reveals such love. Jesus said, "If you love Me, keep My commandments" (John 14:15). "If you keep My commandments, you will abide in My love, just as I have kept My Father's commandments and abide in His love" (John 15:10). Similarly, if we love God's people, we love God and "keep His commandments" (1 John 2:3).

Only through abiding in Christ can we render heartfelt obedience. "As the branch cannot bear fruit of itself, unless it abides in the vine," He said, "Neither can you, unless you abide in Me...He who abides in Me, and I in Him, bears much fruit; for without Me you can do nothing" (John 15:4, 5). To abide in Christ we must be crucified with Him and experience what Paul wrote of: "It is no longer I who live, but Christ lives in me" (Gal. 2:20). For those in this condition Christ can fulfill His new covenant promise: "I will put My laws in their mind and write them on their hearts; and I will be their God, and they shall be My people" (Heb. 8:10).

Blessings of Obedience. Obedience develops Christian character and produces a sense of well-being, causing believers to grow up as "newborn babes" and to be transformed into Christ's image (see 1 Peter 2:2; 2 Cor. 3:18). This transformation from sinner to God's child witnesses effectively to Christ's power.

Scripture pronounces "blessed" all "who walk in the law of the Lord" (Ps. 119:1), whose "delight is in the law of the Lord" and who meditate "in His law...day and night" (Ps. 1:2). The blessings of obedience are many: (1) insight and wisdom (Ps. 119:98, 99); (2) peace (Ps. 119:165; Isa. 48:18); (3) righteousness (Deut. 6:25; Isa. 48:18); (4) a pure and moral life (Prov. 7:1-5); (5) knowledge of the truth (John 7:17); (6) protection against disease (Ex. 15:26); (7) longevity (Prov. 3:1, 2; 4:10, 22); and (8) the assurance that one's prayers will be answered (1 John 3:22; cf. Ps. 66:18).

Inviting us to obedience, God promises abundant blessings (Lev. 26:3-10; Deut. 28:1-12). When we respond positively, we become His "special treasure"—a "kingdom of priests and a holy nation" (Ex. 19:5, 6; cf. 1 Peter 2:5, 9), elevated "above all nations of the earth," "the head and not the tail" (Deut. 28:1, 13).

References

1. Holbrook, "What God's Law Means to Me," *Adventist Review*, Jan. 15, 1987, p. 16.

2. Ellen G. White, *Selected Messages*, book 1, p. 235.

3. *Ibid.*, p. 218.

4. Cf. The Westminster Confession of Faith, A.D. 1647, Chapter XIX, in Philip Schaff, *The Creeds of Christendom*, vol. 3, pp. 640-644.

5. See Taylor G. Bunch, *The Ten Commandments* (Washington, D.C.: Review and Herald, 1944), pp. 35, 36.

6. "Ten Commandments," *SDA Bible Dictionary*, rev. ed., p. 1106.

7. The law of Moses can also refer to a division of the Old Testament called the Pentateuch—the first five books of the Bible (Luke 24:44; Acts 28:23).

8. Included in the book of the covenant were certain civil and ceremonial regulations. The civil precepts were not an addition to those of the Decalogue but merely specific applications of its broad principles. The ceremonial precepts symbolize the gospel by providing the means of grace to sinners. Thus it is the Decalogue that dominates the covenant. Cf. Jer. 7:21-23; Francis D. Nichol, *Answers to Objections* (Washington, D.C.: Review and Herald, 1952), pp. 62-68.

9. Arnold V. Wallenkampf, "Is Conscience a Safe Guide?" *Review and Herald*, April 11, 1983, p. 6.

10. Some have interpreted Paul's statement that "Christ is the end of the law for righteousness to every one who believes" to mean that the end or purpose of the law is to bring us to the point where we can see our sinfulness and come to Christ for pardon and receive through faith His righteousness. (This use of the word *end* [Greek, *telos*], is also found in 1 Tim. 1:5; James 5:11, and 1 Peter 1:9.) See also note 23.

11. Cf. *SDA Bible Commentary*, rev. ed., vol. 6, p. 961; White, *Selected Messages*, book 1, p. 233. The ceremonial law was also a schoolmaster bringing the individual to Christ but through different means. The sanctuary services with their sacrificial offerings pointed sinners to the forgiveness of sin that the blood of the coming Lamb of God, Jesus Christ, would provide, thus bringing them understanding of the grace of the gospel. It was designed to create love for the law of God, while the sacrificial offerings were to be a dramatic illustration of God's love in Christ.

12. *Ibid.*, p. 213.

13. White, *The Desire of Ages*, p. 329.

14. Cf. White, *Education*, pp. 173-184.

15. The historic confessions of faith upholding its validity are "The Waldensean Catechism, c. A.D. 1500; Luther's Small Catechism, A.D. 1529; the Anglican Catechism, A.D. 1549 and 1662; the Scottish Confession of Faith, A.D. 1560 (Reformed); the Heidelberg Catechism, A.D. 1563 (Reformed); the Second Helvetic Confession, A.D. 1566 (Reformed); the Thirty-nine Articles of Religion, A.D. 1571 (Church of England); the Formula of Concord, A.D. 1576 (Lutheran); the Irish Articles of Faith, A.D. 1615 (Irish Episcopal Church); The Westminster Confession of Faith, A.D. 1647; the Westminster Shorter Catechism, A.D. 1647; the Confession of the Waldenses, A.D. 1655; the

Savoy Declaration, A.D. 1658 (Congregational); the Confession of the Society of Friends, A.D. 1675 (Quakers); the Philadelphia Confession, A.D. 1688 (Baptist); the Twenty-five Articles of Religion, A.D. 1784 (Methodist); the New Hampshire Conference, A.D. 1833 (Baptist); the Longer Catechism of the Orthodox, Catholic, Eastern Church, A.D. 1839 (Greek-Russian Church), as quoted in *The Creeds of Christendom*, ed. Philip Schaff, rev. by David S. Schaff (Grand Rapids: Baker Book House, 1983), vols. 1-3.

16. For references to the first and second commandments see Gen. 35:1-4; the fourth, Gen. 2:1-3; the fifth, Gen. 18:19; the sixth, Gen. 4:8-11; the seventh, Gen. 39:7-9; 19:1-10; the eighth, Gen. 44:8; the ninth, Gen. 12:11-20; 20:1-10; and the tenth, Genesis 27.

17. Froom, *Prophetic Faith of Our Fathers*, vol. 1, pp. 456, 894; vol. 2, pp. 528, 784; vol. 3, pp. 252, 744; vol. 4, pp. 392, 846.

18. *Questions on Doctrine*, p. 142.

19. Cain and Abel were fully acquainted with the sacrificial system (Gen. 4:3-5; Heb. 11:4). It is most likely that Adam and Eve obtained their first clothes (Gen. 3:21) from the skins of the animals sacrificed to make atonement for their sins.

20. See, e. g., the following historic confessions of faith: The Westminster Confession of Faith, the Irish Articles of Religion; the Savoy Declaration, the Philadelphia Confession, and the Methodist Articles of Religion.

21. Cf. *The SDA Bible Commentary*, rev. ed., vol. 6, pp. 541, 542.

22. Calvin, *Commenting on a Harmony of the Evangelists*, trans. by William Pringle (Grand Rapids: Wm. B. Eerdmans, 1949), vol. 1, p. 277.

23. *The SDA Bible Commentary*, rev. ed., vol. 6, pp. 541, 542.

24. Others have interpreted Christ as the end of the law to mean that Christ is the goal or aim of the law (cf. Gal. 3:24) or the fulfillment of the law (cf. Matt. 5:17). However, the view that Christ is the termination of the law as a means of salvation (cf. Rom. 6:14) seems best to fit the context of Romans 10:4. "Paul is contrasting God's way of righteousness by faith with man's attempt at righteousness by law. The message of the gospel is that Christ is the end of the law as a way of righteousness to everyone who has faith" (*The SDA Bible Commentary*, rev. ed., vol. 6, p. 595). Cf. White, *Selected Messages*, book 1, p. 394.

25. Nichol, *Answers to Objections*, pp. 100, 101.

The Sabbath

20

The beneficent Creator, after the six days of Creation, rested on the seventh day and instituted the Sabbath for all people as a memorial of Creation. The fourth commandment of God's unchangeable law requires the observance of this seventh-day Sabbath as the day of rest, worship, and ministry in harmony with the teaching and practice of Jesus, the Lord of the Sabbath. The Sabbath is a day of delightful communion with God and one another. It is a symbol of our redemption in Christ, a sign of our sanctification, a token of our allegiance, and a foretaste of our eternal future in God's kingdom. The Sabbath is God's perpetual sign of His eternal covenant between Him and His people. Joyful observance of this holy time from evening to evening, sunset to sunset, is a celebration of God's creative and redemptive acts. (Gen. 2:1-3; Ex. 20:8-11; Luke 4:16; Isa. 56:5, 6; 58:13, 14; Matt. 12:1-12; Ex. 31:13-17; Ezek. 20:12, 20; Deut. 5:12-15; Heb. 4:1-11; Lev. 23:32; Mark 1:32.)

WITH GOD, ADAM AND EVE EXPLORED their paradise home. The scenery was breathtaking beyond description. As the sun slowly set on that Friday, the sixth day of Creation, and the stars began to appear, "God saw everything that He had made, and indeed it was very good" (Gen. 1:31). Thus God finished His creation of "the heavens and the earth, and all the host of them" (Gen. 2:1).

But as beautiful as was the world He had just completed, the greatest gift God could give to the newly created couple was the privilege of a personal relationship with Him. So He gave them the Sabbath, a day of special blessing, fellowship, and communion with their Creator.

The Sabbath Throughout the Bible

The Sabbath is central to our worship of God. The memorial of Creation, it reveals the reason God is to be worshiped: He is the Creator, and we are His creatures. "The Sabbath, therefore, lies at the very foundation of divine worship, for it teaches this great truth in the most impressive manner, and no other institution does this. The true ground of divine worship, not of that on the seventh day merely, but of all worship, is found in the distinction between the Creator and His creatures. This great fact can never become obsolete, and must never be forgotten."[1] It was to keep this truth forever before the human race that God instituted the Sabbath.

The Sabbath at Creation. The Sabbath comes to us from a sinless world. It is God's special gift, enabling the human race to experience the reality of heaven on earth. Three distinct divine acts established the Sabbath.

1. God rested on the Sabbath. On the seventh day God "rested and was refreshed" (Ex. 31:17), yet He did not rest because He needed it (Isa. 40:28). The verb "rested," *shabath*, means literally "to cease" from labor or activity (cf. Gen. 8:22). "God's rest was the result of neither exhaustion nor fatigue, but a cessation from previous occupation."[2]

God rested because He expected humans to rest; He set an example for human beings to follow (Ex. 20:11).

If God finished the Creation on the sixth day (Gen. 2:1), what does Scripture mean when it says that He "ended His work" on the seventh day (Gen. 2:2)? God had finished the creation of the heavens and the earth in those six days, but He had yet to make the Sabbath. It was by resting on the Sabbath that He made it. The Sabbath was His finishing touch, ending His work.

2. God blessed the Sabbath. God not only made the Sabbath, He blessed it. "The blessing on the seventh day implied that it was thereby declared to be a special object of divine favor and a day that would bring blessing to His creatures."[3]

3. God sanctified the Sabbath. To sanctify something means to make it sacred or holy or to set it apart as holy and for holy use—to consecrate it. People, places (such as a sanctuary, temple, or church), and time (holy days) can be sanctified. The fact that God sanctified the seventh day means that this day is holy—that He set apart it for the lofty purpose of enriching the divine-human relationship.

God blessed and sanctified the seventh-day Sabbath *because* He rested on this day from all His works. He blessed and sanctified it for humanity, not for Himself. It is His personal presence that brings to the Sabbath God's blessing and sanctification.

The Sabbath at Sinai. The events following the Israelites' departure from Egypt show that they had largely lost sight of the Sabbath. The rigorous requirements of slavery seem to have made Sabbath observance very difficult. Soon after they gained their freedom, God strongly reminded them, through the miracle of the manna and the proclamation of the Ten Commandments, of their obligation to observe the seventh-day Sabbath.

1. The Sabbath and the manna. One month before He proclaimed the law from Sinai, God promised the people protection against disease if they would diligently give attention to "His commandments and keep all His statutes" (Ex. 15:26; cf. Gen. 26:5). Soon after making this promise God reminded the Israelites of the sacredness of the Sabbath. Through the miracle of the manna He taught them in concrete terms how important He considered their resting on the seventh day to be.

Each weekday God gave the Israelites enough manna to meet their needs for that day. They were not to save any till the next day, for it would spoil if they did (Ex. 16:4, 16-19). On the sixth day they were to gather twice as much as usual so that they would have enough for their needs on both that day and the Sabbath. Teaching that the sixth day was to be a day of preparation and also how the Sabbath was to be kept, God said, "Tomorrow is to be a day of rest, a holy Sabbath to the Lord. So bake what you want to bake and boil what you want to boil. Save whatever is left and keep it until morning" (Ex. 16:23, NIV). Only on the seventh day could the manna be kept without spoiling (Ex. 16:24). In language similar to that of the fourth commandment, Moses said, "Six days you shall gather it, but on the seventh day, which is the Sabbath, there will be none" (Ex. 16:26).

For the forty years—or more than 2,000 successive weekly Sabbaths—that the Israelites were in the wilderness, the miracle of the manna reminded them of this pattern of six days of work and the seventh day of rest.

2. The Sabbath and the law. God placed the Sabbath command in the center of the Decalogue. It reads as follows:

"Remember the Sabbath day, to keep it holy. Six days you shall labor and do all your work, but the seventh day is the Sabbath of the Lord your God. In it you shall do no work: you, nor your son, nor your daughter, nor your manservant, nor your maidservant, nor your cattle, nor your stranger who is within your gates. For in six days the Lord made the heavens and the earth, the sea, and all that is in them, and rested the seventh day. Therefore the Lord blessed the Sabbath day and hallowed it" (Ex. 20:8-11).

All of the commandments of the Decalogue are vital, and none are to be neglected (James 2:10), yet God distinguished the Sabbath command from all others. Regarding it, He commanded, "Remember," alerting humanity to the danger of forgetting its importance.

The words with which the commandment begins—"Remember the Sabbath day, to keep it holy" –show that the Sabbath was not first instituted at Sinai. Those words indicated that it had originated earlier—in fact, at Creation, as the rest of the commandment reveals. God intended that we observe the Sabbath as His memorial of Creation. It defines the time for rest and worship, directing us to contemplate God and His works.

As the memorial of Creation, Sabbath observance is an antidote for idolatry. By reminding us that God created heaven and earth, it distinguishes Him from all false gods. Keeping the Sabbath, then, becomes the sign of our allegiance to the true God—a sign that we acknowledge His sovereignty as Creator and King.

The Sabbath commandment functions as the seal of God's law.[4] Generally, seals contain three elements: the name of the owner of the seal, his title, and jurisdiction. Official seals are used to validate documents of great import. The document takes on the authority of the official whose seal is placed upon it. The seal implies that the official himself approved of the legislation and that all the power of his office stands behind it.

Among the Ten Commandments, it is the Sabbath command that contains the vital elements of a seal. It is the only one of the ten that identifies the true God by giving His name: "the Lord your God;" His title: the One who made—the Creator; and His territory: "the heavens and the earth" (Ex. 20:10, 11). Since only the fourth commandment shows by whose authority the Ten Commandments were given, it therefore "contains the seal of God," attached to His law as evidence of its authenticity and binding force.[5]

Indeed, God made the Sabbath as "a reminder or sign of His power and authority in a world unspotted by sin and rebellion. It was to be an institution of perpetual personal obligation enjoined by the admonition 'remember the Sabbath day, to keep it holy' (Ex. 20:8)."[6]

This commandment divides the week into two parts. God gave humanity six days in which to "labor and do all your work," but the seventh day, "you shall do no work" (Ex. 20:9, 10). "Six days, says the command, are *work* days, but "*the* seventh day" is a *rest* day. That "the seventh day" is uniquely God's rest day is made evident in the opening words of the command: "Remember *the* Sabbath [rest] day, to keep it holy."[7]

Although human beings require physical rest to refresh their bodies, God bases His command that we rest on the Sabbath on His example. Since He rested from His activities of the world's first week, so we are to rest.

3. The Sabbath and the covenant. As God's law was central to the covenant (Ex. 34:27), so the Sabbath, located in the heart of that law, is prominent in His covenant. God declared the Sabbath a "sign between...[you] and Me, that...[you] may know that I am the Lord who sanctifies...[you]" (Eze. 20:12; cf. Eze. 20:20; Ex. 31:17). Therefore, He said, Sabbathkeeping is a "perpetual covenant" (Ex. 31:16). "Just as the covenant is based on God's love for His people (Deut. 7:7, 8), so the Sabbath, as the sign of that covenant, is a sign of divine love."[8]

4. The annual Sabbaths. In addition to the weekly Sabbaths (Lev. 23:3), there were seven annual, ceremonial Sabbaths scattered through Israel's religious calendar. These yearly Sabbaths were not directly related to the seventh-day Sabbath or the weekly cycle. These sabbaths, "beside the Sabbaths of the Lord" (Lev. 23:38), were the first and last days of the Feast of Unleavened Bread, the Day of Pentecost, the Feast of Trumpets, the Day of Atonement, and the first and last days of the Feast of Tabernacles (cf. Lev. 23:7, 8, 21, 24, 25, 27, 28, 35, 36).

Because the reckoning of these sabbaths depended on the beginning of the sacred year, which was based on the lunar calendar, they could fall on any day of the week. When they coincided with the weekly Sabbath, they were called "high days" (cf. John 19:31). "While the weekly Sabbath was ordained at the close of Creation week for all mankind, the annual sabbaths were an integral part of the Jewish system of rites and ceremonies instituted at Mount Sinai,...which pointed forward to the coming of the Messiah, and the observance of which terminated with His death on the cross."[9]

The Sabbath and Christ. Scripture reveals that, as truly as the Father, Christ was the Creator (see 1 Cor. 8:6; Heb. 1:1, 2; John 1:3). So He was the One who set the seventh day apart as a day of rest for humanity.

In time Christ associated the Sabbath with His redemptive as well as His creative work. As the great "I AM" (John 8:58; Ex. 3:14) He incorporated the Sabbath in the Decalogue as a forceful reminder of this weekly worship appointment with the Creator. And He added another reason for the observance of the Sabbath: the redemption of His people (Deut. 5:14, 15). So the Sabbath marks those who have accepted Jesus as Creator and Saviour.

Christ's twofold role as Creator and Redeemer makes obvious why He claimed that as the Son of Man, He "is also Lord of the Sabbath" (Mark 2:28). With such authority, He could have disposed of the Sabbath if He had wanted to, but He did not. On the contrary He applied it to all human beings, saying, "The Sabbath was made for man" (verse 27).

Throughout His earthly ministry Christ exemplified for us faithful Sabbathkeeping. It was "His custom" to worship on the Sabbath (Luke 4:16). His participation in Sabbath services reveals that He endorsed it as a day of worship.

So concerned was Christ for the sacredness of the Sabbath that when He spoke about the persecution to take place after His ascension, He counseled His disciples regarding it. "Pray," He said, "that your flight may not be in winter or on the Sabbath" (Matt. 24:20). This clearly implied, as Jonathon Edwards noted, "that even then Christians were bound to a strict observance of the Sabbath."[10]

When Christ finished His work of Creation—His first great act in world history—He rested on the seventh day. This rest signified completion and accomplishment. He did much the same at the end of His earthly ministry, when He completed His second great act in history. On Friday afternoon, the sixth day of the week, Christ finished His redemptive mission on earth. His last words were, "It is finished!" (John 19:30). Scripture emphasizes that when He died, "it was Preparation Day, and the Sabbath was about to begin" (Luke 23:54, NIV). Following His death, He rested in a tomb, thus symbolizing that He had accomplished the redemption of the human race.[11]

So the Sabbath testifies to Christ's works of Creation and redemption. Through observing it His followers rejoice with Him over His accomplishments for humanity.[12]

The Sabbath and the Apostles. The disciples greatly respected the Sabbath. This was evident at the time of Christ's death. When the Sabbath arrived, they interrupted their burial preparations and "rested on the Sabbath according to the commandment," with plans to continue this work on Sunday, "the first day of the week" (Luke 23:56; 24:1).

As had Christ, the apostles worshiped on the seventh-day Sabbath. In his evangelistic travels Paul attended the synagogue on the Sabbath and preached Christ (Acts 13:14; 17:1, 2; 18:4). Even the Gentiles invited him to preach the Word of God on the Sabbath (Acts 13:42, 44). In localities where there was no synagogue, he searched for the place customary for Sabbath worship (Acts 16:13). As Christ's participation in Sabbath services indicated His acceptance of the seventh day as the special day for worship, so did Paul's.

This apostle's faithful observance of the weekly Sabbath stood in sharp contrast to his attitude toward the annual ceremonial sabbaths. He made clear that Christians were under no obligation to keep these yearly rest days, because Christ had nailed the ceremonial laws to the cross (see chapter 19 of this book). Said he, "Therefore let no one judge you in food or in drink, or regarding a festival or a new moon or sabbaths, which are a shadow of things to come, but the substance is of Christ" (Col. 2:16, 17). Since "the context [of this passage] deals with ritual matters, the sabbaths here referred to are the ceremonial sabbaths of the Jewish annual festivals 'which are a shadow,' or type, of which the fulfillments were to come in Christ."[13]

Likewise, in Galatians Paul remonstrated against the observing of the requirements of the ceremonial law. He said, "You observe days, and months, and seasons, and years! I am afraid I have labored over you in vain" (Gal. 4:10, 11, RSV).

Many are under the impression that John was referring to Sunday when he stated he was "in the Spirit on the Lord's day" (Rev. 1:10). In the Bible, however, the only day referred to as the Lord's special possession is the Sabbath. Christ stated, "The seventh day is the Sabbath of the Lord your God" (Ex. 20:10), later calling it "My holy day" (Isa. 58:13). And Christ called Himself "Lord of the Sabbath" (Mark 2:28). Since, in the Scripture, the only day the Lord calls His own is the seventh-day Sabbath, it seem logical to conclude that it was the Sabbath to which John was referring. Certainly there is no biblical precedent to indicate he would apply that term to the first day of the week, or Sunday.[14]

Nowhere does the Bible command us to observe any weekly day other than the Sabbath. It declares no other weekly day blessed or holy. Nor does the New Testament indicate that God has changed the Sabbath to any other day of the week.

On the contrary, Scripture reveals that God intended that His people should observe the Sabbath throughout eternity: "As the new heavens and the New Earth which I will make will remain before me," says the Lord, "so shall your descendants and your name remain....From one New Moon to another, and from one Sabbath to another, all flesh shall come to worship before Me," says the Lord" (Isa. 66:22, 23).

The Meaning of the Sabbath. The Sabbath has broad significance and is filled with deep and rich spirituality.

1. A perpetual memorial of Creation. As we have seen, the fundamental significance the Ten Commandments attach to the Sabbath is that it memorializes the creation of the world (Ex. 20:11, 12). The command to observe the seventh day as the Sabbath is "linked inseparably to the act of Creation, the institution of the Sabbath and the command to observe it being a direct consequence of the act of Creation. Furthermore, the entire human family owes its existence to the divine act of Creation thus memorialized; accordingly, the obligation to comply with the Sabbath command as a memorial of the creative power of God devolves upon the entire human race."[15] Strong calls the Sabbath "a perpetual obligation as God's appointed memorial of his creating activity."[16]

Those who observed it as a memorial of Creation would be doing so as a grateful acknowledgment "that God was their Creator and their rightful Sovereign; that they were the works of His hands, and the subject of His authority. Thus the institution was wholly commemorative and given to all mankind. There was nothing in it shadowy, or of restricted application to any people."[17] And as long as we worship God because He is our Creator, so long will the Sabbath function as the sign and memorial of Creation.

2. A symbol of redemption. When God delivered Israel from bondage in Egypt, the Sabbath, which was already the memorial of Creation, became a memorial of deliverance as well (Deut. 5:15). "The Lord intended that the weekly Sabbath rest, if properly observed, would constantly release man from the bondage of an Egypt not limited to any country or century but which includes every land and every age. Man today needs escape from the bondage that comes from greediness, from gain and power, from social inequality, and from sin and selfishness."[18]

When we view the cross, the Sabbath rest stands out as a special symbol of redemption. "It is the memorial of the exodus from the bondage of sin under the leadership of Emmanuel. The greatest burden we carry is the guilt of our disobedience. The Sabbath rest, by pointing back to Christ's rest in the tomb, the rest of victory over sin, offers to the Christian a tangible opportunity to accept and experience Christ's forgiveness, peace, and rest."[19]

3. A sign of sanctification. The Sabbath is a sign of God's transforming power, a sign of holiness and sanctification. The Lord declared, "Surely My Sabbaths you shall keep, for it is a sign between Me and you throughout your generations, that you may know that I am the Lord who sanctifies you" (Ex. 31:13; cf. Eze. 20:20). The Sabbath, therefore, is also a sign of God as the Sanctifier. As people are sanctified by Christ's blood (Heb. 13:12), the Sabbath is also a sign of the believer's acceptance of His blood for the forgiveness of sins.

Just as God has set the Sabbath aside for a holy purpose, so He has set His people apart for a holy purpose—to be His special witnesses. Their communion with Him on that day leads to holiness; they learn to depend not on their own resources but on the God who sanctifies them.

"The power that created all things is the power that re-created the soul in His own likeness. To those who keep holy the Sabbath day it is the sign of sanctification. True sanctification is harmony with God, oneness with Him in character. It is received through obedience to those principles that are the transcript of His character. And the Sabbath is the sign of obedience. He who from the heart obeys the fourth commandment will obey the whole law. He is sanctified through obedience."[20]

4. A sign of loyalty. As Adam and Eve's loyalty was tested by the Tree of the Knowledge of Good and Evil placed in the midst of the Garden of Eden, so every human being's loyalty to God will be tested by the Sabbath command placed in the midst of the Decalogue.

Scripture reveals that before the Second Advent the whole world will be divided into two classes: those who are loyal and "keep the commandments of God and the faith of Jesus," and those who worship "the beast and his image" (Rev. 14:12, 9). At that time God's truth will be magnified before the world, and it will be clear to all that the obedient observance of the seventh-day Sabbath of Scripture gives evidence of loyalty to the Creator.

5. A time of fellowship. God created the animals to be humanity's companions (Gen. 1:24, 25). And for a higher level of companionship God gave the man and woman to each other (Gen. 2:18-25). But in the Sabbath, God gave humanity a gift offering the highest form of companionship—companionship with Him. Human beings were not made to associate just with the animals, nor even with other humans. They were made for God.

On the Sabbath we can especially experience God's presence among us. Without the Sabbath all would be labor and sweat without end. Every day would be alike, devoted to secular pursuits. The arrival of the Sabbath, however, brings hope, joy, meaning, and courage. It provides time to commune with God through worship, prayer, song, the study of and meditation on the Word, and sharing the gospel with others. The Sabbath is our opportunity to experience God's presence.

6. A sign of righteousness by faith. Christians recognize that through the guidance of an enlightened conscience non-Christians who honestly search for truth can be led by the Holy Spirit to an understanding of the general principles of God's law (Rom. 2:14-16). This explains why the nine commandments other than the fourth have been, to a degree, practiced outside of Christianity. But this is not the case with the Sabbath commandment.

Many people can see the reason for a weekly day of rest, but they often have a difficult time understanding why work that, when done on any other day of the week would be right and commendable, is a sin when done on the seventh day. Nature does not offer any ground for keeping the seventh day. Planets move in their respective orbits, vegetation grows, rain and sunshine alternate, and beasts carry on as if every day were the same. Why, then, should humans keep the seventh-day Sabbath? "To the Christian there is only one reason, and no other; but that reason is enough: God has spoken."[21]

Only on the basis of God's special revelation can people understand the reasonableness of observing the seventh day. Those who keep the seventh day, then, do so out of faith and implicit trust in Christ, who has enjoined its observance. By observing the Sabbath, believers reveal a willingness to accept God's will for their lives instead of depending on their own judgment.

In keeping the seventh day, believers are not trying to make themselves righteous. Rather, they observe the Sabbath as the result of their relationship with Christ the Creator and Redeemer.[22] Sabbathkeeping is the product of His righteousness in justification and sanctification, signifying that they have been delivered from the bondage of sin and have received His perfect righteousness.

"An apple tree does not become an apple tree by bearing apples. It first has to be an apple tree. Then the apples come as a natural fruitage. So the true Christian does not keep the Sabbath or the other nine precepts to make himself righteous. Rather, this is the natural fruitage of the righteousness Christ shares with him. He who keeps the Sabbath in this way is not a legalist, for the outward keeping of the seventh day betokens the believer's inner experience in justification and sanctification. Hence, the true Sabbathkeeper does not refrain from forbidden actions on the Sabbath in order to win God's favor but because he loves God and wants to make the Sabbath count for the most for closer fellowship with [Him]."[23]

Sabbathkeeping reveals that we have ceased depending on our own works—that we realize that only Christ the Creator can save us. Indeed, "the spirit of true Sabbathkeeping reveals a supreme love for Jesus Christ, the Creator and Saviour, who is making us into new persons. It makes the keeping of the right day in the right way a sign of righteousness by faith."[24]

7. A symbol of resting in Christ. The Sabbath, a memorial of God's delivering Israel from Egypt to the rest of the earthly Canaan, distinguished the redeemed of that time from the surrounding nations. In a similar way the Sabbath is a sign of the deliverance from sin to God's rest, setting the redeemed apart from the world.

All who enter into the rest to which God invites them "have ceased from...[their] works as God did from His" (Heb. 4:10). "This rest is a spiritual rest, a rest from our 'own works,' a ceasing from sin. It is into this rest that God calls His people, and it is of this rest that both the Sabbath and Canaan are symbols."[25]

When God completed His work of Creation and rested on the seventh day, He provided Adam and Eve, in the Sabbath, an opportunity to rest in Him. Though they failed, God's original purpose of offering that rest to humanity remains unchanged. After the Fall the Sabbath continued as a reminder of that rest. "The observance of the seventh-day Sabbath thus testifies not only to faith in God as the Creator of all things, but also to faith in His power to transform the life and qualify men and women for entering that eternal 'rest' He originally intended for the inhabitants of this earth."[26]

God had promised this spiritual rest to literal Israel. Despite their failure to enter it, God's invitation still stands: "There remains, then, a Sabbath-rest for the people of God" (Heb. 4:9, NIV). All who desire to enter that rest "must first enter, by faith, into His spiritual 'rest,' the rest of the soul from sin and from its own efforts at salvation."[27]

The New Testament appeals for the Christian not to wait to experience this rest of grace and faith, for "today" is the opportune time to enter it (Heb. 4:7; 3:13). All who have entered this rest—the saving grace received by faith in Jesus Christ—have ceased every effort to achieve righteousness by their own works. In this way, observing the seventh-day Sabbath is a symbol of the believer's entering into the gospel rest.

Attempts to Change the Day of Worship

Since the Sabbath plays a vital role in the worship of God as Creator and Redeemer, it should not be surprising that Satan has waged an all-out war to overthrow this sacred institution.

Nowhere does the Bible authorize a change from the day of worship God made in Eden and restated on Sinai. Other Christians, Sundaykeepers themselves, have recognized this. Catholic Cardinal James Gibbons once wrote, "You may read the Bible from Genesis to Revelation, and you will not find a single line authorizing the sanctification of Sunday. The Scriptures enforce the religious observance of Saturday."[28]

A. T. Lincoln, a Protestant, admitted that "it cannot be argued that the New Testament itself provides warrant for the belief that since the Resurrection God appointed the first day to be observed as the Sabbath."[29] He acknowledged: "To become a seventh-day Sabbatarian is the only consistent course of action for anyone who holds that the whole Decalogue is binding as moral law."[30]

If there is no biblical evidence that Christ or His disciples changed the day of worship from the seventh day, then how did so many Christians come to accept Sunday in its place?

The Rise of Sunday Observance. The change from Sabbath to Sunday worship came gradually. There is no evidence of Christian weekly Sunday worship before the second century, but the evidence indicates that by the middle of that century some Christians were voluntarily observing Sunday as a day of worship, not a day of rest.[31]

The church of Rome, largely made up of Gentile believers (Rom. 11:13), led in the trend toward Sunday worship. In Rome, the capital of the empire, strong anti-Jewish sentiments arose, becoming even stronger as time passed. Reacting to these sentiments, the Christians in that city attempted to distinguish themselves from the Jews. They dropped some practices held in common with the Jews and initiated a trend away from the veneration of the Sabbath, moving toward the exclusive observance of Sunday.[32]

From the second to the fifth centuries, while Sunday was rising in influence, Christians continued to observe the seventh-day Sabbath nearly everywhere throughout the Roman Empire. The fifth-century historian Socrates wrote, "Almost all the churches throughout the world celebrate the sacred mysteries on the sabbath of every week, yet the Christians of Alexandria and at Rome, on account of some ancient tradition, have ceased to do this."[33]

In the fourth and fifth centuries many Christians worshiped on both Sabbath and Sunday. Sozomen, another historian of that period, wrote, "The people of Constantinople, and almost everywhere, assemble together on the Sabbath, as well as on the first day of the week, which custom is never observed at Rome or at Alexandria."[34] These references demonstrate Rome's leading role in disregarding Sabbath observance.

Why did those who were turning from worship on the seventh day choose Sunday and not another day of the week? A major reason was that Christ was resurrected on Sunday; in fact, it was alleged that He had authorized worship on that day. "But, strange as it may seem, *not one writer of the second and third centuries ever cited a single Bible verse as authority* for the observance of Sunday in the place of the Sabbath. Neither Barnabas, nor Ignatius, nor Justin, nor Irenaeus, nor Tertullian, nor Clement of Rome, nor Clement of Alexandria, nor Origen, nor Cyprian, nor Victorinus, nor any other author who lived near to the time when Jesus lived knew of any such instruction from Jesus or from any part of the Bible."[35]

The popularity and influence that the sun worship of the pagan Romans accorded Sunday undoubtedly contributed to its growing acceptance as a day of worship. Sun worship played an important role throughout the ancient world. It was "one of the oldest components of the Roman religion."

Because of the Eastern sun cults, "from the early part of the second century A.D., the cult of *Sol Invictus* was dominant in Rome and in other parts of the Empire."[36]

This popular religion made its impact on the early church through the new converts. "Christian converts from paganism were constantly attracted toward the veneration of the Sun. This indicated not only by the frequent condemnation of this practice by the [Church] Fathers but also by significant reflexes of Sun worship in the Christian liturgy"[37]

The fourth century saw the introduction of Sunday laws. First, Sunday laws of a civil nature were issued; then came Sunday laws of a religious character. The emperor Constantine decreed the first civil Sunday law on March 7, A.D. 321. In view of Sunday's popularity among the pagan sun worshipers and the esteem with which many Christians regarded it, Constantine hoped that, by making Sunday a holiday, he could ensure the support of these two constituencies for his government.[38]

Constantine's Sunday law reflected his background as a sun worshiper. It read: "On the venerable Day of the Sun [*venerability die Solis*] let the magistrates and people residing in cities rest, and let all workshops be closed. In the country, however, persons engaged in agriculture may freely and lawfully continue their pursuits."[39]

Several decades later the church followed his example. The Council of Laodicea (c. A.D. 364), which was not a universal council but a Roman Catholic one, issued the first ecclesiastical Sunday law. In canon 29 the church stipulated that Christians should honor Sunday and "if possible, do no work on that day," while it denounced the practice of resting on the Sabbath, instructing that Christians should not "be idle on Saturday [Greek *sabbaton*, "the Sabbath"], but shall work on that day."[40]

In A.D. 538, the year marked as the beginning of the 1260-year prophecy (see chapter 13 of this book), the Roman Catholic Third Council of Orleans issued a law even more severe than that of Constantine. Canon 28 of that council says that on Sunday even "agricultural labor ought to be laid aside, in order that the people may not be prevented from attending church."[41]

The Change Prophesied. The Bible reveals that the observance of Sunday as a Christian institution had its origin in "the mystery of lawlessness" (2 Thess. 2:7), which was already at work in Paul's day (see chapter 13 of this book). Through the prophecy of Daniel 7 God revealed His foreknowledge of the change of the day of worship.

Daniel's vision depicts an attack on God's people and on His law. The attacking power, represented by a little horn (and by a beast in Revelation 13:1-10), brings about the great apostasy within the Christian church (see chapter 13 of this book). Arising from the fourth beast and becoming a major persecuting power after the fall of Rome (see chapter 19 of this book), the little horn attempts to "change the times and law" (Dan. 7:25). This apostate power is very successful at deceiving most of the world, but at the end the judgment will decide against it (Dan. 7:11, 22, 26). During the final tribulation God will intervene on behalf of His people and deliver them (Dan. 12:1-3).

This prophecy fits only one power within Christianity. Only one religious organization claims to possess the prerogatives of modifying divine laws. Note what, throughout history, Roman Catholic authorities have claimed:

About A.D. 1400 Petrus de Ancharano asserted that "the pope can modify divine law, since his power is not of man, but of God, and he acts in the place of God upon earth, with the fullest power of binding and loosing his sheep."[42]

The impact of this astonishing assertion was demonstrated during the Reformation. Luther claimed that the Holy Scripture and not the tradition of the church was his guide in life. His slogan was *sola scriptura*—"the Bible and the Bible only." John Eck, one of the foremost defenders of the Roman Catholic faith, attacked Luther on this point by claiming that the authority of the church was above the Bible. He challenged Luther on the observance of Sunday in place of the Bible Sabbath. Said Eck, "Scripture teaches: "Remember to hallow the Sabbath day; six days shall you labor and do all your work, but the seventh day is the Sabbath day of the Lord your God," etc. Yet, the church has changed the Sabbath into Sunday on its own authority, on which you [Luther] have no Scripture."[43]

At the Council of Trent (1545-1563), convened by the pope to counter Protestantism, Gaspare de Fosso, archbishop of Reggio, brought up the issue again. "The authority of the church," he said, "then, is illustrated most clearly by the Scriptures; for while on the one hand she [the church] recommends them, declares them to be divine, [and] offers them to us to be read, ...on the other hand, the legal precepts in the Scriptures taught by the Lord have ceased by virtue Christ's teaching (for He says He has come to fulfill the law, not to destroy it), but they have been changed by the authority of the church."[44]

Does that church still maintain this position? The 1977 edition of *The Convert's Catechism of Catholic Doctrine* contains this series of questions and answers:

"Q. **Which is the Sabbath day?**
"A. Saturday is the Sabbath day.
"Q. **Why do we observe Sunday instead of Saturday?**
"A. We observe Sunday instead of Saturday because the Catholic Church transferred the solemnity from Saturday to Sunday."[45]

In his best seller, *The Faith of Millions* (1974), the Roman Catholic scholar John A. O'Brien came to this compelling conclusion: "Since Saturday, not Sunday, is specified in the Bible, isn't it curious that non-Catholics who profess to take their religion directly from the Bible and not from the Church, observe Sunday instead of Saturday? Yes, of course, it is inconsistent." The custom of Sunday observance, he said, "rests upon the authority of the Catholic Church and not upon an explicit text in the Bible. That observance remains as a reminder of the Mother Church from which the non-Catholic sects broke away—like a boy running away from home but still carrying in his pocket a picture of his mother or a lock of her hair."[46]

The claims to these prerogatives fulfill prophecy and contribute to the identification of the little-horn power.

The Restoration of the Sabbath. In Isaiah 56 and 58 God calls Israel to a Sabbath reform. Revealing the glories of the future gathering of the Gentiles into His fold (Isa. 56:8), He associates the success of this mission of salvation with keeping the Sabbath holy (Isa. 56:1, 2, 6, 7).

He carefully outlines the specific work of His people. Though their mission is worldwide, it is especially directed to a class of people who profess to be believers but who have in reality departed from His precepts (Isa. 58:1, 2). He expresses their mission to those professed believers in these terms: "You shall raise up the foundations of many generations; and you shall be called the Repairer of the Breach, the Restorer of Streets to Dwell In. If you turn away your foot from the Sabbath, from doing your pleasure on My holy day, and call the Sabbath a delight, the holy day of the Lord honorable, and shall honor Him, not doing your own ways, nor finding your own pleasure, nor speaking your own words, then you shall delight yourself in the Lord" (Isa. 58:12-14).

The mission of spiritual Israel parallels that of ancient Israel. God's law was breached when the little-horn power changed the Sabbath. Just as the downtrodden Sabbath was to be restored in Israel, so in modern times the divine institution of the Sabbath is to be restored and the breach in the wall of God's law repaired.[47]

The proclamation of the message of Revelation 14:6-12 in connection with the everlasting gospel accomplishes this work of restoring and magnifying the law. And the proclaiming of this message is the mission of God's church at the time of the Second Advent (see chapter 13 of this book). This message is to arouse the world, inviting everyone to prepare for the judgment.

The wording of the summons to worship the Creator, "Him who made heaven and earth, the sea and springs of water" (Rev. 14:7), is a direct reference to the fourth commandment of God's eternal law. Its inclusion in this final warning confirms God's special concern to have His widely forgotten Sabbath restored before the Second Advent.

The delivering of this message will precipitate a conflict that will involve the whole world. The central issue will be obedience to God's law and the observance of the Sabbath. In the face of this conflict everyone must decide whether to keep God's commandments or those of men. This message will produce a people who keep the commandments of God and the faith of Jesus. Those who reject it will eventually receive the mark of the beast (Rev. 14:9, 12; see chapter 13 of this book).

To successfully accomplish this mission of magnifying God's law and honoring His neglected Sabbath, God's people must set a consistent, loving example of Sabbathkeeping.

The Observance of the Sabbath

To "*remember* the Sabbath day, to keep it holy" (Ex. 20:8), we must think of the Sabbath throughout the week and make the preparations necessary to observe it in a manner pleasing to God. We should be careful not to so exhaust our energies during the week that we cannot engage in His service on the Sabbath.

Because the Sabbath is a day of special communion with God in which we are invited to joyously celebrate His gracious activities in Creation and redemption, it is important that we avoid anything that tends to diminish its sacred atmosphere. The Bible specifies that on the Sabbath we should cease our secular work (Ex. 20:10), avoiding all work done to earn a living and all business transactions (Neh. 13:15-22). We are to honor God, "not doing your own ways, nor finding your own pleasure, nor speaking your own words" (Isa. 58:13). Devoting this day to pleasing ourselves, to being involved in secular interests, conversations, and thoughts or to be engaging in sports would detract from communion with our Creator and violate the sacredness of the Sabbath.[48] Our concern for the Sabbath command should extend to all who are under our jurisdiction—our children, those who work for us, and even our visitors and animals (Ex. 20:10), so that they may also enjoy the blessings of the Sabbath.

The Sabbath begins at sunset on Friday evening and ends at sunset Saturday evening (see Gen. 1:5; cf. Mark 1:32).[49] Scripture calls the day before the Sabbath (Friday) the preparation day (Mark 15:42)—a day to prepare for the Sabbath so that nothing will spoil its sacredness. On this day those who make the family's meals should prepare food for the Sabbath so that during its sacred hours they also can rest from their labors (see Ex. 16:23).

When the holy hours of the Sabbath approach, it is well for family members or groups of believers to gather together just before the setting of the sun on Friday evening to sing, pray, and read God's Word, thus inviting the

Spirit of Christ as a welcome guest. Similarly, they should mark its close by uniting in worship toward the close of the Sabbath on Saturday evening, requesting God's presence and guidance through the ensuing week.

The Lord calls upon His people to make the Sabbath a day of delight (Isa. 58:13). How can they do this? Only as they follow the example of Christ, the Lord of the Sabbath, can they ever hope to experience the real joy and satisfaction that God has for them on this day.

Christ regularly worshiped on the Sabbath, took part in the services, and gave religious instruction (Mark 1:21; 3:1-4; Luke 4:16-27; 13:10). But He did more than just worship. He fellowshipped with others (Mark 1:29-31; Luke 14:1), spent time outdoors (Mark 2:23), and went about doing holy deeds of mercy. Wherever He could, He healed the sick and afflicted (Mark 1:21-31; 3:1-5; Luke 13:10-17; 14:2-4; John 5:1-15; 9:1-14).

When criticized for His work of alleviating suffering, Jesus replied, "It is lawful to do good on the Sabbath" (Matt. 12:12). His healing activities neither broke the Sabbath nor abolished it. But they did terminate the burdensome regulations that had distorted the meaning of the Sabbath as God's instrument of spiritual refreshment and delight.[50] God intended the Sabbath for humanity's spiritual enrichment. Activities that enhance communication with God are proper; those which distract from that purpose and turn the Sabbath into a holiday are improper.

The Lord of the Sabbath invites all to follow His example. Those who accept His call experience the Sabbath as a delight and spiritual feast—a foretaste of heaven. They discover that "the Sabbath is designed by God to prevent spiritual discouragement. Week by week the seventh day comforts our conscience, assuring us that despite our unfinished characters we stand complete in Christ. His accomplishment at Calvary counts as our atonement. We enter His rest."[51]

References

1. John N. Andrews, *History of the Sabbath*, 2nd ed., enl. (Battle Creek, MI: Seventh-day Adventist Publishing Assn., 1873), 3rd ed., enl. p. 575.

2. *SDA Bible Commentary*, rev. ed., vol. 1, p. 220.

3. *Ibid.*

4. J. L. Shuler, *God's Everlasting Sign* (Nashville: Southern Pub. Assn., 1972), pp. 114-116; M. L. Andreason, *The Sabbath* (Washington, D.C.: Review and Herald, 1942), p. 248; A.V. Wallenkampf, "The Baptism, Seal, and Fullness of the Holy Spirit" (unpublished manuscript), p. 48; Ellen G. White, *Patriarchs and Prophets*, p. 307; White, *The Great Controversy*, pp. 613, 640.

5. White, *Patriarchs and Prophets*, p. 307.

6. Wallenkampf, "Baptism, Seal, and the Fullness of the Holy Spirit," p. 48.

7. *SDA Bible Commentary*, rev. ed., vol. 1, p. 605.

8. "Sabbath," *SDA Encyclopedia*, rev. ed., vol. 1, p. 1239.

9. "Sabbath, Annual," *Ibid*, p. 1265.

10. Jonathon Edwards, *The Works of President Edwards* (New York: Leavitt & Allen, 1852 repr. of the Worcester ed.), vol. 4, p. 622. The Puritans considered Sunday to be the Christian Sabbath.

11. Interestingly, it was on a "high day" (John 19:31) that Jesus rested in the tomb—for that Sabbath was both the seventh day of the week and the first sabbath of the Week of Unleavened Bread. The "it is good" of Creation merges with the "it is finished" of redemption as the Author and Finisher once again *rests* in completion.

12. Samuele Bacchiocchi, *Rest for Modern Man* (Nashville: Southern Pub. Assn., 1976), pp. 8, 9.

13. "Sabbath," *SDA Encyclopedia*, rev. ed., p. 1244. See also *SDA Bible Commentary*, rev. ed., vol. 7, pp. 205, 206; cf. White, "The Australia Camp Meeting," *Review and Herald*, Jan. 7, 1896, p. 2.

14. See *SDA Bible Commentary*, rev., ed., vol. 7, pp. 735, 736. Cf. White, *Acts of the Apostles* (Mountain View, CA: Pacific Press, 1911), p. 581.

15. "Sabbath," *SDA Encyclopedia*, p. 1237.

16. A. H. Strong, *Systemic Theology*, p. 408.

17. White, *Patriarchs and Prophets*, p. 48.

18. Bacchiocchi, *Rest for Modern Man*, p. 15.

19. *Ibid.*, p. 19.

20. White, *Testimonies*, vol. 6, p. 350.

21. Andreasen, *Sabbath*, p. 25.

22. Legalism can be defined as "attempts to earn salvation by individual effort. It is conforming to the law and certain observances as a means of justification before God. This is wrong, because 'by the deeds of the law there shall no flesh be justified in his sight' (Romans 3:20)" (Shuler, *God's Everlasting Sign*, p. 90). Shuler continues, "Those who denounce Sabbath observance as legalism need to consider this: If a born-again Christian refrains from worshiping false gods and maintains reverence as commanded by the first and third precepts, is he opposed to salvation by grace? Are purity, honesty, and truthfulness, as advocated by the seventh, eight, and ninth commandments opposed to free grace? The answer is No to both questions. Even so, the keeping of the seventh day by a renewed soul is not legalism, nor is it contrary to salvation only by grace. In fact, the commandment is the only pre-

cept in the law that stands as a sign of deliverance from sin and sanctification by grace alone" (*Ibid*).

23. *Ibid.*, p. 89.

24. *Ibid.*, p. 94.

25. Andreasen, *Sabbath*, p. 105.

26. *SDA Bible Commentary*, rev. ed., vol. 7, p. 420.

27. *Ibid.*

28. James Gibbons, *The Faith of Our Fathers*, 47th rev. enl. ed. (Baltimore: John Murphy & Co., 1895), pp. 111, 112. R. W. Dale, a Congregationalist, said, "It is quite clear that however rigidly or devoutly we may spend Sunday, we are not keeping the Sabbath....The Sabbath was founded on a specific divine command. We can plead no such command for the obligation to observe Sunday" (R. W. Dale, *The Ten Commandments*, 4th ed. [London: Hodder and Stoughton, 1884], p. 100.

29. Andrew T. Lincoln, "From Sabbath to Lord's Day: A Biblical and Theological Perspective," In *From Sabbath to Lord's Day: A Biblical, Historical, and Theological Investigation*, ed. D. A. Carson (Grand Rapids: Zondervan, 1982), p. 386.

30. *Ibid.*, p. 392.

31. See Justin Martyr, *First Apology*, in *Ante-Nicene Fathers* (Grand Rapids: Wm. B. Eerdmans, 1979), vol. 1, p. 186; Maxwell, *God Cares* (Mountain View, CA: Pacific Press, 1981), vol. 1, p. 130.

32. See, e.g., Bacchiocchi, "The Rise of Sunday Observance in Early Christianity," in *The Sabbath in Scripture and History*, ed. Kenneth A. Strand (Washington, D.C.: Review and Herald, 1982), p. 137; Bacchiocchi, *From Sabbath to Sunday* (Rome: Pontifical Gregorian University Press, 1977), pp. 223-232.

33. Socrates, *Ecclesiastical History*, book 7, chap. 19, trans. in *Nicene and Post-Nicene Fathers*, 2nd series, vol. 2, p. 390.

34. Sozomen, *Ecclesiastical History*, book 7, chap. 19, trans. in *Nicene and Post-Nicene Fathers*, 2nd series, vol. 2, p. 390.

35. Maxwell, *God Cares*, vol. 1, p. 131.

36. Gaston H. Halsberghe, *The Cult of Sol Invictus* (Leiden: E. J. Brill, 1972), pp. 26, 44. See also Bacchiocchi, "Rise of Sunday Observance," p. 139.

37. Bacchiocchi, "Rise of Sunday Observance, p. 140. See also Bacchiocci, *From Sabbath to Sunday*, pp. 252, 253.

38. See, e.g., Maxwell, *God Cares*, vol. 1, p. 129; H. G. Heggtveit, *Illustreret Kirkehistorie* (Christiana [Oslo]: Cammermeyers Boghandel, 1891-1895), p. 202, as trans. in Schaff, *History of the Christian Church* 5th ed. (New York: Charles Scribner, 1902), vol. 3, p. 380, note 1.

39. *Codex Justinianus*, book 3, title 12,3, trans. In Schaff, *History of the Christian Church*, 5th ed. (New York: Charles Scribner, 1902), vol. 3, p. 380, note 1.

40. Council of Laodicea, Canon 29, in Charles J. Hefele, *A History of the Councils of the Church From the Original Documents*, trans. and ed. by Henry N. Oxenham (Edinburgh: T and T Clark, 1876), vol. 2, p. 316. See also *SDA Bible Students' Source Book*, rev. ed., p. 885.

41. Giovanni Domenico Mansi, ed., *Sacrorum Conciliorum*, vol. 9, col. 919, as quoted by Maxwell, *God Cares*, vol. 1, p. 129. Cited in part in Andrews, *History of the Sabbath and First Day of the Week*, p. 374.

42. Lucius Ferraris, "Papa," art. 2, *Prompta Bibliotheca* (Venetiis [Venice]: Caspa Storti, 1772), vol. 6, p. 29, as trans. in *SDA Bible Students' Source Book*, rev. ed., p. 680.

43. John Eck, *Enchiridion of Commonplaces Against Luther and Other Enemies of the Church*, trans. Ford L. Battles, 3rd ed. (Grand Rapids: Baker, 1979), p. 13.

44. Gaspare [Ricciulli] de Fosso, Address in the 17th Session of the Council of Trent, Jan, 18, 1562, in Mansi, *Sacrorum Conciliorum*, vol. 33, cols. 529, 530, as trans. in *SDA Bible Students' Source Book*, rev. ed., p. 887.

45. Peter Geiermann, *The Convert's Catechism of Catholic Doctrine* (Rockford, IL: Tan Books and Publishers, 1977), p. 50.

46. John A. O'Brien, *The Faith of Millions*, rev. ed. (Huntington, IN: Our Sunday Visitor Inc., 1974), pp. 400, 401.

47. Cf. White, *The Great Controversy*, pp. 451-453.

48. White, *Selected Messages*, book 3, p. 258.

49. In Scripture, as the Creation story makes clear, days were marked from sunset to sunset. See also Lev. 23:32.

50. Does Christ's example mandate that Christian hospitals should stay open for seven days without providing any Sabbath rest for their staff? Realizing the needs of hospital personnel, White said, "The Saviour has shown us by His example that it is right to relieve suffering on this day; but physicians and nurses should not do any unnecessary work. Ordinary treatment, and operations that can wait, should be deferred till the next day. Let the patients know that physicians must have one day for rest" (*Medical Ministry* [Mountain View, CA: Pacific Press, 1963], p. 214).

   The fees for these medical services on the Sabbath are to be put aside for charity work. White wrote, "It may be necessary to devote even the hours of the holy Sabbath to the relief of suffering humanity. But the fee for such labor should be put into the treasury of the Lord, to be used for the worthy poor, who need medical skill but cannot afford to pay for it" (*Ibid*, p. 216).

51. George E. Vandeman, *When God Made Rest* (Boise, ID: Pacific Press, 1987), p. 21.

Stewardship

21

We are God's stewards, entrusted by Him with time and opportunities, abilities and possessions, and the blessings of the earth and its resources. We are responsible to Him for their proper use. We acknowledge God's ownership by faithful service to Him and our fellowmen and by returning tithes and giving offerings for the proclamation of His gospel and the support and growth of His church. Stewardship is a privilege given to us by God for nurture in love and the victory over selfishness and covetousness. The steward rejoices in the blessings that come to others as a result of his faithfulness. (Gen. 1:26-28; 2:15; 1 Chron. 29:14; Hag. 1:3-11; Mal. 3:8-12; 1 Cor. 9:9-14; Matt. 23:23; 2 Cor. 8:1-15; Rom. 15:26, 27.)

MORE THAN ANYTHING ELSE, living a Christian life means surrender—a giving up of ourselves and an accepting of Christ. As we see how Jesus surrendered and gave Himself up for us, we cry out, "What can I do for you?"

Then, just when we think we have made a full commitment, a full surrender, something happens that demonstrates how shallow our commitment is. As we discover new areas of our lives to turn over to God, our commitment grows. Then, ever so gently, He brings to our attention another area where self needs to surrender. So life goes on through a series of Christian recommitments that go deeper and deeper into our very selves, our lifestyles, how we act and react.

When we give all that we are and have to God, to whom it all belongs anyway (1 Cor. 3:21-4:2), He accepts it but then puts us back in charge of it, making us stewards, or caretakers, of everything that we "possess." Then our tendency to live comfortable, selfish lives is broken by our realization that our Lord was naked, imprisoned, and a stranger. And His enduring "Go ye therefore, and teach all nations" makes the church's activities— sharing, teaching, preaching, baptizing—more precious to us. Because of Him we seek to be faithful stewards.

What Is Stewardship?

"Do you not know that your body is the temple of the Holy Spirit...and you are not your own? For you were bought at a price; therefore glorify God in your body and in your spirit, which are God's" (1 Cor. 6:19, 20). At high cost we were purchased, redeemed. We belong to God. But such was mere *reclaiming*, for He made us; we have belonged to Him from the beginning because "In the beginning God created..." (Gen. 1:1). The Scriptures clearly state that "the earth is the Lord's, and all its fullness, the world and those who dwell therein" (Ps. 24:1).

At Creation God shared His possessions with humanity, and He continues to be the true owner of the world, its inhabitants, and its goods (Ps. 24:1). At the cross He reclaimed as His own that which man had surrendered to Satan at the Fall (1 Cor. 6:19, 20). He has now appointed His people to serve as stewards of His possessions.

A steward is a person "entrusted with the management of the household or estate of another." Stewardship is "the position, duties, or service of a steward."[1]

To the Christian, stewardship means "man's responsibility for, and use of, everything entrusted to him by God—life, physical being, time, talents and abilities, material possessions, opportunities to be of service to others, and his knowledge of the truth."[2] Christians serve as managers over God's possessions and view life as a divine opportunity "to learn to be faithful stewards, thereby qualifying for the higher stewardship of eternal things in the future life."[3]

In its larger dimensions, then, stewardship "involves the wise and unselfish use of life."[4]

Ways to Acknowledge God's Ownership

Life can be divided into four basic areas, each a gift from God. He gave us a body, abilities, time, and material possessions. In addition, we must care for the world around us, over which we were given dominion.

Stewardship of the Body. God's people are stewards of themselves. We are to love God with all our heart, and with all our soul, and with all our strength, and with all our mind (Luke 10:27).

Christians are privileged to develop their physical and mental powers to the best of their ability and opportunities. In so doing they bring honor to God and can prove a greater blessing to their fellow beings (see chapter 22).

Stewardship of Abilities. Each person has special aptitudes. One may be talented in the musical realm; another in manual trades such as sewing or auto mechanics. Some may make friends easily and mingle well with others, while others may naturally tend toward more solitary pursuits.

Every talent can be used to glorify either the one who possesses it or its original Bestower. A person can diligently perfect a talent for God's glory—or for personal selfishness.

We ought to cultivate the gifts the Holy Spirit gives each of us in order to multiply these gifts (Matt. 25). Good stewards use their gifts liberally in order to bring fuller benefit to their master.

Stewardship of Time. As faithful stewards, we glorify God by a wise use of time. "Whatever you do, work at it with all your heart, as working for the Lord, not for men, since you know that you will receive an inheritance from the Lord as a reward. It is the Lord Christ you are serving" (Col. 3:23, 24, NIV).

The Bible admonishes us not to behave "as fools but as wise, redeeming the time, because the days are evil" (Eph. 5:15, 16). Like Jesus, we must be about our Father's business (Luke 2:49). Because time is God's gift, each moment is precious. It is given to form character for eternal life. Faithful stewardship of our time means using it to get to know our Lord, to help our fellowmen, and to share the gospel.

When, at Creation, God gave time to us, He reserved the seventh-day Sabbath as holy time for communion with Him. But six days were provided for the human family to engage in useful employment.

Stewardship of Material Possessions. God gave our first parents the responsibility of subduing the earth, governing the animal kingdom, and caring for the Garden of Eden (Gen. 1:28; 2:15). All this was theirs not only to enjoy but to manage.

One restriction was placed on them. They were not to eat of the Tree of the Knowledge of Good and Evil. This tree provided a constant reminder that God was the owner and final authority over the earth. Respecting this restriction, the first pair demonstrated their faith in and loyalty to Him.

After the Fall, God could no longer test through the Tree of Knowledge.

But humanity still needed a constant reminder that God is the source of every good and perfect gift (James 1:17) and that it is He who provides us with the power to get wealth (Deut. 8:18). To remind us that He is the source of every blessing, God instituted a system of tithes and offerings.

This system eventually provided the financial means for supporting the priesthood of the Israelite temple. Seventh-day Adventists have adopted the Levitical model as a sound, biblical method for financing a worldwide outreach of the gospel. God has ordained that sharing the good news is to be dependent on the efforts and offerings of His people. He calls them to become unselfish co-laborers with Him by giving tithes and offerings to Him.

1. Tithes. As one seventh of our time (the Sabbath) belongs to God, so does one tenth of all material things we acquire. Scripture tells us that the tithe is "holy to the Lord," symbolizing God's ownership of everything (Lev. 27:30, 32). It is to be returned to Him as His own.

The tithing system is beautiful in its simplicity. Its equity is revealed in its proportional claim on the rich and on the poor. In proportion as God has given us the use of His property, so we are to return to Him a tithe.

When God calls for the tithe (Mal. 3:10), He makes no appeal to gratitude or generosity. Although gratitude should be a part of all our expressions to God, we tithe because God has commanded it. The tithe belongs to the Lord, and He requests that we return it to Him.

a. Examples of tithing. Tithing is an accepted practice throughout Scripture. Abraham gave Melchizedek, the priest of God Most High, "a tithe of all" (Gen. 14:20). By doing so, he acknowledged Melchizadek's divine priesthood and showed that he was well acquainted with this sacred institution. This casual reference to tithing indicates that it was already an established custom at that early date.

Evidently, Jacob also understood the tithing requirement. As an exile and fugitive, he vowed to the Lord, "Of all that You give me I will surely give a tenth to You" (Gen. 28:22). And after the Exodus, when Israel was established as a nation, God reaffirmed the law of tithing as a divine institution on which Israel's prosperity depended (Lev. 27:30-32; Num. 18:24, 26, 28; Deut. 12:6, 11, 17).

Far from abrogating this institution, the New Testament assumes its validity. Jesus approved of tithing and condemned those who violate its spirit (Matt. 23:23). While the ceremonial laws regulating the sacrificial offerings symbolizing Christ's atoning sacrifice ended at His death, the tithing law did not.

Because Abraham is the father of all believers, he is the model for tithe paying for Christians. As Abraham paid tithe to Melchizedek, the priest of the Most High God, so New Testament believers give tithe to Christ, our High Priest according to the order of Melchizedek (Heb. 5:9, 10; 7:1-22).[5]

b. Use of tithes. Tithes are sacred and are to be used for sacred purposes only. The Lord commanded, "A tithe of everything from the land, whether grain from the soil or fruit from the trees, belongs to the Lord; it is holy to the Lord....The entire tithe of the herd and flock...will be holy to the Lord" (Lev. 27:30-32, NIV). "Bring all the tithes into the storehouse," He said, "that there may be food in My house" (Mal. 3:10).

In Israel the tithe was used exclusively for the Levites, who, having received no tribal allotment, were to use all their time in fostering Israel's worship, ministering at the sanctuary, and instructing the people in the law of the Lord (Num. 18:21, 24).

After the Crucifixion, when the divinely directed role of the Levitical priesthood ended, tithes were still to be used to support the ministry of God's church. Paul illustrated the principle underlying this by drawing a parallel between the Levitical service and the newly established gospel ministry. He stated, "If we have sown spiritual seed among you, is it too much if we reap a material harvest from you? If others have this right of support from you, shouldn't we have it all the more?...Don't you know that those who work in the temple get their food from the temple, and those who serve at the altar share in what is offered on the altar? In the same way the Lord has commanded that those who preach the gospel should receive their living from the gospel" (1 Cor. 9:11-14, NIV).

Church members, then, willingly bring their tithes to the "storehouse, that there may be food in My house" (Mal. 3:10)—in other words, so that there are enough funds in God's church to provide a living for its ministry and to carry forward the outreach of the gospel.[6, 7]

2. Offerings. Grateful Christians cannot limit their contributions to the church to tithe. In Israel, the tabernacle, and later, the Temple, were built from "free will offerings"—offerings given from willing hearts (Ex. 36:2-7; cf. 1 Chron. 29:14). And special offerings covered the maintenance expenses of these places of worship (Ex.30:12-16; 2 Kings 12:4, 5; 2 Chron. 24:4-13; Neh. 10:32, 33). The Israelites probably contributed as much as one fourth to one third of their income to religious and charitable purposes. Did such heavy contributions lead to poverty? On the contrary, God promised to bless them in their faithfulness (Mal. 3:10-12).[8]

Today too, the Lord calls for liberal giving as He has prospered us. Offerings are needed to build, maintain, and operate churches and to set up medical missionary work, demonstrating the practical significance of the gospel.

Should we give as much as did the Israelites, or are their patterns of giving no longer applicable? In the New Testament Christ laid down the principle of true stewardship—that our gifts to God should be in proportion to the light and privileges we have enjoyed. He said, "For everyone to whom much is given, from him much will be required; and to whom much has been committed, of him they will ask more" (Luke 12:48). When Christ sent His followers on a mission, He said, "Freely you have received, freely give" (Matt. 10:8). This principle applies to the sharing of our financial blessings as well.

Nowhere does the New Testament repeal or relax this system. As we compare our privileges and blessings with those of the Israelites, we see that in Jesus our share has clearly been greater. Our gratitude will find a corresponding expression through a greater liberality so that the gospel of salvation can be extended to others.[9] The more widely the gospel is proclaimed, the greater support it needs.

3. The remaining principle. The principle of stewardship applies to what we retain as well as to what we give. While the tithe is the basic test of our stewardship of our temporal material possessions,[10] the use we make of the remaining principal tests us as well.

Our use of material goods reveals how much we love God and our neighbors. Money can be a power for good: in our hands it can provide food for the hungry, drink for the thirsty, and clothing for the naked (Matt. 25:34-40). From God's perspective money has value mainly as it is used to provide the necessities of life, to bless others, and to support His work.

4. Unfaithfulness in tithe and offerings. Generally speaking, people are ignorant of and neglect the divine principles of stewardship. Even among Christians few acknowledge their role as stewards. God's response to Israel's unfaithfulness gives a clear insight into how He regards this matter. When they used the tithes and offerings for their own benefit, He warned that it amounted to theft (Mal. 3:8) and attributed their lack of prosperity to their fiscal unfaithfulness: "You are cursed with a curse, for you have robbed Me, even this whole nation" (Mal. 3:9).

The Lord revealed His patience, love, and mercy by prefacing His warning with an offer of grace: "Return to Me, and I will return to you" (Mal. 3:7). He offered them abundant blessing and challenged them to test His faithfulness. "Bring the whole tithe into the storehouse, that there may be food in my house. Test me in this,' says the Lord Almighty, 'and see if I will not throw open the floodgates of heaven and pour out so much blessing that you will not have room enough for it. I will prevent pests from devouring your crops, and the vines in your fields will not cast their fruit,' says the Lord Almighty. 'Then all the nations will call you blessed, for yours will be a delightful land,' says the Lord Almighty" (Mal. 3:10-12, NIV).

Stewardship of the Earth. Modern science has made Earth one vast laboratory for research and experimentation. Such research yields many benefits, but the industrial revolution has also resulted in air, water, and land pollution. Technology, in some instances, has manipulated nature rather than managing it wisely.

We are stewards of this world and should do everything to maintain life on all levels by keeping the ecological balance intact. In His coming advent, Christ will "destroy those who destroy the earth" (Rev. 11:18). From this perspective Christian stewards are responsible not only for their own possessions but for the world around them.

Christ as Steward

Proper stewardship is selflessness—complete self-giving to God and service to humanity. Because of His love for us Christ endured the cruelty of the cross, the even deeper pain of rejection by His own, and abysmal God-forsakenness. In comparison to this gift, what could we ever give? His was a gift, not of what He had—even though He had everything—but of Himself. Such is stewardship. To gaze on that greatest gift is to be drawn out of ourselves—to become like Him. It will move us to become the caring church, caring for both those within the communion of believers and those without. Since Christ died for the world, stewardship, in its broadest sense, is for the world.

The Blessings of Stewardship

God has placed us in the role of stewards for our benefit, not for His.

A Personal Blessing. One reason God asks us continually to consecrate to Him our entire life—time, abilities, body, and material possessions—is to encourage our own spiritual growth and character development. As we are kept aware of God's ownership of everything and the ceaseless love He bestows on us, our love and gratitude are nurtured.

Faithful stewardship also assists us in gaining victory over covetousness and selfishness. Covetousness, one of man's greatest enemies, is condemned in the Decalogue. Jesus also warned of it: "Take heed and beware of covetousness, for one's life does not consist in the abundance of the things he possesses" (Luke 12:15). Our giving on a regular basis helps root out covetousness and selfishness from our lives.

Stewardship leads to the development of habits of economy and efficiency. Having "crucified the flesh with its passions and desires" (Gal. 5:24), we will use nothing for selfish gratification. "When the principles of stewardship are given mastery in the life, the soul is illuminated, the purpose is fixed, social pleasures are pruned of unwholesome features, the business life is conducted under the sway of the golden rule, and soul winning becomes the passion. Such are the bountiful blessings of God's provisions in a life of faith and faithfulness."[11]

A deep satisfaction and joy comes from the assurance that on everything invested for the salvation of those for whom He died, the Master inscribes, "Inasmuch as you did it to one of the least of these My brethren, you did it to Me" (Matt. 25:40). "There is nothing too precious for us to give to Jesus. If we return to Him the talents of means which He has entrusted to our keeping, He will give more into our hands. Every effort we make for Christ will be rewarded by Him, and every duty we perform in His name will minister to our own happiness."[12]

A Blessing to Others. True stewards bless all whom they contact. They execute Paul's stewardship injunction, "Command them to do good, to be rich in good deeds, and to be generous and willing to share. In this way they will lay up treasure for themselves as a firm foundation for the coming age, so that they may take hold of the life that is truly life" (1 Tim. 6:18, 19, NIV).

Stewardship involves service to others and being willing to share anything God has graciously bestowed that might benefit another. This means that "no longer do we consider that life consists of how much money we have, the titles we possess, the important people we know, the house and neighborhood we live in, and the position and influence we think we possess."[13] Real life is knowing God, developing loving and generous attributes like His, and giving what we can, according as He has prospered us. To really give in Christ's spirit is to really live.

A Blessing to the Church. The adoption of the biblical plan of stewardship is indispensable for the church. The continual participation of its members in giving is like exercise—it results in a strong church body, involved in sharing the blessings Christ has bestowed on it and ready to respond to whatever needs there are in God's cause. The church will have adequate funds to support the ministry, to expand God's kingdom in its immediate vicinity, and to extend it to the remote places of the earth. It will willingly make time, talents, and means available to God in love and gratitude for His blessings.

In view of Christ's assurance that He will return when the gospel of the kingdom has been proclaimed as "a witness to all the nations" (Matt. 24:14), all are invited to be stewards and co-workers with Him. Thus the church's witness will be a powerful blessing to the world, and its faithful stewards will be made glad as they see the blessings of the gospel extended to others.

References

1. *Webster's New Universal Unabridged Dictionary*, 2nd ed., 1979, p. 1786.

2. *SDA Encyclopedia*, rev. ed., p. 1425.

3. *Ibid.*

4. Paul G. Smith, *Managing God's Goods* (Nashville: Southern Pub. Assn., 1973), p. 21.

5. See C. G. Tuland, "Tithing in the New Testament," *Ministry*, October 1961, p. 12.

6. E.g., in Exodus 27:20 the Lord gave special instructions that olive oil was to be provided for the lamps. Supplying the oil for the place of worship so that it could function properly was a continual obligation—but this operating expense did not come from the tithe. See also White, *Counsels on Stewardship* (Washington, D.C.: Review and Herald, 1940), pp. 102, 103. She says that Bible teachers in church-operated schools should be paid from the tithe (*Ibid.*, p. 103), but that it must not be used for other "school purposes," student loans, or for supporting canvassers and colporteurs (White, *Testimonies*, vol. 9, pp. 248, 249; White, *Selected Messages*, book 2, p. 209). These phases of God's work are to be supported from the offerings.

7. T. H. Jemison made some very practical suggestions on how to calculate tithes. He wrote, "Tithe on salary is easy to figure. Ordinarily there are no 'business expenses'—that is, actual expenses in producing the income—to be deducted. Ten percent of the salary is tithe....

   "Tithing business income has some variations from tithing a salary. A wholesale or retail merchant will deduct the expenses necessary to conduct his business before figuring the tithe. This includes the cost of hired help, heat, light, insurance, rent or property taxes, and similar items. These deductions do not, of course, include any of his personal or family living expenses.

   "The farmer deducts his costs—wages, fertilizer, repairs, interest, taxes, and the like. However, the farmer should consider in his income farm produce used by the family, as this reduces family living costs and serves as income.

   "Comparable procedures can be followed by the manufacturer, the investor, or the professional man. The accurate accounting that is necessary these days in all businesses makes it easy to compute the tithe on the increase, or profit, from the business. Some businessmen include their tithe calculation in their regular bookkeeping system.

   "Sometimes a woman whose husband is not a tithepayer finds it difficult to know how to relate herself to tithe paying. In some cases she can pay tithe on the money given her for household expenses. In other instances this has been forbidden. In such cases she may be able to tithe only what extra money she may earn or receive as a gift. 'For if there be first a willing mind, it is accepted according to that a man hath, and not according to that he hath not." 2 Corinthians 8:12" (*Christian Beliefs*, p. 267).

8. Some Bible students believe that Israel contributed at least two tithes (some think three) in addition to various offerings. Regarding the first tithe the Lord had said, "I have given the children of Levi all the tithe in Israel as an inheritance in return for the work which they perform" (Num. 18:21). But as to the second tithe, He said, "You shall eat before the Lord your God, in the place where He chooses to make His name abide, the tithe of your grain and your new wine and your oil, of the firstlings of your herds and your flocks, that you may learn to fear the Lord your God always" (Deut. 14:23). For two years out of three, the Israelites were to bring this tithe, or its equivalent in money, to the sanctuary. There, it would be used to celebrate the religious festivals and also to provide for the Levites, strangers, fatherless, and widows. Every third year the Israelites were to use the second tithe at home to entertain the Levites, strangers, fatherless, and widows. So the second tithe was used for charity and hospitality (Deut. 14:27-29; 26:12). See White, *Patriarchs and Prophets*, p. 530; "Tithe," *SDA Bible Dictionary*, rev. ed., p. 1127.

9. Cf. White, *Testimonies*, vol. 3, p. 392.

10. From a biblical perspective possession is not ownership. Our attitude toward tithing indicates whether we acknowledge that we are only managers or whether we pretend to be owners.

11. Froom, "Stewardship in Its Larger Aspects," *Ministry*, June 1960, p. 20.

12. White, *Testimonies*, vol. 4, p. 19.

13. P. G. Smith, p. 72.

Christian Behavior

22

We are called to be a godly people who think, feel, and act in harmony with the principles of heaven. For the Spirit to recreate in us the character of our Lord we involve ourselves only in those things which will produce Christlike purity, health, and joy in our lives. This means that our amusement and entertainment should meet the highest standards of Christian taste and beauty. While recognizing cultural differences, our dress is to be simple, modest, and neat, befitting those whose true beauty does not consist of outward adornment but in the imperishable ornament of a gentle and quiet spirit. It also means that because our bodies are the temples of the Holy Spirit, we are to care for them intelligently. Along with adequate exercise and rest, we are to adopt the most healthful diet possible and abstain from the unclean foods identified in the Scriptures. Since alcoholic beverages, tobacco, and the irresponsible use of drugs and narcotics are harmful to our bodies, we are to abstain from them as well. Instead, we are to engage in whatever brings our thoughts and bodies into the discipline of Christ, who desires our wholesomeness, joy, and goodness. (Rom. 12:1, 2; 1 John

2:6; Eph. 5:1-21; Phil. 4:8; 2 Cor. 10:5; 6:14 – 7:1; 1 Pet. 3:1-4; 1 Cor. 6:19, 20; 10:31; Lev. 11:1-47; 3 John 2.)

CHRISTIAN BEHAVIOR—THE LIFESTYLE of a follower of God—arises as a grateful response to God's magnificent salvation through Christ. Paul appeals to all Christians: "I beseech you therefore, brethren, by the mercies of God, that you present your bodies as a living sacrifice, holy, acceptable to God, which is your reasonable service. And do not be conformed to this world, but be transformed by the renewing of your mind, that you may prove which is that good and acceptable and perfect will of God" (Rom. 12:1, 2). So Christians willingly protect and develop their mental, physical, and spiritual faculties in order that they may honor their Creator and Redeemer.

Christ prayed, "I do not pray that You should take them out of the world, but that You should keep them from the evil one. They are not of the world, just as I am not of the world" (John 17:15, 16). How can a Christian be both in the world and separate from it? How should the Christian lifestyle differ from that of the world?

Christians should adopt a different lifestyle, not for the sake of being different, but because God has called them to live by principle. The lifestyle to which He has called them enables them to reach their full potential as His creation, making them efficient in His service. Being different also advances their mission: to serve the world—to be salt in it, light to it. Of what value would salt be without taste, or light that didn't differ from darkness?

Christ is our example. He lived so thoroughly in the world that people accused Him of being "a glutton and a drunkard" (Matt. 11:19, NIV), though He was not. He so consistently lived out God's principles that no one could prove Him guilty of sin (John 8:46, NIV).

Behavior and Salvation

In determining what is appropriate behavior, we should avoid two extremes. The first is accepting the rules and applications of principles as a means of salvation. Paul sums up this extreme with the words, "You who are trying to be justified by law have been alienated from Christ; you have fallen away from grace" (Gal. 5:4, NIV).

The opposite extreme is believing that since works do not save, they are therefore unimportant—that what a person does really doesn't matter. Paul spoke to this extreme too: "You, my brothers, were called to be free. But do not use your freedom to indulge the sinful nature" (Gal. 5:13,

NIV). When each member follows his or her own conscience, "there is no mutual disciplining of fellow Christians in keeping with Matthew 18 and Galatians 6:1, 2. The church becomes not the body of Christ, within which there is mutual love and care, but a collection of atomistic individuals, each of whom goes his or her own way without taking any responsibility for one's fellows or accepting any concern for them."[1]

While our behavior and our spirituality are closely related, we can never earn salvation by correct behavior. Rather, Christian behavior is a natural fruit of salvation and is grounded in what Christ has already accomplished for us at Calvary.

Temples of the Holy Spirit

Not only the church but the individual Christian is a temple for the indwelling of the Holy Spirit: "Do you not know that your body is the temple of the Holy Spirit who is in you, whom you have from God, and you are not your own?" (1 Cor. 6:19).

Christians, then, practice good health habits to protect the command center of their body temples—the mind, the dwelling place of the Spirit of Christ. For this reason Seventh-day Adventists—throughout the past 100 years—have stressed the importance of proper health habits.[2] And this emphasis has been paying off: Recent research reveals that Adventists are less likely than the general population to develop almost any of the major diseases.[3]

As Christians, we are concerned with both the spiritual and the physical aspects of people's lives. Jesus, our pattern, healed "every disease and sickness among the people" (Matt. 4:23, NIV).

The Bible views human beings as a unit (chapter 7). "The dichotomy between spiritual and material is foreign to the Bible."[4] So God's call to holiness involves a call to physical as well as spiritual health. Susannah Wesley, mother of the founder of Methodism, aptly summarized this principle: "Whatever weakens your reason, impairs the tenderness of your conscience, obscures your sense of God, decreases the strength and authority of your mind over your body—that thing is wrong, however innocent it may be in itself."[5]

God's laws, which include the laws of health, are not arbitrary but are designed by our Creator to enable us to enjoy life at its best. Satan, the enemy, wants to steal our health, our joy, our peace of mind, and ultimately to destroy us (see John 10:10).

God's Blessings for Total Health

Attaining this health depends upon practicing a few rather simple but effective God-given principles. Some of these are obvious and quite agreeable to most people. Others, such as proper diet, are more difficult to accept since they involve orientations and habits so basic to our lifestyles. For this reason, we will devote more space to those principles that are either misunderstood, debated, or rejected.[6]

The Blessing of Exercise. Regular exercise is the simple formula for increased energy, a firm body, stress relief, healthier skin, more self-confidence, effective weight control, improved digestion and regularity, and reduced depression and the risk of heart disease and cancer. Exercise is not merely an option, it is essential to maintaining optimal health—both physical and mental.[7]

Useful activity tends to prosperity; inactivity and laziness tend to adversity (Prov. 6:6-13; 14:23). God prescribed activity for the first man and woman—care for their garden home in the open air (Gen. 2:5, 15; 3:19). Christ Himself set an example of physical activity. For most of His life He was engaged in manual labor as a carpenter, and during His ministry He walked the roads of Palestine.[8]

The Blessing of Sunlight. Light is essential to life (Gen. 1:3). It powers the process that produces the nutrients that nourish and energize our bodies and that releases the oxygen we must have to live. Sunshine promotes health and healing.

The Blessing of Water. The human body is 75 percent water, but this vital fluid is continuously being lost through exhaled air, perspiration, and waste products. Drinking six to eight glasses of pure water a day would aid in maintaining efficient, happy well-being. Another important function of water is its use for cleanliness and the relaxation it affords.

The Blessing of Fresh Air. An environment of impure air, in or outside the home, causes the blood to carry less oxygen than is required for the optimal function of every cell. This tends to make a person less alert and responsive. It is therefore important to do everything possible to secure a generous supply of fresh air daily.

The Blessing of Temperate, Drug-Free, Stimulant-Free Living. Drugs have saturated our society because they offer stimulation and release from stress and pain. The Christian is surrounded with seductive invitations to use drugs. Even many innocent-appearing, popular beverages contain drugs: Coffee, tea, and colas contain caffeine,[9] and fruit-flavored wine coolers contain alcohol. Research has shown that the milder gateway drugs tend to lead progressively to stronger mind-altering drugs. The wise Christian will abstain from all that is harmful, using in moderation only that which is good.

1. Tobacco. In any form tobacco is a slow poison that has a harmful effect on the physical, mental, and moral powers. At first its effects are hardly noticeable. It excites and then paralyzes the nerves, weakening and clouding the brain.

Those who use tobacco are slowly committing suicide,[10] transgressing the sixth commandment: "Thou shalt not kill" (Ex. 20:13, KJV).

2. Alcoholic beverages. Alcohol is one of the most widely used drugs on Planet Earth. It has devastated untold millions. Not only does it hurt those who use it, but it exacts its toll from society in general—through broken homes, accidental deaths, and poverty.

Since God communicates with us only through our minds, it is well to remember that alcohol adversely affects their every function. As the level of alcohol in the system rises, the drinker progresses through loss of coordination, confusion, disorientation, stupor, anesthesia, coma, and death. Drinking alcoholic beverages on a regular basis will eventually produce loss of memory, judgment, and learning ability.[11]

Scriptural stories involving the use of alcoholic beverages may give the impression that God approved of their use. However, Scripture also indicates that God's people participated in such social practices as divorce, polygamy, and slavery—practices that God certainly did not condone. In interpreting such Scriptural passages, it is helpful to keep in mind that God does not necessarily endorse all that He permits.

Jesus' answer to the query as to why Moses permitted divorce points to this principle of interpretation. He said, "Moses, because of the hardness of your hearts, permitted you to divorce your wives, but from the beginning it was not so" (Matt. 19:8).[12] Eden is the divine model to which the gospel would restore us. As is true of these other practices, the use of alcohol was not a part of God's original plan.[13]

3. Other drugs and narcotics. There are many other harmful drugs and narcotics through which Satan destroys human lives.[14] True Christians, beholding Christ, will continually glorify God with their bodies, realizing that they are His prized possessions, bought with His precious blood.

The Blessing of Rest. Proper rest is essential for health of body and mind. Christ extends to us the compassionate directive He gave His weary disciples: "Come with me by yourselves to a quiet place and get some rest" (Mark 6:31, NIV). Periods of rest provide much-needed quietness for communion with God: "Be still, and know that I am God" (Ps. 46:10). God stressed our need for rest by setting aside the seventh day of the week as the day of rest (Ex. 20:10).

Rest is more than sleeping or ceasing our regular work. It involves the way we spend our leisure time. Weariness is not always caused by stress or by working too hard or too long: Our minds can be wearied by overstimulation through the media, sickness, or various personal problems.

Recreation is re-creation in the truest sense of the word. It strengthens, builds up, and refreshes the mind and body, thus preparing believers to go back to their vocations with new vigor. To live life at its best, Christians should pursue only those forms of recreation and entertainment that strengthen their bond with Christ and improve health.

Scripture lays down the following principle, which will help Christians select good recreation: "Do not love the world or the things in the world. If anyone loves the world, the love of the Father is not in him. For all that is in the world—the lust of the flesh, the lust of the eyes, and the pride of life—is not of the Father but is of the world" (1 John 2:15, 16).

1. Movies, television, radio and videos. These media can be great educational agencies. They have "changed the whole atmosphere of our modern world and have brought us within easy contact with the life, thought, and activities of the entire globe."[15] The Christian will remember that television and videos make a greater impact on the life of an individual than does any other single activity.

Unfortunately, video and television, with their almost continuous theatrical performances, bring influences into the home that are neither wholesome nor uplifting. If we are not discriminating and decisive, "they will turn our homes into theaters and minstrel shows of a cheap and sordid kind."[16] The committed Christian will turn away from unwholesome, violent, sensual movies and television programs.

Visual and audio media are not evil in themselves. The same channels that portray the depths of human wickedness convey the preaching of the gospel of salvation. And many other worthwhile programs are broadcast. But people can use even the good programs to avoid the responsibilities of life. Christians will not only desire to establish principles for determining what to watch but will also set time limits on their watching, so that social relationship and the responsibilities of life will not suffer. If we cannot discriminate or if we lack the power to control our media, it is much better to dispense with them altogether than to have them rule our lives either by polluting the mind or consuming excessive amounts of time (see Matt. 5:29, 30).

Regarding our contemplation of Christ, an important biblical principle states that "by beholding we are becoming transformed into His likeness with ever-increasing glory" (2 Cor. 3:18, NIV). Beholding brings change. But Christians must continually remember that this principle works on the negative side, too. Films graphically portraying the sins and crimes of humanity—murder, adultery, robbery, and other degrading acts—are contributing to the present breakdown of morality.

Paul's advice in Philippians 4:8 lays out a principle that helps identify the forms of recreation that have value: "Finally, brethren, whatever things are true, whatever things are noble, whatever things are just, whatever things are pure, whatever things are lovely, whatever things are of good report, if there is any virtue and if there is anything praiseworthy—meditate on these things."

2. Reading and music. These same high standards apply to the Christian's reading and music. Music is a gift of God to inspire pure, noble, and elevated thoughts. Good music, then, enhances the finest qualities of character.

Debased music, on the other hand, "destroys the rhythm of the soul and breaks down morality." So Christ's followers will shun "any melody partaking of the nature of jazz, rock, or related hybrid forms, or any language expressing foolish or trivial sentiments."[17] The Christian does not listen to music with suggestive lyrics or melodies (Rom. 13:11-14; 1 Peter 2:11).[18]

Reading offers much that is valuable too. There is a wealth of good literature that cultivates and expands the mind. Yet there is also a "flood of evil literature, often in most attractive guise but damaging to mind and morals. The tales of wild adventure and of moral laxness, whether fact or fiction," are unfit for believers because they create a distaste for a noble, honest, and pure lifestyle and hinder the development of a union with Christ.[19]

3. Unacceptable activities. Adventists also teach that gambling, card playing, theater going, and dancing are to be avoided (1 John 2:15-17). They question spending time watching violent sporting events (Phil. 4:8). Any activity that weakens our relationship with our Lord and causes us to lose sight of eternal interests helps bind Satan's chains about our souls. Christians will rather participate in those wholesome forms of leisure activities that will truly refresh their physical, mental, and spiritual natures.

The Blessing of Nutritious Food. To the first couple, the Creator gave the ideal diet: "I give you every seed-bearing plant on the face of the whole earth and every tree that has fruit with seed in it. They will be yours for food" (Gen. 1:29, NIV). After the Fall, God added to their diet "the plants of the fields" (Gen. 3:18, NIV).

Today's health problems tend to center on the degenerative type of diseases directly traceable to diet and lifestyle. The diet God planned, consisting of grains, fruits, nuts, and vegetables, offers the right nutritional ingredients to support optimum health.

1. The original diet. The Bible does not condemn the eating of clean animals. But God's original diet for man did not include flesh foods, because He did not envision the taking of any animal's life and because a balanced vegetarian diet is the best for health—a fact for which science offers mounting evidence.[20] People consuming animal products that contain bacteria or viruses that cause disease may have their health impaired.[21] It is estimated that every year, in the United States alone, millions suffer from poultry food poisoning because inspection fails to detect contamination by salmonella and other microorganisms.[22] Several experts feel that "bacterial contamination poses a far greater risk than chemical additives and preservatives in food" and expect the incidence of the diseases caused by these bacteria to rise.[23]

Furthermore, studies conducted in recent years indicate that increased meat consumption can cause an increase of atherosclerosis, cancer, kidney disorders, osteoporosis, and trichinosis and can decrease the life expectancy.[24]

The diet God ordained in the Garden of Eden—the vegetarian diet—is the ideal, but sometimes we cannot have the ideal. In those circumstances, in any given situation or locale, those who wish to stay in optimum health will eat the best food that they can obtain.

2. Clean and unclean flesh foods. Only after the Flood did God introduce flesh as food. With all vegetation destroyed, God gave Noah and his family permission to eat flesh foods, stipulating that they were not to eat the blood in the meat (Gen. 9:3-5).

Another stipulation Scripture implies that God gave Noah was that he and his family were to eat only what God identified as clean animals. It was because Noah and his family needed the clean animals for food as well as for sacrifices (Gen. 8:20) that God instructed Noah to take seven pairs of each kind of clean animal, in contrast to only one pair of each kind of unclean, with him into the ark (Gen. 7:2, 3). Leviticus 11 and Deuteronomy 14 provide extensive expositions on clean and unclean food.[25]

By nature, unclean animals do not constitute the best food. Many are either scavengers or predators—from the lion and swine to the vulture and the bottom-dwelling, sucker-type fish. Because of their habits, they are more apt to be carriers of disease.

Studies have revealed that "in addition to the moderate amounts of cholesterol found in both pork and shellfish, both foods contain a number of toxins and contaminants which are associated with human poisoning."[26]

By abstaining from unclean foods, God's people demonstrated their gratefulness for their redemption from the corrupt, unclean world around them (Lev. 20:24-26; Deut. 14:2). To introduce anything unclean into the body temple where God's Spirit dwells is less than God's ideal.

The New Testament did not abolish the distinction between the clean and unclean flesh foods. Some believe that because these dietary laws are mentioned in Leviticus, they are merely ceremonial or ritualistic, so are no longer valid for Christians. Yet the distinction between clean and unclean animals dates back to Noah's day—long before Israel existed. As principles of health, these dietary laws carry with them an ongoing obligation.[27]

3. Regularity, simplicity, and balance. Successful dietary reforms are progressive and must be approached intelligently. Eventually, we should learn to eliminate, or use only sparingly, food with high fat and/or sugar content.

Furthermore, we should prepare the foods we eat in as simple and natural a way as possible and for optimum benefit, should eat at regular intervals. Complex, stimulating diets are not the most healthful. Many condiments and spices irritate the digestive tract,[28] and their habitual use is associated with a number of health problems.

The Blessing of Christian Dress. God provided the first clothing for Adam and Eve and knows that we have need of suitable clothing today (Matt. 6:25-33). We should base our choice of clothing on the principles of simplicity, modesty, practicality, health, and attractiveness.

1. Simple. As it does in all other areas of our lives, the Christian call to simplicity impinges upon how we dress. "Christian witness calls for simplicity.

"The way we dress demonstrates to the world who we are and what we are—not as a legal requirement handed down from the Victorian era, but as an expression of our love for Jesus."[30]

2. Of high moral virtue. Christians will not mar the beauty of their characters with styles that arouse the "lust of the flesh" (1 John 2:16). Because they want to witness to others, they will dress and act modestly, not accentuating the parts of the body that stimulate sexual desires. Modesty promotes moral health. The Christian's aim is to glorify God, not self.

3. Practical and economical. Because they are stewards of the money God has entrusted to them, Christians will practice economy, avoiding "gold or pearls or costly clothing" (1 Tim. 2:9). Practicing economy, however, does not necessarily mean purchasing the cheapest clothing available. Often higher quality items are more economical in the long run.

4. Healthful. It is not only diet that affects a person's health. Christians will avoid clothing styles that do not adequately protect the body or that constrict it or otherwise affect it in such ways as to cause the health to deteriorate.

5. Characterized by grace and natural beauty. Christians understand the warning against "the pride of life" (1 John 2:16). Referring to the lilies, Christ said, "even Solomon in all his glory was not arrayed like one of these" (Matt. 6:29). Thus He illustrated that Heaven's perception of beauty is characterized by grace, simplicity, purity, and natural beauty. Worldly display, as seen in transient fashions, has no value in God's eyes (1 Tim. 2:9).

Christians win unbelievers, not by looking and behaving like the world, but by revealing an attractive and refreshing difference. Peter said unbelieving spouses "may be won by the conduct of their wives, when they observe your chaste conduct accompanied by fear." Instead of adorning the exterior, he counseled, let believers concentrate on developing "the hidden person of the heart, with the incorruptible ornament of a gentle and quiet spirit, which is very precious in the sight of God" (1 Pet. 3:1-4). Scripture teaches that:

a. The character shows forth one's true beauty. Both Peter and Paul set forth the basic principle for guiding Christian men and women in the area of adornment: "Your beauty should not come from outward adornment such as...the wearing of gold jewelry and fine clothes" (1 Peter 3:3, NIV). "I also want women to dress modestly with decency and propriety, not with braided hair or gold or pearls or expensive clothes, but with good deeds, appropriate for women who profess to worship God" (1 Tim. 2:9, 10, NIV).

b. Simplicity harmonizes with reformation and revival. When Jacob called his family to dedicate themselves to God, they gave up "all the foreign gods which were in their hands, and all their earrings which were in their ears," and Jacob buried them (Gen. 35:2, 4).[31]

After Israel's apostasy with the golden calf, God commanded them, "Take off your ornaments, that I may know what to do to you." In penitence they "stripped themselves of their ornaments" (Ex. 33:5, 6). Paul clearly states that Scripture records this apostasy "as warnings for us, on whom the fulfillment of the ages has come" (1 Cor. 10:11, NIV).

c. Good stewardship requires sacrificial living. While much of the world is undernourished, materialism lays before Christians temptations ranging from expensive clothes, cars, and jewelry to luxurious homes. Simplicity of lifestyle and appearance sets Christians in stark contrast to the greed, materialism, and gaudiness of pagan, twenty-first-century society, where values focus on material things rather than on people.

In view of these Scriptural teachings and the principles laid out above, we believe that Christians ought not to adorn themselves with jewelry. We understand this to mean that the wearing of rings, earrings, necklaces, and bracelets, and showy tie tacks, cuff links, and pins—and any other type of jewelry that has as its main function display—is unnecessary and not in harmony with the simplicity of adornment urged by Scripture.[32]

The Bible associates gaudy cosmetics with paganism and apostasy (2 Kings 9:30; Jer. 4:30). As to cosmetics, therefore, we believe that Christians should maintain a natural, healthy appearance. If we lift up the Saviour in the way we speak, act, and dress, we become like magnets, drawing people to Him.[33]

Principles of Christian Standards

In all its manifestations, the Christian lifestyle is a response to salvation through Christ. The Christian desires to honor God and to live as Jesus would live. Although some view the Christian lifestyle as a list of don'ts, we should rather see it as a series of positive principles active in the framework of salvation. Jesus emphasized that He came that we might have life and have it more abundantly. What are the principles that guide us to the full life? When the Holy Spirit comes into the life of an individual, a decided change takes place that is evident to those around that person (John 3:8). The Spirit not only makes an initial change in the life, His effects are ongoing. The fruit of the Spirit is love (Galatians 5:22, 23). The most powerful argument for the validity of Christianity is a loving and lovable Christian.

Living With the Mind of Christ. "Let this mind be in you which was also in Christ Jesus" (Phil. 2:5). Under all circumstances, favorable or adverse, we should seek to understand and live in harmony with the will and mind of Christ (1 Cor. 2:16).

Ellen White has noted the beautiful results of a life that is lived in this kind of relationship with Christ: "All true obedience comes from the heart. It was heart work with Christ. And if we consent, He will so identify Himself with our thoughts and aims, so blend our hearts and minds into conformity to His will, that when obeying Him we shall be but carrying out our own impulses. The will, refined and sanctified, will find its highest delight in doing His service. When we know God as it is our privilege to know Him, our life will be a life of continual obedience. Through an appreciation of the character of Christ, through communion with God, sin will become hateful to us."[34]

Living to Praise and Glorify God. God has done so much for us. One way in which we can show our gratitude is through the praise that we give Him.

The Psalms strongly emphasize this side of the spiritual life: "I have seen you in the sanctuary and beheld your power and your glory. Because your love is better than life, my lips will glorify you. I will praise you as long as I live, and in your name I will lift up my hands. My soul will be satisfied as with the richest of foods; with singing lips my mouth will praise you" (Ps. 63:2-5, NIV).

For the Christian, such an attitude of praise will keep life's other affairs in appropriate perspective. In looking upon our crucified Saviour who redeemed us from the penalty and delivers us from the power of sin, we are motivated to do only "those things that are pleasing in His sight" (1 John 3:22; cf. Eph. 5:10, NIV). Christians "live no longer for themselves but for Him who died for them and rose again" (2 Cor. 5:15). Every true Christian puts God first in all he does, in all he thinks, in all he speaks, and in all that he desires. He has no other gods before His Redeemer (1 Cor. 10:31).

Living to Be an Example. Paul said to "give no offense" to anyone (1 Cor. 10:32). "I myself always strive to have a conscience without offense toward God and men" (Acts 24:16). If our example leads others to sin, we become stumblingblocks to those for whom Christ died. "Whoever claims to live in him must walk as Jesus did" (1 John 2:6, NIV).

Living to Minister. A major reason Christians live as they do is to save lost men and women. Said Paul, "I try to please everybody in every way. For I am not seeking my own good but the good of many, so that they may be saved" (1 Cor. 10:33, NIV; cf. Matt. 20:28).

Requirements and Guidelines

Because of the impact a person's lifestyle makes upon his spiritual experience and his witness, as a church organization we have set certain lifestyle standards as minimal requirements for becoming members. These standards include abstention from tobacco, alcoholic beverages, mind-altering chemicals, unclean flesh foods and a growing Christian experience in matters of dress and the use of leisure time. These minimal standards do not comprehend all of God's ideal for the believer. They simply signify essential first steps in developing a growing, radiant Christian experience. Such standards also provide the foundation essential to unity within the community of believers.

The development of Christian behavior—"God-likeness"—is progressive, involving a lifelong union with Christ. Holy living is nothing less than a daily yielding of the will to Christ's control and a daily conformity to His teachings as He reveals them to us in our Bible study and in prayer. Because we mature at different rates, it is important that we refrain from judging weaker brothers or sisters (Rom. 14:1; 15:1).

Christians in union with the Saviour have but one ideal—that they shall do their best to honor the heavenly Father, who has provided such a rich plan for their salvation. "Therefore, whether you eat or drink, or whatever you do, do all to the glory of God" (1 Cor. 10:31).

References

1. L. A. King, "Legalism or Permissiveness: An Inescapable Dilemma?" *The Christian Century,* April 16, 1980, p. 436.

2. For the development of the biblical basis of healthful living in the SDA Church, see Damsteegt, *Foundations of the Seventh-day Adventist Message and Mission,* pp. 221-240; Damsteegt, "Health Reforms and the Bible in Early Sabbatarian Adventism," *Adventist Heritage,* Winter 1978, pp. 13-21.

3. Lewis R. Walter, Jo Ellen Walton, John A. Scharffenberg, *How You Can Live Six Extra Years* (Santa Barbara, CA: Woodbridge Press, 1981), p. 4; D. C. Nieman, and H. J. Stanton, "The Adventist Lifestyle—a Better Way to Live," *Vibrant Life,* March/April 1988, pp. 14-18.

4. *Zondervan Pictorial Encyclopedia of the Bible* (Grand Rapids, MI: Zondervan Publishers, 1975), vol. 1, p. 884.

5. C. B. Haynes, "Church Standards—No. 5," *Review and Herald,* Oct. 30, 1941, p. 7.

6. For a fuller treatment of these simple health rules, see V. W. Foster, *New Start!* (Santa Barbara, CA: Woodbridge Press, 1988).

7. See, e.g., Kenneth H. Cooper, *Aerobics Program for Total Well Being* (New York: M. Evans, 1982); *Physical Fitness Education Syllabus* (Loma Linda, CA: Department of Health Science, School of Health, Loma Linda University, 1976-1977); John Dignam, "Walking Into Shape," *Signs of the Times,* July 1987, p. 16; B. E. Baldwin, "Exercise," *Journal of Health and Healing 11,* no. 4 (1987): 20-23; Jeanne Wiesseman, *Physical Fitness,* Abundant Living Health Series, vol. 5 (Loma Linda, CA: School of Health, Loma Linda University, n.d.), pp. 21, 37, 38, 45. See also Dianne-Jo Moore, "Walk Your Tensions Away," *Your Life and Health,* No. 4 (1984): 12, 13.

8. Among the various forms of exercise, walking ranks as one of the best. See J. A. Scharffenberg, "Adventist Responsibility in Exercise" (unpublished manuscript); White, *Testimonies,* vol. 3, p. 78; White, "Temperance," *Health Reformer,* April 1872, p.122; Dignam, "Walking Into Shape," pp. 16, 17.

9. Caffeine has also been found to contribute to increased blood cholesterol, high blood pressure, increased gastric secretions, and peptic ulcers. It has

been implicated in heart disease, diabetes, and cancers of the colon, bladder, and pancreas. Its heavy use during pregnancy increases the risk of birth defects and low-birth-weight infants. See Robert O'Brien and Sidney Cohen, "Caffeine," *Encyclopedia of Drug Abuse* (New York: Facts on File, 1984), pp. 50, 51; Marjorie V. Baldwin, "Caffeine on Trial," *Life and Health*, October 1973, pp. 10-13; E. D. Gorham, L. F. Garland, F. C. Garland, *et al*, "Coffee and Pancreatic Cancer in a Rural California County," *Western Journal of Medicine*, January 1988, pp. 48-53; B. K. Jacobsen, and D. S. Thelle, "The Tromso" Heart Study: Is Coffee Drinking an Indicator of a Lifestyle With High Risk for Ischemic Heart Disease?" *Acta Medica Scandinavica 222*, No. 3 (1987), 215-221; J. D. Curb, D. M. Reed, J. A. Kautz, and K. Yano, "Coffee, Caffeine and Serum Cholesterol in Japanese Living in Hawaii," *American Journal of Epidemiology*, April 1986, pp. 648-655. High consumers of coffee are also "less active in religion" (B. S. Victor, M. Lubetsky, and J. F. Greden, "Somatic Manifestations of Caffeinism," *Journal of Clinical Psychiatry*, May 1981, p. 186). For the caffeine content of the various beverages, see "The Latest Caffeine Scoreboard," *FDA Consumer*, March 1984, pp. 14-16; Bosley, "Caffeine: Is It So Harmless?" *Ministry*, August 1986, p. 28; Winston J. Craig and Thuy T. Nguyen, "Caffeine and Theobromine Levels in Cocoa and Carob Products," *Journal of Food Science*, January-February, 1984, pp. 302-303, 305.

10. Regarding the circulatory system, tobacco increases the risk of heart attacks, high blood pressure, and peripheral vascular disease such as Buerger's disease, which necessitates the amputation of fingers and toes. As to the respiratory system, tobacco brings an increase of deaths as a result of lung cancer, chronic bronchitis, and emphysema. It paralyzes the bronchial cilia that cleanse the lung and bronchi of impurities and is associated with cancer of the larynx, mouth, esophagus, urinary bladder, kidney, and pancreas. It is also associated with an increase of duodenal ulcers and deaths from complications resulting from ulcers. See e.g., *Smoking and Health: A Report of the Surgeon General* (Washington, D.C.; U.S. Department of Health, Education, and Welfare, 1979).

11. See, e.g., Galen C. Bosley, "The Effects of Small Quantities of Alcohol," *Ministry*, May 1986, pp. 24-27. Among social drinkers alcohol causes shrinkage of the frontal lobes, the center of moral discernment (L. A. Cala, B. Jones, P. Burns, et. al, "Results of Computerized Tomography, Psychometric Testing and Dietary Studies in Social Drinkers, With Emphasis on Reversibility After Abstinence," *Medical Journal of Australia*, Sept. 17, 1983, pp. 264-269). Cf. Bosley, "Why a Health Message," *Adventist Review*, July 30, 1987, p. 15. Psychological testing of social drinkers showed that their mental abilities and intellectual performance were significantly impaired (D. A. Parker, E. S. Parker, J. A. Brody, and R. Schoenberg, "Alcohol Use and Cognitive Loss Among Employed Men and Women" *American Journal of Public Health*, May 1983, pp. 521-526). As alcohol intake increases, church attendance decreases (A. M. Edward, R. Wolfe, P. Moll, and E. Harburg, "Psychosocial and Behavioral Factors Differentiating Past Drinkers and Lifelong Abstainers," *American Journal of Public Health*, January 1986, p. 69.

12. See Chapter 16, footnote 8 for a discussion of wine at the Lord's Supper.

13. In the Old Testament, the general term for wine is *yayin*. This term designates the juice of the grape in all its stages from unfermented to fermented, though it is frequently used for fully aged wine that contains alcohol. The usual word for unfermented wine is *tirosh*. It is frequently translated as "new wine," which is freshly pressed grape juice. Both terms are rendered *oinos* in the Septuagint Greek translation of the Old Testament (LXX). *Oinos* is the term generally used for wine in the New Testament and refers to both fermented and unfermented wine, depending on the context. (For the Old Testament see Robert P. Teachout, "The Use of 'Wine' in the Old Testament" (Th.D. dissertation, 1979, available through University Microfilms International, Ann Arbor, MI); Lael O. Caesar, "The Meaning of *Yayin*" (unpublished M.A. thesis, Andrews University, Berrien Springs, MI, 1986; William Patton, *Bible Wines* (Oklahoma City, OK: Sane Press, n.d.), pp. 54-64.

    The same expression "strong drink" (*shekar* in Hebrew) signifies a sweet drink, usually fermented, and generally made from sources other than grapes. It includes products like beer (from barley, millet, or wheat), and date or palm wine. The expression does not refer to distilled liquors because distillation was unknown to the Israelites (Patton, pp. 57, 58, 62).

    Fermented wine. Scripture condemns alcoholic wine because it brings violence, misery, and destruction (Prov. 4:17; 23:29, 35). It causes religious leaders to be oppressive (Isa. 56:10-12) and was associated with the perversion of judgment of Israel's leaders (Isa. 28:7) and of King Belshazzar (Dan. 5:1-30).

    Unfermented wine. The Bible speaks favorably of unfermented wine or juice and recommends it as a great blessing. It is to be presented as an offering to God (Num. 18:12, 13; Neh. 10:37-39; 13:12, 13). It is one of God's blessings (Gen. 27:28, NIV "new wine"; Deut. 7:13, 11:14; Prov. 3:10; Isa. 65:8; Joel 3:18), "cheers both God and men" (Judges 9:13), and symbolizes spiritual blessings (Isa. 55:1, 2; Prov. 9:2, 3). It also is a healthful drink (1 Tim. 5:23).

14. See, e.g., Drug Enforcement Administration, *Drugs of Abuse*, 3rd ed. (Washington, D.C.: United States Department of Justice, n.d.); Dan Sperling, "Drug Roundup," *Adventist Review*, Apr. 9, 1987, pp. 12, 13.

15. *SDA Church Manual*, p. 147.

16. *Ibid.*

17. *Ibid.*, p. 148. For examples of degradation in much modern music and entertainment, see Tipper Gore, *Raising PG Kids in an X-rated Society*, (Nashville, TN: Abingdon Press, 1987).

18. "Another form of amusement that has an evil influence is social dancing. "The amusement of dancing, as conducted at the present day, is a school of depravity, a fearful curse to society."—*Messages to Young People*, p. 399 (See also p. 192). (See 2 Cor. 6:15-18; 1 John 2:15-17; James 4:4; 2 Tim. 2:19-22; Eph. 5:8-11; Col. 3:5-10.)" In view of these influences to sin, Christians

would do well not to "patronize the commercialized amusements, joining with the worldly, careless, pleasure-loving multitudes who are 'lovers of pleasures more than lovers of God' [2 Tim. 3:4]" (*SDA Church Manual*, p. 148).

19. *Ibid.*, pp. 146, 147.

20. On the adequacy of a vegetarian diet, see S. Havala, J. Dwyer, "Position of the American Dietetic Association: Vegetarian Diets—Technical Support Paper," *Journal of American Dietetic Association*, March 1988, pp. 352-355; Terry D. Shultz, Winston J. Craig, *et al*, "Vegetarianism and Health" in *Nutrition Update*, vol. 2, 1985, pp. 131-141; U. D. Register and L. M. Sonnenberg, "The Vegetarian Diet," *Journal of the American Dietetic Association*, March 1973, pp. 253-261.

21. See Committee on the Scientific Basis of the Nation's Meat and Poultry Inspection Program, *Meat and Poultry Inspection*, (Washington, D.C.: National Academy Press, 1985), pp. 21-42; John A. Scharffenberg, *Problems With Meat* (Santa Barbara, CA: Woodbridge Press, 1979), pp. 32-35.

22. See, e.g., Committee on Meat and Poultry Inspection, *Meat and Poultry Inspection*, pp. 68-123; Robert M. Andrews, "Meat Inspector: 'Eat at Own Risk,' *Washington Post*, May 16, 1987.

23. Frank Young, Commissioner of the Food and Drug Administration and Sanford Miller, director of the FDA's Center for Food Safety and Applied Nutrition, as quoted by Carole Sugarman, "Rising Fears Over Food Safety," *Washington Post*, July 23, 1986. Cf. White, *Counsels on Diet and Foods* (Washington, D.C.: Review and Herald, 1946), pp. 384, 385.

24. Scharffenberg, *Problems With Meat*, pp. 12-58.

25. See Shea, "Clean and Unclean Meats." (unpublished manuscript, Biblical Research Institute, General Conference of SDA).

26. Winston J. Craig, "Pork and Shellfish—How Safe Are They?" *Health and Healing* 12, No. 1, (1988): pp. 10-12.

27. The New Testament concern for holiness is consistent with that of the Old Testament. There is a spiritual as well as a physical interest in people's well-being (Matt. 4:23; 1 Thess. 5:23; 1 Peter 1:15, 16).

Mark's statement that Jesus "declared all foods clean" (Mark 7:19, RSV) does not mean that He abolished the distinction between clean and unclean foods. The discussion between Jesus and the Pharisees and scribes had nothing to do with the *kind* of food, but with the *manner* in which the disciples ate. The issue was whether or not the ritual washing of hands before meals was necessary (Mark 7:2-5). In effect, Jesus said what defiles a person is not the food eaten with unwashed hands but the wicked things from the heart (Mark 7:20-23), because the food "does not enter his heart but his stomach, and is eliminated." Thus Jesus declared that all foods eaten with unwashed hands are "clean" (Mark 7:19). The Greek word for "food" (*bromata*) used here is the general term for food that refers to all kinds of foods for human consumption; it does not designate just flesh foods.

Peter's vision of the animals, recorded in Acts 10, did not teach that unclean animals had become fit for food; instead, it taught that Gentiles were not unclean and that he could associate with them without being contaminated. Peter himself understood the vision in this way, explaining, "You know how unlawful it is for a Jewish man to keep company with or go to one of another nation. But God has shown me that I should not call nay man uncommon or unclean" (Acts 10:28).

In his letters to the Romans and Corinthians (Rom. 14; 1 Cor. 8:4-13; 10:25-28) Paul addressed the implications for Christians of the widespread practice in the Gentile world of offering flesh foods to idols. The issue among the early Christians was whether the eating of food offered to idols was an act of worship. Those strong in their faith did not believe it was, and thus they would eat all edible things offered to idols. Those who did not have such strong faith used only vegetables, which were not offered to idols. Paul urged that no one should despise those who eat vegetables, or judge those who "eat all things" suitable for food (Rom. 14:2).

Paul warned against future heresies that would forbid believers to partake of the two things God gave humanity at Creation—marriage and food. The foods involved are all food God had created for human consumption. Paul's words here should not be taken to mean that unclean foods were "created to be received with thanksgiving by those who believe and know the truth" (1 Tim. 4:3).

28. Pepper, spices, mustard, pickles, and similar substances hurt the stomach. At first they irritate the lining of the stomach. Then they break down its mucous barrier, destroying its resistance to injury. Irritation of the stomach affects the brain, which in turn influences the temperament, often producing irritability. Cf. M. A. Schneider et al., "The Effect of Spice Ingestion on the Stomach," *American Journal of Gastroenterology* 26 (1956): 722, as quoted in "Physiological Effects of Spices and Condiments," (Loma Linda, CA: Department of Nutrition, School of Health, Loma Linda University [mimeographed]). White, *Counsels on Diet and Foods*, pp. 339-345.

29. Condiments and spices can also produce inflammation of the esophagus and destroy the mucous barrier of the small intestine and colon. They irritate the kidneys and may contribute to hypertension. Some contain carcinogens. See Kenneth I. Burke and Ann Burke, "How Nice Is Spice?" *Adventist Review*, Jan. 8, 1987, pp. 14, 15; Department of Nutrition, "Spices and Condiments"; Marjorie V. Baldwin and Bernell E. Baldwin, "Spices—Recipes for Trouble," *Wildwood Echoes*, Winter 1978-79, pp. 8-11.

30. William G. Johnsson, "On Behalf of Simplicity," *Adventist Review*, March 20, 1986, p. 4.

31. *The SDA Bible Commentary*, vol. 1, p. 417.

32. See Year-End Meeting Actions of the North American Division of Seventh-day Adventists (1986), pp. 23-25.

33. The use of cosmetics is not totally harmless. Some of the chemicals used in their preparation can enter the blood circulation through absorption by the skin and, depending on the chemical and the sensitivity of the person, may injure the health. See N. Shafer, R. W. Shafer, "Potential Carcinogenic Effect of Hair Dyes," *New York State Journal of Medicine*, March 1976, pp. 394-396; Samuel J. Taub, "Cosmetic Allergies: What Goes on Under Your Makeup," *Eye, Ears, Nose, and Throat*, April 1976, pp. 131, 132; S. J. Taub, "Contaminated Cosmetics and Cause of Eye Infections," *Eye, Ear, Nose, and Throat*, Feb. 1976, pp. 81, 82; Cf. White, "Words to Christian Mothers," *Review and Herald*, Oct. 17, 1871.

34. White, *The Desire of Ages*, p. 668.

23 *Marriage and the Family*

Marriage was divinely established in Eden and affirmed by Jesus to be a lifelong union between a man and a woman in loving companionship. For the Christian a marriage commitment is to God as well as to the spouse and should be entered into only between partners who share a common faith. Mutual love, honor, respect, and responsibility are the fabric of this relationship, which is to reflect the love, sanctity, closeness, and permanence of the relationship between Christ and His church. Regarding divorce, Jesus taught that the person who divorces a spouse, except for fornication, and marries another, commits adultery. Although some family relationships may fall short of the ideal, marriage partners who fully commit themselves to each other in Christ may achieve loving unity through the guidance of the Spirit and the nurture of the church. God blesses the family and intends that its members shall assist each other toward complete maturity. Parents are to bring up their children to love and obey the Lord. By their example and their words, they are to teach them that Christ is a loving disciplinarian, ever tender and caring, who wants them to become members of His body, the family of God. Increasing family closeness

is one of the earmarks of the final gospel message. (Gen. 2:18-25; Matt. 19:3-9; John 2:1-11; 2 Cor. 6:14; Eph. 5: 21-33; Matt. 5:31, 32; Mark 10:11, 12; Luke 16:18; 1 Cor. 7:10, 11; Ex. 20:12; Eph. 6:1-4; Deut. 6:5-9; Prov. 22:6; Mal. 4:5, 6.)

THE HOME IS A PRIMARY SETTING for the restoration of the image of God in men and women. Within the family, father, mother, and children can express themselves fully, meeting each other's needs for belonging, love, and intimacy. Here, identity is established and feelings of personal worth are developed. The home is also the place where, by God's grace, the principles of real Christianity are put into practice and its values transmitted from one generation to the next.

The family can be a place of great happiness. It can also be the scene of terrible hurt. Harmonious family life demonstrates the principles of Christianity truly lived out, revealing the character of God. Unfortunately, the manifestation of these characteristics is altogether too rare in modern homes. Instead, many families demonstrate the thoughts and intents of the selfish human heart—quarreling, rebelliousness, rivalry, anger, impropriety, and even cruelty. Yet these characteristics were not part of God's original plan. Jesus said, "From the beginning it was not so" (Matt. 19:8).

From the Beginning

The Sabbath and marriage are two of God's original gifts to the human family. They were intended to provide the joys of rest and belonging regardless of time, place, and culture. The establishment of these two institutions culminated God's creation of this earth. They were His finale—the best of the exceedingly good gifts He gave humanity at Creation. In establishing the Sabbath, God gave human beings a time of rest and renewal, a time for fellowship with Him. In forming the first family, He established the basic social unity for humanity, giving them a sense of belonging and providing them with an opportunity to develop as well-rounded persons in service to God and others.

Male and Female in the Image of God. Genesis 1:26, 27 describes God's creation of the human beings who were to inhabit this earth: "Then God said, 'Let Us make man in Our image, according to Our likeness'...So God created man in His own image; in the image of God created he him; male and female created he them." The term *man* is used here (in both the

Hebrew and the English) in the generic sense, as it is more than 500 times elsewhere in the Old Testament. This term includes both male and female. The text makes clear that it was not a case of the male being created in the image of God and the female in the image of the man.[1] On the contrary, both were made in the image of God.

Just as Father, Son, and Holy Spirit are God, male and female together are to make up "man." And like the Godhead, though they are to be one, they are not the same in function. They are equal in being, in worth, but not identical in person (cf. John 10:30; 1 Cor. 11:3). Their physiques are complementary, their functions cooperative.

Both genders are good (Gen. 1:31), as are their different roles. The family and the home are built upon the fact of sexual differentiation. God could have propagated life on earth without creating male and female, as is demonstrated in the asexual reproduction of some forms of animal life. But God made "two individuals, identical in general form and characteristics, but each containing within itself something lacking in the other and complementary to the other."[2] A world made up exclusively of members of either sex would not be complete. True fulfillment can come only in a society that involves both male and female. Equality is no question here, for both are essential.

During his first day, Adam, the firstborn and thus the head of the human race,[3] sensed his uniqueness—there was no other like him. "But for Adam there was not found a helper comparable to him" (Gen. 2:20). God was sensitive to this lack, for He said, "It is not good that man should be alone; I will make him a helper comparable to him" (Gen. 2:18).

The Hebrew word *neged*, translated "comparable" here, is a noun related to the preposition that means to stand "before, in front of, opposite, corresponding to" someone or something. In this case the person who was to stand in front of Adam was to complement him, corresponding to him as his counterpart. So God "caused a deep sleep to fall on Adam," and taking "one of his ribs" (Gen. 2:21, 22), shaped his companion.[4]

Upon awakening, Adam instantly recognized the close and intimate relationship that this specific act of creation made possible. He exclaimed, "At last, here is one of my own kind—bone taken from my bone, and flesh from my flesh. 'Woman' is her name because she was taken out of man" (Gen. 2:23, TEV; cf. 1 Cor. 11:8).

Marriage. From the diversity of male and female God brought order—oneness. That first Friday He performed the first marriage, joining these two, the epitome of His image, to make them one. And marriage has been the foundation of the family, the foundation of society itself, ever since.

Scripture describes marriage as a decisive act of both detachment and attachment: One shall "leave his father and his mother, and shall cleave unto his wife; and they shall be one flesh" (Gen. 2:24, KJV).

1. Leaving. Vital to the marriage relationship is a leaving behind of the former primary relationships. The marriage relationship is to supercede that of the parent and child. In this sense, "leaving" one's relationship with one's parents allows one to "cleave" to another. Without this process, there is no firm foundation for marriage.

2. Cleaving. The Hebrew term translated "cleave" comes from a word that means "to stick to, to fasten, to join, to hold onto." As a noun, it can even be used for brazing and soldering (Isa. 41:7). The closeness and strength of this bond illustrates the nature of the bond of marriage. Any attempt to break up this union would injure individuals bound this closely together. That this human bond is a close one is also emphasized by the fact that the same verb is used to convey the bond between God and His people: "Him shalt thou serve, and to him shalt thou cleave, and swear by his name" (Deut. 10:20, KJV).

3. Covenanting. In Scripture this pledge, this promise by which married couples are bound together, is spoken of as a "covenant"—the term used for the most solemn and binding agreement known in God's Word (Mal. 2:14; Prov. 2:16, 17). The relationship between husband and wife is to be patterned after God's everlasting covenant with His people, the church (Eph. 5:21-33). Their commitment to each other is to take on the faithfulness and endurance that characterize God's covenant (Ps. 89:34; Lam. 3:23).

God and the couple's family, friends, and community witness the covenant that they make with each other. That covenant is ratified in heaven. "What God has joined together, let not man separate" (Matt. 19:6). The Christian couple understand that in marrying, they have covenanted to be faithful to each other for as long as they both live.[5]

4. Becoming one flesh. The leaving and covenanting to cleave results in a union that is a mystery. Here is a oneness in the full sense—the married couple walk together, stand together, and share a deep intimacy. At the outset this oneness refers to the physical union of marriage. But beyond that it also refers to the intimate bond of mind and emotions that undergirds this physical side of the relationship.

a. Walking together. Of His relationship with His people, God asks, "Can two walk together, except they be agreed? (Amos 3:3, KJV). That query is appropriate also of those who would become one flesh.

God instructed the Israelites not to intermarry with the neighboring nations, "for they will turn your sons away from following Me, to serve other gods" (Deut. 7:4; cf. Joshua 23:11-13). When the Israelites ignored these instructions, they met with disastrous consequences (Judges 14-16; 1 Kings 11:1-10; Ezra 9; 10).

Paul reiterated this principle in broad terms: "Do not be unequally yoked together with unbelievers. For what fellowship has righteousness with lawlessness? And what communion has light with darkness? And what accord has Christ with Belial? Or what part has a believer with an unbeliever? And what agreement has the temple of God with idols? For you are the temple of the living God" (2 Cor. 6:14-16; cf. vss. 17, 18).

Clearly, Scripture intends that believers should marry only believers. But the principle extends even beyond this. True oneness demands an agreement as to beliefs and practices. Differences in religious experience lead to differences in lifestyle that can create deep tensions and rifts in marriage. To achieve the oneness Scripture speaks of, then, people should marry others within their own communion.[6]

b. Standing together. To become one flesh, two people must become completely loyal to each other. When one marries, one risks everything and accepts everything that comes with one's mate. Those who marry proclaim their willingness to share their mates' accountability, to stand with their mates against anything. Marriage requires an active, pursuing love that will not give up.

"Two persons share everything they have, not only their bodies, not only their material possessions, but also their thinking and their feeling, their joy and their suffering, their hopes and their fears, their successes and their failures. 'To become one flesh' means that two persons become completely one with body, soul, and spirit, and yet there remain two different persons."[7]

c. Intimacy. Becoming one flesh involves sexual union: "Adam *knew* Eve his wife, and she conceived" (Gen. 4:1). In their drive to be joined together, a drive that men and women have felt since the days of Adam and Eve, each couple reenacts the first love story. The act of sexual intimacy is the nearest thing to a physical union possible for them; it represents the closeness the couple can know emotionally and spiritually as well. Christian married love should be characterized by warmth, joy, and delight (Prov. 5:18, 19).

"Marriage is honorable among all, and the bed undefiled" (Heb. 13:4). "The Scriptures tell us clearly that the joyous sexual expression of love between husband and wife is God's plan. It is, as the writer of Hebrews emphasizes, *undefiled*, not sinful, not soiled. It is a place of great honor in marriage—the holy of holies where husband and wife meet privately to celebrate their love for each other. It is a time meant to be both holy and intensely enjoyable."[8]

5. Biblical love. Marital love is an unconditional, affectionate, and intimate devotion to each other that encourages mutual growth in the image of God in all aspects of the person: physical, emotional, intellectual, and spiritual. Different types of love operate in marriage: it has its romantic, passionate times; its comfortable times; its companionable and sense-of-belonging times. But it is the *agape* love described in the New Testament—the selfless, all-for-other love—that comprises the foundation of true, lasting marital love.

Jesus manifested the highest form of this kind of love when, accepting both the guilt and the consequences for our sins, He went to the cross. "Having loved His own who were in the world, He loved them to the end" (John 13:1, NASB). He loved us in spite of the end to which our sins brought Him. This was and is the unconditional *agape* love of Jesus Christ.

Describing this love, Paul said: "Love suffers long and is kind; love does not envy; love does not parade itself, is not puffed up; does not behave rudely, does not seek its own, is not provoked, thinks no evil; does not rejoice in iniquity, but rejoices in the truth; bears all things, believes all things, hopes all things, endures all things. Love never fails" (1 Cor. 13:4-8).

Commenting on this passage, Ed Wheat wrote: "*Agape* love is plugged into an eternal power source and it can go on operating when every other kind of love fails....It loves, no matter what. No matter how unlovable the other person is, *agape* can keep on flowing. *Agape* is as unconditional as God's love for us. It is a mental attitude based on a deliberate choice of the will."[9]

6. Individual spiritual responsibility. Though marriage partners have made a covenant to each other, they must each individually bear the responsibility for the choices that they make (2 Cor. 5:10). Taking such responsibility means that they will never blame the other person for what they themselves have done. They must also accept the responsibility for their own spiritual growth—no one can rely upon another's spiritual strength. Yet, on the other hand, each one's relationship with God can serve as a source of strength and encouragement to the other.

The Effects of the Fall Upon Marriage

The distortion of humanity's reflection of God's image that sin brought had its effect upon marriage as certainly as it did on any other area of human experience. Self-interest intruded where perfect love and unity once reigned. Selfishness is the primary motivator of all those not compelled by the love of Christ. Running counter to all the principles of surrender, servanthood, and giving that the gospel represents, it is the common denominator of all Christian failure.

By their disobedience, Adam and Eve contravened the purpose of their creation. Before they sinned, they had lived in full openness before God. After, instead of joyfully coming to Him, they fearfully hid from Him, attempting to conceal the truth about themselves and denying their responsibility for their actions. Pervaded with a deep sense of guilt that their rationalizations could not erase, they could not meet the eye of God and the holy angels. Since then this evasion and self-justifying denial has been the common pattern of human relationships with God.

The fear that drove them to concealment distorted not only Adam's and Eve's relation to God but also to each other. When God questioned them, they both sought to protect themselves at the expense of another. Their accusations give evidence of the serious breakdown that had occurred in the loving relationship God had established at Creation.

After sin, God told the woman, "Your desire shall be for your husband, and he shall rule over you" (Gen. 3:16). He intended this principle, which did not change the basic equality of the man and woman, to benefit both that first couple and married couples thereafter.[10] Unfortunately, this principle became distorted. Since that time dominance through power, manipulation, and destruction of individuality has characterized marriage through the ages. Self-centeredness has left acceptance and appreciation of one another in short supply.

The essence of Christianity is living in the self-denying harmony that characterized marriage before the Fall, which destroyed this harmony. The affections of husband and wife are to contribute to each other's happiness. Each is to cultivate the happiness of the other. They are to blend as one, yet neither of them is to lose his or her individuality, which belongs to God.[11]

Deviations From God's Ideal

Polygamy. The practice of one mate's maintaining several spouses runs contrary to the oneness and union that God established with the first marriage in Eden. In polygamy there is no forsaking of all others. Although Scripture describes plural marriages as a cultural reality in the time of the patriarchs, its description clearly shows that those marriages did not attain the divine ideal. The various subunits within those marriages became involved in power struggles, bitter resentments, and alienation (see Gen. 16; cf. 29:16-30:24, etc.), using the children as emotional weapons to injure other members of the family.

Monogamous marriage provides couples with a sense of belonging that strengthens their intimacy and bonding. They realize that their relationship is unique and that no one else can share what they do. The monogamous relationship reflects most clearly the relationship between Christ and His church and between the individual and God.[12]

Fornication and Adultery. Current thinking and practice make light of lasting commitments in which both spouses are sexually faithful to each other until death. But Scripture regards any sexual relations outside of marriage as sin. The seventh commandment remains in effect and unchanged: "Thou shalt not commit adultery" (Ex. 20:14, KJV). No qualifiers or disqualifiers are mentioned here. This commandment is a principle that jealously guards the marriage relationship.

The full import of the biblical view of fornication and adultery stands in direct contrast to today's tolerance of such activities by "consenting adults." Many passages in both the Old and the New Testament condemn such practices (Lev. 20:10-12; Prov. 6:24-32; 7:6-27; 1 Cor. 6:9, 13, 18; Gal. 5:19; Eph. 5:3; 1 Thess. 4:3; etc.).

Such liaisons can have far-reaching and long-lasting effects. They defraud the legitimate sexual partner and may harm him or her physically, emotionally, financially, legally, and socially. They hurt the extended family, and if children are involved, they particularly injure them. These liaisons may result in the transmission of venereal diseases and the birth of illegitimate babies. Then, too, the cloud of lies and dishonesty that hovers over such affairs so destroys trust that it may never be restored. Even aside from the biblical injunctions against these forms of immorality, the train of unfortunate consequences that result should provide ample warning against engaging in them.

Impurity of Thought. Sin is not merely the outward act; rather, it is also a matter of the heart that reaches deeply into the thought patterns. If the springs are polluted, the rivers are not likely to be clean. Jesus saw that the inner reservoir of the mind motivated human behavior, "for out of the heart came evil thoughts, murder, adultery, fornication, theft, false witness, slander" (Matt 15:19, RSV). In this vein He traced the act of unfaithfulness to the thoughts and emotions: "You have heard that it was said to those of old, 'You shall not commit adultery,' But I say to you that whoever looks at a woman to lust for her has already committed adultery with her in his heart" (Matt. 5:27, 28).

An entire industry has developed to capitalize upon the perversion of the imagination. The sensual films and books it produces have no place in the Christian life. They not only encourage illicit relationships, they also reduce men and women to mere sexual objects, thus distorting the true meaning of sexuality and obscuring the image of God. Christians are called upon to think pure thoughts and live pure lives, because they are preparing to live in a pure society throughout all eternity.

Incest. Some parents cross the boundary that demarcates the healthy expression of affection to their children, becoming physically and emotionally intimate with them. Often this results when the normal husband-wife relationship has been neglected and one of the children has been chosen to play the role of the spouse. This blurring of boundaries may also occur between siblings and extended family members.

Incest was forbidden in the Old Testament (Lev. 18:6-29; Deut. 27:20-23) and condemned in the New (1 Cor. 5:1-5). This kind of abuse damages the child's developing sexuality and creates in him or her an unwarranted burden of shame and guilt that he or she may bring into marriage later in life. When parents transgress those boundaries, they damage the child's developing sense of trust—so vital to faith in God.

Divorce. A statement Jesus made sums up the biblical teaching on divorce: "What God has joined together, let not man separate" (Matt. 19:6; Mark 10:7-9). Marriage is sacred because God has consecrated it. Ultimately, it is God who joins the husband and wife, not mere human words or the sexual act. So it is He who has sealed their union. The Christian understanding of divorce and remarriage, then, must be based on scriptural grounds.

Jesus' statement makes clear the basic scriptural principle that undergirds a Christian understanding of divorce: God intended marriage to be indissoluble. When the Pharisees asked Him whether marital incompatibility was reason enough for divorce, He affirmed the Eden model of marriage as a permanent union. When they pressed Him further about Moses' law of divorce, He answered, "Moses, because of the hardness of your hearts, permitted you to divorce your wives, but from the beginning it was not so" (Matt. 19:8). He went on to stipulate that the only legitimate reason for divorce was sexual infidelity (Matt. 5:32; 19:9).

His response to the Pharisees makes clear that Jesus had a far deeper understanding of fidelity than they did. From what He said, and from the principles regarding marriage in both the Old and New Testaments, it can be affirmed that God intends those who marry to reflect the image of God in a permanent union.

Even the unfaithfulness of one's spouse does not necessarily mean that the marriage must end in divorce. The way of the cross encourages deep repentance and forgiveness, the putting away of the roots of bitterness. Even in the case of adultery, through forgiveness and the reconciling power of God, the injured spouse should seek to maintain God's original purpose in Creation. "Biblically speaking, adultery need be no more destructive to your marriage than any other sin....When you are ready to forgive and let go of your negative attitudes, God will be more than ready to heal you and renew your love for each other."[13]

While the divine ideal for marriage is that of a loving and permanent union that continues until the death of one partner, at times a legal separation becomes necessary because of offenses such as physical abuse to spouse or child. "In some civil jurisdictions such a separation can be secured only by divorce, which under these circumstances would not be condemned. But such a separation or divorce, in which 'unfaithfulness to the marriage vow' is not involved, does not give either one the scriptural right to remarry, unless in the meantime the other party has remarried, committed adultery or fornication, or been removed by death."[14]

Because marriage is a divine institution, the church has a unique and solemn responsibility both to prevent divorce and, should divorce occur, to heal as far as possible the wounds it causes.

Homosexuality. God created male and female to differ from and yet to complement each other. And when He did so, He oriented their sexual feelings toward those of the opposite sex. The differentiation and connectedness that characterize people are manifested in the attraction that draws the two sexes to each other in order to form a whole relationship.

In some cases, sin has affected even this basic orientation, bringing about a phenomenon that has been termed inversion. In such cases, the natural orientation toward the opposite sex appears inverted, producing a basic sexual orientation toward people of the same gender.

Scripture condemns homosexual practices in strongly negative terms (Gen. 19:4-10; cf. Jude 7, 8; Lev. 18:22; 20:13; Rom. 1:26-28; 1 Tim. 1:8-10). Practices of this type produce a serious distortion of the image of God in men and women.

Because "all have sinned, and come short of the glory of God" (Rom. 3:23, KJV), Christians will deal redemptively with those who are afflicted with this disorder. They will reflect the attitude Christ took toward the woman taken in adultery: "Neither do I condemn thee: go, and sin no more" (John 8:11, KJV). Not only those with homosexual tendencies—but all persons trapped in behaviors or relationships that cause anxiety, shame, and guilt—need the sympathetic ear of a trained and experienced Christian counselor. No behavior is beyond the reach of God's healing grace.[15]

The Family

After God created Adam and Eve, He gave them dominion over the world (Gen. 1:26; 2:15). They made up the first family, the first church, and marked the beginning of society. Thus society was built upon marriage and the family. Because they were the only human inhabitants of the earth, God commanded them to "Be fruitful and multiply; fill the earth and subdue it" (Gen. 1:28).

As world population statistics indicate, an unpopulated earth no longer cries out to be filled and subdued. But those married Christian couples who decide to bring children into the world still have the obligation of rearing their children in the nurture and admonition of the Lord (Eph. 6:4). Before a married couple sets out upon that course, they should consider God's ideal for the family.

Parents

1. The father. Scripture has given the husband and father the responsibility of being head and priest of the household (Col. 3:18-21; 1 Peter 3:1-8). He becomes a type of Christ, the head of the church. "For the husband is head of the wife, as also Christ is head of the church; and He is the Saviour of the body. Therefore, just as the church is subject to Christ, so let the wives be to their own husbands in everything. Husbands, love your wives, just as Christ also loved the church and gave Himself for it, that He might sanctify and cleanse it with the washing of water by the word, that He might present it to Himself a glorious church, not having spot or wrinkle or any such thing, but that it should be holy and without blemish. So husbands ought to love their own wives as their own bodies; he who loves his wife loves himself" (Eph. 5:23-28).

As Christ leads the church, husband and wife "both should be yielding, but the Word of God gives preference to the judgment of the husband" where it is not a matter of conscience.[16] At the same time he has the responsibility to treat her individuality with utmost respect.

As Christ demonstrated a gentle rulership that went to the cross in servanthood, so the husband is to lead sacrificially. "Christ's rule is one of wisdom and love, and when husbands fulfill their obligations to their wives, they will use their authority with the same tenderness as Christ uses toward the church. When the Spirit of Christ controls the husband, the wife's subjection will only result in rest and benefit, for he will require from her only that which will result in good, and in the same way that Christ requires submission from the church....Let those who stand as husbands study the words of Christ, not to find out how complete must be the subjection of the wife, but how he may have the mind of Christ, and become purified, refined, and fit to be the lord of his household."[17]

As priest of the family, like Abraham, the father will gather his family about at the beginning of the day and commit them to the Lord's care. In the evening he will lead them into praising Him and thanking Him for the blessings bestowed. This family worship will be the tie that binds—the time that gives God priority in the family.[18]

The wise father spends time with his children. A child may learn many lessons from the father, such as respect and love for their mother, love for God, the importance of prayer, love for other people, the way to work, modesty, love for nature and the things God has made. But if the father is never home, the child is deprived of this privilege and joy.

2. *The mother.* Motherhood is the closest thing on earth to being in partnership with God. "The king upon his throne has no higher work than has the mother. The mother is queen of her household. She has in her power the molding of her children's characters, that they may be fitted for the higher, immortal life. An angel could not ask for a higher mission; for in doing this work she is doing service for God....Let her realize the worth of her work and put on the whole armor of God, that she may resist the temptation to conform to the world's standard. Her work is for time and for eternity."[19]

Somebody in the family must bear the ultimate responsibility for the character of the children. Child training cannot be haphazard or delegated to others, for no one feels quite the same about a child as do its parents. God created the mother with the ability to carry the child within her own body, to suckle the child, and to nurture and love it. Except for the extenuating circumstances of severe financial burdens or of being a single parent,[20] if she will accept it, a mother has the unique privilege of remaining with her children all day; she can enjoy working with the Creator in shaping their characters for eternity.

"*Someone* in a relationship needs to consider the family as a career.... Taking on the career of being a mother and wife is a fabulously rare life-work in the twentieth century, and a very challenging job. A wasted effort? A thankless job? An undignified slave? No, a most exciting possibility of turning the tide, of saving the species, of affecting history, of doing something that will be *felt* and *heard* in ever-widening circles."[21]

In Old Testament times a person's name conveyed a short statement about the person who bore it. Eve received her name after the Fall (Gen. 3:20). Because she was to become the mother of all human beings, her name (Hebrew *chawwah*) was derived from the word for "living" (Hebrew *chay*). It reflects the extraordinary position of honor that she occupies in the history of the human race.

Just as procreation was not the sole and exclusive right of either Adam or Eve, so neither was parenthood. The latter was also to be a shared responsibility. So it should be now, not only in the bearing of children, but also in the rearing of them. Each parent has certain responsibilities, and they are to be carried out as to the Lord. "Lo, children are a heritage of the Lord: and the fruit of the womb is his reward" (Ps. 127:3, KJV).

Children

1. A priority. Other than their commitments to the Lord and their spouses, parents have no higher responsibility than to the children they have brought into the world. They must put their children's interests before their own advancement and comfort; the children did not choose to come into the world, and they must be given the best possible start in life. Since prenatal influences vitally affect one's spiritual, mental, and physical health, making the child's welfare a priority should begin even before birth.[22]

2. Love. A parent's love should be unconditional and sacrificial. Even though it may never be completely reciprocated, children must have it to have a good self-image and emotional health throughout life. Children who have to win love or who feel rejected and unimportant will try to obtain their parents' love through undesirable behaviors that become ingrained and habitual.[23]

Children who are secure in their parents' love will reach out to others. They can be taught to give as well as to receive and that there is a reason for existence beyond self. As children develop, they can learn to glorify God.

3. Commitment. Christian parents are to dedicate their children to God's service at the earliest possible moment of life. Seventh-day Adventist congregations provide for such a dedication with a simple ceremony in which, before the congregation, parents present their children to God in prayer, much as Joseph and Mary presented the infant Jesus to the Lord in the Temple (Luke 2:22-39). In this manner the child begins life as a part of an extended spiritual family. Members of the congregation participate in the social and spiritual development of the young one as a child of God and as a member of the body of Christ.

In this service the parents also dedicate themselves to educate the child in the way of the Lord so that the image of God will be formed in the child. To reach this goal, parents will bring their children to Sabbath school and church regularly so that the little ones become a part of the body of Christ early in life. Then, as the child reaches school age, the parents and church will make every effort to enable him or her to have the Christian education that will nurture that child's love for the Lord even further.

4. Constancy. The spiritual teaching the parents do is an ongoing process that enters into every phase of the child's life. "You shall teach them [the Lord's commands] diligently to your children, and shall talk of them when you sit in your house, when you walk by the way, when you lie down, and when you rise up. You shall bind them as a sign on your hand, and they shall be as frontlets between your eyes. You shall write them on the door-posts of your house and on your gates" (Deut. 6:7-9; 11:18 ff).

The child is influenced by the whole atmosphere of the home. The parents cannot convey spirituality through family worship alone. It must come through their continual trusting in Jesus; it must be manifested in their lifestyles, clothing, and even home decorations. Knowing God as a loving parent is vital to the child's Christian growth.

5. Learning obedience. "Train up a child in the way he should go, and when he is old he will not depart from it" (Prov. 22:6). What does this training entail? Discipline implies far more than punishment. Punishment usually deals with the past, whereas discipline looks to the future. Discipline is a discipling process in which a young one is apprenticed to the parent for training, guidance, and example. It means teaching important principles such as loyalty, truth, equity, consistency, patience, order, mercy, generosity, and work.

When children learn early to obey their parents implicitly, authority poses no problem to them in life. But the type of obedience learned is important also. True obedience comes not simply because it is required but because it springs from within. The secret of this kind of obedience lies in the new birth.

"The man who attempts to keep the commandments of God from a sense of obligation—merely because he is required to do so—will never enter into the joy of obedience. He does not obey....True obedience is the outworking of a principle within. It springs from the love of righteousness, the love of the law of God. The essence of all righteousness is loyalty to our Redeemer. This will lead us to do right because it is right—because right-doing is pleasing to God."[24]

6. Socialization and language development. Within the family children are socialized as members of the human race, with all the responsibilities and privileges that entails. Socialization is the process by which children learn the basic skills with which to function in society. Language with all its nuances of communication is one of the first skills the child learns. The language used in the home needs careful monitoring, then, so that it reveals God's character. The child should hear frequent joyous and spontaneous expressions of affection among family members, and praise to God.

7. Gender identity. In the home, through wholesome interaction with the males and females that make up the entire family system, children learn to function as male or female within society. Adults need to teach them the beauty of their developing sexuality through correct and appropriate information. It is also their responsibility to safeguard the children from sexual abuse.

8. Learning values. A basic socializing function of the home is to provide for the assimilation of the values espoused by the family. The family's values and religious concepts do not always coincide. Parents may claim to adhere to certain religious principles, but the values that they model before the child may not be in accordance with those principles. It is important that parents be consistent.

The Extended Family. Marriage, as God designed it, is exclusive; family is not. In a highly mobile society one rarely finds extended family—grandparents, siblings, and cousins—all living in close proximity. The church family can help those far from or without kin find a true sense of worth and belonging. Here, too, single parents can find a comfortable place in which to rear their children with love and tender cherishing. And the church may supply appropriate role models that may be lacking in the home.

Through learning to love the old people in the congregation, children can learn respect. And those who are old can experience the satisfaction of having a little one to love and enjoy. "Now also when I am old and grayheaded, O God, do not forsake me, until I declare Your strength to this generation, Your power to everyone who is to come" (Ps. 71:18).

God gives special consideration to the elderly, saying, "The silverhaired head is a crown of glory, if it is found in the way of righteousness" (Prov. 16:31), and "Even to your old age, I am He, and even to gray hairs I will carry you! I have made, and I will bear; even I will carry, and will deliver you" (Isa. 46:4).

In the church, singles may find a special place to be loved and cherished and to share their love and energies as well. Through its ministry they can come to sense God's care for them: "Yes, I have loved you with an everlasting love; therefore with lovingkindness I have drawn you" (Jer. 31:3).

It is part of "pure religion" to give special care to those in need (James 1:27; Ex. 22:22; Deut. 24:17; 26:12; Prov. 23:10; Isa. 1:17). The church family has a special opportunity to provide a haven, a shelter, a place of belonging to those who do not have a family; it may surround and include each member in the special unity that Christ said would be the mark of Christianity itself (John 17:20-23).

The Turning

Since the family is the very soul of the church and society, the Christian family itself will be the instrument of winning and holding its members for the Lord. The very last verses of the Old Testament are a prophecy of what will take place before the Lord returns: "Behold, I will send you Elijah the prophet before the coming of the great and dreadful day of the Lord. And he will turn the hearts of the fathers to the children, and the hearts of the children to their fathers" (Mal. 4:5, 6). While many forces today attempt to pull the members from the family, God's call is to be a reuniting, a re-solidifying, a turning and restoration. And those families that respond to His call will have a strength that will reveal real Christianity. The churches made up of those families will grow, their young people will not leave, and they will portray to the world a clear picture of God.

References

1. Cf. Ellen G. White, *Education*, p. 20.

2. A. W. Spalding, *Makers of the Home* (Mountain View, CA: Pacific Press, 1928), p. 58.

3. That Adam was responsible for the planet is evidence that God held him accountable for sin even though he was not the first to transgress (Gen. 3:9). The New Testament, also, as it compares the two "Adams," holds the first Adam liable for the entrance of sin and death (Rom. 5:12; 1 Cor. 15:22; cf. White, *Great Controversy*, p. 647).

4. "God Himself gave Adam a companion. He provided 'an help meet for him'—a helper corresponding to him—one who was fitted to be his companion, and who could be one with him in love and sympathy. Eve was created from a rib taken from the side of Adam, signifying that she was not to control him as the head, nor to be trampled under his feet as an inferior, but to stand by his side as an equal, to be loved and protected by him" (White, *Patriarchs and Prophets*, p. 46).

5. For more on the convenantal aspects of marriage, see 'Marriage as Covenant" in *Covenant and Marriage: Partnership and Commitment* (Leader's Notebook) (Nashville: Family Ministry Department, Sunday School Board of the Southern Baptist Convention, 1987), pp. 51-60.

6. See *SDA Church Manual*, pp. 150, 151; F. M. Wilcox, "Marrying Unbelievers," *Review and Herald*, July 2, 1914, pp. 9, 10; G. B. Thompson, "Marrying Unbelievers: 'Can Two Walk Together, Except They Be Agreed?'" *Review and Herald*, July 31, 1941, pp. 2, 12-14; F. M. Wilcox, "The Marriage Relationship, Following the Divine Order," *Review and Herald*, May 4, 1944, pp. 1-4; White, *Testimonies*, vol. 4, pp. 503-508.

7. Walter Trobisch, *I Married You* (New York, N.Y.: Harper and Row, 1971), p. 18.

8. Ed. Wheat, *Love Life for Every Married Couple* (Grand Rapids: Zondervan,

1980), p. 72.

9. *Ibid.*, p. 62.

10. White, *Patriarchs and Prophets*, pp. 58, 59.

11. E.g., see White, *The Ministry of Healing*, p. 361; White, *Messages to Young People* (Nashville: Southern Pub. Assn., 1930), p. 451.

12. See also White, *Patriarchs and Prophets*, pp. 145, 208, 337, 338; White, *Spiritual Gifts*, vol. 3, pp. 104, 105; vol. 4a, 0. 86.

13. Wheat, *Love Life for Every Married Couple*, p. 202. See also "The Divorce Court or the Cross," in Roy Hession, *Forgotten Factors...An Aid to Deeper Repentance of the Forgotten Factors of Sexual Misbehavior* (Fort Washington, PA: Christian Literature Crusade, 1976); Wheat, "How to Save Your Marriage Alone," in *Love Life*, and Gary Chapman, *Hope for the Separated: Wounded Marriages Can Be Healed* (Chicago: Moody Press, 1982).

14. *SDA Church Manual*, p. 175.

15. See Hession, *Forgotten Factors*. In helping transgressors to repent and find forgiveness in a loving God, this excellent volume carefully delineates the deeper issues of sexual immorality.

16. White, *Testimonies*, vol. 1, p. 307. She also wrote, "We women must remember that God has placed us subject to the husband. He is the head and our judgment and views and reasonings must agree with his if possible. If not, the preference in God's Word is given to the husband where it is not a matter of conscience. We must yield to the head" (E. G. White letter 5, 1861).

17. E. G. White Manuscript 17, 1891. See also Larry Christenson, *The Christian Family* (Minneapolis, MN: Bethany Fellowship, 1970).

18. For ideas on how to have a dynamic family worship, see John and Millie Youngberg, *Heart Tuning: A Guide to Better Family Worship* (Washington, D.C.: Review and Herald, 1985); Christenson, *The Christian Family*, pp. 157-197.

19. White, *The Adventist Home*, pp. 231, 232.

20. Parents who must place a child under another's care should choose someone who holds similar values to theirs so that there can be full cooperation in rearing the child in the love and "admonition of the Lord." The parents should also carefully observe the other children with whom their child would be associated. Do they want their child to be like those children? Children learn so much so quickly and so indelibly—all aspects of child care need to be conscientiously explored.

21. Edith Schaefer, *What Is a Family?* (Old Tappan, NJ: Fleming H. Revell Co., 1975), p. 47.

22. See White, *The Desire of Ages*, p. 512; White, *The Adventist Home*, pp. 255-259.

23. See Gary Smalley and John Trent, *The Blessing* (Nashville: Thomas Nelson Publishers, 1986). The authors carefully depict how parents' bestowal or withholding of unconditional love is the key to the emotional and psychological wellness of the developing child.

24. White, *Christ's Object Lessons*, p. 97.

24

Christ's Ministry in the Heavenly Sanctuary

There is a sanctuary in heaven—the true tabernacle which the Lord set up and not man. In it Christ ministers on our behalf, making available to believers the benefits of His atoning sacrifice offered once for all on the cross. He was inaugurated as our great High Priest and began His intercessory ministry at the time of His ascension. In 1844, at the end of the prophetic period of 2300 days, He entered the second and last phase of His atoning ministry. It is a work of investigative judgment which is part of the ultimate disposition of all sin, typified by the cleansing of the ancient Hebrew sanctuary on the Day of Atonement. In that typical service the sanctuary was cleansed with the blood of animal sacrifices, but the heavenly things are purified with the perfect sacrifice of the blood of Jesus. The investigative judgment reveals to heavenly intelligences who among the dead are asleep in Christ and therefore, in Him, are deemed worthy to have part in the first resurrection. It also makes manifest who among the living are abiding in Christ, keeping the commandments of God and the faith of Jesus, and in Him, therefore, are ready for translation into His everlasting kingdom. This judgment vindicates the justice of God in saving those who believe in Jesus. It declares that those who have remained loyal to God shall receive the kingdom. The completion of this ministry of Christ will mark the close of human probation before the Second Advent. (Heb. 8:1-5; 4:14-16; 9:11-28; 10:19-22; 1:3; 2:16, 17; Dan. 7:9-27; 8:13, 14; 9:24-27; Num. 14:34; Ezek. 4:6; Lev. 16; Rev. 14:6, 7; 20:12; 14:12; 22:12.)

THE HOUR OF THE EVENING SACRIFICE ARRIVES. The priest stands in the court of the Temple in Jerusalem ready to offer the lamb as sacrifice. As he raises the knife to kill the victim, the earth convulses. Terrified, he drops the knife, and the lamb escapes. Over the din of the earthquake he hears a loud ripping noise as an unseen hand rends the veil of the Temple from top to bottom.

Across town, black clouds enshroud a cross. When Jesus, the Passover Lamb of God, calls out, "It is finished!" He dies for the sins of the world.

Type has met antitype. The very event the Temple services have pointed to through the centuries has taken place. The Saviour has completed His atoning sacrifice, and because symbol has met reality, the rituals foreshadowing this sacrifice have been superceded. Thus the rent veil, the dropped knife, the escaped lamb.

But there is more to salvation history. It reaches beyond the cross. Jesus' resurrection and ascension direct our attention to the heavenly sanctuary, where, no longer the Lamb, He ministers as Priest. The once-for-all sacrifice has been offered (Heb. 9:28); now He makes available to all the benefits of this atoning sacrifice.

The Sanctuary in Heaven

God instructed Moses to build, as His earthly dwelling place (Ex. 25:8), the first sanctuary that functioned under the first (old) covenant (Heb. 9:1). This was a place where people were taught the way of salvation. About 400 years later the permanent Temple in Jerusalem built by King Solomon replaced Moses' portable tabernacle. After Nebuchadnezzar destroyed that Temple, the exiles who returned from Babylonian captivity built the second Temple, which Herod the Great beautified and which the Romans destroyed in A.D. 70.

The New Testament reveals that the new covenant also has a sanctuary—one that is in heaven. In it Christ functions as High Priest "at the right hand of the throne of the Majesty." This sanctuary is the "true tabernacle which the Lord erected, and not man" (Heb. 8:1, 2).[1] At Mount Sinai Moses was shown "the pattern," copy, or miniature model of the heavenly sanctuary (see Ex. 25:9, 40).[2] Scripture calls the sanctuary he built "the copies of the things in the heavens," and its "holy places...copies of the true" (Heb. 9:23, 24). The earthly sanctuary and its services, then, give us special insight into the role of the heavenly sanctuary.

Throughout, Scripture presumes the existence of a heavenly sanctuary or temple (e.g., Ps. 11:4; 102:19, Micah 1:2, 3).[3] In vision, John the Revelator saw the heavenly sanctuary. He described it as "the temple of the tabernacle of the testimony in heaven" (Rev. 15:5) and "the temple of God... in heaven" (Rev. 11:19). There he saw the items that the furnishings of the holy place of the earthly sanctuary were modeled after, such as seven lampstands (Rev. 1:12) and an altar of incense (Rev. 8:3). And he saw there also the ark of the covenant which was like the one in the earthly Holy of Holies (Rev. 11:19).

The heavenly altar of incense is located before God's throne (Rev. 8:3; 9:13), which is in the heavenly temple of God (Rev. 4:2; 7:15; 16:17). Thus the heavenly throne room scene (Dan. 7:9, 10) is in the heavenly temple or sanctuary. This is why the final judgments issue from God's temple (Rev. 15:5-8).

It is clear, therefore, that the Scriptures present the heavenly sanctuary as a real place (Heb. 8:2, NEB), not a metaphor or abstraction.[4] The heavenly sanctuary is the primary dwelling place of God.

The Ministry in the Heavenly Sanctuary

The message of the sanctuary was a message of salvation. God used its services to proclaim the gospel (Heb. 4:2). The earthly sanctuary services were "a symbol [*parabole* in Greek—a parable] for the present time"—until Christ's first advent (Heb. 9:9, 10, NASB). "Through symbol and ritual God purposed by means of this gospel-parable to focus the faith of Israel upon the sacrifice and priestly ministry of the world's Redeemer, the 'Lamb of God,' who would take away the sin of the world (Gal. 3:23; John 1:29)."[5]

The sanctuary illustrated three phases of Christ's ministry: (1) the substitutionary sacrifice, (2) the priestly mediation, and (3) the final judgment.

The Substitutionary Sacrifice. Every sanctuary sacrifice symbolized Jesus' death for the forgiveness of sin, revealing the truth that "without shedding of blood there is no remission" (Heb. 9:22). Those sacrifices illustrated the following truths:

1. God's judgment on sin. Because sin is a deep-seated rebellion against all that is good, pure, and true, it cannot be ignored. "The wages of sin is death" (Rom. 6:23).

2. Christ's substitutionary death. "All we like sheep have gone astray;... and the Lord has laid on Him the iniquity of us all" (Isa. 53:6). "Christ died for our sins according to the Scriptures" (1 Cor. 15:3).

3. God provides the atoning sacrifice. That sacrifice is "Christ Jesus, whom God set forth to be a propitiation by His blood, through faith" (Rom. 3:24, 25). "For He [God] made Him [Christ] who knew no sin to be sin for us, that we might become the righteousness of God in Him" (2 Cor. 5:21). Christ the Redeemer took the judgment of sin upon Himself. Therefore, "Christ was treated as we deserve, that we might be treated as He deserves. He was condemned for our sins, in which He had no share, that we might be justified by His righteousness, in which we had no share. He suffered the death which was ours, that we might receive the life which was His. 'With his stripes we are healed' (Isa. 53:5)."[6]

The sacrifices of the earthly sanctuary were repetitive. Like a story, this ritual parable of redemption was told and retold year after year. By contrast, the Antitype—the actual atoning death of our Lord—took place at Calvary *once for all time* (Heb. 9:26-28; 10:10-14).

On the cross the penalty for human sin was fully paid. Divine justice was satisfied. From a legal perspective the world was restored to favor with God (Rom. 5:18). The atonement, or reconciliation, was completed on the cross as foreshadowed by the sacrifices, and the penitent believer can trust in this finished work of our Lord.[7]

The Priestly Mediator. If the sacrifice atoned for sin, why was a priest necessary?

The priest's role drew attention to the need for mediation between sinners and a holy God. Priestly mediation reveals the seriousness of sin and the estrangement it brought between a sinless God and a sinful creature. "Just as every sacrifice foreshadowed Christ's death, so every priest foreshadowed Christ's mediatorial ministry as high priest in the heavenly sanctuary. 'For there is one God, and one Mediator between God and men, the Man Christ Jesus' (1 Tim. 2:5)."[8]

1. Mediator and atonement. The application of the atoning blood during the mediatorial ministry of the priest was also seen as a form of atonement (Lev. 4:35). The English term *atonement* implies a reconciliation between two estranged parties. As the atoning death of Christ reconciled the world to God, so His mediation, or the application of the merits of His sinless life and substitutionary death, makes reconciliation or atonement with God a personal reality for the believer.

The Levitical priesthood illustrates the saving ministry Christ has carried on since His death. Our High Priest, serving "at the right hand of the throne of the Majesty in the heavens," functions as a "Minister of the sanctuary and of the true tabernacle which the Lord erected, and not man" (Heb. 8:1, 2).

The heavenly sanctuary is the great command center where Christ conducts His priestly ministry for our salvation. He is able "to save to the uttermost those who come to God through Him, since He ever lives to make intercession for them" (Heb. 7:25). Therefore, we are encouraged to come "boldly to the throne of grace, that we may obtain mercy and find grace to help in time of need" (Heb. 4:16).

In the earthly sanctuary the priests carried out two distinct ministries—a daily ministry in the holy place, or first apartment (see chapter 4 of this book) and a yearly ministry in the Most Holy Place, or second apartment. Those services illustrated Christ's priestly ministry.[9]

2. The ministry in the holy place. The priestly ministry in the holy place of the sanctuary could be characterized as a ministry of intercession, forgiveness, reconciliation, and restoration. A continual ministry, it provided constant access to God through the priest.[10] It symbolized the truth that the repentant sinner has immediate and constant access to God through Christ's priestly ministry as Intercessor and Mediator (Eph. 2:18; Heb. 4:14-16; 7:25; 9:24; 10:19-22).

When the penitent sinner[11] came to the sanctuary with a sacrifice, he laid his hands on the head of the innocent animal and confessed his sins. This act symbolically transferred his sin and its penalty to the victim. As a result, he obtained forgiveness of sins.[12] As *The Jewish Encyclopedia* states: "The laying of hands upon the victim's head is an ordinary rite by which the substitution and transfer of sins are effected." "In every sacrifice there is the idea of substitution; the victim takes the place of the human sinner."[13]

The blood of the sin offering was applied in one of two ways: a. If it was taken into the holy place, it was sprinkled before the inner veil and placed on the horns of the altar of incense (Lev. 4:6, 7, 17, 18). b. If it was not taken into the sanctuary, it was placed on the horns of the altar of burnt offering in the court (Lev. 4: 25, 30). In that case the priest ate part of the flesh of the sacrifice (Lev. 6:25, 26, 30). In either case, the participants understood that their sins and accountability were transferred to the sanctuary and its priesthood.[14]

"In this ritual parable *the sanctuary assumed the penitent's guilt and accountability*—for the time being at least—when the penitent offered a sin offering, confessing his errors. He went away forgiven, assured of God's acceptance. So in the antitypical experience, when a sinner is drawn in penitence by the Holy Spirit to accept Christ as his Saviour and Lord, *Christ assumes his sins and accountability.* He is freely forgiven. Christ is the believer's Surety as well as his Substitute."[15]

In type and antitype the holy place ministry primarily centers on the individual. Christ's priestly ministry provides for the sinner's forgiveness and reconciliation to God (Heb. 7:25). "For Christ's sake God forgives the repentant sinner, imputes to him the righteous character and obedience of His Son, pardons his sins, and records his name in the book of life as one of His children (Eph. 4:32; 1 John 1:9; 2 Cor. 5:21; Rom. 3:24; Luke 10:20). And as the believer abides in Christ, spiritual grace is mediated to him by our Lord through the Holy Spirit so that he matures spiritually and develops the virtues and graces that reflect the divine character (2 Peter 3:18; Gal. 5:22, 23)."[16]

The ministry in the holy place brings about the believer's justification and sanctification.

The Final Judgment. The events on the Day of Atonement illustrate the three phases of God's final judgment. They are (1) the "premillennial judgment" (or "the investigative judgment") which is also called the "pre-Advent judgment"; (2) the "millennial judgment"; and (3) the "executive judgment" which takes place at the end of the millennium.

1. The ministry in the Most Holy Place. The second division of the priestly ministry is primarily sanctuary-centered, revolving around the cleansing of the sanctuary and of God's people. This form of ministry, which focused on the Most Holy Place of the sanctuary and which only the high priest could perform, was limited to one day of the religious year.

The cleansing of the sanctuary required two gifts—the Lord's goat and the scapegoat (*Azazel* in Hebrew). Sacrificing the Lord's goat, the high priest made atonement for "the Holy Place [actually the Most Holy Place in this chapter], the tabernacle of meeting [the holy place], and the altar [of the court]" (Lev. 16:20; cf. 16:16-18).

Taking the blood of the Lord's goat, which represented the blood of Christ, into the Most Holy Place, the high priest applied it directly, in the very presence of God, to the mercy seat—the cover of the ark containing the Ten Commandments—to satisfy the claims of God's holy law. His action symbolized the immeasurable price Christ had to pay for our sins, revealing how eager God is to reconcile His people to Himself (cf. 2 Cor. 5:19). Then he applied this blood to the altar of incense, which on every day of the year had been sprinkled with the blood representing confessed sins. The high priest thereby made an atonement for the sanctuary, as well as the people, and brought about cleansing of both (Lev. 16:16-20, 30-33).

PLAN OF THE HEBREW SANCTUARY

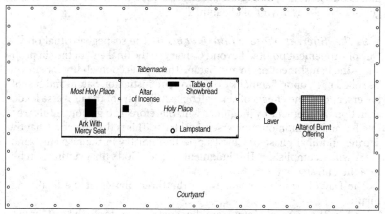

Next, representing Christ as mediator, the high priest took upon himself the sins that had polluted the sanctuary and transferred them to the live goat, Azazel, which was then led away from the camp of God's people. This action removed the sins of the people that had been symbolically transferred from the repentant believers to the sanctuary through the blood or flesh of the sacrifices of the daily ministry of forgiveness. In this way the sanctuary was cleansed and prepared for another year's work of ministry (Lev. 16:16-20, 30-33).[17] And thus all things were set right between God and His people.[18]

The Day of Atonement, then, illustrates the judgment process that deals with the eradication of sin. The atonement performed on this day "foreshadowed the final application of the merits of Christ to banish the presence of sin for all eternity and to accomplish the full reconciliation of the universe into one harmonious government under God."[19]

2. Azazel, the scapegoat. The translation "scapegoat" (escape goat) of the Hebrew *azazel* comes from the Vulgate *caper emissaries,* "goat sent away" (Lev. 16:8, RSV, KJV, margin).[20] A careful examination of Leviticus 16 reveals that Azazel represents Satan, not Christ, as some have thought. The arguments supporting this interpretation are: "(1) the scapegoat was not slain as a sacrifice and thus could not be used as a means of bringing forgiveness. For 'without shedding of blood is no remission' (Heb. 9:22); (2) the sanctuary was entirely cleansed by the blood of the Lord's goat *before* the scapegoat was introduced into the ritual (Lev. 16:20); (3) the passage treats the scapegoat as a personal being who is the opposite of, and opposed to, God (Leviticus 16:8 reads literally, 'One to Yahweh and the other to Azazel'). Therefore, in the setting of the sanctuary parable, it is more consistent to see the Lord's goat as a symbol of Christ and the scape-goat—Azazel—as a symbol of Satan."[21]

3. The different phases of the judgment. The scapegoat ritual on the Day of Atonement pointed beyond Calvary to the final end of the sin prob-lem—the banishment of sin and Satan. The "full accountability for sin will be rolled back upon Satan, its originator and instigator. Satan, and his fol-lowers, and all the effects of sin, will be banished from the universe by de-struction. Atonement by judgment will, therefore, bring about a fully rec-onciled and harmonious universe (Eph. 1:10). This is the objective that the second and final phase of Christ's priestly ministry in the heavenly sanc-tuary will accomplish."[22] This judgment will see God's final vindication be-fore the universe.[23]

The Day of Atonement portrayed the three phases of the final judg-ment:

a. The removal of sins from the sanctuary relates to the first, or pre-Advent, investigative phase of the judgment. It "focuses on the names recorded in the book of Life just as the Day of Atonement focused on the removal of the confessed sins of the penitent from the sanctuary. False believers will be sifted out; the faith of true believers and their union with Christ will be reaffirmed before the loyal universe, and the records of their sins will be blotted out."[24]

b. The banishment of the scapegoat to the wilderness symbolizes Satan's millennial imprisonment on this desolated earth, which begins at the Second Advent and coincides with the second phase of the final judgment, which takes place in heaven (Rev. 20:4; 1 Cor. 6:1-3). This millennial judgment involves a review of the judgment on the wicked and will benefit the redeemed by giving them insight into God's deal-ings with sin and those sinners who were not saved. It will answer all the questions the redeemed may have about God's mercy and justice (see chapter 27 of this book).

c. The clean camp symbolizes the results of the third, or executive, phase of the judgment, when fire destroys the wicked and cleanses the earth (Rev. 20:11-15; Matt. 25:31-46; 2 Peter 3:7-13—see chapter 27 of this book).

The Heavenly Sanctuary in Prophecy

In the above discussion we focused on the sanctuary from the type-an-titype perspective. Now we will look at it in prophecy.

The Anointing of the Heavenly Sanctuary. The seventy-week prophecy of Daniel 9 pointed to the inauguration of Christ's priestly ministry in the heavenly sanctuary. One of the last events to take place during the 490 years was the anointing of the "Most Holy" (Dan. 9:24—see chapter 4 of this book). The Hebrew *qodesh qodeshim* that has been translated as "Most Holy" literally means "Holy of Holies." It would therefore be better to translate the phrase "to anoint a Holy of Holies" or "to anoint the most holy place" (NASB).

As during the inauguration of the earthly sanctuary, it was anointed with holy oil to consecrate it for its services, so in its inauguration, the heavenly sanctuary was to be anointed to consecrate it for Christ's intercessory ministry. With His ascension soon after His death (Dan. 9:27)[25] Christ began His ministry as our High Priest and Intercessor.

The Cleansing of the Heavenly Sanctuary. Speaking of the cleansing of the heavenly sanctuary, the book of Hebrews says, "Almost all things are purged with blood, and without shedding of blood there is no remission. Therefore it was necessary that the copies of the things in the heavens [the earthly sanctuary] should be purified with these [the blood of animals], but the heavenly things themselves [the heavenly sanctuary] with better sacrifices than these"—the precious blood of Christ (Heb. 9:22, 23).

Various commentators have noted this biblical teaching. Henry Alford remarked that "*the heaven itself needed, and obtained, purification* by the atoning blood of Christ."[26] B. F. Westcott commented, "It may be said that even 'heavenly things,' so far as they embody the conditions of man's future life, contracted by the Fall something which required cleansing." It was Christ's blood, he said, that was available "for the cleansing of the heavenly archetype of the earthly sanctuary."[27]

As the sins of God's people were by faith placed upon the sin offering and then symbolically transferred to the earthly sanctuary, so under the new covenant the confessed sins of the penitent are by faith placed on Christ.[28]

And as during the typical Day of Atonement the cleansing of the earthly sanctuary removed the sins accumulated there, so the heavenly sanctuary is cleansed by the final removal of the record of sins in the heavenly books. But before the records are finally cleared, they will be examined to determine who through repentance and faith in Christ is entitled to enter His eternal kingdom. The cleansing of the heavenly sanctuary, therefore, involves a work of investigation or judgment[29] that fully reflects the nature of the Day of Atonement as a day of judgment.[30] This judgment, which ratifies the decision as to who will be saved and who will be lost, must take place before the Second Advent, for at that time Christ returns with His reward, "to give to every one according to his work" (Rev. 22:12). Then, also, Satan's accusations will be answered (cf. Rev. 12:10).

All who have truly repented and by faith claimed the blood of Christ's atoning sacrifice have received pardon. When their names come up in this judgment, and they are found clothed with the robe of Christ's righteousness, their sins are blotted out, and they are accounted worthy of eternal life (Luke 20:35). "He who overcomes," Jesus said, "shall be clothed in white garments, and I will not blot out his name from the Book of Life; but I will confess his name before My Father and before His angels" (Rev. 3:5).

The prophet Daniel reveals the nature of this investigative judgment. While the apostate power symbolized by the little horn carries on its blasphemous and persecuting work against God and His people on earth (Dan. 7:8, 20, 21, 25), thrones are set in place, and God presides over the final judgment. This judgment takes place in the throne room of the heavenly sanctuary and is attended by multitudes of heavenly witnesses. When the court is seated, the books are opened, signaling the beginning of an investigative procedure (Dan. 7:9, 10). It is not until after this judgment that the apostate power is destroyed (Dan. 7:11).[31]

The Time of the Judgment. Both Christ and the Father are involved in the investigative judgment. Before He returns to the earth on the "clouds of heaven," Christ as the "Son of Man" comes "with the clouds of heaven" to the "Ancient of Days," God the Father, and stands before Him (Dan. 7:13). Ever since His ascension Christ has functioned as High Priest, our Intercessor before God (Heb. 7:25). But at this time He comes to receive the kingdom (Dan. 7:14).

1. The eclipse of Christ's priestly ministry. Daniel 8 tells us about the controversy between good and evil and God's final triumph. This chapter reveals that between the inauguration of Christ's high-priestly ministry and the cleansing of the heavenly sanctuary an earthly power would obscure Christ's ministry.

The ram in this vision represented the Medo-Persian empire (Dan. 8:3)—the two horns, the higher coming up last, clearly depicting its two phases, the dominant Persian part of the of the kingdom emerging last. As Daniel predicted, this eastern kingdom did extend its power "westward, northward, and southward," becoming "great" (Dan. 8:4).

The male goat coming from the west symbolized Greece, with the great horn, its "first king," representing Alexander the Great (Dan. 8:21). Coming "from the west" Alexander swiftly defeated Persia. Then, within a few years of his death, the empire was divided into "four kingdoms" (Dan. 8:8, 22)—the kingdoms of Cassander, Lysimachus, Seleucus, and Ptolemy.

At "the latter time of their kingdom" (Dan. 8:23), in other words, toward the end of the divided Greek empire, "a little horn" would arise (Dan. 8:9). Some consider Antiochus Epiphanes, a Syrian king who ruled over Palestine for a short period in the second century B.C., the fulfillment of this part of the prophecy. Others, including many of the Reformers, have identified this little horn as Rome in both its pagan and papal phases. This last interpretation fits exactly the specifications Daniel gave, whereas the other does not.[32] Notice the following points:

a. The little horn power extends from the fall of the Greek empire till the "time of the end" (Dan. 8:17). Only Rome, pagan and papal, meets these time specifications.

b. The prophecies of Daniel 2, 7, and 8 parallel each other (see prophetic parallel chart at the end of this chapter). The four metals of the image of Daniel 2 and the four beasts of Daniel 7 represent the same world empires: Babylon, Medo-Persia, Greece, and Rome. Both the feet of iron and clay and the ten horns of the fourth beast represent the divisions of Rome—those divided states were to continue to exist until the Second Advent. Note that both prophecies point to Rome as the successor of Greece and as the last empire before the Second Advent and final judgment. The little horn in Daniel 8 fits in the same slot—it follows Greece and is supernaturally destroyed or "broken without human hand" (Dan. 8:25; cf. Dan. 2:34).[33]

c. Medo-Persia is called "great," Greece is described as "exceedingly great," and the little horn "grew exceedingly" (Dan. 8:4, 8, 9). Rome, one of the greatest world empires, fits this specification.

d. Only Rome expanded its empire to the south (Egypt), the east (Macedonia and Asia Minor), and "the Glorious Land" (Palestine), just as the prophecy predicted (Dan. 8:9).

e. Rome stood up against the "Prince of the host," the "Prince of princes" (Dan. 8:11, 25), who is none other than Jesus Christ. "Against Him and His people, as well as His sanctuary, the power of Rome fought a most amazing warfare. This description covers both the pagan and papal phases of Rome. While pagan Rome withstood Christ and did indeed destroy the Temple in Jerusalem, papal Rome effectively obscured the priestly, mediatorial ministry of Christ in behalf of sinners in the heavenly sanctuary (see Heb. 8:1, 2) by substituting a priesthood that purports to offer forgiveness through the mediation of men."[34] (See chapter 13 of this book.) This apostate power would be quite successful, for "he cast truth down to the ground. He did all this and prospered" (Dan. 8:12).

2. The time of restoration, cleansing, and judgment. God would not permit the eclipse of truth of Christ's high-priestly ministry to go on indefinitely. Through faithful, God-fearing men and women He revived His cause. The Reformation's partial rediscovery of Christ's role as our Mediator caused a great revival within the Christian world. Yet there was still more truth to be revealed about Christ's heavenly ministry.

Daniel's vision indicated that Christ's role as our High Priest would be made especially prominent toward "the time of the end" (Dan. 8:17), when He would begin His special work of cleansing and judgment in addition to His continual intercessory ministry (Heb. 7:25).[35] The vision specifies when Christ was to begin this antitypical day of atonement ministry—the work of the investigative judgment (Dan. 7) and cleansing of the sanctuary—"Unto two thousand and three hundred days; then shall the sanctuary be cleansed" (Dan. 8:14, KJV).[36] Because the vision refers to the time of the end, the sanctuary it speaks of cannot be the earthly sanctuary—for it was destroyed in A.D. 70. The prophecy must therefore refer to the new covenant sanctuary in heaven—the place where Christ ministers for our salvation.

What are the 2300 days or "2,300 evenings-mornings," as the original Hebrew reads?[37] According to Genesis 1, an "evening and morning" is a day. As we have seen in chapters 4 and 13 of this book, a time period in symbolic prophecy is also symbolic—a prophetic day represents a year. So, as many Christians throughout the centuries have believed, the 2300 days of Daniel 8 signify 2300 literal years.[38]

a. Daniel 9 is the key to unlocking Daniel 8. God commissioned the angel Gabriel to make Daniel "understand the vision" (Dan. 8:16). But its impact was so shocking that Daniel became ill and Gabriel had to discontinue his explanation. At the close of the chapter Daniel remarked: "I was appalled by the vision and did not understand it" (Dan. 8:27, RSV).

Because of this interruption, Gabriel had to delay his explanation of the time period—the only aspect of the vision he had not yet explained. Daniel 9 describes his return to complete this responsibility. Daniel 8 and 9, then, are connected, the latter being the key to unlocking the mystery of the 2300 days.[39] When Gabriel appeared, he said to Daniel: "I have come forth to give you skill to understand....therefore consider the matter, and understand the vision" (Dan. 9:23). Here he refers back to the vision of the 2300 days. His desire to explain the time elements of the vision Daniel 8 makes clear why he introduces his explanation with the seventy-week prophecy.

The seventy weeks, or 490 years, were "determined," or "decreed" (RSV, NASB, NIV), for the Jews and Jerusalem (Dan. 9:24). The underlying Hebrew verb is *chathak*. Although this verb is used only once in the

Scriptures, its meaning can be understood from Hebrew sources.[40] The well-known Hebrew English dictionary by Gesenius states that properly it means "to cut" or "to divide."[41]

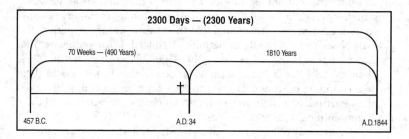

With this background, Gabriel's comments are very revealing. He tells Daniel that 490 years were to be cut off from the longer period of 2300 years. As the starting point for the 490 years, Gabriel points to "the going forth of the command to restore and build Jerusalem" (Dan. 9:25), which took place in 457 B.C., the seventh year of Artaxerxes (see chapter 4 of this book).[42]

The 490 years ended in A.D. 34. When we cut off 490 years from the 2300 years, we are left with 1810 years. Since the 2300 years were to extend 1810 years beyond A.D. 34, they reach to the year 1844.[43]

b. Toward a fuller understanding of Christ's ministry. During the early part of the nineteenth century many Christians—including Baptists, Presbyterians, Methodists, Lutherans, Anglicans, Episcopalians, Congregationalists, and Disciples of Christ—gave intensive study to the prophecy of Daniel 8.[44] All these Bible students expected some very significant events to take place at the end of the 2300 years. Depending on their understanding of the little horn power and the sanctuary, they anticipated this prophetic period to terminate in the purification of the church, the liberation of Palestine and Jerusalem, the return of the Jews, the fall of the Turkish or Muslim power, the destruction of the papacy, the restoration of true worship, the beginning of the earthly millennium, the day of judgment, the cleansing of the earth by fire, or the Second Advent.[45]

None of these predictions materialized, and all who believed them were disappointed. Yet the severity of their disappointment was in proportion to the nature of the predicted event. Obviously, the disappointment of those who expected Christ to return in 1844 was more traumatic than that of those who looked for the return of the Jews to Palestine.[46]

As a result of their disappointment, many gave up the study of prophecy or turned from the historicist method of interpreting prophecy, which had led to these conclusions.[47] Some, however, continued to study this prophecy and the subject of the sanctuary with much prayer and intensity, continuing to look to Christ's ministry in the heavenly sanctuary on their behalf. Rich new insights into that ministry rewarded their efforts. They discovered that the historic prophetic faith of the early church and of the Reformation was still valid. The prophetic time calculations was indeed correct. The 2300 years had ended in 1844. Their mistake—and that of all interpreters of that time—was in their understanding of what event was to take place at the end of that prophetic period. New light from Christ's sanctuary ministry turned their disappointment into hope and joy.[48]

Their study of biblical teachings on the sanctuary revealed that in 1844 Christ came to the Ancient of Days and began the final phase of His high-priestly ministry in the heavenly sanctuary. This ministry was the antitype of the Day of Atonement cleansing of the sanctuary that Daniel 7 depicts as the pre-Advent investigative judgment.

This new insight into Christ's heavenly ministry "is not a departure from the historic Christian faith. It is, instead, the logical completion and inevitable consummation of that faith. It is simply the last-day appearance and fulfillment of the prophesied emphasis characterizing the everlasting gospel—in the closing segment of its witness to the world."[49]

The Significance Within the Great Controversy

The prophecies of Daniel 7 and 8 disclose the broader perspectives of the final outcome of the great controversy between God and Satan.

The Vindication of God's Character. Through the activities of the little horn, Satan has attempted to challenge God's authority. The acts of that power have reproached and trampled upon the heavenly sanctuary, the center of God's government. Daniel's visions point to a pre-Advent judgment in which God will secure a verdict of condemnation upon the little horn, and thus upon Satan himself. In the light of Calvary all Satan's challenges will be refuted. All come to understand and agree that God is right—that He has no responsibility for the sin problem. His character will emerge unassailable, and His government of love will be reaffirmed.

The Vindication of God's People. While the judgment brings condemnation upon the apostate little horn power, it is "made in favor of the saints of the Most High" (Dan. 7:22). Indeed, this judgment not only vindicated God before the universe but His people, as well. Though the saints have been despised and persecuted for their faith in Christ as they may have been throughout the centuries, this judgment puts things right. God's people will realize Christ's promise: "Therefore whoever confesses Me before men, him I will also confess before My Father who is in heaven" (Matt. 10:32; cf. Luke 12:8, 9; Rev. 3:5).

The Judgment and Salvation. Does the investigative judgment jeopardize the salvation of those who believe in Jesus Christ? Not at all. Genuine believers live in union with Christ, trusting in Him as intercessor (Rom. 8:34). Their assurance is in the promise that "we have an Advocate with the Father, Jesus Christ the righteous" (1 John 2:1).

Why, then, a pre-Advent investigative judgment? This judgment is not for the benefit of the Godhead. It is primarily for the benefit of the universe, answering the charges of Satan and giving assurance to the unfallen creation that God will allow into His kingdom only those who truly have been converted. So God opens the books of record for impartial inspection (Dan. 7:9,10).

Human beings belong to one of three classes: (1) the wicked, who reject God's authority; (2) genuine believers, who, trusting in the merits of Christ through faith, live in obedience to God's law; and (3) those who appear to be genuine believers but are not.

The unfallen beings can readily discern the first class. But who is a genuine believer and who is not? Both groups are written in the Book of Life, which contains the names of all who have entered God's service (Luke 10:20; Phil. 4:3; Dan. 12:1; Rev. 21:27). The church itself contains genuine and false believers, the wheat and the tares (Matt. 13:28-30).

God's unfallen creatures are not omniscient—they cannot read the heart. "So a judgment is needed—*before* the second coming of Christ—to sift the true from the false and to demonstrate to the interested universe God's justice in saving the sincere believer. The issue is with God and the universe, not between God and the true child. This calls for the opening of the books of record, the disclosing of those who have professed faith and whose names have been entered into the book of life."[50]

Christ depicted this judgment in His parable of the wedding guests who responded to the generous gospel invitation. Because not all who choose to be Christian are genuine disciples, the king comes to inspect the guests and see who has the wedding garment. This garment represents "the pure, spotless character which Christ's true followers will possess. To the church is given "that she should be arrayed in fine linen, clean and white,' 'not having spot, or wrinkle, or any such thing." (Rev. 19:8; Eph. 5:27). The fine linen, says the Scripture, "is the righteousness of saints" (Rev. 19:8). It is the righteousness of Christ, His own unblemished character, that through faith is imparted to all who receive Him as their personal Saviour."[51] When the king inspects the guests, only those who have put on the robe of Christ's righteousness so generously offered in the gospel invitation are accepted as genuine believers. Those who profess to be followers of God but who are living in disobedience and are not covered by Christ's righteousness will be blotted from the book of life (see Ex. 32:33).

The concept of an investigative judgment of all who profess faith in Christ does not contradict the biblical teaching of salvation by faith through grace.

Paul knew that one day he would face the judgment. He therefore expressed the desire to "be found in Him, not having my own righteousness, which is from the law, but that which is through faith in Christ, the righteousness which is from God by faith" (Phil. 3:9). All who are united with Christ are assured of salvation. In the pre-Advent phase of the last judgment genuine believers, those who have a saving relationship with Christ are affirmed before the unfallen universe.

Christ, however, cannot assure salvation for those who only profess to be Christians on the basis of how many good deeds they have performed (see Matt. 7:21-23). The heavenly records, therefore, are more than just a tool for sifting the genuine from the false. They also are the foundation for confirming the genuine believers before the angels.

"Far from robbing the believer of his assurance with Christ, the doctrine of the sanctuary sustains it. It illustrates and clarifies to his mind the plan of salvation. His penitent heart rejoices to grasp the reality of Christ's substitutionary death for his sins as prefigured in its sacrifices. Furthermore, his faith reaches upward to find its meaning in a *living* Christ, his priestly Advocate in the very presence of the holy God."[52]

A Time to Be Ready. God intends this good news of Christ's closing ministry of salvation to go to all the world before Christ's return. Central to this message is the everlasting gospel, which is to be proclaimed with a sense of urgency because "the hour of His [God's] judgment has come" (Rev. 14:7). This call warns the world that God's judgment is taking place now.

Today we are living in the great antitypical Day of Atonement. As the Israelites were called to afflict their souls on that day (Lev. 23:27), so God calls upon all His people to experience heartfelt repentance. All who wish to retain their names in the Book of Life must make things right with God and their fellow man during this time of God's judgment (Rev. 14:7).

Christ's work as High Priest is nearing its completion. The years of human probation[53] are slipping away. No one knows just when God's voice will proclaim, "It is finished." "Take heed," Christ said, "watch and pray, for you do not know when the time is" (Mark 13:33).

Although we live in the awesome time of the antitypical Day of Atonement, we have no need to fear. Jesus Christ, in His twofold capacity of Sacrifice and Priest, ministers in the heavenly sanctuary on our behalf. Because "we have a great High Priest who has passed through the heavens, Jesus the Son of God, let us hold fast our confession. For we do not have a High Priest who cannot sympathize with our weaknesses, but was in all points tempted as we are, yet without sin. Let us therefore come boldly to the throne of grace, that we may obtain mercy and find grace to help in time of need" (Heb. 4:14-16).

References

1. The book of Hebrews reveals a real sanctuary in heaven. In Hebrews 8:2 the word *sanctuary* is a translation of the Greek *ta hagia*—plural form of the holy place (thing). Additional usages of this plural term can be found, e.g., in Hebrews 9:8, 12, 24, 25; 10:19; 13:11. The various translations give the impression that Christ ministers only in the Most Holy Place or the holy place (see KJV, NKJV, NIV, and NASB), not the sanctuary. This is because the translators consider *ta hagia* an intensive plural, translatable as a singular. But a study of the Septuagint and Josephus shows that the term *ta hagia* does consistently refer to "holy things" or the "holy places"—i.e., to the sanctuary itself. It is the general term used to refer to the entire sanctuary, with its Holy and Most Holy places.

   That Hebrew uses *ta hagia* to refer to the entire sanctuary has strong exegetical support in the epistle itself. The first use of *ta hagia* in Hebrews occurs in 8:2 and is in apposition to "the true tent." Since it is clear from 8:5 that "tent" (*skene*) indicates the entire sanctuary, in Hebrews 8:2 *ta hagia* likewise must designate the entire heavenly sanctuary. There is no reason to translate the plural *ta hagia* in Hebrews as the Most Holy Place. In most cases the context favors the translation of *ta hagia* as "the sanctuary" ("Christ and His High Priestly Ministry," *Ministry*, October 1980, p. 49).

   From their study of the earthly sanctuary and *ta hagia*, the Adventist pioneers concluded that the heavenly sanctuary also has two apartments. This understanding was basic to the development of their teachings on the sanctuary (Damsteegt, "The Historical Development of the Sanctuary Doctrine in Early Adventist Thought" [unpublished manuscript, Biblical Research Institute of the General Conference of Seventh-day Adventists, 1983]; cf. White, *The Great Controversy*, pp. 413-415, 423-432).

2. See *The SDA Bible Commentary*, rev. ed., Ellen G. White Comments, vol. 6, p. 1082.

3. Ancient Jewish writings reveal that some rabbis also believed in a real heavenly sanctuary. Commenting on Exodus 15:17, one rabbi said, "The [position of the terrestrial] Sanctuary corresponds with that of the heavenly Sanctuary and the [position of the] ark with that of the heavenly Throne"

(*Midrash Rabbah. Numbers*, repr. ed. [London: Soncino Press, 1961] vol. 1, chap. 4, sec. 13, p. 110, brackets in original. Another rabbi quoted in the Babylonian Talmud spoke about "the heavenly and the earthly Temple" (*Sanhedrin*, 99b, I. Epstein, ed. [London: Soncino Press, 1969]). Still another commented: "There is no difference of opinion that the sanctuary below is the counterpart of the sanctuary above" (Leon Nemoy, ed., *The Midrash on Psalms*, trans. By William G. Braude [New Haven, Conn.: Yale University Press, 1959], Psalm 30, sec. 1, p. 386).

4. The book of Hebrews depicts a real sanctuary in heaven: "The reality of the heavenly sanctuary is further underlined by the adjective 'true' in Hebrews 8:2. The heavenly sanctuary is the 'true' or better 'real' one. The Greek term used here and in 9:24 where it is also applied to the heavenly sphere is *alethinos*. This Greek adjective means 'real,' as opposed to merely 'apparent.' On account of its classical distinction to the Greek adjective *alethes*, which means 'true,' as opposed to 'false,' the adjective *alethinos*, which is used twice of the heavenly sanctuary, points seemingly unequivocally to the actual reality of a sanctuary in heaven. As God is described as 'real' in John 17:3 and consistently by Paul, as for example, in 1 Thessalonians 1:9, with the usage of *alethinos*, so other entities possess reality insofar as they are associated with His reality. As the heavenly sanctuary is associated with God's reality, so it is as real as God is real" (Hasel, "Christ's Atoning Ministry in Heaven," *Ministry*, January 1976, special insert, p. 21c).

5. Holbrook, "Sanctuary of Salvation," *Ministry*, January 1983, p. 14.

6. White, *The Desire of Ages*, p. 25.

7. Holbrook, "Light in the Shadows," *Journal of Adventist Education*, October-November 1983, p. 27.

8. *Ibid.*, p. 28.

9. "As Christ's ministration was to consist of two great divisions, each occupying a period of time and having a distinctive place in the heavenly sanctuary, so the typical ministration consisted of two divisions, the daily and yearly service, and to each a department of the tabernacle was devoted' (White, *Patriarchs and Prophets*, p. 357).

10. In the daily morning and evening sacrifice the priest represents the whole nation.

11. The father of the family represented his wife and children, who did not offer sacrifices.

12. See, e.g., Angel M. Rodriguez, "Sacrificial Substitution and the Old Testament Sacrifices," in *Sanctuary and the Atonement*, pp. 134-156; A. M. Rodriguez, "Transfer of Sin in Leviticus," in *70 Weeks, Leviticus, and the Nature of Prophecy*, ed. F. B. Holbrook (Washington, DC.: Biblical Research Institute of the General Conference of Seventh-day Adventists, 1986), pp. 169-197.

13. "Atonement, Day of" in *The Jewish Encyclopedia*, ed. Isidore Singer (New York: Funk and Wagnalls Co., 1903), p. 286. See also Hasel, "Studies in Bibli-

cal Atonement I: Continual Sacrifice, Defilement/Cleansing and Sanctuary," in *Sanctuary and the Atonement*, pp. 97-99.

14. Hasel, "Studies in Biblical Atonement I," pp. 99-107; Alberto R. Treiyer, "The Day of Atonement as Related to the Contamination and Purification of the Sanctuary," *70 Weeks, Leviticus, Nature of Prophecy*, p. 253.

15. Holbrook, "Light in the Shadows," p. 27.

16. *Ibid.*, p. 29.

17. See, e.g., Hasel, "Studies in Biblical Atonement II: The Day of Atonement," in *Sanctuary and Atonement*, pp. 115-125.

18. Cf. Hasel, "The 'Little Horn,' the Saints, and the Sanctuary in Daniel 8," in *Sanctuary and Atonement*, pp. 206, 207; Treiyer, "Day of Atonement," pp. 252, 253.

19. Holbrook, "Light in the Shadows," p. 29.

20. Cf. "Azazel," *SDA Bible Dictionary*, rev. ed., p. 102.

21. Holbrook, "Sanctuary and Salvation," p. 16. Throughout the centuries Bible expositors have come to similar conclusions. In the Septuagint *azazel* is rendered *apopompaios*, a Greek word for a malign deity. Ancient Jewish writers and the early Church Fathers referred to him as the devil (*SDA Encyclopedia*, rev. ed., pp. 1291, 1292). Nineteenth- and twentieth-century expositors with similar views include Samuel M. Zwemer, William Milligan, James Hastings, and William Smith, of the Presbyterian Church; E. W. Hengstenberg, Elmer Flack, and H. C. Alleman, of the Lutheran Church; William Jenks, Charles Beecher, and F. N. PeLoubet of the Congregational Church; John M'Clintock and James Strong, of the Methodist Church; James M. Gray, of the Reformed Episcopal Church; J. B. Rotherhorn, of the Disciples of Christ; and George A. Barton, of the Society of Friends. Many others have expressed similar views (*Questions on Doctrine*, pp. 394, 395).

If Azazel represents Satan, how can Scripture (see Lev. 16:10) connect him with the atonement? As the high priest, after having cleansed the sanctuary, placed the sins on Azazel, who was forever removed from God's people, so Christ, after having cleansed the heavenly sanctuary, will place the confessed and forgiven sins of His people on Satan, who will then be forever removed from the saved. "How fitting that the closing act of the drama of God's dealings with sin should be a returning upon the head of Satan of all the sin and guilt that, issuing from him originally, once brought such tragedy to the lives of those now freed of sin by Christ's atoning blood. Thus the cycle is completed, the drama ended. Only when Satan, the instigator of all sin, is finally removed can it truly be said that sin is forever blotted out of God's universe. In this accommodated sense we may understand that the scapegoat has a part in the 'atonement' (Lev. 16:10). With the righteous saved, the wicked 'cut off,' and Satan no more, then, not till then, will the universe be in a state of perfect harmony as it was originally before sin entered" (*The SDA Bible Commentary*, rev. ed., vol. 1, p. 778).

22. Holbrook, "Sanctuary of Salvation," p. 16.

23. Treiyer, "Day of Atonement," p. 245.

24. Holbrook, "Light in the Shadows," p. 30.

25. See chapter 4.

26. Henry Alford, *The Greek Testament*, 3rd ed. (London: Deighton, Bell and Co., 1864), vol. 4, p. 179.

27. B. F. Westcott, *Epistle to the Hebrews*, pp. 272, 271.

28. By placing these confessed sins on Christ, they are "transferred, in fact, to the heavenly sanctuary" (White, *The Great Controversy*, p. 421).

29. This judgment deals with the professed followers of God. "In the typical service only those who had come before God with confession and repentance, and whose sins, through the blood of the sin offering, were transferred to the sanctuary, had a part in the service of the Day of Atonement. So in the great day of final atonement and investigative judgment the only cases considered are those of the professed people of God. The judgment of the wicked is a distinct and separate work, and takes place at a later period. 'Judgment must begin at the house of God: and if it first begin with us, what shall the end be of them that obey not the gospel?' (1 Peter 4:17)" (*Ibid.*, p. 480).

30. Jewish tradition has long portrayed Yom Kippur as the day of judgment—a day when God sits on His throne and judges the world. The books of records are opened, everyone passes before Him, and their destiny is sealed. See "Atonement, Day of," *The Jewish Encyclopedia*; Morris Silverman, comp. and ed., *High Holyday Prayer Book* (Hartford, Conn.: Prayer Book Press, 1951), pp. 147, 164. Yom Kippur brings also comfort and assurance to the believers, for it is "the day on which the fearful anticipation of a judgment to come finally gives place to the confident affirmation that God does not condemn, but will abundantly pardon those who turn to him in penitence and humility" (William W. Simpson, *Jewish Prayer and Worship* [New York: Seabury Press, 1965], pp. 57, 58).

31. See Arthur J. Ferch, "The Judgment Scene in Daniel 7," in *Sanctuary and Atonement*, pp. 163-166, 169.

32. On the problems of the Antiochus interpretation in Daniel, see W. H. Shea, *Selected Studies on Prophetic Interpretation*, pp. 22-55.

33. Shea, "Unity of Daniel," in *Symposium on Daniel*, ed. F. B. Holbrook (Washington, D.C.: Biblical Research Institute of the General Conference of Seventh-day Adventists, 1986), pp. 165-219.

34. "The Amazing Prophecies of Daniel and Revelation," *These Times*, April 1979, p. 18. See also Maxwell, *God Cares*, vol. 1, pp. 166-173; and chapter 13.

35. In the earthly sanctuary, on the Day of Atonement the high priest entered the Most Holy Place, ceasing his ministry in the first apartment. "So when

Christ entered the holy of holies to perform the closing work of the atonement, He ceased His ministration in the first apartment. But when the ministration in the first apartment ended, the ministration in the second apartment began. So Christ had only completed one part of His work as our intercessor, to enter upon another of the work, and He still pleaded His blood before the Father in behalf of sinners" (White, *The Great Controversy*, pp. 428, 429).

36. The translations of the KJV and NKJV render the Hebrew term *nitsdaq*, "shall be cleansed." The New American Bible translates it as "shall be purified." The term *cleansed* is also found in the earliest English translations such as the Bishop's Bible (A.D. 1566), the Geneva Bible (A.D. 1560), Taverner Bible (A.D. 1551), Great Bible (A.D. 1539), Matthew Bible (A.D. 1537), Coverdale (A.D. 1537), and Wycliffe (A.D. 1382). This translation comes from the Latin Vulgate, which reads *mundabitur*, "cleansed," and is rooted in the earliest Greek versions of the Old Testament—the Septuagint and Theodotion—which read *Katharisthesetai*, "shall be cleansed."

Most modern versions do not reflect this traditional rendering. Because *nitsdaq* is derived from the verbal root *tsadaq*, which covers a range of meanings, including "to make right," "being right," "righteous," "justified," and "vindicated," these translations render *tsadaq* as "restored to its rightful state" (RSV), "properly restored" (NASB), "reconsecrated" (NIV), and "restored" (TEV). OT poetic parallelism gives evidence that *tsadaq* can be synonymous with *taher*, "to be clean, pure" (Job 4:17; 17:9 NIV), with *zakah*, "to be pure, clean" (Job 15:14; 25:4), and *bor*, "cleanness" (Ps. 18:20). *Nitsdaq*, then, "includes within its semantic range such meanings as 'cleansing, vindicating, justifying, setting right, restoring.' In whatever way one renders the Hebrew term in a modern language, the 'cleansing' of the sanctuary includes actual cleansing as well as activities of vindicating, justifying, and restoring." (Hasel, "Little Horn,' the Heavenly Sanctuary and the Time of the End: A Study of Daniel 8:9-14," in *Symposium on Daniel*, p. 453). See also *Ibid.*, pp. 448-458; Hasel, "The 'Little Horn,' the Saints, and the Sanctuary in Daniel 8," in *Sanctuary and Atonement*, pp. 203-208; Niels-Erik Andreasen, "Translation of Nisdaq/Katharisthesetai in Daniel 8:14," in *Symposium on Daniel*, pp. 475-496; Maxwell, *God Cares*, vol. 1, p. 175; "Christ and His High Priestly Ministry," *Ministry*, October 1980, pp. 34, 35.

37. Some have interpreted the "2300 evenings-mornings" as only 1150 literal days (e.g., TEV). But this is contrary to Hebrew usage. Carl F. Keil, editor of the Keil and Delitzsch commentary, wrote: "When the Hebrews wish to express separately day and night, the component parts of a day of a week, then the number of both is expressed. They say, e.g., 40 days and 40 nights (Gen. 7:4, 12; Ex. 24:18; 1 Kings 19:8), and three days and three nights (Jonah 2:1; Matt. 12:40), but not 80 or six days-and-nights, when they wish to speak of 40 or three full days. A Hebrew reader could not possibly understand the period of time 2300 evening-mornings of 2300 half days or 1150 whole days, because evening and morning at the creation constituted not the half but the whole day....We must therefore take the words as they are, i.e., understand them of 2300 whole days" (C. F. Keil, *Biblical Commentary*

on the Book of Daniel, trans. M. G. Easton, in C. F. Keil and F. Delitzsch, *Biblical Commentary on the Old Testament* [Grand Rapids: Wm. B. Eerdmans, 1959], vol. 25, pp. 303, 304). For additional arguments, see Hasel, "Sanctuary of Daniel 8," in *Sanctuary and Atonement*, p. 195; Hasel, "The 'Little Horn,' the Heavenly Sanctuary and the Time of the End," in *Symposium on Daniel*, pp. 430-433; Siegfried J. Schwantes, "Ereb Boqer of Daniel 8:14 Re-Examined," in *Symposium on Daniel*, pp. 462-474); Maxwell, *God Cares*, vol. 1, p. 174.

38. Froom, *Prophetic Faith of Our Fathers*, vol. 2, p. 985; vol. 3, pp. 252, 743; vol. 4, pp. 397, 404. For the principle that a prophetic day represents a literal year, see Shea, *Selective Studies on Prophetic Interpretation*, pp. 56-93.

39. See, e.g., Hasel, "Sanctuary in Daniel 8," in *Sanctuary and Atonement*, pp. 196, 197; Shea, "Unity of Daniel," in *Symposium on Daniel*, pp. 220-230.

40. Analysis of Hebrew writings such as the Mishnah reveals that although *chathak* can mean "determine," the more common meaning has "to do with the idea of cutting" (Shea, "The Relationship Between the Prophecies of Daniel 8 and Daniel 9," in *Sanctuary and Atonement*, p. 242).

41. Gesenius, *Hebrew and Chaldee Lexicon to the Old Testament Scripture*, trans. Samuel P. Tregelles (Grand Rapids: W. B. Eerdmans, reprint, ed., 1950), p. 314.

42. See Ferch, "Commencement Date for the Seventy Week Prophecy," in *70 Weeks, Leviticus, and the Nature of Prophecy*, pp. 64-74.

43. From Daniel 8 it is clear that the 2300 days have to cover a long span of years. The question is asked, "How long will the *vision* be?" (Dan. 8:13). The term *vision* is the same as used in verses 1, 2. So when the question "How long is the vision?" is raised by the heavenly angel, he is expecting an answer that covers the entire vision from the first animal symbol through the second animal symbol through the horn symbol to the end of time as is indicated in verses 17 and 19 of Daniel 8. That the 2300 evenings and mornings answers this question indicates rather clearly that they must cover the period from the Medo-Persian empire to the end of time, implying that they represent years.

44. Cf. Damsteegt, *Foundations of the Seventh-day Adventist Message and Mission*, pp. 14, 15; Froom, *Prophetic Faith of Our Fathers*, vol. 4.

45. Froom, *Prophetic Faith of Our Fathers*, vol. 4, p. 404.

46. See, e.g., Francis D. Nichol, *The Midnight Cry* (Washington, D.C.: Review and Herald, 1944).

47. See Froom, *Prophetic Faith of Our Fathers*, vols. 1-4; Damsteegt, *Foundations of the Seventh-day Adventist Message and Mission*, pp. 16-20.

48. See Damsteegt, *Foundations of the Seventh-day Adventist Message and Mission*, pp. 103-146; White, *The Great Controversy*, pp. 423-432.

49. Froom, *Movement of Destiny*, p. 543.

50. Holbrook, "Light in the Shadows," p. 34.

51. White, *Christ's Object Lessons*, p. 310.

52. Holbrook, "Light in the Shadows," p. 35.

53. The end of human probation is the time when repentance is no longer possible. A person's probation can close in any of three ways: (1) at death; (2) when the unpardonable sin has been committed (Matt. 12:31, 32; Luke 12:10); (3) when probation is closed for all just before the Second Advent. As long as Christ functions as High Priest and Mediator between God and man, mercy is available. "No judgments therefore can be inflicted without mercy till Christ's work as priest has ended. But the seven last plagues are poured out without mixture of mercy [Rev. 14:10; 15:1], hence they are poured out after Christ has ceased His pleading, and probation has ended" (U. Smith, in *SDA Encyclopedia*, rev. ed., p. 1152).

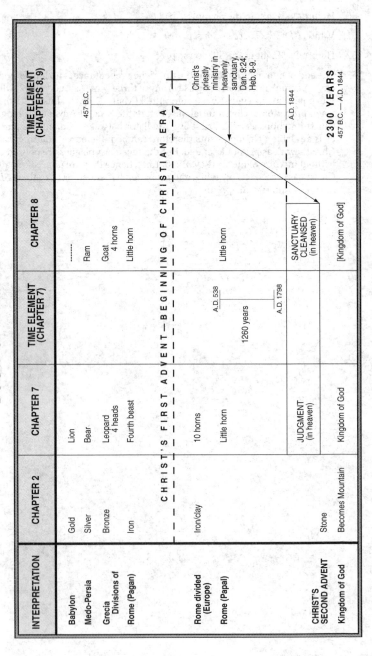

BOOK OF DANIEL

INTERPRETATION	CHAPTER 2	CHAPTER 7	TIME ELEMENT (CHAPTER 7)	CHAPTER 8	TIME ELEMENT (CHAPTERS 8, 9)
Babylon	Gold	Lion		------	457 B.C.
Medo-Persia	Silver	Bear		Ram	
Grecia	Bronze	Leopard 4 heads		Goat 4 horns	
Divisions of					
Rome (Pagan)	Iron	Fourth beast		Little horn	
CHRIST'S FIRST ADVENT—BEGINNING OF CHRISTIAN ERA					Christ's priestly ministry in heavenly sanctuary, Dan. 9:24; Heb. 8-9.
Rome divided (Europe)	Iron/clay	10 horns	A.D. 538	Little horn	
Rome (Papal)		Little horn	1260 years		
			A.D. 1798		A.D. 1844
		JUDGMENT (in heaven)		SANCTUARY CLEANSED (in heaven)	
CHRIST'S SECOND ADVENT	Stone	Kingdom of God		[Kingdom of God]	
Kingdom of God	Becomes Mountain				**2300 YEARS** 457 B.C. — A.D. 1844

The Second Coming of Christ

25

The second coming of Christ is the blessed hope of the church—the grand climax of the gospel. The Saviour's coming will be literal, personal, visible, and worldwide. When He returns, the righteous dead will be resurrected and, together with the righteous living, will be glorified and taken to heaven, but the unrighteous will die. The almost complete fulfillment of most lines of prophecy, together with the present condition of the world, indicates that Christ's coming is imminent. The time of that event has not been revealed, and we are therefore exhorted to be ready at all times. (Titus 2:13; Heb. 9:28; John 14:1-3; Acts 1:9-11; Matt. 24:14; Rev. 1:7; Matt. 24:43, 44; 1 Thess. 4:13-18; 1 Cor. 15:51-54; 2 Thess. 1:7-10; 2:8; Rev. 14:14-20; 19:11-21; Matt. 24; Mark 13; Luke 21; 2 Tim. 3:1-5; 1 Thess. 5:1-6.)

"MOMMY," A LITTLE ONE CONFIDED at bedtime, "I'm so lonely for my friend Jesus. When is He going to come?

That child could hardly know that her little heart's desire has been the longing of the ages. The final words of the Bible give promise of a soon return: "Surely I am coming quickly." And John the Revelator, the loyal companion of Jesus, adds, "Amen. Even so, come, Lord Jesus!" (Rev. 22:20).

To see Jesus! To unite forever with Him who loves us more than we can imagine! To have an end of all earthly suffering! To enjoy eternity with resurrected loved ones now at rest! No wonder that since Christ's ascension His friends have looked forward to that day.

One day He will come, though even to the saints His coming will be an overwhelming surprise—for all slumber and sleep in their long wait (Matt. 25:5). At "midnight," in earth's darkest hour, God will manifest His power to deliver His people. Scripture describes the events: "A loud voice" comes out of the "temple of heaven, from the throne, saying, 'It is done!'" This voice shakes the earth, causing such "a mighty and great earthquake as has not occurred since men were on the earth" (Rev. 16:17, 18). The mountains shake, rocks are scattered everywhere, and the whole earth heaves like the waves of the ocean. Its surface breaks up, "and the cities of the nations fell....Then every island fled away, and the mountains were not found" (verses 19, 20). "The sky receded as a scroll when it is rolled up, and every mountain and island was moved out of its place" (Rev. 6:14).

Despite the chaos descending upon the physical world, God's people take courage as they see "the sign of the Son of Man" (Matt. 24:30). As He descends on the clouds of heaven, every eye sees the Prince of life. He comes, this time, not as a man of sorrows, but as victor and conqueror to claim His own. In place of the crown of thorns, He wears a crown of glory, and "on His robe and on His thigh a name written: KING OF KINGS AND LORD OF LORDS" (Rev. 19:12, 16).

At His coming great despair grips those who have refused to acknowledge Jesus as Saviour and Lord and have rejected the claim of His law on their lives. Nothing makes the rejecters of His grace so aware of their guilt as that voice that had pleaded so patiently, "Turn, turn from your evil ways! For why should you die?" (Eze. 33:11). And the kings of the earth, the great men, the rich men, the commanders, the mighty men, every slave and every free man, hid themselves in the caves and in the rocks of the mountains, and said to the mountains and rocks, 'Fall on us and hide us from the face of Him who sits on the throne and from the wrath of the Lamb! For the great day of His wrath has come, and who is able to stand?" (Rev. 6:15-17).

But the joy of those who have long looked for Him overshadows the despair of the wicked. The coming of the Redeemer brings to its glorious climax the history of God's people—it is the moment of their deliverance. With thrilling adoration they cry out: "Behold, this is our God; we have waited for Him, and He will save us. This is the Lord; we have waited for Him; we will be glad and rejoice in His salvation" (Isa. 25:9).

As Jesus draws near, He calls His sleeping saints from the graves and commissions His angels to "gather together His elect from the four winds, from one end of heaven to the other" (Matt. 24:31). Around the world the righteous dead hear His voice and rise from their graves—what a glad moment!

Then the living righteous are changed "in a moment, in the twinkling of an eye" (1 Cor. 15:52). Glorified and given immortality, together with the resurrected saints they are caught up to meet their Lord in the air to remain with Him forever (1 Thess. 4:16, 17).

The Certainty of Christ's Return

The apostles and early Christians considered Christ's return "the blessed hope" (Titus 2:13; cf. Heb. 9:28). They expected all the prophecies and promises of Scripture to be fulfilled at the Second Advent (see 2 Peter 3:13; cf. Isa. 65:17), for it is the very goal of the Christian pilgrimage. All who love Christ look forward eagerly to the day when they will be able to share face-to-face fellowship with Him—and with the Father, the Holy Spirit, and the angels.

The Testimony of Scripture. The certainty of the Second Advent is rooted in the trustworthiness of the Scripture. Just before His death Jesus told His disciples that He would be returning to His Father to prepare a place for them. But He promised, "I will come again" (John 14:3).

As Christ's first coming to this earth had been prophesied, so His second coming is also foretold through all of Scripture. Even before the Flood God told Enoch that it was Christ's coming in glory that would end sin. He prophesied, "Behold, the Lord comes with ten thousands of His saints, to execute judgment on all, to convict all who are ungodly among them of all their ungodly deeds which they have committed in an ungodly way, and of all the harsh things which ungodly sinners have spoken against Him" (Jude 14, 15).

One thousand years before Christ, the psalmist spoke of the Lord's coming to gather His people, saying, "Our God shall come, and shall not keep silent; a fire shall devour before Him, and it shall be very tempestuous all around Him. He shall call to the heavens from above, and to the earth, that He may judge His people: 'Gather My saints together to Me, those who have made a covenant with Me by sacrifice" (Ps. 50:3-5).

Christ's disciples rejoiced in the promise of His return. Amid all the difficulties they encountered, the assurance this promise brought never failed to renew their courage and strength. Their Master was coming back to take them to His Father's house!

The Guarantee the First Advent Provides. The Second Advent is closely tied to Christ's first advent. If Christ had not come the first time and won a decisive victory over sin and Satan (Col. 2:15), then we would have no reason to believe that He will eventually come to end Satan's dominion of this world and to restore it to its original perfection. But since we have the evidence that He "appeared to put away sin by the sacrifice of Himself," we have reason to believe that He "will appear a second time, apart from sin, for salvation" (Heb. 9:26, 28).

Christ's Heavenly Ministry. Christ's revelation to John makes it clear that the heavenly sanctuary is central to the plan of salvation (Rev. 1:12, 13; 3:12; 4:1-5; 5:8; 7:15; 8:3; 11:1, 19; 14:15, 17; 15:5, 6, 8; 16:1, 17). The prophecies that indicate that He has begun His final ministry on behalf of sinners add to the assurance that soon He will return to take His people home (see chapter 24 of this book). The confidence that Christ is actively working to bring to consummation the redemption already accomplished at the cross has brought great encouragement to Christians looking forward to His return.

The Manner of Christ's Return

As Christ spoke about the signs that would indicate that His coming was near, He also indicated concern that His people not be deceived by false claims. He warned that before the Second Advent "false christs and false prophets will arise and show great signs and wonders, so as to deceive, if possible, even the elect." He said, "If anyone says to you, 'Look, here is the Christ!' Or 'There!' do not believe it" (Matt. 24:23, 24). Forewarned is forearmed. To enable believers to distinguish between the genuine event and a false coming, several biblical passages reveal details of the manner in which Christ will return.

A Literal and Personal Return. When Jesus ascended in a cloud, two angels addressed the disciples, who were still gazing up after their departed Lord: "Men of Galilee, why do you stand gazing up into heaven? This same Jesus, who was taken up from you into heaven, will so come in like manner as you saw Him go into heaven" (Acts 1:11).

In other words, they said that the same Lord who had just left them—a real and tangible person, not some spirit entity (Luke 24:36-43)—would return to earth. And His Second Advent would be as literal and personal as His departure.

A Visible Return. Christ's coming will not be an inward, invisible experience but a real meeting with a visible Person. Leaving no room whatsoever for doubt as to the visibility of His return, Jesus warned His disciples against being taken in by a secret second coming by comparing His return to the brilliance of lightning (Matt. 24:27).

Scripture clearly states that the righteous and the wicked will simultaneously witness His coming. John wrote, "Behold, He is coming with clouds, and every eye will see Him" (Rev. 1:7), and Christ noted the response of the wicked: "All the tribes of the earth will mourn, and they will see the Son of Man coming on the clouds of heaven with power and great glory" (Matt. 24:30).

An Audible Return. Adding to the picture of the universal awareness of Christ's return is the biblical assertion that His coming will be made known by sound as well as sight: "The Lord Himself will descend from heaven with a shout, with the voice of an archangel, and with the trumpet of God" (1 Thess. 4:16). The "great sound of a trumpet" (Matt. 24:31) accompanies the gathering of His people. There is no secrecy here.

A Glorious Return. When Christ returns, He comes as a conqueror, with power and "in the glory of His Father with His angels" (Matt. 16:27). John the Revelator portrays the glory of Christ's return in a most dramatic way. He pictures Christ riding on a white horse and leading the innumerable armies of heaven. The supernatural splendor of the glorified Christ is apparent (Rev. 19:11-16).

A Sudden, Unexpected Return. Christian believers, longing and looking for Christ's return, will be aware when it draws near (1 Thess. 5:4-6). But for the inhabitants of the world in general, Paul wrote, "The day of the Lord so comes as a thief in the night. For when they say, 'Peace and safety!' then sudden destruction comes upon them, as labor pains upon a pregnant woman. And they shall not escape" (1 Thess. 5:2, 3; cf. Matt. 24:43).

Some have concluded that Paul's comparison of Christ's coming to that of a thief indicates that He will come in some secret, invisible manner. However, such a view contradicts the biblical picture of Christ's return in glory and splendor in view of everyone (Rev. 1:7). Paul's point is not that Christ's coming is secret, but that, for the worldly minded, it is as unexpected as that of a thief.

Christ makes the same point by comparing His coming with the unexpected destruction of the antediluvian world by the Flood. "For as in the days before the flood, people were eating and drinking, marrying and giving in marriage, up to the day Noah entered the ark; and they knew nothing about what would happen until the flood came and took them all away. That is how it will be at the coming of the Son of Man" (Matt. 24:38, 39, NIV). Though Noah had preached for many years about a coming flood, it took most people by surprise. There were two classes of people living. One class believed Noah's word and went into the ark and was saved—the other chose to stay outside the ark, and the "flood came and took them all away" (Matt. 24:39).

A Cataclysmic Event. Like the simile of the Flood, Nebuchadnezzar's dream of the metal image depicts the cataclysmic manner in which Christ will establish His kingdom of glory (see chapter 4 of this book). Nebuchadnezzar saw a great image whose "head was of fine gold, its chest and arms of silver, its belly and thighs of bronze, its legs of iron, its feet partly of iron and partly of clay." Then "a stone was cut out without hands, which struck the image on its feet of iron and clay, and broke them in pieces. Then the iron, the clay, the bronze, the silver, and the gold were crushed together, and became like chaff from the summer threshing floors; the wind carried them away so that no trace of them was found. And the stone that struck the image became a great mountain and filled the whole earth" (Dan. 2:32-35).

Through this dream God gave Nebuchadnezzar a synopsis of world history. Between his day and the establishment of Christ's everlasting kingdom (the stone), four major kingdoms or empires and then a conglomeration of weak and strong nations would consecutively occupy the world's stage.

Ever since the days of Christ interpreters have identified the empires as Babylon (605-539 B.C.), Medo-Persia (539-331 B.C.), Greece (331-168 B.C.), and Rome (168 B.C.-A.D. 476).[1] As prophesied, no other empire succeeded Rome. During the fourth and fifth centuries A.D. it broke into a number of smaller kingdoms that later became the nations of Europe. Through the centuries, powerful rulers—Charlemagne, Charles V, Napoleon, Kaiser Wilhelm, and Hitler—have tried to establish another world empire. Each failed, just as the prophecy said: "They will not adhere to one another, just as iron does not mix with clay" (Dan. 2:43).

Finally, the dream focuses on the dramatic climax: the setting up of God's everlasting kingdom. The stone cut out without hands represents Christ's kingdom of glory (Dan. 7:14; Rev. 11:15), which will be established without human effort at the Second Advent.

Christ's kingdom is not to exist simultaneously with any human empire. When He was on earth during the sway of the Roman Empire, the stone kingdom that crushes all nations had not yet come. Only after the phase of the iron and clay feet—the period of the divided nations—would it arrive. It is to be set up at the Second Advent when Christ separates the righteous from the wicked (Matt. 25:31-34).

When it comes, this stone or kingdom will strike the "image on its feet of iron and clay," and "it shall break in pieces and consume all these kingdoms," leaving not a trace of them (Dan. 2:34, 35, 44). Indeed, the Second Advent is an earth-shaking event.

The Second Advent and the Human Race

Christ's second advent will touch both of the great divisions of humanity: those who have accepted Him and the salvation He brings—and those who have turned from Him.

The Gathering of the Elect. An important aspect of the establishment of Christ's eternal kingdom is the gathering of all the redeemed (Matt. 24:31; 25:32-34; Mark 13:27) to the heavenly home Christ has prepared (John 14:3).

When a head of state visits another country, only a few persons can be part of the welcoming party. But when Christ comes, every believer who has ever lived, regardless of age, gender, education, economic status, or race, will participate in the grand Advent celebration. Two events make possible this universal gathering: the resurrection of the righteous dead and the translation of the living saints.

1. The resurrection of the dead in Christ. At the sound of the trumpet announcing Christ's return, the righteous dead will be raised incorruptible and immortal (1 Cor. 15:52, 53). At that moment the "dead in Christ will rise first" (1 Thess. 4:16). In other words, they are raised *before* the living righteous are caught up to be with the Lord.

Resurrected ones reunite with those who sorrowed at their departure. Now they exult, "O death, where is thy sting? O grave, where is thy victory?" (1 Cor. 15:55, KJV).

It is not the diseased, aged, mutilated bodies that went down into the grave that come up in the resurrection but new, immortal, perfect bodies, no longer marked by the sin that caused their decay. The resurrected saints experience the completion of Christ's work of restoration, reflecting the perfect image of God in mind, soul, and body (1 Cor. 15:42-54—see chapter 26 of this book).

2. The translation of the living believers. When the righteous dead are resurrected, the righteous living on the earth at the Second Coming will be changed. "For this corruptible must put on incorruption, and this mortal must put on immortality" (1 Cor. 15:53).

At Christ's return no group of believers takes precedence over any other believers. Paul reveals that the living and transformed believers "shall be caught up together with them [the resurrected believers] in the clouds to meet the Lord in the air. And thus we shall always be with the Lord" (1 Thess. 4:17; cf. Heb. 11:39, 40). So all the believers will be present at the grand Advent gathering—both the resurrected saints of all ages and those who are alive at Christ's return.

The Death of the Unbelievers. To the saved the Second Advent is a time of joy and exhilaration, but to the lost it will be a time of devastating terror. They have resisted Christ's love and His invitations to salvation so long that they have become ensnared in deceptive delusions (see 2 Thess. 2:9-12; Rom. 1:28-32). When they see the One they have rejected coming as King of kings and Lord of lords, they know the hour of their doom has struck. Overwhelmed with terror and despair, they call upon the inanimate creation to shelter them (Rev. 6:16, 17).

At this time God will destroy Babylon, the union of all apostate religions. "She will be utterly burned with fire" (Rev. 18:8). The leader of this confederation—the mystery of iniquity, the lawless one—"the Lord will consume with the breath of His mouth and destroy with the brightness of His coming" (2 Thess. 2:8). The powers responsible for enforcing the mark of the beast (see chapter 13 of this book) will be cast "into the lake of fire burning with brimstone." And the rest of the wicked will be "killed with the sword which proceeded from the mouth of Him who sat on the horse"— Jesus Christ the Lord (Rev. 19:20, 21).

The Signs of Christ's Soon Return

The Scriptures not only reveal the manner and object of Christ's coming, they also describe the signs that tell of the nearness of this climactic event. The first signs announcing the Second Advent took place more than 1700 years after Christ's ascension, and others have followed, contributing to the evidence that His return is very near.

Signs in the Natural World. Christ predicted that there would "be signs in the sun, in the moon, and in the stars" (Luke 21:25), specifying that "the sun will be darkened, and the moon will not give its light; the stars of heaven will fall, and the powers in heaven will be shaken. Then they will see the Son of Man coming in the clouds with great power and glory" (Mark 13:24-26). In addition, John saw that a great earthquake would precede the signs in the heavens (Rev. 6:12). All of these signs would mark the end of the 1260 years of persecution (see chapter 13 of this book).

1. The witness of the earth. In fulfillment of this prophecy "the largest known earthquake,"[2] occurred on November 1, 1755. Known as the Lisbon earthquake, its effects were observed in Europe, Africa, and America, covering an area of about four million square miles. Its destruction centered on Lisbon, Portugal, where, in a matter of minutes, it leveled public and residential buildings, causing scores of thousands of deaths.[3]

While the earthquake's physical effects were large, its impact on the thought of the time was just as significant. Many living then recognized it as a prophetic sign of the end[4] and began to give serious consideration to the judgment of God and the last days. The Lisbon earthquake gave an impetus to the study of prophecy.

2. The witness of the sun and moon. Twenty-five years later the next sign mentioned in prophecy took place—the darkening of the sun and moon. Christ had pointed out the time of the fulfillment of this sign, noting that it was to follow the great tribulation—the 1260 years of papal persecution spoken of elsewhere in Scripture (Matt. 24:29—see chapter 13 of this book). But Christ said that the tribulation that was to precede these signs would be shortened (Matt. 24:21, 22). Through the influence of the Reformation and the movements that grew out of it, the papal persecution was indeed shortened, so that by the middle of the eighteenth century it had almost wholly ceased.

In fulfillment of this prophecy on May 19, 1780, an extraordinary darkness descended upon the northeastern part of the North American continent.[5]

Recalling this event, Timothy Dwight, president of Yale University, said, "The 19th of May, 1780, was a remarkable day. Candles were lighted in many houses; the birds were silent and disappeared, and the fowls retired to roost....A very general opinion prevailed, that the day of judgment was at hand."[6]

Samuel Williams of Harvard reported that the darkness "approached with the clouds from the southwest 'between the hours of 10:00 and 11:00 A.M., and continued until the middle of the next night,' varying in degree and duration in different localities. In some places 'persons could not see to read common print in the open air.'"[7] In Samuel Tenny's opinion "the darkness of *the following evening* was probably as gross as ever has been observed since the Almighty fiat gave birth to light....If every luminous body in the universe had been shrouded in impenetrable shades, or struck out of existence, the darkness could not have been more complete."[8]

At 9:00 that night a full moon rose, but the darkness persisted until after midnight. When the moon became visible, it had the appearance of blood.

John the Revelator had prophesied the extraordinary events of that day. After the earthquake, he wrote, the sun would become "black as sackcloth of hair, and the moon...like blood" (Rev. 6:12).

3. The witness of the stars. Both Christ and John had also spoken about a falling of the stars that would indicate that Christ's coming was near (Rev. 6:13; cf. Matt. 24:29). The great meteoric shower of November 13, 1833—the most extensive display of falling stars on record—fulfilled this prophecy. It was estimated that a single observer could see an average of 60,000 meteors per hour.[9] It was seen from Canada to Mexico and from the mid-Atlantic to the Pacific,[10] many Christians recognizing in it the fulfillment of the Bible prophecy.[11]

An eyewitness said that "there was scarcely a space in the firmament which was not filled at every instant with these falling stars, nor on it, could you in general perceive any particular difference, in appearance; still at times they would shower down in groups—calling to mind the 'fig tree, casting her untimely figs when shaken by a mighty wind.'"[12]

Christ gave these signs to alert Christians to the nearness of His coming so that they might rejoice in their expectation and be fully prepared for it. "Now when these things begin to happen," He said, "look up and lift up your heads, because your redemption draws near." He added, "Look at the fig tree, and all the trees. When they are already budding, you see and know for yourselves that summer is now near. So you, likewise, when you see these things happening, know that the kingdom of God is near" (Luke 21:28-31).

This unique witness of earth, sun, moon, and stars, which came in the precise sequence and at the time Christ had predicted, directed the attention of many toward the prophecies of the Second Advent.

Signs in the Religious World. Scripture predicts that a number of significant signs in the religious world will mark the time just preceding Christ's return.

1. A great religious awakening. The book of Revelation reveals the rise of a great, worldwide religious movement before the Second Advent. In John's vision, an angel heralding Christ's return symbolized this movement: "I saw an angel flying in the midst of heaven having the everlasting gospel to preach to those who dwell on the earth and to every nation, tribe, tongue, and people—saying with a loud voice, 'Fear God and give glory to Him, for the hour His judgment has come; and worship Him who made heaven and earth, the sea and springs of water'" (Rev. 14:6, 7).

The message itself indicates when it is to be proclaimed. The everlasting gospel has been preached throughout all ages. But this message, emphasizing the judgment aspect of the gospel, could only be proclaimed in the time of the end, for it warns that the "hour of His judgment has come."

The book of Daniel informs us that in the time of the end its prophecies would be unsealed (Dan. 12:4). At that time people would understand its mysteries. The unsealing took place as the 1260-year period of papal dominance came to its end with the captivity of the pope in 1798. The combination of the exile of the pope and the signs in the natural world led many Christians to study the prophecies about the events leading to the Second Advent, which resulted in a new depth of understanding of these prophecies.

This focus on the Second Advent also brought about a worldwide revival of the Advent hope. As the Reformation sprang up independently in various countries throughout the Christian world, so did the Advent movement. The worldwide nature of this movement is one of the clearest signs that Christ's return is drawing near. As John the Baptist prepared the way for Christ's first advent, so the Advent movement is preparing the way for His Second Advent—proclaiming the message of Revelation 14:6-

12, God's final call to get ready for the glorious return of the Saviour (see chapters 13 and 24 of this book).[13]

2. Preaching of the Gospel. God "has appointed a day on which He will judge the world in righteousness" (Acts 17:31). In warning us of that day, Christ did not say that it would come when all the world is converted, but that the "gospel of the kingdom will be preached in all the world as a witness to all the nations, and then the end will come" (Matt. 24:14). Thus Peter encourages believers to be "looking for and hastening the coming of the day of God" (2 Peter 3:12).

Statistics on the translation and distribution of the Bible in this century reveal the growth of the gospel witness. In 1900, the Bible was available in 537 languages. By 1980, it had been translated, in full or in part, into 1,811 languages, representing nearly 96 percent of the world population. Similarly, the annual distribution of the Scriptures has risen from 5.4 million Bibles in 1900 to 36.8 million Bibles and nearly half a billion Bible portions by 1980.[14]

In addition, Christianity now has at its disposal an unprecedented variety of resources for use in its mission: service agencies, educational and medical institutions, national and foreign workers, radio and television broadcasting, and impressive financial means. Today, powerful shortwave radio stations can beam the gospel to practically every country around the globe. Used under the guidance of the Holy Spirit, these unparalleled resources make realistic the goal of evangelizing the world in our time.

Seventh-day Adventists, with a membership that represents about 700 languages and 1,000 dialects, are proclaiming the gospel in 204 countries. Almost 93 percent of these members live outside of North America. A total of 347 languages and dialects are used in publications—and 882 languages and dialects are used in both publications *and* oral work. Believing that medical and educational work play essential roles in fulfilling the gospel commission, we operate 698 hospitals, nursing homes, clinics and dispensaries, 34 orphanages and children's homes, 10 medical launches, 28 health food factories, 101 colleges and universities, 1,385 secondary schools, 5,322 elementary schools, 125 Bible correspondence schools, and 33 language institutes. Our 57 publishing houses produce literature in 190 languages and 157 dialects, and our shortwave radio stations broadcast to approximately 75 percent of the world population. In addition, 5,512 radio stations are used each week—as well as 2,252 television stations. The Holy Spirit has abundantly blessed our mission thrust.

3. Religious Decline. The widespread proclamation of the gospel does not necessarily mean a massive growth of genuine Christianity. Instead, the Scriptures predict a decline of true spirituality toward the end of time. Paul said that "in the last days perilous times will come: for men will be lovers of themselves, lovers of money, boasters, proud, blasphemers, disobedient to parents, unthankful, unholy, unloving, unforgiving, slanderers, without self-control, brutal, despisers of good, traitors, headstrong, haughty, lovers of pleasure, rather than lovers of God, having a form of godliness but denying its power" (2 Tim. 3:1-5).

So today, love of self, material things, and the world has supplanted the Spirit of Christ in many hearts. People no longer allow God's principles and His laws to direct their lives; lawlessness has taken over. "And because lawlessness will abound, the love of many will grow cold" (Matt. 24:12).

4. A Resurgence of the Papacy. According to biblical prophecy, at the end of the 1260 years the papacy would receive "a deadly wound that would heal. The papacy would experience a great renewal of influence and respect—"all the world marveled and followed the beast" (Rev. 13:3). Already today, many view the pope as the moral leader of the world.

To a large extent, the papacy's rising influence has come as Christians have substituted traditions, human standards, and science for the authority of the Bible. In doing so, they have become vulnerable to "the lawless one," who works "with all power, signs, and lying wonders" (2 Thess. 2:9). Satan and his instruments will bring about a confederation of evil, symbolized by the unholy trinity of the dragon, the beast, and the false prophet, that will deceive the world (Rev. 16:13, 14; cf. 13:13, 14). Only those whose guide is the Bible and who "keep the commandments of God and the faith of Jesus" (Rev. 14:12) can successfully resist the overwhelming deception this confederation brings.

5. Decline of Religious Freedom. The revival of the papacy will affect Christianity dramatically. The religious liberty obtained at great cost, guaranteed by the separation between church and state, will erode and finally be abolished. With the support of powerful civil governments, this apostate power will attempt to force its form of worship on all people. Everyone will have to choose between loyalty to God and His commandments or loyalty to the beast and his image (Rev. 14:6-12).

The pressure to conform will include economic coercion: "No one may buy or sell except one who has the mark or the name of the beast, or the number of his name" (Rev. 13:17). Eventually, those who refuse to go along will face a death penalty (Rev.13:15). During this final time of trouble God will intervene for His people and deliver everyone whose name is written in the book of life (Dan. 12:1; cf. Rev. 3:5; 20:15).

Increase of Wickedness. The spiritual decline within Christianity and the revival of the man of lawlessness have led to a growing neglect of God's law in the church and in the lives of believers. Many have come to believe that Christ has abolished the law and that Christians are no longer obliged to observe it. This disregard of God's law has led to an increase in crime and immoral behavior.

1. Surge in world crime. The disrespect for God's law current within much of Christianity has contributed to modern society's contempt for law and order. Throughout the world, crime is skyrocketing out of control. A report filed by correspondents from several world capitals stated: "Just as in the United States, crime is on the rise in almost every country around the world." "From London to Moscow to Johannesburg, crime is fast becoming a major menace that is changing the way in which many people live."[15]

2. Sexual revolution. Disregard for God's law has also broken down the restraints of modesty and purity, resulting in a surge of immorality. Today sex is idolized and marketed through films, television, video, songs, magazines, and advertisements.

The sexual revolution has resulted in the shocking rise of the rate of divorce, aberrations like "open marriage" or mate swapping, the sexual abuse of children, an appalling number of abortions, widespread homosexuality and lesbianism, an epidemic of venereal diseases, and the recently surfaced AIDS (acquired immune deficiency syndrome).

Wars and Calamities. Before His return, Jesus said, "Nation will rise against nation, and kingdom against kingdom. And there will be great earthquakes in various places, and famines and pestilences; and there will be fearful sights and great signs from heaven" (Luke 21:10, 11; cf. Mark 13:7, 8; Matt. 24:7). As the end draws near and the conflict between the satanic and divine forces intensifies, these calamities will also intensify in severity and frequency and find an unprecedented fulfillment in our time.

1. Wars. Although wars have plagued humanity throughout history, never before have they been so global and so destructive. World Wars I and II caused more casualties and suffering than all previous wars combined.[16]

Many see the prospect of another worldwide conflict. World War II did not eradicate war. Since it ended, there have been some "140 conflicts fought with conventional weapons, in which up to ten million people have died."[17]

2. Natural disasters. Disasters appear to have increased significantly in recent years. Recent cataclysms of earth and weather, coming one on top of another, have caused some to wonder whether nature has gone berserk—and if the world is experiencing profound changes in climate and structure that will intensify in the future.[18]

3. Famines. Famines have occurred many times in the past, but they have not occurred on the scale with which they have in this century. Never before has the world had millions of people suffering from either starvation or malnutrition.[19] The prospects for the future are hardly brighter. The unprecedented extent of starvation clearly signals that Christ's return is imminent.

Be Ready at All Times

The Bible repeatedly assures us that Jesus will return. But will He come a year from now? Five years? Ten years? Twenty years? No one knows for sure. Jesus Himself declared, "Of that day and hour no one knows, no, not even the angels of heaven, but My Father only" (Matt. 24:36).

At the end of His earthly ministry Christ told the parable of the ten virgins to illustrate the experience of the church of the last days. The two classes of virgins represent the two kinds of believers who profess to be waiting for their Lord. They are called virgins because they profess a pure faith. Their lamps represent the Word of God; the oil symbolizes the Holy Spirit.

Superficially, these two groups appear alike: both go out to meet the Bridegroom, both have oil in their lamps, and their behavior doesn't seem to differ. They have all heard the message of Christ's soon coming and are looking forward to it. But then comes an apparent delay—their faith is to be tested.

Suddenly, at midnight—in the darkest hour of earth's history—they hear the cry, "Behold, the bridegroom is coming; go out to meet him!" (Matt. 25:6). Now the difference between the two groups becomes apparent—some are not ready to meet the Bridegroom. These "foolish" virgins are not hypocrites—they respect the truth, the Word of God. But they lack the oil—they have not been sealed by the Holy Spirit (cf. Rev. 7:1-3). They have been content with superficial work and have not fallen on Jesus Christ the Rock. They have a form of godliness but are destitute of God's power.

When the Bridegroom comes, only those who are ready go in with Him to the marriage celebration, and the door is shut. Eventually the foolish virgins, who had gone to purchase more oil, return and call, "Lord, Lord, open to us!" But the Bridegroom answers, "I do not know you" (Matt. 25:11-12).

How sad that when Christ returns to this earth, He will have to speak these words to some whom He loves. He warned, "Many will say to Me in that day, "Lord, Lord, have we not prophesied in Your name, cast out demons in Your name, and done many wonders in Your name?" And then I will declare to them, "I never knew you; depart from Me, you who practice lawlessness!" (Matt. 7:22, 23).

Before the Flood, God sent Noah to alert the antediluvian world to the coming destruction. In a similar way, God is sending a threefold message of warning to prepare the world for Christ's return (see Rev. 14:6-16).

All who accept God's message of mercy will rejoice at the prospect of the Second Advent. Theirs is the assurance, "Blessed are those who are called to the marriage supper of the Lamb!" (Rev. 19:9). Indeed, "to those who eagerly wait for Him He will appear a second time, apart from sin, for salvation" (Heb. 9:28).

The Redeemer's return brings to a glorious climax the history of God's people. It is the moment of their deliverance, and with joy and adoration, they cry out, "Behold this is our God; we have waited for Him…we will be glad and rejoice in His salvation" (Isa. 25:9).

References

1. Froom, *Prophetic Faith of Our Fathers*, vol. 1, pp. 456, 894; vol. 2, pp. 528, 784; vol. 3, pp. 252, 744; vol. 4, pp. 396, 846. See also chapter 24 of this book.

2. G. I. Eiby, *Earthquakes* (New York, NY: Van Nostrand Reinholdt Co., 1980), p. 164.

3. See, e.g., Sir Charles Lyell, *Principles of Geology* (Philadelphia: James Kay, Jun. & Brother, 1837), vol. 1, pp. 416-419; "Lisbon," *Encyclopedia Americana*, ed. Francis Lieber (Philadelphia, PA: Carey and Lea, 1831), p. 10; W. H. Hobbs, *Earthquakes*, (New York: D. Appleton and Co., 1907), p. 143; Thomas Hunter, *An Historical Account of Earthquakes Extracted from the Most Authentic Historians* (Liverpool: R. Williamson, 1756), pp. 54-90; cf. White, *The Great Controversy*, pp. 304, 305. Early reports mentioned 100,000 dead. Modern encyclopedias may give 60,000.

4. See John Biddolf, *A Poem on the Earthquake at Lisbon* (London: W. Owen, 1755), p. 9, quoted in *Source Book*, p. 358; Froom, *Prophetic Faith of Our Fathers*, vol. 2, pp. 674-677. On February 6, 1756, the Anglican Church held a day of fasting and humiliation in memory of this earthquake (*Ibid*). See also T. D. Kendrick, *The Lisbon Earthquake* (London: Methuen & Co. Ltd., 1955), pp. 72-164.

5. Cf. White, *The Great Controversy*, pp. 306-308.

6. Timothy Dwight, quoted in *Connecticut Historical Collections*, comp. John W. Barber, 2nd ed. (New Haven, CT: Durrie & Peck and J. W. Barber, 1836), p. 403; cited in *Source Book*, p. 316.

7. Samuel Williams, "An Account of a Very Uncommon Darkness in the State

of New England, May 19, 1780," in *Memoirs of the American Academy of Arts and Sciences: to the End of the Year 1783* (Boston, MA: Adams and Nourse, 1785), vol. 1, pp. 234, 235. Cf. *Source Book*, p. 315.

8. Letter of Samuel Tenny, Exeter, [NH], Dec. 1785, in *Collections of the Massachusetts Historical Society for the Year 1792* (Boston, MA: Belknap and Hall, 1792), vol. 1, p. 97.

9. Peter M. Millman, "The Falling of the Stars," *The Telescope*, 7 (May-June, 1940, p. 60). See also Froom, *Prophetic Faith of Our Fathers*, vol. 4, p. 295.

10. Denison Olmsted, *Letters on Astronomy*, 1840 ed., pp. 348, 349, in *Source Book*, pp. 410, 411.

11. Froom, *Prophetic Faith of Our Fathers*, vol. 4, pp. 297-300; cf. White, *The Great Controversy*, pp. 333, 334.

12. Phenomena as observed at Bowling Green, Missouri, reported in the *Salt River Journal*, Nov. 20, 1780 as quoted in *American Journal of Science and Arts*, ed., Benjamin Silliman, 25 (1834): p. 382.

13. See Froom, *Prophetic Faith of Our Fathers*, vol. 4; Damsteegt, *Foundations of the Seventh-day Adventist Message and Mission*.

14. David B. Barrett, ed., *World Christian Encyclopedia. A Comparative Study of Churches and Religions in the Modern World A. D. 1900-2000* (Oxford: Oxford University Press, 1982), p. 13.

15. "Abroad, Too, Fear Grips the Cities," *U.S. News & World Report*, Febr. 23, 1981, p. 65.

16. David Singer and Melvin Small, *The Wages of War: 1816-1965. A Statistical Handbook* (New York, NY: John Wiley & Sons, 1972), pp. 66, 67.

17. Margaret Thatcher, as quoted in Ernest W. Lefever and E. Stephen Hung, *The Apocalypse Premise* (Washington, D.C.: Ethics and Public Policy Center, 1982), p. 394.

18. See Paul Recer, "Is Mother Nature Going Beserk?" *U.S. News & World Report*, Feb. 22, 1982, p. 66.

19. A special supplement to the United Nations publication *Development Forum*, entitled "Facts on Food," (Nov. 1974) said that "half the world population, 2,000 million is badly nourished," cited in Ronald J. Sider, *Rich Christians in an Age of Hunger* (New York, NY: Paulist Press, 1977), p. 228, n. 4. Cf. p. 16.

26

Death and Resurrection

The wages of sin is death. But God, who alone is immortal, will grant eternal life to His redeemed. Until that day death is an unconscious state for all people. When Christ, who is our life, appears, the resurrected righteous and the living righteous will be glorified and caught up to meet their Lord. The second resurrection, a resurrection of the unrighteous, will take place a thousand years later. (Rom. 6:23; 1 Tim. 6:15, 16; Eccl. 9:5, 6; Ps. 146:3, 4; John 11:11-14; Col. 3:4; 1 Cor. 15:51-54; 1 Thess. 4:13-17; John 5:28, 29; Rev. 20:1-10.)

THE PHILISTINE ARMY MOVED into Shunem, set up its camp, and made ready to attack Israel. His mood far from optimistic, King Saul positioned Israel's army on nearby Mount Gilboa. In the past, the assurance of God's presence had enabled Saul to lead Israel against its foes fearlessly. But he had turned from serving the Lord, and when the apostate king had tried to contact God about the outcome of the impending battle, God had refused to communicate with him.

The ominous fear of the unknown morrow weighed heavily upon Saul. If only Samuel were here. But Samuel was dead and could no longer counsel him. Or could he?

Locating a medium who had escaped his earlier witch hunts, the tall king stooped to inquiring through her about the outcome of the next day's battle. He requested, "Bring up Samuel to me." During the séance the medium "saw a spirit ascending out of the earth." This spirit informed the hapless king that not only would Israel lose the war but that he and his sons would be killed (see 1 Samuel 28).

The prediction came true. But was it really Samuel's spirit that made the prediction? How could a medium, condemned by God, have power over the spirit of Samuel—God's prophet? And where did Samuel come from—why did his spirit arise "out of the earth"? What had death brought to Samuel? If it wasn't Samuel's spirit that spoke to Saul, who was it? Let us see what the Bible teaches on the subject of death, communication with the dead, and the resurrection.

Immortality and Death

Immortality is the state or quality of not being subject to death. The translators of Scripture used the word *immortality* to translate the Greek terms *athanasia*, "deathlessness," and *aphtharsia*, "incorruptibility." How does this concept relate to God and human beings?

Immortality. Scripture reveals that the eternal God is immortal (1 Tim. 1:17). In fact, He "alone has immortality" (1 Tim. 6:16). He is uncreated, self-existent, and has no beginning and no end (see chapter 2 of this book).

"The Scriptures nowhere describe immortality as a quality or state that man—or his 'soul' or 'spirit'—possesses inherently. The terms usually rendered 'soul' and 'spirit'...in the Bible occur more than 1,600 times, but never in association with the words 'immortal' or 'immortality'" (see chapter 7 of this book).[1]

In contrast to God, then, human beings are mortal. Scripture compares their lives with "a vapor that appears for a little time and then vanishes away" (James 4:14). They are "but flesh, a breath that passes away and does not come again" (Ps. 78:39). Man "comes forth like a flower and fades away; he flees like a shadow and does not continue" (Job 14:2).

God and human beings differ markedly. God is infinite—they are finite. God is immortal—they are mortal. God is eternal—they are transitory.

Conditional Immortality. At Creation "God formed man of the dust of the ground, and breathed into his nostrils the breath of life; and man became a living being" (Gen. 2:7). The Creation account reveals that humanity derived life from God (cf. Acts 17:25, 28; Col. 1:16, 17). The corollary of this basic fact is that immortality is not innate to humanity but is God's gift.

When God created Adam and Eve, He gave them free will—the power of choice. They could obey or disobey, and their continued existence depended upon continual obedience through God's power. So their possession of the gift of immortality was conditional.

God carefully spelled out the condition upon which they would forfeit this gift—eating of "the tree of the knowledge of good and evil." God warned them, when "you eat of it you shall surely die" (Gen. 2:17).[2]

Death: The Wages of Sin. Contradicting God's warning that disobedience would bring death, Satan asserted, "You will not surely die" (Gen. 3:4). But after they transgressed God's command, Adam and Eve discovered that the wages of sin is, indeed, death (Rom. 6:23). Their sin brought this sentence: You shall "return to the ground, for out of it you were taken; for dust you are, and to dust you shall return" (Gen. 3:19). These words do not point to a continuation of life but to its cessation.

After giving this sentence, God barred the sinful couple from the Tree of Life so that they could not "eat, and live forever" (Gen. 3:22). His action made it clear that the immortality promised on condition of obedience was lost through sin. They had now become mortal—subject to death. And because Adam could not transmit what he no longer possessed, "death spread to all men, because all had sinned" (Rom. 5:12).

It was only God's mercy that kept Adam and Eve from dying immediately. The Son of God had offered to give His life so that they might have another opportunity—a second chance. He was "the Lamb slain from the foundation of the world" (Rev. 13:8).

Hope for Humanity. Although people are born mortal, the Bible encourages them to seek immortality (see, e.g., Rom. 2:7). Jesus Christ is the source of this immortality: "The gift of God is eternal life in Christ Jesus our Lord" (Rom. 6:23; cf. 1 John 5:11). He "has abolished death and brought life and immortality to light" (2 Tim. 1:10). "For as in Adam all die, even so in Christ all shall be made alive (1 Cor. 15:22). Christ Himself said that His voice would open graves and resurrect the dead (John 5:28, 29).

If Christ had not come, the human situation would have been hopeless, and all who died would have perished eternally. Because of Him, however, no one need perish. Said John, "For God so loved the world that He gave His only begotten Son, that whoever believes in Him should not perish but have everlasting life" (John 3:16). So belief in Christ not only abolishes the penalty for sin, but it also secures for believers the priceless gift of immortality.

Christ brought "immortality to light through the gospel" (2 Tim. 1:10). Paul assures us that it is the Holy Scriptures that are able to make us "wise for salvation through faith which is in Christ Jesus" (2 Tim. 3:15). Those who do not accept the gospel will not receive immortality.

The Receiving of Immortality. The moment of the bestowal of the gift of immortality is described by Paul: "Behold, I tell you a mystery: We shall not all sleep, but we shall all be changed—in a moment, in the twinkling of an eye, at the last trumpet. For the trumpet will sound, and the dead will be raised incorruptible, and we shall be changed. For this corruptible must put on incorruption, and this mortal must put on immortality. So when this corruptible has put on incorruption, and this mortal has put on immortality, then shall be brought to pass the saying that is written: 'Death is swallowed up in victory'" (1 Cor. 15:51-54). This makes very clear that God does not bestow immortality upon the believer at death but at the resurrection, when "the last trumpet" sounds. *Then* "this mortal" shall "put on immortality." While John points out that we receive the gift of eternal life when we accept Jesus Christ as personal Saviour (1 John 5:11-13), the actual realization of this gift will take place when Christ returns. Only then will we be changed from mortal to immortal, from corruptible to incorruptible.

The Nature of Death

If death is the cessation of life, what does the Bible say about a person's condition in death? What makes it important that Christians understand this biblical teaching?

Death Is a Sleep. Death is not complete annihilation—it is only a state of temporary unconsciousness while the person awaits the resurrection. The Bible repeatedly calls this intermediate state a sleep.

Referring to their deaths, the Old Testament describes David, Solomon, and the other kings of Israel and Judah as sleeping with their forefathers (1 Kings 2:10; 11:43; 14:20, 31; 15:8; 2 Chron. 21:1; 26:23; etc.). Job called death a sleep (Job 14:10-12), as did David (Ps. 13:3), Jeremiah (Jer. 51:39, 57), and Daniel (Dan. 12:2).

The New Testament uses the same imagery. In describing the condition of Jairus' daughter, who was dead, Christ said that she was sleeping (Matt. 9:24; Mark 5:39). He referred to the deceased Lazarus in a similar manner (John 11:11-14). Matthew wrote that many "saints who had fallen asleep were raised" after Christ's resurrection (Matt. 27:52), and in recording Stephen's martyrdom, Luke wrote that "he fell asleep" (Acts 7:60). Both Paul and Peter also called death a sleep (1 Cor. 15:51, 52; 1 Thess. 4:13-17; 2 Peter 3:4).

The biblical representation of death as a sleep clearly fits its nature, as the following comparisons demonstrate: 1. Those who sleep are unconscious. "The dead know nothing" (Eccl. 9:5). 2. In sleep, conscious thinking ceases. "His breath goeth forth,...in that very day his thoughts perish" (Ps. 146:4, KJV). 3. Sleep brings an end to all the day's activities. "There is no work or device or knowledge or wisdom in the grave where you are going" (Eccl. 9:10). 4. Sleep disassociates us from those who are awake and from their activities. "Nevermore will they have a share in anything done under the sun" (verse 6). 5. Normal sleep renders the emotions inactive. "Their love, their hatred, and their envy have now perished" (verse 6). 6. In sleep men do not praise God. "The dead do not praise the Lord" (Ps. 115:17). 7. Sleep presupposes an awakening. "The hour is coming in which all who are in the graves will hear His voice and come forth" (John 5:28, 29).[3]

The Person Returns to Dust. To understand what happens to a person at death, one must understand what makes up his or her nature. The Bible portrays a person as an organic unit (see chapter 7 of this book). At times it uses the word *soul* to refer to the whole person and at other times to the affections and emotions. But it does not teach that man comprises two separate parts. Body and soul only exist together—they form an indivisible union.

At humanity's creation, the union of the dust of the ground (earth's elements) and the breath of life produced a living being or soul. Adam did not receive a soul as a separate entity—he *became* a living soul (Gen. 2:7—see also chapter 7 of this book). At death the inverse takes place: the dust of the ground minus the breath of life yields a dead person or dead soul without any consciousness (Ps. 146:4). The elements that made up the body return to the earth from which they came (Gen. 3:19). The soul has no conscious existence apart from the body, and no scripture indicates that at death the soul survives as a conscious entity. Indeed, "the soul who sins shall die" (Eze. 18:20).

The Abode of the Dead. The Old Testament calls the place where people go at death *sheol* (Hebrew), and the New Testament *hades* (Greek). In the Scripture, *sheol* most often simply means the grave.[4] The meaning of *hades* is similar to that of *sheol.*[5]

All the dead go into this place (Ps. 89:48), both the righteous and the wicked. Jacob said, "I shall go down in the grave [*sheol*]" (Gen. 37:35). When the earth opened "its mouth" to swallow the wicked Korah and his company, they went "down alive into the pit [*sheol*]" (Num. 16:30).

Sheol receives the whole person at death. When Christ died, He went into the grave (*hades*) but at the Resurrection His soul left the grave (*hades*, Acts 2:27, 31, or *sheol*, Ps. 16:10). When David thanked God for healing, he testified that his soul was saved "from the grave [*sheol*]" (Ps. 30:3).

The grave is not a place of consciousness.[6] Since death is a sleep, the dead will remain in a state of unconsciousness in the grave until the resurrection, when the grave (*hades*) gives up its dead (Rev. 20:13).

The Spirit Returns to God. Though the body returns to dust, the spirit returns to God. Solomon said that at death "the dust will return to the earth as it was, and the spirit will return to God who gave it" (Eccl. 12:7). This is true of all, both the righteous and the wicked.

Many have thought that this text gives evidence that the essence of the person continues to live after death. But in the Bible neither the Hebrew nor the Greek term for *spirit* (*ruach* and *pneuma*, respectively) refers to an intelligent entity capable of a conscious existence apart from the body. Rather, these terms refer to the "breath"—the spark of life essential to individual existence, the life principle that animates animals and human beings (see chapter 7 of this book).

Solomon wrote, "Man's fate is like that of the animals; the same fate awaits them both: As one dies, so dies the other. All have the same breath ["spirit," margin; *ruach*]; man has no advantage over the animal. . . .All go to the same place; all come from dust, and to dust all return. Who knows if the spirit [*ruach*] of man rises upward and if the spirit [*ruach*] of the animal goes down into the earth?" (Eccl. 3:19-21, NIV). So according to Solomon, at death there is no difference between the spirits of man and beast.

Solomon's statement that the spirit (*ruach*) returns to God who gave it indicates that what returns to God is simply the life principle that He imparted. There is no indication that the spirit, or breath, was a conscious entity separate from the body. This *ruach* can be equated with the "breath of life" that God breathed into the first human being to animate his lifeless body (cf. Gen. 2:7).

Harmony Throughout the Scriptures. Many honest Christians who have not studied the complete teaching of the Bible on death have been unaware that death is a sleep until the resurrection. They have assumed that various passages support the idea that the spirit or soul has a conscious existence after death. Careful study reveals that the consistent teaching of the Bible is that death causes the cessation of consciousness.[7]

Spiritualism. If the dead are completely insensate, with whom or what do spiritualist mediums communicate?

Every honest person will admit that at least some of these phenomena are fraudulent; but others cannot be explained as such. There obviously is some supernatural power connected with spiritualism. What does the Bible teach on this point?

1. The basis of spiritualism. Spiritualism originated with Satan's first lie to Eve—"You will not surely die" (Gen. 3:4). His words were the first sermon on the immortality of the soul. Today, throughout the world, religions of all sorts unwittingly repeat this error. For many, the divine sentence that "the soul who sins shall die" (Eze. 18:20) has been reversed to say, "the soul, even though it sins, shall live eternally."

This erroneous doctrine of natural immortality has led to belief in consciousness in death. As we have seen, these positions directly contradict the biblical teaching on this subject. They were incorporated into the Christian faith from pagan philosophy—particularly that of Plato—during the time of the great apostasy (see chapter 13 of this book). These beliefs became the prevailing view within Christianity and continue to be the dominant view today.

Belief that the dead are conscious has prepared many Christians to accept spiritualism. If the dead are alive and in the presence of God, why could they not return to earth as ministering spirits? And if they can, why not try to communicate with them to receive their counsel and instruction, to avoid misfortune, or to receive comfort in sorrow?

Building on this line of reasoning, Satan and his angels (Rev. 12:4, 9) have established a channel of communication through which they can accomplish their deception. Through such means as spiritualistic séances they impersonate departed loved ones, bring supposed comfort and assurance to the living. At times they predict future events, which, when proved to be accurate, give them credibility. Then the dangerous heresies they proclaim take on the patina of authenticity, even though they contradict the Bible and God's law. Having removed the barriers against evil, Satan has free rein to lead people away from God and to certain destruction.

2. *Warning against spiritualism.* No one need be deceived by spiritualism. The Bible clearly exposes its claims as false. As we have seen, the Bible tells us that the dead do not know anything—that they lie unconscious in the grave.

The Bible also strongly forbids any attempt to communicate with the dead or the spirit world. It says that those who claim to communicate with the dead, as spiritualistic mediums do today, are actually communicating with "familiar spirits" that are "spirits of devils." The Lord said these activities were abominations and that those who perpetrated them were to be punished by death (Lev. 19:31; 20:27; cf. Deut. 18:10, 11).

Isaiah expressed well the foolishness of spiritualism: "When they say to you, 'Seek those who are mediums and wizards, who whisper and mutter,' should not a people seek their God? Should they seek the dead on behalf of the living? To the law and to the testimony! If they do not speak according to this word, it is because there is no light in them" (Isa. 8:19, 20). Indeed, only the teachings of the Bible can safeguard Christians against this overwhelming deception.

3. *Manifestations of spiritualism.* The Bible records a number of spiritualistic activities—from the magicians of Pharaoh and the magicians, astrologers, and sorcerers of Ninevah and Babylon to the witches and mediums of Israel—and condemns them all. One example is the séance the witch of Endor conjured for Saul, with which we began this chapter.

Scripture says, "When Saul inquired of the Lord, the Lord did not answer him, either by dreams or by Urim or by the prophets" (1 Sam. 28:6). God, then, had nothing to do with what happened at Endor. Saul was deceived by a demon impersonating the dead Samuel; he never saw the real Samuel. The witch saw the form of an old man while Saul only "perceived" or concluded it was Samuel (verse 14).

If we are to believe that that apparition truly was Samuel, we must be prepared to believe that witches, wizards, necromancers, sorcerers, spiritualists, or mediums can call the righteous dead from wherever they go when they die. We must also accept that the godly Samuel existed in a conscious state in the earth, because the old man ascended "out of the earth" (verse 13).

This séance brought Saul despair, not hope. The next day he committed suicide (1 Sam. 31:4). Yet the so-called Samuel had predicted that on that day Saul and his sons would be with him (1 Sam. 28:19). If he were correct, we would have to conclude that after death the disobedient Saul and righteous Samuel dwelt together. Instead, we must conclude that an evil angel brought about the deceptive events that occurred at this séance.

4. *The final delusion.* In the past the manifestations of spiritualism were confined to the realm of the occult, but more recently spiritualism has taken on a "Christian" appearance so that it might deceive the Christian world. In professing to accept Christ and the Bible, spiritualism has become an extremely dangerous enemy to believers. Its effects are subtle and deceptive. Through the influence of spiritualism "the Bible is interpreted in a manner that is pleasing to the unrenewed heart, while its solemn and vital truths are made of no effect. Love is dwelt upon as the chief attribute of God, but it is degraded to a weak sentimentalism, making little distinction between good and evil. God's justice, His denunciations of sin, the requirements of His holy law, are all kept out of sight. The people are taught to regard the Decalogue as a dead letter. Pleasing, bewitching fables captivate the sense and lead men to reject the Bible as the foundation of their faith."[8]

Through this means right and wrong become relative, and each person, or situation, or culture becomes the norm as to what is "truth." In essence each person becomes a god, fulfilling Satan's promise that "ye shall be as gods" (Gen. 3:5, KJV).

Before us is "the hour of trial which shall come upon the whole world, to test those who dwell on the earth" (Rev. 3:10). Satan is about to use great signs and miracles in his final effort to deceive the world. Speaking of this masterful delusion, John said, "I saw three unclean spirits like frogs. They are spirits of demons, performing signs, which go out to the kings of the earth and of the whole world, to gather them to the battle of that great day of God Almighty" (Rev. 16:13, 14; cf. 13:13, 14).

Only those who are kept by the power of God, having their minds fortified with the truths of Scripture, accepting it as their only authority, will be able to escape. All others have no protection and will be swept away by this delusion.

The First and Second Deaths. The second death is the final punishment of unrepentant sinners—all whose names are not written in the Book of Life—that takes place at the end of the 1,000 years (see chapter 27 of this book). From this death there is no resurrection. With the destruction of Satan and the unrighteous, sin is eradicated, and death itself is destroyed (1 Cor. 15:26; Rev. 20:14; 21:8). Christ has given the assurance that everyone "who overcomes shall not be hurt by the second death" (Rev. 2:11).

Based on what Scripture has designated the second death, we can assume that the first death is what every person—except those who are translated—experiences as a result of Adam's transgression. It is "the normal outworking on humanity of the degenerative effects of sin."[9]

Resurrection

Resurrection is "the restoration of life, together with fullness of being and personality, subsequent to death."[10] Because humanity is subject to death, there must be a resurrection if they are to experience life beyond the grave. Throughout the Old and New Testaments, God's messengers have expressed hope in a resurrection (Job 14:13-15; 19:25-29; Ps. 49:15; 73:24; Isa. 26:19; 1 Cor. 15).

The hope of the resurrection, for which we have solid evidence, encourages us that we can enjoy a better future beyond this present world in which death is the destiny of all.

Christ's Resurrection. The resurrection of the righteous dead to immortality is closely associated with Christ's resurrection because it is the resurrected Christ who eventually will raise up the dead (John 5:28, 29).

1. Its importance. What would have happened if Christ had not been resurrected? Paul summarizes the consequences: a. There would be no use in preaching the gospel: "If Christ is not risen, then our preaching is vain" (1 Cor. 15:14). b. There would be no forgiveness of sins: "And if Christ is not risen,...you are still in your sins!" (verse 17). c. There would be no purpose in believing in Jesus: "And if Christ is not risen, your faith is futile" (verse 17). d. There would be no general resurrection from the dead: "Now if Christ preached that He has been raised from the dead, how do some among you say that there is no resurrection of the dead?" (verse 12). e. There would be no hope beyond the grave: "If Christ is not risen, ...Then also those who have fallen asleep in Christ have perished" (verses 17, 18).[11]

2. A bodily resurrection. The Christ who came from the tomb was the *same* Jesus who lived here in the flesh. Now He had a glorified body, but it was still a real body. It was so real that others did not even notice a difference (Luke 24:13-27; John 20:14-18).

Jesus Himself denied that He was some kind of spirit or ghost. Speaking to His disciples, He said, "Behold My hands and My feet...Handle Me and see, for a spirit does not have flesh and bones as you see I have" (Luke 24:39). To prove the physical reality of His resurrection, He also ate in their presence (verse 43).

3. Its impact. The Resurrection had an electrifying impact on Christ's disciples. It transformed a group of weak and frightened men into valiant apostles ready to do anything for their Lord (Phil. 3:10, 11; Acts 4:33). The mission they undertook as a result of it shook the Roman Empire and turned the world upside down (Acts 17:6).

"It was the certainty of Christ's resurrection that brought point and power to the preaching of the gospel (cf. Phil. 3:10, 11). Peter speaks of the 'resurrection of Jesus Christ from the dead' as producing a 'lively hope' in believers (1 Peter 1:3). The apostles considered themselves ordained to be witnesses 'of his resurrection' (Acts 1:22), and based their teaching of the resurrection of Christ on the Messianic predictions of the Old Testament (Acts 2:31). It was their personal knowledge of 'the resurrection of the Lord Jesus' that gave 'great power' to their witness (Acts 4:33). The apostles drew the opposition of the Jewish leaders when they went forth preaching 'through Jesus the resurrection from the dead' (verse 2)....When arraigned before the Sanhedrin, Paul declared that it was because of his 'hope and resurrection of the dead' that he had been 'called in question' before them (Acts 23:6; cf. 24:21). To the Romans, Paul wrote that Jesus Christ was 'declared to be the Son of God with power...by the resurrection from the dead' (Rom. 1:4). In baptism, he explained, the Christian testifies to his faith in the resurrection of Christ (Rom. 6:4, 5)."[12]

The Two Resurrections. Christ taught that there are two general resurrections: a "resurrection of life" for the just and a "resurrection of condemnation" for the unjust (John 5:28, 29; Acts 24:15). The 1,000 years separates these resurrections (Rev. 20:4, 5).

1. The resurrection of life. Those who are raised in the first resurrection are called "blessed and holy" (Rev. 20:6). They will not experience the second death in the lake of fire at the close of the 1,000 years (verse 14). This resurrection to life and immortality (John 5:29; 1 Cor. 15:52, 53) takes place at the Second Advent (1 Cor. 15:22, 23; 1 Thess. 4:15-18). Those who experience it cannot die anymore (Luke 20:36). They are united with Christ forever.

What will the resurrected body be like? Like Christ, the resurrected saints will have real bodies. And as Christ arose a glorified being, so will the righteous. Paul said that Christ "will transform our lowly body that it may be conformed to His glorious body" (Phil. 3:21). He calls the unglorified body and the glorified one the "natural body" and the "spiritual body," respectively; the former being mortal and corruptible, the latter immortal and imperishable. The change from mortality to immortality takes place instantaneously at the resurrection (see 1 Cor. 15:42-54).

2. The resurrection of condemnation. The unrighteous are raised in the second general resurrection, which takes place at the end of the 1,000 years (see chapter 27 of this book). This resurrection proceeds to the final judgment and condemnation (John 5:29). Those whose names are not found in the Book of Life will be raised at this time and "cast into the lake of fire" and experience the second death (Rev. 20:14, 15).

They could have avoided this tragic end. In unmistakable language Scripture presents God's way to escape: "Repent! Turn away from all your offenses; then sin will not be your downfall. Rid yourselves of all the offenses you have committed, and get a new heart and a new spirit. Why will you die?...For I take no pleasure in the death of anyone, declares the Sovereign Lord. Repent and live!" (Eze. 18:30-32, NIV).

Christ promises that "he who overcomes shall not be hurt at all by the second death" (Rev. 2:11). Those who accept Jesus and the salvation He brings will experience an indescribable joy at His climactic return. In never-fading happiness, they will spend eternity fellowshipping with their Lord and Saviour.

References

1. "Immortality," *SDA Bible Encyclopedia*, rev. ed., p. 621.

2. Throughout the centuries prominent Christians of many faiths—Lutheran, Reformed, Anglican, Baptist, Congregationalist, Presbyterian, Methodist, etc.—have expounded the biblical teaching of conditional immortality. Among the most prominent were the following: sixteenth century—Mar-

tin Luther, William Tyndale, John Frith, George Wishart; seventeenth century—Robert Overton, Samuel Richardson, John Milton, George Wither, John Jackson, John Canne, Archbishop John Tillotson, Dr. Isaac Barrow; eighteenth century—Dr. William Coward, Henry Layton, Joseph N. Scott, M.D., Dr. Joseph Priestly, Peter Pecard, Archdeacon Francis Blackburne, Bishop William Warburton, Samuel Bourn, Dr. William Whiston, Dr. John Tottie, Prof. Henry Dodwell; nineteenth century—Bishop Timothy Kendrick, Dr. William Thomson, Dr. Edward White, Dr. John Thomas, H. H. Dobney, Archbishop Richard Whately, Dean Henry Alford, James Panton Ham, Charles F. Hudson, Dr. Robert W. Dale, Dean Frederick W. Farrar, Hermann Olshausen, Canon Henry Constable, William Gladstone, Joseph Parker, Bishop John J. S. Perowne, Sir George G. Stokes, Dr. W. A. Brown, Dr. J. Agar Beet, Dr. R. F. Weymouth, Dr. Lyman Abbott, Dr. Edward Beecher, Dr. Emmanuel Petavel-Olliff, Dr. Franz Delitzsch, Bishop Charles J. Ellicott, Dr. George Dana Boardman, J. H. Pettingell; twentieth century—Canon William H. M. Hay Aitken, Eric Lewis, Dr. William Temple, Dr. Gerardus van der Leeuw, Dr. Aubrey R. Vine, Dr. Martin J. Heinecken, David R. Davies, Dr. Basil F. C. Atkinson, Dr. Emil Brunner, Dr. Reinhold Niebuhr, Dr. T. A. Kantonen, Dr. D. R. G. Owen. See *Questions on Doctrine*, pp. 571-609; Froom, *The Conditionalist Faith of Our Fathers* (Washington, D.C.; Review and Herald, 1965, 1966), vols. 1 and 2.

3. See "Death," *SDA Bible Dictionary*, rev. ed., pp. 277, 278,

4. R. L. Harris, "The Meaning of the Word Sheol as Shown by Parallels in Poetic Texts," *Journal of the Evangelical Theological Society*, Dec. 1961, pp. 129-135; see also *SDA Bible Commentary*, rev. ed., vol. 3, p. 999.

5. See, e.g., *SDA Bible Commentary*, rev. ed., vol. 5, p. 387.

6. The only exception is when *sheol* is used figuratively (see Eze. 32:21) or *hades* in a parable (Luke 16:23). *Sheol* occurs more than sixty times in the Old Testament, but nowhere does it refer to a place of punishment after death. That idea was later attached to *gehenna* (Mark 9:43-48), not to *hades*. There is only one exception (Luke 16:23). See also *SDA Bible Commentary*, rev. ed., vol. 3, p. 999.

7. The following passages have been thought to pose problems for this view of the Scriptures' teachings on the nature of death. But a closer look shows them to be in full harmony with the rest of Scripture.

a. Rachel's death. Referring to Rachel's death, Scripture says that "her soul was departing" (Gen. 35:18). This expression simply indicates that in her last moments of consciousness and with her last breath she gave her son a name. Thus other translations read: "As she breathed her last" (NIV).

b. Elijah and the dead boy. When Elijah prayed that the soul of the dead son of the widow of Zarephath would return, God answered him by reviving the boy (1 Kings 17:21, 22). This was the result of the union of the life principle with the body, neither of which was alive or conscious when apart.

c. Moses' appearance on the mountain. Moses' appearance on the Mount of

Transfiguration does not provide evidence of the existence of conscious spirits or the presence of all righteous dead in heaven. Shortly before this event Jesus told His disciples that before they would die some of them would see the Son of man in His kingdom. This promise was fulfilled to Peter, James, and John (Matt. 16:28-17:3).

On the mountain Christ revealed to them a miniature of God's kingdom of glory. There was Christ, the glorious King, together with Moses and Elijah—representatives of the two types of subjects of the kingdom. Moses represented the righteous dead who are to be resurrected from the grave at the Second Advent, and Elijah represented the righteous living who are to be translated to heaven without seeing death (2 Kings 2:11).

Jude provides the evidence of Moses' special resurrection. After Moses died and was buried (Deut. 34:5, 6), there was a dispute between Michael and the devil about the body of Moses (Jude 9). From Moses' appearance on the mountain it can be concluded that the devil lost the contest and Moses was resurrected from his grave, making him the first known subject of Christ's resurrecting power. This event does not provide evidence for the doctrine of the immortality of the soul. Rather, it presents support for the doctrine of the bodily resurrection.

d. Parable of the rich man and Lazarus. Christ's story of the rich man and Lazarus has been used to teach the consciousness of the dead (Luke 16:19-31). Unfortunately, those who interpret it in this way have not recognized that this story is a parable that, taken literally in every detail, would be absurd. The dead would go to their reward as real beings with bodily parts such as eyes, tongue, and fingers. All the righteous would be on Abraham's bosom, and heaven and hell would be within speaking distance. Both classes would receive their reward at death, in contrast to Christ's teaching that they will receive it at the Second Advent (Matt. 25:31-41; Rev. 22:12).

This story, however, is a parable—one of Christ's favorite methods of teaching. Each parable was meant to teach a lesson, and what Christ was teaching had nothing to do with the state of the dead. The moral of this parable is the importance of living by the Word of God. Jesus showed that the rich man was preoccupied with materialism and neglected to care for those in need. Eternal destiny is decided in this present life, and there is no second probation. Scripture is the guide to repentance and salvation, and if we will not heed the warnings of God's Word, nothing can reach us. Thus Christ ended the parable with the words, "If they do not hear Moses and the prophets, neither will they be persuaded though one rise from the dead" (Luke 16:31).

Christ simply employed elements of a common Jewish story in which the dead carry on a conversation. (The parable's concept of Abraham's bosom and Hades was very similar to Jewish tradition. See "Discourse on the Greeks Concerning Hades," *Josephus' Complete Works*, trans. By William Whiston [Grand Rapids: Kregel, 1960], p. 637.) Similarly, we find in the Bible a parable in which trees talk (Judges 9:7-15; cf. 2 Kings 14:9). No one would use this parable to prove that trees can talk. So one should refrain from giving

Christ's parable a meaning that would contradict the abundant scriptural evidence and Christ's personal teaching that death is a sleep.

e. *Christ's promise to the thief.* Christ promised the thief at the cross, "Assuredly, I say to you, today you will be with Me in Paradise" (Luke 23:43). Paradise obviously is synonymous with heaven (2 Cor. 12:4; Rev. 2:7). As the translated text reads, Christ would go to heaven that Friday to be in the very presence of God, as would the thief. Yet on Resurrection morning Christ Himself said to Mary as she fell at His feet to worship Him, "Touch me not; for I am not yet ascended to my Father: but go to my brethren, and say unto them, I ascend unto my Father, and your Father; and to my God, and your God" (John 20:17, KJV). That Christ remained in the grave over the weekend is indicated by the words of the angel: "Come, see the place where the Lord lay" (Matt 28:6).

Did Christ contradict Himself? Not at all. The solution to the understanding of the text involves its punctuation. The early manuscripts of the Bible did not have any commas or spaces between the words. Insertion of punctuation and word divisions can make considerable difference in the meaning of the text. Bible translators use their best judgment in placing punctuation marks, but their work is certainly not inspired.

If the translators, who did such excellent work in general, had placed the comma in Luke 23:43 *after* "today" instead of *before* it, this passage would not contradict the teaching of the rest of the Bible on death. Christ's words would then be properly understood to mean: "Assuredly, I say to you today [this day, when I am dying as a criminal], you will be with Me in paradise." In harmony with the biblical teaching, Jesus assured the thief that he would be with Him in Paradise—a promise that will be fulfilled following the resurrection of the just at His second coming.

f. *To depart and be with Christ.* "For to me, to live is Christ, and to die is gain," Paul said. "For I am hard pressed between the two, having a desire to depart and be with Christ, which is far better" (Phil. 1:21, 23). Did Paul expect to enter heaven immediately at death?

Paul wrote much on the subject of being with Christ. In another letter he wrote about those "who sleep in Jesus." At the Second Advent, he said, the righteous dead will be resurrected, and together with the living righteous they will be "caught up together...to meet the Lord in the air. And thus we shall always be with the Lord" (1 Thess. 4:14, 17).

Against this background we see that in his letter to the Philippians, Paul is not giving a detailed exposition on what happens at death. He is simply expressing his desire to leave his present troubled existence and to be with Christ, without giving any reference or explanation as to the period of time between death and the resurrection. His hope is centered on the promised personal companionship with Jesus throughout eternity. For those who die there is no long interval between the time when they close their eyes in death and when they open them at the resurrection. Since the dead are not conscious and have no awareness of the passing of time, the resurrection morning will seem to come the moment after death. For the Christian, death is gain: no more temptations, trials, and sorrows, and at the resurrection the gift of a glorious immortality.

8.   White, *The Great Controversy*, p. 558.

9.   "Death," *SDA Bible Dictionary*, rev. ed., p. 278; cf. *Questions on Doctrine*, p. 524.

10.   "Resurrection," *SDA Bible Dictionary*, rev. ed., p. 935.

11.   *Questions on Doctrine*, pp. 67, 68.

12.   "Resurrection," *SDA Bible Dictionary*, rev. ed., p. 936.

27 The Millennium and the End of Sin

The millennium is the thousand-year reign of Christ with His saints in heaven between the first and second resurrections. During this time the wicked dead will be judged; the earth will be utterly desolate, without living human inhabitants but occupied by Satan and his angels. At its close Christ with His saints and the Holy City will descend from heaven to earth. The unrighteous dead will then be resurrected and, with Satan and his angels, will surround the city—but fire from God will consume them and cleanse the earth. The universe will thus be freed of sin and sinners forever. (Rev. 20; 1 Cor. 6:2, 3; Jer. 4:23-26; Rev. 21:1-5; Mal. 4:1; Ezek. 28:19, 20.)

THROUGHOUT HISTORY THERE HAVE BEEN those who have waxed eloquent about the horrors of hell, playing on people's fear in an attempt to bring them to worship God. But what kind of god do they portray?

How will God finally get rid of evil? What will happen to Satan? What will keep sin from erecting its ugly head once more? How can a just God also be loving?

Events at the Beginning of the Millennium

During the millennium, the thousand-year period of which the twentieth chapter of Revelation speaks, Satan's influence over the earth will be restricted, and Christ will reign with His saints (Rev. 20:1-4).

The Second Advent. Revelation 19 and 20 belong together—there is no break between these chapters. They describe Christ's coming (Rev. 19:11-21) and immediately continue with the millennium, their sequence indicating that the millennium begins when Christ returns.

Revelation represents the three powers that gather the nations of the world to oppose Christ's work and His people immediately before the Second Advent as a dragon, a beast, and a false prophet (Rev. 16:13). When "the beast, the kings of the earth, and their armies" assemble to make war against Christ at the time of His return, the beast and the false prophet are destroyed (Rev. 19:19, 20). What follows in Revelation 20, the chapter on the millennium, deals with the fate of the third member of the demonic trio—the dragon. He is taken captive and cast into the bottomless pit, where he remains for 1,000 years.[1]

As we saw in chapter 25, it is with Christ's Second Advent, when the kingdoms of this world are destroyed, that God sets up His kingdom of glory—a kingdom that will last forever (Dan. 2:44). Then, His people will begin their reign.

The First Resurrection. At the Second Advent the first resurrection takes place. The righteous, the "blessed and holy," are raised—for "over such the second death has no power, but they shall be priests of God and Christ, and shall reign with Him a thousand years" (Rev. 20:6—see chapter 26 of this book).

The Righteous Go to Heaven. After the resurrection of the righteous dead, they and the living saints are caught up "to meet the Lord in the air" (1 Thess. 4:17). Then Christ will fulfill the promise He made just before He left this world: "I go to prepare a place for you. And if I go to prepare a place for you, I will come again and receive you to Myself; that where I am, there you may be also" (John 14:2, 3). Jesus described the place to which He will take His followers as "My Father's house," where there are "many mansions," or dwelling places (John 14:2). Here Jesus refers to the New Jerusalem, which does not come to this earth until the end of the millennium. At the Second Advent, then, when the righteous "meet the Lord in the air," their destination is heaven—not the earth that they have just left.[2] Christ does not establish His kingdom of glory on the earth at this time. He does that at the end of the millennium.

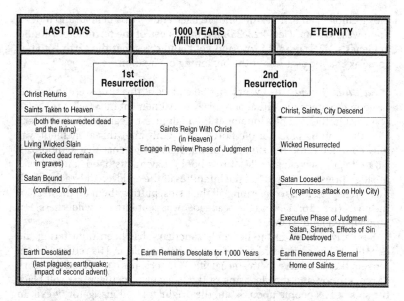

LAST DAYS	1000 YEARS (Millennium)	ETERNITY
1st Resurrection		**2nd Resurrection**
Christ Returns		
Saints Taken to Heaven		Christ, Saints, City Descend
(both the resurrected dead and the living)	Saints Reign With Christ (in Heaven) Engage in Review Phase of Judgment	
Living Wicked Slain		Wicked Resurrected
(wicked dead remain in graves)		
Satan Bound		Satan Loosed
(confined to earth)		(organizes attack on Holy City)
		Executive Phase of Judgment Satan, Sinners, Effects of Sin Are Destroyed
Earth Desolated	Earth Remains Desolate for 1,000 Years	Earth Renewed As Eternal
(last plagues; earthquake; impact of second advent)		Home of Saints

Christ's Enemies Are Slain. Christ compared His return to what happened at the Flood and in the destruction of Sodom and Gomorrah (Matt. 24:37-39; Luke 17:28-30). His comparison makes two points: first, that the destruction that came caught the wicked by surprise; and second, that what came was *destruction*—the Flood "took them all away" (Matt. 24:39). The fire and brimstone that rained down upon Sodom "destroyed them all" (Luke 17:29; see also Matt. 13:38-40). At the Second Advent Christ will descend from heaven with His armies as the rider on the white horse whose name is "King of Kings and Lord of Lords" and strike the rebellious nations of the world. After the beast and the false prophet are destroyed, "the rest" of Satan's followers will die, and there will be no survivors, for they "were killed with the sword which proceeded from the mouth of Him who sat on the horse. And all the birds were filled with their flesh" (Rev. 19:21).[3]

Describing this scene, Scripture has said, "The Lord comes out of His place to punish the inhabitants of the earth for their iniquity; the earth will also disclose her blood, and will no more cover her slain" (Isa. 26:21).

The Earth Becomes Desolate. Since the righteous ascend to be with the Lord, and the wicked are destroyed at His appearing, the earth stands for a time without human inhabitants. Scripture points to such a situation. Jeremiah said, "I beheld the earth, and indeed it was without form, and void; and the heavens, they had no light. I beheld the mountains, and indeed they trembled, and all the hills moved back and forth. I beheld, and indeed there was no man" (Jer. 4:23-25). Jeremiah's use of the terminology found in Genesis 1:2, "without form, and void," indicates that the earth is to become as chaotic as it was at the beginning of Creation.

Satan Is Bound. The events that take place at this time were foreshadowed in the scapegoat ritual of the Day of Atonement in Israel's sanctuary service. On the Day of Atonement the high priest cleansed the sanctuary with the atoning blood of the Lord's goat. Only after this atonement was fully completed did the ritual involving Azazel, the goat that symbolized Satan, begin (see chapter 24 of this book). Laying his hands on its head, the high priest confessed "all the iniquities of the children of Israel, and all their transgressions, concerning all their sins, putting them on the head of the goat" (Lev. 16:21). And the scapegoat was sent into the wilderness, "an uninhabited land" (Lev. 16:22).

Similarly, Christ, in the heavenly sanctuary, has been ministering the benefits of His completed atonement to His people; at His return He will redeem them and give them eternal life. When He has completed this work of redemption and the cleansing of the heavenly sanctuary, He will place the sins of His people upon Satan, the originator and instigator of evil. In no way can it be said that Satan atones for the sins of believers—Christ has fully done that. But Satan must bear the responsibility of all the sin he has caused those who are saved to commit. And as "a fit man" led the scapegoat into an uninhabited land, so God will banish Satan to the desolate and uninhabited earth (see chapter 24 of this book).[4]

John's vision of the millennium vividly portrayed the banishment of Satan. He saw that at the beginning of the thousand years "the dragon, that serpent of old, who is the Devil and Satan" is chained and confined to "the bottomless pit" (Rev. 20:2, 3). This symbolically conveys the temporary ending of Satan's activities of persecution and deception: "He should deceive the nations no more till the thousand years were finished" (Rev. 20:3).

The term John uses—*bottomless pit* (Greek, *abussos*)—appropriately describes the earth's condition at this time.[5] Battered by the seven plagues that immediately precede Christ's coming (see particularly Rev. 16:18-21) and covered with the bodies of the wicked, the earth is a scene of utter desolation.

Confined to this earth, Satan is "bound" by a chain of circumstances. Since the earth is devoid of any human life, Satan has no one to tempt or to persecute. He is bound in the sense that he has nothing to do.

Events During the Millennium

Christ in Heaven With the Redeemed. At His Second Advent Christ takes His followers to heaven—to the dwelling places He has prepared for them in the New Jerusalem. Like Moses and the Israelites, the redeemed, filled with gratitude, sing a song of their deliverance—"the song of Moses, the servant of God, and the song of the Lamb, saying: 'Great and marvelous are Your works, Lord God Almighty! Just and true are Your ways, O King of the saints!'" (Rev. 15:3).

The Saints Reign With Christ. During the millennium Christ will fulfill His promise to give the overcomers "power over the nations" (Rev. 2:26). Daniel saw that after the destruction of Christ's enemies "the kingdom and dominion, and the greatness of the kingdoms under the whole heaven, shall be given to the people, the saints of the Most High" (Dan. 7:27). Those whom Christ raises in the first resurrection will reign with Him for a thousand years (Rev. 20:4).

But in what sense can the saints be said to reign if they are in heaven, and all the wicked are dead? Their reign will consist of involvement in an important phase of Christ's governing.[6]

The Judgment of the Wicked. John saw that during the millennium the saints would be involved in judgment—he saw "thrones, and they sat on them, and judgment was committed to them" (Rev. 20:4). This is the time of the judgment of Satan and his angels that Scripture notes (2 Peter 2:4; Jude 6). It's the time when Paul's declaration that the saints would judge the world and even the angels (1 Cor. 6:2, 3) will come to pass.[7]

The millennial judgment does not decide who is to be saved or lost. God makes that decision before the Second Advent—all those who were not either resurrected or translated then are forever lost. The judgment in which the righteous participate serves the purpose of answering any questions the righteous may have as to why the wicked are lost. God wants those to whom He has given eternal life to have full confidence in His leadership, so He will reveal to them the operations of His mercy and justice.

Imagine you were in heaven, and you found that one of your loved ones whom you certainly expected to be there was not. Such a case might cause you to question God's justice—and that kind of doubt lies at the very base of sin. To lay to rest forever any occasion for such doubts—and to ensure that sin will never rise again—God will provide the answers to these questions during this review phase of the millennial judgment.

In this work the redeemed fulfill a crucial role in the great controversy between good and evil. "They will confirm to their eternal satisfaction how earnestly and patiently God cared for lost sinners. They will perceive how heedlessly and stubbornly sinners spurned and rejected His love. They will discover that even seemingly mild sinners secretly cherished ugly selfishness rather than accept the value system of their Lord and Saviour."[8]

Satan's Time for Reflection. During the millennium Satan will suffer intensely. Confined with his angels to a desolate earth, he cannot carry on the deceptions that had constantly occupied his time. He is forced to view the results of his rebellion against God and His law—he must contemplate the part he has played in the controversy between good and evil. He can only look to the future with fear for the dreadful penalty he must suffer because of all the evil for which he is responsible.

Events at the End of the Millennium

At the end of the thousand years "the rest of the dead"—the wicked—will be resurrected, thus releasing Satan from the inactivity that has imprisoned him (Rev. 20:5, 7). Deceiving the wicked once again, he leads them against "the camp of the saints and the beloved city [the New Jerusalem]" (Rev. 20:9), which, with Christ, have descended from heaven by this time.[9]

Christ, the Saints, and the City Descend. Christ descends to earth again, with the saints and the New Jerusalem, for two purposes. He will end the great controversy by executing the decision of the millennial judgment, and He will purify and renew the earth so that He can establish on it His eternal kingdom. Then, in the fullest sense, "the Lord shall be King over all the earth" (Zech. 14:9).

The Resurrection of Condemnation. Now the moment has arrived that will complete the fulfillment of Christ's promise that "all who are in the graves will hear His voice" (John 5:28). At His Second Advent Christ brought the righteous dead from their graves in the first resurrection—"the resurrection of life." Now the other resurrection Jesus spoke of will take place—"the resurrection of condemnation" (John 5:29). Revelation also refers to this resurrection: "The rest of the dead [those who were not raised in the first resurrection] did not live again *until the thousand years were finished*" (Rev. 20:5).

Satan's Captivity Ends. The resurrection of the wicked at the end of the thousand years releases Satan from his captivity "for a little while" (Rev. 20:3). In his last attempt to challenge God's government he "will go out to deceive the nations which are in the four corners of the earth" (Rev. 20:8). Since the wicked are raised with the same rebellious spirit they each possessed when they died, his work will not be difficult.

The Attack on the City. In his final deception Satan seeks to inspire the wicked with the hope of capturing the kingdom of God by force. Gathering the nations of the world, he leads them against the beloved city (Rev. 20:8, 9).[10] "The wicked who stubbornly refused an entrance into the City of

God through the merits of Christ's sacrificial atonement, now determine to gain admission and control by siege and battle."[11]

The fact that the wicked, as soon as God gives them life again, turn against Him and attempt to overthrow His kingdom confirms the decision He has made about their fate. In this way His name and character, which Satan has sought to besmirch, will be fully vindicated before all.[12]

The Great White Throne Judgment. John indicates that when God's enemies have surrounded the city and are ready to attack it, God sets up His great white throne. As the entire human race meets around this throne—some secure inside the city, others outside, terrified in the presence of the Judge—God will carry out the last phase of judgment. This is the time Christ spoke of when He said, "There will be weeping and gnashing of teeth, when you see Abraham and Isaac and Jacob and all the prophets in the kingdom of God, and yourselves thrust out" (Luke 13:28).

To carry out this executive phase of the judgment, God's record books will be opened. "And another book was opened, which is the Book of Life. And the dead were judged according to their works, by the things which were written in the books" (Rev. 20:12). Then God pronounces the sentence of doom.

Why does God raise these people to life only to end their existence again? During the millennium, the redeemed have had an opportunity to examine the justice of God's treatment of every intelligent being in the universe. Now the lost themselves—including Satan and his angels—will confirm the justice of God's ways.

At this great white throne judgment Paul's words, "We shall all stand before the judgment seat of Christ" (Rom. 14:10), will be fulfilled. There, all creatures—unfallen and fallen, saved and lost—bow the knee and confess that Jesus Christ is Lord (Phil. 2:10, 11; cf. Isa. 45:22, 23). Then the question of God's justice will have been forever resolved. Those who receive eternal life will have an unshakable faith in Him. Never again will sin mar the universe or wreak havoc on its inhabitants.

Satan and Sinners Destroyed. Immediately upon their sentencing, Satan, his angels, and his human followers receive their punishment. They are to die an eternal death. "Fire came down from God out of heaven and devoured" all the unsaved (Rev. 20:9). The very surface of the earth outside the city appears to melt, becoming a vast lake of fire for the "judgment and perdition of ungodly men" (2 Peter 3:7). The "day of the Lord's vengeance" (Isa. 34:8), upon which He will perform "his strange act" (Isa. 28:21, KJV) of destroying His enemies, has arrived. Said John: "And anyone not found written in the Book of Life was cast into the lake of fire" (Rev. 20:15). The devil and his associates also suffer this fate (Rev. 20:10).

The context of the entire Bible makes clear that this "second death" (Rev. 21:8) that the wicked suffer means their total destruction. What then of the concept of an eternally burning hell? Careful study shows that the Bible teaches no such hell or torment.

1. Hell. Biblically, hell is "the place and state of punishment and destruction, by eternal fire in the second death, of those who reject God and the offer of salvation in Jesus Christ."[13]

English versions of the Bible frequently use the word *hell* to translate the Hebrew word *sheol* and the Greek *hades*. These terms generally refer to the grave where the dead—both righteous and wicked—await, in a state of unconsciousness, the resurrection (see chapter 26 of this book). Because today's concept of hell differs so greatly from what these Hebrew and Greek terms imply, a number of modern versions avoid the word *hell*, simply transliterating the Hebrew word as "Sheol" and the Greek as "Hades."

In contrast, the Greek word *geenna*, which English versions of the New Testament also translate with the word *hell*, denotes a place of fiery punishment for the impenitent. In the Bible, then, "hell" does not always have the same meaning—and the failure to note this distinction has often led to great confusion.

Geenna is derived from the Hebrew *Ge Hinnom*, "Valley of Hinnom"—a gorge on the south side of Jerusalem. Here, Israel had conducted the heathen rite of burning children to Molech (2 Chron. 28:3; 33:1, 6; 2 Kings 23:10). Jeremiah predicted that because of this sin the Lord would make the valley a "Valley of Slaughter," where the corpses of the Israelites would be buried till there was no more place for them. The remaining bodies were to be "food for the birds" (Jer. 7:32, 33; 19:6; Isa. 30:33). Jeremiah's prophecy undoubtedly led Israel to view *Ge Hinnom* as a place of judgment of the wicked, a place of abhorrence, punishment, and shame.[14] Later rabbinical tradition considers it a place for burning carcasses and rubbish.

Jesus used the fires of Hinnom as a representation of hellfire (e.g., Matt. 5:22; 18:9). So the fires of Hinnom symbolized the consuming fire of the last judgment. He stated that it was an experience beyond death (Luke 12:5) and that hell would destroy both body and soul (Matt. 10:28).

What is the nature of hellfire? Do people in hell burn forever?

2. The fate of the wicked. According to the Scriptures, God promises eternal life only to the righteous. The wages of sin is *death*, not eternal life in hell (Rom. 6:23).

The Scriptures teach that the wicked will be "cut off" (Ps. 37:9, 34)—that they will perish (Ps. 37:20; 68:2). They will not live in a state of consciousness forever but will be burned up (Mal. 4:1; Matt. 13:30, 40; 2 Peter 3:10). They will be destroyed (Ps. 145:20; 2 Thess. 1:9; Heb. 2:14), consumed (Ps. 104:35).

3. Everlasting punishment. In speaking of the punishment of the wicked, the New Testament uses the terms *everlasting* and *eternal*. These terms translate the Greek word *aionios* and apply to God as well as to man. To avoid misunderstanding, one must remember that *aionios* is a relative term—its meaning is determined by the object it modifies. So when Scripture uses *aionios* ("everlasting," "eternal") of God, it does mean that He possesses infinite existence—for God is immortal. But when it uses this word of mortal human beings or perishable things, it means as long as the person lives or the thing exists. Jude 7, for example, says that Sodom and Gomorrah suffered "the vengeance of eternal fire." Yet those cities are not burning today. Peter said that that fire turned those cities into ashes, condemning them to destruction (2 Peter 2:6). The "eternal" fire burned until there was nothing left to burn, and then it went out (see also Jer. 17:27; 2 Chron. 36:19).

Similarly, when Christ assigns the wicked to "everlasting fire" (Matt. 25:41), that fire that will burn up the wicked will be "unquenchable" (Matt. 3:12). Only when there is nothing to burn will it go out.[15]

When Christ spoke of "everlasting punishment" (Matt. 25:46), He did not mean everlasting *punishing*. He meant that as the "eternal life [the righteous will enjoy] will continue throughout the ceaseless ages of eternity; and the punishment [the wicked will suffer] will also be eternal—not eternal duration of conscious suffering, however, but punishment that is complete and final. The end of those who thus suffer is the second death. This death will be eternal, from which there will not, and cannot, be any resurrection."[16]

When the Bible speaks of "eternal redemption" (Heb. 9:12) and "eternal judgment" (Heb. 6:2), it is referring to the eternal results of the redemption and the judgment—not to an endless process of redemption and judgment. In the same way, when it speaks of eternal or everlasting punishment, it is speaking of the results and not of the process of that punishment. The death the wicked die will be final and everlasting.

4. Tormented forever and ever. Scripture's use of the expression "forever and ever" (Rev. 14:11; 19:3; 20:10) has also contributed to the conclusion that the process of punishing Satan and the wicked will go on throughout eternity. But like "everlasting," the object it modifies determines the meaning of the word *forever*. When associated with God, its meaning is absolute—for God is immortal; when associated with mortal humans, its meaning is limited.

Scripture's description of God's punishment of Edom yields a good example of this usage. Isaiah says that God would turn that country into burning pitch that would "not be quenched night or day" and that its smoke was to "ascend forever. From generation to generation it shall lie waste; no one shall pass through it forever and ever" (Isa. 34:9, 10). Edom was destroyed, but it is not still burning. The "forever" lasted until its destruction was complete.

Throughout Scripture it is clear that "forever" has its limits. The Old Testament says that a slave could serve his master "forever" (Ex. 21:6), that the child Samuel was to abide in the tabernacle "forever" (1 Sam. 1:22), and that Jonah thought he would be in the belly of the great fish "forever" (Jonah 2:6). The New Testament uses this term in a similar way: Paul, for example, counseled Philemon to receive Onesimus "forever" (Philemon 15). In all these instances "forever" means "as long as the person lives."

Psalm 92:7 says that the wicked will be destroyed forever. And prophesying of the great final conflagration, Malachi said, "The day is coming, burning like an oven, and all the proud, yes, all who do wickedly will be stubble. And the day which is coming shall burn them up,' says the Lord of hosts, 'that will leave them neither root nor branch'" (Mal. 4:1).

Once the wicked—Satan, evil angels, and impenitent people—are all destroyed by fire, both root and branch, there will be no further use for death or hades (see chapter 26 of this book). These also God will eternally destroy (Rev. 20:14).

So the Bible makes very clear that the *punishment*, not the *punishing*, is everlasting—is the second death. From this punishment there is no resurrection—its effects are eternal.

Archbishop William Temple was right when he asserted, "One thing we can say with confidence: Everlasting torment is to be ruled out. If men had not imported the Greek and unbiblical notion of natural indestructibility of the individual soul, and then read the New Testament with that already in their minds, they would have drawn from it [the New Testament] a belief, not in everlasting torment, but in annihilation. It is the fire that is called aeonian [everlasting], not the life cast into it."[17]

The full penalty of God's law having been executed, the demands of justice are satisfied. Now heaven and earth proclaim the righteousness of the Lord.

5. *The principle of punishment.* Death is the ultimate penalty for sin. As a result of their sin, all who refuse the salvation God offers will die eternally. But some have sinned flagrantly, demonic in the delight they have taken in causing others to suffer. Others have lived relatively moral, peaceful lives, their guilt mainly that of rejecting the salvation provided in Christ. Is it fair that they suffer the same punishment?

Christ said, the "servant who knows his master's will and does not get ready or does not do what his master wants will be beaten with many blows. But the one who does not know and does things deserving punishment will be beaten with few blows. From everyone who has been given much, much will be demanded; and from the one who has been entrusted much, much will be asked" (Luke 12:47, 48, NIV).

Undoubtedly, those who have rebelled against God the most will suffer more than those who have not. But we should understand their ultimate suffering in terms of Christ's "second death" experience on the cross. There, He bore the sins of the world. And it was the awful separation from His Father that sin brought that caused the agony He suffered—a mental anguish beyond description. So with lost sinners. They reap what they sow not only during this life but in the final destruction. In God's presence, the guilt they feel because of the sins they have committed will cause them to suffer an indescribable agony. And the greater the guilt, the greater the agony. Satan, the instigator and promoter of sin, will suffer the most.[18]

The Cleansing of the Earth. Describing the day of the Lord, when all traces of sin will be eliminated, Peter said, "The heavens will pass away with a great noise, and the elements will melt with fervent heat; both the earth and the works that are in it will be burned up" (2 Peter 3:10).

The fire that destroys the wicked purifies the earth from the pollution of sin. Out of the ruins of this earth God will bring "a new heaven and a New Earth, for the first heaven and the first earth had passed away" (Rev. 21:1). From this cleansed, re-created earth—the eternal home of the redeemed—God will forever banish mourning, pain, and death (Rev. 21:4). Finally, the curse sin brought will have been lifted (Rev. 22:3).

In view of the coming day of the Lord, in which sin and impenitent sinners will be destroyed, Peter says to all, "What kind of people ought you to be? You ought to live holy and godly lives as you look forward to the day of God and speed its coming." Basing his hope on the promise of Christ's return, he affirmed, "We are looking forward to a new heaven and a New Earth, the home of righteousness. So then, dear friends, since you are looking forward to this, make every effort to be found spotless, blameless and at peace with him" (2 Peter 3:11, 13, 14, NIV).

References

1. See *SDA Bible Commentary*, rev. ed., vol. 7, p. 885.

2. See *Questions on Doctrine*, p. 495.

3. "When the beast and the false prophet are cast into the lake of fire (Rev. 19:20), 'the remnant' (Rev. 19:21) or 'the rest,' of their followers are slain by the sword of Christ. These are the kings, captains, mighty men, and 'all men, both free and bond' (Rev. 19:18). The same classes are mentioned under the sixth seal, as seeking to hide from the face of the Lamb (Rev. 6:14-17) when the heavens depart as a scroll and every mountain and island is moved. Obviously these scriptures depict the same earth-shattering event, the second advent of Christ.

"How many are involved in the death of 'the remnant' (Rev. 19:21)? According to Rev. 13:8 there will be only two classes on earth at the time of the advent: 'all that dwell upon the earth shall worship him [the beast], whose names are not written in the book of life.' It is evident, therefore, that when 'the remnant' are 'slain with the sword' (Rev. 19:21), there are no survivors except those who have withstood the beast, namely, those who are written in the book of life (Rev. 13:8)" (*SDA Bible Commentary*, rev. ed., vol. 7, p. 885).

4. Cf. *Questions on Doctrine*, p. 500. The scapegoat is not the Saviour of the righteous.

5. The Septuagint uses this expression to translate the Hebrew word *tehom*, "deep," in Genesis 1:2. This indicates that the condition of the earth during the millennium reflects at least in part the condition of the earth in the beginning when it was "without form, and void; and darkness was on the face of the deep." See *SDA Bible Commentary*, rev. ed., vol. 7, p. 879.

6. The fact that they reign or have dominion does not necessarily mean that there must be wicked living on the earth. In the beginning, God gave Adam and Eve a dominion to rule (Gen. 1:26). Before they sinned, they reigned over the part of the creation that God had assigned them. One need not have unruly subjects in order to reign.

7. *SDA Bible Commentary*, rev. ed., vol. 7, p. 880.

8. Maxwell, *God Cares* (Boise, ID: Pacific Press, 1985), vol. 2, p. 500.

9. Revelation's portrayal of the descent of the New Jerusalem does not necessarily indicate the exact time of the descent, for in the previous chapter we see that "beloved city" surrounded by the armies of the devil. This scenario leads to the conclusion that that New Jerusalem must have originally descended before the rejuvenation of the earth.

10. The names *Gog* and *Magog* were associated with the enemies of Israel, who were to attack God's people and Jerusalem after the exile (see Eze. 38:2, 14-16). Various of the Old Testament prophecies regarding Israel were not fulfilled. They will meet their fulfillment in spiritual Israel. So the mighty enemy confederation Ezekiel spoke of as coming against Jerusalem will find its fulfillment when God allows Satan, with his armies of the unsaved, to come against His people and His beloved city for the final battle of the great controversy.

11. *Questions on Doctrine*, p. 505.

12. Cf. *SDA Bible Commentary*, rev. ed., vol. 4, p. 708.

13. "Hell," *SDA Encyclopedia*, rev. ed., p. 579.

14. See "Hell," *SDA Dictionary*, rev. ed., p. 475.

15. Cf. Jeremiah's prophecy of the destruction of Jerusalem by unquenchable fire (Jer. 17:27), fulfilled when Nebuchadnezzar took the city (2 Chron. 36:19). The fire burned until the city was destroyed and then went out.

16. *Questions on Doctrine*, p. 539.

17. William Temple, *Christian Faith and Life* (New York: Macmillan, 1931), p. 81.

18. Cf. "Hell," *SDA Bible Dictionary*, rev. ed., p. 475.

The New Earth

28

On the New Earth, in which righteousness dwells, God will provide an eternal home for the redeemed and a perfect environment for everlasting life, love, joy, and learning in His presence. For here God Himself will dwell with His people, and suffering and death will have passed away. The great controversy will be ended, and sin will be no more. All things, animate and inanimate, will declare that God is love, and He shall reign forever. Amen. (2 Pet. 3:13; Isa. 35; 65:17-25; Matt. 5:5; Rev. 21:1-7; 22:1-5; 11:15.)

AFTER A CLOSE BRUSH WITH DEATH a boy said in relief, "My home's in heaven, but I'm not homesick." Like him, many feel that at death heaven is a preferable alternative to the "other place," but that it runs a poor second to the reality and stimulus of life here and now. If the views many have about the hereafter were true, this feeling would be justifiable. But from the descriptions and hints Scripture provides, what God is preparing for the redeemed to enjoy so outshines the life we live now that few would hesitate to give up this world for the new one.

The Nature of the New Earth

A Tangible Reality. The first two chapters of the Bible tell of God's creation of a perfect world as a home for the human beings He created. The

Bible's last two chapters also speak of God's creating a perfect world for humanity—but this time it's a re-creation, a restoration of the earth from the ravages sin brought.

Over and over the Bible declares that this eternal home of the redeemed will be a real place, a locality that real people with bodies and brains can see, hear, touch, taste, smell, measure, picture, test, and fully experience. It is on the New Earth that God will locate this real heaven.

Second Peter 3 tersely summarizes the scriptural background of this concept. Peter speaks of the antediluvian world as "the world that then existed" and was destroyed by water. The second world is "the earth which now exists"—a world that will be cleansed by fire to make way for the third world, "a New Earth in which righteousness dwells" (verses 6, 7, 13).[1] The "third" world will be as real as the first two.

Continuity and Difference. The term "New Earth" expresses both a continuity with and difference from the present earth.[2] Peter and John envision the old earth cleansed by fire from all defilement and then renovated (2 Peter 3:10-13; Rev. 21:1).[3] The New Earth is, then, first of all, *this* earth, not some alien place. Though renewed, it will remain familiar, known—home. That's good! It is, however, new in the sense that God will remove from the earth every blemish that sin has caused.

The New Jerusalem

The New Jerusalem is the capital city of this New Earth. In the Hebrew language, *Jerusalem* means "city of peace." The earthly Jerusalem has seldom lived up to its name, but the name *New Jerusalem* will accurately reflect reality.

A Connecting Link. In one sense that city links heaven and the New Earth. Primarily, the term *heaven* means "sky." Scripture uses it to refer to (1) the atmospheric heavens (Gen. 1:20), (2) the starry heavens (Gen. 1:14-17), and (3) the "third heaven," where Paradise is located (2 Cor. 12:2-4). From this connection of "heaven" with Paradise, it became synonymous with Paradise, the place of God's throne and dwelling. Hence, by extension, Scripture terms God's realm and rulership and the people who willingly accept His rule the "kingdom of heaven."

God answers beyond all expectations the petition in the Lord's Prayer, "Thy kingdom come. Thy will be done in earth, as it is in heaven" when He relocates the New Jerusalem to Planet Earth (Rev. 21:1, 2). He not only refurbishes the earth, He exalts it. Transcending its pre-Fall status, it becomes the capital of the universe.

The Physical Description. John uses romantic terms to convey the beauty of the New Jerusalem: The city is like a "bride adorned for her husband" (Rev. 21:2). His description of the physical attributes of the city portray to us its reality.

1. Its light. The first specific attribute John noticed as he viewed "the bride, the Lamb's wife" was "her light" (Rev. 21:9, 11). God's glory illuminates the city, making the light of sun and moon superfluous (Rev. 21:23, 24). No dark alleys will mar the New Jerusalem, for the walls and streets are translucent and "there shall be no night there" (Rev. 21:25). "They need no lamp, nor light of the sun, for the Lord God gives them light" (Rev. 22:5).

2. Its construction. God has used only the very finest materials in building the city. The wall is of jasper, a "most precious stone" (Rev. 21:11, 18). The foundations are adorned with twelve different gems: jasper, sapphire, chalcedony, emerald, sardonyx, sardius, chrysolite, beryl, topaz, chrysoprase, jacinth, and amethyst (Rev. 21:19, 20).

These gems are not, however, the most valuable part. God has made the city—its buildings and streets—of gold (Rev. 21:18, 21), using that precious metal as freely as people now use concrete. This gold is finer than any now known, for John calls it "pure gold, like clear glass" (Rev. 21:18).

Twelve gates, each made of a single pearl, grant access to the city. "Pearls are the product of suffering: a tiny irritant slips inside an oyster's shell, and as the little creature suffers, it transforms that irritant into a lustrous gem. The gates are of pearl. Your entrance, my entrance, God provided at infinite personal suffering as in Christ He reconciled all things to Himself."[4]

Just as meaningful today as the list of materials that went into the construction of the city is the fact that the angel who showed the city to John measured its walls. That they could be measured, that they have height and length and thickness, conveys to the modern, data-oriented mentality the city's reality.

3. Its food and water supply. From the throne of God in the center of the city flows the "river of water of life" (Rev. 22:1). And like a banyan tree with multiple trunks, the Tree of Life grows "on either side of the river." Its twelve fruits contain the vital element the human race has gone without since Adam and Eve had to leave Eden—the antidote for aging, burnout, and simple fatigue (Rev. 22:2; Gen. 3:22). Those who eat the fruit of this tree need no night in which to rest (cf. Rev. 21:25), for in the New Earth they will never feel tired.

Our Eternal Home

The Bible makes clear that ultimately the saved will inherit this earth (Matt. 5:5; Ps. 37:9, 29: 115:16). Jesus promised to prepare for His followers "dwelling places" in His Father's house (John 14:1-3). As we have noted, Scripture locates the Father's throne and heavenly headquarters in the New Jerusalem, which will descend to this earth (Rev. 21:2, 3, 5).

City Home. The New Jerusalem is the city for which Abraham looked (Heb. 11:10). Within that vast city Christ is preparing "mansions" (John 14:2), or as the original word indicates, "abiding places"—real homes.

Country Homes. But the redeemed will not be confined within the walls of the New Jerusalem. They will inherit the earth. From their city homes the redeemed will go out into the country to design and build their dream homes, to plant crops, and harvest and eat them (Isa. 65:21).

At Home With God and Christ. On the New Earth the promise Jesus made to His disciples will find eternal fulfillment: "That where I am there you may be also" (John 14:3). The purpose of the Incarnation, "God with us," will have finally reached its goal. "Behold, the tabernacle of God is with men, and He will dwell with them, and they shall be His people, and God Himself will be with them and be their God" (Rev. 21:3). Here, the saved have the privilege of living in the presence of the Father and the Son, of fellowshipping with them.

Life in the New Earth

What will life on the New Earth be like?

Reigning With God and Christ. God will involve the redeemed in the affairs of His kingdom. "The throne of God and of the Lamb will be in the city, and his servants will serve him....And they will reign for ever and ever" (Rev. 22:3-5, NIV; cf. 5:10).

We do not know the extent of their rule. However, we may safely assume that as an important part of their role in the kingdom, the redeemed will serve as Christ's ambassadors to the universe, testifying to their experience of God's love. Their greatest delight will be to glorify God.

Physical Activities in the New Earth. Life in the New Earth will challenge the most ambitious for eternity. The glimpses of the categories of the activities available to the redeemed there whet our appetites but do not even begin to delimit the possibilities.

We have already seen the scriptural promises that the redeemed will "build houses and inhabit them" (see Isa. 65:21). Building implies design, construction, furnishing, and the potential for remodeling or rebuilding. And from the word *inhabit* we may infer a whole spectrum of activities relating to daily life.

The underlying motif of the entire New Earth existence is the restoration of what God had planned for His original creation. In Eden God gave the first human beings a garden to "tend and keep" (Gen. 2:15). If, as Isaiah said, in the New Earth they shall plant vineyards, why not orchards and grain fields? If, as Revelation indicates, they shall play harps, why not trumpets and other instruments? It was, after all, God Himself who implanted in humanity the creative urge and placed them in a world of unlimited potential (Gen. 1:28-31).

Social Life in the New Earth. We will realize no small part of our joy in eternity in relationships.

1. Friends and family. Will we recognize our friends and family after we have been glorified, changed into Jesus' image? After Christ's resurrection His disciples had no trouble recognizing Him. Mary recognized His voice (John 20:11-16), Thomas His physical appearance (John 20:27, 28), and the disciples from Emmaus His mannerisms (Luke 24:30, 31, 35). In the kingdom of heaven, Abraham, Isaac, and Jacob still bear their individual names and identity (Matt. 8:11). We may safely assume that on the New Earth we will continue our relationships with those we know and love now.

In fact, it is the relationships we will enjoy there—and not just those with family and current friends—that makes heaven our hope. Its many material benefits "will seem as nothing compared with the eternal values of relationships with God the Father; with our Saviour; with the Holy Spirit; with angels; with the saints from every kindred, nation, tongue, and people; and with our families....No more shattered personalities, fractured families, or disrupted communion. Wholeness and wholesomeness will be universal. Physical and mental integration will make heaven and eternity the perfect fulfillment."[5]

"The loves and sympathies which God Himself has planted in the soul shall there find truest and sweetest exercise. The pure communion with holy beings, the harmonious social life with the blessed angels and with the faithful ones of all ages...—these help to constitute the happiness of the redeemed."[6]

2. Marriage? Some of Christ's contemporaries related the case of a woman repeatedly widowed who had had seven husbands in all. They asked Him whose wife she would be after the resurrection. It takes but little imagination to see the endless complications that would be introduced if the marriage relationships of this earth were renewed in heaven. Christ's answer reveals the divine wisdom: "In resurrection they neither marry; nor are given in marriage, but are as the angels of God in heaven" (Matt. 22:29, 30, KJV).

Then will the redeemed be deprived of the benefits now associated with marriage? In the New Earth the redeemed will not be *deprived* of any good thing! God has promised that "no good thing will He withhold from those who walk uprightly" (Ps. 84:11). If that is true in this life, how much more will it be true in the next.

The quintessence of marriage is love. The epitome of joy is in the expression of love. Scripture says, "God is love," and "in Your presence is fullness of joy; at Your right hand are pleasures forevermore" (1 John 4:8; Ps. 16:11). In the New Earth no one will lack for either love or joy or pleasure. No one there will feel lonely, empty, or unloved.

We can trust that the loving Creator who designed marriage to bring joy in this present world will have something even better in the next—something that will be as superior to marriage as His new world will be to this one.

Intellectual Life in the New Earth

Mental restoration. "The leaves of the tree [of life] were for the healing of the nations" (Rev. 22:2). The healing Revelation speaks of means more than "cure"—it means "restoration," since no one there will ever become sick (Isa. 33.24, 20). As they eat of the tree of life, the redeemed will outgrow the physical and mental dwarfing that centuries of sin have brought about—they will be restored into the image of God.

Unlimited potential. Eternity offers unlimited intellectual horizons. In the New Earth "immortal minds will contemplate with never-failing delight the wonders of creative power, the mysteries of redeeming love. There will be no cruel, deceiving foe to tempt to forgetfulness of God. Every faculty will be developed, every capacity increased. The acquirement of knowledge will not weary the mind or exhaust the energies. There the grandest enterprises may be carried forward, the loftiest aspirations reached, the highest ambitions realized; and still there will arise new heights to surmount, new wonders to admire, new truths to comprehend, fresh objects to call forth the powers of mind and soul and body."[7]

Spiritual Pursuits in the New Earth. Apart from Christ, everlasting life would be meaningless. Throughout eternity the redeemed will ever hunger and thirst for more of Jesus—for greater understanding of His life and work, for more communion with Him, for more time to witness to unfallen worlds about His matchless love, for a character that reflects His more closely. The redeemed will live for and with Christ. They will rest, fully satisfied, in Him forever!

Christ Himself lived to serve (Matt. 20:28), and He called His followers to the same life. Working with Him now is, in itself, rewarding. And the relationship it engenders offers in addition the greater blessing and privilege of working with Him on the New Earth. There, with great joy and satisfaction, "His servants shall serve Him" (Rev. 22:3).

Although the redeemed will have the opportunity of investigating God's treasure house of nature, the most popular science will be the science of the cross. With intellects restored to the acuity God intended them to possess and with the blindness of sin removed, they will be able to perceive spiritual truth in a way they can only long for here. They will make the subject of salvation—a subject that contains a depth, a height, and a breadth that surpasses all imagination—their study and song throughout eternity. Through this study the redeemed will see ever-greater vistas of the truth as it is in Jesus.

Week by week the saved will meet together for Sabbath worship: "'And from one Sabbath to another, all flesh shall come to worship before Me,' says the Lord" (Isa. 66:23).

There Shall Be No More...

Every Evil Eradicated. Some of the most cheering promises about the New Earth concern what will *not* be there. "There shall be no more death, neither sorrow, nor crying, neither shall there be any more pain: for the former things are passed away" (Rev. 21:4, KJV).

All these evils will disappear forever because God will eradicate every form of sin, the cause of all evil. Scripture mentions the Tree of Life as part of the New Earth, but not once does it include there the Tree of Knowledge of Good and Evil or any other source of temptation. In that good land the Christian will never have to battle the world, the flesh, or the devil.

The guarantee that the New Earth will remain "new" despite the influx of immigrants from the sin-polluted, old Planet Earth is the fact that God will exclude the "vile, the murderers, the sexually immoral, those who practice magic arts, the idolaters and all liars" (Rev. 21:8, NIV; 22:15). He must—for whatever sin enters, it ruins.

"Every trace of the curse is swept away....One reminder alone remains: Our Redeemer will ever bear the marks of His crucifixion. Upon His wounded head, upon His side, His hands and feet, are the only traces of the cruel work that sin has wrought. Says the prophet, beholding Christ in His glory: 'He had bright beams coming out of his hand: and there was the hiding of his power.' Habakkuk 3:4, margin...Through the eternal ages the wounds of Calvary will show forth His praise and declare His power."[8]

The Former Shall Not Be Remembered. On the New Earth, Isaiah says, "the former shall not be remembered, nor come into mind" (Isa. 65:17, KJV). Read in context, however, it becomes evident that it is the troubles of the old life that the redeemed will forget (see Isa. 65:16). They will not forget the good things God has done, the abundant grace by which He saved them, else this whole sin struggle would be in vain. The saints' own experience of Christ's saving grace is the essence of their witness throughout eternity.

In addition, the history of sin forms an important element of assurance that "affliction will not rise up a second time" (Nahum 1:9). Thoughts of the sad results sin has produced will serve as an eternal deterrent to anyone ever tempted to choose that suicidal path again. But while the events of the past serve an important purpose, heaven's atmosphere cleanses those terrible memories of their pain. The promise is that their memories will not evoke in the redeemed remorse, regret, disappointment, grief, or vexation.

Value of Belief in a New Creation

Belief in the doctrine of the New Earth brings a number of very practical benefits to the Christian.

It Gives an Incentive to Endure. Christ Himself, "for the joy that was set before Him endured the cross, despising the shame" (Heb. 12:2). Paul renewed his courage by contemplating the future glory: "Therefore we do not lose heart....For our light affliction, which is but for a moment, is working for us as far more exceeding and eternal weight of glory" (2 Cor. 4:16, 17).

It Brings the Joys and Certainty of a Reward. Christ Himself said, "Rejoice, and be exceedingly glad, for great is your reward in heaven" (Matt. 5:12). Paul reiterates, "If any man's work abide,...he shall receive a reward" (1 Cor. 3:14, KJV).

It Gives Strength Against Temptation. Moses was enabled to walk away from the "pleasures of sin" and the "treasures of Egypt" because he "looked to the reward" (Heb. 11:26).

It Provides a Foretaste of Heaven. The Christian's reward is not *only* future. Christ Himself, by the Holy Spirit, comes to the Christian and dwells in him as an "earnest" or down payment guaranteeing the blessings to come (2 Cor. 1:22; 5:5; Eph. 1:14). Christ says, "If anyone hears My voice and opens the door, I will come in" (Rev. 3:20). "And when Christ comes He always brings heaven with Him." Communing with Him "is heaven in the heart; it is glory begun; it is salvation anticipated."[9]

It Leads to Greater Effectiveness. Some view Christians as being so heavenly minded as to be of no earthly value. But it is that very belief in the hereafter that gives Christians a solid base from which to move the world. As C. S. Lewis observed: "If you read history you will find that the Christians who did most for the present world were just those who thought most of the next....It is since Christians have largely ceased to think of the other world that they have become so ineffective in this. Aim at heaven and you will get earth 'thrown in'; aim at earth and you will get neither."[10]

"The wise man will give more care to the carving of a statue in marble than to the building of a snowman."[11] The Christian, who plans on living forever, will naturally structure his life with more care (and thus impact society more constructively) than the person who thinks he's disposable—born only to be thrown away.

The "occupation with celestial themes, which the Holy Spirit fosters, has a mighty assimilating power. By it the soul is elevated and ennobled. Its field and its powers of vision are enlarged, and the relative proportions and value of things seen and unseen are more clearly appreciated."[12]

It Reveals God's Character. The world as we now see it grossly misrepresents both God's character and His original plan for this planet. Sin has so damaged earth's physical ecosystems that many can scarcely imagine a connection between this world and the paradise portrayed in Genesis 1 and 2. Now a constant struggle for survival characterizes life. Even the life of the believer, who must do battle with the world, the flesh, and the devil, does not accurately portray God's original plan. In what God has planned for the redeemed—a world untouched by Satan's influence, a world in which God's purpose rules alone—we have a truer representation of His character.

It Draws Us to God. Ultimately, the Bible describes the New Earth *in order to attract the nonreligious person to Christ.* One person, on hearing that "the earth restored to its Eden beauty, as real as 'the earth that now is,' was to be the final home of the saints," where they would be "free from all sorrow, pain, and death, and know and see each other face-to-face," strenuously objected.

"Why," said he, "that cannot be: that is just what would suit the world; that is just what the wicked would like."

Many "seem to think that religion, with...its final reward, must be something for which the world could have no desire; hence when any state of happiness is named, for which the heart of man, in his fallen condition, would truly long, they think it can be no part of true religion."[13] Nothing could be further from the truth.

God's very purpose in making known what He has prepared for those who love Him is to attract individuals from their preoccupation with this world—to help them discern the value of the next and glimpse in the beautiful things prepared by the Father's heart of love.

Forever New

In this old earth it is often said that "all good things come to an end." The best of the good news regarding the New Earth is that it will never come to an end. Then will come to pass those lyrics from the "Hallelujah Chorus": "The kingdom of this world is become the kingdom of our Lord, and of His Christ; and He shall reign forever and ever" (see Rev. 11:15; cf. Dan. 2:44; 7:27). And, Scripture says, every creature will join in the anthem: "Blessing, and honour, and glory, and power, be unto him that sitteth upon the throne, and unto the Lamb for ever and ever" (Rev. 5:13, KJV).

"The great controversy is ended. Sin and sinners are no more. The entire universe is clean. One pulse of harmony and gladness beats through the vast creation. From Him who created all flow life and light and gladness throughout the realms of illimitable space. From the minutest atom to the greatest world, all things, animate and inanimate, in their unshadowed beauty and perfect joy, declare that God is love."[14]

References

1. See James White, "The New Earth. The Dominion Lost in Adam Restored Through Christ," *Review and Herald*, Mar. 22, 1877, pp. 92, 93.

2. The English word *new* translates two Greek words used in the New Testament. *Neos* "expresses the idea of newness in respect to time, and may be translated 'new,' 'recent,' 'young.' It is the opposite of *archaios*, 'old,' 'original,' 'ancient.'" *Kainos*, on the other hand, connotes "newness as to form or quality, and may be translated 'new,' 'fresh,' 'different as to nature.' It is opposed to *palaios*, 'old,' 'aged,' 'worn out,' 'marred.' *Kainos* is the term that is used to describe the 'New Earth'" ("New Earth," *SDA Bible Dictionary*, rev. ed., p. 792).

3. *Ibid.*

4. Richard W. Coffen, "New Life, New Heaven, New Earth," *These Times*, Sept. 1969, p. 7.

5. Neal C. Wilson, "God's Family Reunited," *Adventist Review*, Oct. 8, 1981, p. 23.

6. White, *The Great Controversy*, p. 677.

7. *Ibid.*

8. *Ibid.*, p. 674.

9. "Clusters of Eschol," *Review and Herald*, Nov. 14, 1854, pp. 111, 112.

10. C. S. Lewis, *Mere Christianity* (Westwood, NJ: Barbour and Co., 1952), p. 113.

11. Fagal, *Heaven Is for You*, p. 37.

12. "Clusters of Eschol," pp. 111, 112.

13. Uriah Smith, "The Popular Hope, and Ours," *Review and Herald*, Feb. 7, 1854, p. 20.

14. White, *The Great Controversy*, p. 678.

INDEX

#

1260-year prophecy 185, 190, 192, 196, 379, 380
2300-day prophecy 358
   2300 evenings-mornings 358, 367, 368
   and cleansing of the sanctuary 358
   ended in 1844 359
   seventy weeks, or 490 years 358

A

Aaron 14, 98
Abihu 98
Abraham 17, 46, 52, 65, 108, 109, 110, 115, 136, 137, 142, 165, 420, 421
   faith of 136
Acceptance with God
   ground of our 146
Adam 44, 53, 54, 57, 58, 65, 80, 81, 83, 85, 86, 88, 92, 93, 98, 100, 101, 102, 103, 104, 105, 106, 123, 128, 165, 388, 389, 391, 395
   the "first man" 54
Adam and Eve 17, 44, 72, 81, 92, 93, 100, 101, 102, 103, 113, 115, 123, 270, 272, 273, 279, 281, 289, 291, 388, 389, 414
Adoption 145
   as God's sons and daughters 133
   into God's family 138
Advent movement 192, 380, 381
Alexander the Great 356
   kingdom divided among Cassander, Lysimachus, Seleucus, and Ptolemy. 356
Alford, Henry 355
Ananias 70
Ancient of Days 356, 360
Angels 49, 51, 53, 59, 98, 100, 106, 113, 114, 116, 120

Animal sacrifices 45, 61, 273
Antiochus Epiphanes 357
Arianism 184
Ark of the covenant 272, 273
Artaxerxes 48, 64, 359
Assurance of salvation. *See* Salvation, assurance of
Atonement 31, 61, 121, 125, 126, 127, 273, 350, 351, 352, 353, 354, 358, 365, 366, 367, 406, 409
Augustine 184
   The City of God 184
Azazel, the scapegoat 352, 353, 354, 365, 406. *See also* Christ's ministry in the heavenly sanctuary; The priestly Mediator; Azazel the scapegoat

B

Babylon 47, 376, 378, 394
   fallen 194
   fornication of, through church-state alliances 195
   Satan's city 194
   wine of, representing false teachings 195
Babylon, king of 114
Babylonian Talmud 364
Balaam 15
Baptism 211–224
   and salvation 213
   and the resurrection 223
   by dipping, sprinkling, or pouring 213
   by immersion 211
      Essenes at Qumran immersed 214
      example of Jesus immersed in Jordan River 214
      John the Baptist practiced 214
      Philip and the Ethiopian eunuch 214

Word *baptize* means "to immerse" 214
commandment of Jesus 212
examining candidates for 219
example of Jesus 212
for the dead 223
fruit of 220
in name of Father, Son, and Holy Spirit 212
in the New Testament 214
meaning of 215
  symbol of believer's death, burial, and resurrection 215
  symbol of Christ's death and resurrection 215
  symbol of consecration to Christ's service 217
  symbol of covenant relationship 216
  symbol of entrance into the church 218
  of infants and children 219
one baptism 213
qualifications for 218
  faith 218
  repentance 218
  showing fruits of repentance 218
rebaptism 221
through history 214
Baptism by immersion 189
Beast
  called "man of sin" 196
Beast, the 194, 195, 382, 404. *See also* Three angels' messages; Third angel's message
  church-state union 196
  image of 194, 195, 197
  mark of 196
Belisarius 184
Berkhof, L. 93
Berthier, General 185
Bethlehem 40, 46, 47, 88, 122
Bible 11–22
  accuracy of 17
  authority of 18
    Holy Spirit and 19
    Jesus and 18
    scope of 20

authorship of 13
claims of 18
focus of 13
inspiration of 14
  and history 16
  process 14
translation and distribution of 381
unity of 20
writers of 15
Bishop of Rome 184
Blood of Christ 347, 349, 350, 351, 352, 353, 355, 356, 365, 366, 367
Book of Life 354, 356, 361, 362
Born again. *See* New birth
Bottomless pit 406
Bruce, F. F. 56

C

Calvary 13, 23, 28, 32, 40, 49, 72, 73, 83, 88, 105, 106, 107, 117, 125, 127, 129, 130, 139, 146, 186, 193, 232, 350, 354, 360, 423
Calvin, John 146
Ceremonial law 273, 274, 278
  as schoolmaster 278
  came to an end at Christ's death 274
Character
  holiness of 144
  transformation of 140
Christ. *See* Jesus Christ
Christ's ministry in the heavenly sanctuary 347–370. *See also* Sanctuary
  the final judgment 352
    the ministry in the Most Holy Place 352
      the Lord's goat and Azazel the scapegoat 352
  the heavenly sanctuary in prophecy 354
    the anointing of the heavenly sanctuary 354
    the cleansing of the heavenly sanctuary 355
    the time of the judgment 356
      the eclipse of Christ's priestly ministry 356
      the time of restoration, cleansing,

and judgment 358
The priestly Mediator 350
  Azazel the scapegoat 353
  Mediator and atonement 350
  the different phases of the judg-
    ment 354
  the ministry in the holy place 351
  Sin offering 351
the sanctuary in heaven 348
  altar of incense 349
  seven lampstands 349
the significance within the great
    controversy 360
  a time to be ready 362
  the judgment and salvation 361
  the vindication of God's character
    360
  the vindication of God's people
    360
the substitutionary Sacrifice 349
  Christ's substitutionary death 350
  God's judgment on sin 350
  God provides the atoning sacrifice
    350
two divisions: holy place ministry
    and Most Holy Place ministry
    352
Christianity 24, 32
Christian behavior 311–328
  and its relation to salvation 312
  Christian dress 319
    adornment and jewelry 320
    principles of 319
  healthful living 313
    avoidance of alcoholic or caffein-
      ated beverages 314
    avoidance of harmful drugs 315
    avoidance of tobacco 315
    a nutritious diet 317
      clean and unclean flesh foods
      318
      regularity, simplicity, and balance
      319
      the original diet 318
  is our grateful response to God's sav-
    ing us 312
  our bodies as temples of Holy Spirit
    313

  principles of Christian standards
    321
  recreation and entertainment 316
    choice of movies, TV, radio, and
      videos 316
    reading and music 317
    some unacceptable activities 317
  requirements and guidelines 322
Christian growth. See Growing in
    Christ
Church, the 163–180
  as "Jerusalem above" 168
  as army, militant and triumphant
    170
  as pillar and foundation of truth 169
  a temple 167
  Bible the guiding authority of 175
  Biblical meaning of 165
  body of Christ 163, 167.
  bride of Christ 163, 168
  built on the Rock 165
  Christ the Head of 175
  deacons and deaconesses 177
  defined 163
  discipline 178
    dealing with divisive persons 179
    disfellowshipping 178
    private offenses 178
    public offenses 178
    restoration of offenders 179
  elders 176
    attitude toward 177
    qualifications of 176
    responsibility and authority of 177
  family of God 163, 169
  government of 174
    principles of 175
  great apostasy of 182
    rise of "man of sin" 183
  invisible 171
  is true Israel 166
  membership in 169, 172
    qualifications for 172
  nature of 165
  officers of 176
  ordinances of 174
  organization of 172
    functions of 173

persecution of 183
  for 1260 years 184
persecution of, in the wilderness 182
roots of 165
the suffering church 184
visible 171
Church and state 173, 382
  united in unholy alliance 184
Church discipline. *See* Church, the;
  Discipline
Church of Rome
  as spiritual Babylon 194
Church ordinances 221
  baptism and Lord's Supper 221
  foot washing 226
  Lord's Supper 226
  sacraments and 221
Communion service 225. *See also* Lord's Supper
  includes foot washing and Lord's
  Supper 226
Confession 134, 135, 137
Constantine. emperor
  and Sunday law 293
Conversion 135, 268
Council of Laodicea
  enjoined honoring of Sunday 293
Council of Orleans
  and Sunday legislation 293
Council of Trent 294
Counter-Reformation, Catholic 185
Covenant 36, 38, 107, 108, 109, 111,
  273, 278, 285. *See also* Grace;
  Covenant of
  Abrahamic covenant 109
  circumcision as symbol of covenant
    relationship 216
  covenant relationship 45
  first covenant 109
  given at the Fall 107
  God's law the basis for 268
  new 109, 349
  old 110, 111, 348
  renewed through Abraham 108
  Sinaitic covenant 109, 110
Creation 36, 39, 40, 69, 71, 79–90, 93,
  94, 97, 99, 106, 107, 108, 194,
  281, 282, 284, 285, 286, 287,

  288, 291, 296, 298, 300, 388
  6,000 years since 81, 82, 87
  and preexisting matter 80
  and salvation 87
  completed in six days 79, 87
  days of 80, 81
    literal, 24-hour days 81
  God's creative Word in 80
  God rested on seventh day 79
  purpose of 83
    to populate the world 84
    to reveal God's glory 83
  significance of 84
    antidote to idolatry 84
    basis for true fellowship 85
    basis for true self-worth 85
    basis of personal stewardship 85
    emphasized the sacredness of life
      86
    foundation of true worship 84
    marriage as a divine institution 85
    memorial of Creation 84
    provided remedy for pessimism,
      loneliness, and meaningless-
      ness 86
    revealed holiness of God's Law 86
    showed the dignity of manual labor
      85
    showed worth of the physical uni-
      verse 85
  the Bible account of 81

D

Daniel 47, 48, 98, 355, 356, 357, 358,
  359, 360, 365, 366, 367, 368
Dark day of May 19, 1780 379
Darwin, Charles 194
  Origin of Species 194
David 37, 76, 99, 103, 104, 106, 107,
  122, 135, 144, 146, 164, 390,
  391, 398
  throne of 63
Day of Atonement 347, 352, 353, 354,
  355, 360, 362, 365, 366, 406
Death. *See* Death and resurrection
Death and resurrection 387–402
  immortality and death 388. *See
    also* Immortality

conditional immortality 388
death: the wages of sin 389
hope for humanity 389
immortality 388
the receiving of immortality 390
resurrection 395
Christ's resurrection 395. *See
also* Jesus Christ; Resurrection
of
a bodily resurrection 396
its impact 396
its importance 395
the two resurrections 396
the resurrection of condemnation 397
the resurrection of life 397
the nature of death 390
death is a sleep 390
harmony throughout the Scriptures 392
spiritualism 392
manifestations of spiritualism
394
the basis of spiritualism 392
the final delusion 394
warning against spiritualism 393
the abode of the dead 391
the person returns to dust 391
the spirit returns to God 392
Decalogue. *See* Law of God
Destruction of the wicked 405, 411
De Ancharano, Petrus 294
De Fosso, Gaspare 294
Divine nature, the
partaking of 140
Dragon 382, 404, 406
Dwight, Timothy 379

E

Eck, John 294
Edom 412
Edwards, Jonathon 286
Egypt 36, 45
Elihu 71
Elijah 19, 64, 118, 398, 399
Emmaus 421
Enoch 373
Esau 28

Eternal life 389
gift of 139
Europe
divided nations of 376
Eve 92, 93, 98, 100, 101, 102, 103, 105,
113, 115, 117
Evolution 105, 106
theistic 105
Evolution, theory of 194
Exodus, the 36, 37
Experience of salvation, the 133–148
and the future 144
and the past 134
and the present 139
Extreme unction, Catholic practice of
188
Ezekiel 13, 16, 18

F

Faith
and works 136, 137
based on evidence 25
in Christ's sacrifice 45
salvation by 144
that works 137
False prophet 382, 404
Farrar, Frederic W. 189
Fellowship 163, 169, 173
Flood, the 17, 103, 373, 375, 376, 385,
405
Foot washing 225
an ordinance of the Church 226
example of Jesus in washing disciples' feet 226
Jesus washed disciples' feet 202
meaning of the ordinance 227
a fellowship of forgiveness 228
a fellowship with Christ and believers 228
a type of higher cleansing 227
memorial of Christ's condescension 227
spiritual preparation for 226
Forgiveness 37, 38, 45, 121, 125, 127,
134, 135, 137, 152, 273, 349, 351
French Revolution 192

G

Gabriel 62, 358, 359
Garden of Eden 81, 87
Garden of Gethsemane 202
Gehenna, or Geenna 410
General revelation 12
Gentiles 166, 180
Gesenius 359, 368
Gethsemane, 151
Gibbons, Cardinal James 291
Gift of prophecy, the 247–262
　an identifying mark of remnant
　　church 247
　functions of, in New Testament 249
　　assisted in founding of the Church
　　　249
　　confirmed faith in times of contro-
　　　versy 249
　　edified the Church 249
　　initiated the Church's mission
　　　outreach 249
　　united and protected Church 249
　　warned of future difficulties 249
　in Bible times 248
　in the last days 250
　　a continuation of spiritual gifts 250
　　help in the final crisis 251
　　prophetic gift in the remnant
　　　church 251
　　prophetic gift just before the Sec-
　　　ond Advent 250
　in the Seventh-day Adventist Church
　　255
　　as manifested in ministry of El-
　　　len G. White 247, 255. See
　　　also White, Ellen G.
　　application of prophetic tests to
　　　her ministry 255
　　influence of her ministry 256
　　relation of her writings to the
　　　Bible 258
　　she foresaw Protestant-Catholic
　　　cooperation 256
　　she foresaw rise of modern spiri-
　　　tualism 256
　　she never assumed title of proph-
　　　etess 255
　one of the spiritual gifts 247

postbiblical prophets and the Bible
　　253
　　prophets whose testimonies were
　　　not included in Bible 253
　testing the prophetic gift 254
　　does the message agree with Bible?
　　　254
　　do the predictions come true? 254
　　is Christ's incarnation recognized?
　　　254
　　what fruit does the prophet bear?
　　　254
Glorification 144, 145
God
　activities of 26
　attributes of 27
　　omnipotent 27
　　omnipresent 27
　　omniscient 27
　　self-existent 27
　　unchangeable 27
　cares for those He made 82
　character of 12, 43, 123, 185, 425
　　blends mercy and justice 123
　　vindication of 360
　creative work of, continues today 86
　existence of 12, 23, 25
　faithfulness of 38
　Father, Son and Holy Spirit, 23
　goodness of 38
　grace of 44
　knowledge of 23, 24
　love of 40, 43, 44
　　seen in Creation 83
　mercy of 38
　names of 26
　self-revelation of 12, 23, 24, 25
　　method and content 16
　sovereignty of 27
　takes initiative to save us 123, 124
　throne of 122
　truth about 12
　unconditional love of 38
　vengeance of 38
　wrath of against sin 123
Godhead, the 23–34, 65
　all members involved in Creation 83
　fullness of 49

God the Father 35–42
  Ancient of Days, the 35, 98
  views of 35
    in the Old Testament 36
God the Holy Spirit 69–78
  creative and re-creative work of 71
  fulfills role of executor 71
God the Son 43–68
  oneness of 29, 30
  plurality Within 29
  relationship Within 29
Gog and Magog 414
Gospel, the 273
Gospel commission 238
Grace
  cheap grace 155
  covenant of 107, 108, 109, 110
  free, but costly 155
  God's saving 122
Grant, Robert M. 189
Great Controversy, the 44, 113–120,
    356, 360, 426
  as revealed in, Book of Job 116
  central issue of 116
    Christ and obedience to the Law
      116
    God's Law and government 116
  Earth, the theater of the universe
    115
  impact on human race 115
  moved from Heaven to Earth 115
  origin of 114
    angelic rebellion 114
    rebellion of Lucifer 114
    war in Heaven 114
  over the truth as it is in Jesus 117
  showdown at Calvary 117
  significance of doctrine of 119
    displays Christ's present loving
      concern for world 120
    explains mystery of suffering 119
    produces a constant state of watch-
      fulness 119
    reveals cosmic significance of the
      Cross 120
Growing in Christ 149–162
  Christian life begins with death 154
  death to self 153
  hallmarks of 155
    a life of fruit bearing 159
    a life of love and unity 156
    a life of prayer 158
    a life of Spirit 155
    a life of spiritual warfare 160
    a life of study 158
    a life of worship, witness, and hope
      161
  living the new life 154

H

Hades 391, 410
Hallelujah Chorus 426
Heaven 122, 424
Hell 403, 410
  do wicked burn forever in? 411
Herod the Great 348
Holy Ghost. *See* Holy Spirit
Holy See 184
Holy Spirit 11, 13, 14, 15, 16, 18, 19,
    20, 23, 24, 25, 29, 30, 31, 35, 38,
    39, 43, 47, 48, 49, 50, 52, 56, 63,
    92, 97, 109, 202, 203, 206, 207,
    210, 373, 381, 384, 421, 424, 425
  as Paraclete: Comforter, Advocate,
    Helper 74
  baptism of 72, 76, 238
  bestows spiritual gifts 75
  brings presence of Christ 74
  brings truth of Christ 74
  guides operation of Church 75
  infilling of. *See* Baptism of
  is a person, not a force 70
  is truly God 70
  mission of 73
    to bring conviction of sin 73
    to lead to repentance 74
    to urge acceptance of Christ's righ-
      teousness 73
    to warn of judgment 73
  outpouring of 238, 251
  Spirit-filled life 139, 142
  true Vicar of Christ on earth 75
  walking in the Spirit 210
Holy water, Catholic use of 188
Howard, J. K. 214
Huss 188

I

Immortality 99, 140, 146, 189, 387, 388, 389
  conditional 99, 388, 397
  erroneous doctrine of natural immortality 393
  God alone has 388
  man is mortal 388
Imparted righteousness. *See* Righteousness; Imparted
Imputed righteousness. *See* Righteousness; Imputed
Incarnation 44
Indulgences 187
Infallibility, doctrine of papal 186, 198
Inquisition, the 188
Isaac 137, 421

J

Jacob 28, 29, 59, 62, 421
  dream of the ladder 59
Jahaziel 248
Jairus, daughter of 390
James 136, 137, 143
Jehoshaphat 247, 248, 259
Jeremiah 18, 19, 118
Jerome 188
Jerusalem 47, 48, 63, 64
  God's city 194
Jesus Christ
  and temptation 54
  ascension of 63, 174, 238, 286, 355, 356, 372
  as our Ransom 127, 128
  baptism of 30
  betrayal of 47, 222
  Bridegroom 384
  Creator 49, 118
    active agent in Creation 83
  Cross of 13, 31, 32, 43, 44, 63, 83, 106, 108, 126, 135, 149, 150, 151, 152, 153, 166, 182, 208, 232, 274
    Christ's promise to thief on the cross 400
  Crucifixion of 47, 69, 72, 88, 182, 222, 423
  equal with the Father 49
  experienced temptation as a human being 43
  first Advent of 29
  forty-day fast in the wilderness 117
  High priestly ministry of 186
  His ministry of reconciliation 124
  Immanuel 47, 51
  incarnation of 30, 44, 49, 59, 69, 75, 106, 140, 254
    is a mystery 49
  Lamb of God 49, 61, 122, 196, 278, 348, 389
  life, death, and resurrection of 121–132
  Mediator 30, 31, 61, 350, 353, 358, 369
  meditating on His life 140
  Messiah 13, 43, 45, 46, 47, 48, 49, 57, 60, 61, 62, 63, 164, 166, 182, 191, 216, 274
  ministry of 47
  miracles of 43
    never performed for Himself 52
  offices of 60
    King 62
      kingdom of glory 64
      kingdom of grace 62, 63, 64
    Priest 60
      earthly priesthood 61
      heavenly priesthood 61
    Prophet 60
  omnipresent through Holy Spirit 75
  Only-begotten Son 65
  our Example 57, 58, 133
  our High Priest 57, 61, 125, 186, 349, 351, 355, 356, 358, 362, 363, 369
  our Intercessor 356
  our Mediator 188
  our Substitute 133, 137
  our vicarious sin-bearer 126
  parables of 41
    lost coin 41
    lost sheep 41
    prodigal son 41
    rich man and Lazarus 222, 399
    talents 238
    ten virgins 384

wedding garment 129, 361
wheat and tares 170
Paschal Lamb 229
Promised One 45
Redeemer 13, 45, 46, 264, 286, 349, 423
resurrection of 43, 49, 69, 71, 72, 121, 129, 130, 166, 391, 395
reveals the Father 39
righteousness of 126, 129, 137, 143, 146, 361
role of His blood 127
saving life and death of 128, 129
saving ministry of 130
   brings justification 131
   brings reconciliation throughout universe 130
   motivates for mission 131
   provides a new relationship with God 131
   shows futility of salvation by works 131
   vindicates God's Law 130
Saviour 45, 49
   predictions concerning 45
Second Adam 53, 54, 57, 58, 88, 106, 128
Son of David 46
Son of Man 53
Suffering Servant 61
supernatural birth of 46
temptations in the wilderness 117
the Center of Bible doctrines 118
the propitiation for sin 126, 132
the Representative of humanity 128
the Rock 164
transfiguration of 142
trial of 63
triumphal entry 63
two Natures of 49
   truly and fully God 50
      divine attributes 50
      divine names 51
      divine nature cannot die 57
      divine powers and prerogatives 50
   truly and fully man 52

'the likeness of sinful flesh" 53
   divinity clothed with humanity 54
   evidences of Christ's humanity 52
   no evil propensities or inclinations 57, 66, 67
   one with human race except in sin 56
   sinlessness of His humanity 54, 56, 66
   union of 58
Word of God 51, 65, 80
Jewish nation 48, 166
Job 142
Joel 251
John 12, 14, 15, 16, 17, 19, 70, 71, 72, 73, 74, 75, 76, 122, 124, 126, 127, 131, 182, 183, 188, 190, 191, 193, 195, 198
John the Baptist 72, 380
Jonah 16, 17, 18
Josephus 363
Joshua 137
Judah 247, 248
Judas 47, 227, 234
Judgment, Day of 35
Judgment, the 133, 193, 263, 352, 361
   executive judgment 352, 354
   investigative judgment 352, 354, 358, 360, 361, 362
      also called pre-Advent or premillennial judgment 352
   millennial judgment 352, 354
Justification 133, 134, 135, 136, 137, 138, 139, 144, 145, 188, 197, 352
   by faith 137
   daily 144
   defined 136
   experience of 137
Justinian 184, 198
   Code of 184

K

Kingdom of Glory 64, 376, 404
   of grace 62, 63, 219
Koinonia (fellowship) 169

L

Ladd, G. E. 124
Latter rain, the 251
Law and grace. *See* Law of God; and
    God's grace
Law of God 263–280, 352, 393
    and God's grace 275
    and the Cross of Christ 274
    a reflection of God's character 270
    blessings of obeying 277
    Christ and 276
        He did not destroy, but fulfilled the
            law 276
    Christ has removed curse of 275
    law and the gospel 272
        after the Cross 274
        at Sinai 273
        before Sinai 272
    nature of 265
        a delightful law 267
        a law of principles 266
        a moral law 265
        a positive law 265
        a simple law 266
        a spiritual law 265
        a unique law 267
        reflection of Lawgiver's character
            265
    never abolished 275
    perpetuity of 270
        law at Sinai 270
        law before Christ's return 271
            God's judgments and the law 272
            saints defend the law 271
            the law under attack 271
        law before Sinai 270
    purpose of 267
        basis of God's covenant 268
        is an agent in conversion 268
        points out sin 268
        provides true freedom 269
        restrains evil and brings blessings
            269
        reveals God's will for humanity
            267
    two divisions of 266
Lazarus 390, 399
Levitical priesthood 351

Lewis, C. S. 425
Lincoln, A. T. 291
Lisbon earthquake of 1755 378
Little-horn power 293, 295, 357, 360
    Bible identifies as papacy 294
    sought to change times and laws
        294
Lord's Supper 163, 186, 225–236
    and the question of fermented wine
        235
    celebration of 229
    frequency of observing 235
    meaning of 229
        anticipation of the Second Advent
            232
        commemoration of deliverance
            from sin 225
        corporate communion with Christ
            231
        symbolism of bread and fruit of the
            vine 229
    qualifications for participating in
        233
        for believing Christians 233
    relationship to baptism 23
    self-examination prior to 234
Love
    defined in 1 Corinthians 13 30
    God's, displayed in Creation 83
    Jesus is 202
    ours in response to God's 124
Lucifer 100, 114, 120
Luther, Martin 141, 188
    his ninety-five theses 141

M

Man
    created for relationships 98
    creation of 92
        a little lower than the angels 98
        dust plus breath = living soul 94,
            388, 391
        from dust of the ground 92
        God breathed into Adam the
            breath of life 93
        in God's image 91, 93, 97, 98, 99
    doctrine of 109
    fall of 100, 105, 106, 107, 115, 355

free will of 28, 98, 388
Man, nature of 91–112
  biblical meaning of soul 94
  biblical meaning of spirit 95
  Greek word pneuma 96
  Greek word psuche 95
  Hebrew word nephesh 95
  Hebrew word ruach 95, 96
  unity of 94, 96, 97, 98
Mark of the Beast. See Beast, the;
    Mark of
Marriage and the family 329–346
  marriage
    as God designed it from the begin-
        ning 330
      becoming one flesh 332
      cleaving 332
      covenanting 332
      leaving 332
      male and female, in the image of
          God 330
    deviations from God's ideal 335
      divorce 337
      fornication and adultery 336
      homosexuality 338
      impurity of thought 336
      incest 337
      polygamy 335
    effects of the Fall on 334
    institution of 84, 85
    marital intimacy 333
    marital love 334
    marriage in the New Earth 421
  the family 338
    children 341
      a priority 341
      commitment 341
      constancy 341
      gender identity 342
      learning obedience 342
      learning values 343
      love 341
      socialization and language devel-
          opment 342
    parents 339
      the father 339
      the mother 340
    the extended family 343

the turning of hearts 343
Mary 30, 43, 47, 50, 52, 62, 71, 75, 96,
    187, 188, 421
Melchizedek 304, 305
Michelangelo 92
Millennium and the end of sin, the 28,
    64, 354, 396, 403–416
  events at the beginning of the mil-
      lennium 404
    Christ's enemies are slain 405
    Satan is bound 406
    the earth becomes desolate 405
    the first resurrection 404
    the righteous go to heaven 404
    the Second Advent 404
  events at the end of the millennium
      408
    Christ, the saints, and the City
        descend 408
    everlasting punishment 411
    hell 410
    Satan's captivity ends 408
    the attack on the City 408
    the cleansing of the earth 413
    the fate of the wicked 410
    the great white throne judgment
        409
    the principle of punishment 412
    the resurrection of condemnation
        408
    tormented forever and ever 411
  events during the millennium 406
    Christ in heaven with the re-
        deemed 406
    Satan's time for reflection 408
    the judgment of the wicked 407
    the saints reign with Christ 407
Mishnah 368
Moses 14, 17, 19, 21, 44, 45, 60, 64,
    98, 123, 164, 264, 267, 268, 270,
    272, 273, 278, 348, 349, 398,
    399, 407
Most Holy Place 351, 352, 363, 366
Mount Gilboa 387
Mount of Transfiguration 64, 399
Mount Sinai 264, 271, 273, 349
Mount Zion 190, 196

N

Nadab 98
Napoleon 185
Nazareth 212
Nebuchadnezzar 348, 376, 415
New birth 62, 105, 133, 134, 155
New Earth, the 417–428
  forever new 426
  life in the New Earth 420
    intellectual life in the New Earth 422
      mental restoration 422
      spiritual pursuits in the New Earth 422
      unlimited potential 422
    physical activities in the New Earth 420
    reigning with God and Christ 420
    social life in the New Earth 421
      friends and family 421
      marriage in 421
  our eternal home 419
    at home with God and Christ 420
    city home 420
    country homes 420
  there shall be no more ... 423
    every evil eradicated 423
    the former shall not be remembered 424
  the nature of the New Earth 417
    a tangible reality 417
    continuity and difference 418
  the New Jerusalem 418
    a connecting link 418
    the physical description 418
      its construction 419
      its food and water supply 419
      its light 419
  value of belief in a new creation 424
    it brings the joys and certainty of a reward 424
    it draws us to God 425
    it gives an incentive to endure 424
    it gives strength against temptation 424
    it leads to greater effectiveness 425
    it provides a foretaste of Heaven 424

    it reveals God's character 425
New Jerusalem 64. *See also* New Earth, the; The New Jerusalem
New Testament 12, 13, 14, 18, 21, 36, 39, 41, 45, 46, 94, 95, 96, 104, 110, 126, 127, 132, 142, 147
Ninevah 394
Noah 37, 94, 115, 142, 165, 213, 375, 385

O

O'Brien, John A. 295
Obedience 28, 31, 263, 266, 267, 269, 270, 273, 275, 276, 277
  of faith 263
Offerings 305
Onesimus 412
Ordinances. *See* Church ordinances
Origin of sin. *See* Sin; Origin of
Orr, James 105
Ostrogoths 184

P

Palestine 166
Papacy 184, 382
  claims of 199
  deadly wound of 198, 382
Papal system 189
  reformers identified as man of sin, mystery of iniquity, and little horn 189
Paradise 400, 418
Pardon from sin 137, 138
Passover 49, 225, 226, 229, 230, 234, 235, 348
Penance, Catholic doctrine of 187, 188
Pentecost 71, 72, 75, 134, 251
  our own internal 134
Perfection 143, 145
  biblical 142
  in Christ 143
  of Christ 142
Pharaoh 14, 28, 394
Philemon 412
Pilate 63
Plan of redemption 62
Plato 393

Pneuma 392
Pope 184
Pope, Alexander 106
Prayer 141, 144

Prayers for the dead, Catholic doctrine of 188
Predestination 27, 33
and human freedom (free will) 27
God's foreknowledge and 28, 29
our, to adoption by Christ 107
Priesthood of all believers 172
Probation 369
Promised Land 164
Prophecy, gift of 191
Prophecy of Daniel 2 376
great image of 357
Prophecy of Daniel 7
four beasts of 357
ten horns of the fourth beast 357
Prophecy of Daniel 8 356
goat representing Greece 356
Alexander the Great 356
his kingdom divided into four kingdoms 356
ram representing Medo-Persia 356
Prophecy of Daniel 9. *See* 2300-day prophecy
Protestantism 256, 261
departure of, from Reformation truths 195
Protestant Reformation. *See* Reformation, the
Purgatory, Catholic doctrine of 185, 187, 188
Purification from sin 139

R

Rachel 398
Rafael 141
his painting of the Transfiguration 141
Reconciliation 350, 351, 352, 353
Redemption 134, 138, 143, 145, 273, 286, 288, 374, 406
Reformation, the 141, 185, 256, 358, 360
birth of 185
doctrinal issues of 185
eclipse of Christ's high-priestly mediatorial ministry 186
head of the church on earth is the vicar of Christ 185
infallibility of the church and its head 186
meritorious nature of good works 186
penance and indulgences 187
ultimate authority resides in the church 187
doctrine of Bible and Bible only 189
stagnated 189
uncovered long-forgotten truths 188
Religious liberty 189, 382
Remnant, the 190
characteristics of 190
defined 190
emergence in last days 191
have faith of Jesus 191
have testimony of Jesus 191
keep commandments of God 191
mission of 192
origin of 199
proclaim a message to prepare world for Christ's return 197
Remnant and its mission, the 181–200
Repentance 133, 134, 138, 369
defined 135
motivation for 135
qualification for baptism 218
the gift of God 135
Restoration
to the image of God 140
Resurrection
first 404
Return of Jesus Christ. *See* Second Advent of Jesus Christ
Rich man and Lazarus 399
Righteousness
imparted 138
our fitness for heaven 138
imputed 137
our title to heaven 138
robe of 143
Righteousness by faith 193, 196, 279, 289

Roman Catholic Church 185
  celibacy of the priesthood 188
  the mass 186, 188
    substituted for Lord's Supper 186

Rome
  Bible prophecies concerning 357
  pagan and papal 357
Rosary, Catholic use of 188
Ruach 392

S

Sabbath 79, 81, 82, 84, 281–300
  as seal of God's law 284
  attempts to change day of worship
      291
    Catholic catechism and change of
        the Sabbath to Sunday 294
    nowhere does Bible authorize 291
    rise of Sunday observance 292
    the change prophesied 293
  ceremonial Sabbaths 285
  change of 199
  fourth of Ten Commandments 281
  God sanctified at Creation 84
  meaning of
    perpetual memorial of Creation
        287
    sign of loyalty 289
    sign of righteousness by faith 289
    sign of sanctification 281, 288
    symbol of redemption 288
    symbol of resting in Christ 290
    time of fellowship 289
  memorial of Creation 84, 281
  observance of 296. *See also* Sabbath-
      keeping
    from sunset Friday to sunset Satur-
        day 296
  restoration of true 295
  seventh-day 79, 81, 84, 189
  throughout the Bible 282
    at Creation 282
      God blessed the Sabbath 282
      God rested on the Sabbath 282
      God sanctified the Sabbath 283
    at Sinai 283
    Sabbath and the covenant 285

Sabbath and the Law 284
Sabbath and the manna 283
the annual Sabbaths 285
Sabbath and Christ 285
  Christ's custom was to worship
      on Sabbath 286
  Christ is Lord of the Sabbath 286
  Christ rested on Sabbath, after
      Creation and after His death
      286
Sabbath and the apostles 286
to be observed throughout eternity
    287
Sabbathkeeping 290, 296, 300
  is not legalism 298
Sabbath rest 291
Sacrificial offerings 45
Saints, Cathlic doctrine of veneration
    of 188
Salvation 38, 43, 44, 47, 59, 65, 70, 71,
    122, 123, 124, 127, 128, 129,
    130, 131, 133, 145, 191, 312,
    348, 349, 351, 358, 361, 362
  assurance of 133, 138
  dramatized in prophecy 45
  plan of 141, 150, 374
Samaritan woman 202
Samuel 16, 387, 388, 394, 398
Sanctification 133, 134, 137, 139, 143,
    144, 352
  a lifelong process 145
  defined 138
  holy living 139
  is progressive 141
  living a sanctified life 139, 143
  Sabbath as sign of 288
  three phases of 138
Sanctuary
  cleansing of 352, 353, 355, 356
  earthly 44, 45, 49, 127, 186, 273
    altar of burnt offering 61, 351
    altar of incense 351, 352
    a gospel-parable 349
    daily and yearly ministries of 351
    Most Holy Place 351
    patterned after the heavenly sanc-
        tuary 349
    sacrificial system 49, 61, 127, 273,
        274

began in Eden 279
type and antitype in 274
services of 45, 127, 273
heavenly 43, 64, 172, 272, 374, 406.
    See also Christ's ministry in the
    heavenly sanctuary
    Most Holy Place 355
    throne room of 356
Sanhedrin 63, 396
Satan 44, 45, 58, 59, 61, 100, 101, 102,
        105, 107, 113, 114, 115, 116,
        117, 118, 119, 120, 122, 124,
        137, 142, 146, 182–200, 353,
        354, 355, 360, 361, 365, 373,
        382, 389, 392, 393, 394, 395,
        403, 404, 405, 406, 407, 408,
        409, 411, 412, 413, 414
    final delusions of
        signs and miracles 395
    first lie of 392
    the accuser 137
    the dragon 181
Saul 387, 388, 394
Schaff, Philip 56, 130
Scriptures. *See* Bible
Scroll with seven seals 122
Seal of God
    contains three elements 284
    Sabbath as 284
Second Advent of Jesus Christ 28, 41,
        64, 139, 140, 144, 170, 232, 250,
        251, 253, 271, 354, 355, 357,
        369, 373, 374, 376, 377, 378,
        380, 385, 404
    signs of its nearness 73, 192, 378
Second coming of Christ, the 371–
        386. *See also* Second Advent of
        Jesus Christ
    be ready at all times 384
    biblical description of 372
    the "Blessed Hope" 371
    the certainty of Christ's return 373
        Christ's heavenly ministry 374
        the guarantee the first advent pro-
            vides 373
        the testimony of Scripture 373
    the manner of Christ's return 374
        an audible return 375

a cataclysmic event 376
a glorious return 375
a literal and personal return 374
a sudden, unexpected return 375
a visible return 374
the Second Advent and the human
        race 376
    the death of the unbelievers 377
    the gathering of the elect 377
        the resurrection of the dead in
            Christ 377
        the translation of the living be-
            lievers 377
the signs of Christ's soon return 378
    increase of wickedness 382
        sexual revolution 383
        surge in world crime 383
    Lisbon earthquake, Dark day, Fall-
        ing of the stars 378
    signs in the natural world 378
        the witness of the earth 378
        the witness of the stars 379
        the witness of the sun and moon
            378
    signs in the religious world 380
        a great religious awakening 380
        a resurgence of the papacy 382
        decline of religious freedom 382
        preaching of the gospel 381
        religious decline 381
    wars and calamities 383
        famines 384
        natural disasters 383
        wars 383
Second death, the 413
Septuagint 363, 365, 367
Serpent 44, 53, 105
    bronze 44
    Satan in form of 101, 102, 115
    seed of 44
    symbol of Satan 44
    tempted Eve 82
Seth 165
Seventh-day Adventist Church 381
    statistics concerning 381
Seventy-week prophecy. *See* 2300-day
    prophecy
Seventy elders, the 98

Seventy weeks 47, 48
  seventieth week 48
  sixty-nine weeks 48
Seven last plagues 196, 272, 369, 406
Shem 165
Sheol 391, 398
Shepherd of Hermas 133, 140
Sin 350
  and guilt 103
  character of 102
  consequences of man's 101
    blaming 101
    fear 101
    shame 101
  death the wages of 387, 389
  definition of 102
  deliverance from, through Christ 44
  effects of on humanity 103
  eradication of sinful behavior 104
  heart as control center of 103
  inherited or acquired? 104
  involves thoughts, as well as actions 102
  nature of 152
  origin of 100
    is God author of sin? 100
  penalty of 45, 135
  separates us from God 30, 72
  the end of 403
  transgression of God's Law 45
Sinai 36, 123, 264, 269, 270, 271, 272, 273, 276, 283, 284, 285, 291
Sin offering 351, 355, 366
Smith, Wilbur M. 130
Sodom and Gomorrah 405, 411
Sola Scriptura 294
Solomon 103, 146, 348, 390, 392
Song of Moses and the Lamb 407
Sozomen 292, 299
Special revelation 12
Spiritualism 392
  familiar spirits 393
  spiritualistic mediums 393
Spiritual gifts 69, 70, 71, 206, 237
  and the Body of Christ 239
  bestowed by Holy Spirit 237
  Bible listing of 241
  discovering 243

confirmation from the body 244
openness to providential guidance 244
spiritual preparaion for 243
study of Scripture 244
implications of 242
  a common ministry 242
  failure to use 243
  for gifts and mission 242
  for the role of the clergy 242
  unity in diversity, not uniformity 243
  witnessing: The purpose for the gifts 243
purpose of 239
  growth of the Church 241
  to bring harmony in the Church 239
Spiritual gifts and ministries 237–246
Spiritual maturity 143
Spiritual transformation 139, 140, 141, 145, 146
Spirit of God. *See* Holy Spirit
Spirit of prophecy 253, 258. *See also* Gift of prophecy, the
Stars, falling of, on November 13, 1833 379
Stewardship 301–310
  areas of 302
    abilities or talents 303
    material possessions 303
    the body 303
    time 303
  blessings of 307
  defined 302
  man given stewardship of environ-ment at Creation 99
  tithes
    how to calculate 309
    tithing in Israel 310
Study of the Word 141

T

Tabernacle
  Old Testament 45
Taylor, Vincent 125
Temple, Old Testament 274, 348, 357
  veil of, torn in two at Christ's death 274

Temple, William 412
Temple of the Holy Spirit
  body as 193
Ten Commandments 15, 81, 194, 263,
        264, 265, 266, 267, 268, 269,
        270, 272, 273, 275, 278, 283,
        284, 287, 299, 352
  quoted from Exodus 264
Testimony of Jesus Christ 190, 253,
        260
Theology
  function of 118
Thief on the cross 400
Thomas 421
Three angels' messages 190
  first angel's message 192, 380
    call to worship the Creator 193
    everlasting gospel to the world 192
    judgment-hour message 193
  second angel's message 194
    Babylon is fallen 194
      message repeated in Revelation
        18 195
  third angel's message 195, 362
    sets forth issue of true and false
        worship 196
    warning against worshipping beast
        and his image 195
Time of trouble 382
Time prophecy 48, 49
Tithes 304, 305
  examples of tithing 304
  one-tenth of all that we acquire 304
  use of 305
Torrance, T. F. 134
Tower of Babel 115
Tradition, Catholic doctrine of 188
Translation 144
Transubstatiation, Catholic doctrine
        of 188
Tree of Knowledge of Good and Evil
        92, 100, 101
Tree of Life 92, 99, 102, 389, 419, 423
Trinity 29, 31, 32
Tyre, king of 114

U

Ullman, Karl 56

Unfaithfulness in tithes and offerings
        306
Unity in the Body of Christ 201–210
  achievement of unity 206
    Christ's commandment to love 207
    Holy Spirit as Source of unity 206
    role of spiritual gifts in 206
    steps to 208
    unity at the Cross 208
  Bible unity and the Church 202
    the extent of unity 203
    unity in diversity 204
      many gifts, one Spirit 204
      unity is not uniformity 204
      vine and branches 204
    unity of faith 204
    unity of the Spirit 202
  Christ's prayer for 202
  importance of 205
    unity makes the Church's efforts
        effective 205
    unity reveals reality of God's king-
        dom 205
    unity shows strength of the Church
        205
  seven-fold "one-ness" 203
Unpardonable sin, the 70, 369
Use of remainder after tithes and of-
        ferings 306

V

Vatican II Council 256
Verduin, Leonard 105
Victorious living 59, 138, 139
Vulgate 353, 367

W

Wesley, Susannah 313
Westcott, B. F. 355
Wheat, Ed 334
White, Ellen G. 247. See also Gift of
        prophecy, the
  Books by
    Five-volume Conflict of the Ages
        series 257
    Steps to Christ 256, 257
    Testimonies for the Church 258
    The Desire of Ages 256

wrote more than 80 titles 257
brief overview of her life 255
brief sketch of her accomplishments
257
known as "the Lord's messenger"
247
Will, the 142
Williams, Samuel 379
Woman
representing God's true church 134,
182
representing people of God 44, 181
Seed of 44, 107, 273
Woman, wicked
representing apostate religion 194
Word of God 11–22
World Council of Churches 256
Worship 163, 173
Wycliffe, John 188
Morning Star of the Reformation
188

Y

Year-day principle 48, 64, 358
Yom Kippur 366

Z

Zechariah 16, 137